Frommer's

Paris 2005

W9-AWD-927

La Tour Eiffel, stretching 317m (1,056 ft.), symbolizes and shines over the City of Light.
© Hollenbeck Photography.

Even public works can be art works in Paris. The subway entrance at Port Dauphine is in the Art Nouveau style. © *Stephen Studd/Tony Stone Images.*

The Basilisque du Sacré-Coeur crowns Montmartre, a neighborhood that offers hidden treasures on its side streets. For a walking tour of the area, see chapter 8, "Strolling Around Paris." © *John Elk III Photography.*

Pick up a fresh baguette if you're planning a Parisian picnic, and complete your feast with a bottle of wine and a pastry or chocolate treat. For the best places to shop for an alfresco lunch, see chapter 9, "Shopping." *Top: © Steven Rothfeld/Tony Stone Images; bottom: © Bill Gallery/Viesti Associates, Inc.*

This ugly fellow seems to contemplate the long history of Paris from his perch atop the Cathédrale de Notre-Dame. See "Top Attractions" in chapter 7, "Exploring Paris." © Harald Sund/Image Bank.

Paris is filled with great museums, from the Louvre to the Musée d'Orsay to the Musée Picasso, which contains the world's greatest collection of works by the Spanish master. See "The Major Museums," in chapter 7. © Catherine Karnow Photography.

The parks of Paris, in particular the Jardin des Tuileries, are a favorite spot for young and old to enjoy the city and each others' company. See "Parks & Gardens," in chapter 7.
© Bryan F. Peterson/The Stock Market.

An hour northwest of Paris is Giverny, where the Impressionist Claude Monet captured the beauty and color of his famous water lilies. See chapter 11, "Side Trips from Paris."
© Robert Holmes Photography.

A bronze Dionysus looks over the great palace of Versailles, home of some of the grandest and most opulent European royal courts. See "Versailles," in chapter 11.
© Robert Holmes Photography.

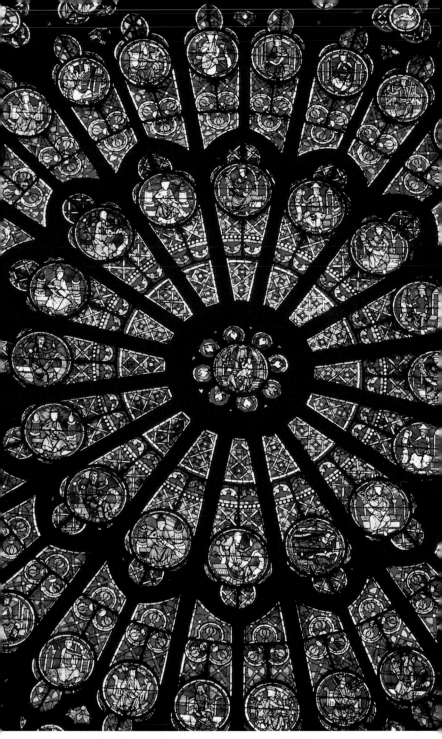

Light streams through the dazzling rose window at the Cathédral de Notre-Dame.
See chapter 7, "Exploring Paris." © John Elk III Photography.

A New Star-Rating System & Other Exciting News from Frommer's!

In our continuing effort to publish the savviest, most up-to-date, and most appealing travel guides available, we've added some great new features.

Frommer's guides now include a new **star-rating system.** Every hotel, restaurant, and attraction is rated from 0 to 3 stars to help you set priorities and organize your time.

We've also added **seven brand-new features** that point you to the great deals, in-the-know advice, and unique experiences that separate travelers from tourists. Throughout the guide, look for:

Finds	Special finds—those places only insiders know about
Fun Fact	Fun facts—details that make travelers more informed and their trips more fun
Kids	Best bets for kids—advice for the whole family
Moments	Special moments—those experiences that memories are made of
Overrated	Places or experiences not worth your time or money
Tips	Insider tips—some great ways to save time and money
Value	Great values—where to get the best deals

We've also added a **"What's New"** section in every guide—a timely crash course in what's hot and what's not in every destination we cover.

Here's what the critics say about Frommer's:

Other Great Guides for Your Trip:

Frommer's France 2003
Frommer's Born to Shop Paris
Frommer's Irreverent Guide to Paris
Frommer's Memorable Walks in Paris
Frommer's Paris from $80 a Day
Frommer's Portable Paris 2003
Unofficial Guide to Paris

Paris

2003

by Darwin Porter & Danforth Prince

Wiley Publishing, Inc.

About the Authors

Darwin Porter, a native of North Carolina, and **Danforth Prince** lived in France for many years. Darwin worked in television advertising and as a bureau chief for the Miami *Herald*. Danforth, who began his association with Darwin in 1982, worked for the Paris bureau of the *New York Times*. They are also the authors of *Frommer's France 2003*, and *Frommer's Provence & the Riviera*.

Published by:

Wiley Publishing, Inc.

909 Third Ave.
New York, NY 10022

ISBN 0-7645-6623-7
ISSN 0899-3203

Editor: Kathleen Warnock
Production Editor: Bethany André
Design by Michele Laseau
Cartographer: Nicholas Trotter
Photo Editor: Richard Fox
Production by Wiley Indianapolis Composition Services

For information on our other products and services or to obtain technical support, please contact our Customer Care Department within the U.S. at 800-762-2974, outside the U.S. at 317-572-3993 or fax 317-572-4002.

Wiley also publishes its books in a variety of electronic formats. Some content that appears in print may not be available in electronic formats.

Manufactured in the United States of America

5   4   3   2   1

Contents

7 Exploring Paris 172

8 Strolling Around Paris 234

9 Shopping 246

10 Paris After Dark 270

11 Side Trips from Paris 290

List of Maps

An Invitation to the Reader

In researching this book, we discovered many wonderful places—hotels, restaurants, shops, and more. We're sure you'll find others. Please tell us about them, so we can share the information with your fellow travelers in upcoming editions. If you were disappointed with a recommendation, we'd love to know that, too. Please write to:

Frommer's Paris 2003
Wiley Publishing, Inc. • 909 Third Ave. • New York, NY 10022

An Additional Note

Please be advised that travel information is subject to change at any time—and this is especially true of prices. We therefore suggest that you write or call ahead for confirmation when making your travel plans. The authors, editors, and publisher cannot be held responsible for the experiences of readers while traveling. Your safety is important to us, however, so we encourage you to stay alert and be aware of your surroundings. Keep a close eye on cameras, purses, and wallets, all favorite targets of thieves and pickpockets.

New! Frommer's Star Ratings & Icons

Every hotel, restaurant, and attraction listing in this guide has been ranked for quality, value, service, amenities, and special features using a star-rating scale. In country, state, and regional guides, we also rate towns and regions to help you narrow down your choices and budget your time accordingly. Hotels and restaurants in the Very Expensive and Expensive categories are rated on a scale of one (highly recommended) to three stars (exceptional). Those in the Moderate and Inexpensive categories rate from zero (recommended) to two stars (very highly recommended). Attractions, towns, and regions are rated according to the following scale: zero stars (recommended), one star (highly recommended), two stars (very highly recommended), and three stars (must-see).

In addition to the rating system, we also use seven icons to highlight insider information, useful tips, special bargains, hidden gems, memorable experiences, kid-friendly venues, places to avoid, and other useful information:

(Finds   (Fun Fact   (Kids   (Moments   (Overrated   (Tips   (Value

The following abbreviations are used for credit cards:

AE	American Express	DISC	Discover	V	Visa
DC	Diners Club	MC	MasterCard	

FROMMERS.COM

Now that you have the guidebook to a great trip, visit our website at **www.frommers.com** for travel information on nearly 2,500 destinations. With features updated regularly, we give you instant access to the most current trip-planning information available. At Frommers.com, you'll also find the best prices on airfares, accommodations, and car rentals—and you can even book travel online through our travel booking partners. At Frommers.com, you'll also find the following:

- Online updates to our most popular guidebooks
- Vacation sweepstakes and contest giveaways
- Newsletter highlighting the hottest travel trends
- Online travel message boards with featured travel discussions

What's New in Paris

The talk in Paris for 2002 was the changeover from the historic French franc to the euro, a currency Paris (and France) now shares with 11 other European Union countries, including Germany, Italy, and Spain. Most businesses adjusted relatively easily (though the changeover was costly in some cases), but there was much grumbling among Parisians, especially older people, many of whom put little trust in the new currency and often were uncertain of its value. Counterfeiters and swindlers, of course, had a field day.

As for the city itself, Paris continues to reinvent itself. We visit again for the memories and the evocative cityscapes, but we are forever searching for what is new. Paris is a city of contradiction—one that remains the same, one that is eternal, but one that is forever changing.

ACCOMMODATIONS Paris continues to upgrade tired old properties, to renovate, and to add private bathrooms, which means hotel prices are on the rise, especially in the cheaper digs. Because of the favorable dollar/euro rate, many moderate choices remain. Inexpensive rooms are getting harder to come by.

On the deluxe front, a charmer has opened off the Champs-Elysées: **Hotel François 1er,** 7 rue Magellan, 75008 Paris (© **01-47-23-44-04**). Occupying swanky real estate, this boutique hotel is like a private town house, the pet project of a famed French architect.

Once a favorite of such stars as Elizabeth Taylor, the **Hotel Lancaster,** 7 rue de Berri, 75008 Paris (© **800/223-6800** in the U.S., or 01-40-76-40-76), has been considerably improved. Its well-upholstered accommodations are again attracting the upmarket clients who once made it an oasis of Anglo-Saxon charm.

The major hotel opening in Paris was the launching of **Hyatt Regency Paris-Madeleine,** 24 bd. Malesherbes, 75008 Paris (© **01-55-27-12-34**), in the heart of the financial district. Designed for the busy man or woman on the move, this Hyatt offers spacious rooms and deluxe service.

On the Left Bank, excitement was generated by the comeback of **L'Hôtel,** 13 rue des Beaux-Artes, 75006 Paris (© **01-44-41-99-00**). This once-seedy hotel where Oscar Wilde died has returned to its former glory of the 1960s. Those cramped rooms are now bigger due to a reduction in the number of rooms, and the Victorian and baroque styling remains nostalgic.

On a more modestly priced front, **Best Western Aramais Saint-Germain,** 124 rue de Rennes, 76006 Paris (© **01-45-48-03-75**), between Saint-Germain-des-Prés and Montparnasse, has been beautifully renovated and modernized.

DINING It's so old it's new again. There's a buzz about a long-established Alsatian restaurant, **Jenny,** 39 bd. du Temple, 3e (© **01-44-54-39-00**), as many Parisians in these uncertain times return to comfort food. In this case, it's sauerkraut piled high with tender pork knuckles, ham slices, and sausages.

Following a trend of cooking like *maman* used to make, **Bath's,** 9 rue de la Trémoille, 8e (℡ **01-40-70-01-09**), is enjoying tremendous vogue for its provincial cuisine from the Auvergnat region in central France. Parisians flock here to partake of such dishes as cream of lentil soup studded with foie gras and ravioli filled with the pungent Cantal cheese of the district.

Installed on the seventh floor of the Théâtre des Champs-Elysées, **La Maison Blanche,** 15 av. Montaigne, 8e (℡ **01-47-23-55-99**), is a showcase for the culinary finesse of twin brothers Jacques and Laurent Pourcel. Chic Paris is drawn here for the sublime Provençal cuisine.

Famed chef Jean-Georges Vongerichten, who has scored big hits in New York and London, returns to Paris with his fusion cuisine at the chic **Market,** 15 av. Matignon, 8e (℡ **01-56-43-40-90**). In postmodern decor, this place is super-hip and is awakening the sleepy and somewhat jaded palates of those who live along this avenue, one of the most expensive addresses in the world.

Finally, another stylishly hip place is **Korova,** 33 rue Marbeuf, 8e (℡ **01-53-89-93-93**), recognized for its international cuisine. It's like a private club with Zen simplicity. One of its owners, Fréderick Grasser Hermé, is known in France for his "shocking" cookbooks. Make up your own mind after you've tried his chicken cooked with Coca-Cola.

SIGHTSEEING It took 2 centuries, but the most famous lady in Paris, *Mona Lisa,* is finally getting her own room at the **Louvre,** 34-36 quai du Louvre, 1er (℡ **01-40-20-51-51**). Maybe in her own quarters, her smile will be even more enigmatic.

Visitors heading for Paris's fabled **Petit Palais** along avenue Winston-Churchill will find the doors locked in 2003. This palace of art has shut down for much needed renovations.

All the attention focused on the Arab world is luring more visitors to the newly reorganized **Musée de l'Institut,** 1 rue des Fossés St-Bernard, 5e (℡ **01-40-51-38-38**). Its exhibits evoke French nostalgia for their "lost colonies" in North Africa.

SHOPPING Yves Saint Laurent may have retired, but like the late Coco Chanel, his name and fashion inspiration lives on at his major outlet in Paris: **Yves Saint Haute Couture** at 5 av. Marceau, 16e (℡ **01-44-31-64-00**), and other outlets.

In these tight economic times, discount and retail houses are the rage among Paris shoppers. Gaining increasing attention for their bargains on clothing are **Annexe des Créateurs,** 19 rue Godot de Mauroy, 9e (℡ **01-42-65-46-40**).

AFTER DARK The *literati* in Paris show up at the hip bar **La Belle Hortense,** 31 rue Vieille-du-Temple, 4e (℡ **01-48-04-71-60**), in the increasingly chic Marais district. This ersatz literary salon even maintains a bookstore at the rear of the premises. On the Left Bank, **Le Bar de L'Hôtel,** 13 rue des Beaux-Arts, 6e (℡ **01-44-41-99-00**), is in fashion again now that this boutique hotel has been beautifully restored.

SIDE TRIPS Those visiting the cathedral in Chartres will find a sublime new restaurant: **La Vieille Maison,** 5 rue au Lait (℡ **02-37-34-10-67**). Installed in a 14th-century building, the modern French cuisine reflects the best seasonal ingredients and is a culinary showcase for some fine regionally inspired cookery.

The latest attraction at Disneyland Paris is **Walt Disney Studios** (℡ **01-60-30-60-53**), next to Disneyland Park. This tour offers a behind-the-scenes look at how the Mickey Mouse people create characters to entertain the world. You learn Disney "trade secrets" and are plunged into the center of the action in a film shoot.

The Best of Paris

Discovering the City of Light and making it your own has always been the most compelling reason to visit Paris. If you're a first-timer, everything, of course, will be new to you. If you've been away for a while, expect changes: Taxi drivers may no longer correct your fractured French but address you in English—tantamount to a revolution. More Parisians have a rudimentary knowledge of the language, and the country, at least at first glance, seems less xenophobic than in past years—as you spend your much-needed euros, you likely won't be looked at as an "ugly American." Part of this new rapprochement derives from Parisians' interest in music, videos, and films from foreign countries, and in part from France's growing awareness of its role within a united Europe.

Security is tighter than ever in the wake of the terrorist attacks in New York and Washington, D.C., on September 11, 2001. Paris has fully activated its antiterrorist campaign first launched in the mid-1990s when France was the target of a spate of Algerian terrorist attacks.

Expect to see far more police in bulletproof vests at all transport hubs and government buildings, as well as at high-profile sites such as the Eiffel Tower.

Metal detectors at Paris's airports are turned up so high that the zipper on a pair of trousers can trigger an alarm. Often, you have to do a virtual striptease before security will give you the green light.

As Paris and the country itself moves deeper into the millennium, there is a fear among the French of a loss of identity. France continues to attract record numbers of immigrants from its former colonies. Many native-born French have expressed concern that the country will lose the battle to keep its language distinct and unadulterated by foreign (particularly American) slang or catchwords (*le weekend* or *le software*). In fact, the rancor of France's collective xenophobia has been increasingly redirected toward the many immigrants seeking better lives in Paris, where the infrastructure has nearly been stretched to its limits.

Though Paris is in flux culturally and socially, it lures travelers for the same reasons it always has. You'll still find classic sights like the Tour Eiffel, Notre-Dame, the Arc de Triomphe, Sacré-Coeur, and all those atmospheric cafes, as well as trendy new projects like the Grand Arche de La Défense, the Cité des Sciences et de l'Industrie, the Cité de la Musique, and the Bibliothèque François-Mitterrand. And don't forget the parks, gardens, and squares; the Champs-Elysées and other grand boulevards; the river Seine and its quays. Paris's beauty is still overwhelming, especially at night, when it truly is the City of Light.

1 Frommer's Favorite Paris Experiences

- **Whiling Away an Afternoon in a Parisian Cafe:** The cafe is where passionate meetings of writers, artists, philosophers, thinkers, and revolutionaries once took place— and perhaps still do. Parisians stop by their favorite cafes to meet current lovers and friends, to make new ones, or sit in solitude with a newspaper or book. Whether you order a small coffee or the most expensive cognac in the house, nobody will hurry you from this quintessentially Parisian activity. For our recommendations, see "The Top Cafes" in chapter 6, "Where to Dine."

• **Taking Afternoon Tea à la Française:** Drinking tea in London has its charm, but the Parisian *salon de thé* is unique. Skip over those cucumber-and-watercress sandwiches and delve into a luscious dessert like the Mont Blanc, a creamy purée of sweetened chestnuts and meringue. The grandest Parisian tea salon is **Angélina,** but you might want to stop by **Berthillon,** for one of their scrumptious ice creams, or the **Restaurant/Salon de Thé Bernardaud,** if you want your tea served on gorgeous Bernardaud porcelain. See chapter 6, "Where to Dine" for details.

• **Strolling Along the Seine:** Such painters as Sisley, Turner, and Monet have fallen under the Seine's spell. On its banks, lovers still walk hand in hand, anglers cast their lines, and *bouquinistes* (secondhand-book dealers) peddle their mix of postcards, 100-year-old pornography, and tattered histories of Indochina. Clochards seek a home for the night under its bridges, and the Bateaux-Mouches ply its waters. For a spectacular view of the Louvre, cross the city's first iron bridge, the pont des Arts, one of only four pedestrian bridges. Paris's oldest and most famous bridge is the ironically named pont Neuf (New Bridge), from which you have an excellent view of the Palais de Justice and Sainte-Chapelle on Ile de la Cité. For more details about sights and moments of Paris, see chapter 7, "Exploring Paris."

• **Spending a Day at the Races:** Paris boasts eight tracks for horse racing. The most famous and the classiest is **Longchamp,** in the Bois de Boulogne, the site of the Prix de l'Arc de Triomphe and Grand Prix (see p. 223). These and other top races are major social events, so you'll have to dress up (buy your outfit on rue du Faubourg St-Honoré). Take the Métro to Porte d'Auteuil, then a bus from there to the track. The racing newspaper *Paris Turf* and weekly entertainment magazines have details about race times.

• **Calling on the Dead:** You don't have to be a ghoul to be thrilled by a visit to Europe's most famous cemetery, **Père-Lachaise** (see p. 218).You can pay your respects to the earthly remains of Jim Morrison, Gertrude Stein and Alice B. Toklas, Oscar Wilde, Yves Montand and Simone Signoret, Edith Piaf, Isadora Duncan, Abélard and Héloïse, Frédéric Chopin, Marcel Proust, Eugène Delacroix, and others. The tomb designs are intriguing and often eerie. Laid out in 1803 on a hill in Ménilmontant, the cemetery offers surprises with its bizarre monuments, unexpected views, and ornate sculpture.

• **Discovering Hidden Montmartre:** This is Paris's most touristy area. However, far removed from the area's top draw, Sacré-Coeur, is the neighborhood of the true Montmartrois. Wander the back streets away from the souvenir shops. Arm yourself with a good map and seek out such streets as rue Lepic (refresh yourself at the Lux Bar at no. 12), rue Constance, rue Tholozé (with its view over the Paris rooftops), rue des Abbesses, and rue Germain-Pilon. None of these is famous, but each boasts buildings whose detailing shows the pride and care permeating Paris's architecture. Discover dozens of other streets on your own. At dusk, sit on Sacré-Coeur's top steps and watch as Paris turns into the City of Light. For a walking tour of Montmartre, see chapter 8, "Strolling Around Paris."

- **Checking Out the Marchés:** A daily Parisian ritual is ambling through one of the open-air markets to buy fresh food—perhaps a properly creamy Camembert or a pumpkin-gold cantaloupe—to be eaten before sundown. You can take part in this time-honored tradition by purchasing the makings for a picnic in a park or even in your room. Like artists, the vendors arrange their wares into a mosaic of vibrant colors: Sanguine, an Italian citrus with juice the color of a brilliant orange sunset; ruby-red peppers; and golden-yellow bananas from Martinique all dazzle the eye. Our favorite market is on rue Montorgueil, beginning at rue Rambuteau, 1er (Métro: Les Halles). On mornings spent at this grubby little cluster of food stalls, we've spotted some of France's finest chefs stocking up for the day. For more details on shops and shopping, refer to chapter 9, "Shopping."

- **Window-Shopping in the Faubourg St-Honoré:** In the 1700s, the wealthiest of Parisians resided in the Faubourg St-Honoré; today the quarter is home to stores catering to the rich, particularly on rue du Faubourg St-Honoré and avenue Montaigne. Even if you don't buy anything, it's great to window-shop big names like Hermès, Dior, Laroche, Courrèges, Cardin, and Saint Laurent. If you want to browse in the stores, be sure to dress the part. See chapter 9, "Shopping" for the lowdown on these boutiques.

- **Exploring Ile de la Cité's Flower Market:** A fine finish to any day (Mon–Sat) spent meandering along the Seine is a stroll through the **Marché aux Fleurs,** place Louis-Lépine (see p. 264). You can buy rare flowers, the gems of the French Riviera—bouquets that have inspired artists throughout the centuries. Even the most basic hotel room will feel like a luxury suite once you fill it with bunches of carnations, lavender, roses, tulips, and the like. On Sundays, the area is transformed into the **Marché aux Oiseaux,** where you can admire rare birds from around the world.

- **Going Gourmet at Fauchon:** An exotic world of food, **Fauchon** (p. 260) offers more than 20,000 products from around the globe. Everything you never knew you were missing is in aisle after aisle of coffees, spices, pastries, fruits, vegetables, rare Armagnacs, and much more. Take your pick: Tonganese mangoes, Scottish smoked salmon, preserved cocks' combs, Romanian rose-petal jelly, blue-red Indian pomegranates, golden Tunisian dates, larks stuffed with foie gras, dark morels from France's rich soil, Finnish reindeer's tongue, century-old eggs from China, and a Creole punch from Martinique reputed to be the best anywhere.

- **Attending a Free Concert:** Summer brings one of the joys of Paris: free concerts in parks and churches all over the city. Pick up an entertainment weekly for details. Some of the best concerts are held at the **American Church in Paris,** 65 quai d'Orsay, 7e

(© **01-40-62-05-00**; Métro: Alma-Marceau; RER: Pont de l'Alma). **Sainte-Chapelle** is known for its splendid concerts several times a week; call the box office at 4 bd. du Palais, 1er (© **01-53-73-78-50**; Métro: Cité). For more concerts, refer to chapter 10, "Paris After Dark."

- **Attending a Ballet or an Opera:** In 1989, the **Opéra Bastille** (p. 271) was inaugurated to compete with the *grande dame* of the music scene, the **Opéra Garnier** (p. 272), which then was solely for dance and soon closed for renovations. The Garnier reopened a few years ago, and opera has joined dance in the rococo splendor created by Charles Garnier, beneath a controversial ceiling by Chagall. The modern Bastille, France's largest opera house, with curtains by designer Issey Miyake, features opera and symphony performances in four concert halls (its main hall seats 2,700). Whether for a performance of Bizet or Tharp, dress with pomp and circumstance.

- **Watching the Show at the Folies-Bergère:** Often denounced, the campy showcase at the **Folies-Bergère** (p. 274) has been pleasing audiences since 1868, even though classic acts like Maurice Chevalier, Mistinguett, and Josephine Baker (who performed her famous banana dance here) vanished long ago. True, the Tour Eiffel cancan is a bit corny and the show has become less daring, but those ladies in their sequins, feathers, and pom-poms still evoke a Paris of days gone by, immortalized on a Manet canvas. The show, tacky or not, seems to go on forever.

- **Sipping Cocktails at Willi's:** Back in the early 1970s, the first-timer to Paris might have arrived with a copy of Hemingway's *A Moveable Feast* and, taking the author's endorsement to heart, headed for Harry's Bar at "Sank roo doe Noo." Harry's is still around but now draws an older, conservative clientele. Today's chic younger expats head for Willi's Wine Bar, where the longhaired young bartenders are mostly English, as are the waitresses, dressed in Laura Ashley garb. The place is like an informal club for Brits, Australians, and Yanks, especially in the afternoon. Some 300 wines await your selection. See page 284.

2 Best Hotel Bets

For full details on the following hotels, see chapter 5, "Where to Stay."

- **Best Newcomer:** A boutique charmer near the Champs-Elysées, **Hotel François 1er,** 7 rue Magellan, 8e (© **01-47-23-44-04**), occupies platinum real estate. Inside, the hotel is a nugget of Parisian styling and chic, like your own private town house in Paris. See p. 90.

- **Best for Business Travelers:** Corporate types from all over the world converge at the **Hôtel Balzac,** 6 rue Balzac, 8e (© **800/457-4000** in the U.S. and Canada),a Belle Epoque town house with a good business center, 2 blocks from many of the offices along the Champs-Elysées. Its restaurant serves some of the best food in town and is suitable for entertaining clients. See p. 90.

- **Best for Families:** An affordable Left Bank choice is the **Hôtel de Fleurie,** 32-34 rue Grégoire-de-Tours, 6e (© **01-53-73-70-00**), in the heart of St-Germain-des-Prés. The accommodations are thoughtfully appointed, and many connecting rooms with two large beds are perfect for families. Children under 12 stay free with their parents. See p. 100.

- **Best Value:** Not far from the Champs-Elysées, the **Résidence Lord Byron,** 5 rue de Chateaubriand, 8e (© **01-43-59- 89-98**), is a classy little getaway that's far from opulent but is clean and comfortable and worth every euro. See p. 92.

- **Best Location:** Only a 2-minute walk from Paris's most historic and beautiful square, **Hôtel de la Place des Vosges,** 12 rue de Birague, 4e (© **01-42-72-60-46**), is a little charmer. In a building 350 years old, it is small scale and inviting, with some decorative touches that evoke the era of Louis XIII. See p. 84.

- **Best View:** Of the 32 rooms at the **Hôtel du Quai-Voltaire,** 19 quai Voltaire, 7e (© **01-42-61-50-91**), 28 open onto views of the Seine. If you stay here, you'll be following in the footsteps of Wilde, Baudelaire, and Wagner. This 17th-century abbey was transformed into a hotel back in 1856 and has been welcoming guests who appreciate its tattered charms ever since. See p. 108.

- **Best for Nostalgia:** If you yearn for a Left Bank "literary" address, make it the **Odéon-Hôtel,** 3 rue de l'Odéon, 6e (© **01-43-25-90-67**), in the heart of the 6th arrondissement, filled with the ghosts of Gide, Hemingway, Fitzgerald, Joyce, and Stein and Toklas. Evoking a Norman country inn, this charming hotel lures guests with its high, crooked ceilings, exposed beams, and memories of yesterday. See p. 101.

- **Best for Stargazing:** The tycoons, hot stars, and hotter mistresses of yesterday—Douglas Fairbanks and Mary Pickford, William Randolph Hearst and Marion Davies—knew where to stay back then. Tom Cruise and his ilk know *the* address in Paris is still the **Hôtel de Crillon,** 10 place de la Concorde, 8e (© **800/223-6800** in the U.S. and Canada), once the palace of the duc de Crillon. If you want its grandest suite and have a discriminating taste for the macabre, ask for the Marie Antoinette Apartment—it exhibits Antoinette-style elegance, and its namesake was beheaded practically at the doorstep of this deluxe citadel. See p. 88.

- **Best for Opulence:** Now owned by Mohammed al-Fayed, the **Hôtel Ritz,** 15 place Vendôme, 1er (© **800/223-6800** in the U.S. and Canada), has dripped with wealth, luxury, and decadence since César Ritz opened it in 1898. Barbara Hutton, Coco Chanel, and Marcel Proust are just a few names inscribed in its glorious guest book; if you're into romantic tragedy, remember this was where Princess Diana and Dodi al-Fayed had their last meal. You can join the Saudi oil princes, Milanese divas, and movie legends staying here—if you have big bucks. See p. 78.

- **Best-Kept Secret:** Built in 1913 and long in a seedy state, the fully restored **Terrass Hôtel,** 12-14 rue Joseph-de-Maistre, 18e (© **01-46-06-72-85**), is now the only four-star choice in Montmartre, an area not known for luxury accommodations. Its rooms take in far-ranging views of the Tour Eiffel, Arc de Triomphe, and Opéra Garnier. See p. 86.

- **Best Historic Hotel:** Inaugurated by Napoleon III in 1855, the **Hôtel du Louvre,** place André-Malraux, 1er (© **800/888-4747** in the U.S. and Canada), was once described by a French journalist as "a palace of the people, rising adjacent to the palace of kings." Today, the hotel offers luxurious accommodations and panoramic views down avenue de l'Opéra. See p. 75.

- **Best for Romance:** Until the 1970s, **L'Hôtel,** 13 rue des Beaux-Arts, 6e (© **01-44-41-99-00**), was a fleabag filled with drunks and addicts (in 1900, Oscar Wilde died here penniless). Millions of francs of renovations later, the rooms that were once cramped and claustrophobic are now ravishingly romantic, wrought like small jewel boxes. See p. 101.

- **Most Trendy Hotel:** A converted town house, the **Hôtel Costes,** 239 rue St-Honoré, 1er (© **01-42-44-50-50**), evokes the imperial heyday of Napoleon III. Fashion headliners especially like it— Costes is the choice of many a model, as the Paris offices of *Harper's Bazaar* are close at hand. If you're into swags, patterned fabrics, jewel-tone colors, and lavish accessories, this can be your Gilded Age address. See p. 75.

- **Best Service:** Though you can't fault the flawless decor of the **Hôtel Plaza Athénée,** 25 av. Montaigne, 8e (© **866/732-1106** in the U.S. and Canada), the billionaires check in because they get the royal treatment from the jaded but indulgent and ever-so-polite staff. In an upscale neighborhood between the Seine and the Champs-Elysées, the Plaza Athénée offers service that's impeccable. See p. 88.

3 Best Dining Bets

For full listings of the following restaurants, see chapter 6, "Where to Dine."

- **Best Chef:** Proud owner of five Michelin stars, **Alain Ducasse,** at the Restaurant Plaza Athénée, 25 av. Montaigne, 8e (© **01-53-67-65-00**), has taken Paris by storm, assuming the throne of semiretired Joël Robuchon now that he splits his time between his restaurant here and the one in Monte Carlo. He combines produce from every French region in a cuisine that's contemporary but not quite new, embracing the Mediterranean without abandoning France. See p. 142.

- **Best Haute Cuisine Restaurant:** Named for a 14th-century chef who wrote one of the oldest known books on French cookery, **Taillevent,** 15 rue Lamennais, 8e (© **01-44-95-15-01**), occupies a 19th-century town house off the Champs-Elysées. Though its owner likes to keep about 60% of the crowd French, we suggest you try for a reservation at Paris's most outstanding all-around restaurant. See p. 142.

- **Best Newcomer:** A bastion of French modern cookery, **L'Astrance,** 4 rue Beethoven, 16e (© **01-40-50-84-40**), is small and charming. Chef Pascal Barbot is creating a media event in Paris with creative cuisine that includes such delights as an "oyster cappuccino" or his "ravioli" in which the "pasta" is made with avocados and not flour. See p. 147.

- **Best Modern French Cuisine:** A temple of gastronomy is found at **Carré des Feuillants,** 14 rue de Castiglione, 1er (© **01-42-86-82-82**), near Place Vendôme and the Tuileries. Alain Dutournier is one of the leading chefs of France, and he restored this 17th-century convent, turning it into a citadel of refined cuisine and mouthwatering specialties. See p. 119.

- **Best Provençal Cuisine:** Now that Michelin has bestowed a coveted two stars, **Les Elysées du Vernet,** 25 rue Vernet, 8e (© 01-44-31-98-98), is hosting *tout Paris* and the media. Montpellier-born chef Alain Solivérès is emerging as one of the greatest in Paris, challenging some big-name chefs. His Provençal cookery is the freshest and among the best in the whole country. See p. 140.

- **Best Old-Fashioned Bistro:** Established in 1931 and bouncing back from a period of decline, **Allard,** 41 rue St-André-des-Arts, 6e (© 01-43-26-48-23), is better than ever, from its zinc bar to its repertoire of French classics—escargots, frogs' legs, foie gras, boeuf à la mode, and cassoulet. This is a good bet for real Left Bank bistro ambience. See p. 156.

- **Best Underappreciated Restaurant:** Henri Faugeron may no longer be the media darling he once was, but his **Relais Gourmand Faugeron,** 52 rue de Longchamp, 16e (© 01-47-04-24-53), is as stunning as ever, though the dishes may not be as "revolutionary" as he proclaims. The food is outstanding and uses only the freshest of ingredients, handled with skill by a stellar kitchen staff. See p. 147.

- **Best Decor:** Declared a French national treasure, the Belle Epoque **Le Train Bleu** in the Gare de Lyon, 12e (© 01-43-43-09-06), evokes the heyday of the Gilded Age. Completely restored, the restaurant boasts heavy purple-velvet hangings, boxes sprinkled with green plants, Napoleon III antiques, gleaming brass, and lighting fixtures made of bronze and Bohemia opaline-shaped glass cups. Incidentally, we said this restaurant had the best decor in Paris—not the finest cuisine. See p. 138.

- **Best View:** A penthouse restaurant, **La Tour d'Argent,** 15-17 quai de la Tournelle, 5e (© 01-43-54-23-31), is owned by ex-playboy Claude Terrail, who pays part of Notre-Dame's electric bill to illuminate the cathedral at night for his diners' pleasure. Dining here is a theatrical event. See p. 151.

- **Best Provincial Restaurant:** The cuisine of the Auvergne in central France is showcased at **Bath's,** 9 rue de la Trémoille, 8e (© 01-40-70-01-09). In a cozy, elegant setting, you can dine on the best dishes of this province, including ravioli stuffed with Cantal cheese, and filet of beef with lentils. See p. 142.

- **Best for Stargazing:** No, it's not Taillevent or even Alain Ducasse. On the see-and-be-seen circuit, the star is the **Buddha Bar,** 8 rue Boissy d'Anglas, 8e (© 01-53-05-90-00). The crowd doesn't come for the cuisine, though its fusion of French and Pacific Rim is exceedingly well executed. If you don't want to dine, stop by the hip lacquered bar across from the dining room. See p. 143.

- **Worst-Kept Secret:** In the heart of the Latin Quarter, **Perraudin,** 157 rue St-Jacques, 5e (© 01-46-33-15-75), duplicates the allure of an early-1900s bistro. You get the feeling Emile Zola could walk in any minute. It offers great food and great value, an old-fashioned dining experience that's rapidly disappearing from the city. See p. 155.

- **Best Brasserie:** Head for the Left Bank and the **Brasserie Balzar,** 49 rue des Ecoles, 5e (© 01-43-54-13-67), opened in 1898. If you dine on the familiar French food here, you'll be following in the footsteps of Sartre and Camus and others. You can even have a complete dinner in the middle of the afternoon. See p. 152.

- **Best Baby Bistro:** A few years ago, several great French chefs realized the average visitor can't afford the haute cuisine served at their restaurants, so they created "baby bistros" to serve superb food at affordable prices. The best of these is a sideshow created by one of the grandest chefs, Jacques Cagna: **La Rôtisserie d'Armaillé,** 6 rue d'Armaillé, 17e (© **01-42-27-19-20**), near place d'Etoile. See p. 151.

- **Best Seafood:** The fattest lobsters and prawns in the Rungis market emerge on platters at **Goumard,** 9 rue Duphot, 1er (© **01-42-60-36-07**), so chic that even the toilets are historic monuments. Nothing is allowed to interfere with the taste of the sea: You'll have to fly to the Riviera to find a better bouillabaisse. See p. 122.

- **Best *Cuisine Bourgeoise* (Comfort Food):** If Joyce, Verlaine, Valéry, and Hemingway rose from the grave today and strode into the **Crémerie-Restaurant Polidor,** 41 rue Monsieur-le-Prince, 6e (© **01-43-26-95-34**), they wouldn't notice any difference, not even on the menu, but would ask for their napkins, which are locked in a cabinet in back with their names on them. See p. 158.

- **Best Atmosphere:** A favorite of Colette and Cocteau, the world-famous **Le Grand Véfour,** 17 rue de Beaujolais, 1er (© **01-42-96-56-27**), at the Palais-Royal, has an interior classified as a historic monument. Incidentally, it serves some of the most refined cuisine in Paris. See p. 122.

- **Best Lyonnais Cuisine:** Lyon is hailed as France's gastronomic capital, and the best place in Paris to introduce yourself to its cuisine is **Aux Lyonnais,** 32 rue St-Marc, 2e (© **01-42-96-65-04**). This fin-de-siècle bistro turns out the dishes for which Lyon is famous, from perfect pike dumplings to Lyonnais sausages—all washed down, of course, with Beaujolais. See p. 127.

- **Best Kosher Food:** If corned beef, pastrami, herring, and dill pickles thrill you, head to **rue des Rosiers** in the 4th arrondissement (Métro: St-Paul). John Russel wrote that rue des Rosiers is the "last sanctuary of certain ways of life; what you see there in miniature is Warsaw before the ghetto was razed." North African overtones reflect the long-ago arrival of Jews from Morocco, Tunisia, and Algeria. The best time to go is Sunday morning: You can wander the streets eating as you go—apple strudel, Jewish rye bread, pickled lemons, smoked salmon, and *merguez,* a spicy smoked sausage from Algeria. Many spots offer sit-down meals, like **Chez Jo Goldenberg,** 7 rue des Rosiers, 4e ((© **01-48-87-20-16**), where the *carpe farcie* (stuffed carp) is outstanding and beef goulash a fine runner-up. See p. 132.

- **Best American Cuisine:** A Yankee outpost in Les Halles, **Joe Allen,** 30 rue Pierre-Lescot, 1er (© **01-42-36-70-13**), serves the finest burgers in Paris. Desserts include New York cheesecake, pecan pie made with pecans imported from the United States, and the inspired cultural fusion of American brownies made with French chocolate. See p. 125.

- **Best Vegetarian Cuisine:** One of the best-known veggie restaurants in the Marais is **Aquarius,** 54 rue Ste-Croix-de-la-Bretonnerie, 4e (© **01-48-87-48-71**). Choose from the array of soups and salads or have a mushroom tart or a galette of wheat with raw vegetables. In this rustic 17th-century setting, you can expect flavorful, wholesome, and generous meals. See p. 131.

- **Best Wine Cellar:** At the elegant **Lasserre,** 17 av. Franklin-D-Roosevelt, 8e (© **01-43-59-53-43**), you'll find not only wonderful food but also one of the great wine cellars of France, with some 180,000 bottles. See p. 139.

- **Best for Cheese:** Cheese is king at **Androuët,** 49 rue St-Roch, 1er (© **01-42-97-57-39**). Many cheese lovers opt for a bottle of wine, a green salad, and all-you-can-eat choices from the most sophisticated *dégustation de fromages* in the world. See p. 124.

- **Best on the Champs-Elysées:** The specialties of Denmark are served with flair at the **Restaurant Copenhague/Flora Danica,** 142 av. des Champs-Elysées, 8e (© **01-44-13-86-26**). In summer you can dine on the terrace of this "Maison du Danemark." See p. 144.

- **Best Late-Night Dining:** There's no place better in Paris to get a good meal at 3am than **Au Pied de Cochon,** 6 rue Coquillière, 1er (© **01-40-13-77-00**). Though everyone lauds its grilled pig's feet with béarnaise sauce, few have noticed you can also find some of the freshest oysters in town here. See p. 122.

- **Best for Tea:** Try **Angélina,** 226 rue de Rivoli, 1er (© **01-42-60-82-00**), for a view of haute couture's lionesses having their tea. The house specialty is the Mont Blanc, a combination of chestnut cream and meringue. See p. 123. If you're looking for luscious ice cream along with your tea, try **Berthillon,** 31 rue St-Louis-en-l'Ile, 4e (© **01-43-54-31-61**). See p. 130.

- **Best for Picnic Fare:** For the most elegant picnic fixings in town, go to **Fauchon,** 26 place de la Madeleine, 8e (© **01-47-42-60-11**), where you'll find a complete charcuterie and famous pastry shop. It's said to offer 20,000 kinds of imported fruits, vegetables, and other exotic delicacies, snacks, salads, and canapés, all packed to take out. See p. 260.

- **Best Champagne Julep:** While you wait for a table at **Closerie des Lilas,** 171 bd. du Montparnasse, 6e (© **01-40-51-34-50**), savor the best champagne julep in the world at the bar. See p. 155.

4 The Best Cafes

For full details on the following cafes, turn to chapter 6, "Where to Dine."

- **Most Evocative Left Bank Cafe:** Old bohemia still lives at the old-fashioned cafe **La Palette,** 43 rue de Seine, 6e (© **01-43-26-68-15**), where patrons still down the same Ricard and Pernod they did back in the 1930s. It's a battered but artistic Quartier Latin cafe. See p. 169.

- **Most Historical Cafe:** Fans of French history flock to **Le Procope,** 13 rue de l'Ancienne-Comédie, 6e (© **01-40-46-79-00**), where such luminaries as Voltaire, Oscar Wilde, and Napoleon used to hang out. The ground floor is outfitted like an antique library. See p. 170.

- **Most Legendary Hangout:** Once a gathering place for French intellectuals, **Les Deux Magots,** 6 place St-Germain-des-Prés, 6e (© **01-45-48-55-25**), is still going strong, with tourists now sitting at tables where Gore Vidal and James Baldwin once did. See p. 170.

- **Most Chic Cafe of Today:** Today's equivalent of La Coupole or even the Deux Magots is **Café Cosmos,** 101 bd. du Montparnasse 6e (② **01-43-26-74-36**). In days of yore, you might have seen literary masterpieces being scribbled, by hand, at some of the tables of this crowded cafe. Today in an age where most novels are written at home with word processors, it's where the hip media crowd gathers to discuss the film scripts and modeling contracts they're cultivating at the moment. See p. 168.

- **Most Quintessential Paris Left Bank Cafe:** Vying with Deux Magots (see above), **Café de Flore,** 172 bd. St-Germain, 6e (② **01-45-48-55-26**), basks in its memories of its famous visitors, who included Camus, Picasso, and Apollinaire. Even though tourists now take up the tables here, Café de Flore still pulls off a Left Bank aura. See p. 167.

Tips **The Best Websites for Paris**

Surf to these recommended websites for information on the City of Light:

- **Bonjour Paris, www.bparis.com**, is one of the most comprehensive and fun sites about life in Paris, written from an American expatriate point of view. You can also subscribe to a regular e-newsletter.

- **Paris Digest, www.parisdigest.com**, is an independent site containing articles that link to restaurants, hotels, museums, monuments, parks, and activities. It includes city history and tips for getting around.

- **Paris France Guide, www.parisfranceguide.com**, is produced by the publishers of such magazines as *Living in France, Study in France,* and *What's On in France.* This site has lots of useful information, such as articles and current listings for nightlife, events, theater, and music.

- **Paris Voice, www.parisvoice.com**, is the online version of the monthly *Paris Voice,* a hip and opinionated guide for "English-speaking Parisians." The calendar of events includes music, movies, and performance-art listings. There are also restaurant reviews and guides like "Where to Kiss in Paris."

- **Paris Pages, www.paris.org**, offers a wealth of information on Paris for a widespread audience. The lodging reviews are organized by area and by the nearby monuments. The guide includes an event calendar, shop listings, a map of attractions with details about each, and photo tours.

- **Paris Tourist Office, www.paris-touristoffice.com**, offers information on city events arranged by week, month, favorites, and year, plus the closest Métro stops for museums, lodgings, restaurants, and nightlife. You can tour parks and gardens and discover Paris's trendy districts.

A Traveler's Guide to Paris's Art & Architecture

by Reid Bramblett

Paris is one of the artistic capitals of Europe. For centuries the city has produced, and been home to, countless artists and artistic movements. This chapter will help you find the best examples of each period in the city's museums and architecture.

GOTHIC (1100–1400)

Almost all artistic expression in medieval France was church-related. Paris retains almost no art from the Classical or Romanesque eras, but much remains from the medieval Gothic era when artists created sculpture and stained glass for churches.

Because Mass was in Latin, many images were used to communicate the Bible's most important lessons to the mostly illiterate populace. **Bas reliefs** (sculpture that projects slightly from a flat surface) were used to illustrate key tales that inspired faith in God and fear of sin (*Last Judgments* were favorites). These reliefs were wrapped around column capitals, festooned onto facades, and fitted into the **tympanum** (the arched spaces above doorways; the complete door, tympanum, arch, and supporting pillars assemblage is the **portal**).

The French were also becoming masters of **stained glass.** Many painterly conventions began in this era on windowpanes, or as elaborate doodles in the margins of **illuminated manuscripts,** which developed into altarpieces of the colorful **International Gothic** style.

In both Gothic painting and sculpture, figures tend to be highly stylized, flowing, and rhythmic. The figures' features and gestures are exaggerated for symbolic or emotional emphasis.

Outstanding examples and artists include:

- **Cathédrale de Chartres** (1194–1220). A day trip from Paris, Cathédrale de Chartres boasts magnificent sculpture and some of the best stained glass in Europe.
- **Cathédrale de Notre-Dame** (1163–1250). The Gothic high points of this cathedral are the sculpture on the facade, an interior choir screen lined with deep-relief carvings, and three rose windows filled with stained glass.
- **Sainte-Chapelle** (1240–50). The finest stained glass in the world adorns this tiny chapel.
- **Unicorn Tapestries** (1499–1514). These famed tapestries shine brightly as a final statement of medieval sensibilities while borrowing some burgeoning Renaissance conventions. Find them in the **Musée de Cluny.**

THE RENAISSANCE (1400–1600)

Renaissance means "rebirth," in this case the return of Classical ideals originating in Greece and Rome. Humanist thinkers rediscovered the wisdom of the ancients, while artists strove for greater naturalism, using newly developed techniques such as linear perspective to achieve new heights of realism. Famous practitioners of the style include **Michelangelo** (1475–1564) and **Leonardo da Vinci** (1452–1519). **Mannerism,** the late 16th-century branch of the High Renaissance, took Michelangelo's bright color palate and twisting figures to extremes and exhausted the movement.

Aside from collecting Italian art, the French had little to do with the Renaissance, which started in Italy and was quickly picked up in Germany and the Low Countries. France owes many of its early Renaissance treasures to **François I,** who imported art (paintings by Raphael and Titian) and artists (Leonardo da Vinci). Henri II's Florentine wife, **Catherine de Médici,** also collected 16th-century Italian masterpieces.

Significant artists and examples to look for in Paris include:

- **Italian Artists.** Many works by Italy's finest reside in the **Louvre,** including paintings by **Giotto, Fra' Angelico,** and **Veronese;** sculptures by **Michelangelo;** and a handful of works by **Leonardo da Vinci,** who moved to a Loire Valley château for the last 3 years of his life and whose *Mona Lisa* (1503–05), perhaps the world's most famous painting, hangs here.
- **The School of Fontainebleau.** This group of artists working on the **Palais de Fontainebleau** outside Paris from 1530 to 1560 were imported Italian Mannerists who combined painting, stucco, sculpture, and woodwork to decorate the château's Galerie François I. They included **Niccolò dell'Abbate, Benvenuto Cellini, Primaticcio,** and **Rosso Fiorentino.** (If you don't make it out to Fontainebleau, check out Cellini's sculpture *Diana of Fontainebleau* [1543–44] in the Louvre.)

THE BAROQUE (1600–1800)

The 17th-century **baroque style** is hard to pin down. In some ways it was a result of the Catholic Counter-Reformation, reaffirming spirituality in a simplified, monumental, and religious version of Renaissance ideals. In other ways it delved even deeper into Classical modes and a kind of super-realism based on using peasants as models and the exaggerated *chiaroscuro* (interplay or contrast of light and dark) of Italian painter Caravaggio.

Some view those two movements as extensions of Renaissance experiments, and find the true baroque in later compositions—all explosions of dynamic fury, movement, color, and figures—that are well-balanced, but in such cluttered abundance as to appear untamed. **Rococo** is this later baroque art gone awry, frothy, and chaotic.

Significant practitioners of the baroque with examples in the **Louvre** include:

- **Nicolas Poussin** (1594–1665). The most Classical French painter, Poussin created mythological scenes that presaged the Romantic movement. His balance and predilection to paint from nature influenced French Impressionists such as Cézanne.
- **Antoine Watteau** (1684–1721). Watteau indulged in the wild, untamed complexity of the rococo. Cruise the Louvre for his colorful, theatrical works. He began the short-lived *fête galante* style that featured china-doll figures against stylized landscapes of woodlands or ballrooms.

- **François Boucher** (1703–70). Louis XV's rococo court painter, Boucher studied Watteau and produced lots of decorative landscapes and genre works.
- **Jean Honoré Fragonard** (1732–1806). Boucher's student and the master of rococo, Fragonard painted an overindulgence of pink-cheeked, genteel lovers frolicking against billowing treescapes. The Louvre hangs his famous *The Bathers.*

NEOCLASSICAL & ROMANTIC (1770–1890)

As the baroque got excessive, the rococo got cute, and the somber Counter-Reformation got serious about the limits on religious art, several artists looked for relief to the ancients. Viewing new excavations of Greek and Roman sites (Pompeii and Paestum) and statuary became integral parts of the Grand Tour through Italy, while the Enlightenment (and growing Revolutionary) interest in Greek democracy beat an intellectual path to the distant past. This gave rise to a **neoclassical** artistic style that emphasized symmetry, austerity, clean lines, and Classical themes, such as depictions of events from history or mythology.

The **Romantics,** on the other hand, felt both the ancients and the Renaissance had gotten it wrong and that the Middle Ages was the place to be. They idealized Romantic tales of chivalry and held a deep respect for nature, human rights, and the nobility of peasantry, and a suspicion of progress. Their paintings were heroic, historic, and (melo)dramatic, and quested for beauty.

Some great artists and movements of the era, all with examples in the **Louvre,** include:

- **Jacques Louis David** (1748–1825). David dropped the baroque after a year of study in Rome exposed him to neoclassicism, which he brought back to Paris and displayed in such paintings as *The Oath of the Horatii* (1784) and *Coronation of Napoléon and Josephine* (1805–08).
- **Jean Ingres** (1780–1867). Trained with David, Ingres become a defender of the neoclassicists and the Royal French Academy, and opposed the Romantics. His *Grand Odalisque* (1814) hangs in the Louvre.
- **Theodore Géricault** (1791–1824). One of the great early Romantics, Géricault painted the large, dramatic history painting *The Raft of the Medusa* (1819), which served as a model for the movement.
- **Eugène Delacroix** (1798–1863). His *Liberty Leading the People* (1830) was painted in the Romantic style, but the artist was also experimenting with color and brushstroke.
- **The Barbizon School.** This school of landscape painters, founded in the 1830s by **Théodore Rousseau** (1812–67), painted directly from nature at Barbizon near Paris. **Jean François Millet** (1814–75) preferred classical scenes and local peasants; his works are at the **Musée d'Orsay. Jean Baptiste Camille Corot** (1796–1875), the third Barbizon great, was a sort of idealistic proto-Impressionist.

IMPRESSIONISM (1870–1920)

Formal, rigid neoclassicism and idealized Romanticism rankled some late 19th-century artists interested in painting directly from nature. Seeking to capture the *impression* light made reflecting off objects, they adopted a free, open style; deceptively loose compositions; swift, visible brushwork; and often light colors. For subject matter, they turned away from the Classical themes of previous styles to landscapes and scenes of modern life. Unless specified below, you'll find some of the best examples of their works in the **Musée d'Orsay.**

Impressionist greats include:

- **Edouard Manet** (1832–83). His groundbreaking *Picnic on the Grass* (1863) and *Olympia* (1863) weren't Impressionism proper, but they helped inspire the movement with their harsh realism, visible brushstrokes, and thick outlines.
- **Claude Monet** (1840–1926). The Impressionist movement officially began with an 1874 exhibition in which Monet exhibited his loose, Turner-inspired *Impression, Sunrise* (1874), now in the **Musée Marmottan,** which one critic picked to lambaste the whole exhibition, deriding it all as "Impressionist." Far from being insulted, the anti-establishment artists in the show adopted the word for their exhibits, held through the 1880s.
- **Pierre Auguste Renoir** (1841–1919). Originally, Renoir was a porcelain painter, which helps explain his figures' ivory skin and chubby pink cheeks.
- **Edgar Degas** (1834–1917). Degas was an accomplished painter, sculptor, and draughtsman—his pastels of dancers and bathers are particularly memorable.
- **Auguste Rodin** (1840–1917). The greatest Impressionist-era sculptor, Rodin crafted remarkably expressive bronzes, refusing to idealize the human figure as had his neoclassical predecessors. The **Musée Rodin,** his former Paris studio, contains, among other works, his *Burghers of Calais* (1886), *The Kiss* (1886–98), and *The Thinker* (1880).

POST-IMPRESSIONISM (1880–1930)

Few experimental French artists of the late 19th century were technically Impressionists, though many were friends with those in the movement. The smaller movements or styles are usually lumped together as "Post-Impressionist."

Again, you'll find the best examples of their works at the **Musée d'Orsay,** though you'll find pieces by Matisse, Chagall, and the Cubists, including Picasso, in the **Centre Pompidou.** Important Post-Impressionists include:

- **Paul Cézanne** (1839–1906). He adopted the short brushstrokes, love of landscape, and light color palate of his Impressionist friends, but Cézanne was more formal and deliberate in his style. He sought to give his art monumentality and permanence, even if the subjects were simple still-lifes, portraits, or landscapes.
- **Paul Gauguin** (1848–1903). Gauguin could never settle himself or his work, trying Brittany first, where he developed **Synthetism** (black outlines around solid colors), and later hopping around the South Pacific, where he was inspired by local styles and colors.
- **Georges Seurat** (1859–91), **Paul Signac** (1863–1935), and **Camille Jacob Pissarro** (1830–1903). Together these artists developed **Divisionism** and its more formal cousin **pointillism.** Rather than mixing, say, yellow and blue paint together to make green, they applied tiny dots of yellow and blue right next to each other so that the viewer's eye mixes them together to make green.
- **Henri de Toulouse-Lautrec** (1864–1901). Most famous for his work with thinned-down oils, Toulouse-Lautrec created paintings and posters of wispy, fluid lines anticipating Art Nouveau and often depicting the bohemian life of Paris's dance halls and cafes. In Montmartre you can still visit the **Moulin Rouge,** the cabaret he immortalized on canvas.

- **Vincent van Gogh** (1853–90) spent most of his tortured artistic career in France. He combined Divisionism, Synthetism, and a touch of Japanese influence, and painted with thick, short strokes. Never particularly accepted by any artistic circle, he is the most popular painter in the world today (his paintings fetch record sums at auction, and he sells more postcards and posters than any other artist), even though he sold only one painting in his short life.

- **Henri Matisse** (1869–1954). He took a hint from Synthetism and added wild colors and strong patterns to create **Fauvism** (a critic described those who used the style as *fauves,* meaning "wild beasts"). Matisse continued exploring these themes even when most artists were turning to Cubism. When his health failed, he began assembling brightly colored collages of paper cutouts.

- **Pablo Picasso** (1881–1973). Along with **Georges Braque** (1882–1963), this Barcelona-born artist painted objects from all points of view at once, rather than use optical tricks like perspective to fool viewers into seeing three dimensions. The fractured result was **Cubism** and was expanded upon by the likes of **Fernand Léger** (1881–1955) and **Juan Gris** (1887–1927), while Picasso moved on to other styles. You can see all of his periods at the **Musée Picasso** in the Marais.

2 Architecture 101

While each architectural era has its distinctive features, there are some elements, general floor plans, and terms common to many.

From the Romanesque period on, most **churches** consist either of a single wide **aisle,** or a wide central **nave** flanked by two narrow aisles. A row of **columns,** or square stacks of masonry called **piers,** connected by **arches,** separates the aisles from the nave.

This main nave/aisle assemblage is usually crossed by a perpendicular corridor called a **transept** near the far, east end of the church so that the floor plan looks like a Latin cross (shaped like a lowercase "t"). At the east end sits the holy **altar.** This is usually on a raised dais and in the entrance to—or, especially later, just in front of—the large **chapel** formed by the shorter, far end of the cross. If this large, main chapel is rounded off on the end, it is called an **apse;** it is often elongated and filled with the stalls of the **choir.** Some churches, especially after the Renaissance when mathematical proportion became important, were built on a Greek Cross plan, each axis the same length, like a giant "+."

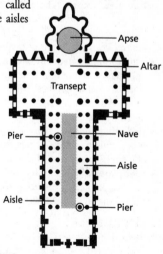

Church Floor Plan

It's worth pointing out that very few buildings (especially churches) were built in one particular style. These massive, expensive structures often took centuries to complete, during which time tastes would change and plans would be altered.

ANCIENT ROMAN (BC 125–450 AD)

France was Rome's first transalpine conquest, and the legions of Julius Caesar quickly subdued the Celtic tribes across France, converting it into Roman Gaul and importing Roman building concepts.

IDENTIFIABLE FEATURES
- The **load-bearing arch.**
- The use of **concrete and brick.**

BEST EXAMPLES
- **Parvis Archaeological Excavations.** The Romanized village of Lutèce, later renamed after its native *Parisii* tribe of Celtic Gauls, is partially excavated under place du Parvis in front of Notre-Dame.
- **Musée de Cluny.** This medieval monastery was built on top of a **Roman baths complex,** remnants of which are still visible on the grounds outside and in the huge preserved *frigidarium* (the cold water bath) that is now a room of the museum. The museum itself also contains ancient statuary.

ROMANESQUE (800–1100)

Romanesque architects concentrated on building large churches with wide aisles to accommodate the population that came to hear Mass and worship at the altars of various saints. The Romanesque took its inspiration from ancient Rome (hence the name). Early Christians in Italy had adapted the basilica (ancient Roman law-court buildings) to become churches. Few examples of the Romanesque remain in Paris, however, with most churches having been rebuilt in later eras.

IDENTIFIABLE FEATURES
- **Rounded arches.** These load-bearing architectural devices allowed the architects to open up wide naves and spaces, channeling all that weight of the stone walls and ceiling across the curve of the arch and down into the ground via the columns or pilasters.
- **Thick walls, infrequent and small windows, and huge piers.** These were necessary to support the weight of all that masonry, giving Romanesque churches a dark, somber, mysterious, and often oppressive feeling.
- **Apse.** This rounded space behind the altar in many Romanesque churches opens up the holiest, east end of the church.
- **Radiating chapels.** These smaller chapels began to sprout off the east end of the church, especially later in the Romanesque period, often in the form of a fan of minichapels radiating off the **apse** (see above).
- **Ambulatory.** This curving corridor separates the altar and choir area from the ring of smaller, **radiating chapels** (see above). This, too, was a convention of the later Romanesque and carried into the Gothic.

BEST EXAMPLES
- **St-Germain-des-Prés.** The overall building is Romanesque, including the fine sculpted column capitals near the entrance of the left aisle; only the far left corner is original, the others are copies. By the time builders got to creating the choir, the early Gothic was on—note the pointy arches. Over the (early Renaissance) portal is a Romanesque carving of the *Last Judgment.*
- **St-Julien-le-Pauvre.** This small church has a general Romanesque plan overwritten by later Gothic embellishments, including the facade.

GOTHIC (1100–1500)

By the 12th century, engineering developments freed church architecture from the heavy, thick walls of Romanesque structures and allowed ceilings to soar, walls to thin, and windows to proliferate.

Instead of dark, somber, relatively unadorned Romanesque interiors that forced the eyes of the faithful toward the altar, the Gothic interior enticed the churchgoers' gaze upward to high ceilings filled with light. The priests still conducted Mass in Latin, but now peasants could "read" the stories told in pictures in the stained glass windows.

The squat, brooding exteriors of the Romanesque fortresses of God were replaced by graceful buttresses and spires that soared above town centers.

IDENTIFIABLE FEATURES

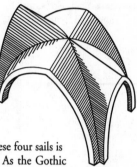

Cross Vault

- **Pointed arches.** The most significant development of the Gothic era was the discovery that pointed arches could carry far more weight than rounded ones.
- **Cross vaults.** Instead of being flat, the square patch of ceiling between four columns arches up to a point in the center, creating four sail shapes, sort of like the underside of a pyramid. The **X** separating these four sails is often reinforced with ridges called **ribbing.** As the Gothic progressed, four-sided cross vaults became six- or eight-sided as architects played with the angles.
- **Flying buttresses.** These free-standing exterior pillars connected by graceful, thin arms of stone help channel the weight of the building and its roof out and down into the ground. To help counter the cross forces involved in this engineering sleight of hand, the piers of buttresses were often topped by heavy pinnacles, which took the form of minispires or statues.
- **Spires.** These pinnacles of masonry seem to defy gravity and reach toward heaven itself.
- **Gargoyles.** Disguised as wide-mouthed creatures, gargoyles are actually drain spouts.
- **Tracery.** These lacy spider webs of carved stone grace the pointy ends of windows and sometimes the spans of ceiling vaults.
- **Stained glass.** Because pointy arches can carry more weight than rounded ones, windows could be larger and more numerous. They were often filled with Bible stories and symbolism writ in the colorful patterns of stained glass.
- **Rose windows.** Huge circular windows filled with **tracery** (see above) and "petals" of stained glass, rose windows often appear as the centerpiece of facades and, in some larger churches, at the ends of transepts as well.

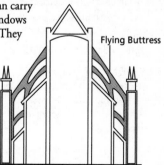

Flying Buttress

Cross Section of Gothic Church

- **Ambulatory.** The Gothic made much greater use of this corridor of space wrapping behind the apse and often around a **choir** (the boxed-off area, usually behind the altar, where the choir sat and sang).
- **Choir screen.** Serving as the inner wall of the ambulatory and the outer wall of the choir section, choir screens are often decorated with carvings or tombs.

BEST EXAMPLES

- **Basilique St-Denis** (1140–1144). Today you'll find the world's first Gothic cathedral in a Paris suburb.
- **Cathédrale de Chartres** (1194–1220). This Gothic masterpiece boasts good statuary, a soaring spire, and some 150 glorious stained glass windows.
- **Cathédrale de Notre-Dame** (1163–1250). This famous cathedral possesses pinnacled flying buttresses, a trio of France's best rose windows, good portal carvings, a choir screen of deeply carved reliefs, and spiffy gargoyles (though many of those are actually 19th-century Neo-Gothic).

Cathédrale de Chartres

RENAISSANCE (1500–1630)

In architecture, as in painting, the Renaissance came from Italy and was only slowly Frenchified. And, as in painting, its rules stressed proportion, order, Classical inspiration, and precision to create unified, balanced structures.

IDENTIFIABLE FEATURES

- **Proportion and symmetry.** Other than a close eye to these Renaissance ideals, little specifically identifies buildings of this period.
- **Steeply pitched roofs.** Many roofs are of pale stone with dark gray tiles. This feature is a throwback to medieval sensibilities, but because almost no medieval mansions survive in Paris, the buildings that *do* sport steep roofs tend to be Renaissance.
- **Dormer windows.** These tend to be tall and made of stone, which differentiates them from the less extravagant, wooden ones of later periods.

BEST EXAMPLES

- **Hôtel Carnavalet** (1544). Another example of a Renaissance mansion, this is the only 16th-century hotel left in Paris. It contains the **Musée Carnavalet,** a museum devoted to the history of Paris and the French Revolution.

- **Place des Vosges.** This square is lined by Renaissance mansions rising above a lovely arcaded corridor that wraps all the way around.

CLASSICISM & ROCOCO (1630–1800)

While Italy and Germany embraced the opulent baroque, France took the fundamentals of Renaissance **Classicism** even further, becoming more imitative of ancient models—this represents a change from the Renaissance preference to find inspiration in the Classic era.

During the reign of Louis XIV, art and architecture were subservient to political ends. Buildings were grandiose and severely ordered on the Versailles model. Opulence was saved for interior decoration, which increasingly (especially from 1715 to 1750, after the death of Louis XIV) became an excessively detailed and self-indulgent **rococo** (*rocaille* in French). Externally, this later style is only noticeable by a greater elegance and delicacy.

Rococo tastes didn't last long, though, and soon a **neoclassical** movement was raising structures, such as Paris's **Panthéon** (1758), even more strictly based on ancient models than the earlier Classicism was.

IDENTIFIABLE FEATURES

- **Symmetrical, rectangular structures.** French Classicism concentrated on horizontal and vertical lines and simple proportions.

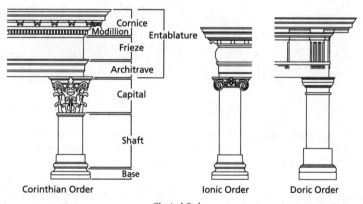

Cornice
Modillion
Entablature
Frieze
Architrave
Capital
Shaft
Base

Corinthian Order   Ionic Order   Doric Order

Classical Orders

- **Classical throwbacks.** Classicism was favored for the very fact that it brought back such elements as Classical orders (Doric, Ionic, and Corinthian) and projecting central sections topped by triangular pediments.
- **Mansard roofs.** A defining feature and true French trademark developed by **François Mansart** (1598–1666) in the early 15th century, a mansard roof has a double slope, the lower being longer and steeper than the upper.

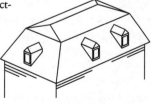

Mansard Roof

- **Dormer windows.** Unlike the larger Renaissance ones flanked by showy stone scrolls, later dormers tended to be lower, less extravagant, and wooden.
- *Oeil-de-bouef* **windows.** These small, round "ox-eye" windows poke out of the roof's slope.
- **Excessive detail.** Rococo interior decoration is often asymmetrical and abstract with shell-like forms and many **C**- and **S**-curves. Naturalistic flowers and trees are sometimes playfully introduced.

BEST EXAMPLES

- **Palais du Louvre** (1650–1670). A collaborative Classical masterpiece, the Louvre was designed as a palace. **Le Vau** (1612–70) was its chief architect, along with collaborators **François Mansart,** the interior decorator **Charles Le Brun** (1619–90), and the unparalleled landscape gardener **André Le Nôtre** (1613–1700). The structure subsequently had several purposes (see chapter 7 for the complete history) before becoming a museum.
- **Château de Versailles** (1669–1685). Versailles is France's—indeed, Europe's—grandest palace, the Divine Monarchy writ as a statement of fussily decorative, politically charged Classical architecture, though the interior was redecorated in more flamboyant styles. The chief architects of its complete overhaul under Louis XIV were the oft-used team (see Palais du Lou-

Château de Versailles

vre, above) of Le Vau, Mansart, Le Brun, and Le Nôtre. Mansart's grand-nephew (and Louis XIV's chief architect) **Jules Hardouin-Mansart** (1646–1708) took over after Le Vau's death, changing much of the exterior look. The **Clock Room** is a good example of rococo interior decoration.
- **Panthéon** (1758). This Left Bank monument is a perfect example of the strict neoclassical style.

THE 19TH CENTURY

Architectural styles in 19th-century Paris were eclectic, beginning in a severe Classical mode and ending with an identity crisis torn between Industrial Age technology and Art Nouveau organic. The "Identifiable Features" section explores the main facets of competing styles during this turbulent century.

IDENTIFIABLE FEATURES

- **First Empire.** Elegant, neoclassical furnishings—distinguished by strong lines often accented with a simple curve—became the rage during Napoleon's reign.
- **Second Empire.** Napoleon III's reign saw the eclectic Second Empire reinterpret Classicism in an ornate, dramatic mode. Urban planning was the architectural rage, and Paris became a city of wide boulevards courtesy of **Baron Georges-Eugène Haussmann** (1809–91), commissioned by

Napoleon III in 1852 to redesign the city. Paris owes much of its remarkably unified look to Haussmann, who drew his beloved thoroughfares directly across the city, tearing down existing structures along the way. He lined the boulevards with simple, six-story apartment blocks, like elongated 18th-century town houses with continuous balconies wrapping around the third and sixth floors and mansard roofs with dormer windows.

- **Third Republic.** Expositions in 1878, 1889, and 1900 were the catalysts for constructing huge glass-and-steel structures that showed off modern techniques and the engineering prowess of the Industrial Revolution. This produced such Parisian monuments as the Tour Eiffel and Sacré-Coeur.
- **Art Nouveau.** These architects and decorators rebelled against the Third Republic era of mass production by stressing the uniqueness of craft. They created asymmetrical, curvaceous designs based on organic inspiration (plants and flowers) in such mediums as wrought iron, stained glass, tile, and hand-painted wallpaper.

BEST EXAMPLES

- **Palais de Fontainebleau.** Napoleon spent his Imperial decade (1804–14) refurbishing his quarters in this palace in First Empire style.
- **Arc de Triomphe** (1836). Napoleon's oversize imitation of a Roman triumphal arch is the ultimate paean to the Classical era. The arch presides over **L'Etoile,** an intersection of 12 wide boulevards laid out by Baron Haussmann in the Second Empire.
- **Tour Eiffel** (1889). Under the Third Republic, the French wanted to show how far they had come in the 100 years since the Revolution. They hired **Gustave Eiffel** (1832–1923) to slap together the world's tallest structure, a temporary 1,051-foot tower made of riveted steel girders. Everyone agreed it was tall; most thought it was ugly and completely lacking in aesthetics. Its usefulness as a radio transmitter saved Eiffel's tower from being torn down.
- **Métro station entrances.** Art Nouveau was less an architectural mode than a decorative movement. You can still find some of the original Art Nouveau Métro entrances designed by **Hector Guimard** (1867–1942). (A recently renovated entrance is at the Porte Dauphine station on the No. 2 line.)

THE 20TH CENTURY

France commissioned some ambitious architectural projects in the

Tour Eiffel

last century, most of them the *grand projets* of the late François Mitterrand. The majority were considered controversial or even offensive when completed. Only slowly have structures such as the Centre Pompidou or Louvre's glass pyramids become accepted. Over time, a lucky few may even become as beloved as the once-despised Tour Eiffel.

IDENTIFIABLE FEATURES

Other than a concerted effort to be unique, break convention, and look stunningly modern, nothing communally identifies France's recent architecture.

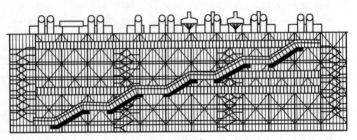

Centre Pompidou

BEST EXAMPLES

- **Centre Pompidou** (1977). Brit Richard Rogers (b. 1933) and Italian Renzo Piano (b. 1937) turned architecture inside out—literally—to craft Paris's eye-popping modern-art museum. Exposed pipes, steel supports, and plastic-tube escalators wrap around the exterior.
- **Louvre's glass pyramids** (1989). Chinese-American architect I. M. Pei (b. 1917) was called in to cap the Louvre's new underground entrance with the pyramids in the center of the Palais du Louvre's 17th-century courtyard.
- **Opera Bastille** (1989). In 1989, Paris's opera company moved into this curvaceous, dark glass mound of space designed by Canadian Carlos Ott. (Unfortunately, the acoustics have been lambasted.)

3

Planning Your Trip to Paris

This chapter provides the nuts-and-bolts details you need before setting off for Paris—everything from information sources to money matters to the major airlines and how to save money on your flight.

1 Visitor Information

TOURIST OFFICES

Your best source of information is the **French Government Tourist Office,** which you can reach at the following addresses:

IN THE UNITED STATES 444 Madison Ave., 16th Floor, New York, NY 10022 (© 212/838-7800; fax 212/838-7855); 676 N. Michigan Ave., Suite 3360, Chicago, IL 60611 (© 312/751-7800; fax 312/337-6339); 9454 Wilshire Blvd., Suite 715, Beverly Hills, CA 90212 (© 310/271-6665; fax 310/276-2835). To request information at any of these offices, call the **France on Call** hot line at © 900/990-0040.

IN CANADA Maison de la France/French Government Tourist Office, 1981 av. McGill College, Suite 490, Montréal, PQ H3A 2W9 (© 514/876-9881; fax 514/845-4868).

IN THE UNITED KINGDOM Maison de la France /French Government Tourist Office, 178 Piccadilly, London, W1J 9AL (© 090/6824-4123; fax 020/7943-6594).

IN IRELAND Maison de la France/French Government Tourist Office, 10 Suffolk St., Dublin 2, Ireland (© 01/679-0813; fax 01/880-7772).

IN AUSTRALIA French Tourist Bureau, 25 Bligh St., Sydney, NSW 2000 (© 02/9231-5244; fax 02/9221-8682).

WEBSITES

The French Government Tourist Office's home on the Internet is at www.francetourism.com.

For general information, see "Planning Your Trip Online" later in this chapter. For more Paris-related websites, see "The Best Websites for Paris" box on p. 12.

2 Entry Requirements & Customs Regulations

ENTRY REQUIREMENTS

All non-French nationals need a **valid passport** to enter France (check its expiration date). The French government no longer requires visas for **U.S. citizens,** provided they're staying less than 90 days. For longer stays, they must apply for a long-term visa, residence card, or temporary-stay visa.

Each requires proof of income or a viable means of support in France and a legitimate purpose for remaining in the country. Applications are available from the **Consulate Section of the French Embassy,** 4101 Reservoir Rd. NW, Washington, DC 20007 (© 202/944-6000), or from the **Visa Section of the French Consulate,** 10 E. 74th

> ### ⓒ Destination: Paris—Red Alert Checklist
>
> - Citizens of EU countries can cross into France for as long as they wish. Citizens of other countries must have a passport.
> - If you purchased traveler's checks, have you recorded the check numbers and stored the documentation separately from the checks?
> - Did you pack your camera and an extra set of camera batteries, and purchase enough film? If you packed film in your checked baggage, did you invest in protective pouches to shield film from airport x-rays?
> - Did you bring your ID cards that could entitle you to discounts such as AAA and AARP cards, student IDs, etc.?
> - Did you bring copies of your drug prescriptions, extra glasses, and/ or contact lenses?
> - Do you have your credit-card PINs?
> - If you have an E-ticket, do you have documentation?
> - Did you leave a copy of your itinerary with someone at home?
> - Did you check to see if any travel advisories have been issued by the **U.S. State Department** (http://travel.state.gov/travel_warnings.html) regarding your destination?
> - Do you have the address and phone number of your country's embassy with you?

St., New York, NY 10021 (ⓒ **212/ 606-3689**). Visas are required for students planning to study in France even if the stay is less than 90 days.

At this writing, citizens of Australia, Canada, New Zealand, Switzerland, Japan, and European Union countries do not need visas.

If your passport is lost or stolen, go to your consulate as soon as possible for a replacement.

Passport applications can be downloaded at these websites: http:// travel. state.gov (U.S.); www.dfait-maeci.gc. ca/passport (Canada); http://www. passport.gov.uk/ (U.K.); http://www. irlgov.ie/iveagh/services/passports/pass portforms.htm (Ireland); www.dfat. gov.au/passports (Australia).

CUSTOMS REGULATIONS
WHAT YOU CAN BRING INTO
FRANCE   Customs restrictions differ for citizens of European Union (EU) countries and non-EU countries.

For Non-EU Nationals   You can bring in, duty-free, 200 cigarettes, 20 cigarillos, 50 cigars, or 250 grams of smoking tobacco. This amount is doubled if you live outside Europe. You can also bring in 2 liters of wine and either 1 liter of alcohol over 22 proof or 2 liters of wine under 22 proof. In addition, you can bring in 50 grams (1.75 oz.) of perfume, a quarter liter (250ml) of eau de toilette, 500 grams (1 lb.) of coffee, and 200 grams (half pound) of tea. Visitors 15 and over may bring in other goods totaling 182.40€ ($163); the allowance for those 14 and under is 91.20€ ($81). (Customs officials tend to be lenient about general merchandise, realizing the limits are unrealistically low.)

For EU Citizens   Visitors from European Union countries can bring into France any amount of goods as long as they're intended for their personal use—not for resale.

WHAT YOU CAN BRING HOME

U.S. Citizens If you've been out of the country for 48 hours or more, you can bring back $400 worth of goods (per person) without paying a duty. On the first $1,000 worth of goods over $400 you pay a flat 10%. Beyond that, it works on an item-by-item basis. There are a few restrictions on amount: 1 liter of alcohol (you must be over 21), 200 cigarettes, and 100 cigars. Antiques over 100 years old and works of art are exempt from the $400 limit, as is anything you mail home. Once per day, you can mail yourself $200 worth of goods duty-free; mark the package "For Personal Use." You can mail other people up to $100 worth of goods per person per day; label each package "Unsolicited Gift." Any package must state on the exterior a description of the contents and their values. You can't mail alcohol, perfume (it contains alcohol), or tobacco products.

For more details on regulations, visit the **U.S. Customs Service** website at www.customs.ustreas.gov or contact the office at P.O. Box 7407, Washington, DC 20044 (*©* **202/354-1000**), to request the free *Know Before You Go* pamphlet.

To prevent the spread of diseases, you can't bring in any plants, fruits, vegetables, meats, or other foodstuffs. This includes cured meats like salami. You may bring in the following: baked goods, all but the softest cheeses (the rule is vague, but if the cheese is at all spreadable, don't risk confiscation), candies, roasted coffee beans and dried tea, fish (packaged salmon is okay), seeds for veggies and flowers (but not for trees), and mushrooms. Check out the USDA's website at www.aphis. usda.gov/oa/travel.html for more details.

For Canadian Citizens For a summary of Canadian rules, write for the booklet *I Declare,* issued by the **Canadian Customs and Revenue Agency,** 333 Dunsmuir St., Vancouver, B.C., V6B 5R4 CANADA (*©* **800/461-9999**), or check out the website www. ccra-adrc.gc.ca. Canada allows its citizens a $750 exemption if you're gone more than 7 days ($200 if you're gone between 48 hr. and 7 days), and you're allowed to bring back, duty-free, 200 cigarettes, 50 cigars, and 1.5 liters of wine *or* 1.14 liters of liquor *or* 8.5 liters of beer or ale. You're also allowed to mail gifts to Canada at the rate of $60 a day, provided they're unsolicited and aren't alcohol or tobacco (write on the package "Unsolicited Gift, Under $60 Value").

For U.K. Citizens You'll go through a separate Customs exit (the "Blue Exit") especially for EU travelers. You can bring home almost as much as you like of any goods from any EU country (theoretical limits run along the lines of "90 litres of wine"). If you're returning home from a non-EU country, you're allowed to bring home 200 cigarettes, 2 liters of table wine plus 1 liter of spirits or 2 liters of fortified or sparkling wine, 60 milliliters/cubic centimeters of perfume, 250 milliliters/cubic centimeters of toilet water, and a total of £145 in other goods. For more information, get in touch with **Her Majesty's Customs and Excise Office,** Berkeley House, 304 Regents Park Rd., Finchley, London N3 2JY (*©* **0845/010-9000** in central London; call 020/7202-4227 for other locations), or check out its website at www.open.gov.uk.

For Australian Citizens The duty-free allowance in Australia is A$400 or for those under 18, A$200. Upon returning to Australia, citizens can bring in 250 cigarettes or 250 grams of loose tobacco and 1.125 liters of alcohol. A brochure available from Australian consulates or Customs offices is *Know Before You Go.* For more information, contact **Australian Customs Service,** GPO Box 8, Sydney NSW 2001 (*©* **02-921-32-000**

within Australia or 02/6275-6666 from overseas; www.customs.gov.au).

For New Zealand Citizens The duty-free allowance for New Zealand is NZ$700. Citizens over 17 can bring back 200 cigarettes or 50 cigars or 250 grams of tobacco (or a mix of all three of these if their combined weight does not exceed 250g); plus 4.5 liters of wine or beer, plus 1.125 liters of liquor. Most questions are answered in a free pamphlet that's available at New Zealand consulates and Customs offices entitled *New Zealand Customs Guide for Travelers, Notice no. 4.* For more information, contact **New Zealand Customs,** 50 Anzac Ave., P.O. Box 29, Auckland (℃ **09/359-6655**).

3 Money

CURRENCY

The **euro,** the new single European currency, became the official currency of France and 11 other participating countries on January 1, 1999.

The euro didn't go into general circulation until January 1, 2002. The old currency, the French franc, disappeared into history on March 1, 2002, replaced by the euro, which is officially abbreviated as "EUR," or €. Exchange rates of participating countries are locked into a common currency fluctuating against the dollar.

For more details on the euro, check out www.europa.eu.int/euro.

ATMS

ATMs are prevalent in Paris and its outlying regions. ATMs are linked to a national network that most likely includes your bank at home. Both the **Cirrus** (℃ **800/424-7787;** www.mastercard.com) and the **Plus** (℃ **800/843-7587;** www.visa.com) networks have automated ATM locators listing the banks in France that'll accept your card. Or, just search out any machine with your network's symbol emblazoned on it.

Important note: Make sure that the PINs on your bank cards and credit cards will work in France. You'll need

The U.S. Dollar, the British Pound & the Euro

Euro	U.S.$	U.K.£	Euro	U.S.$	U.K.£
1	0.89	0.70	75	66.98	52.50
2	1.79	1.40	100	89.30	70.00
3	2.68	2.10	125	111.63	87.50
4	3.57	2.80	150	133.95	105.00
5	4.47	3.50	175	156.28	122.50
6	5.36	4.20	200	178.60	140.00
7	6.25	4.90	225	200.93	157.50
8	7.14	5.60	250	223.25	175.00
9	8.04	6.30	275	245.58	192.50
10	8.93	7.00	300	267.90	210.00
15	13.40	10.50	350	312.55	245.00
20	17.86	14.00	400	357.20	280.00
25	22.33	17.50	500	446.50	350.00
50	44.65	35.00	1,000	893.00	700.00

Fun Fact **Introducing the Euro (€)**

In January of 2002, the largest money-changing operation in history led to the deliberate obsolescence of many of Europe's currencies, including the French franc. Replacing the franc is the euro, a currency that, at this writing, was based on the fiscal participation of a dozen European nations.

For Americans: One euro equals approximately U.S.89¢, and U.S.$1 equals approximately 1.12€. This is the approximate rate of exchange used to calculate the dollar values throughout this book. Amounts have been rounded off.

For Britons: Great Britain still uses the pound sterling, with 1€ equaling approximately 70 pence, and £1 equaling approximately 1.43€. This was the rate of exchange used to calculate the pound sterling values laid out in the table "The U.S. Dollar, the British Pound & the Euro."

Note: The relative value of the euro fluctuates against the U.S. dollar, the pound sterling, and most of the world's other currencies, and its value might not be the same by the time you travel to France. Consequently, this table should be used as an indication of approximate values.

Exchange rates are more favorable at the point of arrival. Nevertheless, it's helpful to exchange a little money before leaving (standing in line at the **cambio** [exchange bureau] in the Paris airport could make you miss the next bus leaving for downtown). Check with your local American Express or Thomas Cook offices or major banks. Or, order euros in advance from **American Express** (© 800/221-7282; www. americanexpress.com), **Thomas Cook** (© 800/223-7373; www.thomas cook.com), or **Capital for Foreign Exchange** (© 888/842-0880).

It's best to exchange currency or traveler's checks at a bank, not a cambio, hotel, or shop. Currency and traveler's checks (for which you'll receive a better rate than cash) can be changed at all principal airports and at some travel agencies, such as American Express and Thomas Cook. Note the rates and ask about commission fees; it can sometimes pay to shop around and ask the right questions.

a **four-digit code** (six digits won't work), so if you have a six-digit code, you'll have to go into your bank and get a new PIN for your trip. If you're unsure about this, contact Cirrus or Plus (see above). Be sure to check the daily withdrawal limit at the same time.

TRAVELER'S CHECKS

These days, traveler's checks seem less necessary in Paris, as there are many 24-hour ATMs that allow you to withdraw small amounts of cash as needed. But if you prefer the security of the tried and true, you might want to stick with traveler's checks—provided that you don't mind showing ID every time you want to cash a check.

You can get traveler's checks at almost any bank. **American Express** offers denominations of $20, $50, $100, $500, and (for cardholders only) $1,000. You'll pay a service charge

---

> **_Tips_ Fast Cash in an Emergency**
>
> If you need emergency cash over the weekend when all banks and American Express offices are closed, you can have money wired to you from **Western Union** (© 800/325-6000; www.westernunion.com), which has dozens of locations in Paris.

---

ranging from 1% to 4%. You can also get American Express traveler's checks over the phone by calling © 800/221-7782; Amex gold and platinum cardholders who use this number are exempt from the 1% fee. AAA members can obtain checks without a fee at most AAA offices.

Visa offers traveler's checks at Citibank locations nationwide, and at other banks. The service charge ranges between 1.5% and 2%; checks come in denominations of $20, $50, $100, $500, and $1,000. Call © 800/732-1322 for information. **MasterCard** also offers traveler's checks. Call

© 800/ 223-9920 for a location near you.

CREDIT CARDS

Credit cards are invaluable when traveling—they're a safe way to carry money and a convenient record of all your expenses. You can also withdraw cash advances from your cards at any bank (although this should be reserved for emergencies because you'll start paying hefty interest the moment you receive the cash).

Note that many banks, including Chase and Citibank, charge a 2% to 3% service fee for transactions in a foreign currency.

---

4 When to Go

In August, Parisians traditionally leave for their annual holiday and put the city on a skeleton staff to serve visitors. July has also become a popular vacation month, with many restaurateurs taking a holiday then.

Hotels, especially first-class and deluxe, are easy to come by in July and August. Budget hotels, on the other hand, are likely to be full during these months of student invasion. You might also try to avoid the first 2 weeks in October, when the annual auto show attracts thousands of enthusiasts.

THE WEATHER: APRIL IN PARIS?

Balmy weather in Paris has prompted more popular songs and love ballads than weather conditions in any other city. But the weather here is actually quite fickle. Rain is more common than snow throughout the winter, prompting longtime residents to complain about the occasional bone-chilling dampness.

In recent years, Paris has had about 15 snow days a year, and there are only a few oppressively hot days (over 86°F) in summer. What will most likely chill a Parisian heart, however, are the winds that sweep along the city's boulevards, channeled by bordering buildings. Other than the occasional winds and rain (which add an undeniable drama to many of the city's panoramas), Paris offers some of the most pleasant weather of any capital in Europe, with an average temperature of 53°F.

Paris's Average Daytime Temperature & Rainfall

	Jan	Feb	Mar	Apr	May	June	July	Aug	Sept	Oct	Nov	Dec
Temp. °F	38	39	46	51	58	64	66	66	61	53	45	40
Rainfall (in.)	3.2	2.9	2.4	2.7	3.2	3.5	3.3	3.7	3.3	3.0	3.5	3.1

HOLIDAYS

Holidays in France are known as *jours fériés.* Shops and banks are closed, as well as many (but not all) restaurants and museums. Major holidays include January 1 (New Year's Day), April 20 (Easter), Ascension Day (40 days after Easter), Pentecost (seventh Sun after Easter), May 1 (May Day), May 8 (VE Day), July 14 (Bastille Day), August 15 (Assumption of the Virgin Mary), November 1 (All Saints' Day), November 11 (Armistice Day), and December 25 (Christmas).

PARIS CALENDAR OF EVENTS

Check the Paris Tourist Office website at **www.paris-touristoffice.com** and other websites listed in chapter 1 for up-to-the-minute details on these and other events.

January

International Ready-to-Wear Fashion Shows (Salon International de Prêt-à-Porter), Parc des Expositions, 15th arrondissement. Hundreds of designers, from the giants to the unknown, unveil their visions (hallucinations?) of what you will be wearing in 6 months. The event in the Porte de Versailles convention facilities is geared to wholesalers, retailers, buyers, journalists, and industry professionals, but for the 15€ to 23€ ($13–$20) entrance fee, the rules are usually bent for the merely fashion-conscious. Much more exclusive are the *défilés* (fashion shows) at the headquarters of houses like Lagerfeld, Lanvin, Courrèges, and Valentino. For details, call © 01-44-94-70-00. January 25 to January 28, 2003.

February

Special Exhibitions, Special Concerts: During Paris's grayest month, look for a splash of expositions and concerts designed to perk up the city. Concerts and theaters spring up at such diverse sites as the **Cité de la Musique,** 221 av. Jean-Jaurès, 19e (© 01-44-84-45-00; Métro: Porte-de-Pantin); the **Théâtre des Champs-Elysées,** 15 av. Montaigne, 8e (© 01-49-52-50-50; Métro: Alma-Marceau); and the **Maison Radio-France,** 116 av. du Président-Kennedy, 16e (© 01-56-40-15-16; Métro: Passy-Ranelagh). Also look for openings of new operas at the **Opéra Bastille,** 2 place de la Bastille, 4e (© 08-92-69-78-68; Métro: Bastille), operas and dance at the **Opéra Garnier,** place de l'Opéra, 9e (© 08-92-69-78-65), and concerts at the **Auditorium du Louvre,** 1er (© 01-40-20-51-51; Métro: Musée du Louvre), and the **Salle Cortot,** 78 rue Cardinet, 17e (© 01-47-63-85-72; Métro: Malesherbes). A copy of *Pariscope* or *L'Officiel des Spectacles* is the best info source.

March

Foire du Trône, Bois de Vincennes, 12e. A mammoth amusement park that its fans call France's largest country fair, the Foire du Trône boasts origins dating from 957, when merchants met with farmers to exchange grain and wine. This high-tech continuation of that tradition, held on the lawns of the Pelouse de Reuilly, has a Ferris wheel, carousels, acrobats, fire eaters, and diversions that seem like a Gallic Coney Island. It's open Sunday from noon to 1am, Monday to

Thursday from 2pm to midnight, and Friday and Saturday from 2pm to 1am. Call ☎ **01-46-27-52-29.** March 23 to May 23, 2003.

April

Fête de Jazz de Paris, citywide. Some of the world's best-known jazz artists descend on Paris for this 14-day fest. Clubs both high- and lowbrow throw open their doors. The atmosphere is dark and smoky, the crowds hip. For details, call ☎ **01-47-83-33-58.** April 30 to May 12, 2003.

International Marathon of Paris. Beginning on the Champs-Elysées at 9am, runners take over Paris's boulevards in a race that draws competitors from around the world. Depending on their speed and endurance, participants arrive at the finishing point on avenue Foch, 16th arrondissement, beginning about 2½ hours later. For details, call ☎ **01-41-33-15-68.** April 7, 2003.

Les Grandes Eaux Musicales, Versailles. These musical events are intended to re-create the atmosphere of the ancient regime. The fountains around the palace are turned on, with special emphasis on the Neptune Fountain, which sits squarely in front of the best view of the château. You can promenade in the garden and listen to the music of French composers (Couperin, Charpentier, and Lully) and others (Mozart or Haydn) whose careers thrived during the years of the palace's construction. The music is generally recorded, but live concerts take place every Sunday from 11:15am to 5:30pm. For details, call ☎ **01-30-83-78-00.** April to early October.

May

VE Day, citywide. The celebration commemorating the capitulation of the Nazis on May 7, 1945, lasts 4 days in Paris, with a parade along the Champs-Elysées and additional ceremonies in Reims. Pro-American sentiments are probably higher during this festival than at any other time of year. May 5 to May 8.

Grand Steeplechase de Paris, Auteuil and Longchamp racetracks, Bois de Boulogne. This is a counterpoint to the horse races conducted at Chantilly (see below). For details, call ☎ **01-49-10-20-30.** May 26, 2003.

French Open Tennis Championship, Stade Roland-Garros, 16th arrondissement. The Open features 10 days of Grand Slam men's and women's tennis, with European and South American players traditionally dominating on the hot, dusty red courts. For details, call ☎ **01-47-43-48-00.** May 27 to June 9, 2003.

Fête de St-Denis, St-Denis. This series presents a month of artfully contrived music in the burial place of the French kings, a grim early Gothic monument in this industrialized northern suburb. For details, call ☎ **01-48-13-12-10.** May 29 to June 29, 2003.

June

Prix du Jockey Club (first week of June) **& Prix Diane-Hermès** (second week of June), Hippodrome de Chantilly. Thoroughbreds from as far away as Kentucky and Brunei, as well as mounts sponsored by Europe's old and new fortunes, compete in a very civil competition broadcast around France and talked about in horsey circles around the world. On race days, as many as 30 trains depart from Paris's Gare du Nord for Chantilly, where they're met by free shuttle buses to the track. For details on this and all other equine events in this calendar, call ☎ **01-49-10-20-30.**

Paris Air Show, Le Bourget. This is where France's military-industrial complex shows off enough high-tech hardware to make anyone think twice about invading La Patrie. Fans, competitors, and industrial spies mob the airport's exhibition halls for a taste of what Gallic technocrats have wrought. For details, call ✆ **01-53-23-33-33.** June 15 to June 22, 2003.

Fête Chopin, Orangerie du Parc de Bagatelle, Versailles. Hear all the Chopin you ever wanted at these piano recitals from the works of the Polish exile who lived most of his life in Paris. For details, call ✆ **01-45-00-22-19.** June 19 to July 14.

Fête de la Musique, citywide. This celebration at the summer solstice is the one day that noise laws don't apply in Paris. Musicians and wannabes pour into the streets, where you can make music with anything, even if it means banging two garbage cans together or driving around blowing your car horn (illegal otherwise). You might hear anything from Russians playing balalaikas to Cubans playing salsa rhythms. There are musical parties in virtually all the open spaces, with more organized concerts at place de la Bastille and place de la République and in La Villette and the Latin Quarter. For details, call ✆ **01-40-03-94-70.** June 21, 2003.

Festival Musique en l'Ile. A series of concerts, most including dignified masses composed from the 17th to the late 19th centuries, are presented at the Church Saint Louis en l'Ile and the Church Saint-Germain-des-Prés. For more information, call La Toison d'Art at ✆ **01-44-62-00-55.** June 27 to September 1, 2003.

La Course des Garçons de Café, throughout the city. There's no more amusing race in Paris. Balancing heavy trays, the *garçons* (both waiters and waitresses) line up in front of the Hôtel de Ville in the 4th arrondissement, then race for 8km (5 miles) through the streets, ending at the Hôtel de Ville. Some obviously don't make it. A Sunday in the last week of June or first week of July.

La Villette Jazz Festival, La Villette. This homage to the art of jazz incorporates 50 concerts in churches, auditoriums, and concert halls in all neighborhoods of this Paris suburb. Past festivals have included Herbie Hancock, Shirley Horn, Michel Portal, and other artists from around the world. For details, call ✆ **08-03-30-63-06.** Late June to the first week in July.

July

Gay Pride Parade, place de la République to place de la Bastille. A week of expositions and parties climaxes in a parade patterned after those in New York and San Francisco. It's followed by a dance at the Palais de Bercy, a convention hall/sports arena. For details, see www.gaypride.fr. July 7, 2003.

Tour de France. This is Europe's most visible, highly contested, and overabundantly televised bicycle race. Crews of wind-tunnel–tested athletes speed along an itinerary tracing the six sides of the French "hexagon," detouring deep into the Massif Central and across the Swiss Alps. The race is decided at a finish line drawn across the Champs-Elysées. For details, call ✆ **01-41-33-15-00.** July 6 to July 28, 2003.

Bastille Day, citywide. This celebration of the 1789 storming of the Bastille is the birth date of modern France, and festivities reach their peak in Paris with street fairs, pageants, fireworks, and feasts. The day begins with a parade down the

Champs-Elysées and ends with fireworks in Montmartre. Wherever you are, before the end of the day you'll hear Piaf warbling "La Foule" ("The Crowd"), the song that celebrated her passion for the stranger she met and later lost in a crowd on Bastille Day, and lots of people singing "La Marseillaise." July 14, 2003.

Paris Quartier d'Eté, Latin Quarter. For 4 weeks the Arènes de Lutèce or the Sorbonne's Cour d'Honneur host pop orchestral concerts. The dozen or so concerts are grander than the outdoor setting would imply and include performances by the Orchestre de Paris, Orchestre National de France, and Baroque Orchestra of the European Union. On the fringes you can find plays, jazz, and parades in the Tuileries. For details, call ℂ **01-44-94-98-00** or fax 01-44-94-98-01. July 14 to August 15, 2003.

August

International Ready-to-Wear Fashion Shows (Salon International de Prêt-à-Porter), Parc des Expositions, 15th arrondissement. More of what took place at the fashion shows in January (see above), with an emphasis on what *le beau monde* will be wearing next spring. For details, call **01-44-94-70-00.** Late August to early September.

September

Biennale des Antiquaires, Carrousel du Louvre, 99 rue de Rivoli, 1er. Antiques dealers and lovers from all over gather at this gilded event in even-numbered years. Precious furnishings and objets d'art are displayed in the underground exhibit halls linked to the Louvre or perhaps in the Grand Palais once it's restored. For details, call ℂ **01-44-51-74-74;** www.biennale-antiquaires.com. Usually third week in September.

Fête d'Automne (Autumn Festival), citywide. Paris welcomes the return of its residents from their August holidays with an ongoing and eclectic festival of modern music, ballet, theater, and modern art. Venues include art galleries, churches, concert halls, auditoriums, and parks throughout Paris. There's an emphasis on experimental works, which the festival's promoters scatter judiciously between more traditional productions. Depending on the event, tickets cost from 15€ to 73€ ($13–$65). For details, contact the **Festival d'Automne,** 156 rue de Rivoli, 75001 Paris (ℂ **01-53-45-17-00;** fax 01-53-45-17-01; www.festival-automne.com). Mid-September to late December.

Paris Auto Show, Parc des Expositions, 15th arrondissement. Glitzy attendees and lots of hype attend this showcase for European car design. The show takes place in even-numbered years near the Porte de Versailles. In addition, a permanent exhibit on French auto design at the Cité des Sciences et de l'Industrie is upgraded and enriched during October. For details, call ℂ **01-56-88-22-40.** September 28 to October 13, 2004.

October

Prix de l'Arc de Triomphe, Hippodrome de Longchamp, 16th arrondissement. France's answer to England's Ascot is the country's most prestigious horse race, culminating the equine season in Europe. For details, call ℂ **01-49-10-20-30.** Early October.

November

Armistice Day, citywide. The signing of the controversial document that ended World War I is celebrated with a military parade from the Arc de Triomphe to the Hôtel des Invalides. November 11.

Fête d'Art Sacré (Festival of Sacred Art). A series of classical concerts is held in five of the oldest churches of Paris. For details, call ℂ 01-44-70-64-10. Mid-November to mid-December.

Release of the Beaujolais Nouveau, citywide. Parisians eagerly await the yearly release of the first new Beaujolais, that fruity wine from Burgundy. Signs are posted in bistros, wine bars, and cafes—these places report their heaviest patronage of the year during this celebration of the grape. Third Thursday in November.

December

Paris Boat Show (Salon International de la Navigation de Plaisance), Parc des Expositions, 15th arrondissement. This is Europe's most visible exposition of what's afloat and of interest to wholesalers, retailers, boat owners (or wannabes), and anyone involved in the business of waterborne holidaymaking. For details, call ℂ 01-41-90-47-22, or check on the Web at www.salon nautiqueparis.com. Eight days in early December.

Fête de St-Sylvestre (New Year's Eve), citywide. It's most boisterously celebrated in the Latin Quarter around the Sorbonne. At midnight, the city explodes. Strangers kiss strangers, and boulevard St-Michel and the Champs-Elysées become virtual pedestrian malls. December 31.

5 Health & Insurance

TRAVEL INSURANCE AT A GLANCE

Since France is far from home for most of us, and a number of things could go wrong—lost luggage, trip cancellation, a medical emergency—consider the following types of insurance.

Check your current policies before you buy insurance for trip cancellation, lost luggage, medical expenses, or car-rental insurance. You're likely to have partial or complete coverage. But if you need some, ask your travel agent. The price varies, depending on the cost and length of your trip, your age and health, and the type of trip. Insurance for extreme sports or adventure travel, for example, will cost more than for a cruise. Some insurers provide packages for specialty vacations, such as skiing or backpacking. More dangerous activities may be excluded from basic policies.

For information in the United States, contact one of the following insurers:

• Access America (ℂ 800/284-8300; www.accessamerica.com/)

• Travel Assistance International (ℂ 800/821-2828; www.travel assistance.com)
• Travel Guard International (ℂ 800/826-1300; www.travel guard.com)
• Travel Insured International (ℂ 800/243-3174; www.travel insured.com)
• Travelex Insurance Services (ℂ 800/228-9792; www.travelex-insurance.com)

For information in Great Britain, contact the following agency:

• Columbus Direct, 17 Devonshire Sq., London, EC2 M4S (ℂ 020/7375-0011; www.columbusdirect.com)

TRIP-CANCELLATION INSURANCE (TCI)

There are three major types of trip-cancellation insurance: one, in the event that you prepay a tour that gets cancelled, and you can't get your money back; a second when you or someone in your family gets sick or dies, and you can't travel (but beware that you may not be covered for a pre-existing condition); and a third, when bad weather makes travel impossible. Some insurers provide coverage for events like jury duty; natural disasters, like floods or fire; even the loss of a job. A few have added provisions for cancellations because of terrorist activities. Check the fine print before signing on, and don't buy trip-cancellation insurance from the tour operator who may be responsible for the cancellation; buy it from a reputable agency. Don't overbuy. You won't be reimbursed for more than the cost of your trip.

MEDICAL INSURANCE

Most health insurance policies cover you if you get sick away from home—but check, particularly if an HMO insures you. With the exception of certain HMOs and Medicare/Medicaid, your medical insurance should cover emergency medical treatment—even hospital care—overseas. However, most out-of-country hospitals make you pay your bills up front, and send you a refund after you've returned home and filed the paperwork. Members of **Blue Cross/Blue Shield** can use their cards at select hospitals in most major cities worldwide. Call ℂ **800/810-BLUE** or go to www.bluecares.com for a list.

Some credit cards (American Express, certain gold and platinum Visa and MasterCards) offer automatic flight insurance against death or dismemberment in case of an airplane crash if you charged your ticket.

If you require additional insurance, try one of the following companies:

- **MEDEX International,** 9515 Deereco Rd., Timonium, MD 21093-5375 (ℂ **888/MEDEX-00** or 410/453-6300; fax 410/453-6301; www.medexassist.com)
- **Travel Assistance International,** 9200 Keystone Crossing, Suite 300, Indianapolis, IN 46240

(ℂ **800/821-2828;** www.travelassistance.com; for general information on services, call the company's Worldwide Assistance Services, Inc., at ℂ 800/777-8710).

The cost of travel medical insurance varies. Check your existing policies before you buy additional coverage. Also, check to see if your medical insurance covers you for emergency medical evacuation. If you have to buy a one-way same-day ticket home and forfeit your nonrefundable round-trip ticket, you may be out big money.

LOST-LUGGAGE INSURANCE

On International flights (including U.S. portions of international trips), reimbursement for lost baggage is limited to approximately $9.07 per pound, up to approximately $635 per checked bag. If you plan to check items more valuable than the standard liability, you may purchase "excess valuation" coverage from the airline, up to $5,000. Be sure to take any valuables or irreplaceable items with you in your carry-on luggage. If you file a lost-luggage claim, be prepared to answer detailed questions about the contents of your baggage, and be sure to file a claim immediately, as most airlines enforce a 21-day deadline. Before you leave home, compile an inventory of all packed items and an estimate of the total value to ensure you're properly compensated if your luggage is lost. You will only be reimbursed for what you lost, no more. Once you've filed a complaint, persist in securing your reimbursement; there are no laws governing the length of time it takes for a carrier to reimburse you. If you arrive at a destination without your bags, ask the airline to forward them to your hotel or your next destination; they will usually comply. If your bag is delayed or lost, the airline may reimburse you for reasonable expenses, such as a toothbrush or clothing, but the airline is under no legal obligation to do so.

Your homeowners or renters policy may also cover lost luggage. Many platinum and gold credit cards cover you as well. If you choose to purchase additional lost-luggage insurance, be sure not to buy more than you need. Buy in advance from the insurer or a trusted agent (prices will be much higher at the airport).

CAR-RENTAL INSURANCE (LOSS/DAMAGE WAIVER OR COLLISION DAMAGE WAIVER)

If you hold a private auto insurance policy, you probably are covered in the United States, but not abroad, for loss or damage to the car, and liability in case a passenger is injured. The credit card you used to rent the car also may provide some coverage.

Car-rental insurance probably does not cover liability if you caused the accident. Check your own auto insurance policy, the rental company policy, and your credit-card coverage for the extent of coverage. Is your destination covered? Are other drivers covered? How much liability is covered if a passenger is injured? (If you rely on your credit card for coverage, you may want to bring a second credit card with you, as damages may be charged to your card and you may find yourself stranded with no money.)

Car-rental insurance in Paris starts at about $16.50 a day for compact cars.

THE HEALTHY TRAVELER

In general, Paris is a "safe" destination, although problems can and do occur anywhere. You don't need shots; most foodstuff is safe and the water in Paris is potable. If you're concerned, order bottled water. It is easy to get a prescription filled in French towns and cities, and nearly all places contain English-speaking doctors at hospitals with well-trained medical staffs, which are found throughout France.

In other words, France is part of the civilized world.

The vegetarian can go into almost any restaurant in Paris, even those specializing in meat and fish, and order a heaping plate of fresh vegetables.

Regarding the outbreaks of mad cow disease and foot-and-mouth disease, the World Health Organization recently reported that the current risk in the United Kingdom appears to be extremely small, perhaps about "1 case per billion" servings. They also reported that in France, "this risk, if it exists at all, would be perhaps even less than in the United Kingdom."

Nonetheless, France is leery of U.K. beef despite the "all clear" signals coming from the EU. France even flaunted EU laws and banned U.K. beef, which is causing problems for France in the EU Court of Justice.

As for foot-and-mouth disease, which is not passed on to humans, there is little concern. The U.S. Department of Agriculture in 2001 added France to its list of countries said to be free of foot-and-mouth disease.

WHAT TO DO IF YOU GET SICK AWAY FROM HOME

If you worry about getting sick away from home, consider purchasing **medical travel insurance** and carry your ID card in your purse or wallet. In most cases, your existing health plan will provide the coverage you need. See the section on insurance, above, for more information.

If you suffer from a chronic illness, consult your doctor before your departure. For conditions like epilepsy, diabetes, or heart problems, wear a **MedicAlert Identification Tag** (© **800/825-3785;** www.medicalert. org), which will alert doctors to your condition and give them access to your records through Medic Alert's 24-hour hot line.

Pack **prescription medications** in your carry-on luggage, and keep prescription medications in their original containers. Also bring along copies of your prescriptions in case you lose your pills or run out. Carry the generic names of prescription medicines, in case a local pharmacist is unfamiliar with the brand name.

Don't forget sunglasses, sunscreen if you're going to be spending time outdoors, and an extra pair of contact lenses or prescription glasses.

Contact the **International Association for Medical Assistance to Travelers** (IAMAT) (© 716/754-4883 or 519/836-3412; www.sentex.net/~iamat) for tips on travel and health concerns in Paris or France and lists of local, English-speaking doctors. In Canada, call 519/836-0102. The United States **Centers for Disease Control and Prevention** (© 800/311-3435; www.cdc.gov) provides up-to-date information on necessary vaccines and health hazards by region or country (their booklet, *Health Information for International Travel*, costs $25 by mail; on the Internet, it's free). Any foreign consulate can provide a list of area doctors who speak English. If you get sick, consider asking your hotel concierge to recommend a local doctor—even his or her own.

THE SAFE TRAVELER

The most common menace, especially in large cities, particularly Paris, is the plague of pickpockets and roving gangs of Gypsy children who surround you, distract you, and steal your purse or wallet. Never leave valuables in a car, and never travel with your car unlocked. A U.S. State Department travel advisory warns that every car (whether parked, stopped at a traffic light, or moving) can be a potential target for armed robbery. In these uncertain times, it is prudent to check the U.S. State Department's travel advisories at http://travel.state.gov/travel_warnings.html.

6 Tips for Travelers with Special Needs

TRAVELERS WITH DISABILITIES

Facilities in Paris for travelers with disabilities are certainly better than you'll find in most cities. Nearly all modern hotels in France now have rooms designed especially for persons with disabilities. Older hotels, unless renovated, may not provide important features like elevators, special toilet facilities, or ramps for wheelchair accessibility. Depending on your needs, it's best to contact each hotel directly and make your special needs known before you arrive.

Most high-speed trains in France can deal with wheelchairs, and guide dogs ride free. Older trains have compartments for wheelchair boarding. On the Paris Métro, persons with disabilities can sit in wider seats. Some stations don't have escalators or elevators, however, and this may present problems.

AGENCIES/OPERATORS

- **Flying Wheels Travel** (© 800/535-6790; www.flyingwheels travel. com) offers escorted tours and cruises that emphasize sports and private tours in minivans with lifts.
- **Access Adventures** (© 716/889-9096), a Rochester, New York-based agency, offers customized itineraries for a variety of travelers with disabilities.
- **Accessible Journeys** (© 800/TINGLES or 610/521-0339; www.disabilitytravel.com) caters specifically to slow walkers and wheelchair travelers and their families and friends.

ORGANIZATIONS

- **The Moss Rehab Hospital** (© 215/456-5995; www.moss resourcenet.org) provides helpful phone assistance through its **Travel Information Service.**

- The **Society for Accessible Travel and Hospitality** (✆ **212/447-7285;** fax 212/725-8253; www.sath.org/) offers a wealth of travel resources for all types of disabilities and informed recommendations on destinations, access guides, travel agents, tour operators, vehicle rentals, and companion services. Annual membership costs $45 for adults, $30 for seniors and students.

- The **American Foundation for the Blind** (✆ **800/232-5463;** www.afb.org) provides information on traveling with Seeing Eye dogs.

PUBLICATIONS

- **Mobility International USA** (✆ **541/343-1284;** www.miusa.org) publishes *A World of Options,* a 658-page book of resources on everything from biking trips to scuba outfitters, and a newsletter called *Over the Rainbow.* Annual membership costs $35.

- **Twin Peaks Press** (✆ **360/694-2462)** publishes travel-related books for travelers with special needs.

- *Open World for Disability and Mature Travel* magazine, published by the Society for Accessible Travel and Hospitality (see above), is full of resources and information. A year's subscription costs $13 ($21 outside the U.S.).

FOR BRITISH TRAVELERS

The **Royal Association for Disability and Rehabilitation** (RADAR), Unit 12, City Forum, 250 City Rd., London EC1V 8AF (✆ **020/7250-3222;** www.radar.org.uk), publishes three holiday "fact packs" for £2 each or £5 for all three. The first provides general information, including tips for planning and booking a holiday, obtaining insurance, and handling finances; the second outlines transportation available when going abroad and equipment for rent; the third deals with specialized accommodations. Another good resource is **Holiday Care,** Imperial Building, 2nd Floor, Victoria Road, Horley, Surrey RH6 7PZ (✆ **01293/774-535;** www.holidaycare.org.uk), a national charity advising on accessible accommodations for the elderly and persons with disabilities. Annual membership costs £30.

GAYS & LESBIANS

France is one of the world's most tolerant countries toward gays and lesbians, and no special laws discriminate against them. "Gay Paree" boasts a large gay population, with dozens of gay clubs, restaurants, organizations, and services.

In Paris **SOS Ecoute Gay** (✆ 01-44-93-01-02) is a gay hot line designed to creatively counsel persons with gay-related problems. Volunteers, some of whom are more helpful than others, answer the phones. A phone counselor responds to calls Monday and Wednesday from 8 to 10pm and Tuesday, Thursday, and Friday from 6 to 8pm. Also helpful is **La Maison des Femmes,** 163 rue de Charenton, 12e (✆ **01-43-43-41-13;** Métro: Reuilly-Diderot), offering information about Paris for lesbians and bisexual women, and sometimes sponsoring informal dinners and get-togethers. Call anytime for a recorded announcement that gives the hours that someone will be available for that particular week.

Lesbian or bisexual women might also like to pick up a copy of *Lesbia,* if only to check out the ads. These and other publications are available at Paris's largest gay bookstore, **Les Mots à la Bouche,** 6 rue Ste-Croix-de-la-Bretonnerie, 4e (✆ **01-42-78-88-30**). Hours are Monday to Saturday from 11am to 11pm and Sunday from 2 to 8pm. Both French- and English-language publications are available.

AGENCIES/OPERATORS

- **Above and Beyond Tours** (© 800/397-2681; www.above beyondtours.com) offers gay and lesbian tours worldwide and is the exclusive gay and lesbian tour operator for United Airlines.
- **Now, Voyager** (© 800/255-6951; www.nowvoyager.com) is a San Francisco–based gay-owned and -operated travel service.
- **Olivia Cruises & Resorts** (© 800/631-6277 or 510/655-0364; http://oliviatravel.com) charters resorts and ships for lesbian vacations all over the world.

PUBLICATIONS

- *Frommer's Gay & Lesbian Europe* is an excellent resource, with an entire chapter about Paris.
- *Out & About* (© 800/929-2268 or 415/644-8044; www.outand about.com) offers guidebooks and a newsletter 10 times a year with information on the global gay and lesbian scene.
- *Spartacus International Gay Guide* and *Odysseus* are annual English-language guidebooks for gay men, with some information for lesbians. You can get them from most gay and lesbian bookstores, or order them from **Giovanni's Room** bookstore, 1145 Pine St., Philadelphia, PA 19107 (© **215/923-2960;** www.giovannis room.com).

SENIOR TRAVEL

Mention that you're a senior citizen when you make your reservations. All major airlines and many French hotels offer discounts for seniors.

Members of **AARP** (formerly known as the American Association of Retired Persons), 601 E St. NW, Washington, DC 10049 (© **800/424-3410** or 202/434-2277; www.aarp. org), get discounts on hotels, airfares, and car rentals. AARP offers members a range of benefits, including *Modern Maturity of My Generation* magazine and a monthly newsletter. Anyone over 50 can join.

The **Alliance for Retired Americans,** 8403 Colesville Rd., Suite 1200, Silver Spring, MD 20910 (© **301/578-8422;** www.retiredamericans.org), offers a newsletter six times a year and discounts on hotel and auto rentals; annual dues are $13 per person or couple. *Note:* Members of the former National Council of Senior Citizens receive membership in the Alliance.

AGENCIES/OPERATORS

- **Grand Circle Travel** (© 800/221-2610 or 617/350-7500; www.gct.com) offers package deals for the 50-plus market, mostly of the tour-bus variety, with free trips thrown in for those who organize groups of 10 or more.
- **SAGA Holidays** (© 800/343-0273; www.sagaholidays.com) offers inclusive tours and cruises for those 50 and older. SAGA also offers a number of single-traveler tours and sponsors the "Road Scholar Tours" (© 800/621-2151; sales info@sagaholidays. com), vacations with an educational bent. Order a free brochure from the website.
- **Elderhostel** (© 877/426-8056; www.elderhostel.org) arranges study programs for those age 55 and over (and a spouse or companion of any age) in the United States and in more than 80 countries around the world, including France. Most courses last 5 to 7 days in the United States (2–4 weeks abroad), and many include airfare, accommodations in university dormitories or modest inns, meals, and tuition.
- **Interhostel** (© 800/733-9753; www.learn.unh.edu/interhostel), organized by the University of New Hampshire, also offers educational travel for senior citizens.

On these escorted tours, the days are packed with seminars, lectures, and field trips, with sightseeing led by academic experts. **Interhostel** takes travelers 50 and over (with companions over 40), and offers 1- and 2-week trips, mostly international.

PUBLICATIONS

- *The Book of Deals* is a collection of more than 1,000 senior discounts on airlines, lodging, tours, and attractions around the country; it's available for $9.95 by calling © 800/460-6676.
- *101 Tips for the Mature Traveler* is available from Grand Circle Travel (© 800/221-2610 or 617/350-7500; fax 617/346-6700).
- *The 50+ Traveler's Guidebook* (St. Martin's Press).
- *Unbelievably Good Deals and Great Adventures That You Absolutely Can't Get Unless You're Over 50* (Contemporary Publishing Co.).

STUDENT TRAVEL

Paris offers student discounts on nearly everything, from museums to movies. The best resource for students is the **Council on International Educational Exchange** (CIEE) (© 212/822-2700). It can set you up with an ID card (see below), and its travel branch, **Council Travel Service** (© 888/2COUNCIL; www.counciltravel.com), is the biggest student travel agency operation in the world. It can get you discounts on plane tickets, rail passes, and the like.

From CIEE you can obtain the student traveler's best friend, the $22 **International Student Identity Card** (ISIC). It's the only officially acceptable form of student ID, good for cut rates on rail passes, plane tickets, and other discounts. It also provides you with basic health and life insurance and a 24-hour help line. If you're no longer a student but are still under 26, you can get from the same people a **GO 25 card,** which will get you the insurance and some of the discounts.

In Canada, **Travel CUTS,** 200 Ronson Drive, Suite 320, Toronto, ONT, M9W 5Z9 (© 800/667-2887 or 416/614-2887; www.travelcuts.com), offers similar services.

USIT Campus, 52 Grosvenor Gardens, London SW1W 0AG (© 0870/240-1010; www.usitworld.com), opposite Victoria Station, is Britain's specialist in student and youth travel.

PUBLICATIONS

Hanging Out in France (www.frommers.com/hangingout/), is the French entry in the top student travel series for students, covering everything from adrenaline sports to the hottest club and music scenes.

7 Getting There

BY PLANE

High season on most airlines' routes to Paris is usually June to the beginning of September. This is the most expensive and most crowded time to travel. **Shoulder season** is April to May, early September to October, and December 15 to 24. **Low season** is November 1 to December 14 and December 25 to March 31.

THE MAJOR AIRLINES

FROM NORTH AMERICA One of the best choices for travelers in the southeastern United States and Midwest is **Delta Airlines** (© 800/221-1222; www.delta.com). Delta flies direct to Paris from Atlanta, which is a hub for frequent flights from cities like New Orleans, Phoenix, Columbia (S.C.), and

Nashville. Delta also operates daily nonstop flights to Paris from Cincinnati and New York.

Another excellent choice is **United Airlines** (© 800/241-6522; www.ual.com), with nonstop flights from Chicago, Washington, D.C., and San Francisco to Paris. United also offers discounted fares in the low and shoulder seasons to London from five major North American hubs. From London, it's an easy train and Hovercraft or Chunnel connection to Paris, a fact that tempts many to spend a weekend in London either before or after their visit to Paris.

Another good option is **Continental Airlines** (© 800/525-0280; www.continental.com), serving the Northeast and much of the Southwest through its busy hubs in Newark and Houston. From both cities, Continental provides nonstop flights to Paris.

The French flag carrier, **Air France** (© 800/237-2747; www.airfrance.com), offers daily or several-times-a-week flights to Paris from Newark; Washington, D.C.; Miami; Chicago; New York; Houston; San Francisco; Los Angeles; Boston; Cincinnati; Atlanta; Montréal; Toronto; and Mexico City. In 2001, Air France resumed flights of the Concorde between New York and Paris. The jets have been revamped to address safety concerns, following a crash outside Paris on July 25, 2000.

American Airlines (© 800/433-7300; www.aa.com) provides daily nonstop flights to Paris from Dallas/Fort Worth, Chicago, Miami, Boston, and New York. American Airlines now flies into Roissy-Charles de Gaulle instead of Orly Airport. Facilities at its new terminal 2A include a deluxe Admirals Club, plus a mammoth Arrivals Lounge complete with 10 showers.

US Airways (© 800/428-4322; www.usairways.com) offers daily nonstop service from Philadelphia to Paris.

If you'd like to see London before traveling on to Paris, there are dozens of **British Airways** (© 800/247-9297; www.british-airways.com) flights from North American cities to London. You can fly first from, say, New York to London, and then take the BA shuttle flight to Paris following a holiday in England.

Canadians usually choose **Air Canada** (© 888/247-2262 from the U.S. and Canada; www.aircanada.ca) for flights to Paris from Toronto and Montréal. Nonstop flights from Montréal and Toronto depart every evening. Two of the nonstop flights from Toronto are shared with Air France and feature Air France aircraft.

FROM THE UNITED KINGDOM
From London, **Air France** (© 0845/084-5111; www.airfrance.com) and **British Airways** (© 0845/773-3377 in the U.K.; www.british-airways.com) fly frequently to Paris, offering up to 17 flights daily from Heathrow. **Aer Lingus** (© 866/IRISH-FLY; www.aerlingus.com) has frequent direct flights from Dublin to Paris throughout the day. Many commercial travelers also use regular flights from the London City Airport in the Docklands. There are also direct flights to Paris from major cities such

---

Fun Fact Sample Flying Times

The flying time to Paris from New York is about 7 hours; from Chicago, 9 hours; from Los Angeles, 11 hours; from Atlanta, about 8 hours; from Washington, D.C., about 7½ hours; from London, about 1 hour; from Edinburgh, 2 hours; from Dublin, 2 hours; from Sydney, 21½ hours; from Auckland, 23¼ hours.

as Manchester, Edinburgh, and Southampton. For more information, contact Air France, British Airways, or **British Midland** (© 0870/607-0555; www.flybmi.com).

FROM AUSTRALIA Getting to Paris from Australia is rather difficult, because **Air France** (© 02-92-44-21-00; www.airfrance.com) has discontinued all direct flights to and from that country, requiring transfers through, among others, Singapore, with ongoing service to Sydney provided by Qantas. Consequently, on virtually any route, and with any airline you take, you have to change planes at least once en route. **British Airways** (© 02-89-04-88-00; www.british-airways.com) flies daily from both Sydney and Melbourne to London in time for any of several connecting flights to Paris. **Qantas** (© 08-03-84-68-46; www.qantas.com) can route passengers from Australia into London, where plentiful connections exist for the hop across the Channel.

NEW AIR TRAVEL SECURITY MEASURES

In the wake of the terrorist attacks of September 11, 2001, the airline industry began implementing sweeping security measures in airports. Expect a lengthy check-in process and extensive delays. Although regulations vary from airline to airline, you can expedite the process by taking the following steps:

- **Arrive early.** Arrive at the airport at least 2 hours before your scheduled flight.
- **Try not to drive your car to the airport.** Parking and curbside access to the terminal may be limited. Call ahead and check.
- **Don't count on curbside check-in.** Some airlines and airports have stopped curbside check-in, while others offer it on a limited basis. Check with the individual airline for up-to-date information.

- **Be sure to carry plenty of documentation.** A government-issued photo ID (federal, state, or local) is now required. And of course, you will need your passport to enter France. You may need to show ID at various checkpoints. With an E-ticket, you may be required to have printed confirmation of purchase, and perhaps even the credit card with which you bought your ticket (see "All about E-Ticketing" below). This varies from airline to airline, so call ahead to make sure you have the proper documentation. And be sure that your ID is **up-to-date;** an expired driver's license or passport may keep you from boarding the plane altogether.
- **Know what you can carry on—and what you can't.** Travelers in the United States are now limited to one carry-on bag, plus one personal bag (like a purse or a briefcase). The Transportation Safety Administration (TSA) has also issued a list of restricted carry-on items; see the box "What You Can Carry On—And What You Can't."
- **Prepare to be searched.** Electronic items, such as laptops or cell phones, should be readied for additional screening. Limit the metal items you wear.
- **It's no joke.** When a check-in agent asks if someone other than you packed your bag, don't decide to be a comedian. The agents will not hesitate to call an alarm.
- **No ticket, no gate access.** Only ticketed passengers will be allowed beyond the screener checkpoints, except for those people with specific medical or parental needs.

FLYING FOR LESS: TIPS FOR GETTING THE BEST AIRFARE

Passengers within the same airplane cabin are rarely paying the same fare. Business travelers who need to purchase tickets at the last minute, change their itinerary at a moment's notice, or

---

Tips   **What You Can Carry On—And What You Can't**

The Transportation Safety Administration (TSA), the government agency that now handles all aspects of airport security, has devised new restrictions for carry-on baggage, to expedite the screening process and prevent potential weapons from passing through security. Passengers are now limited to bringing just one carry-on bag and one personal item onto the aircraft (previous regulations allowed two carry-on bags and one personal item, like a briefcase or purse). For more information, go to the TSA's website (www.tsa.gov). The agency has released an updated list of items you are not allowed to carry onto an aircraft.

Not permitted: knives and box cutters, corkscrews, straight razors, metal scissors, golf clubs, baseball bats, pool cues, hockey sticks, ski poles, ice picks.

Permitted: nail clippers, nail files, tweezers, eyelash curlers, safety razors (including disposable razors), syringes (with documented proof of medical need), walking canes and umbrellas (must be inspected first).

The airline you fly may have **additional restrictions** on items you can and cannot carry onboard. Call ahead to avoid problems.

---

get home for the weekend pay the premium rate. Passengers who can book their ticket well in advance, stay over Saturday night, or who are willing to travel on a Tuesday, Wednesday, or Thursday after 7pm, will pay a fraction of the full fare. Here are a few other easy ways to save.

- **Take advantage of APEX fares.** Advance-purchase booking, or APEX, fares are often the key to getting the lowest fare. You generally must be willing to make your plans and buy your tickets as far ahead as possible. The 14-day APEX fare is the most popular fare. Second in importance and popularity is the 21-Day APEX fare. Because the number of seats allocated to APEX fares is sometimes less than 25% of plane capacity, the early bird gets the low-cost seat. There's often a surcharge for flying on a weekend, and cancellation and refund policies can be strict.

- **Watch for sales.** You'll almost never see sales during July and August or the Thanksgiving or Christmas seasons, but at other times you can get great deals. In the last couple of years, there have been amazing prices on winter flights to Paris. If you already hold a ticket when a sale breaks, it might pay to exchange it, even if you incur a $50 to $75 penalty charge. Note that the lowest-priced fares are often nonrefundable, require advance purchase of 1 to 3 weeks and a certain length of stay, and carry penalties for changing dates of travel. Make sure you know exactly what the restrictions are before you commit.

- If your schedule is flexible, ask if you can secure a cheaper fare by **staying an extra day** or by **flying midweek.** (Many airlines won't volunteer this information.)

- **Consolidators,** also known as "bucket shops," are a good place to find low fares, often below even the airlines' discounted rates. Basically, they're travel agents who get discounts for buying in bulk and pass some of the savings on to you. Before you pay, however, be aware that consolidator tickets are usually nonrefundable or come with stiff cancellation penalties.

We've gotten great deals on many occasions from **Cheap Tickets** ★ (© 800/377-1000; www.cheaptickets.com).

Council Travel (© 800/ 2 COUNCIL; www.counciltravel. com) and **STA Travel** (© 800/ 781-4040; www.statravel.com) cater especially to young travelers, but their bargain-basement prices are available to people of all ages. Other reliable consolidators include **Lowestfare.com** (© 888/ 278-8830; www.lowestfare.com); **Cheap Seats** (© 800/451-7200; www.cheapseatstravel.com); and **1-800/FLY-CHEAP** (www.fly cheap. com).

• Join a travel club such as **Moment's Notice** (© 718/234-6295; www.moments-notice. com) or **Sears Discount Travel Club** (© 800/433-9383, or 800/255-1487 to join; www.travelers advantage.com), which supply unsold tickets at discounted prices. You pay an annual membership fee to use the club's hot-line number.

Of course, you're limited to what's available, so you have to be flexible.

• Join **frequent-flier clubs.** It's best to accrue miles on one program so you can rack up free flights and achieve elite status faster. But it makes sense to open as many accounts as possible, no matter how seldom you fly an airline. It's free, and you'll get the best choice of seats, faster response to phone inquiries, and prompter service if your luggage is stolen, your flight canceled or delayed, or if you want to change your seat. Some airlines offer you the opportunity to buy miles if your total is close to that for a free flight or upgrade.

• Search the **Internet** for cheap fares—though it's still best to compare your findings with the research of a dedicated travel agent, if you're lucky enough to have one, especially when you're booking more than just a flight. Among the better-respected virtual travel agents are **Travelocity** (www.travelocity.com), **Expedia** (www.expedia.com), and **Yahoo! Travel** (http://travel.yahoo.com).

PARIS AIRPORTS

Paris has two international airports: **Orly** (© 01-49-75-15-15), 14km (8½ miles) south of the city, and

---

(**Tips** **All About E-Ticketing**

Only yesterday **electronic tickets (E-tickets)** were the fast, easy ticket-free alternative to paper tickets. E-tickets allowed passengers to avoid long lines at airport check-in while saving the airlines money on postage and labor. With increased security measures in airports, an E-ticket no longer guarantees accelerated check-in. You often can't go straight to the boarding gate, even if you have no bags to check. You'll probably need to show your printed E-ticket receipt or confirmation of purchase, as well as a photo ID, and sometimes the credit card with which you purchased your E-ticket. That said, buying an E-ticket is still a fast, convenient way to book a flight; instead of having to wait for a paper ticket in the mail, you can book your fare by phone or on the computer, and the airline will immediately confirm by fax or e-mail. In addition, airlines often offer incentives like frequent-flier miles for electronic bookings.

Tips Changing Plans (and Planes)

If your flight is cancelled, don't head for the nearest ticket counter. Call the airline directly from the nearest phone to reschedule. You may be able to quickly rebook while other passengers are still waiting in line to speak to a harried customer service rep.

Charles de Gaulle (Roissy) (© 01-48-62-22-80), 23km (14¼ miles) northeast. A 12€ ($11) Air France shuttle operates between the two every 30 minutes, taking 50 to 75 minutes.

CHARLES DE GAULLE AIRPORT (ROISSY) At Charles de Gaulle, foreign carriers use Aérogare 1 and Air France uses Aérogare 2. From Aérogare 1, take a walkway to the passport checkpoint and the Customs area. A **shuttle bus** (*navette*) links the terminals.

The free shuttle bus connecting Aérogare 1 with Aérogare 2 also transports passengers to the Roissy rail station, from which fast **RER trains** (Line B) leave every 15 minutes daily between 5am to midnight for such Métro stations as Gare du Nord, Châtelet, Luxembourg, Port Royal, and Denfert-Rochereau. A typical RER fare from Roissy to any point in central Paris is 11€ ($9.80) in first class or 7.45€ ($6.65) in second.

You can also take either of two Air France shuttle buses, both of which depart from Roissy for points within central Paris. Line 2 departs at 12-minute intervals every day between 5:45am and 11pm, charging 9.90€ ($8.80) each way for the 40-minute transit to the Place de l'Etoile, with a stop en route at Porte Maillot. Line 4 departs at 30-minute intervals every day between 7am and 9:30pm, charging 11€ ($10) for the 50-minute trip to the Gare Montparnasse, making an intermediate stop at the Gare de Lyon en route. From any of those points within central Paris, Métro lines can carry you on to virtually any other point within the city.

Another option, the **Roissybus** (© 01-48-04-18-24), departs from a point near the corner of the rue Scribe and place de l'Opéra every 15 minutes from 5:45am to 11pm. The cost for the 50-minute ride is 7.30€ ($6.50).

Taxis from Roissy into the city run about 38€ ($34) on the meter. At night (8pm–7am), fares are about 40% higher. Long queues of both taxis and passengers form outside each of the airport's terminals in a surprisingly orderly fashion.

ORLY AIRPORT Orly has two terminals: Orly Sud (south) for international flights and Orly Ouest (west) for domestic flights. A free shuttle bus links them together.

Air France buses leave from exit E of Orly Ouest and from exit K, Platform 5 of Orly Sud every 12 minutes from 5:45am to 11pm, for Gare des Invalides in central Paris at a cost of 7.60€ ($6.75) one-way. Other buses depart for place Denfert-Rochereau in the south of Paris at a cost of 5.60€ ($5).

An alternative method for reaching central Paris involves taking a monorail (**Orly Val**) to the RER station of Anthony, then the RER train into downtown Paris. The Orly Val makes stops at the north and south terminals, and continues at 8-minute intervals for the 10-minute ride to the Anthony RER station. At Anthony, you'll board an RER train (Line B) for the 30-minute ride into the city. The cost of the Orly Val monorail plus the RER (Line B) transit into Paris is 8.65€ ($7.70), a fare that might seem a bit expensive, but which offsets the horrendous construction costs of a monorail that sails above the congested roadways encircling the airport.

A **taxi** from Orly to the center of Paris costs about 30€ ($27), more at night and on weekends. Returning to the airport, **buses** to Orly leave from the Invalides terminal to either Orly Sud or Orly Ouest every 15 minutes, taking about 30 minutes.

Caution: Don't take a meterless taxi from Orly Sud or Orly Ouest—it's much safer (and usually cheaper) to hire a metered cab from the taxi queues, which are under the scrutiny of a police officer.

BY CAR

Driving in Paris is definitely not recommended. Parking is difficult, traffic is dense, and networks of one-way streets make navigation, even with the best of maps, a problem. If you do drive, remember that Paris is encircled by a ring road called the *périphérique.* Always obtain detailed directions to your destination, including the name of the exit on the périphérique you're looking for (exits aren't numbered). Avoid rush hours. Few hotels, except the luxury ones, have garages, but the staff will usually be able to direct you to one nearby.

The **major highways** into Paris are the A1 from the north (Great Britain and Benelux); A13 from Rouen, Normandy, and northwest France; A10

from Bordeaux, the Pyrénées, France's southwest, and Spain; A6 from Lyon, the French Alps, the Riviera, and Italy; and A4 from Metz, Nancy, and Strasbourg in eastern France.

BY TRAIN

If you're already in Europe, you might decide to travel to Paris by train, especially if you have a **Eurailpass.** Rail passes or individual rail tickets within Europe are available at most travel agencies, at any office of **Rail Europe** (© **800/848-7245** in the U.S., 800/361-RAIL in Canada; www.raileurope.com), or at **Eurostar** (© **800/EUROSTAR** in the U.S., 0870/584-8848 in London, 01-44-51-06-02 in Paris; www.eurostar.com).

There are six major train stations in Paris: **Gare d'Austerlitz,** 55 quai d'Austerlitz, 13e (serving the southwest, with trains from the Loire Valley, the Bordeaux country, and the Pyrénées); **Gare de l'Est,** place du 11 Novembre 1918, 10e (serving the east, with trains from Strasbourg, Nancy, Reims, and beyond to Zurich, Basel, Luxembourg, and Austria); **Gare de Lyon,** 20 bd. Diderot, 12e (serving the southeast with trains from the Côte d'Azur and Provence to Geneva, Lausanne, and Italy); **Gare Montparnasse,** 17 bd. Vaugirard, 15e (serving the west, with trains from Brittany); **Gare du Nord,** 18 rue de Dunkerque,

15e (serving the north, with trains from Holland, Denmark, Belgium, and Germany); and **Gare St-Lazare,** 13 rue d'Amsterdam, 8e (serving the northwest, with trains from Normandy).

For general train information and to make reservations, call © **08-36-35-35-35** daily from 7am to 8pm. Buses operate between rail stations. Each of these stations has a Métro stop, making the whole city easily accessible. Taxis are also available at designated stands at every station. Look for the sign that says TETE DE STATION. Be alert in train stations, especially at night.

BY BUS

Bus travel to Paris is available from London and many other cities on the Continent. In the early 1990s, the French government established strong incentives for long-haul buses not to drive into the center of Paris, so the arrival/departure point for Europe's largest bus operator, **Eurolines France,** is a 35-minute Métro ride from central Paris, at the terminus of Métro line 3 (Gallieni), in the eastern suburb of Bagnolet. Despite this inconvenience, many people prefer bus travel. Eurolines France is at 28 av. du Général-de-Gaulle, 93541 Bagnolet (© **08-36-69-52-52**).

Long-haul buses are equipped with toilets, and they stop at mealtimes for rest and refreshment. The price of a round-trip ticket between Paris and London (a 7-hr. trip) is 53€ to 73€ ($47–$65) for passengers 26 or over, and 53€ to 66€ ($47–$59) for passengers under 26.

Because Eurolines doesn't have a U.S.-based sales agent, most people wait until they reach Europe to buy their tickets. Any European travel agent can arrange these purchases. If you're traveling to Paris from London, contact **Eurolines (U.K.) Ltd.,** 52 Grosvenor Gardens, Victoria, London SW1 (© **0870/514-3219**), for information or credit-card sales.

BY FERRY FROM ENGLAND

Despite competition from the Chunnel, services aboard ferries and hydrofoils operate day and night in all seasons, with the exception of last-minute cancellations during storms. Many channel crossings are timed to coincide with the arrival/departure of major trains (especially those between London and Paris); trains let you off a short walk from the piers. Most ferries carry cars, trucks, and massive amounts of freight, but some hydrofoils take passengers only. The major routes include at least 12 trips a day between Dover or Folkestone and Calais or Boulogne. Hovercraft and hydrofoils make the trip from Dover to Calais, the shortest distance across the Channel, in 40 minutes during good weather; the slower-moving ferries might take several hours, depending on weather and tides. If you're bringing a car, it's important to make reservations, as space below decks is usually crowded. Timetables can vary depending on the weather and many other factors.

The leading operator of ferries across the Channel is **P&O Stena Lines** (call BritRail for reservations at © **800/677-8585** in North America or 0870/600-0611 in England). It operates car and passenger ferries between Portsmouth, England, and Cherbourg, France (three departures a day; 4¼ hr. each way during daylight hours, 7 hr. each way at night); between Portsmouth and Le Havre, France (three a day; 5½ hr. each way). The most popular routes are between Dover and Calais, France (25 sailings a day; 75 min. each way), which costs £26 one-way for adults; children under 4 go free.

The shortest and most popular route is between Calais and Dover. **Hoverspeed** operates at least 12 hovercraft crossings daily; the trip takes 35 minutes. It also runs a SeaCat (a catamaran propelled by jet engines) that takes longer, just under 1 hour, between Dover and Calais. For reservations and information, call Hoverspeed (℡ **800/677-8585** in North America or 0870/240-8070 in England). Typical one-way fares are £25 ($38) per person.

If you plan to transport a rental car between England and France, check in advance with the rental company about license and insurance requirements and additional drop-off charges. And be aware that many car-rental companies, for insurance reasons, forbid transport of one of their vehicles over the water between England and France. Transport of a car each way begins at £109 ($164).

UNDER THE CHANNEL

One of the great engineering feats of our time, the $15-billion Channel Tunnel (Chunnel) opened in 1994, and the **Eurostar Express** now has daily service from London to both Paris and Brussels. The 50km (31-mile) journey takes 35 minutes, though actual time spent in the Chunnel is only 19 minutes. Stores selling duty-free goods, restaurants, service stations, and bilingual staffs are available to travelers on both sides of the Channel.

Eurostar tickets are available through **Rail Europe** (℡ **800/4-EURAIL;** www.raileurope.com). In Great Britain, make reservations for Eurostar at ℡ **0870/584-8848;** in the United States, call ℡ **800/EURO STAR.** Chunnel train traffic is roughly competitive with air travel, if you calculate door-to-door travel time. Trains leave from London's Waterloo Station and arrive in Paris at the Gare du Nord.

The tunnel also accommodates passenger cars, charter buses, taxis, and motorcycles, transporting them under the Channel from Folkestone, England, to Calais, France. It operates 24

hours a day, running every 15 minutes during peak travel times and at least once an hour at night. You can buy tickets at the tollbooth at the tunnel's entrance. With **Le Shuttle** (℡ **0870/5353-535;** www.eurotunnel. com), gone are the days of weather-related delays, seasickness, and advance reservations.

Before they board Le Shuttle, motorists stop at a tollbooth and pass through British and French immigration at the same time. Then they drive onto a 1km (½) long train and travel through the tunnel. During the ride, motorists stay in air-conditioned carriages, remaining inside their cars or stepping outside to stretch their legs. When the trip is completed, they simply drive off. Total travel time is about an hour. Once on French soil, British drivers must remember to drive on the right-hand side of the road.

Before you start your search for the lowest airfare, you may want to consider booking your flight as part of a package. What you lose in adventure, you'll gain in time and money saved in accommodations, and maybe even food and entertainment, along with your flight.

ESCORTED TOURS

The two largest tour operators conducting escorted tours of France and Europe are **Globus/Cosmos** (℡ **800/ 221-0090;** www.globusandcosmos. com) and **Trafalgar** (www.trafalgar tours.com). Both companies have first-class tours that run about $100 a day and budget tours for about $75 a day. The differences are mainly in hotel location and the number of activities. There's little difference in the companies' services, so choose your tour based on the itinerary and preferred date of departure. Brochures are available at travel agencies, and all tours must be booked through travel agents.

PACKAGE TOURS FOR INDEPENDENT TRAVELERS

Package tours are not the same thing as escorted tours. With a package tour, you travel independently but pay a group rate. Packages usually include airfare, a choice of hotels, and car rentals, and packagers often offer several options at different prices. In many cases, a package that includes airfare, hotel, and transportation to and from the airport will cost you less than just the hotel alone if you booked it yourself. That's because packages are sold in bulk to tour operators—who resell them to the public at a cost that drastically undercuts standard rates.

FINDING A GENERAL PACKAGE

The best place to start your search is the travel section of your local Sunday newspaper. Also check the ads in the back of national travel magazines such as *Travel & Leisure, National Geographic Traveler,* and *Condé Nast Traveler.*

Liberty Travel (© 888/271-1584 to be connected with the agent closest to you; www.libertytravel.com), one of the biggest packagers in the Northeast, often runs a full-page ad in the Sunday papers. You won't get much in the way of service, but you will get a good deal. American Express Travel (© 800/941-2639; www.american express.com) is another option. Check out its Last Minute Travel Bargains (www.lastminute.com) site, offered in conjunction with Continental Airlines, with discounted vacation packages and reduced fares that differ from the E-savers bargains Continental e-mails weekly to subscribers. Northwest Airlines (www.nwa.com) offers a similar service. Posted on Northwest's website every Wednesday, its Cyber Saver Bargain Alerts offers special hotel rates, package deals, and discounted airline fares.

Another good resource is the airlines themselves, which often package their flights together with accommodations. Among the airline packagers, your options are American Airlines Vacations (© 800/321-2121; www.aa vacations.com) and US Airways Vacations (© 800/455-0123; www.usair waysvacations.com).

The French Experience, 370 Lexington Ave., Room 511, New York, NY 10017 (© 800/283-7262 or 212/986-1115; fax 212/986-3808; www.frenchexperience.com), offers inexpensive tickets to Paris on most scheduled airlines and arranges tours and stays in various types and categories of country inns, hotels, private châteaus, and B&Bs. In addition, it takes reservations for about 38 small hotels in Paris and arranges short-term apartment rentals in the city or farmhouse rentals in the countryside and offers all-inclusive packages in Paris and prearranged package tours of various regions of France. Tours can be adapted to suit individual needs.

FINDING A SPECIALTY PACKAGE

What about special-interest tours? For a city as diverse and popular as Paris, there are only a few specialty tours.

One outfit that coordinates hotel stays with major musical events, usually within at least one (and often both) of the city's opera houses, is Dailey-Thorp Tours, 475 Park Ave. S., New York, NY 10016 (© 800/998-4677; or 212/307-1555; fax 212/974-1420; www.daileythorp.com). Stays in Paris last between 3 and 7 days and, in many cases, are tied in with opera performances in other cities (usually London, Berlin, or Milan) as well. Expect accommodations in deluxe hotels such as the Grand, the Louvre, or the Scribe, and a staff that has made arrangements for all the nuts-and-bolts of your arrival in, and artistic exposure to, Paris.

Die-hard tennis fans set their calendars by the events that transpire each year in Paris's Roland-Garros stadium at the French Open. You can compile your hotel bookings and tickets to the event, but if you're unsure about how to match the dates of your visit with tennis tournaments that will be watched around the world, consider the California-based company that specializes in this issue: **Advantage Tennis Tours,** 33 White Sail Drive, Suite 100, Laguna Niguel, CA 92677 (© **800/341-8687;** www.advantage tennistours.com). Packages usually include either 5 or 6 nights of hotel accommodations in Paris, 2 or 3 days on Center Court, the organizational skills of a bilingual hostess, and a chance to meet and mingle, at any of at least one catered lunch, with tennis fans of many different nationalities. There will even be an opportunity to grab a racquet and play some tennis on your own, in between bouts of sightseeing. Rates, per person, without airfare, begin at $2,600, double occupancy, depending on your choice of hotel and the duration of your visit.

8 Planning Your Trip Online

Researching and booking your trip online can save time and money. Then again, it might not. It is simply not true that you always get the best deal online. Most booking engines do not include schedules and prices for budget airlines, and from time to time you'll get a better last-minute price by calling the airline directly, so it's best to call the airline to see if you can do better before booking online.

On the plus side, Internet users can tap into the same travel-planning databases that were once accessible only to travel agents—and do it at the same speed. Sites such as **Frommers. com, Travelocity.com, Expedia.com,** and **Orbitz.com** allow consumers to comparison-shop for airfares, access special bargains, book flights, and reserve hotel rooms and rental cars.

But don't fire your travel agent yet. Although online booking sites offer tips and hard data to help you bargain-shop, they cannot endow you with the hard-earned experience that makes a reliable travel agent an invaluable resource, even in the Internet age. And for consumers with a complex itinerary, a trusty travel agent is still the best way to arrange the most direct flights to and from the best airports.

 Frommers.com: The Complete Travel Resource

For an excellent travel-planning resource, we highly recommend Frommers.com (www.frommers.com). We're a little biased, of course, but we guarantee you'll find the travel tips, reviews, monthly vacation giveaways, and online-booking capabilities indispensable. Among the features are our popular Message Boards, where Frommer's readers post queries and share advice (sometimes even our authors show up to answer questions); the Frommers.com Newsletter, for the latest travel bargains and inside travel secrets; and Frommer's Destinations Section, where you'll get expert travel tips, hotel and dining recommendations, and advice on the sights to see for more than 2,500 destinations around the globe. When your research is done, the Online Reservation System (www.frommers.com/booktravelnow) takes you to Frommer's favorite sites for booking your vacation at affordable prices.

Some sites, such as Expedia.com, will send you **e-mail notification** when a cheap fare becomes available to your favorite destination. Some will also tell you when fares to a particular destination are lowest.

Keep in mind that because several airlines no longer pay commissions on tickets sold by online travel agencies, these agencies may either add a $10 surcharge to your bill if you book on that carrier or neglect to offer those carriers' schedules.

The list of sites below is selective, not comprehensive. Some sites will have evolved or disappeared by the time you read this.

TRAVEL PLANNING & BOOKING SITES

- **Travelocity** (www.travelocity.com) and **Expedia** (www.expedia.com) are among the most popular sites, each offering an excellent range of options. Travelers search by destination, dates, and cost.
- **Qixo** (www.qixo.com) is another powerful search engine that allows you to search for flights and accommodations from some 20 airline and travel-planning sites (such as Travelocity) at once. Qixo sorts results by price.

SMART E-SHOPPING

The savvy traveler is one armed with good information. Here are a few tips to help you navigate the Internet successfully and safely.

- **Know when sales start.** Last-minute deals may vanish in minutes. If you have a favorite site or airline, find out when last-minute deals are released to the public. (For example, Southwest's specials are posted every Tues at 12:01am Central Time.)
- **Shop around.** Compare results from different sites and airlines—and against a travel agent's best fare, if you can. If possible, try a

range of times and airports before you make a purchase.
- **Follow the rules of the trade.** Book in advance, and choose an off-peak time and date if possible. Some sites tell you when fares to a destination tend to be cheapest.
- **Stay secure.** Book tickets only through secure sites (some airline sites are not secure). Look for a key icon (Netscape) or a padlock (Internet Explorer) at the bottom of your Web browser before you enter credit-card information or other personal data.
- **Avoid online auctions.** Sites that auction airline tickets and frequent-flier miles are the No. 1 perpetrators of Internet fraud, according to the National Consumers League.
- **Maintain a paper trail.** If you book an E-ticket, print out a confirmation, or write down your confirmation number, and keep it safe and accessible—or your trip could be a virtual one!

ONLINE TRAVELER'S TOOLBOX

Veteran travelers usually carry some essential items to make their trips easier. Following is a selection of online tools to bookmark and use.

- **Visa ATM Locator** (www.visa.com) or **MasterCard ATM Locator** (www.mastercard.com). Find ATMs in hundreds of cities in the United States and around the world.
- **Foreign Languages for Travelers** (www.travlang.com). Learn basic terms in more than 70 languages and click on any underlined phrase to hear what it sounds like. *Note:* Free audio software and your own speakers are required.
- **Intellicast** (www.intellicast.com). Weather forecasts for all 50 states and cities around the world. *Note:* Temperatures are in Celsius for many international destinations.

- **MapQuest** (www.mapquest.com). The best of the mapping sites, MapQuest lets you choose a specific address or destination, and in seconds, it returns a map and detailed directions.
- **Cybercafes.com** (www.cybercafes.com) or **Internet Café Guide** (www.netcafeguide.com). Locate Internet cafes at hundreds of locations around the globe. Catch up on your e-mail and log on to the Web for a few dollars per hour.
- **Universal Currency Converter** (www.xe.com). See what your dollar or pound is worth in more than 100 other countries.
- **U.S. State Department Travel Warnings** (www.travel.state.gov). Reports on places where health concerns or unrest might threaten U.S. travelers. It also lists the locations of U.S. embassies around the world.

9 Recommended Reading

BOOKS   There are numerous books on all aspects of French history and society—ranging from the very general, such as the section on France in the *Encyclopedia Americana,* International Edition (Grolier, 1989), which presents an excellent, illustrated overview of the French people and their way of life, to the very specific, such as Judi Culbertson and Tom Randall's *Permanent Parisians: An Illustrated Guide to the Cemeteries of Paris* (Chelsea Green, 1986), which depicts the lives of famous French and expatriates who are buried in Paris.

HISTORY   In addition to the encyclopedia reference above, a broad overview of French history can be found in other encyclopedias and general history books. One very good one is *History of France* by Guillaume de Bertier de Savigny and David H. Pinkney (Forum Press, 1983), a comprehensive history with illustrations and plenty of obscure but interesting facts.

Two books that present French life and society in the 17th century are Warren Lewis's *The Splendid Century* (William Morrow, 1978) and Madame de Sévigne's *Selected Letters,* edited by Leonard W. Tancock (Penguin, 1982), which contains imaginative and witty letters written to her daughter during the reign of Louis XIV.

Simon Schama's *Citizens* (Alfred A. Knopf, 1989) is "a magnificent and electrifyingly new history of the French Revolution"—long, but enjoyable.

Moving into the 20th century, *Pleasure of the Belle Epoque: Entertainment and Festivity in Turn-of-the-Century France,* by Charles Rearick (Yale University Press, 1985), depicts public diversions in the changing and troubled times of the Third Republic. *Paris Was Yesterday, 1925-1939* (Harcourt Brace Jovanovich, 1988) is a fascinating collection of excerpts from Janet Flanner's "Letters from Paris" column of the *New Yorker.* Larry Collins and Dominique Lapierre have written a popular history of the liberation of Paris in 1944 called *Is Paris Burning?* (Warner Books, 1991).

Finally, two unusual approaches to French history are Rudolph Chleminski's *The French at Table* (William Morrow, 1985), a funny and honest history of why the French know how to eat better than anyone and how they go about it, and *Paris: A Century of Change, 1878-1978,* by Normal Evenson (Yale University Press, 1979), a notable study of the urban development of Paris.

TRAVEL   In *The Flâneur, A Stroll Through the Paradoxes of Paris* (Bloomsbury, 2001), Edmund White wants the reader to experience Paris as

Parisians do. Hard to translate exactly, *a flâneur* is someone who strolls, loafs, or idles. With White, you can circumnavigate Paris as whim dictates.

BIOGRAPHY   You can get a more intimate look at history through biographies of historical figures. Hugh Ross Williamson brings to life Catherine de Médici in his *Catherine de Medici* (Viking Press, 1973) by combining text and magnificent illustrations from the art of the 16th century. This queen of France was the dominant personality during her nation's religious wars and mother of three kings of France, a queen of Spain, and a queen of Navarre.

Representing a very different era are *A Moveable Feast* (Collier Books, 1987), Ernest Hemingway's recollections of Paris during the 1920s, and Morley Callaghan's *That Summer in Paris: Memories of Tangled Friendships with Hemingway, Fitzgerald and Some Others* (1963), an anecdotal account of the same period. Another interesting read is *The Autobiography of Alice B. Toklas,* by Gertrude Stein (Vintage Books, 1990). It's not only the account of 30 years in Paris, but also the biography of Gertrude Stein.

Simone de Beauvoir, by Deirdre Bair (Summit Books, 1990), was described by one critic as a biography *"à l'Americaine"*—that is to say, long, with all the warts of its subject unsparingly described." The story of the great feminist intellectual was based in part on tape-recorded conversations and unpublished letters.

Colette: A Life, by Herbert R. Lottman (Little, Brown, 1991), is a painstakingly researched biography of the celebrated French writer and her fascinating life—which included not only writing novels and appearing in cabarets but also dabbling in lesbianism and perhaps even collaborating with the enemy during the Nazi occupation.

THE ARTS   Much of France's beauty can be found in its art. Three books that approach France from this perspective are *The History of Impressionism,* by John Rewald (Museum of Modern Art, 1973), which is a collection of writings about and quotations from the artists, illuminating this period in art; *The French Through Their Films,* by Robin Buss (Ungar, 1988), an exploration of more than 100 widely circulated films; and *The Studios of Paris: The Capital of Art in the Late Nineteenth Century,* by John Milner (Yale University Press, 1988). In the last, Milner presents the dynamic forces that made Paris one of the most complex centers of the art world in the early modern era.

Nightlife of Paris: The Art of Toulouse-Lautrec, by Patrick O'Connor (Universe, 1992), is an enchanting 80-page book with anecdotes about the hedonistic luminaries of Belle Epoque Paris, with paintings, sketches, and lithographs by the artist.

Olympia: Paris in the Age of Manet, by Otto Friedrich (Harper-Collins, 1992), takes its inspiration from the celebrated artwork in the Musée d'Orsay in Paris. From here the book takes off on an anecdote-rich gossipy chain of historical associations, tracing the rise of the Impressionist school of modern painting, but incorporating social commentary, too, such as the pattern of prostitution and venereal disease in 19th-century France.

FICTION   The *Chanson de Roland,* edited by F. Whitehead (2nd ed.; Basil Blackwell, 1942), written between the 11th and 14th centuries, is the earliest and most celebrated of the "songs of heroic exploits." *The Misanthrope* and *Tartuffe* (Harcourt, Brace and World, 1965) are two masterful satires on the frivolity of the 17th century by the great comic dramatist Molière. François-Marie Arouet Voltaire's *Candide* (Bantam Classics, 1981) is a classic satire attacking the philosophy of optimism and the abuses of the ancient regime.

A few of the masterpieces of the 19th century are *Madame Bovary,* by Gustave Flaubert (Random House, 1982), in which the carefully wrought characters, setting, and plot attest to the genius of Flaubert in presenting the tragedy of Emma Bovary; Victor Hugo's *Les Misérables* (Modern Library, 1983), a classic tale of social oppression and human courage set in the era of Napoleon I; and *Selected Stories* by the master of short stories, Guy de Maupassant (New American Library, 1984).

Honoré de Balzac's *La comédie humaine* depicts life in France from the fall of Napoleon to 1848. Henry James's *The Ambassadors* and *The American* both take place in Paris. *The Vagabond,* by Colette, evokes the life of a French music-hall performer.

Tropic of Cancer is the semiautobiographical story of Henry Miller's years in Paris. One of France's leading thinkers, Jean-Paul Sartre, shows individuals struggling against their freedom in *No Exit and Three Other Plays.*

4

Getting to Know the City of Light

Ernest Hemingway called the many splendors of Paris a "moveable feast" and wrote, "There is never any ending to Paris, and the memory of each person who has lived in it differs from that of any other." It's this aura of personal discovery that has always been the most compelling reason to come to Paris. Perhaps that's why France has been called *le deuxième pays de tout le monde*—"everybody's second country."

The Seine not only divides Paris into the Right Bank and the Left Bank but seems to split the city into two vastly different sections and ways of life. Depending on your time, interest, and budget, you may quickly decide which section of Paris suits you best.

In the very heart of Paris, the old clichés about the Left Bank being for poor, struggling artists, and the Right Bank being for the well heeled were broken down long ago. The very heart of the Left Bank, including the areas around Odéon and St-Germain-des-Prés, are as chic as anything on the Right Bank—and just as expensive.

The history of Paris repeats itself. In the old days, Montmartre was the artists' quarter until prices and tourism drove these "bohemians" to less expensive *quartiers* such as Montparnasse. But Montparnasse long ago became gold-plated real estate.

So where does the struggling artist go today? Not to the central core of the Right or Left Bank, but farther afield. First, it was the Marais, until that district, too, saw rents spiral and the average visitor carrying a gold American Express card. Now, it's farther east, into the 11th (arrondissement), a blue-collar neighborhood between the Marais, Ménilmontant, and République. The heartbeat of this area is rue Oberkampf. If you'd like to see this newly gentrified area before it, too, changes forever, refer to the box, "A Bar Crawl in Trendy Ménilmontant" in chapter 10, "Paris After Dark."

1 Essentials

VISITOR INFORMATION

At the airports are small **info offices,** which, for a fee, will help you make a hotel reservation. But the prime source is the **Office de Tourisme de Paris,** 127 av. des Champs-Elysées, 8e (© **08-36-68-31-12;** fax 01-49-52-53-00; www.paris touristoffice.com; Métro: Charles de Gaulle-Etoile or George V), where you can obtain info about Paris and the provinces. It's open April to October daily from 9am to 8pm. From November to March, hours are Monday to Saturday from 9am to 8pm and Sunday from 11am to 7pm. The staff will make an accommodations reservation for you on the same day you want a room: 1.20€ ($1.05) for hostels and *foyers* ("homes"), 3.05€ ($2.70) one-star hotels, 3.80€ ($3.40)

Tips **Country & City Telephone Codes**

The country code for France is **33**. The city code for Paris (as well as for all cities in the Ile de France region) is **1**; use this code if you're calling from outside France. If you're calling Paris from within Parisor from anywhere else in France, use 01, which is now built into all phone numbers in the Ile de France, making them 10 digits long.

---

two-star hotels, and 6.10€ ($5.45) three-star hotels. (Stars refer to government ratings, rather than those used in this book.) It's often very busy in summer, so you'll probably have to wait in line.

There is a tourist office, **Bureau Gare de Lyon,** at the major rail terminus, Gare de Lyon, 12th arrondissement, serving rail passengers arriving by train. It is not accessible by phone but is available to walk-in clients. It is open Monday to Saturday from 8am to 8pm. Métro: Gare de Lyon.

There are **other branches** in the base of the Eiffel Tower (open May–Sept daily 11am–6:40pm) and in the arrivals hall of the Gare de Lyon (open year-round Mon–Sat 8am–8pm). These offices will give you free copies of the English-language *Time Out* and *Paris User's Guide.*

CITY LAYOUT

Paris is surprisingly compact. Occupying 1,119 km² (432 sq. miles), it's home to more than 10 million people. The city is divided into 20 municipal wards called **arrondissements,** each with its own mayor, city hall, police station, and central post office. Some even have remnants of market squares.

The river Seine divides Paris into the **Right Bank** (Rive Droite) to the north and the **Left Bank** (Rive Gauche) to the south. These designations make sense when you stand on a bridge and face downstream; watching the water flow out toward the sea, to your right is the north bank, to your left the south. Thirty-two bridges link the banks of the Seine, some providing access to the two small islands at the heart of the city, **Ile de la Cité,** the city's birthplace and site of Notre-Dame, and **Ile St-Louis,** a moat-guarded oasis of sober 17th-century mansions. These islands can cause some confusion to walkers who think they've just crossed a bridge from one bank to the other, only to find themselves caught up in an almost medieval maze of narrow streets and old buildings.

As part of Napoleon III's massive urban redevelopment project, Baron Georges-Eugène Haussmann forever changed the look of Paris between 1860 and 1870 by creating the **legendary boulevards:** St-Michel, St-Germain, Haussmann, Malesherbes, Sébastopol, Magenta, Voltaire, and Strasbourg.

The "main street" on the Right Bank is the **Champs-Elysées,** beginning at the Arc de Triomphe and running to place de la Concorde. Haussmann also created avenue de l'Opéra (as well as the Opéra), and the 12 avenues that radiate starlike from the Arc de Triomphe, giving it its original name, place de l'Etoile (*étoile* means "star"); it was renamed place Charles de Gaulle following the general's death and is often referred to as **place Charles de Gaulle-Etoile.**

Haussmann also cleared Ile de la Cité of its medieval buildings, transforming it into a showcase for Notre-Dame. Finally, he laid out two elegant parks on the western and southeastern fringes of the city: the **Bois de Boulogne** and **Bois de Vincennes.**

FINDING AN ADDRESS

The key to finding any address in Paris is looking for the arrondissement number, rendered either as a number followed by "e" or "er" (1er, 2e, and so on) or more formally as part of the postal code (the last two digits indicate the arrondissement—75007 indicates the 7th arrondissement, 75017 the 17th). Numbers on buildings running parallel to the Seine usually follow the course of the river—east to west. On north-south streets, numbering begins at the river.

If you're staying more than 2 or 3 days, buy an inexpensive little book that includes the *plan de Paris* by arrondissement, available at all major newsstands and bookshops. If you can find it, the forest-green *Paris Classique l'Indispensable* is a thorough, well-indexed, and accurate guide to the city and its suburbs. Most map guides provide you with a Métro map, a foldout map of the city, and indexed maps of each arrondissement, with all streets listed and keyed. We've given you a head start by including a **free full-color foldout map** at the back of this guide.

ARRONDISSEMENTS IN BRIEF

Each of Paris's 20 arrondissements possesses a unique style and flavor. You'll want to decide which district appeals most to you and then try to find accommodations there. Later on, try to visit as many areas as you can so you get the full taste of Paris.

1ST ARRONDISSEMENT (MUSEE DU LOUVRE/LES HALLES) "I never knew what a palace was until I had a glimpse of the Louvre," wrote Nathaniel Hawthorne. Perhaps the world's greatest art museum, the **Louvre,** a former royal residence, still lures visitors to the 1st arrondissement. Walk through the **Jardin des Tuileries,** Paris's most formal garden (laid out by Le Nôtre, gardener to Louis XIV). Pause to take in the classic beauty of **place Vendôme,** the opulent home of the Hôtel Ritz. Zola's "belly of Paris" (Les Halles) is no longer the food-and-meat market of Paris (traders moved to the new, more accessible suburb of Rungis); today the **Forum des Halles** is a center of shopping, entertainment, and culture.

2ND ARRONDISSEMENT (LA BOURSE) Home to the **Bourse** (stock exchange), this Right Bank district lies between the Grands Boulevards and rue Etienne-Marcel. From Monday to Friday, brokers play the market until it's time to break for lunch, when the movers and shakers of French capitalism channel their hysteria into the area restaurants. Much of the eastern end of the arrondissement (**Le Sentier**) is devoted to wholesale outlets of the Paris garment district, where thousands of garments are sold (usually in bulk) to buyers from clothing stores throughout Europe. "Everything that exists elsewhere exists in Paris," wrote Victor Hugo in *Les Misérables,* and this district provides ample evidence of that.

3RD ARRONDISSEMENT (LE MARAIS) This district embraces much of *Le Marais* (the swamp), one of the best loved Right Bank neighborhoods. (It extends into the 4th as well.) After decades of decay, Le Marais recently made a comeback, though it may never again enjoy the prosperity of its 17th-century aristocratic heyday; today it contains Paris's **gay neighborhood,** with lots of gay/lesbian restaurants, bars, and stores, as well as the remains of the old Jewish quarter, centered on **rue des Rosiers.** Two of the district's chief attractions are the **Musée Picasso,** a kind of pirate's ransom of painting and sculpture the Picasso estate had to turn over to the French government in lieu of the artist's astronomical death duties, and the **Musée Carnavalet,** which brings to life the history of Paris from prehistoric times to the present.

4TH ARRONDISSEMENT (ILE DE LA CITE/ILE ST-LOUIS & BEAUBOURG) At times it seems as if the 4th has it all: Notre-Dame on Ile de la Cité, Ile St-Louis and its aristocratic town houses, courtyards, and antiques shops. **Ile St-Louis,** a former cow pasture and dueling ground, is home to dozens of 17th-century mansions and 6,000 lucky Louisiens, its permanent residents. Seek out **Ile de la Cité's** two Gothic churches, **Sainte-Chapelle** and **Notre-Dame,** a majestic structure that, according to poet e. e. cummings, doesn't budge an inch for all the idiocies of this world. You'll find France's finest bird and flower markets along with the nation's law courts, which Balzac described as a "cathedral of chicanery." It was here that Marie Antoinette was sentenced to death in 1793. The 4th is also home to the freshly renovated **Centre Pompidou,** one of the top three attractions in France. After all this pomp and glory, you can retreat to **place des Vosges,** a square of perfect harmony and beauty where Victor Hugo lived from 1832 to 1848 and penned many of his famous masterpieces. (His house is now a museum—see p. 173.)

5TH ARRONDISSEMENT (LATIN QUARTER) The Quartier Latin is the intellectual heart and soul of Paris. Bookstores, schools, churches, clubs, student dives, Roman ruins, publishing houses, and expensive and boutiques characterize the district. Discussions of Artaud or Molière over cups of coffee may be more rare than in the past, but they aren't out of place. Beginning with the founding of the **Sorbonne** in 1253, the quarter was called Latin because students and professors spoke the language. You'll follow in the footsteps of Descartes, Verlaine, Camus, Sartre, James Thurber, Elliot Paul, and Hemingway as you explore. Changing times have brought Greek, Moroccan, and Vietnamese immigrants, among others, offering everything from couscous to fiery-hot spring rolls and souvlaki. The 5th borders the Seine, and you'll want to stroll along quai de Montebello, inspecting the inventories of the bouquinistes, who sell everything from antique Daumier prints to yellowing copies of Balzac's *Père Goriot,* in the shadow of Notre-Dame. The 5th also has the **Panthéon,** built by Louis XV after he recovered from the gout and wanted to do something nice for Ste-Geneviève, Paris's patron saint. It's the resting place of Rousseau, Gambetta, Zola, Braille, Hugo, Voltaire, and Jean Moulin, the World War II Resistance leader whom the Gestapo tortured to death.

6TH ARRONDISSEMENT (ST-GERMAIN/LUXEMBOURG) This is the heartland of Paris publishing and, for some, the most colorful Left Bank quarter, where waves of young artists still emerge from the Ecole des Beaux-Arts. The secret of the district lies in discovering its narrow streets, hidden squares, and magnificent gardens. To be really authentic, stroll with an unwrapped loaf of sourdough bread from the wood-fired ovens of **Poilâne** at 8 rue du Cherche-Midi. Everywhere you turn, you'll encounter historic and literary associations, none more so than on **rue Jacob.** At no. 7, Racine lived with his uncle as a teenager; Richard Wagner resided at no. 14 from

Paris Arrondissements

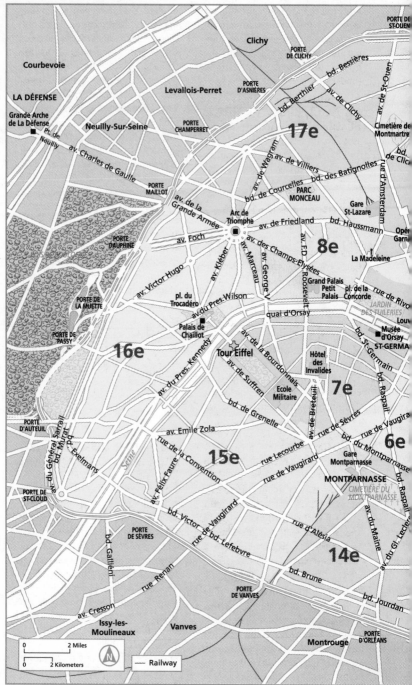

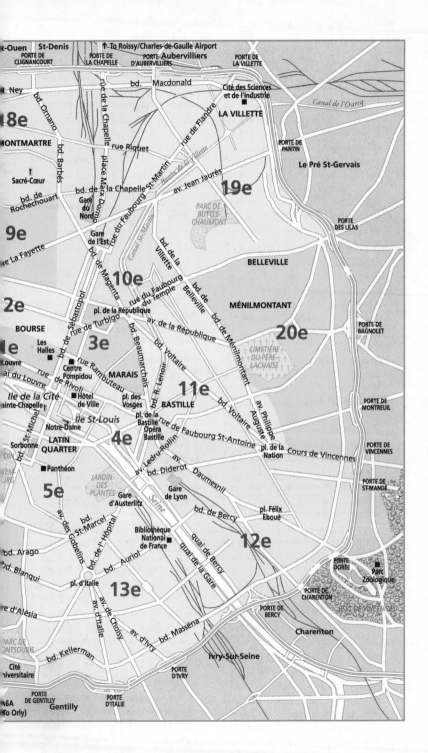

1841 to 1842; Ingres once lived at no. 27 (now it's the office of the French publishing house Editions du Seuil); and Hemingway once occupied a tiny upstairs room at no. 44. The 6th takes in the **Jardin du Luxembourg,** a 60-acre playground where Isadora Duncan went dancing in the predawn hours and a destitute Ernest Hemingway went looking for pigeons for lunch, carrying them in a baby carriage back to his humble flat for cooking.

7TH   ARRONDISSEMENT (EIFFEL   TOWER/MUSEE D'ORSAY)   Paris's most famous symbol, **la Tour Eiffel,** dominates Paris and especially the 7th, a Left Bank district of residences and offices. The tower is one of the most recognizable landmarks in the world, despite the fact that many Parisians (especially its nearest neighbors) hated it when it was unveiled in 1889. Many of Paris's most imposing monuments are in the 7th, like the **Hôtel des Invalides,** which contains Napoleon's Tomb and the Musée de l'Armée, and the **Musée d'Orsay,** the world's premier showcase of 19th-century French art and culture, housed in the old Gare d'Orsay. But there's much hidden charm here as well. **Rue du Bac** was home to the swashbuckling heroes of Dumas's *The Three Musketeers* and to James McNeill Whistler, who moved to no. 110 after selling *Mother.* Auguste Rodin lived at what's now the **Musée Rodin,** 77 rue de Varenne, until his death in 1917.

8TH   ARRONDISSEMENT (CHAMPS-ELYSEES/ MADELEINE)   The showcase of the 8th is the **Champs-Elysées,** stretching from the **Arc de Triomphe** to the Egyptian obelisk on **place de la Concorde.** By the 1980s, the Champs-Elysées had become a garish strip, with too much traffic, fast-food joints, and panhandlers. In the 1990s, Jacques Chirac, then the Gaullist mayor, launched a cleanup, broadening the sidewalks and planting new trees. Now you'll find fashion houses, elegant hotels, restaurants, and shops. Everything in the 8th is the city's "best, grandest, and most impressive": It has the best restaurant (**Taillevent**), the sexiest strip joint (**Crazy Horse Saloon**), the most splendid square (**place de la Concorde**), the best rooftop cafe (**La Samaritaine**), the grandest hotel (the **Crillon**), the most impressive arch (**Arc de Triomphe**), the most expensive residential street (**avenue Montaigne**), the world's oldest subway station (**Franklin D. Roosevelt**), and the most ancient monument (the 3,300-year-old **Obelisk of Luxor**).

9TH   ARRONDISSEMENT (OPERA   GARNIER/PIGALLE) From the Quartier de l'Opéra to the strip joints of Pigalle (the infamous "Pig Alley" for World War II GIs), the 9th endures, even if fashion prefers other addresses. Over the decades, the 9th has been celebrated in literature and song for the music halls that brought gaiety to the city. No. 17 bd. de la Madeleine was where Marie Duplessis, who gained fame as the heroine Marguerite Gautier in Alexandre Dumas the younger's *La Dame aux camellias,* died. (Greta Garbo played her in the film *Camille.*) At **place Pigalle,** gone is the cafe La Nouvelle Athènes, where Degas, Pissarro, and Manet used to meet. Today, you're more likely to find nightclubs. Other attractions include the **Folies-Bergère,** where cancan dancers have been high-kicking since 1868. It is the rococo **Opéra Garnier** (home of the Phantom) that made the 9th the last hurrah of

Second Empire opulence. Renoir hated it, but generations later, Chagall did the ceilings. Pavlova danced *Swan Lake* here, and Nijinsky took the night off to go cruising.

10TH ARRONDISSEMENT (GARE DU NORD/GARE DE L'EST)

The **Gare du Nord** and **Gare de l'Est,** along with porno houses and dreary commercial zones, make the 10th one of the least desirable arrondissements for living, dining, or sightseeing. We try to avoid it, except for two long-time favorite restaurants (see chapter 6): **Brasserie Flo,** 7 cour des Petites-Ecuries, best known for its formidable *choucroute,* a heap of sauerkraut garnished with everything; and **Julien,** 16 rue du Faubourg St-Denis, called the poor man's Maxim's for its Belle Epoque interiors and moderate prices.

11TH ARRONDISSEMENT (OPERA BASTILLE)

For many years, this quarter seemed to sink lower and lower into decay, overcrowded by working-class immigrants from the far reaches of the former Empire. The opening of the **Opéra Bastille,** however, has given the 11th new hope and new life. The facility, called the "people's opera house," stands on the landmark place de la Bastille, where on July 14, 1789, 633 Parisians stormed the fortress and seized the ammunition depot, as the French Revolution swept across the city. Over the years, the prison held Voltaire, the Marquis de Sade, and the mysterious "Man in the Iron Mask." The area between the Marais, Ménilmontant, and République is now being called "blue-collar chic," as the *artistes* of Paris have been driven from the costlier sections of the Marais and can now be found walking the gritty sidewalks of rue Oberkampf. Hip Parisians in search of a more cutting-edge experience are now found living and working among the decaying 19th-century apartments and the 1960s public housing with graffiti-splattered walls.

12TH ARRONDISSEMENT (BOIS DE VINCENNES/GARE DE LYON)

Very few out-of-towners came here until a French chef opened a restaurant called **Au Trou Gascon** (see p. 137). The 12th's major attraction remains the **Bois de Vincennes,** sprawling on the eastern periphery of Paris. This park is a longtime favorite of French families, who enjoy its zoos and museums, its royal château and boating lakes, and its **Parc Floral de Paris,** a celebrated flower garden boasting springtime rhododendrons and autumn dahlias. Venture into the dreary **Gare de Lyon** for **Le Train Bleu,** a restaurant whose ceiling frescoes and Art Nouveau decor are national artistic treasures; the food's good, too (see p. 138). The 12th, once a depressing urban wasteland, has been singled out for budgetary resuscitation and is beginning to sport new housing, shops, gardens, and restaurants. Many will occupy the site of the former Reuilly rail tracks.

13TH ARRONDISSEMENT (GARE D'AUSTERLITZ)

Centered around the grimy **Gare d'Austerlitz,** the 13th might have its devotees, but we've yet to meet one. British snobs who flitted in and out of the train station were among the first of the district's foreign visitors and wrote the 13th off as a dreary working-class counterpart of London's East End. The 13th is also home to Paris's **Chinatown,** stretching for 13 square blocks around the Tolbiac Métro stop. It emerged out of the refugee crisis at the end of the Vietnam War, taking over a neighborhood that had held mostly Arab-speaking peoples. Today, recognizing the overcrowding in the district, the Paris civic authorities are imposing new, not particularly welcome, restrictions on population densities.

14TH ARRONDISSEMENT (MONTPARNASSE) The northern end of this large arrondissement is devoted to **Montparnasse,** home of the "lost generation" and stamping ground of Stein, Toklas, Hemingway, and other American expats of the 1920s. After World War II, it ceased to be the center of intellectual life, but the memory lingers in its cafes. One of the monuments that sets the tone of the neighborhood is **Rodin's statue of Balzac** at the junction of boulevards Montparnasse and Raspail. At this corner are some of the world's most famous **literary cafes,** including La Rotonde, Le Select, La Dôme, and La Coupole. Though Gertrude Stein avoided them (she loathed cafes), the other American expatriates, including Hemingway and Fitzgerald, had no qualms about enjoying a drink here (or quite a few of them, for that matter). Stein stayed at home (27 rue de Fleurus) with Alice B. Toklas, collecting paintings, including those of Picasso, and entertaining the likes of Max Jacob, Apollinaire, T. S. Eliot, and Matisse.

15TH ARRONDISSEMENT (GARE MONTPARNASSE/ INSTITUT PASTEUR) This is a mostly residential district beginning at **Gare Montparnasse,** stretching all the way to the Seine. In size and population, it's the largest quarter of Paris but attracts few tourists and has few attractions, except for the **Parc des Expositions,** the **Cimetière du Montparnasse,** and the **Institut Pasteur.** In the early 20th century, many artists—like Chagall, Léger, and Modigliani—lived here in a shared atelier known as "The Beehive."

16TH ARRONDISSEMENT (TROCADERO/BOIS DE BOULOGNE) Originally the village of Passy, where Benjamin Franklin lived during most of his time in Paris, this district is still reminiscent of Proust's world. Highlights include the **Bois de Boulogne;** the **Jardin du Trocadéro;** the **Maison de Balzac;** the **Musée Guimet** (famous for its Asian collections); and the **Cimetière de Passy,** resting place of Manet, Talleyrand, Giraudoux, and Debussy. One of the largest arrondissements, it's known today for its well-heeled bourgeoisie, its upscale rents, and some rather posh (and, according to its critics, rather smug) residential boulevards. The arrondissement also has the best vantage point to view the Eiffel Tower, **place du Trocadéro.**

17TH ARRONDISSEMENT (PARC MONCEAU/PLACE CLICHY) Flanking the northern periphery of Paris, the 17th incorporates neighborhoods of bourgeois respectability (in its west end) and less affluent neighborhoods in its east end. It boasts two of the great restaurants of Paris, **Guy Savoy** and **Michel Rostang** (see chapter 6, "Where to Dine").

18TH ARRONDISSEMENT (MONTMARTRE) The 18th is the most famous outer quarter of Paris, containing **Montmartre,** the **Moulin Rouge, Sacré-Coeur,** and ultratouristy **place du Tertre.** Utrillo was its native son, Renoir lived here, and Toulouse-Lautrec adopted the area as his own. The most famous enclave of artists in Paris's history, the **Bateau-Lavoir,** of Picasso fame, gathered here. Max Jacob, Matisse, and Braque were all frequent visitors. Today, place Blanche is known for its prostitutes, and Montmartre is filled with honky-tonks, souvenir shops, and terrible restaurants. You can still find pockets of quiet beauty, though. The city's most famous flea market, the **Marché aux Puces de Clignancourt,** is another landmark.

19TH ARRONDISSEMENT (LA VILLETTE) Today, visitors come to what was once the village of La Villette to see the angular **Cité des Sciences et de l'Industrie,** a spectacular science museum and park built on a site that for years was devoted to the city's slaughterhouses. Mostly residential, and not at all upscale, the district is one of the most ethnically diverse in Paris, the home of people from all parts of the former Empire. A highlight is

Les Buttes Chaumont, a park where kids can enjoy puppet shows and donkey rides.

20TH ARRONDISSEMENT (PERE-LACHAISE CEMETERY) The 20th's greatest landmark is **Père-Lachaise Cemetery,** the resting place of Jim Morrison, Edith Piaf, Marcel Proust, Oscar Wilde, Isadora Duncan, Sarah Bernhardt, Gertrude Stein and Alice B. Toklas, Colette, and many others. Otherwise, the 20th arrondissement is a dreary and sometimes volatile melting pot comprising residents from France's former colonies. Though nostalgia buffs sometimes head here to visit Piaf's former neighborhood, **Ménilmontant-Belleville,** it has been almost totally bulldozed and rebuilt since the bad old days when she grew up here.

2 Getting Around

Paris is a city for strollers whose greatest joy is rambling through unexpected alleyways and squares. Only when you're dead tired and can't walk another step, or have to go all the way across town in a hurry, should you consider using the Métro, a swift but dull means of urban transport.

For information on the city's public transportation, call ✆ **08-36-68-77-14.**

BY METRO & RER

A century old, the **Paris Métro** will soon become one of the most modern and efficient in the world. At its centenary in the summer of 2000, the Métro announced a gigantic overhaul program to refurbish some 200 of the system's nearly 300 stations by 2003. The **Métro** (✆ **08-36-68-77-14**) is the easiest and most efficient way to get around Paris. Most stations display a map of the system at the entrance. Within Paris, you can transfer between the subway and the RER regional trains for no additional cost. To make sure you catch the right train, find your destination, and then visually follow the line it's on to the end of the route and note its name. This is the sign you look for in the stations and the name you'll see on the train. Transfer stations are known as *correspondances* (note that some require long walks—Châtelet-Les Halles is the most notorious).

Few trips will require more than one transfer. Some stations have maps with push-button indicators that'll help you plot your route by lighting up when you press the button for your destination. A ride on the urban lines costs 1.30€ ($1.15) to any point within the 20 arrondissements of Paris, as well as to many of its nearby suburbs. A bulk purchase of 10 tickets (which are bound together into what the French refer to as a *carnet*) costs 9.25€ ($8.25). Métro fares to outlying suburbs on the Sceaux, the Noissy-St-Léger, and St-Germain-en-Laye lines cost more and are sold on an individual basis depending on the distance you travel. At the entrance to the Métro station, insert your ticket into the

(Value) Money-Saving Public Transportation Passes

You can buy a **Paris Visite pass,** valid for 1, 2, 3, or 5 days on the public transport system, including the Métro, the city buses, the RER (regional express) trains within Paris city limits, and even the funicular to the top of Montmartre. (The RER has both first- and second-class compartments, and the pass lets you travel in first class.) The cost is 8.35€ ($7.45) for a 1-day pass, 14€ ($12) for a 2-day pass, 18€ ($16) for a 3-day pass, or 27€ ($24) for 5 days. The card is available at the **Services Touristiques de la Régie Autonome des Transports Parisiens** (RATP), with offices at place de la Madeleine, 8e (Métro: Madeleine); and 54 quai de la Rapée, 12e (Métro: Gare de Lyon). For information about these passes or any aspect of public transport in or around Paris, call ℂ **08-36-68-41-14** for information in English, or ℂ **08-36-68-77-14** for information in French; or consult their website at www.ratp.fr. Passes are sold at either of the addresses immediately above, at the Champs-Elysées branch of the Paris Tourist office (see above), or at the ticket counter of any Métro station.

Another, more economical pass that's available to visitors is the **Carte Mobilis,** allowing unlimited travel on bus, Métro, and RER lines in Paris during a 1-day period. Depending on the zone you want to travel within, it will cost a minimum of 5€ ($4.45) for travel within a short distance beyond the 20 arrondissements of Paris. Other variations exist in denominations of 6.70€ ($5.95); 8.50€ ($7.55) (which will carry you from central Paris to Versailles); and 11€ ($10) for a 1-day pass that will include transit to the far-flung site of Marne-la-Vallée, site of Euro Disney. You can buy these passes at any Métro or RER station in Greater Paris.

Most economical for anyone planning a full week's visit to Paris with a lot of public transport is a **Carte Orange.** Sold at any Métro station, it allows 1 full week of unlimited Métro or bus transit within Paris (the 20 arrondissements plus a wide swath of the outlying suburbs) for 13€ ($12). To get one, you'll have to submit a passport-size photo. Cartes Oranges are valid from any Monday to the following Sunday, they're sold only on Monday, Tuesday, Wednesday, and Thursday of any given week, and they're valid only for the week in which they're sold.

Officially, Cartes Oranges can only be sold to residents of the Ile de France, but according to a spokesperson at the RATP, 99% of RATP salespeople never ask for a *carte d'identité,* and the sale of Cartes Oranges slipped long ago into general usage, including by smart out-of-town visitors.

turnstile and pass through. Take the ticket back, because it may be checked by uniformed police officers when you leave the subway. There are also occasional ticket checks on the trains, platforms, and passageways. If you're changing trains, get out and determine which direction (final destination) on the next line you want, then follow the bright orange CORRESPONDANCE signs until you reach the proper platform. Don't follow a SORTIE sign, which means "exit." If you exit, you'll have to pay another fare to resume your journey.

The Paris Métro runs daily from 5:30am to 1am, at which time all underground trains reach their final terminus at the end of each of their respective lines. Be alert that the last train may pass through central Paris as much as an hour before that time. The subways are reasonably safe at any hour, but beware of pickpockets.

BY BUS

Bus travel is much slower than the subway. Most buses run from 7am to 8:30pm (a few operate to 12:30am, and 10 operate during the early morning hours). Service is limited on Sundays and holidays. Bus and Métro fares are the same and you can use the same *carnet* tickets on both. At certain stops, signs list the destinations and numbers of the buses serving that point. Destinations are usually listed north to south and east to west. Most stops along the way are also posted on the sides of the buses. To catch a bus, wait in line at the bus stop. Signal the driver to stop the bus and board.

Most bus rides (including any that begin and end within Paris's 20 arrondissements and nearby suburbs) require one ticket (the same that's used within the Métro). For bus travel to some of the more distant suburbs, an additional ticket might be required. If you intend to use the buses a lot, pick up an **RATP bus map** at its offices on place de la Madeleine and quai de la Rapée (see the "Money-Saving Public Transportation Passes" box) or at any tourist office. For details on bus and Métro routes, call ℃ **08-36-68-77-14** for information in French, or ℃ **08-36-68-41-14** for information in English.

The same entity that maintains Paris's network of Métros and buses, the **RATP** (℃ **08-36-68-77-14**), has initiated a motorized mode of transport designed as a means of appreciating the city's visual grandeur. Known as the **Balabus,** it's a fleet of big-windowed orange-and-white motor coaches whose major drawback is their limited hours—they run only on Sunday and national holidays from noon to 9pm, April to September. The coaches journey in both directions between the Gare de Lyon and the Grande Arche de La Défense, encompassing some of the city's most monumental vistas and making regular stops. Presentation of two Métro tickets, each priced at 1.30€ ($1.15), a valid Carte Mobilis (see box above), or a valid Paris Visite pass (see the "Money-Saving Public Transportation Passes" box) will take you along the entire route. You'll recognize the bus and the route it follows by the "Bb" symbol on each bus's side and on signs posted beside the route it follows.

BY CAR

Again, don't even think about driving in Paris. The streets are narrow, with confusing one-way designations, and parking is next to impossible. Besides, most visitors don't have the ruthlessness required to survive in Parisian traffic. Think about renting a car only if you plan to explore the Ile de France and beyond.

You can rent cars from locally based agencies like **Autorent,** 98 rue de la Convention, 15e (℃ **01-45-54-22-45;** Métro: Boucicaut), or from competitors like **Rent-a-Car,** 62 bd. Malesherbes, 8e (℃ **01-45-22-28-28;** Métro: Gare St-Lazare) and **Inter Touring Service,** 117 bd. Auguste-Blanqui, 13e (℃ **01-45-88-52-37;** Métro: Glacière). **Budget** (℃ **800/472-3325** in the U.S. and Canada; www.budget.com) maintains about 30 locations in Paris, with its largest branch at 81 av. Kléber, 16e (℃ **08-25-00-35-64;** Métro: Trocadéro). **Hertz** (℃ **800/654-3001** in the U.S. and Canada; www.hertz.com) maintains about 15 locations in Paris, including offices at the airports and the main office at 27 place St-Ferdinand, 17e (℃ **01-45-74-97-39;** Métro: Argentine). Be sure to ask about promotional discounts. **Avis** (© 800/331-2112 in the U.S. and Canada; www.avis.com) has offices at both airports, as well as a headquarters at 5 rue Bixio, 7e (© **01-44-18-10-50;** Métro: Ecole Militaire), near the Eiffel Tower. **National** (© **800/227-3876** in the U.S. and Canada; www.nationalcar. com) is represented in Paris by **National Citer,** whose largest office is at 165 bis rue de Vaugirard, 15e (© **01-44-38-61-61;** Métro: Pasteur). It has offices at both airports as well.

BY TAXI

Taxi drivers are organized into an effective lobby to keep their number limited to around 15,000, and it's nearly impossible to get one at rush hour. You can hail regular cabs on the street when their signs read *libre*. Taxis are easier to find at the many stands near Métro stations.

The flag drops at 2.15€ ($1.90), and you pay .60€ (55¢) per kilometer. At night, expect to pay 1.15€ ($1) per kilometer. On airport trips, you're not required to pay for the driver's empty return ride. Be warned that many taxis can refuse to take a fourth passenger except for a child. It is their legal right. Although drivers can refuse a fourth passenger, some taxis are large enough to take up to five. You're allowed several small pieces of luggage free if they're transported inside and don't weigh more than 5 kilograms (11 lb.). Heavier suitcases carried in the trunk cost .90€ (80¢) apiece. Tip 12% to 15%—the latter usually elicits a *merci*. To radio cabs, call © **01-42-03-50-50** or 01-44-52-23-58; you'll be charged from the point where the taxi begins the drive to pick you up.

BY BICYCLE

To bike through the streets and parks of Paris, perhaps with a baguette tucked under your arm, might've been a fantasy of yours since you saw your first Maurice Chevalier film. In recent years, the city has added many miles of right-hand lanes designated for cyclists as well as hundreds of bike racks. (When these aren't available, many Parisians simply chain their bikes to fences or lampposts.) Cycling is especially popular in the larger parks and gardens.

Paris-Vélos, 2 rue du Fer-à-Moulin, 5e (© **01-43-37-59-22;** Métro: Censier-Daubenton), rents bicycles by the day, weekend, or week, charging 14€ to 24€ ($12–$21) per weekday, 24€ to 33€ ($21–$29) Saturday and Sunday, and 68€ to 91€ ($61–$81) per week. You must leave a 304€ ($271) deposit. It's open Monday to Saturday from 10am to 12:30pm and 2 to 7pm.

BY BOAT

From April to mid-October, the **Batobus** (© **01-44-11-33-44**), a series of 150-passenger ferries with big windows for viewing the riverfronts, operates at 25-minute intervals daily from 10am to 7pm. Boats chug along between the quays at the base of the Eiffel Tower and the quays at the base of the Louvre, stopping at the Musée d'Orsay, St-Germain-des-Prés, Notre-Dame, the Hôtel-de-Ville, and what the management refers to as the Champs-Elysées, but which is actually a stop at the base of the Pont Alexandre-III. Transit between any two stops costs 3.05€ ($2.70) for children and adults, and 1.50€ ($1.35) for transit between any additional stops, although passengers who intend to use the boat as a sightseeing opportunity usually opt to pay a flat rate (good all day) of 9.90€ ($8.80) for adults and 5.30€ ($4.70) for persons under 19, and then settle back and watch the monuments. Photo ops are countless aboard this leisurely but panoramic "floating observation platform." Anyone wanting a 2-day exposure to the delights of waterborne Paris can buy a 2-day pass for 12€ ($11) for adults and 6.10€ ($5.45) for children under 12.

FAST FACTS: Paris

American Express From its administrative headquarters in the Paris suburb of Reuil-Malmaison, at 4 rue de Louis-Blériot, 92561 Reuil-Malmaison CEDEX, Amex operates a 24-hour phone line (© **01-47-14-50-00**) that handles questions about American Express services (banking, wire transfers, or emergencies that include lost or stolen Amex cards) within Greater Paris. Tours, mail drop, money exchange, and wire-transfer services are available at 11 rue Scribe, 9e Paris (© **01-47-14-50-00**; Métro: Opéra), and a smaller branch at 38 av. Wagram, 8e (© **01-42-27-58-80**; Métro: Ternes). Both are open for banking services Monday to Saturday from 9am to noon and from 2 to 5pm. Foreign exchange and participation in the company's many guided bus tours in and around Paris are offered at all three branches Monday to Saturday from 9am to 6pm, and Sunday (rue Scribe branch only) from 10am to 4:30pm.

Babysitters The best selection of English-speaking sitters is found at **Kid Services,** 17 rue Molière, 1er (© **01-42-61-90-00**).

Banks Banks in Paris are open Monday to Friday from 9am to 5pm. A few are open on Saturday. Ask at your hotel for the location of the bank nearest you. Shops and most hotels will cash your traveler's checks, but not at the advantageous rate a bank or foreign-exchange office will give you, so if you don't have access to your funds through an ATM, make sure you've allowed enough funds for "le weekend."

Business Hours Opening hours in France are erratic, as befits a nation of individualists. Most museums close 1 day a week (often Tues) and national holidays; hours tend to be from 9:30am to 5pm. Some museums, particularly the smaller ones, close for lunch from noon to 2pm. Most museums are open Saturday, but many close Sunday morning and reopen in the afternoon. (See chapter 7 for specific times.) Generally, **offices** are open Monday to Friday from 9am to 5pm, but don't count on it. Always call first. **Large stores** are open from 9 or 9:30am (often 10am) to 6 or 7pm without a break for lunch. Some **shops,** particularly those operated by non-native French owners, open at 8am and close at 8 or 9pm. In some **small stores,** the lunch break can last 3 hours, beginning at 1pm.

Dentists For emergency dental service, call **S.O.S. Dentaire,** 87 bd. du Port-Royal, 13e (© **01-43-37-51-00**; Métro: Port-Royal), Monday to Friday from 8pm to midnight and Saturday and Sunday from 9:30am to midnight. For 24 hour walk-in relief from a hospital specializing in handling accidents affecting the mouth, teeth, and jaws, as well as agonizing toothaches, we suggest **L'Hôpital Salpetrière,** 47 Bd. De l'Hôpital, 75013 Paris (© **01-42-16-00-00**). You can also call or visit the **American Hospital,** 63 bd. Victor-Hugo, Neuilly (© **01-46-41-25-25**; Métro: Pont de Levallois or Pont de Neuilly; Bus: 82). A 24-hour English/French dental clinic is on the premises.

Drugstores After regular hours, ask at your hotel where the nearest 24-hour *pharmacie* is. You'll also find the address posted on the doors or windows of other drugstores in the neighborhood. One all-night drugstore is the **Pharmacie Derhy,** in La Galerie Les Champs, 84 av. des Champs-Elysées, 8e (© **01-45-62-02-41**; Métro: George V).

Electricity In general, expect 200 volts AC (60 cycles), though you'll encounter 110 and 115 volts in some older establishments. Adapters are needed to fit sockets. Many hotels have two-pin (in some cases, three-pin) sockets for electric razors. It's best to ask at your hotel before plugging in any electrical appliance.

Embassies/Consulates If you have a passport, immigration, legal, or other problem, contact your consulate. Call before you go, as they often keep strange hours and observe both French and home-country holidays.

The Embassy of the **United States,** at 2 av. Gabriel, 8e (© **01-43-12-22-22;** Métro: Concorde), is open Monday to Friday from 9am to 6pm. Passports are issued at its consulate at 2 rue St-Florentin (© **01-36-70-14-88;** Métro: Concorde). Getting a passport replaced costs $55. The Embassy of **Canada** is at 35 av. Montaigne, 8e (© **01-44-43-29-00;** Métro: F. D. Roosevelt or Alma-Marceau); open Monday to Friday from 9am to noon and 2 to 4pm. The Canadian consulate is at the embassy. The Embassy of the **United Kingdom** is at 35 rue du Faubourg St-Honoré, 8e (© **01-44-51-31-00;** Métro: Concorde or Madeleine); open Monday to Friday from 9:30am to 12:30pm and 2:30 to 5pm. The consulate is at the same address. The Embassy of **Australia** is at 4 rue Jean-Rey, 15e (© **01-40-59-33-00;** Métro: Bir Hakeim); open Monday to Friday from 9:15am to noon and 2:30 to 4:30pm. The Embassy of **New Zealand** is at 7 ter rue Léonard-de-Vinci, 16e (© **01-45-00-24-11;** Métro: Victor Hugo); open Monday to Friday from 9am to 1pm and 2:30 to 6pm. The Embassy of **Ireland** is at 4 rue Rude, 16e (© **01-44-17-67-00;** Métro: Etoile); open Monday to Friday from 9:30am to noon.

Emergencies For the police, call © **17;** to report a fire, call © **18.** For an ambulance, call the fire department at © **01-45-78-74-52;** a fire vehicle rushes patients to the nearest emergency room. For **S.A.M.U.,** an independently operated, privately owned ambulance company, call © **15.** For less urgent matters, you can reach the police at 9 bd. du Palais, 4e (© **01-53-73-53-71** or 01-53-73-53-73; Métro: Cité).

Hospitals Open Monday to Saturday from 8am to 7pm, **Central Médical Europe,** 44 rue d'Amsterdam, 9e (© **01-42-81-93-33;** Métro: Liège or St-Lazare), maintains contacts with medical and dental practitioners in all fields. Appointments are recommended. Another choice is the **American Hospital of Paris,** 63 bd. Victor-Hugo, Neuilly (© **01-46-41-25-25;** Métro: Pont de Levallois or Pont de Neuilly; Bus: 82), which operates 24-hour medical and dental services. An additional clinic is the **Centre Figuier,** 2 rue du Figuier, 4e (© **01-49-96-62-70;** Métro: St-Paul). Call before visiting.

Internet Access To surf the Net or check your e-mail, try the **Cybercafé Latino,** 13 rue de l'Ecole Polytechnique, 5e (© **01-40-51-86-94;** www.cyber cafelatino.com; Métro: Maubert-Mutualité), open daily from 1pm to 2am, or **Le Rendez-vous Toyota,** 79 av. des Champs-Elysées, 8e (© **01-56-89-29-79;** www.lerendez-voustoyota.com; Métro: George V), open Tuesday to Thursday from 10:30am to 9pm, Friday and Saturday from 10:30am to midnight, and Sunday from 10:30am to 9pm. See also **Le Web Bar** in chapter 10.

Liquor Laws Supermarkets, grocery stores, and cafes sell alcoholic beverages. The legal drinking age is 16, but persons under that age can be served alcohol in a bar or restaurant if accompanied by a parent or legal guardian. Wine and liquor are sold every day of the week, year-round. Hours of cafes vary. Some open at 6am, serving drinks to 3am; others are open 24 hours. Bars and nightclubs may stay open as late as they wish.

The Breathalyzer test is used in France, and a motorist is considered "legally intoxicated" with 0.5 grams of alcohol per liter of blood (the more liberal U.S. law is 1g per liter). If convicted, a motorist faces a stiff fine and a possible prison term of 2 months to 2 years. If bodily injury results, sentences can range from 2 years to life.

Mail/Post Offices Most post offices in Paris are open Monday to Friday from 8am to 7pm and Saturday from 8am to noon. The **main post office** (PTT) for Paris is at 52 rue du Louvre, 75001 Paris (*C* **01-40-28-76-00;** Métro: Louvre). It's open 24 hours a day for the sale of stamps, phone calls, and sending faxes and telegrams, with limited hours (Mon–Fri 8am–5pm and Sat 8am–noon) for services like the sale of money orders. Stamps can usually be purchased at your hotel reception desk and at cafes with red TABAC signs. You can send faxes at the main post office in each arrondissement.

Airmail letters within Europe cost .45€ (40¢); to the United States and Canada, .65€ (60¢); and to Australia and New Zealand, .80€ (70¢). You can have mail sent to you *poste restante* (general delivery) at the main post office for a small fee. Take an ID, such as a passport, to pick up mail. American Express (see above) offers a *poste restante* service, but you may be asked to show an American Express card or traveler's checks.

Newspapers/Magazines English-language newspapers are available at nearly every kiosk. Published Monday to Saturday, the *International Herald-Tribune* is the most popular paper with visiting Americans and Canadians; the *Guardian* provides a British point of view. For those who read in French, the leading domestic newspapers are *Le Monde, Le Figaro,* and *Libération;* the top magazines are *L'Express, Le Point,* and *Le Nouvel Observateur.* Kiosks are generally open daily from 8am to 9pm.

Pets If you have certificates from a vet and proof of rabies vaccination, you can bring most house pets into France.

Police Call *C* **17** for emergencies. The principal Préfecture is at 9 bd. du Palais, 4e (*C* **01-53-71-53-71;** Métro: Cité).

Restrooms If you're in dire need, duck into a cafe or brasserie to use the lavatory. It's customary to make some small purchase if you do so. In the street, the domed self-cleaning lavatories are a decent option if you have small change; Métro stations and underground garages usually have public lavatories, but the degree of cleanliness varies.

Safety In Paris, be especially aware of child pickpockets. They roam the capital, preying on tourists around attractions like the Louvre, Eiffel Tower, and Notre-Dame, and they also often strike in the Métro, sometimes blocking a victim from the escalator. A band of these young thieves can clean your pockets even while you try to fend them off. Their method is to get very close to a target, ask for a handout (sometimes), and deftly help themselves to your money or passport.

Although public safety is not as much a problem in Paris as it is in large American cities, concerns are growing. Robbery at gun- or knifepoint is uncommon here, but not unknown. Be careful.

Telephone Public phones are found in cafes, restaurants, Métro stations, post offices, airports, and train stations, and occasionally on the streets. Finding a coin-operated telephone in France is an arduous task. A simpler and more widely accepted method of payment is the *télécarte*, a prepaid calling card available at kiosks, post offices, and Métro stations and costing 7.45€ to 15€ ($6.65–$13) for 50 and 120 units, respectively. A local call costs one unit, which provides you with 6 to 18 minutes of conversation, depending on the rate. Avoid making calls from your hotel, which might double or triple the charges.

To call **long distance within France,** dial the 10-digit number (9-digit in some cases outside Paris) of the person or place you're calling. To make a **direct international call,** first dial 00, listen for the tone, then slowly dial the country code, the area code, and the local number. The country code for the **USA** and **Canada** is 1; **Great Britain,** 44; **Ireland,** 353; **Australia,** 61; **New Zealand,** 64; **South Africa,** 27.

An easy and relatively inexpensive way to call home is **USA Direct/AT&T World Connect.** From within France, dial any of the following numbers: (© **0800/99-0011,** -1011, -1111, or -1211). Then follow the prompt, which will ask you to punch in the number of either your AT&T credit card or a MasterCard or Visa. Along with the U.S., the countries participating in the system—referred to as World Connect—include **Canada,** the **United Kingdom, Ireland, Australia,** and **New Zealand.** By punching in the number of the party you want in any of these countries, you'll avoid the surcharges imposed by the hotel operator. An AT&T operator will be available to help you with complications arising during the process.

Time France is usually 6 hours ahead of Eastern Standard Time and 9 hours ahead of Pacific Standard Time in the United States. French daylight saving time lasts from around April to September, when clocks are set 1 hour ahead of the standard time.

Tipping By law, all bills show *service compris,* which means the tip is included; additional gratuities are customarily given as follows: For **hotel staff,** tip the porter 1.05€ to 1.50€ (95¢–$1.35) per item of baggage and 1.50€ ($1.35) per day for the chambermaid. You're not obligated to tip the concierge, doorman, or anyone else unless you use his or her services. In **cafes** and **restaurants,** waiter service is usually included, though you can leave some small change, if you like. Tip **taxi drivers** 12% to 15% of the amount on the meter. In **theaters** and **restaurants,** give cloakroom attendants at least .75€ (70¢) per item. Give **restroom attendants** in nightclubs and such places about .30€ (25¢). Tip the **hairdresser** about 15%, and don't forget to tip the person who gives you a shampoo or a manicure 1.50€ ($1.35). For **guides** for group visits to museums and monuments, .75€ to 1.50€ (70¢–$1.35) is a reasonable tip.

Water Drinking water is generally safe, though it has been known to cause diarrhea in some unaccustomed stomachs. If you ask for water in a restaurant, it'll be bottled water (for which you'll pay), unless you specifically request tap water (*l'eau du robinet*).

5

Where to Stay

Paris boasts some 2,000 hotels—with about 80,000 rooms—spread across its 20 arrondissements. They range from the Ritz and the Crillon to dives so repellent even George Orwell, author of *Down and Out in Paris and London,* wouldn't have considered checking in. (Of course, you won't find those in this guide!) We've included deluxe places for those who can afford to live like the Sultan of Brunei as well as a wide range of moderate and inexpensive choices for the rest of us.

Most visitors, at least those from North America, come to Paris in July and August. Many French are on vacation, and trade fairs and conventions come to a halt, so there are usually plenty of rooms, even though these months have traditionally been the peak season for European travel. In most hotels, February as busy as April or September because of the volume of business travelers and the numbers of tourists who've learned to take advantage of off-season discounts.

Because hot weather rarely lasts long in Paris, few hotels, except the deluxe ones, provide air-conditioning. If you're trapped in a garret on a hot summer night, you'll have to sweat it out. You can open your window to get some cooler air, but open windows admit the nuisance of noise pollution. To avoid this, you can request a room in back when reserving.

READING THE GOVERNMENT RATINGS

The French government grades hotels with a star system, ranging from one star for a simple inn to four stars for a deluxe hotel. Moderately priced hotels usually get two or three stars. This system is based on a complex formula of room sizes, facilities, plumbing, elevators, dining options, renovations, and so on. In one-star hotels, the bathrooms are often shared and the facilities extremely limited (such as no elevator), and the rooms may not have phones or TVs; breakfast is often the only meal served. In two- or three-star hotels, there are usually elevators, and rooms will likely have baths, phones, and TVs. In four-star hotels, you'll get the works, with all the amenities plus facilities and services such as room service, 24-hour concierges, elevators, and perhaps even health clubs.

However, the system is a bit misleading. For tax reasons, a four-star hotel might elect to have a three-star rating, which, with the hotel's permission, is granted by the government. The government won't add a star where it's not merited, but will remove one at the hotel's request.

WHICH BANK IS FOR YOU?

The river dividing Paris geographically and culturally demands you make a choice. Are you more **Left Bank,** wanting a room in the heart of St-Germain, where Jean-Paul Sartre and Simone de Beauvoir once spent the night? Or are you more **Right Bank,** preferring sumptuous quarters like those at the Crillon, where Tom Cruise once slept? Would you rather look for that special old curio

A Room in Paris

If you seek accommodations in something more intimate (and in some cases, more restrictive) than a hotel, consider booking a room within a private home. A California-based agency promoting upmarket B&B accommodations in Paris is **European B&B,** 437 J St., Suite 210, San Diego, CA 92101 (© **800/872-2632** in the U.S.; fax 619/531-1686; www.parisbandb.com). In Paris, contact their affiliate **Alcôve & Agapes,** 8 bus rue Coysevox, 75018 Paris (© **01-44-85-06-05;** fax 01-44-85-06-14).

These organizations act as intermediaries between travelers who seek rooms in private homes and Parisians who wish to welcome visitors. Most hosts speak at least some English, range in age from 30 to 75, and have at least some points of view about entertainment and dining options within the neighborhood. Available options include individual bedrooms, usually within large, old-fashioned private apartments, as well as "unhosted" accommodations where the apartment is otherwise empty and without the benefit (or restrictions) of a live-in host.

Rates for occupancy by either one or two persons, with breakfast included, range from 65€ to 157€ ($58–$140) per unit, depending on the apartment, the neighborhood, the setup, and the plumbing. In cases where a client occupies an unhosted apartment, the refrigerators will be stocked with up to 3 days' breakfast supplies, and are replenished at regular intervals if your stay exceeds 3 days.

in a dusty shop on the Left Bank's rue Jacob or inspect the latest Lagerfeld or Dior couture on the Right Bank's avenue Montaigne? Each of Paris's neighborhoods has its own flavor, and your experiences and memories of Paris will likely be formed by where you choose to stay.

If you desire chic surroundings, choose a Right Bank hotel. That puts you near the most elegant shops and within walking distance of major sights like the Arc de Triomphe, place de la Concorde, the Jardin des Tuileries, the Opéra Garnier, and the Louvre. The best Right Bank hotels are near the Arc de Triomphe in the 8th arrondissement, though many first-class lodgings cluster near the Trocadéro and Bois du Boulogne in the 16th or near the Palais des Congrès in the 17th. If you'd like to be near place Vendôme, try for a hotel in the 1st. Also popular are the increasingly fashionable Marais and Bastille in the 3rd and 4th arrondissements, and Les Halles/Beaubourg, home of the Centre Pompidou and Les Halles shopping mall, in the 3rd.

If you want less formality and tiny bohemian streets, head for the Left Bank, where prices are traditionally lower. Hotels that cater to students are found in the 5th and 6th arrondissements, the 5th being known as the Latin Quarter. These areas, with their literary overtones, boast the Sorbonne, the Panthéon, the Jardin du Luxembourg, cafe life, bookstores, and publishing houses. The 7th arrondissement provides a touch of avant-garde St-Germain.

BEST HOTEL BETS
See chapter 1 for a list of our hotel favorites—the best newcomer, the best view, and more.

1 On the Right Bank

We'll begin with the most centrally located arrondissements on the Right Bank, then work our way through the more outlying neighborhoods and to the area around the Arc de Triomphe.

1ST ARRONDISSEMENT
VERY EXPENSIVE

Hôtel Costes ★★★   Grand style and a location close to the headquarters of some of Paris's most upscale shops, as well as the offices of *Harper's Bazaar*, attract high-style fashion types. Don't expect the Ritz, but this is one of the shining stars of Paris hostelries. The town house–style premise was a *maison bourgeoise* for many generations, presenting a dignified facade. In 1996, it was richly adorned with jewel-toned colors, heavy swagged curtains, and lavish Napoleon III accessories. Today, everything about it evokes the rich days of the Gilded Age, especially the guest rooms. Some are small, but they're cozy and ornate, with one or two large beds, CD players, and fax machines. The best units are called Grande Chambre and they contain sitting areas. For the ultimate luxury, ask for one of the duplex units with split-level layouts. Each unit is equipped with a luxurious bathroom with tub-and-shower combo.

239 rue St-Honoré, 75001 Paris. ✆ **01-42-44-50-50.** Fax 01-42-44-50-01. 82 units. 456€–608€ ($406–$541) double; from 1,140€ ($1,015) suite. AE, DC, MC, V. Métro: Tuileries or Concorde. **Amenities:** Restaurant (French); bar; indoor pool; health club; car-rental desk; room service; massage; babysitting; laundry/dry cleaning. *In room:* A/C, TV, minibar, hair dryer.

Hôtel de Vendôme ★★   Once the Embassy of Texas (when that state was a nation), this jewel box opened in 1998 at one of the world's most prestigious addresses. It is comparable to the Costes, but with a less flashy clientele. Though the guest rooms are only moderate in size, you live in opulent comfort. Most of the rooms are in classic Second Empire style with luxurious beds, tasteful fabrics, well-upholstered hand-carved furnishings, and first-rate bathrooms with tubs and showers. The security is fantastic, with TV intercoms. This new version of the hotel replaces a lackluster one that stood here for a century, and its facade and roof are classified as historic monuments by the French government.

1 place Vendôme, 75001 Paris. ✆ **01-55-04-55-00.** Fax 01-49-27-97-89. www.hoteldevendome.com. 29 units. 380€–638€ ($338–$568) double; from 684€ ($609) suite. AE, DC, MC, V. Métro: Concorde or Opéra. **Amenities:** 2 restaurants; piano bar; 24-hr. room service; in-room massage; laundry/dry cleaning. *In room:* A/C, fax, TV, minibar, hair dryer, safe.

Hôtel du Louvre ★★   After a massive overhaul, the hotel is now in a neck-and-neck race with the Regina for neighborhood supremacy. When Napoleon

---

Tips **Cafe and a Croissant?**

Hotel breakfasts are fairly uniform and include your choice of coffee, tea, or hot chocolate; a freshly baked croissant and roll; and limited quantities of butter and jam or jelly. It can be at your door moments after you call for it and is served at almost any hour. (When we mention breakfast charges in our listings, we refer to continental breakfasts only.) Breakfasts with eggs, bacon, ham, or other items must be ordered from the a la carte menu. For a charge, larger hotels serve the full or "English" breakfast, but smaller hotels typically serve only the continental variety.

Where to Stay on the Right Bank (1–4, 9–12 & 18e)

Golden Tulip Opéra
de Noailles **5**
Hôtel Britannique **19**
Hôtel Burgundy **6**
Hôtel Caron de
Beaumarchais **22**
Hôtel Central **21**
Hôtel Concorde St-Lazare **4**

Hôtel Costes **11**
Hôtel de la Place des Vosges **31**
Hôtel de la Tour
d'Auvergne **2**
Hôtel de Lutéce **24**
Hôtel des Chevaliers **30**
Hôtel des Deux-Iles **25**
Hôtel des Tuileries **12**

Hôtel de Vendôme **10**
Hôtel du Jeu de Paume **26**
Hôtel du Louvre **14**
Hôtel du 7e Art **27**
Hôtel Ermitage **1**
Hôtel Henri IV **18**
Hôtel Mansart **8**

Gare de l'Est
GARE DE L'EST
JARDIN VILLEMIN
Hôpital St-Louis
BELLEVILLE Ⓜ
bd. de Belleville
COURONNES
MÉNILMONTANT
10e
rue du Faubourg St-Martin
bd. de Strasbourg
HÂTEAU 'EAU
Canal St-Martin
rue St-Maur
du Temple
av.
GONCOURT
Parmentier
St-Joseph
Fontaine au Roi
rue de Faubourg
rue de la
JACQUES BONSERGENT

Ⓜ Métro Stop
Ⓡ RER Stop
— Railway

PARMENTIER
Oberkampf
ST-MAUR
RÉPUBLIQUE
place de la République
av. de la République
bd. Voltaire
11e
bd. St-Martin
uvelle
rue St-Martin
bd. du Temple
OBERKAMPF
28 29
TEMPLE
Conservatoire des Arts et Métiers
rue de Turbigo
Square du Temple
rue Réaumur
rue de Temple
FILLES DU CALVAIRE
rue St-Sébastien
ST-AMBROISE
RICHARD LENOIR
RÉAUMUR-SÉBASTOPOL
ARTS ET MÉTIERS
rue Beaubourg
3e
rue des Archives
rue Charlot
rue de Turenne
ST-SÉBASTIEN FROISSART
rue St-Sabin
rue Amelot
bd. Richard
rue du Chemin Vert
ETIENNE MARCEL
bd. de Sébastopol
rue St-Denis
rue M Rambuteau
RAMBUTEAU
Centre Pompidou
rue du Renard
rue Vieille du Temple
Musée Picasso
Musée Carnavalet
rue des Francs Bourgeois
CHEMIN VERT Ⓜ
bd. Beaumarchais
rue des Tournelles
BREGUET SABIN
rue Sedaine
Lenoir
30
place des Vosges
31
BASTILLE
BASTILLE Ⓜ
place de la Bastille
32 →
BASTILLE
Opéra Bastille
20
21 22
rue St-Antoine
4e
ST-PAUL
27
rue St-Paul
BASTILLE
bd. Henri IV
bd. Bourbon
bd. de la Bastille
33
12e
19
HÔTEL DE VILLE
Hôtel de Ville
av. Victoria
St-Germain l'Auxerrois
quai de l'Hôtel de Ville
quai des Célestins
PONT MARIE
SULLY-MORLAND
pont au Change
pont Notre Dame
pont d'Arcole
ILE DE LA CITÉ
pont Louis Philippe
pont Marie
pont des Deux Ponts
ILE ST-LOUIS
pont de Sully
Ste-Chapelle
Ⓜ **CITÉ**
rue de la Cité
pont d'Arcole
bd. du Palais
pont St-Louis
r. des Deux Ponts
23 24 25 26
Notre-Dame

Hôtel Pavillon Bastille **33**
Hôtel Regina **13**
Hôtel Ritz **7**
Hôtel Saint-Merry **20**
Hôtel St-Louis **23**
Hôtel Victoires Opéra **16**
Hôtel Williams Opéra **3**

Le Stendhal **9**
Libertel Croix de Malte **29**
Nouvel Hôtel **32**
Relais du Louvre **17**
Résidence Alhambra **28**
Terrass Hôtel **1**
Timhôtel Le Louvre **15**

III inaugurated the hotel in 1855, French journalists described it as "a palace of the people, rising adjacent to the palace of kings." In 1897, Camille Pissarro moved into a room with a view that inspired many of his landscapes. Between the Louvre and the Palais Royal, the hotel has a decor of marble, bronze, and gilt. The guest rooms are quintessentially Parisian, filled with souvenirs of the Belle Epoque. Most were renovated between 1996 and 2000. Some are small, but most are medium-size to spacious—with elegant fabrics and upholstery, excellent carpeting, double-glazed windows, comfortable beds, traditional wood furniture, and tiled bathrooms with a choice of tub or shower.

Place André-Malraux, 75001 Paris. ℂ 800/888-4747 in the U.S. and Canada, or 01-44-58-38-38. Fax 01-44-58-38-01. www.hoteldulouvre.com. 195 units. 420€–515€ ($375–$460) double; 690€–1,070€ ($616–$956) suite. Ask about off-season discounts. AE, DC, MC, V. Parking 18€ ($16). Métro: Palais Royal or Louvre-Rivoli. **Amenities:** restaurant; bar; 24-hr. room service; massage; laundry/dry cleaning; babysitting; business center. *In room:* A/C, TV, minibar, hair dryer, safe.

Hôtel Regina ⭐ Restored to its old-fashioned grandeur, it is adjacent to rue de Rivoli's equestrian statue of Joan of Arc opposite the Louvre. Since 1999, the management has poured millions into a full-fledged renovation, retaining the patina of the Art Nouveau interior and making historically appropriate improvements. The guest rooms are richly decorated and spacious; those overlooking the Tuileries enjoy panoramic views as far away as the Eiffel Tower. The bathrooms, each with tub and shower, are midsize to large, many with stained glass windows. The public areas contain every period of Louis furniture imaginable, Oriental carpets, 18th-century paintings, and bowls of flowers. Fountains play in a flagstone-covered courtyard. There are more grace notes in this hotel than at its closest competitor, Hotel du Louvre.

2 place des Pyramides, 75001 Paris. ℂ 01-42-60-31-10. Fax 01-40-15-95-16. www.regina-hotel.com. 120 units. 318€–415€ ($284–$371) double; 505€–675€ ($451–$603) suite. AE, DC, MC, V. Parking 23€ ($20). Métro: Pyramides or Tuileries. **Amenities:** 2 restaurants (both French); bar; 24-hr. room service; massage; babysitting; laundry/dry cleaning. *In room:* A/C, TV, minibar, hair dryer, safe.

Hôtel Ritz ⭐⭐⭐ The Ritz is Europe's greatest hotel, an enduring symbol of elegance on one of Paris's most beautiful and historic squares. César Ritz, the "little shepherd boy from Niederwald," converted the private Hôtel de Lazun into a luxury hotel that he opened in 1898. With the help of the culinary master Escoffier, he made the Ritz a miracle of luxury living.

In 1979, the Ritz family sold the hotel to Egyptian businessman Mohammed al-Fayed, who refurbished it and added a cooking school. (You may remember that his son Dodi al-Fayed and Princess Diana dined here before they set out on their fateful drive.) Two town houses were annexed, joined by an arcade lined with miniature display cases representing 125 of Paris's leading boutiques. The public salons are furnished with museum-caliber antiques. Each guest room is uniquely decorated, most often with Louis XIV or XV reproductions; all have fine rugs, marble fireplaces, tapestries, brass beds, and more. The marble bathrooms are the city's most luxurious, filled with deluxe toiletries, sumptuous tubs, scales, private phones, cords to summon maids and valets, robes, full-length and makeup mirrors, and dual basins. Ever since Edward VII got stuck in a too-narrow bathtub with his lover of the evening, the tubs at the Ritz have been deep and big.

15 place Vendôme, 75001 Paris. ℂ 800/223-6800 in the U.S. and Canada, or 01-43-16-30-30. Fax 01-43-16-36-68. www.ritzparis.com. 175 units. 550€–730€ ($491–$652) double; from 800€ ($714) suite. AE, DC, MC, V. Parking 35€ ($31). Métro: Opéra, Concorde, or Madeleine. **Amenities:** 2 restaurants (both French); 2 bars; indoor pool; cooking school; health club; shopping arcade; 24-hr. room service; massage; laundry/dry cleaning. *In room:* A/C, TV, fax, minibar, hair dryer, safe.

Fun Fact A Hotel Tale

During Paris's occupation, on August 25, 1944, Ernest Hemingway "liberated" the Ritz. Armed with machine guns, "Papa" and a group of Allied soldiers pulled up to the hotel in a Jeep, intent on capturing Nazis and freeing, if only symbolically, the landmark. After a sweeping inventory that extended from the cellars to the roof, the group discovered the Nazis had fled. Hemingway led his team to the Ritz bar to order a round of dry martinis. In commemoration of the 50th anniversary of the liberation, the renovated Bar Hemingway reopened on August 25, 1994.

EXPENSIVE

Hôtel des Tuileries ✯   On a quiet narrow street, this hotel occupies a 17th-century town house Marie Antoinette used when she left Versailles for unofficial Paris visits. Don't expect mementos of the queen, as all the frippery of her era was long ago stripped away. But in honor of its royal antecedents, the hotel's very limited public areas and guest rooms are filled with copies of 18th- and 19th-century furniture—a bit dowdy, but still dignified and very comfortable. In 2001, major improvements were made to the building structure, including the elevators. Each unit has a full tub-and-shower bathroom.

10 rue St-Hyacinthe, 75001 Paris. ℂ 01-42-61-04-17. Fax 01-49-27-91-56. www.hotel-des-tuileries.com. 26 units. 135€–213€ ($121–$190) double. AE, DC, MC, V. Parking 21€ ($19). Métro: Tuileries or Pyramides. **Amenities:** Room service (7am–midnight); babysitting; laundry/dry cleaning. *In room:* A/C, TV with cable, minibar, hair dryer, safe.

MODERATE

Hôtel Britannique *Value*   Conservatively modern and plush, this is a much-renovated 19th-century hotel near Les Halles, the Pompidou, and Notre-Dame. It was rerated with three government stars after a complete renovation in 2001 and 2002. The place not only is British in name but also seems to have cultivated an English style of graciousness. The guest rooms may be small, but they're immaculate and soundproof, with comfortable beds and well-maintained bathrooms, each with tub and shower. Cable television provides U.S. and U.K. television shows. The reading room is a cozy retreat.

20 av. Victoria, 75001 Paris. ℂ 01-42-33-74-59. Fax 01-42-33-82-65.www.hotel-britannique.fr. 40 units. 149€–171€ ($133–$153) double. AE, DC, MC, V. Parking 15€–20€ ($13–$18). Métro: Châtelet. **Amenities:** Room service (8am–9pm). *In room:* TV, minibar, hair dryer, safe.

Hôtel Burgundy ✯ *Value*   The Burgundy is one of this outrageously expensive area's best values. The frequently renovated building began as two adjacent town houses in the 1830s, one a pension where Baudelaire wrote some of his eerie poetry in the 1860s and the other a bordello. British-born managers, who insisted on using the English name, linked them. Radically renovated in 1992, with continued improvements in 2001, the hotel hosts many North and South Americans and features conservatively decorated rooms with comfortable beds and a tub and shower in each bathroom.

8 rue Duphot, 75001 Paris. ℂ 01-42-60-34-12. Fax 01-47-03-95-20. http://perso.wanadoo.fr/hotel. burgundy. 89 units. 160€–175€ ($143–$156) double; 289€ ($257) suite. AE, DC, MC, V. Métro: Madeleine or Concorde. **Amenities:** Restaurant (French); bar; room service (7–10:30am); babysitting. *In room:* A/C, TV, minibar, hair dryer.

Hôtel Mansart *Value*   After operating as a glorious wreck for decades, this hotel—designed by its namesake—was renovated in 1991 and offers some of the lowest rates in this pricey area. The public rooms contain Louis reproductions and floor-to-ceiling geometric designs inspired by the inlaid marble floors (or formal gardens) of the French Renaissance. The guest rooms are small to medium in size and are both formal and comfortable, though only five suites and most expensive rooms overlook the famous square. Twenty rooms are air-conditioned, and each comes with a tub and shower in the bathroom. Breakfast is the only meal served.

5 rue des Capucines, 75001 Paris. ✆ **01-42-61-50-28.** Fax 01-49-27-97-44. www.esprit-de-france. com. 57 units. 150€–170€ ($134–$152) double; 230€–270€ ($205–$241) suite. AE, DC, MC, V. Métro: Opéra or Madeleine. **Amenities:** Bar; 24-hr. room service for drinks; babysitting; laundry/dry cleaning. *In room:* TV, hair dryer, minibar, safe.

Relais du Louvre   One of the neighborhood's most up-to-date hotels, it opened in 1991, overlooking the neoclassical colonnade at the eastern end of the Louvre. Between 1800 and 1941, its upper floors contained the printing presses that recorded the goings-on in Paris's House of Representatives. Its street level held the Café Momus, favored by Voltaire, Hugo, and intellectuals of the day and is where Puccini set one of the pivotal scenes of *La Bohème*. Bedrooms are outfitted in monochromatic schemes of blue, yellow, or soft reds, usually with copies of Directoire-style (French 1830s) furniture. All units have shower-tub combos except for five of the simplest and smallest singles, which have only shower. Many rooms are a bit small, but others contain roomy sitting areas.

19 rue des Prêtres-St-Germain-l'Auxerrois, 75001 Paris. ✆ **01-40-41-96-42.** Fax 01-40-41-96-44. www.relaisdulouvre.com. 21 units. 145€–180€ ($129–$160) double; 205€–244€ ($183–$218) suite. AE, DC, MC, V. Parking 14€ ($12). Métro: Louvre or Pont Neuf. **Amenities:** 24-hr. room service for drinks; laundry/dry cleaning; babysitting. *In room:* A/C, TV, minibar, hair dryer, safe.

INEXPENSIVE

Hôtel Henri IV *Finds*   This is our funky, fun selection. Four hundred years ago, this decrepit narrow building housed the printing presses used for the edicts of Henri IV. Today one of the most famous and most consistently crowded budget hotels in Europe sits in a dramatic location at the westernmost tip of Ile de la Cité, beside a formal park. The crowd is mostly bargain-conscious academics, journalists, and Francophiles, many of whom reserve rooms as much as 2 months in advance. The low-ceilinged lobby, a flight above street level, is cramped and bleak; the creaky stairway leading to the guest rooms is almost impossibly narrow. The rooms are considered romantically threadbare by many,

---

⌒*Tips* **Splish, Splash . . . Taking a Bath**

Throughout the hotels in this chapter, expect the bathrooms in very expensive and expensive hotels to be a bit larger than normal, with fine toiletries, plush towels, and perhaps bathrobes. The bathrooms in moderate and inexpensive hotels tend to be cramped but still acceptable, with towels that are less plush than those at expensive places.

Be aware that some hotels offer tub/shower combinations; some offer shower stalls, and some offer a mix. If this is important to you, request your preference when reserving. Also be aware that almost all hotels, except the inexpensive ones, include hair dryers in the bathrooms.

and rundown and substandard by others. Five rooms have showers but no toilets.

25 place Dauphine, 75001 Paris. ☏ **01-43-54-44-53**. 20 units, 6 with shower only. 29€–35€ ($26–$31) double without shower; 42€–45€ ($37–$40) double with shower; 55€–69€ ($49–$62) double with complete bathroom. Rates include breakfast. No credit cards. Métro: Pont Neuf. *In room:* No phone.

Timhôtel Le Louvre *(Kids)*   This hotel and its sibling, the Timhôtel Palais-Royal, are mirror images, at least inside; they're part of a new breed of government-rated two-star family-friendly hotels cropping up around France. These Timhôtels share the same manager and temperament, and though the rooms at the Palais-Royal branch are a bit larger than the ones here, this branch is so close to the Louvre as to be almost irresistible. The ambience is standardized modern, with monochromatic guest rooms and wall-to-wall carpeting upgraded in 1998. Each bedroom comes with a full tub and shower in the bathroom.

The 46-room **Timhôtel Palais-Royal** is at 3 rue de la Banque, 75002 Paris (☏ **01-42-61-53-90**; fax 01-42-60-05-39; Métro: Bourse).

4 rue Croix des Petits-Champs, 75001 Paris. ☏ **01-42-60-34-86**. Fax 01-42-60-10-39. www.timhotel.com. 56 units. 115€–138€ ($103–$123) double. AE, DC, MC, V. Métro: Palais Royal. **Amenities:** Babysitting; laundry/dry cleaning. *In room:* A/C, TV.

2ND ARRONDISSEMENT
EXPENSIVE

Hôtel Victoires Opéra *(★)*   Head to this little charmer if you want a reasonably priced place convenient to Les Halles and the Pompidou as well as to the Marais, with its shops and gay and straight restaurants. It's a classically decorated hotel, evoking the era of Louis Philippe. Renovations in 2001 included the addition of a private bathroom for every room. Most of the rooms are alike—comfortable, but a bit tiny. All units come with a tub-shower combination. Skip the hotel breakfast (which costs extra) and cross the street to Stohrer at no. 51, one of Paris's most historic pâtisseries, founded in 1730 by the pâtissier to Louis XV.

56 rue Montorgueil, 75002 Paris. ☏ **01-42-36-41-08**. Fax 01-45-08-08-79. www.hotelvictoiresopera.com. 26 units. 214€–275€ ($191–$246) double; 335€ ($299) junior suite. AE, DC, MC, V. Parking 12€ ($11). Métro: Les Halles. **Amenities:** 24-hr. room service; babysitting; laundry/dry cleaning. *In room:* A/C, TV, minibar, iron/ironing board, safe.

Le Stendhal *(★)*   Opened in 1992, this hotel mixes a young hip style with a sense of tradition. Its location, close to the glamorous place Vendôme jewelry stores, couldn't be grander. The effect is that of a boutique-style *hôtel de luxe* that seems like a Parisian version of an upscale English B&B. The rooms, accessible via a tiny elevator, have vivid color schemes. Most are small but not without their charm, and each bathroom comes with a full tub and shower combo. The red-and-black Stendhal Suite pays homage to the author, who made this his private home for many years and died here in 1842.

22 rue Danielle-Casanova, 75002 Paris. ☏ **01-44-58-52-52**. Fax 01-44-58-52-00. h1610@accor-hotels.com. 20 units. 225€–254€ ($201–$227)double; from 289€ ($258) suite. AE, DC, MC, V. Parking 15€ ($13). Métro: Opéra. **Amenities:** 24-hr. room service; babysitting. *In room:* A/C, TV, minibar, hair dryer, safe.

MODERATE

Golden Tulip Opéra de Noailles   If you're looking for a postmodern hotel in the style of Putman and Starck, book here. Proprietor Martine Falck has turned this old-fashioned place in a great location into a refined Art Deco choice with bold colors and cutting-edge style, yet the prices remain reasonable. The guest rooms come in various shapes and sizes, but all are comfortable; and all come with a tub-and-shower combo. A favorite is no. 601, which has its own terrace.

9 rue de la Michodière, 75002 Paris. © **800/344-1212** in the U.S., or 01-47-42-92-90. Fax 01-49-24-92-71. www.hoteldenoailles.com. 61 units. 182€–198€ ($163–$176) double. Rates include breakfast if booked directly with the hotel. AE, DC, MC, V. Parking 15€ ($13). Métro: 4 Septembre or Opéra. **Amenities:** Bar; health club; sauna; room service (8am–10:30pm); massage; babysitting; laundry/dry cleaning. *In room:* A/C, TV, hair dryer, safe.

3RD ARRONDISSEMENT
MODERATE

Hôtel des Chevaliers   Half a block from the northwestern edge of place des Vosges, this renovated hotel occupies a dramatic corner building whose 17th-century vestiges have been elevated into high art. These include the remnants of a stone-sided well in the cellar, a sweeping stone barrel vault covering the breakfast area, half-timbering artfully exposed in the stairwell, and Louis XIII accessories that'll remind you of the hotel's origins. Each guest room is comfortable and well maintained, and each unit comes with a tub and shower in the bathroom. Rooms on the top floor have artfully exposed ceiling beams.

30 rue de Turenne, 75003 Paris. © **01-42-72-73-47.** Fax 01-42-72-54-10. 53 units. 103€–125€ ($92–$111) double; 143€ ($128) triple. Parking 11€ ($10). Métro: Chemin Vert or St-Paul. *In room:* A/C, TV, minibar, hair dryer, safe.

4TH ARRONDISSEMENT
EXPENSIVE

Hôtel du Jeu de Paume ✸   It's small-scale and charming, with a layout that includes an interconnected pair of 17th-century town houses accessed via a timbered passageway from the street outside. This hotel has rooms that are a bit larger than those within some of its nearby competitors on the Ile St-Louis. It originated as a "clubhouse" that was used by members of the court of Louis XIII, who amused themselves with *Les jeux de paume* (an early form of tennis) nearby. Public areas are outfitted in a simple and unfrilly version of Art Deco. Bedrooms, some under a wood-beamed ceiling, are bright and freshly decorated with contemporary styling, each with elegant raw materials such as oaken floors. All contain well-maintained private bathrooms with tub-and-shower combinations. In terms of mentality and aesthetics, here you'll feel more closely aligned with the pervasive ethic of the Marais than within the Quartier Latin to the south. There's an elevator on the premises, and scads of charm from the well-meaning staff.

54 rue St-Louis-en-l'Isle, 75004 Paris. © **01-43-26-14-18.** Fax 01-40-46-02-76. www.jeudepaumehotel. com. 30 units. 201€–262€ ($179–$234) double; 410€–433€ ($366–$387) suite. AE, DC, MC, V. Parking: 18€ ($16). Métro: Pont-Marie. **Amenities:** Exercise room; sauna; room service (7am–midnight); babysitting; laundry/dry cleaning. *In room:* TV, minibar, hair dryer, safe.

MODERATE

Hôtel Caron de Beaumarchais *Value*   Built in the 18th century and gracefully upgraded in 1998, this good-value choice features floors of artfully worn gray stone, antique reproductions, and elaborate fabrics based on antique patterns. Hotelier Alain Bigeard likes his primrose-colored guest rooms to evoke the taste of the French gentry in the 18th century when the Marais was the scene of high-society dances or even duels. Most rooms retain their original ceiling beams. The smallest units overlook the interior courtyard, and the top-floor rooms are tiny but have panoramic balcony views across the Right Bank. Each of the bedrooms except two comes with a tub-shower combination.

Kids Family-Friendly Hotels

Hôtel de Fleurie (p. 100)   In the heart of St-Germain-des-Prés, this has long been a Left Bank family favorite. The hotel is known for its *chambres familiales*—two connecting rooms with a pair of large beds in each room. Children under 12 stay free with their parents.

Hôtel du Ministère (p. 91)   For the family on a budget that doesn't mind cramped quarters, the Ministère is one of the best bets in this expensive area near the Champs-Elysées.

Résidence Lord Byron (p. 92)   The Byron is not only a good value and an unusually family-oriented place for the swanky 8th arrondissement, but is only a short walk from many major monuments.

Timhôtel Le Louvre (p. 81)   This is an especially convenient choice because it offers some rooms with four beds for the price of a double. And the location near the Louvre is irresistible.

---

12 rue Vieille-du-Temple, 75004 Paris. ✆ **01-42-72-34-12.** Fax 01-42-72-34-63. www.carondebeau marchais.com. 19 units. 128€–142€ ($114–$127) double. AE, DC, MC, V. Métro: St-Paul or Hôtel de Ville. **Amenities:** Babysitting; laundry/dry cleaning. *In room:* A/C, TV, minibar, hair dryer.

Hôtel de Lutèce   This hotel feels like a country house in Brittany. The lounge, with its old fireplace, is furnished with antiques and contemporary paintings. Ranging in size from small to medium, many of the individualized guest rooms boast antiques, adding to a refined atmosphere. Many were renovated in 1998, and each unit comes either with a tub or shower. A few of the rooms, rented to late arrivals, are so small there is hardly space for one's luggage. The breakfast room is also too small and sometimes you have to wait.

65 rue St-Louis-en-l'Ile, 75004 Paris. ✆ **01-43-26-23-52.** Fax 01-43-29-60-25. www.hotel-ile-saintlouis. com. 23 units. 141€–144€ ($126–$129) double. AE, MC, V. Métro: Pont Marie or Cité. **Amenities:** Room service; laundry/dry cleaning. *In room:* A/C, TV, hair dryer, safe.

Hôtel des Deux-Iles ✪   This is a much-restored 18th-century town house. It was an inexpensive hotel until 1976 when an elaborate decor with lots of bamboo and reed furniture and French provincial touches was added. The result is an unpretentious but charming hotel with a great location. The guest rooms are on the small side, however, but each comes with a small, well-maintained private bathroom with shower. A garden of plants and flowers off the lobby leads to a basement breakfast room with a fireplace.

59 rue St-Louis-en-l'Ile, 75004 Paris. ✆ **01-43-26-13-35.** Fax 01-43-29-60-25. www.hotel-ile-saintlouis. com. 17 units. 141€ ($126) double. AE, MC, V. Métro: Pont Marie. **Amenities:** Courtyard garden; room service (7am–8pm); laundry/dry cleaning. *In room:* A/C, TV, hair dryer, safe.

Hôtel Saint-Louis *(Value)*   Proprietors Guy and Andrée Record maintain a charming family atmosphere at this small, antique-filled hotel in a 17th-century town house. A full renovation was completed in 1998. Considering its prime location on Ile St-Louis, the hotel represents an incredible value. Expect cozy, slightly cramped rooms, each with a small private bathroom with tub-and-shower combo. With mansard roofs and old-fashioned moldings, the top-floor rooms sport tiny balconies with sweeping rooftop views. The breakfast room is in the cellar, with 17th-century stone vaulting.

75 rue St-Louis-en-l'Ile, 75004 Paris. © **01-46-34-04-80.** Fax 01-46-34-02-13. www.hotelsaintlouis.com. 19 units. 139€–198€ ($124–$176) double. AE, MC, V. Métro: Pont Marie or RER St-Michel. **Amenities:** Room service (7:30–10am); babysitting; laundry. *In room:* A/C, TV, hair dryer, safe.

Hotel Saint-Merry ★ *Finds*   The rebirth of this once-notorious brothel as a charming, upscale hotel is another example of how the Marais has been gentrified. It contains a dozen rooms, each of them relatively small but charmingly accented with neo-Gothic details, exposed stone, 18th-century ceiling beams, and lots of quirky architectural details, all carefully preserved by a team of architects and decorators. The tiled bathrooms are small, but each comes with a tub-and-shower combo. Expect a clientele that's estimated by the staff as about 50 percent gay and male, the other half straight and involved in the arts scene that flourishes in the surrounding neighborhood. Before it became a bordello, this place was conceived as the presbytery of the nearby Church of Saint-Merry.

78 rue de la Verrerie. 75004 Paris. © **01-42-78-14-15.** Fax 01-40-29-06-82. www.hotelmarais.com. 12 units. 146€–210€ ($130–$188) double; AE, MC, V. 305€ ($272) suite. Métro: Hôtel de Ville or Châtelet. *In room:* TV, hair dryer, safe.

INEXPENSIVE

Hôtel de la Place des Vosges ★★ *Value*   Built about 350 years ago, during the same era as the square it's named after, which lies less than a 2-minute walk away, this is a well-managed, small-scale property with reasonable prices and lots of charm. The structure, which was once used as a stable for the mules of Henri IV, was renovated in 2000. Many of the bedrooms have beamed ceilings, small dimensions, tiled bathrooms (with tub or shower), TV sets hanging from chains in the ceiling, and a sense of cozy, well-ordered efficiency. The most desirable and expensive accommodation is the top-floor room 60, overlooking the rooftops of Paris, with a luxurious private bathroom. There are patches of chiseled stone at parts of the hotel, a decorative touch that helps evoke the era of Louis XIII.

12 rue de Birague, 75004 Paris. © **01-42-72-60-46.** Fax 01-42-72-02-64. hotel.place.des.vosges@gofornet. com. 16 units. 100€–105€ ($90–$94) double; 137€ ($122) room 60. AE, MC, V. Métro: Bastille. **Amenities:** elevator. *In room:* TV, hair dryer.

Hôtel du 7e Art   The building that contains this place is one of many 17th-century buildings classified as historic monuments in this neighborhood. Don't expect grand luxury: Rooms are cramped but clean and outfitted with the simplest furniture, relieved by 1950s-era Hollywood movie posters. Each has white walls, and some—including those under the sloping mansard-style roof

---

Value **Good, Clean Rooms for Under $50 a Night . . .**
C'est possible?

Largely unnoticed by U.S. visitors—as yet—a new French Revolution is quietly taking place. Some two dozen modern, amenity-packed hotels have sprouted up in Paris under the **Ibis Hotel** banner. These cookie-cutter properties have become the McDonald's of French budget lodgings. Operated by Accor Hotels (© **800/221-4542**), they have attractive but tiny rooms and lie near Métro stops a 5-minute ride from the Seine. If you stay at Motel 6 and Red Roof Inns in the United States, it's a comparable experience. You can book a room at an Ibis for the price of two martinis at the George V.

---

on the top floor—have exposed ceiling beams. All have small-size bathrooms with either tub or shower. There's a bar in the lobby and a breakfast room, but be warned in advance that there's no elevator for access to any of this place's five stories (*4 étages*). The hotel is named after the "7th Art," a French reference to filmmaking.

20 rue St-Paul, 75004 Paris. © **01-44-54-85-00.** Fax 01-42-77-69-10. hotel/art@wanadoo.fr. 23 units. 70€–120€ ($63–$107) double. AE, DC, MC, V. Parking: 15€ ($13). Métro: St-Paul. **Amenities:** Laundromat; health club. *In room:* TV, safe.

9TH ARRONDISSEMENT
EXPENSIVE

Hôtel Concorde St-Lazare ⭐ Across from the St-Lazare rail station, this hotel—the area's best—first greeted visitors flocking to the Universal Exposition of 1889. In 2000 each of the guest rooms was elevated to modern standards of comfort and redecorated. Many rooms (medium-size to quite large) have high ceilings, especially those on the lower floors, which also have double-glazed windows to cut down on the noise. The beds are plush and comfortable, and bathrooms come with tub-and-shower combos.

108 rue St-Lazare, 75008 Paris. © **800/888-4747** in the U.S. outside N.Y. State and Canada, 212/752-3900 in N.Y. State, 020/7630-1704 in London, or © 01-40-08-44-44. Fax 01-42-93-01-20. www.concordestlazare-paris.com. 300 units. 400€–490€ ($356–$436) double; 685€–915€ ($612–$817) suite. AE, DC, MC, V. Parking 23€ ($20). Métro: St-Lazare. **Amenities:** Restaurant (French); bar; cafe; 24-hr. room service; babysitting; laundry/dry cleaning. *In room:* A/C, TV, minibar, hair dryer, safe.

INEXPENSIVE

Hôtel de la Tour d'Auvergne Here's a good bet for those who want to be near the Opera or the Gare du Nord. This building was erected before Baron Haussmann reconfigured Paris's avenues around 1870. Later, Modigliani rented a room for 6 months, and the staff will tell you Victor Hugo and Auguste Rodin lived on this street. The interior has been modernized into a glossy internationalism. The guest rooms are meticulously coordinated, yet the small decorative canopies over the headboards make them feel cluttered. Though the views over the back courtyard are uninspired, some guests request rear rooms for their quiet. Every year, five rooms are renovated, so the comfort level is kept at a high standard, and each unit comes with a tub-shower combination.

10 rue de la Tour d'Auvergne, 75009 Paris. © **01-48-78-61-60.** Fax 01-49-95-99-00. 24 units. 132€ ($120) double. AE, DC, MC, V. Métro: Cadet or Anvers. **Amenities:** 24-hr. room service; babysitting. *In room:* TV, minibar, hair dryer.

Hôtel Williams Opéra Even now, this hotel remains relatively unknown. Behind the dignified facade of a 19th-century building, entrepreneurs installed a little hotel in 1992. The guest rooms are clean and uncomplicated, though the decor is a bit cold. Each is soundproof, thanks to double-glazing, and has a safe. The front rooms overlook one of the area's largest public gardens, a verdant oasis in an otherwise congested commercial neighborhood; fifth- and second-floor rooms offer small wrought-iron balconies. About half of the accommodations have tub baths, the rest contain showers.

3 rue Mayran, 75009 Paris. © **01-48-78-68-35.** Fax 01-45-26-08-70. www.hotel-paris-williams.com. 30 units. 103€ ($92) double. AE, MC, V. Parking 9.10€ ($8.10). Métro: Cadet. *In room:* TV, hair dryer.

11TH ARRONDISSEMENT
INEXPENSIVE

Libertel Croix de Malte A member of a nationwide chain of government-rated two-star hotels, this is a well-maintained choice. Business increased thanks to a radical 1992 overhaul and its proximity to the Opéra Bastille and the Marais. The hotel consists of buildings of two and three floors, one of which is accessible through a shared breakfast room. There's a landscaped courtyard in back with access to a lobby bar. The cozy guest rooms contain brightly painted modern furniture accented with vivid green, blue, and pink patterns that flash back to the 1960s. About half of the units contain tubs, the rest are equipped with showers.

5 rue de Malte, 75011 Paris. ⓒ **01-48-05-09-36.** Fax 01-43-57-02-54. www.accor.com. 29 units. 104€ ($93) double. AE, MC, V. Métro: Oberkampf. **Amenities:** Room service (breakfast); babysitting. *In room:* TV, hair dryer.

Résidence Alhambra   Named for the famous cabaret/vaudeville theater that once stood nearby, the Alhambra dates from the 1800s. A radical renovation in 2000 gave the hotel its fine contemporary format. In the rear garden, its two-story chalet offers eight additional guest rooms. The small accommodations are bland but comfortable, each in a monochromatic pastel scheme that includes white and ocher. Ten private bathrooms contain a tub-and-shower combo, the rest showers.

13 rue de Malte, 75011 Paris. ⓒ **01-47-00-35-52.** Fax 01-43-57-98-75. www.hotelalhambra.fr. 58 units. 56€–67€ ($50–$60) double; 71€–90€ ($63–$80) triple. AE, DC, MC, V. Parking 15€ ($13). Métro: Oberkampf. **Amenities:** Garden; babysitting. *In room:* TV.

12TH ARRONDISSEMENT
MODERATE

Hôtel Pavillon Bastille   Hardly your cozy little back-street dig, this is a bold, innovative hotel in a town house across from the Opéra Bastille, a block south of place de la Bastille. A 17th-century fountain graces the courtyard. The guest rooms have twin or double beds, partially mirrored walls, and contemporary built-in furniture. Each unit comes with a tub-shower combo.

65 rue de Lyon, 75012 Paris. ⓒ **01-43-43-65-65.** Fax 01-43-43-96-52. www.pavillon-bastille.com. 25 units. 130€ ($116) double; 213€ ($190) suite. AE, DC, MC, V. Parking 12€ ($11). Métro: Bastille. **Amenities:** Room service; laundry/dry cleaning. *In room:* A/C, TV, minibar, hair dryer, iron/ironing board, safe.

INEXPENSIVE

Nouvel Hôtel   This hotel evokes the French provinces more than urban Paris. Surrounded by greenery in a neighborhood rarely visited by tourists, the Nouvel conjures a day when parts of Paris still seemed like small country towns. The beauty of the place is most visible from the inside courtyard, site of warm-weather breakfasts, the only meal served. Winding halls lead to small guest rooms overlooking the courtyard or, less appealingly, the street. Each contains flowered fabrics and old-fashioned furniture, but only three have tub baths, the rest are equipped with showers.

24 av. du Bel-Air, 75012 Paris. ⓒ **01-43-43-01-81.** Fax 01-43-44-64-13. www.nouvel-hotel-paris.com. 28 units. 63€–76€ ($57–$68) double. Rates include breakfast. AE, DC, MC, V. Métro: Nation. *In room:* TV.

18TH ARRONDISSEMENT
EXPENSIVE

Terrass Hôtel ★★ *Finds*   Built in 1913 and renovated into a plush but traditional style in 2001, this is the only government-rated four-star hotel on the Butte Montmartre. In an area filled with some of Paris's seediest hotels, this place is easily in a class of its own. Its main advantage is its location amid Montmartre's bohemian atmosphere (or what's left of it). Staffed by English-speaking employees, it has a large marble-floored lobby ringed with blond oak paneling and accented with 18th-century antiques and valuable paintings. The guest rooms are high-ceilinged and well upholstered, often featuring views. All the bathrooms are well maintained, each with a shower and about half with both a shower and tub.

12-14 rue Joseph-de-Maistre, 75018 Paris. © 01-46-06-72-85. Fax 01-42-52-29-11. www.terrass-hotel. com. 100 units. 225€–248€ ($201–$221) double; 302€ ($270) suite. Rates include breakfast. AE, DC, MC, V. Parking 15€ ($13). Métro: Place de Clichy or Blanche. **Amenities:** 2 restaurants (both French); bar; room service (7am–11pm); babysitting; laundry/dry cleaning. *In room:* A/C, TV, minibar, hair dryer, safe in some rooms.

INEXPENSIVE

Hôtel Ermitage Built in 1870 of chiseled limestone in the Napoleon III style, this hotel's facade evokes a perfectly proportioned small villa. It's set in a calm area, a brief uphill stroll from Sacré-Coeur. Views extend out over Paris, and there's a verdant garden in the back courtyard. The small guest rooms are like those in a countryside auberge with exposed ceiling beams, flowered wallpaper, and casement windows opening onto the garden or a street seemingly airlifted from the provinces. All the bedrooms come with small tubs and showers.

24 rue Lamarck, 75018 Paris. © 01-42-64-79-22. Fax 01-42-64-10-33. 12 units. 84€ ($75) double. Rates include breakfast. No credit cards. Parking 9.10€ ($8.10). Métro: Lamarck-Caulaincourt. **Amenities:** Garden; babysitting. *In room:* hair dryer.

8TH ARRONDISSEMENT
VERY EXPENSIVE

Four Seasons Hôtel George V ✹✹✹ In its latest reincarnation, with all its glitz and glamour, this hotel is one of the greatest in the world. Both the Bristol and Plaza Athénée accurately claim they have more class, but George V's history is as gilt-edged as they come. It was opened in 1928 in honor of George V (father of the present queen of England) and noted for grandeur that managed to survive the Depression and two world wars. Between the wars, it was an official branch of the League of Nations. After the Liberation of Paris in 1944, it became the war headquarters of General Eisenhower and his staff. After its acquisition by Saudi Prince Al Waleed, and a 2-year shutdown for renovations, it was reopened late in 1999 under the banner of Toronto-based Four Seasons. Rooms are about as close as you'll come to residency within a supremely well upholstered private home. The renovation reduced the number of units from 300 to 245, and they now come in three sizes. The largest are magnificent, the smallest are, in the words of a spokesperson, *"très agreeable."* Each unit comes with a large bathroom with a luxurious tub and shower. The staff-to-guest ratio is the highest in Paris.

31 av. George-V, 75008 Paris. © 800/332-3442 in the U.S. or Canada, or 01-49-52-70-00. Fax 01-49-52-70-10. www.fourseasons.com. 245 units. 630€–1,175€ ($563–$1,049) double; from 1,450€ ($1,295) suite. Parking 45€ ($40). AE, DC, MC, V. Métro: George V. **Amenities:** 2 restaurants (both French); bar; indoor pool; spa; health club; 24-hr. room service. *In room:* A/C, TV, minibar, hair dryer, safe.

Hôtel Bristol ✹✹✹ This palace is near the Palais d'Elysée (home of the French president), on the shopping street parallel to the Champs-Elysées. In terms of style and glamour, here's how the lineup reads in Paris: (1) Ritz, (2) Plaza Athénée, and (3) Bristol. The 18th-century Parisian facade has a glass-and-wrought-iron entryway, where uniformed English-speaking attendants greet you. Hippolyte Jammet founded the Bristol in 1924, installing many antiques and Louis XV and XVI furnishings. The guest rooms are opulent, with antiques or well-made reproductions, inlaid wood, bronze, crystal, Oriental carpets, and original oil paintings. Each room is freshened every 3 years, and each comes with a luxurious bathroom with tub-and-shower combo. Personalized old-world service is rigidly maintained here—some guests find it forbidding, others absolutely adore it.

112 rue du Faubourg St-Honoré, 75008 Paris. ⓒ **01-53-43-43-00.** Fax 01-53-43-43-26. www.hotel-bristol. com. 175 units. 578€–669€ ($514–$595) double; from 1,307€ ($1,163) suite. AE, DC, MC, V. Free parking. Métro: Miromesnil. **Amenities:** 2 restaurants; bar; indoor pool; spa; room service; babysitting; laundry/ dry cleaning. *In room:* A/C, TV, minibar, hair dryer, safe.

Hôtel de Crillon ★★★   One of Europe's grand hotels, the Crillon sits across from the U.S. Embassy. Although some international CEOs and diplomats treat it as a shrine, those seeking less pomposity might prefer the Plaza Athénée or the Ritz. The 200-plus-year-old building, once the palace of the duc de Crillon, has been a hotel since the early 1900s and is now owned by Jean Taittinger of the champagne family. The public salons boast 17th- and 18th-century tapestries, gilt-and-brocade furniture, chandeliers, fine sculpture, and Louis XVI chests and chairs. The guest rooms are large and luxurious. Some are spectacular, like the Leonard Bernstein Suite, which has one of the maestro's pianos and one of the grandest views of any hotel room in Paris. The marble bathrooms are sumptuous as well, with deluxe toiletries, dual sinks, and robes.

10 place de la Concorde, 75008 Paris. ⓒ **800/223-6800** in the U.S. and Canada, or 01-44-71-15-00. Fax 01-44-71-15-02. www.crillon.com. 147 units. 600€–707€ ($536–$631) double; from 1,034€ ($923) suite. AE, DC, MC, V. Free parking. Métro: Concorde. **Amenities:** 2 restaurants; bar; tearoom; exercise room; 24-hr. room service; laundry/dry cleaning. *In room:* A/C, TV, fax, minibar, hair dryer, safe.

Hôtel Meurice ★★★   After a spectacular 2-year renovation, the landmark Meurice, which reopened in mid-2000, is better than ever. The hotel is more media hip and style conscious, in addition to being better located, than the George V, its closest rival. Since the early 1800s, it has welcomed the royal, the rich, and even the radical: The deposed king of Spain, Alfonso XIII, once occupied suite 108; and the mad genius Salvador Dalí made the Meurice his headquarters, as did General von Cholritz, the Nazi who ruled Paris during the occupation. The mosaic floors, elaborate plaster ceilings, hand-carved moldings, and Art Nouveau glass roof atop the Winter Garden look like new. Each guest room is individually decorated with period pieces, fine carpets, Italian and French fabrics, rare marbles, and modern features such as fax and Internet access. Louis XVI and Empire styles predominate. Our favorites and the least expensive are the sixth-floor dormer rooms. Some rooms have painted ceilings of puffy clouds and blue skies along with canopied beds. Each unit comes with a full state-of-the-art bathroom.

228 rue de Rivoli, Paris 75001. ⓒ **01-44-58-10-10.** Fax 01-44-58-10-15. www.meuricehotel.com. 160 units. 640€–740€ ($572–$661) double; from 900€ ($804) suite. Métro: Tuileries or Concorde. Parking 24€ ($22). **Amenities:** 2 restaurants; bar; exercise room; full-service spa; 24-hr. room service; babysitting; in-room massage; laundry/dry cleaning. *In room:* A/C, TV, minibar, hair dryer, safe.

Hôtel Plaza Athénée ★★★   The Plaza Athénée, an 1889 Art Nouveau marvel, is a landmark of discretion and style. In the 8th, only the Bristol can compare. About half the celebrities visiting Paris have been pampered here; in the old days, Mata Hari used to frequent the place. Superbly decorated subdivisions within the hotel include the **Bar Montaigne,** whose audaciously designed countertops are extraordinarily crafted from crystal that's lit from beneath. It's been described as an enormous iceberg that self-illuminates when you touch it. The **Salon Gobelins** (with tapestries against rich paneling) and the **Salon Marie Antoinette,** a richly paneled and grand room, are two public rooms that add to

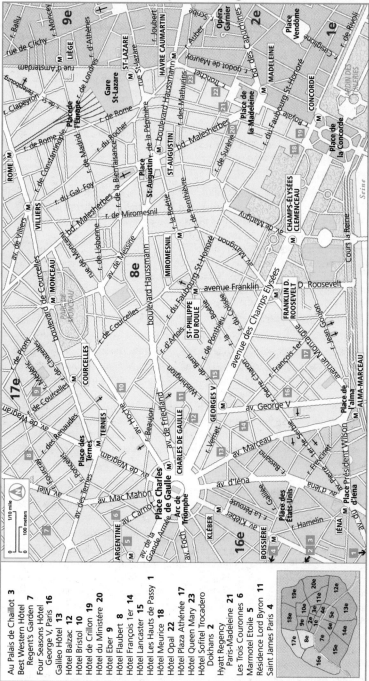

Au Palais de Chaillot **3**
Best Western Hôtel
  Regent's Garden **7**
Four Seasons Hôtel
  George V, Paris **16**
Galileo Hôtel **13**
Hôtel Balzac **12**
Hôtel Bristol **10**
Hôtel de Crillon **19**
Hôtel du Ministère **20**
Hôtel Eber **9**
Hôtel Flaubert **8**
Hôtel François 1er **14**
Hôtel Lancaster **15**
Hôtel Les Hauts de Passy **1**
Hôtel Meurice **18**
Hôtel Opal **22**
Hôtel Plaza Athénée **17**
Hôtel Queen Mary **23**
Hôtel Sofitel Trocadero
  Dokhans **2**
Hyatt Regency
  Paris-Madeleine **21**
Les Trois Couronnes **6**
Marmotel Etoile **5**
Résidence Lord Byron **11**
Saint James Paris **4**

the ambience of this grand hotel. This, coupled with an interior courtyard of calm and quiet, draped with vines and dotted with geraniums. The quietest guest rooms overlook a courtyard with awnings and parasol-shaded tables; they have ample closet space, and their large tiled bathrooms contain double basins. Some rooms overlooking avenue Montaigne have views of the Eiffel Tower. In 1999, the hotel completed a radical overhaul, creating larger rooms out of some of the smaller, less desirable ones.

25 av. Montaigne, 75008 Paris. ✆ 866/732-1106 in the U.S. and Canada, or 01-53-67-66-65. Fax 01-53-67-66-66. www.plaza-athenee-paris.com. 188 units. 458€–671€ ($409–$599) double; from 1,220€ ($1,089) suite. AE, DC, MC, V. Parking 18€ ($16). Métro: F. D. Roosevelt or Alma-Marceau. **Amenities:** 2 restaurants; bar; health club; salon; 24-hr. room service; massage; babysitting; laundry/dry cleaning. *In room:* A/C, TV, minibar, hair dryer, safe.

EXPENSIVE

Hôtel Balzac ✿✿✿   If the Crillon and the Ritz are Rolls Royces, then the Balzac is a Bentley, boasting a well-trained formal staff. Elegant and discreet, it opened in 1986 in a Belle Epoque mansion, then was redecorated in 1994 by English designer Nina Campbell. Most of the guest rooms are medium to spacious, with modern furniture, double-glazing, mirrored closets, and king-size beds. Most rooms have shower/tub bathroom combos; six just have showers.

6 rue Balzac, 75008 Paris. ✆ 800/457-4000 in the U.S. and Canada, or 01-44-35-18-00. Fax 01-44-35-18-05. hbalzac@cybercable.fr. 70 units. 334€395€ ($299–$353) double; from 502€ ($448) suite. AE, DC, MC, V. Parking 23€ ($20). Métro: George V. **Amenities:** Restaurant (French); bar; 24-hr. room service; babysitting; laundry/dry cleaning. *In room:* A/C, TV, minibar, hair dryer.

Hotel François 1er ✿✿   Our favorite boutique hotel off the Champs-Elysées is this beautifully restored charmer a few steps from those swanky avenues of platinum real estate, avenue George V and avenue Montaigne. Inaugurated in 1986 and renovated in 2000, this hotel is like a private town house, the creation of Pierre Yves Rochkon, the architect responsible for the restoration of such landmarks as the Hotel George V. The marbled lobby and sumptuous lounges set a refined and elegant style that's also reflected in the bedrooms, which have true Parisian styling and luxurious bathrooms with tub and shower. At the hotel's bar, with its elegant winter garden, some models and designers from the nearby fashion houses such as Chanel and Christian Dior often meet for drinks.

7 rue Magellan, 75008 Paris. ✆ 01-47-23-44-04. Fax 01-47-23-93-43. www.france-hotel-guide.com/h75008francois1er2.htm. 40 units. 305€–458€ ($272–$409) double; from 535€ ($478) suite. AE, DC, MC, V. Métro: George V. **Amenities:** restaurant; bar; 24-hr. room service; laundry/dry cleaning; in-room massage. *In room:* A/C, TV, minibar, hair dryer, trouser press, safe.

Hotel Lancaster ✿✿   Small-scale, unglitzy, and intensely chic, this hotel is an oasis of Anglo-Saxon charm in the midst of one of the most frenetic neighborhoods in Paris. Built in the 1890s and transformed into a hotel in 1925, it functioned as a not-particularly fashionable dowager with an English-derived decor and a conservative, mostly English, clientele that appreciated its slow rhythms and resistance to change. Much of that changed in 1996, when Grace Leo Andrieu, a style-setter who has evolved into a subject of intense interest to the popular press, hauled in a team of decorators and gutted, then rebuilt, much of the interior. Expect a well-upholstered combination of English, French, and Asian design, a stunning collection of 18th- and 19th-century antiques, a worldly staff, and a feeling that's more akin to a private club than a hotel. This is the kind of hotel where wealthy clients pre-reserve their favorite rooms as much as a year in advance. Each accommodation comes with a luxurious bathroom with tub-and-shower combination. The in-house restaurant is open only to residents of the hotel. Meals and drinks are served in the garden, pending cooperation of the weather.

7 rue de Berri, 75008 Paris. ℂ **800/223-6800** in the U.S. (reservations only), or 01-40-76-40-76. Fax 01-40-76-40-00. www.hotel-lancaster.fr. 71 units. 390€–545€ ($348–$487) double; 750€–1,600€ ($670–$1,429) suite. AE, DC, MC, V. Métro: Georges V. **Amenities:** Restaurant; bar; garden; small fitness center; laundry/dry cleaning. *In room:* A/C, TV, minibar, safe.

Hyatt Regency Paris-Madeleine 🌟🌟   In the heart of the financial district, this is Paris's latest luxury hotel and represents Hyatt's first venture into the heart of the French capital. For clients visiting Paris on business, this is our most recommended choice, as rooms were designed not only for rest but for work—large writing desks, three phones, modem sockets, voice mail, individual fax machines—you name it. As you enter, the hotel evokes a noble, romantic private home with a lavish use of quality materials such as sycamore wood. Bedrooms are spacious with large beds and luxurious, tiled bathrooms with tubs and showers. Some of the units boast an exceptional view over the rooftops of Paris.

24 bd. Malesherbes, 75008 Paris. ℂ **01-55-27-12-34.** Fax 01-55-27-12-35. http://paris.hyatt.com. 81 units. 456€–547€ ($406–$487) double; 669€–973€ ($595–$866) suite. AE, DC, MC, V. Free parking. **Amenities:** 2 restaurants; bar; massage salon; fitness center; 24-hr. business center; 24-hr. room service; babysitting; laundry/dry cleaning. *In room:* A/C, TV, minibar, hair dryer, safe.

MODERATE

Galileo Hôtel 🌟 *(Finds)*   This is one of the 8th's most charming boutique hotels. It's the invention of Roland and Elisabeth Buffat, who have won friends from around the world with their Hotel des Deux-Iles and Hotel de Lutèce on St-Louis-en-l'Ile (listed earlier in this chapter). A short walk from the Champs-Elysées, the town-house hotel is the epitome of French elegance and charm. The guest rooms are medium in size for the most part and a study in understated taste, decorated in various shades of cocoa and beige. The most spacious are nos. 100, 200, 501, and 502, with a glass-covered veranda you can use even in winter. Bathrooms are tiled and beautifully kept with either a tub or shower. For such a tony neighborhood, the prices are moderate.

54 rue Galilée, 75008 Paris. ℂ **01-47-20-66-06.** Fax 01-47-20-67-17. www.hotel-ile-saintlouis.com. 27 units. 132€–149€ ($118–$133) double. AE, DC, MC, V. Parking 23€ ($20). Métro: Charles de Gaulle-Etoile or George V. **Amenities:** Room service (8am–9pm); babysitting; laundry/dry cleaning. *In room:* A/C, TV, minibar, hair dryer, safe.

Hôtel Queen Mary 🌟   Meticulously renovated inside and out, this early-1900s hotel is graced with an iron-and-glass canopy, ornate wrought iron, and the kind of detail normally reserved for more expensive hotels. The public rooms have touches of greenery and reproductions of mid-19th-century antiques; each guest room has an upholstered headboard, comfortable beds, and mahogany furnishings, plus a carafe of sherry. All the rooms, ranging from small to medium, were fully renovated in 1998, and 31 come with tub-and-shower combinations; five are shower-only accommodations.

9 rue Greffulhe, 75008 Paris. ℂ **01-42-66-40-50.** Fax 01-42-66-94-92. www.hotelqueenmary.com. 36 units. 129€–169€ ($115–$151) double; 239€ ($213) suite. AE, DC, MC, V. Parking 15€ ($13). Métro: Madeleine or Havre-Caumartin. **Amenities:** Bar; business center; room service (11am–10pm); babysitting. *In room:* A/C, TV, minibar, hair dryer, safe.

INEXPENSIVE

Hôtel du Ministère 🌟 *(Kids)*   The Ministère is a winning choice near the Champs-Elysées and the American Embassy, though it's far from Paris's cheapest budget hotel. Long a family hotel, new owners began refurbishing it in 1999, completing work in 2001, and the hotel is better than ever. The guest rooms are on the small side, but each is comfortably appointed and well maintained; many have oak beams and fine furnishings. Try to avoid a room on the top floor, as you'll be too cramped. Each unit is equipped with a tub-shower combo.

31 rue de Surène, 75008 Paris. ℭ **01-42-66-21-43.** Fax 01-42-66-96-04. www.ministerehotel.com. 28 units. 151€–181€ ($134–$162) double. AE, MC, V. Parking 17€ ($15). Métro: Madeleine or Miromesnil. **Amenities:** Bar; room service; laundry/dry cleaning. *In room:* A/C, TV, minibar, hair dryer, safe.

Hôtel Opal *Finds* This rejuvenated circa-1900 hotel is a real find behind La Madeleine church and near the Opéra Garnier. The guest rooms are somewhat tight but very clean and comfortable, and many of them are air-conditioned. Those on the top floor are reached by a narrow staircase; some have skylights. Most rooms have twin brass beds, and all of them come with a tub-and-shower combo. Reception will make arrangements for parking at a nearby garage.

19 rue Tronchet, 75008 Paris. ℭ **01-42-65-77-97.** Fax 01-49-24-06-58. www.hotels.fr/opal. 36 units. 144€–167€ ($129–$149) double. Extra bed 15€ ($13). AE, DC, V. Parking 23€ ($20) nearby. Métro: Madeleine. **Amenities:** Bar; room service (breakfast); babysitting; laundry/dry cleaning. *In room:* A/C in some rooms, TV, minibar, hair dryer, safe.

Résidence Lord Byron *Kids* Off the Champs-Elysées on a curving street of handsome buildings, the Lord Byron may not be as grand as other hotels in the neighborhood, but it's more affordable. Unassuming and a bit staid, it's exactly what repeat guests want: a sense of solitude and understatement. The guest rooms are small to medium in size, and come mainly with shower bathrooms. You can eat breakfast in the dining room or in a shaded inner garden. At random, and spontaneously, we witnessed some tender moments of kindness in the breakfast room of this hotel. The scene involved the staff, many of whom have children of their own, who gracefully eased the social strains of the morning breakfast buffet and its proximity to small children, their parents, and other clients. Also, accommodations here are larger than what's usually available within newer hotels, and rooms that are usually marketed as quads for families contain curtains that separate the living area from the sleeping areas (or the sleeping areas of parents from the sleeping areas of children). Although the larger ("family") rooms don't overlook it, there is nonetheless, a small garden in back that provides breathing space for toddlers and adults alike.

5 rue de Chateaubriand, 75008 Paris. ℭ **01-43-59-89-98.** Fax 01-42-89-46-04. www.escapade-paris.com. 31 units. 149€–166€ ($133–$148) double; 239€ ($213) suite. AE, DC, MC, V. Parking 90€ ($80). Métro: George V. RER: Etoile. **Amenities:** Garden; room service; babysitting; dry cleaning. *In room:* A/C, TV, minibar, hair dryer, safe.

16TH ARRONDISSEMENT
VERY EXPENSIVE

Hotel Sofitel Trocadéro Dokhans ★★ Except for the fact that porters walk through its public areas carrying luggage, you might suspect that this well-accessorized hotel was a private home. It's housed within a stately 19th-century building vaguely inspired by Palladio, and it contains the kind of accessories that would look appropriate on the set of a Viennese operetta. This includes antique paneling, lacquered Regency-era armchairs, gilded bronze chandeliers, and a pervasive sense of good, upper-bourgeois taste. Like many a large private home, the bedrooms come in a wide range of sizes from small to spacious, as do the beautifully maintained bathrooms, each with tub and shower. Bedrooms are individually decorated, and each has antiques or good reproductions, ornamental swags and curtains above the headboards, lots of personalized touches, and triple-glazed windows to seal away noises from the neighborhood outside. Each contains a CD player and a personal fax machine. Well-respected decorator Frédéric Méchiche designed and decorated all aspects of this decor.

117 rue Lauriston, 75115 Paris. ℭ **01-53-65-66-99.** Fax 01-53-65-66-88. hotel.trocadero.dokhans@ wanadoo.fr. 45 units. 380€–448€ ($339–$400) double; 760€ ($679) suite. AE, DC, MC, V. Parking 14€ ($12). Métro: Trocadéro. **Amenities:** Restaurant (French, lunch only); champagne bar. *In room:* A/C, TV, minibar, hair dryer.

Saint James Paris ★★★   In an 1892 stone building inspired by a château in the French countryside, the Saint-James is as grand as any of the very expensive hotels in the more visible (and central) neighborhoods of Paris. It's set among the staid yet luxurious residences of the 16th arrondissement, and staying here gives you access to the private restaurant, bar, and fitness center reserved for aristocratic Parisian members. You'll find it intimate and warm, even if exclusivity and snobbery are part of its image. The guest rooms are spacious, the older ones featuring Art Deco detailing, the more newly renovated with sleek contemporary styling. Each contains a luxurious bathroom with tub-and-shower combination.

43 av. Bugeaud, 75016 Paris. ℭ **800/525-4800** in the U.S. and Canada, or 01-44-05-81-81. Fax 01-44-05-81-82. www.saint-james-paris.com. 48 units. 420€ ($375) double; 465€–730€ ($415–$652) suite. AE, DC, MC, V. Free parking. Métro: Porte Dauphine. RER: Av. Foch. **Amenities:** Restaurant; bar; health club; Jacuzzi; sauna; 24-hr. room service; in-room massage; babysitting; laundry/dry cleaning. *In room:* A/C, TV, kitchenette (in 2 units), minibar, hair dryer, safe.

INEXPENSIVE

Au Palais de Chaillot Hôtel   When Thierry and Cyrille Pien, brothers trained in the States, opened this excellent hotel in 1997, budgeters flocked here. Between the Champs-Elysées and Trocadéro, the town house was restored from top to bottom and the result is a contemporary yet informal style of Parisian chic. The guest rooms come in various shapes and sizes, and are furnished with a light touch, with bright colors and wicker. Nos. 61, 62, and 63 afford partial views of the Eiffel Tower. Each unit comes with a neatly tiled shower-only bathroom.

35 av. Raymond-Poincaré, 75016 Paris. ℭ **01-53-70-09-09.** Fax 01-53-70-09-08. www.chaillotel.com. 28 units. 94€ ($84) double; 116€ ($103) triple. AE, DC, MC, V. Parking 18€ ($16). Métro: Victor Hugo or Trocadéro. **Amenities:** Room service (breakfast and drinks 7am–11pm); laundry/dry cleaning. *In room:* TV, hair dryer.

Hôtel Les Hauts de Passy   Across the river from the Eiffel Tower in a chic residential neighborhood, this hotel sits on a pedestrian-only street where an outdoor market is held Tuesday to Sunday. All the rooms were recently renovated and are inviting, with double-glazed windows. The bathrooms, though small, are squeaky clean, with tubs in a few units. Just outside the door is a wonderful boulangerie where you can have breakfast while watching the market bustle.

37 rue de l'Annonciation, 75016 Paris. ℭ **01-42-88-47-28.** Fax 01-42-88-99-09. www.france-hotel-guide. com/. 31 units. 84€–106€ ($75–$95) double. MC, V. Parking 14€ ($13). Métro: La Muette or Passy. **Amenities:** Car-rental desk; breakfast-only room service; laundry/babysitting. *In room:* TV, minibar, hair dryer.

17TH ARRONDISSEMENT
MODERATE

Best Western Hôtel Regent's Garden ★   Near the convention center (Palais des Congrés) and the Arc de Triomphe, the Regent's Garden boasts a proud heritage: Napoleon III built this château for his physician. The interior resembles a classically decorated country house. Fluted columns mark the entryway, which leads to a mix of furniture in the lobby. The guest rooms have flower prints on the walls, traditional French furniture, and tall soundproof windows, plus neatly organized private bathrooms with both a tub and shower. There's a garden with ivy-covered walls and umbrella-shaded tables—a perfect place to meet other guests.

6 rue Pierre-Demours, 75017 Paris. ✆ **01-45-74-07-30.** Fax 01-40-55-01-42. www.hotel-paris-garden.com. 39 units. 130€–230€ ($116–$205) double. AE, DC, MC, V. Parking 10€ ($8.90). Métro: Ternes or Charles de Gaulle-Etoile. **Amenities:** Garden; 24-hr. room service (drinks); babysitting. *In room:* A/C, TV, minibar, hair dryer.

Hôtel Eber Hidden on a quiet side street, this early-1900s government-rated three-star hotel is comfortably rustic, with exposed stone and wood paneling, paneled ceilings, and a Renaissance-style fireplace. The guest rooms are pleasant, and most have armchairs for reading. Every accommodation is contemporary-looking and has a well-maintained private bathroom—half with tubs, half with showers. The courtyard provides an oasis for breakfast and afternoon tea.

18 rue Léon-Jost, 75017 Paris. ✆ **01-46-22-60-70.** Fax 01-47-63-01-01. 18 units. 108€–134€ ($96–$119) double; 198€–228€ ($176–$204) suite. AE, DC, MC, V. Parking 15€ ($13). Métro: Courcelles. **Amenities:** Bar; 24-hr. room service (snacks and drinks); babysitting; laundry/dry cleaning. *In room:* A/C, TV, minibar, hair dryer.

INEXPENSIVE
Hôtel Flaubert For an inexpensive retreat in the 17th, this is as good as it gets. The staff here long ago became accustomed to handling the problems their international guests might have. Terra-cotta tiles and bentwood furniture in the public areas make for an efficient if not lushly comfortable setting for breakfast. Though the climbing plants in the courtyard overshadow the guest rooms, the accommodations are appealing and, particularly those beneath the mansard's eaves, cozy. In 2000, management added about a dozen new rooms, thanks to the acquisition and refurbishment of a building next door. Throughout, rooms are modern, relatively small-scale, and comfortable. About half of the private bathrooms contain tubs, the others showers.

19 rue Rennequin, 75017 Paris. ✆ **01-46-22-44-35.** Fax 01-43-80-32-34. www.hotelflaubert.com. 49 units. 94€ ($84) double. AE, DC, MC, V. Métro: Ternes or Charles de Gaulle-Etoile. **Amenities:** Garden; room service (breakfast). *In room:* TV, minibar, hair dryer.

Les Trois Couronnes This prestigious older hotel in Paris's business hub is within easy access of the Métro and many of the city's attractions. With its blend of Art Deco and Art Nouveau, it was radically redecorated and upgraded in 1995. The cheerful guest rooms, small and old-fashioned, have pleasant views of the surrounding area. Bathrooms are neatly kept and tiled; each contains a private shower, some a tub-shower combo.

30 rue de l'Arc-de-Triomphe, 75017 Paris. ✆ **01-43-80-46-81.** Fax 01-46-22-53-96. www.3couronnes.com. 20 units. 87€–99€ ($77–$88) double. AE, DC, MC, V. Parking 15€ ($13). Métro: Charles de Gaulle-Etoile. **Amenities:** Room service (breakfast). *In room:* TV, minibar, hair dryer, safe.

Marmotel Etoile This hotel is on an inconvenient side of place Charles de Gaulle-Etoile, and you have to ford a river of traffic to get to the Champs-Elysées. The guest rooms are simple and small but comfortable and decorated in a variety of styles that includes rattan, angular modern, and somewhat old-fashioned furnishings. The ones overlooking the carefully landscaped flagstone-covered courtyard benefit from an unexpected oasis of calm; those fronting the avenue's traffic are less peaceful. Bedrooms are equally divided between those that have a shower only or those with a tub-shower combo.

34 av. de la Grande Armée, 75017 Paris. ✆ **01-47-63-57-26.** Fax 01-45-74-25-27. marmotel@aol.com. 23 units. 75€–78€ ($67–$69) double. AE, DC, MC, V. Métro: Argentine. **Amenities:** Room service (breakfast); dry cleaning. *In room:* TV, hair dryer, minibar, safe.

2 On the Left Bank

We'll begin with the most centrally located arrondissements on the Left Bank, then work our way through the more outlying neighborhoods and to the area near the Eiffel Tower.

5TH ARRONDISSEMENT
MODERATE

Grand Hôtel St-Michel   Built in the 19th century, this hotel is larger and more businesslike than many of the town house–style inns nearby. It basks in the reflected glow of Brazilian dissident Georges Amado, whose memoirs (released in 1996) recorded his 2-year literary sojourn in one of the rooms. The public rooms are tasteful, with oil portraits and rich upholsteries. In 1997, the hotel completed a renovation and moved from a government rating of two- to three-star status. All but four of the units have tub-shower combinations. The changes enlarged some rooms, lowering their ceilings and adding modern amenities like minibars, but retained old-fashioned touches such as wrought-iron balconies (fifth floor only). Sixth-floor rooms offer interesting views over the rooftops.

19 rue Cujas, 75005 Paris. ✆ **01-46-33-33-02.** Fax 01-40-46-96-33. www.grand-hotel-st-michel.com. 46 units. 159€ ($142) double; 219€ ($196) triple. AE, DC, MC, V. Métro: Cluny-La Sorbonne. RER: Luxembourg or St-Michel. **Amenities:** Bar; babysitting; room service (breakfast); laundry/dry cleaning. *In room:* TV, minibar, hair dryer, safe.

Hôtel Abbatial St-Germain *Value*   The origins of this hotel run deep: Interior renovations have revealed such 17th-century touches as dovecotes and massive oak beams. In the early 1990s, a restoration made the public areas especially appealing and brought the small rooms, furnished in faux Louis XVI, up to modern standards. Bedrooms were again restored in 2001 and 2002. All windows are double-glazed, and the fifth- and sixth-floor rooms enjoy views over Notre-Dame. The small bathrooms are neatly kept and equipped with showers or tub-and-shower combinations.

46 bd. St-Germain, 75005 Paris. ✆ **01-46-34-02-12.** Fax 01-43-25-47-73. www.abbatial.com. 43 units. 123€–145€ ($110–$130) double. AE, MC, V. Parking 19€ ($17). Métro: Maubert-Mutualité. **Amenities:** Babysitting; laundry/dry cleaning. *In room:* A/C, TV, minibar, hair dryer, safe.

Hôtel Agora St-Germain   One of the best of the neighborhood's moderately priced choices, this hotel occupies a building constructed in the early 1600s, probably to house a group of guardsmen protecting the brother of the king at his lodgings nearby. It's in the heart of artistic/historic Paris and offers compact, soundproof guest rooms that are not particularly fashionably furnished. All but seven of the bedrooms have tub-shower combos, the rest only showers.

42 rue des Bernardins, 75005 Paris. ✆ **01-46-34-13-00.** Fax 01-46-34-75-05. www.france-hotel-guide.com. 39 units. 127€–147€ ($113–$131) double. AE, DC, MC, V. Parking 19€ ($17). Métro: Maubert-Mutualité. **Amenities:** Room service (8am–3pm). *In room:* A/C, TV, minibar, hair dryer, safe.

Hôtel des Arènes *Finds*   In a 19th-century building whose chiseled stone facade evokes old traditions, this hotel offers well-maintained modern guest rooms. Many in back overlook the tree-dotted ruins of Paris's ancient Roman

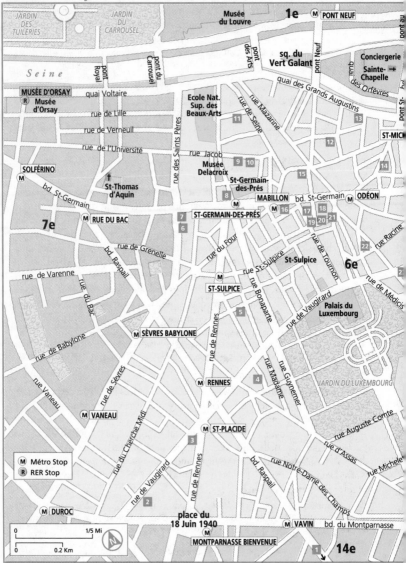

arena, unearthed in 1865. Rooms in back are quiet, almost like living in the country. All accommodations come with a tub-and-shower combo. Although the gardens of the arena do not belong to the hotel, guests have direct access to them.

51 rue Monge, 75005 Paris. ☎ 01-43-25-09-26. Fax 01-43-25-79-56. www.france-hotel-guide.com/h7500 5arenes2.htm. 52 units. 110€ ($98) double; 154€ ($138) triple. AE, MC, V. Parking 15€ ($13). Métro: Monge or Cardinal Lemoine. **Amenities:** Room service (breakfast). *In room:* TV, minibar, hair dryer, safe.

Hôtel des Grands Hommes   Built in the 18th century and renovated in the 1990s, this hotel offers direct profile views (from many rooms) of the Panthéon.

Best Western Aramis Saint-Germain **3**
Familia-Hôtel **34**
Grand Hôtel de L'Univers **17**
Grand Hôtel St-Michel **27**
Hôtel Abbatial St-Germain **32**
Hôtel Agora St-Germain **31**
Hôtel Aviatic **2**
Hôtel Clément **16**
Hôtel de Fleurie **15**
Hôtel de L'Abbaye St-Germain **5**
Hôtel Delavigne **22**
Hôtel des Arénes **36**
Hôtel des Deux Continents **10**
Hôtel des Grandes Ecoles **33**
Hôtel des Grands Hommes **26**
Hôtel des Jardins du Luxembourg **25**
Hôtel des Saints-Péres **6**
Hôtel du Globe **19**
Hôtel du Lys **14**
Hôtel du Parc-Montsouris **1**
Hôtel du Pas-de-Calais **7**
Hôtel du Vert Galant **38**
Hôtel Le Clos Médicis **23**
Hôtel Le Home Latin **30**
Hôtel Le Ste-Beuve **4**
Hôtel Louis II **20**
Hôtel Moderne St-Germain **29**
Hôtel Observatoire-Luxembourg **24**
Hôtel St-Germain-des-Prés **8**
Hôtel Résidence St-Christophe **37**
L'Hôtel **11**
La Villa **9**
Minerve Hôtel **28**
Odéon-Hôtel **21**
Relais Christine **12**
Relais St-Germain **18**
Résidence des Arts **13**
Timhôtel Jardin des Plantes **35**

All but a handful of the accommodations have exposed ceiling beams and pleasantly old-fashioned furnishings that sometimes include brass beds. Fifth- and sixth-floor rooms have small balconies and also the best views. Those with the most space are on the ground floor. In 2001 and 2002, the bedrooms were renovated, and now each comes with a complete tub-and-shower combo.

17 place du Panthéon, 75005 Paris. ☎ **01-46-34-19-60.** Fax 01-43-26-67-32. 32 units. 182€ ($163) double; 243€–381€ ($217–$340) suite. AE, DC, MC, V. Parking 14€ ($12). Métro: Cardinal Lemoine or Luxembourg. **Amenities:** Babysitting; laundry/dry cleaning. *In room:* A/C, TV, minibar, hair dryer.

Hôtel des Jardins du Luxembourg Built during Baron Haussmann's 19th-century overhaul of Paris, this hotel boasts an imposing facade of honey-colored stone accented with ornate iron balconies. The interior is outfitted in strong, clean lines, often with groupings of Art Deco furnishings. The high-ceilinged guest rooms, some with Provençal tiles and ornate moldings, are well-maintained, the size ranging from small to medium. Best of all, they overlook a quiet dead-end alley, ensuring relatively peaceful nights. Some have balconies overlooking the rooftops. In 2000, the carpeting was replaced in all the bedrooms. Each unit comes with a neat, tidily arranged bathroom with a combined tub and shower.

5 impasse Royer-Collard, 75005 Paris. ✆ **01-40-46-08-88.** Fax 01-40-46-02-28. http://www.travel-in-paris. com/jardin-luxembourg/english.htm. 26 units. 130€–140€ ($116–$125) double. AE, DC, MC, V. Parking 15€ ($13). Métro: Cluny-La Sorbonne. RER: Luxembourg. **Amenities:** Room service (7am–4pm); babysitting; laundry/dry cleaning. In room: A/C, TV, minibar, hair dryer, safe.

Hôtel Moderne St-Germain *Value* In the heart of the Latin Quarter, the grand Hôtel Moderne is better than ever because it ended the 20th century with a complete overhaul. Its charming owner, Mme. Gibon, welcomes guests warmly to her spotless rooms. In the units fronting rue des Ecoles, double-glazed aluminum windows hush the traffic. Though the rooms are small, this is still one of the neighborhood's better government-rated three-star hotels. All the bathrooms contain showers, and about half of them also have tubs. Guests enjoy access to the sauna and Jacuzzi at the Hôtel Sully next door.

33 rue des Ecoles, 75005 Paris. ✆ **01-43-54-37-78.** Fax 01-43-29-91-31. www.tulipinn.com. 45 units. 114€–137€ ($102–$122) double; 182€ ($163) triple. AE, DC, MC, V. Parking 23€ ($20). Métro: Maubert-Mutualité. **Amenities:** Use of sauna and Jacuzzi next door; laundry/dry cleaning. In room: A/C, TV, minibar, hair dryer, safe.

Hôtel Observatoire-Luxembourg The hotel's simple Art-Nouveau facade is something of an architectural oddity in this neighborhood. Many of its rooms, especially those on the fifth and sixth floors, overlook either the Jardin du Luxembourg across the street or the nearby St-Jacques church. (Room 507, though not the largest, boasts the best view, encompassing both trees and medieval architecture.) A successful renovation in 2001 upgraded the public areas; they're streamlined and angular but softened by bright colors. Each bedroom has a private shower; half of the units also come with tubs.

107 bd. St-Michel, 75005 Paris. ✆ **01-46-34-10-12.** Fax 01-46-33-73-86. www.hotelconnect.com/france/ paris/observatoire/index.htm. 37 units. 150€ ($134) double. AE, DC, MC, V. Métro: Saint-Michel. RER: Luxembourg. **Amenities:** Babysitting; laundry/dry cleaning. In room: A/C, TV, minibar, hair dryer, safe.

Hôtel-Résidence Saint-Christophe This hotel, in one of the Latin Quarter's undiscovered but charming areas, offers a gracious English-speaking staff. It was created in 1987 when a derelict hotel was connected to a butcher shop. All the small- to medium-size rooms were renovated in 1998, with Louis XV–style furniture and wall-to-wall carpeting. Major improvements to the rooms were also made in 2001. All the bedrooms have private showers and half also have tubs.

17 rue Lacépède, 75005 Paris. ✆ **01-43-31-81-54.** Fax 01-43-31-12-54. www.cybevasion.com/hotels/ france/75/5/hotel-residence-saint-christophe/. 31 units. 96€–112€ ($86–$100) double. AE, DC, MC, V. Parking 15€ ($13). Métro: Place Monge. **Amenities:** Laundry/dry cleaning. In room: TV, minibar, hair dryer.

INEXPENSIVE

Familia-Hôtel As the name implies, this is a hotel that has been family-run for decades. Many personal touches make the place unique, and it was lavishly renovated in 1998. As in many Paris hotels, rooms are quite small and cozy but still comfortable. The walls of 14 rooms are graced with finely executed, sepia-colored frescoes of Parisian scenes. Eight rooms have restored stone walls, and seven have balconies with delightful views over the Latin Quarter. All units have showers, and half of the rooms also come with tubs.

11 rue des Ecoles, 75005 Paris. ℂ **01-43-54-55-27.** Fax 01-43-29-61-77. www.hotel-paris-familia.com/. 30 units. 84€–101€ ($75–$90) double. Rates include breakfast. AE, DC, MC, V. Métro: Jussieu or Maubert-Mutualité. **Amenities:** car-rental desk. *In room:* TV, minibar, hair dryer.

Hôtel des Grandes Ecoles *Value* Few other hotels in the neighborhood offer so much low-key charm at such reasonable prices. It's composed of a trio of high-ceilinged buildings, interconnected via a sheltered courtyard where in warm weather singing birds provide a worthy substitute for the TVs deliberately missing from the rooms. Accommodations, as reflected by the price, range from snug, cozy doubles to more spacious chambers. All units were renovated in 2001, and the small bathrooms with showers were also spruced up. Each room is comfortable, but with a lot of luggage the very smallest would be cramped. The room decor is old-fashioned, with feminine touches such as Laura Ashley–inspired flowered upholsteries and ruffles. Many offer views of a garden whose trellises and flowerbeds evoke the countryside.

75 rue de Cardinal-Lemoine, 75005 Paris. ℂ **01-43-26-79-23.** Fax 01-43-25-28-15. www.hotel-grandes-ecoles.com. 51 units. 95€–125€ ($85–$112) double. MC, V. Parking 25€ ($22). Métro: Cardinal Lemoine or Monge. *In room:* Hair dryer.

Hôtel Le Home Latin *Value* This is one of Paris's most famous budget hotels, known since the 1970s for its simple lodgings. The blandly functional rooms were renovated in 1999; some have small balconies overlooking the street. Those facing the courtyard are quieter than those on the street. The elevator doesn't go above the fifth floor, but to make up for the stair climb, the sixth floor's *chambres mansardées* offer a romantic location under the eaves and panoramic views. Forty-seven units come with showers only; the rest contain a tub-and-shower combo.

15-17 rue du Sommerard, 75005 Paris. ℂ **01-43-26-25-21.** Fax 01-43-29-87-04. www.homelatinhotel.com. 54 units. 90€–99€ ($81–$88) double; 114€ ($102) triple; 131€ ($117) quad. AE, DC, MC, V. Parking 13€ ($12). Métro: St-Michel or Maubert-Mutualité. *In room:* Hair dryers; no phone.

Minerve Hôtel This is a well-managed, government-rated two-star hotel in the heart of the Latin Quarter, with good-size, comfortable rooms and a staff with a sense of humor. Bedrooms have contemporary-looking mahogany furniture and walls covered in fabric. Try for one of 10 rooms with balconies where you can look out over the street life of Paris, and in some cases enjoy a view of Notre Dame. Depending on your room assignment, bathrooms range in dimension from cramped to midsize, each with a tub-and-shower combo. If there's no space at the Minerve, a staff member will arrange an equivalent (and equivalently priced) lodging in its sibling, the Familia next door (see description above).

13 rue des Ecoles, 75005 Paris. ℂ **01-43-26-26-04.** Fax 01-44-07-01-96. www.hotel-paris-minerve.com. 54 units. 77€–113€ ($68–$101) double. AE, MC, V. Métro: Cardinal Lemoine. **Amenities:** Car-rental desk. *In room:* TV, hair dryer.

Timhôtel Jardin des Plantes Opened in 1986 and renovated in 1997, the government-rated two-star Timhôtel is across from the Jardin des Plantes, the gardens created by order of Louis XIII's doctors in 1626 (there are still some 15,000 medicinal herbs in the gardens). Some of the small, well-equipped guest rooms open onto flowered terraces. The bathrooms have tubs and showers and were renovated in 2001. The hotel has a roof terrace and vaulted basement lounge.

5 rue Linné, 75005 Paris. ☎ **01-47-07-06-20**. Fax 01-47-07-62-74. www.timhotel.com. 33 units. 95€–122€ ($85–$109) double. AE, DC, MC, V. Parking 15€ ($13). Métro: Jussieu. Bus: 67 or 89. **Amenities:** Sauna; room service; babysitting; laundry/dry cleaning. *In room:* A/C, TV, hair dryer.

6TH ARRONDISSEMENT
VERY EXPENSIVE

Relais Christine ★★   This hotel welcomes you into what was a 16th-century Augustinian cloister. You enter from a narrow cobblestone street into a symmetrical courtyard, then an elegant reception area with baroque sculpture and Renaissance antiques. Each guest room is uniquely decorated with wooden beams and Louis XIII–style furnishings; the rooms come in a wide range of styles and shapes, and some are among the Left Bank's largest, with extras like mirrored closets, plush carpets, thermostats, and balconies facing the outer courtyard. The least attractive rooms are those in the interior, dim and small. Each comes with a complete tub and shower bathroom.

3 rue Christine, 75006 Paris. ☎ **01-40-51-60-80**. Fax 01-40-51-60-81. www.relais-christine.com. 51 units. 315€–365€ ($281–$326) double; 700€ ($625) duplex or suite. AE, DC, MC, V. Free parking. Métro: Odéon. **Amenities:** Honor bar in lobby; room service; babysitting; in-room massage; laundry/dry cleaning. *In room:* A/C, TV, minibar, hair dryer, safe.

EXPENSIVE

Hôtel de Fleurie ★★ *Kids*   Off boulevard St-Germain on a colorful little street, the Fleurie is one of the best of the "new" old hotels, with its statuary-studded facade recapturing a 17th-century elegance. The stone walls have been exposed in the reception salon, where you check in at a refectory desk. Many guest rooms and tub-and-shower bathrooms were renovated in 1999, and many have elaborate curtains and antique reproductions. All units come with tiled bathrooms with tub and shower, except for five that offer tubs only. This hotel has long been a family favorite—interconnecting doors in certain pairs of rooms create safe havens the hotel refers to as *chambres familiales.*

32-34 rue Grégoire-de-Tours, 75006 Paris. ☎ **01-53-73-70-00**. Fax 01-53-73-70-20. www.hotel-de-fleurie.tm.fr. 29 units. 167€–198€ ($149–$177) double; 244€–274€ ($218–$245) family room. Children 12 and under stay free in parents' room. AE, DC, MC, V. Métro: Odéon or St-Germain-des-Prés. **Amenities:** Bar; car-rental desk; room service (8am–5pm); babysitting; laundry/dry cleaning. *In room:* A/C, TV, minibar, hair dryer, trouser press, safe.

Hôtel de l'Abbaye St-Germain ★   This is one of the district's most charming boutique hotels, having been a convent in the early 18th century. Its brightly colored rooms have traditional furniture like you'd find in a private club, plus touches of sophisticated flair. The more expensive units are quite spacious; the cheaper ones are small but efficiently organized and still quite comfortable. In front is a small garden and in back a verdant courtyard with a fountain, raised flowerbeds, and masses of ivy and climbing vines. If you don't mind the expense, one of the most charming rooms has a terrace overlooking the upper floors of neighboring buildings. Bedrooms come with neatly tiled and complete bathrooms.

10 rue Cassette, 75006 Paris. ☎ **01-45-44-38-11**. Fax 01-45-48-07-86. www.hotel-abbaye.com. 46 units. 195€–284€ ($174–$254) double; 372€–387€ ($332–$346) suite. Rates include breakfast. AE, MC, V. Métro: St-Sulpice. **Amenities:** Garden; room service (7am–midnight); babysitting; laundry/dry cleaning. *In room:* A/C, TV, hair dryer, safe.

La Villa ⭐ This hotel's facade resembles those of many of the other buildings in the neighborhood. Inside, however, the decor is a minimalist ultramodern creation rejecting all traditional French aesthetics. The public areas and guest rooms contain Bauhaus-like furniture; the lobby's angular lines are softened with bouquets of leaves and flowers. Most unusual are the baths, whose stainless steel; pink, black, or beige marble; and chrome surfaces are either post-Sputnik or postmodern, depending on your frame of reference. Everything was renovated in 2000, and all but four units contain a complete tub and shower.

29 rue Jacob, 75006 Paris. ℂ **01-43-26-60-00.** Fax 01-46-34-63-63. www.villa-saintgermain.com. 31 units. 225€–320€ ($201–$286) double; 400€ ($357) suite. AE, DC, MC, V. Métro: St-Germain-des-Prés. **Amenities:** Bar; room service (drinks noon–midnight); babysitting. *In room:* A/C, TV, minibar, hair dryer, safe.

L'Hôtel ⭐⭐ Ranking just a notch below the Relais Christine (see above), this is one of the Left Bank's most charming boutique hotels. It was once a 19th-century fleabag called the Alsace, whose major distinction was that Oscar Wilde died there, broke and in despair. But today's guests aren't anywhere near poverty. The guest rooms vary in size, style, and price, from quite small to deluxe, but all have nonworking fireplaces and fabric-covered walls. An eclectic collection of antiques pops up all over: One spacious room contains the furnishings and memorabilia of stage star Mistinguett, a frequent performer with Maurice Chevalier and his on-again/off-again lover. Her pedestal bed is in the middle of the room, surrounded by mirrors, as she liked to see how she looked or "performed" at all times. In 2000, aesthetic superstar Jacques Garcia redecorated the hotel, retaining its Victorian-baroque sense but outfitting each room differently. Expect to be lodged amid themes that reflect China, Russia, Japan, India, or high-camp Victorian. The Cardinal room is all scarlet, the *Viollet-le-Duc* room is neo-Gothic, and the room where Wilde died is stately, Victorian, respectful, and nostalgia-laden. They installed a small swimming pool and steam bath (*hammam*) in the cellar, renovated the bar (discussed later in "Paris After Dark"), and revitalized the restaurant. About half the bathrooms have showers, the others small tubs.

13 rue des Beaux Arts, 75006 Paris. ℂ **01-44-41-99-00.** Fax 01-43-25-64-81. www.l-hotel.com. 20 units. 260€–595€ ($232–$531) double; from 686€ ($613) suite. AE, DC, MC, V. Métro: St-Germain-des-Prés or Mabillon. **Amenities:** Pool; steam bath; room service (7am–11:30pm); babysitting; laundry/dry cleaning. *In room:* A/C, TV, minibar, hair dryer.

Odéon-Hôtel ⭐⭐ Reminiscent of a modernized Norman country inn, the Odéon offers charming rustic touches such as exposed beams, stone walls, high crooked ceilings, and tapestries mixed with contemporary fabrics, mirrored ceilings, and black leather furnishings. Located near both the Théâtre de l'Odéon and boulevard St-Germain, the Odéon stands on the first street in Paris to have pavements (1779) and gutters. By the turn of the 20th century, this area, which had drawn the original Shakespeare & Co. bookshop, began attracting such writers as Gertrude Stein and her coterie. The guest rooms are small to medium in size but charming, and each comes with a combo tub and shower.

3 rue de l'Odéon, 75006 Paris. ℂ **01-43-25-90-67.** Fax 01-43-25-55-98. www.odeonhotel.fr. 33 units. 144€–228€ ($129–$204) double. AE, DC, MC, V. Parking 18€ ($16). Métro: Odéon. **Amenities:** Room service (drinks only, 24-hr.); babysitting. *In room:* A/C, TV, hair dryer, safe.

Relais St-Germain ⭐ Adapted from a 17th-century building, the St-Germain is an oasis of charm and comfort. It's comparable to the Relais Christine (see above) but with a more accommodating staff. The decor is a medley of traditional and modern, evoking a charming provincial house. All the necessary amenities have been tucked in under the beams, including soundproofing and full bathrooms. Bathrooms range from midsize to roomy, each with a combination tub and shower. Four rooms feature kitchenettes, and the only suite has a terrace.

9 carrefour de l'Odéon, 75006 Paris. ℂ 01-43-29-12-05. Fax 01-46-33-45-30. 22 units. 266€–327€ ($238–$292) double; 357€ ($319) suite. Rates include breakfast. AE, DC, MC, V. Métro: Odéon. **Amenities:** Wine bar; room service (7am–10pm); babysitting; laundry/dry cleaning. *In room:* A/C, TV, minibar, hair dryer, safe.

MODERATE

Best Western Aramais Saint-Germain Between Saint-Germain-des-Prés and Montparnasse, this is a recently renovated hotel that is attractively modernized and gracefully comfortable. Individually decorated bedrooms are midsize and furnished in a sleek, modern fashion, each with a private tiled bathroom with tub and shower. Nine of the bedrooms also contain a private Jacuzzi, and rooms are also soundproofed. The English-speaking staff is most helpful.

124 rue de Rennes, 75006 Paris. ℂ 01-45-48-03-75. Fax 01-45-44-99-29. www.hotel-aramis.com. 42 units. 145€–160€ ($130–$143) double; 175€–190€ ($156–$170) triple. Rooms with Jacuzzi 16€ ($14) extra. AE, DC, MC, V. Métro: Rennes. **Amenities:** Private bar; laundry. *In room:* A/C, TV, minibar.

Grand Hôtel de l'Univers In the 1400s, this was home to a family of the emergent bourgeoisie, and the hotel exudes charm and tranquillity. The pleasantly renovated guest rooms are cramped but well maintained and some have panoramic views over the crooked rooftops. A renovation in 2000 added English-inspired decor to the bedrooms. All units have private bathrooms with tub-shower combos.

6 rue Grégoire-de-Tours, 75006 Paris. ℂ 01-43-29-37-00. Fax 01-40-51-06-45. www.hotel-paris-univers. com. 34 units. 165€–205€ ($147–$183) double. AE, DC, MC, V. Métro: Odéon. **Amenities:** Room service (8am–8pm); babysitting; laundry/dry cleaning. *In room:* A/C, TV, minibar, hair dryer, safe.

Hôtel Aviatic Completely remodeled, this is a bit of old Paris in an interesting section of Montparnasse, with a modest inner courtyard and a vine-covered wall lattice, surrounded by cafes popular with artists, writers, and jazz musicians. It has been a family-run hotel for a century and has an English-speaking staff. The reception lounge boasts marble columns, brass chandeliers, antiques, and a petite salon. The guest rooms, which are midsize and fairly standard throughout, were renovated in stages throughout the 1990s, and each comes with a shower or tub-and-shower combo. Those that were renovated the most recently (management calls them "the millennium rooms") are the most stylish and expensive and have decors that evoke the French Empire period of the 1830s.

105 rue de Vaugirard, 75006 Paris. ℂ 01-53-63-25-50. Fax 01-53-63-25-55. www.aviatic.fr. 43 units. 120€–157€ ($107–$140) double. AE, DC, MC, V. Parking 18€ ($16). Métro: Montparnasse-Bienvenue or Saint-Placide. **Amenities:** Room service (7am–3pm); babysitting; laundry/dry cleaning. *In room:* A/C, TV, minibar, hair dryer, safe.

Hôtel des Deux Continents Built from three interconnected historic buildings, each between three and six stories high, this hotel is a reliable choice with a sense of Latin Quarter style. The carefully coordinated guest rooms, renovated between 1992 and 1998, range from small to medium-size and include reproductions of antique furnishings and soundproof upholstered walls. Each is equipped with a neatly tiled shower bathroom, a third of which also offer tubs.

25 rue Jacob, 75006 Paris. ℂ 01-43-26-72-46. Fax 01-43-25-67-80. www.2continents-hotel.com. 41 units. 144€–152€ ($129–$136) double; 186€ ($166) triple. MC, V. Métro: St-Germain-des-Prés. *In room:* A/C, TV.

Hôtel des Saints-Pères   This hotel off boulevard St-Germain is comparable to the Odéon, and there's no better recommendation than the long list of guests who return again and again (poet Edna St. Vincent Millay loved the camellia-trimmed garden). The hotel, designed by Louis XIV's architect, Jacques-Ange Gabriel, is decorated in part with antique paintings, tapestries, and mirrors. Many of the guest rooms face a quiet courtyard. Most sought-after is the *chambre à la fresque*, with a 17th-century painted ceiling. The hotel has installed new plumbing and replastered and repainted the rooms. All bathrooms have tub-and-shower combos.

65 rue des Sts-Pères, 75006 Paris. © 01-45-44-50-00. Fax 01-45-44-90-83. www.esprit-de-france.com. 39 units. 144€–190€ ($129–$170) double; 274€ ($244) suite. AE, MC, V. Métro: St-Germain-des-Prés or Sèvres-Babylone. **Amenities:** Garden; 24-hr. room service for drinks. *In room:* TV, minibar.

Hôtel du Pas-de-Calais   The Pas-de-Calais goes back to the 17th century. Its elegant facade, with massive wooden doors, has been retained. Romantic novelist Chateaubriand lived here from 1811 to 1814, but its most famous guest was Jean-Paul Sartre, who struggled with the play *Les Mains Sales* (*Dirty Hands*) in room 41. The hotel is a bit weak on style, but as one longtime guest confided, despite the updates, "we still stay here for the memories." The modern guest rooms were renovated in 2000; inner rooms surround a courtyard with two garden tables and several trellises. The inner rooms are the smallest and cheapest; the other rooms range from midsize to spacious. Each bedroom comes with a tub and shower.

59 rue des Sts-Pères, 75006 Paris. © 01-45-48-78-74. Fax 01-45-44-94-57. 40 units. 140€–213€ ($125–$190) double. AE, DC, MC, V. Parking 18€ ($16). Métro: St-Germain-des-Prés or Sèvres-Babylone. **Amenities:** 24-hr. room service for drinks and snacks; babysitting; laundry/dry cleaning. *In room:* A/C, TV, hair dryer, safe.

Hôtel Le Clos Médicis   The location of this hotel across from the Jardin du Luxembourg is a major advantage. You'll find a verdant garden with lattices and exposed stone walls, a lobby with modern spotlights and simple furniture, and a multilingual staff. Decorated in a vaguely Art Nouveau style, the warmly colored guest rooms, small to medium in size, are comfortable, and each comes with a neatly tiled shower-and-tub bathroom.

56 rue Monsieur-le-Prince, 75006 Paris. © 01-43-29-10-80. Fax 01-43-54-26-90. www.closmedicis.com. 38 units. 150€–180€ ($134–$161) double; 190€ ($170) duplex suite. AE, DC, MC, V. Parking 23€ ($20). Métro: Odéon. RER: Luxembourg. **Amenities:** Garden; laundry/dry cleaning; room service (7–11am). *In room:* A/C, TV, minibar, hair dryer, safe.

Hôtel Le Ste-Beuve (★ *Finds*)   The location of this discreet hideaway adds to its charms, on a street that's tucked into a narrow and quiet neighborhood, reeking of respectability, near the Luxembourg Garden. The public areas are outfitted with deep leather armchairs and a midwinter fire that blazes in an open hearth. Bedrooms each contain at least one antique, and each comes in a different color scheme. None is overly large, but all of them (four to a floor) face the quiet street, noises from which are muffled by double-glazing. Full bathrooms are sheathed in dark-brown marble. The aura is one of well-managed comfort and respectability.

9 rue Ste-Beuve, 75006 Paris. © 01-45-48-20-07. Fax 01-45-48-67-52. www.paris-hotel-charme.com. 22 units. 122€–265€ ($109–$237) double; 265€ ($237) suite. Parking 14€ ($12). Métro: Notre-Dame-des-Champs. **Amenities:** Room service (drinks 7am–10pm); dry cleaning; babysitting. *In room:* TV, minibar, safe.

Hôtel Louis II   In an 18th-century building, this hotel offers guest rooms decorated in rustic French tones. Afternoon drinks and morning coffee are served in the reception salon, where gilt-framed mirrors, fresh flowers, and antiques radiate a provincial aura, like something out of Proust. The generally small, soundproof rooms with exposed beams and lace bedding complete the impression. Many visitors ask for the romantic attic rooms. In 2000, the public rooms and bedrooms were renovated in a "hotel de charme" style. About half of the rooms contain tub baths, the rest showers.

2 rue St-Sulpice, 75006 Paris. © **01-46-33-13-80.** Fax 01-46-33-17-29. www.hotel-louis2.com. 22 units. 115€–175€ ($103–$156) double; 220€ ($196) triple. AE, DC, MC, V. Parking 18€ ($16). Métro: Odéon. **Amenities:** Room service (breakfast 7am–1pm); laundry/dry cleaning. *In room:* TV, minibar, hair dryer, safe.

Hôtel St-Germain-des-Prés Most of this hotel's attraction comes from its location in the Latin Quarter, behind a well-known Left Bank street. Janet Flanner, the legendary 1920s *New Yorker* correspondent, lived here for a while. Renovated in 1999, the guest rooms are small but charming, with antique ceiling beams and safes; air-conditioning is available in most. The public areas are severely elegant. Most of the bathrooms contain tubs, and all come with showers.

36 rue Bonaparte, 75006 Paris. © **01-43-26-00-19.** Fax 01-40-46-83-63. www.hotel-st-ger.com. 30 units. 167€–243€ ($149–$217) double; 304€ ($271) suite. Rates include breakfast. AE, MC, V. Métro: St-Germain-des-Prés. **Amenities:** Room service (8am–8pm); babysitting; laundry/dry cleaning. *In room:* A/C, TV, minibar, hair dryer, safe.

Résidence des Arts ✦ A converted 1550 residence, this winner is filled with handsomely decorated suites, studios, and apartments in the heart of the Latin Quarter. The structure was an apartment building until the mid-1990s when it was renovated, with two additional floors added when it opened in 1998. Regular doubles are rented with shower-only bathrooms. Each suite and apartment offers a large sitting room with a hide-a-bed, and a separate bedroom with a king-size bed. Suites and apartments have full bathrooms with tubs and showers, and each apartment comes with a kitchenette. The furnishings are tasteful and comfortable, and the service first-rate. A bistro and restaurant are also connected to the hotel.

14 rue Git-le-Coeur, 75006 Paris. © **01-55-42-71-11.** Fax 01-55-42-71-00. www.hotel-and-paris.com. 11 units. 129€–160€ ($115–$143) double; 228€–251€ ($204–$224) suite for 2–4; 274€–304€ ($244–$271) apt for 2–4; 350€–388€ ($312–$346) apt for 4–6. AE, MC, V. Métro: St-Michel. **Amenities:** Restaurant; bar; room service (8am–11pm); laundry/dry cleaning. *In room:* A/C, TV, safe, kitchenette in some.

INEXPENSIVE

Hôtel Clément This hotel sits on a quiet, narrow street, within sight of the twin towers of St-Sulpice church. From the 1700s, the building was renovated several years ago into a bright, uncomplicated design. Guest rooms are comfortably furnished but often small, although in 2000 some walls for the smaller rooms were broken apart, thereby creating larger but fewer units than before. Most of the bathrooms contain tubs; only two units are shower-only.

6 rue Clément, 75006 Paris. © **01-43-26-53-60.** Fax 01-44-07-06-83. hclement@worldnet.fr. 28 units. 96€–114€ ($86–$102) double; 129€ ($115) suite. AE, DC, V. Métro: Mabillon. *In room:* A/C, TV, hair dryer, safe.

Hôtel Delavigne Despite radical modernization, you still get a sense of the building's 18th-century origins. The public areas feature an attractively rustic use of chiseled stone, some of which is original. The high-ceilinged guest rooms are tasteful, sometimes with wooden furniture, often with upholstered headboards, and some with Spanish-style wrought iron. Those were upgraded and renovated in 2000 and 2001. All of the bathrooms except four have both a tub and shower.

1 rue Casimir-Delavigne, 75006 Paris. ☎ **01-43-29-31-50.** Fax 01-43-29-78-56. www.hoteldelavigne.com. 34 units. 109€–126€ ($98–$113) double; 141€ ($126) triple. MC, V. Métro: Odéon. **Amenities:** 24-hr. room service; babysitting; laundry/dry cleaning. *In room:* TV, hair dryer, safe.

Hôtel du Globe   Located on an evocative street, this 17th-century building has most of its original stonework and dozens of original timbers and beams. There's no elevator (you have to lug your suitcases up a very narrow antique staircase) and no breakfast area (trays are brought to your room). Each guest room is decorated with individual old-fashioned flair. *A tip:* The rooms with tubs are almost twice as large as those with shower stalls. The largest and most desirable rooms are nos. 1, 12 (with a baldachin-style bed), 14, 15, and 16. The room without a bathroom is a single at 50€ ($45).

15 rue des Quatre-Vents, 75006 Paris. ☎ **01-46-33-62-69.** Fax 01-46-33-62-69. hotelglobe@post.club-internet.fr. 20 units, 19 with bathroom. 83€–100€ ($74–$89) double. MC, V. Closed 3 weeks in Aug. Métro: Mabillon, Odéon, or St-Sulpice. **Amenities:** 24-hr. room service (drinks); laundry/dry cleaning. *In room:* TV.

Hôtel du Lys   The tall casement windows and high ceilings are from the 17th century. This cozy place has functioned as a hotel since the turn of the 20th century. There's no elevator, a fact that guarantees you'll make frequent use of the historic staircase. The guest rooms have different patterns of curtains and wallpaper, and about a quarter were renovated in 1998. Only a few units are large (these rent at the higher price); others are small but cozy affairs. Don't expect attentive service; the Lys is like an upscale dorm, with guests pursuing an array of interests and activities in the area. All bathrooms come with showers, and about half of the units also contain tubs.

23 rue Serpente, 75006 Paris. ☎ **01-43-26-97-57.** Fax 01-44-07-34-90. 22 units. 88€–96€ ($79–$86) double; 120€ ($107) triple. Rates include breakfast. MC, V. Métro: Cluny-La Sorbonne or St-Michel. *In room:* TV, hair dryer, safe.

13TH ARRONDISSEMENT
INEXPENSIVE
Hôtel du Vert Galant   Verdant climbing plants and shrubs make this hotel feel like an auberge deep in the French countryside. The smallish guest rooms have tiled or carpeted floors, unfussy furniture, and (in most cases) views of the garden or the public park across the street. All bathrooms have showers and nearly three-fourths of them also contain tubs. One of the place's best aspects is the Basque inn next door, the **Auberge Etchegorry,** sharing the same management; hotel guests receive a discount.

41 rue Croulebarbe, 75013 Paris. ☎ **01-44-08-83-50.** Fax 01-44-08-83-69. 15 units. 76€–84€ ($68–$75) double. AE, DC, MC, V. Parking 7.60€ ($6.75). Métro: Corvisart or Gobelins. **Amenities:** Restaurant (French); bar; room service (7–11am); babysitting. *In room:* TV, minibar, hair dryer.

14TH ARRONDISSEMENT
INEXPENSIVE
Hôtel du Parc-Montsouris   The residential neighborhood is far removed from central Paris's bustle, the staff is a bit absent-minded, and the decor doesn't pretend to be stylish, but the prices are reasonable enough that this government-rated two-star hotel (a simple structure built in the 1930s) attracts loyal repeat guests; they might be parents of students studying at the nearby Cité Universitaire or provincial clothiers attending fashion shows at the nearby Porte de Versailles. The guest rooms are low-key and quiet, each renovated in the late

1990s. Singles and doubles are small, but the triples are spacious, the suites even more so. Bathrooms contain tubs and showers, except for the seven with showers only.

4 rue du Parc de Montsouris, 75014 Paris. ℰ **01-45-89-09-72.** Fax 01-45-80-92-72. http://hotel-parc-montsouris.com. 35 units. 65€ ($58) double; 74€ ($66) triple; 90€ ($80) suite. AE, MC, V. Métro: Porte d'Orléans. RER: Cité-Universitaire. **Amenities:** Room service (7–11am); laundry/dry cleaning. *In room:* TV, hair dryer.

7TH ARRONDISSEMENT
VERY EXPENSIVE

Hôtel Montalembert ★★ Unusually elegant for the Left Bank, the Montalembert dates from 1926 when it was built in the beaux arts style. It was restored between 1989 and 1992 and again in 2001 and hailed as a smashing success, borrowing sophisticated elements of Bauhaus and postmodern design in honey beiges, creams, and golds. The guest rooms are spacious, except for some standard doubles, which are quite small unless you're a very thin model. The full bathrooms are luxurious, with deep tubs, chrome fixtures, Cascais marble, and tall pivoting mirrors.

3 rue de Montalembert, 75007 Paris. ℰ **800/786-6397** in the U.S. and Canada, or 01-45-49-68-68. Fax 01-45-49-69-49. www.montalembert.com. 56 units. 280€–440€ ($250–$393) double; 640€–760€ ($572–$679) suite. AE, DC, MC, V. Parking 18€ ($16). Métro: Rue du Bac. **Amenities:** Restaurant; bar; access to nearby health club; 24-hr. room service; babysitting; laundry/dry cleaning. *In room:* A/C, TV, minibar, hair dryer, safe.

EXPENSIVE

Hôtel de l'Université ★ Long favored by well-heeled parents of North American students studying in Paris, this 300-year-old town house filled with antiques enjoys a location in a discreetly upscale neighborhood. No. 54 is a favorite room, with a rattan bed and period pieces. Another charmer is no. 35—it has a fireplace and opens onto a courtyard with a fountain. The most expensive accommodation has a small terrace overlooking the surrounding rooftops. Most of the bedrooms are midsize or even small, as are the bathrooms, each with a tub and shower. But a few rented at the higher price tag have generous space.

22 rue de l'Université, 75007 Paris. ℰ **01-42-61-09-39.** Fax 01-42-60-40-84. www.hoteluniversite.com. 27 units. 160€–200€ ($143–$178) double. AE, MC, V. Métro: St-Germain-des-Prés. **Amenities:** Babysitting; laundry/dry cleaning. *In room:* A/C, TV, hair dryer, safe.

Le Duc de St-Simon ★ On a quiet residential street, this is the only hotel in the area to pose a challenge to the Montalembert. Two famous cafes, Les Deux Magots and Le Flore, are a few steps away. The small villa has a landscaped courtyard, a rear garden, and a Napoleon III (mid-19th century) decor with trompe l'oeil panels. Climbing wisteria graces the courtyard. Each guest room is sure to include at least one antique; a few are somewhat cramped, but most offer adequate space. Each room, except one with shower only, has a beautifully kept private bathroom with tub-and-shower combo.

14 rue de St-Simon, 75007 Paris. ℰ **01-44-39-20-20.** Fax 01-45-48-68-25. duc.de.saint-simon@wanadoo.fr. 34 units. 210€–265€ ($188–$237) double; 320€–340€ ($286–$304) suite. AE, MC, V. Métro: Rue du Bac. **Amenities:** Garden; bar; room service (7:30am–10pm); babysitting; laundry/dry cleaning. *In room:* hair dryer, safe.

L'Hotel Pont Royal ★ Since the 1920s this hotel has been known as Paris's literary hotel, the haunt of such authors as Huxley, Capote, Arthur Miller, T.S. Eliot, Camus, and Sartre. During its long renovation, local artists painted personal visions of the nearby le Pont Royal. At least one painting of the "Royal

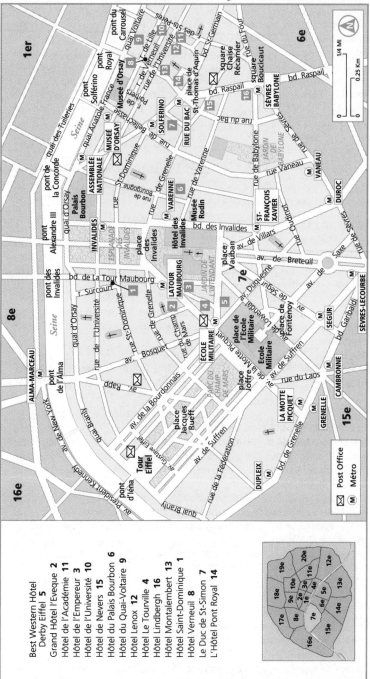

Best Western Hôtel
Derby Eiffel **5**
Grand Hôtel l'Eveque **2**
Hôtel de l'Académie **11**
Hôtel de l'Empereur **3**
Hôtel de l'Université **10**
Hôtel de Nevers **15**
Hôtel du Palais Bourbon **6**
Hôtel du Quai-Voltaire **9**
Hôtel Lenox **12**
Hôtel Le Tourville **4**
Hôtel Lindbergh **16**
Hôtel Montalembert **13**
Hôtel Saint-Dominique **1**
Hôtel Verneuil **8**
Le Duc de St-Simon **7**
L'Hôtel Pont Royal **14**

Bridge" hangs in every unit. In the heart of St-Germain-des-Prés, the government-rated four-star hotel is better than ever, with its refined, contemporary atmosphere and quality materials such as mahogany, silk, and stone. The hotel's top-floor rooms overlook not only the rooftops of Paris but panoramic views from the Eiffel Tower to Sacré-Coeur. What you'll find is a cozy and comfortably paneled setting that's ready, willing, and able to provide a safe and comfortable home for you in this elegant neighborhood. Bedrooms are compact—not overly large, but cozy and woodsy-looking. Views from some of the rooms on the hotel's top floor stretch all the way to Sacré-Coeur. All but two units come with newly installed private bathrooms with tub-and-shower combos. The other two have showers.

5-7 rue de Montalembert, 75007 Paris. ✆ **01-42-84-70-00.** Fax 01-42-84-71-00. www.hotel-pont-royal. com. 75 units. 300€–400€ ($268–$357) double; 500€–540€ ($447–$482) suite. AE, DC, MC, V. Métro: Rue du Bac. **Amenities:** Restaurant (French); bar; room service (7am–11pm); babysitting; laundry/dry cleaning. *In room:* TV, minibar, hair dryer, safe.

MODERATE

Best Western Hôtel Derby Eiffel Upgraded in 2001, this hotel faces the Ecole Militaire and contains airy public areas. Our favorite is a glass-roofed conservatory in back, filled year-round with plants and used as a breakfast area. The soundproof and modern guest rooms employ thick fabrics and soothing neutral colors. Most front-facing rooms offer views of the Eiffel Tower. In 1998, enormous sums were spent upgrading the rooms and bathrooms and improving the hotel's interior aesthetics. All bathrooms have showers and about half of the rooms also contain tubs.

5 av. Duquesne, 75007 Paris. ✆ **800/528-1234** in the U.S. and Canada, or 01-47-05-12-05. Fax 01-47-05-43-43. www.derbyeiffelhotel.com. 43 units. 122€–151€ ($109–$135) double; 153€–206€ ($137–$184) triple; 184€–229€ ($164–$205) suite. AE, DC, MC, V. Métro: Ecole Militaire. **Amenities:** Room service (7–11am); babysitting; laundry/dry cleaning. *In room:* A/C, TV, minibar, hair dryer, safe.

Hôtel de l'Académie ✦✦ The exterior walls and old ceiling beams are all that remain of this 17th-century residence of the duc de Rohan's private guards. Other than its Renaissance origins and associations with the Duc de Rohan, this place is locally famous for having housed poet and novelist Antonio Marchado, "the Victor Hugo of Spain," between 1909 and 1914. In 1999, the hotel was completely renovated to include an elegant reception area. The up-to-date guest rooms have a lush Ile-de-France decor and views over the neighborhood's 18th- and 19th-century buildings. By American standards the rooms are small, but they're average for Paris. All but eight bathrooms have full tub-shower combos.

32 rue des Sts-Pères, 75007 Paris. ✆ **800/246-0041** in the U.S. and Canada, or 01-45-49-80-00. Fax 01-45-44-75-24. www.academiehotel.com. 34 units. 199€–229€ ($178–$205) double; 310€–459€ ($277–$410) suite. AE, DC, MC, V. Parking 23€ ($21). Métro: St-Germain-des-Prés. **Amenities:** Exercise room; business center; room service (7am–11pm); in-room massage; babysitting; dry cleaning. *In room:* A/C, TV, minibar, hair dryer, safe.

Hôtel du Quai-Voltaire ✦✦ Built in the 1600s as an abbey, and transformed into a hotel in 1856, the Quai-Voltaire is best known for its illustrious guests such as Wilde, Richard Wagner, and Baudelaire, who occupied rooms 47, 55, and 56, respectively. Camille Pissarro painted Le Pont Royal from the window of his fourth-floor room. Many rooms in this inn have been renovated, and most overlook the bookstalls and boats of the Seine. Doubles tend to be small, the triples midsize but not spacious. There are bathtubs in all but five of the rooms; those five contain showers only. *Warning:* This hotel is not for everyone, although it has its devotees. The front rooms enjoy one of the greatest views of Paris but are exposed to the roar of traffic. It's also a long walk from any Métro stop.

19 quai Voltaire, 75007 Paris. ✆ **01-42-61-50-91.** Fax 01-42-61-62-26. 33 units. 115€–145€ ($103–$130) double; 155€ ($138) triple. AE, DC, MC, V. Parking 18€ ($16) nearby. Métro: Musée d'Orsay or Rue du Bac. **Amenities:** Bar; room service; laundry. *In room:* TV, hair dryer.

Hôtel Lenox   The Lenox is a favorite for those seeking reasonably priced accommodations in St-Germain-des-Prés. In 1910, T. S. Eliot spent a summer here "on the old man's money" when it was a basic pension. Today this much-improved place offers a helpful staff and cramped but comfortable rooms radically and expensively upgraded in 2000. Rooms evoke the chintzes and furniture of an English country house. Many returning guests request the attic duplex with its tiny balcony and skylight. All bathrooms have showers and half come with tubs, too.

9 rue de l'Université, 75007 Paris. ✆ **01-42-96-10-95.** Fax 01-42-61-52-83. www.lenoxsaintgermain.com. 34 units. 117€–196€ ($105–$175) double; 266€ ($238) duplex suite. AE, DC, MC, V. Métro: Rue du Bac. **Amenities:** Bar; room service (breakfast); laundry/dry cleaning. *In room:* A/C, TV, hair dryer, safe.

Hotel Le Tourville ✿   This is a well-managed, personalized "hotel de charme" that occupies a desirable town house midway between the Eiffel Tower and Les Invalides. It originated in the 1930s as a hotel, and was revitalized and reconfigured during the 1990s into the stylish charmer you see today. Bedrooms contain original artworks, an antique or an antique reproduction, and some kind of traditional wooden furniture covered in modern, sometimes bold, upholsteries. Four of the rooms, including the suite, have private terraces for soaking up the Parisian sunshine. Rooms 16 and 18 are the most desirable. About half the bathrooms are small with shower stalls; the others are more generously endowed with tub-and-shower combinations. The staff is particularly well trained. Breakfast is the only meal served, but you can get a drink in the lobby.

16 av. de Tourville, 75007 Paris. ✆ **01-47-05-62-62.** Fax 01-47-05-43-90. www.hoteltourville.com. 30 units. 145€–220€ ($130–$196) double; 310€ ($277) suite. AE, DC, MC, V. Métro: Ecole Militaire. **Amenities:** Bar; 24-hr. room service; laundry/dry cleaning; in-room massage. *In room:* A/C, TV, hair dryer.

Hôtel Verneuil ✿ *(Finds*   Small-scale and personalized, this hotel, in the words of a recent critic, "combines modernist sympathies with nostalgia for *la vieille France.*" Within what was built in the 1600s as a town house, it offers a creative, intimate jumble of charm and coziness. Expect a mixture of antique and contemporary furniture, lots of books, and in the bedrooms, trompe l'oeil ceilings, antique beams that in some, but not all, cases have been painted white, quilts, and walls covered in fabric. Bathrooms come with combo tubs and showers.

8 rue de Verneuil, 75007 Paris. ✆ **01-42-60-82-14.** Fax 01-42-61-40-38. www.france-hotel-guide.com. 26 units. 135€–175€ ($121–$156) double. AE, DC, MC, V. Parking 18€ ($16). Métro: St-Germain-des-Prés. **Amenities:** Bar; 24-hr. room service (drinks); babysitting; laundry/dry cleaning. *In room:* TV, minibar, hair dryer, safe.

INEXPENSIVE

Grand Hôtel L'Eveque   Built in the 1930s, this hotel draws many English-speaking guests who appreciate its proximity to the Eiffel Tower. In 2000, the interior was completely renovated and repainted and all the carpets changed. The pastel-colored guest rooms retain an Art Deco inspiration, enough space to be comfortable, and double-insulated windows overlooking a courtyard in back or the street in front. The small bathrooms all contain showers but not tubs.

29 rue Cler, 75007 Paris. ℂ **01-47-05-49-15.** Fax 01-45-50-49-36. www.hotel-leveque.com. 50 units. 84€–91€ ($75–$81) double; 106€–114€ ($95–$102) triple. AE, MC, V. Métro: Ecole Militaire. *In room:* A/C, TV, hair dryer, safe.

Hôtel de l'Empereur   This convenient hotel was built in the early 1700s and enjoys a loyal group of repeat visitors. There's an elevator to haul you and your luggage to one of the smallish but attractively decorated guest rooms, with mostly shower-only bathrooms. There's no restaurant or bar, but a nearby restaurant will send up platters of food on request.

2 rue Chevert, 75007 Paris. ℂ **01-45-55-88-02.** Fax 01-45-51-88-54. www.hotelempereur.com. 38 units. 75€–85€ ($67–$76) double; 105€ ($94) triple; 120€ ($107) quad. AE, DC, MC, V. Parking 130€ ($116) across the street. Métro: Latour-Maubourg. **Amenities:** Room service (7–11:30am); laundry/dry cleaning. *In room:* TV, fridge, hair dryer.

Hôtel de Nevers ✦   This is one of the neighborhood's most historic choices—it was a convent from 1627 to 1790, when it was disbanded by the Revolution. The building is *classé*, meaning any restoration must respect the original architecture. That precludes an elevator, so you'll have to use the beautiful wrought-iron staircase. The cozy, pleasant guest rooms contain a mix of antique and reproduced furniture. Rooms 10 and 11 are especially sought-after for their terraces overlooking a corner of rue du Bac or a rear courtyard. There was a major upgrade/refurbishment in 2000. All units have showers, and about half have shower-tub combos.

83 rue du Bac, 75007 Paris. ℂ **01-45-44-61-30.** Fax 01-42-22-29-47. hoteldenevers75@aol.com. 11 units. 79€–90€ ($71–$80) double. No credit cards. Métro: Rue du Bac. *In room:* TV, minibar, hair dryer.

Hôtel du Palais Bourbon   The solid stone walls of this 18th-century building aren't as grand as those of the embassies and stately homes nearby. But don't be put off by the tight entrance hall and rather dark halls: Though the guest rooms on the upper floors are larger, all the rooms are pleasantly decorated, with carefully crafted built-in furniture. Each bathroom contains both a tub and a shower.

49 rue de Bourgogne, 75007 Paris. ℂ **01-44-11-30-70.** Fax 01-45-55-20-21. www.hotel-palais-bourbon. com. 34 units. 109€ ($98) double; 132€ ($117) triple; 140€ ($125) quad. Rate includes breakfast. MC, V. Métro: Varenne. **Amenities:** Room service (7–11am). *In room:* A/C, TV, minibar, hair dryer, safe.

Hôtel Lindbergh   About a 3-minute walk from St-Germain-des-Prés, this hotel offers streamlined and simple, medium-size guest rooms. About two-thirds of the bathrooms contain tubs, although all of them are equipped with showers. Breakfast is the only meal served, but the staff will point out worthy restaurants nearby—an inexpensive bistro, Le Cigale, is a few buildings away.

5 rue Chomel, 75007 Paris. ℂ **01-45-48-35-53.** Fax 01-45-49-31-48. www.hotellindbergh.com. 26 units. 91€–122€ ($81–$109) double; 128€–141€ ($114–$126) triple; 141€–152€ ($126–$136) quad. AE, DC, MC, V. Parking 17€ ($15). Métro: Sèvres-Babylone or St-Sulpice. **Amenities:** Laundry/dry cleaning. *In room:* TV, hair dryer.

Hôtel Saint-Dominique   Part of this place's charm derives from its division into three buildings connected through an open-air courtyard. The most visible of these was an 18th-century convent—you can still see its ceiling beams and structural timbers in the reception area. The guest rooms aren't large, but each is warm and simply decorated; many have wallpaper in nostalgic patterns. Bathrooms are neatly laid out, each with a shower, and there are complete bathrooms in about one-third of the units.

62 rue St-Dominique, 75007 Paris. ℂ **01-47-05-51-44.** Fax 01-47-05-81-28. hotel.saint.dominique@ wanadoo.fr. 34 units. 99€–115€ ($88–$103) double. AE, MC, V. Métro: Latour-Maubourg or Invalides. **Amenities:** Room service (7–10am). *In room:* TV, minibar, hair dryer (in some), safe.

3 Near the Airports
ORLY
EXPENSIVE

Hilton Paris Orly Airport ⭐   Boxy and bland, the Hilton at Orly remains a solid and well-maintained hotel business travelers appreciate for its convenience. Incoming planes can't penetrate the guest rooms' sound barriers, guaranteeing you a shot at a good night's sleep. (Unlike the 24-hour Charles de Gaulle Airport, Orly is closed to arriving flights from midnight to 6am.) The rooms are standard for a chain hotel. Each was renovated in the late 1990s, with a tub-and-shower combo.

Aéroport Orly, 267 Orly Sud, 94544 Orly Aerogare Cedex. ℂ **800/445-8667** in the U.S. and Canada, or 01-45-12-45-12. Fax 01-45-12-45-00. www.hilton.com. 353 units. 112€–142€ ($100–$126) double; 183€ ($163) suite. AE, DC, MC, V. Parking 16€ ($14). Free shuttle bus between hotel and both Orly terminals; 40-min. taxi ride from central Paris, except during rush hours. **Amenities:** Restaurant; bar; health club; sauna; 24-hr. room service; laundry/dry cleaning. *In room:* A/C, TV, minibar, hair dryer.

INEXPENSIVE

Climat de France   Also boxy and contemporary-looking, and interconnected with Orly by frequent 10-minute complimentary shuttle-bus rides, this 1990s hotel offers standardized, not-particularly imaginative bedrooms. Each is comfortable, insulated against noises from the nearby airport, and a bit larger than you might have expected. Each unit comes with a neatly tiled bathroom with tub and shower.

58 voie Nouvelle (near the Parc Georges Mélliès), 94544 Orly. ℂ **01-41-80-75-75.** Fax 01-41-80-12-12. airplus@club-internet.fr. 71 units. 60€–65€ ($54–$58) double. AE, DC, MC, V. Free parking. Transit to and from airport by complimentary shuttle bus. **Amenities:** Restaurant (French); room service (12:30–2:30pm and 7:30–10:30pm). *In room:* TV.

CHARLES-DE-GAULLE
EXPENSIVE

Hôtel Sofitel Paris Aéroport CDG ⭐   Many travelers shuttle happily through this bustling but somewhat anonymous member of the French chain. It employs a multilingual staff that's accustomed to accommodating constantly arriving and departing international business travelers. Renovated in 1998, the conservative monochromatic guest rooms are soundproof havens against the all-night roar of jets. Each unit comes with a tiled bathroom with tub and shower.

Aéroport Charles de Gaulle, Zone Central, B.P. 20248, 95713 Roissy. ℂ **800/221-4542** in the U.S. and Canada, or 01-49-19-29-29. Fax 01-49-19-29-00. www.accor.com. 352 units. 258€–304€ ($231–$271) double; from 486€ ($434) suite. AE, DC, MC, V. Parking 24€ ($22). Free shuttle bus service to/from airport. **Amenities:** Restaurant (French); bar; business center; 24-hr. room service. *In room:* A/C, TV, minibar, hair dryer, safe.

INEXPENSIVE

Hotel Campanile de Roissy   Accommodations here tend to be less expensive than those of its nearby competitors. Its cement-and-glass design is barely masked by a thin overlay of cheerful-looking rustic artifacts, but generally, this is an efficiently decorated, not particularly stylish place to stay, with a well-meaning but overworked staff. Each unit comes with a small, shower-only bathroom.

Parc de Roissy, 95700 Val-d'Oise. ℭ **01-34-29-80-40.** Fax 01-34-29-80-39. www.envergure.fr. 260 units. 69€–84€ ($62–$75) double. Rates include breakfast. AE, DC, MC, V. Free parking. Take free shuttle van to and from Roissy. **Amenities:** Shuttle; restaurant; bar. *In room:* TV.

4 Gay-Friendly Hotels

Any hotel recommended in this guide is at least tolerant of same-sex couples, but this hotel is especially welcoming. For its location, see the "Where to Stay on the Right Bank (1–4, 9–12 & 18e)" map on p. 76. For full coverage of Paris's gay/gay-friendly hotels and restaurants, see *Frommer's Gay & Lesbian Europe.*

INEXPENSIVE

Hôtel Central This is Paris's most famous gay hotel, with rooms on the second, third, and fourth floors of an 18th-century building. If you arrive between 8:30am and 5pm, you'll find a registration staff one floor above street level; otherwise, you'll have to retrieve your room keys and register at the street-level bar, Le Central (see chapter 10). Frankly, many visitors prefer the bar to the guest rooms, but if you want a hotel that'll put you in the middle of the gay scene, this is it. The guest rooms are simple and serviceable but show wear and tear. With a single exception, one private bathroom is shared for every two rooms. Women are welcome but rare.

33 rue Vieille-du-Temple, 75004 Paris. ℭ **01-48-87-99-33.** Fax 01-42-77-06-27. www.hotelcentralmarais. com. 7 units, 1 with bathroom. 84€ ($75) double without bathroom; 100€ ($89) double with bathroom. MC, V. Métro: Hôtel de Ville.

Where to Dine

Welcome to the city that prides itself on being the world's culinary capital. Only in Paris can you turn onto the nearest little crooked side street, enter the first nondescript bistro you see, sit down at a bare, wobbly table, order from an illegibly hand-scrawled menu, and get a truly memorable meal.

See chapter 1 for a list of our favorites—the best chef, the best view, the best baby bistro, and more.

1 Food for Thought

WHAT'S COOKING IN FRANCE   Once you arrive in Paris, you'll find that the word "French," although used frequently, isn't very helpful in describing cuisine. "French" covers such a broad scope that it doesn't prepare you for the offerings of the specialty chefs. Even the Parisians themselves might ask, "What *type* of French cooking?"

Sometimes a chef will include regional specialties, classic dishes, and even modern cuisine all on one menu. In that case, such a restaurant is truly "French." Other chefs prefer a more narrow focus and feature the cooking of one region or one style—classic or modern. Still others prefer to strike a middle ground between classic and modern; they're called "creative."

Regional cuisine showcases the diversity of the provinces of France, from Alsace on the German border to the Basque country at the frontier of Spain. The climate has a lot to do with this diversified offering—olive oil, garlic, and tomatoes from Provence in the south to oysters and saltwater fish from Brittany. Every region is known for special dishes—Burgundy for its escargots plucked off the grape vines; Périgord for its truffles and foie gras; Normandy for its soft, rich cheeses, Calvados, and cream sauces; and Alsace for its sauerkraut and wines. Today, one or more restaurants in Paris represent almost every region of France. You can go on a complete culinary tour of the country and never leave the city limits, although regional dishes always taste better on home turf.

Few chefs today use the expression **"nouvelle cuisine,"** now called "modern." This cooking style, which burst upon us in the early 1970s, is now old hat (or should we say old toque?). It was a rebellion against the fats, butter, and sauces of haute cuisine, and used reductions of foodstuff to create flavor along with vegetable purées and lighter ingredients. Portions were reduced. Diners were shocked to see a piece of *boeuf* (beef) the size of an egg on their plate under a slice of fresh kiwi. Created in the name of innovation, many of these dishes were successful, while others, such as asparagus ice cream, were dismal failures.

From nouvelle cuisine grew *cuisine improvisée,* which is creative cookery based on the freshest ingredients available. Chefs make their selections at the morning market and then rush back to their kitchen to create spontaneous dishes often while dictating the menu of the day to an assistant who rushes it into print.

But fans of the great chef Escoffier can also rest assured. Modern hasn't replaced **classic cuisine,** and France is still awash in béchamel and ablaze with cognac. Haute gastronomie is alive and thriving at restaurants not only in Paris but throughout France. This richly extravagant fare is often lethal in price, but it makes use of expensive ingredients, including fatted ducks, lobster, truffles, and plenty of butter and cream, plus sauces that consume endless time in their preparation. Breaking from Escoffier, many chefs today have forged ahead with a **"new classic cuisine,"** where they have taken classic dishes and branded them with their own distinctive style and flavor, often lightening the calories.

> **Tips Mystifying Menu?**
>
> If you need help distinguishing a *blanquette de veau* from a *crème brûlée,* turn to the glossary in appendix B.

PARIS'S RANGE OF RESTAURANTS Paris boasts a surplus of restaurants and cafes. Ultraexpensive **temples of gastronomy** include Alain Ducasse, L'Astor, Taillevent, Pierre Gagnaire, Lasserre, Jacques Cagna, Le Grand Véfour, and La Tour d'Argent. Savvy diners confine their trips to *luxe* places for special occasions. An array of other choices awaits, including simpler restaurants dispensing cuisines from every province of France and from former colonies like Morocco and Algeria.

Paris has hundreds of restaurants serving exotic **international fare,** reflecting the changing complexion of Paris itself and the city's increasing appreciation for food from other cultures. Your most memorable meal in Paris may turn out to be Vietnamese or West African.

You'll also find hundreds of bistros, brasseries, and cafes. In modern times their designations and roles have become almost meaningless. Traditionally, a **bistro** was a small restaurant, often with mom at the cash register and pop in the kitchen. Menus are most often handwritten or mimeographed, and the selection of dishes tends to be small. They can be chic and elegant, sometimes heavily Mediterranean in style, and often dispensing gutsy fare, including the *pot-au-feu* (beef simmered with vegetables) the chef's grandmother prepared for him as a kid.

French for "brewery," most **brasseries** have an Alsatian connection, and that means lots of beer, although Alsatian wines are also featured. They are almost always brightly lit and open 24 hours. Both snacks and full meals are available. The Alsatian establishments serve sauerkraut with an array of pork products.

The **cafe** is a French institution. Not just places for an aperitif, a café au lait, or a croissant, many serve rib-sticking fare as well, certainly entrecôte with french fries but often classics like *blanquette de veau* (veal in white sauce). For more lore about this French passion, see section 5, "The Top Cafes" later in this chapter.

More attention in the late 1990s focused on the **wine bar,** a host of which we recommend in chapter 10, "Paris After Dark." Originally, wine bars concentrated on their lists of wines, featuring many esoteric choices and ignoring the food except for some *charcuterie* (cold cuts) and cheeses. Today, you're likely to be offered various daily specials, from homemade foie gras to *boeuf à la mode* (marinated beef braised with red wine and served with vegetables).

Tips   Dining Savoir-Faire

- Three-star dining remains quite expensive, with appetizers sometimes priced at $50 and dinners easily costing $200 per person in the top dining rooms of celebrated chefs. But you can get around that high price tag in many places by **dining at lunch** (when prices are always cheaper) or ordering a prix-fixe meal at lunch or dinner.
- The **prix-fixe (fixed-price) menu** or *le menu* is a set meal that the chef prepares that day. It is most often fresh and promptly served and represents a greater bargain than dining a la carte. Of course, it's limited, so you'll have to like the choices provided. Sometimes there are one to three menus, beginning with the less expensive and going up for a more elaborate meal. A lot depends on your pocketbook and appetite.
- In France, **lunch** (as well as dinner) tends to be a full-course meal with meat, vegetables, salad, bread, cheese, dessert, wine, and coffee. It may be difficult to find a restaurant that serves the type of light lunch North Americans usually eat. Cafes, however, offer sandwiches, soup, and salads in a relaxed setting.
- Average visitors head for the old-fashioned family-run **bistro,** and we've ferreted out the best ones. In today's Paris, tradition and nostalgia, along with affordable prices, make these bistros busier than ever, especially because so many are being forced out of existence due to rising rents.
- **Coffee** in France is served after the meal and carries an extra charge. The French consider it barbaric to drink coffee during the meal and, unless you order it with milk (*au lait*), it'll be served black. In more conscientious places, it's prepared as the traditional *café filtre*, a slow but rewarding java draw.
- In years gone by, no man would consider dining out, even at the neighborhood bistro, without a suit and tie, and no woman would be seen without a smart dress or suit. That **dress code** is more relaxed now, except in first-class and *luxe* establishments. Relaxed doesn't mean sloppy jeans and jogging attire, however. Parisians still value style, even when dressing informally.
- Sometimes service is added to your tab—usually 12% to 15%. If not, look for the words *service non compris* on your bill. That means that the cost of service was not added, and you'll be expected to leave a **tip.**

Paris prices may seem extravagant to visitors from other parts of the world, particularly those who don't live in big cities, but there has been an emergence of moderately priced **informal restaurants** here, and we recommend several.

Although they're not as fashionable as they were, still around are **baby bistros,** reasonably priced spin-offs from deluxe restaurants where you can get a taste of a famous chef's cuisine without breaking the bank. We cover the best of them.

2 Restaurants by Cuisine

ALGERIAN
Au Clair de Lune (2e, $, p. 127)
Wally Le Saharien (9e, $$, p. 134)

ALSATIAN
Bofinger ⭐ (4e, $$, p. 130)
Brasserie de l'Ile St-Louis (4e, $,
   p. 132)
Brasserie Flo ⭐ (10e, $$, p. 135)
Jenny (3e, $, p. 128)

AMERICAN
Chicago Pizza Pie Factory ⭐⭐ (8e,
   $, p. 148)
Joe Allen ⭐⭐ (1er, $, p. 125)

ASIAN
Kambodia (16e, $$, p. 147)

AUVERGNAT
Bath's (8e, $$$, p. 142)
L'Ambassade d'Auvergne ⭐ (3e, $,
   p. 129)
Restaurant Bleu (14e, $, p. 160)

BASQUE
Au Bascou ⭐ (3e, $, p. 128)
Auberge Etchegorry (13e, $$,
   p. 159)
Chez l'Ami Jean (7e, $, p. 162)

BRETON
Chez Michel (10e, $, p. 135)

BURGUNDIAN
Chez Pauline ⭐ (1er, $$, p. 122)

CAFES
Brasserie Lipp (6e, $$$, p. 167)
Café Beaubourg (4e, $$, p. 168)
Café Cosmos ⭐⭐ (6e, $$, p. 168)
Café de Flore ⭐⭐ (6e, $$$,
   p. 167)
Café de la Musique (19e, $$,
   p. 168)
Café de l'Industrie (11e, $, p. 170)
Café des Hauteurs (7e, $$, p. 169)
Fouquet's ⭐ (8e, $$$, p. 168)
La Coupole ⭐ (14e, $$, p. 169)
La Palette ⭐⭐ (6e, $$, p. 169)
La Rotonde (6e, $$, p. 169)

Le Gutenberg (1er, $, p. 171)
Le Procope ⭐⭐ (6e, $$, p. 170)
Le Rouquet ⭐ (7e, $$$, p. 168)
Les Deux Magots ⭐⭐ (6e, $$,
   p. 170)
Restaurant/Salon de Thé Bernar-
   daud ⭐⭐ (8e, $$, p. 170)

CAMBODIAN
Kambodia (16e, $$, p. 147)

CENTRAL EUROPEAN
Chez Jo Goldenberg ⭐⭐ (4e, $,
   p. 132)
La Cagouille ⭐ (14e, $$, p. 160)

CHINESE
Chez Vong ⭐ (1er, $, p. 124)
China Club ⭐ (12e, $$, p. 138)
Le Canton (6e, $, p. 158)

CREOLE
Babylone Bis (2e, $, p. 127)

DANISH
Restaurant Copenhague/Flora
   Danica ⭐ (8e, $$$, p. 144)

FRENCH (MODERN)
Alcazar Bar & Restaurant ⭐ (6e,
   $$, p. 156)
Bofinger ⭐ (4e, $$, p. 130)
Buddha Bar ⭐⭐ (8e, $$$, p. 143)
Café la Parisienne (4e, $, p. 132)
Carré des Feuillants ⭐⭐⭐ (1er,
   $$$$, p. 119)
Chez Diane (6e, $, p. 158)
Chez Jean ⭐ (9e, $$$, p. 134)
Jacques Cagna ⭐⭐⭐ (6e, $$$$,
   p. 155)
Julien ⭐ (10e, $, p. 136)
L'Amazonial (1er, $, p. 171)
L'Ambroisie ⭐⭐⭐ (4e, $$$$,
   p. 129)
L'Arpège ⭐⭐⭐ (7e, $$$$, p. 161)
Lasserre ⭐⭐⭐ (8e, $$$$, p. 139)
L'Astor ⭐⭐⭐ (8e, $$$$, p. 139)
L'Astrance ⭐⭐⭐ (16e, $$$,
   p. 147)
Le Bistro d'á Côté ⭐ (17e, $$$,
   p. 150)

Key to Abbreviations: $$$$ = Very Expensive $$$ = Expensive $$ = Moderate $ = Inexpensive

Le Coconnas ✶ (4e, $$, p. 131)
Le Violon d'Ingres ✶✶✶ (7e, $$$, p. 161)
Marty ✶ (5e, $$, p. 153)
Michel Rostang ✶✶✶ (17e, $$$$, p. 150)
Pierre Gagnaire ✶✶✶ (8e, $$$$, p. 140)
Restaurant Plaza Athénée (Alain Ducasse) ✶✶✶ (8e, $$$$, p. 142)
Shozan ✶ (8e, $$$, p. 144)
Taillevent ✶✶✶ (8e, $$$$, p. 142)

FRENCH (TRADITIONAL)

Allard ✶✶ (6e, $$, p. 156)
Angélina ✶✶ (1er, $, p. 123)
A Sousceyrac (11e, $$, p. 136)
Astier ✶ (11e, $$, p. 137)
Au Clair de Lune (2e, $, p. 127)
Au Gourmet de l'Ile ✶ (4e, $, p. 132)
Au Pied de Cochon ✶✶ (1er, $$, p. 122)
Au Pied de Fouet (7e, $, p. 162)
Aux Charpentiers (6e, $, p. 157)
Aux Lyonnais ✶✶ (2e, $, p. 127)
Bath's ✶✶ (8e, $$$, p. 142)
Benoit ✶ (4e, $$$, p. 129)
Bistro de la Grille (6e, $, p. 157)
Bofinger ✶ (4e, $$, p. 130)
Brasserie Balzar ✶✶ (5e, $$, p. 152)
Brasserie de l'Ile St-Louis (4e, $, p. 132)
Cave de l'Os à Moelle (15e, $, p. 166)
Chartier (9e, $, p. 134)
Chez André (8e, $$, p. 145)
Chez Diane (6e, $, p. 158)
Chez Georges (2e, $$, p. 126)
Chez Georges (17e, $$, p. 150)
Chez Gramond ✶ (6e, $$, p. 156)
Chez Jean ✶ (9e, $$$, p. 134)
Chez Pauline ✶ (1er, $$, p. 122)
Clémentine (2e, $, p. 127)
Closerie des Lilas ✶✶ (6e, $$$, p. 155)
Crémerie-Restaurant Polidor ✶✶ (6e, $, p. 158)

Guy Savoy ✶✶✶ (17e, $$$$, p. 149)
Jacques Cagna ✶✶✶ (6e, $$$$, p. 155)
Jamin ✶✶✶ (16e, $$$$, p. 146)
Julien ✶ (10e, $, p. 136)
La Butte Chaillot ✶ (16e, $$, p. 149)
La Cagouille ✶ (14e, $$, p. 160)
Ladurée (8e, $$, p. 145)
La Grille (10e, $$, p. 135)
L'Ambassade d'Auvergne ✶ (3e, $, p. 129)
L'Ambroisie ✶✶✶ (4e, $$$$, p. 129)
L'Ami Louis ✶ (3e, $$$, p. 128)
La Petite Chaise (7e, $$, p. 162)
La Petite Hostellerie ✶ (5e, $, p. 154)
La Poule au Pot (1er, $, p. 125)
La Rose de France ✶ (1er, $, p. 125)
La Rôtisserie d'Armaillé ✶✶ (17e, $$, p. 151)
La Rôtisserie d'en Face ✶ (6e, $$, p. 157)
Lasserre ✶✶✶ (8e, $$$$, p. 139)
La Tour d'Argent ✶✶✶ (5e, $$$$, p. 151)
La Tour de Monthléry (Chez Denise) (1er, $, p. 126)
L'Ebauchoir ✶ (12e, $, p. 138)
Le Berry's (8e, $, p. 146)
Le Bistro d'á Côté ✶ (17e, $$$, p. 150)
Le Bistro de l'Etoile ✶ (16e, $, p. 149)
Le Café du Commerce (15e, $, p. 166)
Le Coconnas ✶ (4e, $$, p. 131)
Le Grand Véfour ✶✶✶ (1er, $$$$, p. 122)
Le Grand Zinc (9e, $, p. 135)
Le Petit Marguery (13e, $$, p. 159)
Lescure ✶ (1er, $, p. 126)
Les Gourmets des Ternes (8e, $, p. 146)
Le Square Trousseau (12e, $, p. 139)

Le Train Bleu ★★ (12e, $$, p. 138)

Le Vaudeville (2e, $$, p. 126)

Le Vieux Bistro ★ (4e, $$, p. 131)

Le Violon d'Ingres ★★★ (7e, $$$, p. 161)

Michel Rostang ★★★ (17e, $$$$, p. 150)

Perraudin ★★ (5e, $, p. 155)

Relais Gourmand Faugeron ★★★ (16e, $$$$, p. 147)

Restaurant Plaza Athénée (Alain Ducasse) ★★★ (8e, $$$$, p. 142)

Taillevent ★★★ (8e, $$$$, p. 142)

Trumilou ★ (4e, $, p. 133)

FUSION

Market ★ (8e, $$$, p. 143)

GASCONY

Au Trou Gascon ★★★ (12e, $$$, p. 137)

INDIAN

Yugaraj (6e, $$, p. 157)

INTERNATIONAL

Georges ★ (4e, $$, p. 130)

Korova ★ (8e, $$, p. 145)

L'Amazonial (1er, $, p. 171)

Le Fumoir ★ (1er, $$, p. 123)

Spoon, Food & Wine ★ (8e, $$$, p. 144)

ITALIAN

Il Cortile ★★ (1er, $$, p. 123)

JAPANESE

Isami (4e, $$, p. 131)

Shozan ★ (8e, $$$, p. 144)

JEWISH

Chez Jo Goldenberg ★★ (4e, $, p. 132)

KOREAN

Shing-Jung (8e, $, p. 146)

LATE NIGHT

Au Pied de Cochon ★★ (1er, $$, p. 122)

Babylone Bis (2e, $, p. 127)

La Poule au Pot (1er, $, p. 125)

La Tour de Monthléry (Chez Denise) (1er, $, p. 126)

Le Vaudeville (2e, $$, p. 126)

LEBANESE

Al Dar (5e, $, p. 154)

LOIRE VALLEY (ANJOU)

Au Petit Riche (9e, $$, p. 134)

LYONNAIS

Aux Lyonnais ★★ (2e, $, p. 127)

MEDITERRANEAN

Il Cortile ★★ (1er, $$, p. 123)

MOROCCAN

Mansouria (11e, $, p. 137)

ORGANIC

Le Grain de Folie (18e, $, p. 139)

PACIFIC RIM

Buddha Bar ★★ (8e, $$$, p. 143)

PIZZA

Chicago Pizza Pie Factory ★★ (8e, $, p. 148)

POITEVINE

Le Petit Marguery (13e, $$, p. 159)

PROVENÇAL

Chez Janou (3e, $, p. 128)

La Bastide Odéon ★ (6e, $, p. 158)

La Maison Blanche ★ (8e, $$$, p. 143)

Les Elysées du Vernet ★★★ (8e, $$$$, p. 140)

PYRENEE

La Fontaine de Mars (7e, $, p. 162)

SEAFOOD

Goumard ★★★ (1er, $$$$, p. 122)

Keryado ★ (13e, $, p. 159)

La Cagouille ★ (14e, $$, p. 160)

La Grille (10e, $$, p. 135)

Paul Minchelli ★ (7e, $$$, p. 161)

SENEGALESE

Le Manguier (11e, $, p. 137)

Paris-Dakar (10e, $, p. 136)

SEYCHELLE ISLANDS
Coco de Mer ⭐ (5e, $, p. 154)

SOUTHWESTERN FRENCH
Chez l'Ami Jean (7e, $, p. 162)
La Fermette du Sud-Ouest ⭐ (1er, $, p. 125)
La Fontaine de Mars (7e, $, p. 162)
La Régalade (14e, $$, p. 160)
L'Assiette (14e, $$, p. 160)
Restaurant du Marché (15e, $$, p. 166)

TEA
Angélina ⭐⭐ (1er, $, p. 123)

THAI
Blue Elephant (11e, $$$, p. 136)

VEGETARIAN
Aquarius ⭐⭐ (4e, $, p. 131)
Le Grain de Folie (18e, $, p. 139)

VIETNAMESE
Kim Anh (15e, $$, p. 165)
Le Canton (6e, $, p. 158)

3 On the Right Bank

We'll begin with the most centrally located arrondissements on the Right Bank, then work our way through the more outlying neighborhoods and to the area around the Arc de Triomphe.

1ST ARRONDISSEMENT
VERY EXPENSIVE

Carré des Feuillants ⭐⭐⭐ MODERN FRENCH   This is a bastion of perfection, an elegant enclave of haute gastronomy between the Place Vendôme and the Tuileries. When leading chef Alain Dutournier turned this 17th-century convent into a restaurant, it was an overnight success. The interior is like an early-1900s bourgeois house with several small salons opening onto a sky-lit courtyard, across from which is a glass-enclosed kitchen. You'll find a sophisticated reinterpretation of cuisine from France's southwest, using seasonally fresh ingredients and lots of know-how. Examples are roasted veal kidneys cooked in their own fat; grilled wood pigeon served with chutney and polenta; crayfish with sweet garlic; and roasted leg of suckling lamb from the Pyrénées with autumn vegetables. Lighter dishes are scallops wrapped in parsley-infused puff pastry served with cabbage and truffles, and mullet-studded risotto with lettuce. For dessert, try a slice of pistachio cream cake with candied tangerines.

14 rue de Castiglione (near place Vendôme and the Tuileries), 1er. ☎ 01-42-86-82-82. Fax 01-42-86-07-71. Reservations required far in advance. Main courses 40€–52€ ($35–$46); fixed-price lunch 58€ ($52); fixed-price dinner 137€ ($122). AE, DC, MC, V. Mon–Fri noon–2:30pm; Mon–Sat 7:30–10pm. Closed Aug. Métro: Tuileries, Concorde, Opéra, or Madeleine.

Tips **Don't Leave Home Without Them**

No matter how long you stay in Paris, we suggest you indulge in at least one break-the-bank French meal at a fabulous restaurant. It will be a memory you'll treasure long after you've recovered from paying the tab. However, to get a table at one of these places, *you must reserve far in advance*—at least a day or two ahead, sometimes even a few weeks or months ahead! We suggest you look over these listings, and call for reservations before you leave or at least as soon as you get into town.

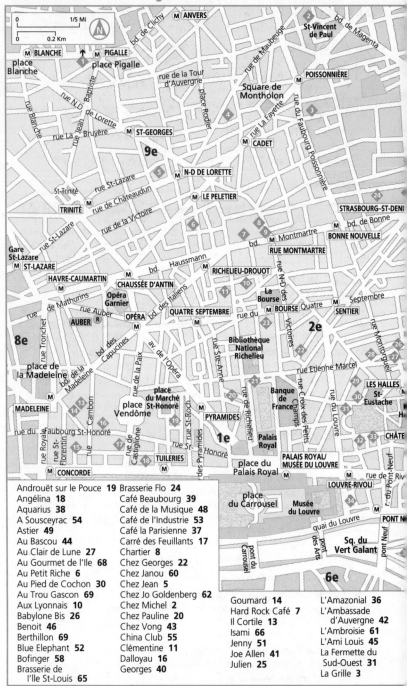

Androuët sur le Pouce **19**
Angélina **18**
Aquarius **38**
A Sousceyrac **54**
Astier **49**
Au Bascou **44**
Au Clair de Lune **27**
Au Gourmet de l'Ile **68**
Au Petit Riche **6**
Au Pied de Cochon **30**
Au Trou Gascon **69**
Aux Lyonnais **10**
Babylone Bis **26**
Benoit **46**
Berthillon **69**
Blue Elephant **52**
Bofinger **58**
Brasserie de
  l'Ile St-Louis **65**

Brasserie Flo **24**
Café Beaubourg **39**
Café de la Musique **48**
Café de l'Industrie **53**
Café la Parisienne **37**
Carré des Feuillants **17**
Chartier **8**
Chez Georges **22**
Chez Janou **60**
Chez Jean **5**
Chez Jo Goldenberg **62**
Chez Michel **2**
Chez Pauline **20**
Chez Vong **43**
China Club **55**
Clémentine **11**
Dalloyau **16**
Georges **40**

Goumard **14**
Hard Rock Café **7**
Il Cortile **13**
Isami **66**
Jenny **51**
Joe Allen **41**
Julien **25**

L'Amazonial **36**
L'Ambassade
  d'Auvergne **42**
L'Ambroisie **61**
L'Ami Louis **45**
La Fermette du
  Sud-Ouest **31**
La Grille **3**

America Online Keyword: Travel

Booked seat 6A, open return.

Rented red 4-wheel drive.

Reserved cabin, no running water.

Discovered space.

over 700 airlines, 50,000 hotels, 50 rental car companies and
0 cruise and vacation packages, you can create the perfect get-
y for you. Choose the car, the room, even the ground you walk on.

Travelocity.com
A Sabre Company
Go Virtually Anywhere.

Book your air, hotel, and transportation all in one place.

Hotel or hostel? Cruise or canoe? Car? Plane? Camel? Wherever you're going, visit Yahoo! Travel and get total control over your arrangements. Even choose your seat assignment. So. One hump or two? travel.yahoo.com

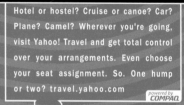

YAHOO!
Travel

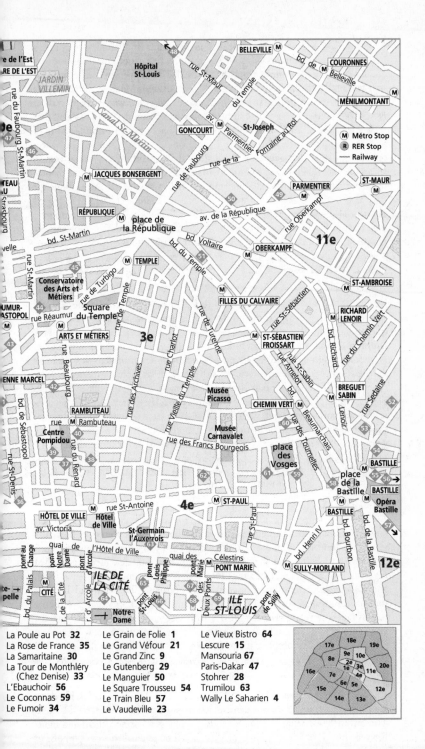

Goumard ★★★ SEAFOOD Opened in 1872, this landmark is one of Paris's leading seafood restaurants. It's so devoted to the fine art of preparing fish that other food is strictly banned from the menu (if you happen to dislike fish, the staff will orally present a limited roster of meat dishes). Much of the seafood is flown in directly from Brittany daily. Examples are a *craquant* (a crispy version of crayfish) in its own herb salad, lobster soup with coconut, grilled sea-wolf filet with a fricassee of artichokes and Provençal pistou, a grilled turbot salad on a bed of artichokes with tarragon, and poached turbot with hollandaise sauce, served with leeks in vinaigrette. In all these dishes, nothing (no excess butter, spices, or salt) is allowed to interfere with the natural flavor of the sea. Be prepared for some unusual food—the staff will help translate the menu items for you. The decor consists of an unusual collection of Lalique crystal fish displayed in artificial aquariums. Even more unusual are the men's and women's restrooms, now classified as historic monuments; the commodes were designed by the Art Nouveau master cabinetmaker Majorelle in the early 1900s.

9 rue Duphot, 1er. © 01-42-60-36-07. Fax 01-42-60-04-54. Reservations required far in advance. Main courses 25€–70€ ($22–$63). AE, DC, MC, V. Mon–Sat 12:30–2:30pm and 7:30–10:30pm. Closed 3 weeks in Aug. Métro: Madeleine or Concorde.

Le Grand Véfour ★★★ TRADITIONAL FRENCH This is the all-time winner: a great, great chef; the most beautiful restaurant decor in Paris, and a gastronomic, history-infused citadel of classic French cuisine. This restaurant has been around since the reign of Louis XV, though not under the same name. Napoleon, Danton, Hugo, Colette, and Cocteau have dined here—as the brass plaques on the tables testify—and it's still a great gastronomic experience. Guy Martin, chef here for the past decade, bases many dishes on recipes from the French Alps. His best dish is sliced lamb in a chocolate-coffee sauce. Other specialties are noisettes of lamb with star anise and Breton lobster and the unusual cabbage sorbet in dark-chocolate sauce. The desserts are often grand, like the *gourmandises au chocolat,* a richness of chocolate served with chocolate sorbet.

17 rue de Beaujolais, 1er. © 01-42-96-56-27. Fax 01-42-86-80-71. Reservations required far in advance. Main courses 65€–84€ ($58–$75); fixed-price menu 68€ ($61) at lunch, 198€ ($176) at dinner. AE, DC, MC, V. Mon–Fri 12:30–2pm; Mon–Thurs 8–10pm. Métro: Louvre-Palais Royal.

MODERATE

Au Pied de Cochon ★★ TRADITIONAL FRENCH/LATE NIGHT Their famous onion soup and namesake specialty (grilled pig's feet with béarnaise sauce) still lure visitors, and where else in Paris can you get a good meal at 3am? Two other specialties are the *tentation* (temptation) platter, including grilled pig's tail, pig's snout, and half a pig's foot with béarnaise and *frites* (french fries), and *andouillette* (chitterling sausages) with béarnaise. Two flavorful but less unusual dishes are a *jarret* (shin) of pork, caramelized in honey and served on a bed of sauerkraut, and grilled pork ribs with sage sauce. On the street outside, you can buy some of the freshest oysters in town. The attendants will give you slices of lemon to accompany them, and you can down them on the spot.

6 rue Coquillière, 1er. © 01-40-13-77-00. Reservations recommended for lunch and dinner hours. Main courses 15€–27€ ($14–$24). AE, DC, MC, V. Daily 24 hr. Métro: Les Halles.

Chez Pauline ★ *Finds* BURGUNDIAN/TRADITIONAL FRENCH Fans say this *bistrot de luxe* is a less expensive, less majestic version of Le Grand Véfour. The early-1900s setting is grand enough to impress a business client and light-hearted enough to attract a roster of VIPs. You'll be ushered to a table on one of two levels, amid polished mirrors, red leather banquettes, and memorabilia of long-ago Paris. The emphasis is on the cuisine of central France, especially Burgundy, as shown by the liberal use of wines in favorites like cassoulet of Burgundian snails with bacon and tomatoes, *boeuf bourguignonne* (braised beef in red-wine sauce) with tagliatelle, terrine of parslied ham, wild-duckling filet with seasonal berries, salmon steak with green peppercorns, and ragout of wild hare in Pouilly aspic. Also wonderful is the roasted Bresse chicken with dauphinois potatoes. Dessert may include a *clafoutis* (pastry) of apricots and raspberries sautéed in sugar as well as caramelized rice pudding. Owner/chef André Genin is an author of children's books, some on the techniques of French cuisine.

5 rue Villedo, 1er. ℂ **01-42-96-20-70.** Reservations recommended. Main courses 21€–33€ ($18–$29); fixed-price menu 38€ ($34). AE, DC, V. Mon–Fri 12:15–2:30pm; Mon–Sat 7:30–10:30pm. Closed Sat–Sun May to late Aug. Métro: Palais Royal.

Il Cortile ★★ ITALIAN/MEDITERRANEAN   Flanking the verdant courtyard of a discreet small hotel, this much-talked-about restaurant serves the best Italian food in Paris. During warm weather, tables are set up in an enclosed patio—a welcome luxury in this congested neighborhood. The cuisine is fresh, inventive, and seasonal. Dishes are from throughout Italy, with emphasis on the north, as shown by a special promotion of wines of Tuscany and the Piedmont. Look for items like farfalle pasta with squid ink and fresh shellfish, fettuccine with *pistou* (pasta in a soup made from various vegetables), and an award-winning version of guinea fowl (spit-roasted and served with artfully shaped slices of the bird's gizzard, heart, and liver; it comes with polenta). The service is virtually flawless: The Italian-speaking staff is diplomatic and good-humored. If you want to see what's cooking, ask for a seat in the dining room with a view of the open rotisserie, where spit-roasted hens and guinea fowl slowly spin.

In the Hôtel Castille, 37 rue Cambon, 1er. ℂ **01-44-58-45-67.** Reservations recommended. Main courses 29€–30€ ($26–$27); fixed-price menu 42€ ($38). AE, DC, DISC, MC, V. Mon–Fri noon–2:30pm and 7:30–10:30pm. Métro: Concorde or Madeleine.

Le Fumoir ★ INTERNATIONAL   Stylish and breezy, this upscale brasserie is set in an antique building a few steps from the Louvre. Currently, it's one of the most fashionable places in Paris to be seen eating or drinking. In a high-ceilinged room of warm but somber browns and indirect lighting, you can order salads, pastries, and drinks at off-hours and platters of more substantial food at conventional mealtimes. Examples are codfish filet with onions and herbs, sliced rack of veal simmered in its own juices with tarragon, calf's liver with onions, lamb chops with grilled tuna steak, and herring in mustard-flavored cream sauce.

6 rue de l'Amiral-Coligny, 1er. ℂ **01-42-92-00-24.** Reservations recommended. Main courses 14€–21€ ($13–$19). AE, V. Salads, pastries, and snacks daily 11am–2pm; complete menu daily noon–3pm and 7–11:30pm. Métro: Louvre-Rivoli.

INEXPENSIVE

Angélina ★★ TRADITIONAL FRENCH/TEA   In the high-rent area near the Inter-Continental (though on a section of rue de Rivoli that's getting scuzzy), this *salon de thé* (tearoom) combines fashion-industry glitter and bourgeois respectability. The carpets are plush, the ceilings are high, and the gilded accessories have the right amount of patina. This place has no equal when it comes to viewing the lionesses of haute couture over tea and delicate sandwiches. The overwrought and slightly snooty waitresses bear silver trays with light platters, pastries, drinks, and tea or coffee to tiny marble-topped tables. Lunch usually offers a salad and a *plat du jour* (special of the day) like chicken salad, steak tartare, *sole*

Moments **Le Grand Fromage**

Cheese is king at **Androuët sur le Pouce** ★★, 49 rue St-Roch, 1er (© **01-42-97-57-39**), where a tradition that began in 1909 has evolved into a "bar à fromage" (cheese bar) that's the modern-day evolution of one of the most famous purveyors of cheese in the world. Gone are the formal meals and dining rituals that used to prevail at Androuët. Since 2002, the venue has included two dining options, both of which have met with screaming approval from the Parisian public. The menu is simple, consisting of either *tartines* (open-faced sandwiches) or cheese platters. Tartines, priced at from 9.10€ to 15€ ($8–$14), include your choice of any kind of cheese and/or a medley of smoked or marinated fish or meats. If you opt for a platter, you'll select from offerings presented on a half-dozen cheese boards, whose categories are organized into such classifications as goat cheeses, triple crèmes, and so on. If you select a portion of five different cheeses from the platters, it will cost 10€ ($9.25); seven cheeses will cost 14€ ($12), 11 cheeses will cost 22€ ($20); and 15 different cheeses (recommended only for serious cheese lovers who won't mind some degree of indigestion) will cost 27€ ($24). Ultrafresh bread and green salads are the only accompaniment for your tartines and cheese platters. There's also a staggering assortment of French wines. It's open Monday to Friday from 11:45am to 2:30pm and 7 to 9:30pm.

Although this organization maintains a total of 10 branches within greater Paris, the most centrally located of the other branches is **Androuët sur le Pouce,** 23 rue des Acacias, 17e (© **01-40-68-00-12;** Métro: Ternes). Charging the same prices and using the same system as the larger branch described above, it's open Monday to Friday from noon to 2:30pm, and Monday to Saturday from 7 to 9:30pm.

Don't expect a full-fledged shop selling cheeses at either of the branches, since the organization's shops are usually separate entities located within walking distance of an Androuët sur le Pouce outlet. The chain's largest sales outlet is Androuët, 23 rue du Villiers, 17e (© **01-47-64-39-20;** Métro: Villiers).

meunière (filet of sole, sautéed in butter with lemon, parsley and other seasonings), or poached salmon. The house specialty, designed to go well with tea, is a Mont Blanc, a combination of chestnut cream and meringue.

226 rue de Rivoli, 1er. © 01-42-60-82-00. Reservations accepted for lunch, not for teatime. Pot of tea for 1 person 5.95€–6.10€ ($5.30–$5.45); sandwiches and salads 11€–14€ ($9.75–$12); main courses 11€–27€ ($9.50–$24). AE, MC, V. Mon–Fri 9am–7pm; Sat–Sun 9am–7:30pm (lunch daily 11:45am–3pm). Métro: Tuileries or Concorde.

Chez Vong ★ CANTONESE   This is the kind of Les Halles restaurant you head for when you've had your fill of grand French cuisine and grander culinary pretensions. The decor is a soothing mix of green and browns, steeped in a Chinese colonial ambience that evokes early-1900s Shanghai. Menu items feature shrimp and scallops served as spicy as you like, including a superhot version with garlic and red peppers, "joyous beef" that mingles sliced filet with pepper sauce, chicken in puff pastry with ginger, and a tempting array of fresh-fish dishes.

10 rue de la Grande-Truanderie, 1er. ✆ **01-40-26-09-36.** Reservations recommended. Main courses 14€–30€ ($12–$27); fixed-price lunch Mon–Fri only, 23€ ($20). AE, DC, MC, V. Mon–Sat noon–2:30pm and 7pm–midnight. Métro: Etienne-Marcel or Les Halles.

Joe Allen ⭐⭐ *Kids* AMERICAN   The first American restaurant to open in Les Halles is aging well. Joe Allen long ago invaded Paris with his hamburger. Though the New York restaurateur admits "it's a silly idea," it works, and it's Paris's best burger. While listening to the jukebox, you can order black-bean soup, chili, juicy sirloin steak, barbecued spareribs, or apple pie. Joe Allen is getting more sophisticated, however, catering to modern tastes with dishes like grilled salmon with coconut rice and sun-dried tomatoes. His saloon is the only place in Paris serving authentic New York cheesecake and pecan pie, and thanks to French chocolate, he feels his brownies are better than those in the States. Giving the brownies tough competition are the California chocolate-mousse pie, strawberries Romanoff, and coconut-cream pie. On a regular night, if you haven't made a reservation for dinner, expect to wait at the New York bar for at least 30 minutes.

30 rue Pierre-Lescot, 1er. ✆ **01-42-36-70-13.** Reservations recommended for dinner. Main courses 13€–19€ ($12–$17); fixed-price menu 22€ ($20). AE, MC, V. Daily noon–12:30am. Métro: Etienne-Marcel.

La Fermette du Sud-Ouest ⭐ SOUTHWESTERN FRENCH   In the heart of one of Paris's most ancient neighborhoods, a stone's throw from Ste-Eustache church, this restaurant occupies the site of a 1500s convent. After the Revolution, the convent was converted into a coaching inn that preserved the original stonework and massive beams. La Fermette prepares rich, savory stews and confits celebrating agrarian France, serving them on the ground floor and on a mezzanine resembling a medieval choir loft. Menu items include an age-old but ever-popular magret of duckling with flap mushrooms, *andouillette* (chitterling sausages), and a sometimes startling array of *cochonailles* (pork products and by-products) you probably need to be French to appreciate. Cassoulet and *pot-au-feu* (beef simmered with vegetables) are enduring specialties.

31 rue Coquillière, 1er. ✆ **01-42-36-73-55.** Reservations recommended. Main courses 12€–21€ ($11–$18); fixed-price lunch 14€–22€ ($13–$20); fixed-price dinner 22€ ($20). MC, V. Mon–Sat noon–2pm and 7:30–10pm. Métro: Les Halles.

La Poule au Pot TRADITIONAL FRENCH/LATE NIGHT   This bistro welcomes late-night carousers and showbiz personalities looking for a meal after a performance. (Past aficionados have included the Rolling Stones, Prince, and Johnny Hallyday.) The decor is authentically Art Deco, the ambience nurturing. The time-tested and savory menu items include a salad of warm goat cheese on toast, onion soup, pan-fried stingray with capers, Burgundy-style snails, country paté on a bed of onion marmalade, and a succulent version of the restaurant's namesake, chicken in a pot with slices of paté and fresh vegetables (in summer, it can be served cold, on a bed of lettuce, with vinaigrette sauce).

9 rue Vauvilliers, 1er. ✆ **01-42-36-32-96.** Reservations recommended. Main courses 18€–30€ ($16–$27); fixed-price menu 27€ ($24). MC, V. Tues–Sun 5pm–5am. Métro: Louvre or Les Halles.

La Rose de France ⭐ *Value* TRADITIONAL FRENCH   At this restaurant on Ile de la Cité near Notre-Dame, around the corner from the Pont Neuf, you'll dine with a crowd of young Parisians who know they can expect a good meal at reasonable prices. Founded more than 30 years ago by its present owner,

M. Cointepas, it can be relied on for fresh food served in a friendly atmosphere. In warm weather, the sidewalk tables overlooking the Palais de Justice are most popular. Main dishes include sweetbreads, veal chop flambéed with Calvados and served with apples, beef filet *en croûte* (wrapped in pastry), and lamb chops seasoned with Provençal herbs and served with gratin of potatoes. For dessert, try the fruit tart of the day or the sorbet of the month.

24 place Dauphine, 1er. ✆ **01-43-54-10-12.** Reservations recommended. Main courses 15€–18€ ($14–$16); menu du jour 21€ ($19) without wine, 27€ ($24) with wine. AE, MC, V. Mon–Fri noon–2pm and 7–10pm. Closed last 3 weeks in Aug and 15 days at end of Dec. Métro: Cité or Pont Neuf.

La Tour de Monthléry (Chez Denise) TRADITIONAL FRENCH/LATE NIGHT   This restaurant is both workaday and stylish—no small feat considering its gregarious owner, Denise Bénariac, has maintained her reign for more than 30 years. Amid a decor that has changed little since 1900 (note the nickel-plated bar near the entrance), you can order hearty cuisine. The food tastes best after a long night of carousing. Menu items include grilled pig's trotters, mutton stew, steak with peppercorns, stuffed cabbage, pot-au-feu, and a golden-velvety paté of chicken livers. Wine goes beautifully with this kind of food, and the restaurant complies by recommending several worthy, unpretentious vintages.

5 rue des Prouvaires, 1er. ✆ **01-42-36-21-82.** Main courses 18€–22€ ($16–$20). MC, V. Open continuously Mon 7am to Sat 7am. Métro: Louvre or Les Halles.

Lescure 🍴 *Finds* TRADITIONAL FRENCH   This animated and appealing minibistro is a major find—one of the few reasonably priced restaurants near place de la Concorde. You'll get a lot for your euro. The tables on the sidewalk are tiny, and there isn't much room inside, but what this place does have is rustic charm. The kitchen is wide open, and the aroma of drying bay leaves, salami, and garlic pigtails hanging from the ceiling fills the room. Expect *cuisine bourgeoise*—nothing innovative, just substantial hearty fare. Perhaps begin with *paté en croûte* (paté in puff pastry). Main-course house specialties include *confit de canard* (duckling), beef bourguignonne, and game dishes from October to January. The chef's fruit tarts are a favorite dessert. In autumn and winter, expect a savory repertoire of game dishes like venison and pheasant.

7 rue de Mondovi, 1er. ✆ **01-42-60-18-91.** Reservations not accepted. Main courses 9.10€–15€ ($8.10–$13); 4-course fixed-price menu 20€ ($18). MC, V. Mon–Fri noon–2:15pm and 7–10:30pm. Closed 3 weeks in Aug. Métro: Concorde.

2ND ARRONDISSEMENT
MODERATE

Chez Georges TRADITIONAL FRENCH   This bistro is a local landmark, opened in 1964 near La Bourse (stock exchange) and run by three generations of the same family. Naturally, at lunch it's packed with stock-exchange members. The owners serve what they call *la cuisine bourgeoise* (comfort food). Waiters bring around bowls of appetizers, like celery rémoulade, to get you started. You can follow with sweetbreads with morels, duck breast with cêpe mushrooms, classic cassoulet, or pot-au-feu. A delight is sole filet with a sauce made from Pouilly wine and crème fraîche. Beaujolais goes great with this hearty food.

1 rue du Mail, 2e. ✆ **01-42-60-07-11.** Reservations required. Main courses 20€–27€ ($18–$24). AE, MC, V. Mon–Sat noon–2:15pm and 7–9:45pm. Closed 3 weeks in Aug. Métro: Bourse.

Le Vaudeville TRADITIONAL FRENCH/LATE NIGHT   Adjacent to La Bourse (stock exchange), this bistro retains its marble walls and Art Deco carvings from 1918. In summer, tables dot a terrace amid banks of geraniums. The place is boisterous and informal, often welcoming groups of six or eight diners at a time. A bar near the entrance provides a perch if your reservation is delayed. The roster of platters includes snails in garlic butter, shellfish, smoked salmon, sauerkraut, and grilled meats. Three dishes reign as enduring favorites: fresh grilled codfish with mashed potatoes and truffle juice, fresh escalope of warm foie gras with grapes, and *tête du veau* (veal's head). The main value is the fixed-price menu.

29 rue Vivienne, 2e. ✆ **01-40-20-04-62.** Reservations recommended in the evenings. Main courses 15€–23€ ($13–$20); fixed-price menu 21€ ($19) at lunch, 30€ ($27) at dinner. AE, DC, MC, V. Daily noon–3pm and 7pm–1am. Métro: Bourse.

INEXPENSIVE

Au Clair de Lune ALGERIAN/TRADITIONAL FRENCH This is a pocket of a long-gone French-colonial ambition. This neighborhood staple has flourished in the heart of Paris's wholesale garment district since the 1930s, when Algeria was a distinct part of the French-speaking world. Today you'll dine in a long narrow room whose walls are hung with colorful Berber carpets and whose patrons are likely to include shop workers from the nearby wholesale clothiers. On the menu is always the Algerian staple of couscous, as well as an array of oft-changing daily specials such as veal stew, shoulder or rack of lamb, grilled fish, and roast chicken. The portions are so large you should take along a ravenous appetite. The wines are from throughout France and North Africa.

13 rue Française, 2e. ✆ **01-42-33-59-10.** Main courses 8.80€–13€ ($7.85–$12). MC, V. Daily noon–2:30pm and 7:30–11pm. Métro: Etienne-Marcel or Les Halles.

Aux Lyonnais ★★ TRADITIONAL FRENCH/LYONNAIS A LYON LE COCHON EST ROI! proclaims the sign. Pig may be king at this fin-de-siècle bistro (with walls molded with roses and garlands, brass globe lamps, potted palms, and etched glass), just behind La Bourse, but the competent kitchen staff does everything well. After a meal here, you'll know why Lyon is called the gastronomic capital of France. Everything is washed down with Beaujolais. Launch your repast with one of the large Lyonnais sausages, though a favorite opener remains a chicory salad with bacon and slices of hot sausages. Poached eggs in red-wine sauce and grilled pig's feet still appear on the menu. Pike dumplings are always prepared to perfection and served classically in white-butter sauce. The upside-down apple pie with crème fraîche is the dessert of choice.

32 rue St-Marc, 2e. ✆ **01-42-96-65-04.** Reservations required. Main courses 12€–15€ ($11–$13). AE, DC, MC, V. Mon–Sat 11:30am–3pm and 6:30–11:30pm. Métro: Bourse or Richelieu-Drouot.

Babylone Bis CREOLE/LATE NIGHT This place honors the French Caribbean island of Guadeloupe with specialties like *accras* (fritters) of codfish and Creole *boudin* (blood sausage), which preface courses like fricassee of shrimp or chicken and *colombo* (stew) of baby goat and pan-fried slices of shark meat. Look for African masks, touches of zebra skin, and photos of the divas and celebs (Diana Ross, Stevie Wonder, French sports stars, and fashion models) who've dined here. Don't think of coming before dark. After 2am or so, the focus shifts away from the hearty Caribbean soul food toward reggae, jazz, and cocktails.

34 rue Tiquetonne, 2e. ✆ **01-42-33-48-35.** Main courses 12€–21€ ($11–$19). V. Daily 8pm–8am. Métro: Etienne-Marcel or Sentier.

Clémentine TRADITIONAL FRENCH In an antique building adjacent to the Musée Grévin, this well-managed bistro serves time-honored food with an occasional individualistic flair. Among early-1900s panels, polished brass, and mirrors, you can order pepper steak, codfish steak studded with lard, oven-braised veal served in its own juices, and an unusual preparation of chicken breast with goat cheese. The *fondant au chocolat* (chocolate candy) seems to be an assiduously guarded, long-cherished family recipe. There's room for barely 25 diners, so advance reservations are important.

5 rue St-Marc, 2e. ✆ **01-40-41-05-65.** Reservations required. Main courses 14€ ($12) each; fixed-price menu 24€ ($22). AE, MC, V. Mon–Fri noon–2:30pm and 7:30–10:30pm. Métro: Bourse or Grands Boulevards.

3RD ARRONDISSEMENT
EXPENSIVE

L'Ami Louis ⭐ TRADITIONAL FRENCH   L'Ami Louis is in one of central Paris's least fashionable neighborhoods, far removed from the part of the Marais that has become chic, and its facade has seen better days. It was one of Paris's most famous brasseries in the 1930s, thanks to its excellent food served in copious portions and its old-fashioned decor. Its traditions, even the hostile waiters, are fervently maintained today. Amid a "brown gravy" decor (the walls retain a smoky patina), dishes like roasted suckling lamb, pheasant, venison, confit of duckling, and endless slices of foie gras may commune on your marble-topped table. Though some whisper that the ingredients aren't as select as they were in the restaurant's heyday, its sauces are as thick as they were between the wars. Don't save room for dessert, which isn't very good.

32 rue du Vertbois, 3e. ✆ **01-48-87-77-48.** Reservations required far in advance. Main courses 38€–68€ ($34–$61). MC, V. Wed–Sun noon–1:30pm and 8–11pm. Closed July 19–Aug 25. Métro: Temple.

INEXPENSIVE

Au Bascou ⭐ *Finds* BASQUE   The succulent cuisine of France's "deep southwest" is the specialty within this restaurant, where art objects and oil paintings celebrate the beauty of the region, and hanging clusters of pimentos add spice to the air. This restaurant serves Basque food as good as it gets. For a ray of sunshine in your life, try the *piperade Basque,* a spicy omelet loaded with peppers and onions; pimentos stuffed with a purée of codfish; and an *axoa* of veal (shoulder of calf served with a pimento-and-pepper–based green sauce). Also noteworthy is thick-sliced filet of cod served with a confit of tomatoes. All starters are priced at 8.35€ ($7.45) and all desserts at 6.10€ ($5.45).

38 rue Réaumur, 3e. ✆ **01-42-72-69-25.** Reservations recommended. All main courses 14€ ($12). AE, DC, MC, V. Tues–Fri noon–3pm; Mon–Sat 8–11pm. Closed 1 week in Aug. Métro: Arts-et-Métiers.

Chez Janou PROVENÇAL   On one of the 17th-century streets behind place des Vosges, this unpretentious bistro operates from a pair of cramped but cozy dining rooms filled with memorabilia from Provence. The service is brusque and sometimes hectic. The food here is like a visit to your French grandmother's kitchen where she'll regale you with her time-tested dishes like large shrimp with pastis sauce, *brouillade des pleurotes* (baked eggs with oyster mushrooms), spinach salad with goat cheese, fondue of ratatouille, gratin of mussels, and a simple but savory magret of duck with rosemary. There's also a covered terrace.

2 rue Roger-Verlomme, 3e. ✆ **01-42-72-28-41.** Reservations recommended. Main courses 10€–16€ ($9.25–$15); 2-course fixed-price menu 13€ ($12). No credit cards. Daily noon–3pm and 7:30pm–midnight. Métro: Chemin-Vert.

Jenny ALSATIAN   One of the city's most famous and popular Alsatian restaurants was established in 1930 by members of the Jenny family, who commissioned one of the noteworthy craftsmen of the era, Spindler, to create marquetry panels for the sheathing of the walls. Today, little has changed since its inauguration, except for the fact that the clientele is a lot more contemporary-looking than in the old days. Up to 220 diners can fit into this nostalgia-laden setting, where Alsatian Gemütlichkeit prevails. An ongoing specialty is the *choucroute* (sauerkraut) *de chez Jenny*, which is piled high with sausages, tender pork knuckles, and slices of ham. Also available are oysters, onion soup, grilled meats, and grilled fish. Any of these taste wonderful accompanied by one of the Alsatian wines (especially Rieslings) that fill the wine list.

39 bd. du Temple, 3e. ☎ **01-44-54-39-00.** Reservations recommended. Main courses 14€–23€ ($13–$20); fixed-price menus 16€–23€ ($14–$20). AE, DC, MC, V. Daily noon–midnight. Métro: République.

L'Ambassade d'Auvergne ⭐ AUVERGNAT/TRADITIONAL FRENCH You enter this rustic tavern through a busy bar with heavy oak beams, hanging hams, and ceramic plates. This favorite showcases the culinary generosity of France's most isolated region, the Auvergne, whose pork products are widely celebrated. The best examples are a chicory salad with apples and pieces of country ham; pork braised with cabbage, turnips, and white beans; grilled tripe sausages with mashed potatoes and Cantal (a strong, hard cheese) with garlic; and pork jowls with green lentils. The cholesterol is intense, but devotees love this type of food. Nonpork specialties are pan-fried duck liver with gingerbread, perch filets steamed in verbena tea, and roasted rack of lamb with wild mushrooms. Dessert might be a poached pear with crispy almonds and caramel sauce or a wine-flavored sorbet.

22 rue de Grenier St-Lazare, 3e. ☎ **01-42-72-31-22.** Reservations recommended. Main courses 14€–18€ ($12–$16); fixed-price menus 26€ ($23). AE, MC, V. Daily noon–2pm and 7:30–11pm. Closed 2 weeks in Aug. Métro: Rambuteau.

4TH ARRONDISSEMENT
VERY EXPENSIVE
L'Ambroisie ⭐⭐⭐ MODERN & TRADITIONAL FRENCH One of Paris's most talented chefs, Bernard Pacaud, draws world attention with his vivid flavors and expert culinary skill. Expect culinary perfection but a cool reception at this early-17th-century town house in Le Marais, with three high-ceilinged salons whose decor vaguely recalls an Italian palazzo. Pacaud's tables are nearly always filled with satisfied diners who come back again and again to see where his imagination will take him next. The dishes change seasonally and may include fricassee of Breton lobster with chestnuts, served with a purée of pumpkin; turbot filet braised with endive, served with a julienne of black truffles; or one of our favorite dishes in all Paris, *poulard de Bresse demi-deuil homage à la Mère Brazier* (chicken roasted with black truffles and truffled vegetables in a style invented by a Lyonnais matron after World War II). An award-winning dessert is the *tarte fine sablée* served with bitter chocolate and vanilla-flavored ice cream.

9 place des Vosges, 4e. ☎ **01-42-78-51-45.** Reservations required far in advance. Main courses 65€–103€ ($58–$92). AE, MC, V. Tues–Sat noon–1:30pm and 8–9:30pm. Métro: St-Paul or Chèmin Vert.

EXPENSIVE
Benoit ⭐ TRADITIONAL FRENCH There's something awesomely traditional and weighty about this old-fashioned historical monument, which has served every mayor of Paris since it was founded in 1912 by the grandfather of the present owner. He's one of the last *bistrotiers* who purchases Beaujolais in casks, and bottles it in his own cellars. The setting is scarlet and theatrical, and the service can be either intensely attentive or very arrogant, depending on a

Moments **Taking an Ice Cream Break at Berthillon**

A landmark on Ile St-Louis after 3 dozen years in business, the *salon de thé* **Berthillon** ★★★, 31 rue St-Louis-en-l'Ile, 4e (℃ **01-43-54-31-61;** Métro: Pont Marie), offers the world's best selection of ice creams. Try gingerbread, bitter-chocolate mousse, rhubarb, melon, kumquat, black currant, or any fresh fruit in season—there are more than 50 flavors and nothing artificial. Parisians have flocked here in such numbers that gendarmes have been called out to direct the traffic of ice cream aficionados. It's open Wednesday to Sunday from 10am to 8pm.

delicate chemistry that only longtime fans of this place really understand. Prices are higher, a lot higher, than you'd expect for bistro fare, but clients just keep coming back for more. Cuisine is rich, full of flavor, and satisfying, based on time-tested classics that rarely get modernized. Traditional crowd-pleasers include salmon that's both marinated and smoked; snails served in their shell with garlic butter; and cassoulet, a white bean and pork dish from France's southwest that's absolutely fabulous on a cold day. A dessert that gets raved about is a *Sainte-Eve,* composed of pears layered with macaroon-flavored cream enclosed in puff pastry.

20 rue St Martin, 4e. ℃ **01-42-72-25-76.** Reservations required. Main courses 24€–38€ ($22–$34); fixed-price lunch 38€ ($34). AE. Daily noon–2pm and 8–10pm. Métro: Châtelet or Hôtel-de-Ville.

MODERATE

Bofinger ★ ALSATIAN/MODERN & TRADITIONAL FRENCH Opened in the 1860s, Bofinger is the oldest Alsatian brasserie in town and one of the best. It's a Belle Epoque palace, resplendent with shiny brass and stained glass. Weather permitting, you can dine on an outdoor terrace. Affiliated today with La Coupole, Julien, and Brasserie Flo, the restaurant has updated its menu, retaining the most popular of its traditional dishes, like choucroute and a sole meunière. Recent additions have included roasted leg of lamb with a fondant of artichoke hearts and a purée of parsley, grilled turbot with a *brandade* (a pounded mixture of fish, olive oil, garlic, milk, and cream) of fennel, and stingray filet with chives and burnt-butter sauce. Shellfish, including an abundance of fresh oysters and lobster, is almost always available in season.

5-7 rue de la Bastille, 4e. ℃ **01-42-72-87-82.** Reservations recommended. Main courses 14€–30€ ($12–$27). AE, DC, MC, V. Mon–Fri noon–3pm and 6:30pm–1am; Sat–Sun noon–1am. Métro: Bastille.

Georges ★ INTERNATIONAL With the establishment of this restaurant, the Centre Pompidou again thrusts itself into the spotlight as the kind of place that artsy Paris is talking about. The venue inhabits a large space on the top floor of Paris's most comprehensive arts complex, with views through bay windows over most of the city. The decor is minimalist and postmodern, incorporating brushed aluminum and stainless steel. Tables are made from sandblasted glass, lit from below, and accessorized with hypermodern cutlery. Menu items are mostly continental, with hints of Asia. Some combinations come as a surprise—macaroni with lobster, for example. Others come as exotic, including roasted ostrich steak. Other than these original dishes, some of the best items on the menu are the roasted scallops given added zest by lemon butter, and a tuna steak spiced up with coriander. There's also a luscious version of sole meunière featured (may that dish never go out of style). To access the place, head for the exterior elevator just to the left of the Centre Pompidou's main entrance, and know in advance that unless you verify your reservation to the security guard, they might not let you up.

On the uppermost (6th) floor of the Centre Georges Pompidou, 19 rue Beaubourg, 4e. ✆ **01-44-78-47-99.** Reservations imperative for dinner, strongly recommended for lunch. Main courses 17€–33€ ($15–$30). AE, DC, MC, V. Wed–Mon 11am–2am. Métro: Châtelet or Rambuteau.

Isami JAPANESE Dining here is guaranteed to evoke a sense of cultural dislocation—the staff is mostly from Japan, and few speak much French or English. That, however, is part of the place's allure for its loyal customers, many of whom work in the arts. The staff is quick to tell you that only authentic Japanese versions of sushi and sashimi are served, with absolutely none of what they call California/Japanese cuisine. Begin a meal with miso soup or some pickled vegetables, as a prelude for the wide array of fish (tuna, salmon, whitefish, fluke, snapper, bluefish, oysters, clams, shrimp, and more) that forms this restaurant's backbone. Lingering isn't encouraged.

4 quai d'Orléans, 4e. ✆ **01-40-46-06-97.** Reservations recommended. Meals 30€–53€ ($27–$48), depending on the fish and how many pieces ordered. Set menu 27€ ($24). AE, DC, DISC, MC, V. Tues–Sat noon–2pm; Mon–Sat 7:30–10pm. Métro: Pont Marie.

Le Coconnas ✿ MODERN & TRADITIONAL FRENCH Claude Terrail (owner of La Tour d'Argent) serves superb cuisine in this restaurant named after the legendary rake whose peccadilloes scandalized place des Vosges. The restaurant features a Louis XIII decor of high-backed chairs and elegantly rustic accessories. Menu items change frequently but present a cost-conscious alternative to the grand cuisine served by other restaurants in the chain. Look for foie gras maison, baked goat's cheese dunked in white wine, roasted pigeon stuffed with pine nuts, coq au vin, *la poule au pot* (stewed chicken), and desserts like crème brûlée with honey. None of these items sets off fireworks, but the ingredients are fresh and harmonious and the prices are fair for the quality.

2 bis place des Vosges, 4e. ✆ **01-42-78-58-16.** Reservations required. Main dishes 24€ ($22); fixed-price menu 23€ ($20). AE, DC, MC, V. Tues–Sun noon–2:30pm and 7:30–10:30pm. Métro: Bastille or St-Paul.

Le Vieux Bistro ✿ *Finds* TRADITIONAL FRENCH This is one of the last old-fashioned bistros still left in the heart of Paris. Few other restaurants offer so close-up, and so forbidding, a view of the massive walls of Paris's largest cathedral, visible through lacy curtains from the windows of the front dining room. To reach it, you'll bypass a dozen souvenir stands, then settle into one of the two old-time dining rooms for a flavorful meal of French staples. The cuisine evokes the kind you're served along a little back-road deep in the heart of France, a bit heavy perhaps, but evocative of food of long ago. The premier specialty remains boeuf bourguignonne, and in winter lots of game dishes. You can order snails with garlic butter, filet mignon roasted in a bag and served with marrow sauce, veal filets, and a classic dessert, *tarte tatin* (studded with apples and sugar, drenched with Calvados, and capped with fresh cream).

14 rue du Cloître-Notre-Dame, 4e. ✆ **01-43-54-18-95.** Main courses 9.90€–23€ ($8.80–$20). MC, V. Daily noon–2pm and 7:30–11pm. Métro: Cité.

INEXPENSIVE

Aquarius ✿✿ VEGETARIAN In a 17th-century building whose original stonework forms part of the earthy decor, this is one of the best-known vegetarian restaurants in Le Marais. The owners serve only a limited array of (strictly organic) wine, and smoking is expressly forbidden. Their flavorful meals are healthfully prepared. Choose from an array of soups and salads; a galette of wheat served with crudités and mushroom tarts; or a country plate composed of fried mushrooms and potatoes, garlic, and goat cheese, served with a salad.

54 rue Ste-Croix-de-la-Bretonnerie, 4e. ℂ **01-48-87-48-71.** Main courses 7.60€–11€ ($6.75–$10); fixed-price menu 11€–15€ ($10–$13). MC, V. Mon–Sat noon–10pm. Métro: Hôtel de Ville. RER: Châtelet-Les Halles.

Au Gourmet de l'Ile ⭐ 𝘝𝘢𝘭𝘶𝘦 TRADITIONAL FRENCH   Locals swear by the cuisine at Au Gourmet de l'Ile, whose fixed-price meals are among Paris's best bargains. The setting is beautiful, with a beamed ceiling, walls from the 1400s, and candlelit tables. In the window is a sign emblazoned with AAAAA, which, roughly translated, stands for the Amiable Association of Amateurs of the Authentic Andouillette. These chitterling sausages are soul food to the French. Popular and tasty too are *la charbonnée de l'Ile* (a savory pork with onions) and stuffed mussels in shallot butter. The fixed-price menu includes a choice of 15 appetizers, 15 main courses, salad or cheese, and 15 desserts.

42 rue St-Louis-en-l'Ile, 4e. ℂ **01-43-26-79-27.** Reservations required. Main courses 12€–20€ ($11–$18); fixed-price menus 25€–30€ ($22–$26). MC, V. Wed–Sun noon–2pm; Tues–Sun 7–10:30pm. Métro: Pont Marie.

Brasserie de l'Ile St-Louis ALSATIAN/TRADITIONAL FRENCH   This is the kind of retro-chic brasserie where the likes of Brigitte Bardot, Elizabeth Taylor, Grace Jones, and John Frankenheimer have scheduled informal meals and rendezvous. Little about the place's patina and paneled decor has changed since the 1880s, giving it an aura modern competitors can only try to imitate. The menu is conservative and well-prepared, including an always-popular version of Alsatian sauerkraut, cassoulet in the old-fashioned style of Toulouse, calf's liver, and a succulent *jarret* (hock) of pork with warm apple marmalade.

55 quai de Bourbon, 4e. ℂ **01-43-54-02-59.** Main courses 6.85€–20€ ($6.10–$18). MC, V. Thurs 5pm–12:30am; Fri–Tues noon–12:30am. Closed Aug. Métro: Pont Marie or Cité.

Café la Parisienne 𝘒𝘪𝘥𝘴 MODERN FRENCH   Whimsical and often chaotic, this appealing restaurant shares something of the avant-garde aesthetic of its neighbor the Centre Pompidou, and was renovated in mid-1999. It was named after the bread rations that were issued here during World War II and has an enviable location beside the St-Merri church and a spinning, spitting, and bobbing fountain by Jean Tingueley and Niki de Saint-Phalle. In fair weather, tables and chairs overlook the charming fountain. You might begin with beef carpaccio with salad, then follow with noisettes of lamb flavored with whiskey and fresh thyme or fricassee of poultry with morels. Finish with *glace Berthillon*, Paris's best ice cream. There's also a beautiful terrace where you can enjoy a breathtaking view.

10 rue Brise-Miche, 4e. ℂ **01-42-78-44-11.** Reservations recommended. Main courses 9.90€–12€ ($8.80–$11). MC, V. Daily 8am–2am. Métro: Rambuteau, Hôtel de Ville, or Châtelet-Les Halles.

Chez Jo Goldenberg ⭐⭐ 𝘍𝘪𝘯𝘥𝘴 CENTRAL EUROPEAN/JEWISH   This is the best-known restaurant on the "Street of the Rose Bushes." Albert Goldenberg, the doyen of Jewish restaurateurs in Paris, long ago moved to choicer surroundings (69 av. de Wagram, 17e), but his brother Joseph has remained here. Dining is on two levels, one for nonsmokers. Look for the collection of samovars, the white fantail pigeon in a wicker cage, and the interesting paintings. The *carpe farcie* (stuffed carp) is a preferred selection, but the beef goulash

> ### *Moments* A Parisian *Pique-nique*
>
> One of the best ways to save money and participate in Parisian life is to picnic. Go to a *fromagerie* for cheese; to a *boulangerie* for a baguette; to a *charcuterie* for paté, sausage, or salad; and to a *pâtisserie* for luscious pastries. Add a bottle of Côtes du Rhone—it goes well with picnics—and you'll have the makings of a delightful, typically French meal you can take to the nearest park or along the banks of the Seine. Pretend you're in Manet's *Déjeuner sur l'herbe* and enjoy! (Don't forget the corkscrew!)
>
> The best spot for a picnic is a cozy nook along one of your favorite views of the **Seine.** Otherwise the best place for picnics (also boating, walks, and jogging) is the **Bois de Boulogne** (Métro: Porte Maillot), covering some 2,000 acres at the western edge of Paris. At night it becomes a twilight zone of sex and drugs, but it's lovely during the day. (See chapter 7 for more on the Bois de Boulogne.) Even though they're in a state of restoration, the splendid gardens of **Versailles** offer another fine picnic spot. You can also enjoy your meal on the grass on a day trip to the cathedral city of **Chartres.** Go to a bucolic spot, Parc André Gagon, only a 5-minute walk northwest of the fabled cathedral.

is also good. We like the eggplant moussaka and the pastrami. The menu also offers Israeli wines, but M. Goldenberg admits they're not as good as French wine. Live Yiddish music is presented every night beginning at 9pm, and special menus are presented during Jewish holidays—reservations are a must.

7 rue des Rosiers, 4e. © **01-48-87-20-16.** Reservations required. Main courses 11€–23€ ($10–$20). AE, DC, MC, V. Daily 11am–1am. Métro: St. Paul.

Trumilou ⭐ TRADITIONAL FRENCH   This is one of the most popular of the restaurants surrounding Paris's Hôtel de Ville and has welcomed most of France's politicians, including George Pompidou, who came here frequently before he was elected president. ("As soon as they become president, they opt for grander restaurants," say the good-natured owners, the Drumonds.) The countrified decor includes a collection of farm implements and family memorabilia. The menu rarely changes and doesn't need to, with chicken Provençal, sweetbreads "in the style of our grandmother," duckling with plums, stuffed cabbage, and *blanquette de veau* (veal in white sauce).

84 quai de l'Hôtel-de-Ville, 4e. © **01-42-77-63-98.** Reservations recommended Sat–Sun. Main courses 11€–15€ ($10–$13); fixed-price menu 16€ ($14). MC, V. Daily noon–3pm and 7–11pm. Métro: Hôtel de Ville.

9TH ARRONDISSEMENT

Like its counterparts from Hong Kong to Reykjavík, the **Hard Rock Cafe,** 14 bd. Montmartre, 9e (© **01-53-24-60-00;** Métro: Grands Boulevards or Richelieu-Drouot), offers musical memorabilia as well as musical selections from 35 years of rock. The crowd appreciates the juicy steaks, hamburgers, veggie burgers, salads, and heaping platters of informal French-inspired food. It's open Monday to Thursday from noon to 1am and Friday and Saturday from noon to 2am.

EXPENSIVE

Chez Jean ✿ MODERN & TRADITIONAL FRENCH The crowd is young, the food is good, and the brassiere aura of the 1950s makes you think that expat novelist James Baldwin will arrive for his table at any minute. There has been a brasserie on this site since around 1900. Amid well-oiled pine-wood panels and polished copper, you can choose from some of grandmother's favorites as well as more modern dishes like risotto with lobster and squid ink, scallops with endive fricassee, lamb roasted with basil, filet of beef with a mushroom risotto, and pavé of duckling with honey sauce and exotic mushroom fricassee. The changing menu attracts fans who consider the food more sophisticated than that served at other brasseries (the chefs gained their experience in upscale restaurants).

8 rue St-Lazare, 9e. ☎ 01-48-78-62-73. Reservations recommended far in advance. Main courses 21€ ($19) each; fixed-price menu 31€ ($28). MC, V. Mon–Fri noon–2:30pm; daily 7–11pm. Métro: Notre-Dame de Lorette, Opéra, or Cadet.

MODERATE

Au Petit Riche LOIRE VALLEY (ANJOU) That's not Flaubert or Balzac walking through the door. But should they miraculously come back, the decor of old Paris with original gas lamps and time-mellowed paneling would make them feel right at home. When it opened in 1865, this bistro was the food outlet for the Café Riche next door; today it offers yesterday's grandeur and simple, well-prepared food. You'll be ushered to one of five areas crafted for maximum intimacy, with velour banquettes, ceilings painted with allegorical themes, and accents of brass and frosted glass. The wine list favors Loire Valley vintages that go well with such dishes as *rillettes* and *rillons* (potted fish or meat, especially pork) in Vouvray wine aspic, poached fish with buttery white-wine sauce, blanquette of chicken, and seasonal game dishes like *civet* (stew) of rabbit.

25 rue Le Peletier, 9e. ☎ 01-47-70-68-68. Reservations recommended. Main courses 14€–25€ ($13–$22); fixed-price menus 25€ ($22) at lunch, 22€–27€ ($20–$24) at dinner. AE, DC, MC, V. Mon–Sat noon–2:15pm and 7pm–midnight. Métro: Le Peletier or Richelieu-Drouot.

Wally Le Saharien ALGERIAN Head to this dining room—lined with desert photos and tribal artifacts crafted from ceramics, wood, and weavings—for an insight into the spicy, slow-cooked cuisine that fueled the colonial expansion of France into North Africa. The fixed-price dinner menu begins with a trio of starters: a spicy soup, stuffed and grilled sardines, and a savory *pastilla* of pigeon in puff pastry. This can be followed by any of several kinds of couscous or a *méchouia* (slow-cooked tart) of lamb dusted with an optional coating of sugar, according to your taste. *Merguez,* the cumin-laden spicy sausage of the North African world, factors importantly into any meal, as do homemade (usually honey-infused) pastries. End your meal with traditional mint-flavored tea.

36 rue Rodier, 9e. ☎ 01-42-85-51-90. Reservations recommended. A la carte main courses (available only at lunch) 18€–24€ ($16–$21); fixed-price dinner 40€ ($36). MC, V. Tues–Sat noon–2pm; Mon–Sat 7–10pm. Métro: Anvers.

INEXPENSIVE

Chartier TRADITIONAL FRENCH Opened in 1896, this unpretentious fin-de-siècle restaurant, long a budget favorite, is now an official monument featuring a whimsical mural with trees, a flowering staircase, and an early depiction of an airplane; it was painted in 1929 by an artist who traded his work for food. The menu follows brasserie-style traditions, including items you might not dare to eat—boiled veal's head, tripe, tongue, sweetbreads, lamb's brains, chitterling sausages—as well as some old-time tempters. The waiter will steer you through dishes like boeuf bourguignonne, pot-au-feu (combining beef, turnips, cabbage, and carrots), pavé of rump steak, and at least five kinds of fish. The prices are low, even for a three-course meal, a fact that as many as 320 diners appreciate at a time.

7 rue de Faubourg Montmartre, 9e. ℭ **01-47-70-86-29.** Main courses 6.55€–8.95€ ($5.85–$8). MC, V. Daily 11:30am–3pm and 6–10pm. Métro: Grands Boulevards or Rue Montmartre.

Le Grand Zinc TRADITIONAL FRENCH   The Paris of the 1880s lives on here. You make your way into the restaurant past baskets of *bélons* (brown-fleshed oysters) from Brittany, a year-round favorite. The specialties of the house are *coq au vin* (chicken in white wine) and old-fashioned savory staples like rack of lamb, rump steak, veal chops with morels, and even a simple form of Provençal bouillabaisse. Nothing ever changes—certainly not the time-tested recipes.

5 rue de Faubourg Montmartre, 9e. ℭ **01-47-70-88-64.** Main courses 12€–24€ ($11–$22); fixed-price menu 16€ ($14) at lunch, 19€ ($17) at dinner. AE, DC, MC, V. Mon–Sat noon–midnight. Closed Aug. Métro: Grands Boulevards.

10TH ARRONDISSEMENT
MODERATE

Brasserie Flo ⭐ ALSATIAN   This restaurant is a bit hard to find, but once you arrive (after walking through passageway after passageway), you'll see that fin-de-siècle Paris lives on. It opened in 1860 and has changed its decor very little since. The house specialty is *la formidable choucroute* (a heaping mound of sauerkraut with boiled ham, bacon, and sausage) for two. The onion soup and sole meunière are always good, as is the warm foie gras and guinea hen with lentils. Look for the plats du jour, ranging from roast pigeon to veal fricassee with sorrel.

7 cour des Petites-Ecuries, 10e. ℭ **01-47-70-13-59.** Reservations recommended. Main courses 13€–27€ ($12–$24); fixed-price menus 27€ ($24) at lunch 30€, ($27) at dinner. AE, DC, MC, V. Daily noon–3pm and 7pm–1:30am. Métro: Château d'Eau or Strasbourg-St-Denis.

La Grille *Value* TRADITIONAL FRENCH/SEAFOOD   Few other moderate restaurants are as hotly pursued by Parisians as this nine-table holdover from another age. For at least a century after the French Revolution, fishermen from Dieppe used this place as a springboard for carousing and cabaret-watching after delivering their fish to Les Halles market. The holy grail at La Grille is an entire turbot prepared tableside with an emulsified white-butter sauce. If the turbot doesn't appeal to you, consider the seafood terrine, boeuf bourguignonne, or marinated sardine filets. The high-calorie, high-satisfaction desserts include chocolate mousse and vanilla custard. (The restaurant name derives not from a grill used for cooking but from the 200-year-old wrought-iron grills in front, classified as national treasures and among the best examples of their kind in Paris.)

80 rue du Faubourg-Poissonière, 10e. ℭ **01-47-70-89-73.** Reservations required. Main courses 15€–29€ ($13–$26). AE, MC, V. Mon–Fri noon–2:30pm and 7:15–10pm. Métro: Poissonière.

INEXPENSIVE

Chez Michel BRETON   Adapting to the tastes and income of its loyal crowd, this restaurant near the Gare du Nord serves generous portions of well-prepared Breton dishes. At least part of this food derives from the northwestern origins of owner/chef Thierry Breton. In a pair of dining rooms accented with exposed wood, you'll enjoy the fruits of the fields and seacoast, densely flavored and traditional; they include veal chops fried in butter and served with gratin of potatoes enriched with calf's foot gelatin and codfish filets served on beds of tomatoes and onions and a tapenade of black olives. The appropriate conclusion to a meal is a snifter of Calvados, the apple-based brandy of the French coast.

10 rue de Belzunce, 10e. ℂ **01-44-53-06-20.** Reservations recommended. Fixed-price menu 28€ ($25); menu dégustation 53€ ($48). MC, V. Tues–Sat noon–2pm and 7pm–midnight. Métro: Gare du Nord.

Julien ⭐ MODERN & TRADITIONAL FRENCH   Julien offers an opportunity to dine in one of the most sumptuous Belle Epoque interiors in Paris. Of special interest are the murals representing the four seasons and the sometimes very fashionable crowd. The food is in the style of *cuisine bourgeoise* but without the heavy sauces. The sumptuous starter courses include eggplant caviar and wild-mushroom salad. Among the main courses are Gascony cassoulet, sliced foie gras with lentils, fresh salmon with sorrel, and chateaubriand béarnaise. The wine list is extensive and reasonably priced.

16 rue du Faubourg St-Denis, 10e. ℂ **01-47-70-12-06.** Reservations required. Main courses 15€–27€ ($13–$24); fixed-price lunch 22€ ($19); 31€ ($27) dinner. AE, DC, MC, V. Daily noon–3pm and 7pm–1:30am. Métro: Strasbourg-St-Denis.

Paris-Dakar SENEGALESE   Named after the rally that carries vehicles across the world's toughest terrain, this restaurant celebrates the culinary traditions of France's former colonies in West Africa. After a genuine welcome, you'll have the option of sampling such Senegalese dishes as *poulet yassa* (chicken braised with limes and onions); *maffé* (beef fried with peanuts, onions, and spice); and the national dish, *thiepbkoudiene* (fish sautéed with rice, fresh vegetables, and fiery chilies). A Senegalese version of the Arab-derived *méchoui* (roasted rack of lamb) is served, as is a fish (*le capitaine*) that flourishes off the coast of West Africa, with a lime-and-sweet-onion sauce. If you're adventurous, ask for a glass of the palm wine, fermented from coconuts in a style common in West Africa.

95 rue du Faubourg St-Martin, 10e. ℂ **01-42-08-16-64.** Reservations recommended. Main courses 12€–15€ ($10–$13); fixed-price menus 23€–30€ ($20–$27). AE, MC, V. Tues–Thurs and Sat–Sun noon–3pm; Tues–Sun 7pm–1am. Métro: Gare de l'Est.

11TH ARRONDISSEMENT
EXPENSIVE

Blue Elephant THAI   At this Paris branch of an international chain of stylish Thai restaurants, the decor artfully evokes the jungles of Southeast Asia, interspersed with Thai sculptures and paintings. The menu items are succulent, infused with lemongrass, curries, and the aromas that make Thai cuisine so distinctive. Examples are a salad made with *pomelo*, a Thai fruit that's larger and tarter than a grapefruit, studded with shrimp and herbs; salmon soufflé served in banana leaves; chicken in green-curry sauce; and grilled fish with passion fruit.

43 rue de la Roquette, 11e. ℂ **01-47-00-42-00.** Reservations recommended far in advance. Main courses 11€–20€ ($10–$18); fixed-price lunch 18€–25€ ($16–$22); fixed-price dinner 38€–43€ ($34–$39). AE, DC, MC, V. Sun–Fri noon–2:30pm; Mon–Sat 7pm–midnight; Sun 7–11pm. Métro: Bastille.

MODERATE

A Sousceyrac TRADITIONAL FRENCH   The name derives from a village in the Lotte region of southwestern France that has always been associated with rich cuisine, traditional values, and literature. (*Le Déjeuner de Sousceyrac* by Père Benoît was a best-selling ode to French nostalgia in the 1970s.) You can capture some of this feeling at this charmer whose decor and menu have changed little since 1925. A writer from *Gourmet* magazine noted, "A Sousceyrac was undoubtedly intended to induce deep nostalgia in Parisians the day it opened;

its southwestern-inflected menu practically reads like a roster of what French-men like to call *'The Patrimony'.* " Classic examples include slices of velvety foie gras; mousse of grouse; and roasted rabbit *à la royale,* cooked in a blend of red wine, a puréed medley of its innards, and its own blood. Dishes like this absolutely demand accompaniment by a strong red wine, of which the restaurant lists many.

26 rue Faidherbe, 11e. (C) 01-43-71-65-30. Reservations recommended. Main courses 20€–29€ ($18–$26). Fixed-price menu 30€ ($26). DC, MC, V. Mon–Fri noon–2pm; Mon–Sat 7:30–9:45pm. Closed 1 week in Mar and all of Aug. Métro: Charonnes or Faidherbe.

Astier (*Finds* TRADITIONAL FRENCH Nobody could accuse this place of being glamorous, understanding that well-prepared hearty food has its own allure. The mandatory set menu is a good value, with at least 10 choices for each of four courses. For some real down-home cookery—French style—order the roasted rabbit with mustard sauce, *rascasse* (scorpionfish) with fresh spinach, or duckling breast with foie gras cream sauce. There's also a superbly varied cheese platter and desserts like crème caramel and chocolate mousse.

44 rue Jean-Pierre-Timbaud, 11e. (C) 01-43-57-16-35. Reservations recommended. Fixed-price menus 20€–24€ ($18–$21) at lunch, 24€ ($21) at dinner. MC, V. Mon–Fri noon–2pm and 8–11pm. Métro: Oberkampf or Parmentier.

INEXPENSIVE

Le Manguier SENEGALESE Many of the patrons who dine here don't know much about Senegalese cuisine, but thanks to a charming welcome and live music presenting African jazz at its most compelling, they tend to come back. The decor evokes a West African fishing village. You can order zesty fare like roast chicken marinated with lime and served with onions, smoked shark meat, and the national dish, *thiebkoudiene* (a delectable blend of fish, rice, and fresh vegetables). The medley is perked up with a selection of fiery sauces you apply yourself. The drinks of choice are beer, a rum-based cocktail (*Le Dakar*), and wine.

67 av. Parmentier, 11e. (C) 01-48-07-03-27. Reservations recommended. Main courses 11€–14€ ($10–$12). AE, MC, V. Mon–Sat noon–3pm and 7pm–2am. Métro: Parmentier.

Mansouria MOROCCAN One of Paris's most charming Moroccan restaurants occupies a much-restored building midway between place de la Bastille and place de la Nation. The minimalist decor combines futuristic architecture with bare white walls accented only with sets of antique doors and portals from the sub-Sahara. The menu items are artfully prepared. Look for six kinds of couscous, including versions with chicken, beef brochettes, or lamb, onions, and almonds. *Tagines* are succulent dishes of chicken or fish prepared with aromatic herbs and slow cooked in clay pots that are carried to your table.

11 rue Faidherbe, 11e. (C) 01-43-71-00-16. Reservations recommended. Main courses 17€–23€ ($15–$21); fixed-price menus 29€–43€ ($26–$39). AE, MC, V. Wed–Sat noon–2pm; Tues–Sat 7:30–11pm. Métro: Faidherbe-Chaligny.

12TH ARRONDISSEMENT
EXPENSIVE

Au Trou Gascon (★★★ GASCONY One of Paris's most acclaimed chefs, Alain Dutournier lures some of the most fashionable palates of Paris to this unchic location in the 12th arrondissement. He launched his cooking career in southwest France's Gascony region. His parents mortgaged their own inn to allow him to open this early-1900s bistro. At first he got little business, but word eventually spread of a savant in the kitchen who practiced authentic *cuisine* *moderne.* His wife, Nicole, is the welcoming hostess, and the wine steward has distinguished himself for his exciting cave containing several little-known wines along with a fabulous collection of Armagnacs. It's estimated the wine cellar has some 800 varieties. Start with fresh duck foie gras cooked in a terrine or Gascony cured ham cut from the bone. The best main courses include fresh tuna with braised cabbage, a superb cassoulet, and chicken from the Chalosse region of Landes, which Dutournier roasts and serves in its own drippings.

40 rue Taine, 12e. ℂ 01-43-44-34-26. Reservations required far in advance. Main courses 24€–30€ ($21–$27); fixed-price lunch 36€ ($32). AE, DC, MC, V. Mon–Fri noon–2pm; Mon–Sat 7:30–10pm. Closed Aug. Métro: Daumesnil.

MODERATE

China Club ✿ CANTONESE/CHINESE   Evoking 1930s Hong Kong, this favorite is still going strong, still laughing at upstart new Asian restaurants, and still serving some of the best Asian cuisine in Paris. The food is mainly Cantonese, prepared with flair and taste. Before dinner you might want to enjoy a drink in the upstairs smoking lounge. Nearly everything is good, especially the sautéed shrimp and calamari, Shanghai chicken, and red rice sautéed with vegetables. The vast menu offers plenty of choices. Downstairs, the Sing Song club has live music, including something called Sino-French jazz, but only on Friday and Saturday.

50 rue de Charenton, 12e. ℂ 01-43-43-82-02. Main courses 11€–29€ ($10–$26); fixed-price dinner 24€ ($22); fixed-price Sun dinner 19€ ($17). AE, MC, V. Sun–Thurs 7pm–2am; Fri–Sat 7pm–3am. Closed Aug. Métro: Bastille or Ledru-Rollin.

Le Train Bleu ✿✿ TRADITIONAL FRENCH   To reach this restaurant, climb the ornate double staircase facing the Gare de Lyon's grimy platforms. The restaurant and station were built along with the Grand Palais, Petit Palais, and pont Alexandre III for the 1900 World Exhibition. Inaugurated by the French president in 1901 and renovated and cleaned at great expense in 1992, Le Train Bleu boasts a decor classified as a national artistic treasure, with a lavishly frescoed ceiling, bronze statues, mosaics, mirrors, banquettes, and 41 Belle Epoque murals (each celebrating the distant corners of the French-speaking world, which join Paris via its rail network). The formally dressed staff is fast and efficient, in case you're about to catch a train. You can choose from well-prepared soufflé of brill, escargots in Chablis sauce, steak tartare, loin of lamb Provençal, veal kidneys in mustard sauce, rib of beef for two, and rum cake with raisins. We have to be honest—this standard brasserie fare doesn't match the decor, but we always like to go here anyway for the setting alone. And the food's not that bad.

In the Gare de Lyon, 12e. ℂ 01-43-43-09-06. Reservations recommended. Main courses 23€–33€ ($20–$30); fixed-price menu 40€ ($35), including wine. AE, DC, MC, V. Daily 11:30am–3pm and 7–11pm. Métro: Gare de Lyon.

INEXPENSIVE

L'Ebauchoir ✿ *Finds* TRADITIONAL FRENCH   Tucked into a neighborhood rarely visited by foreigners and featuring a 1950s decor that has become fashionable again, this bistro attracts carpenters, plumbers, and electricians, as well as an occasional journalist and screenwriter. With buffed aluminum trim and plaster-and-stucco walls tinted dark orange-yellow and blue, the place might remind you of a factory canteen. You can order surprisingly generous and well-prepared stuffed sardines, snapper filet with olive oil and garlic, crabmeat soup, fried calf's liver with coriander and honey, and rack of lamb combined with saddle of lamb.

43 rue de Cîteaux, 12e. ✆ **01-43-42-49-31.** Reservations recommended for dinner. Main courses 11€–18€ ($10–$16); fixed-price lunch 11€–17€ ($10–$15). MC, V. Mon–Sat noon–2:30pm and 8–10:30pm. Métro: Faidherbe-Chaligny.

Le Square Trousseau TRADITIONAL FRENCH   This is a well-recommended bistro, with traditional food and a setting that evokes the best of turn-of-the-20th-century France. Within a circa-1905 decor accented with etched glass, tiles, and banquettes, you'll be presented with dishes that include pot-au-feu, sole meunière, sweetbreads, calf's liver, and steak au poivre. A habitué told us that she comes here for "comfort food," including the terrines and tarts her mother used to prepare for her. But she notes many delicious innovations in the menu, which she calls "winds of change." Among these are some delicious risottos.

1 rue Antoine-Vollon, 12e. ✆ **01-43-43-06-00.** Reservations recommended. Main courses 15€–23€ ($14–$20); fixed-price lunch 20€–24€ ($18–$22). AE, MC, V. Tues–Sat noon–2:30pm and 8–11:30pm. Métro: Ledru-Rollin.

18TH ARRONDISSEMENT
INEXPENSIVE

Le Grain de Folie ORGANIC/VEGETARIAN   Simple and wholesome, the cuisine at this vegetarian restaurant is inspired by France, Greece, California, Turkey, and India. The menu includes an array of theme salads, cereals, tarts, terrines, and casseroles. Dessert selections might include an old-fashioned tart or a fruit salad. The decor includes potted plants and exposed stone. You can choose one of an array of wines or a frothy glass of vegetable juice to accompany your meal. This place may be a bit difficult to find, but it's worth the search.

24 rue de la Vieuville, 18e. ✆ **01-42-58-15-57.** Reservations recommended. Main courses 7.60€–11€ ($6.75–$10); fixed-price menu 8.35€–15€ ($7.45–$13). No credit cards. Mon–Sat noon–2:30pm and 7:30–11pm; Sun 11:30am–11pm. Métro: Abbesses.

8TH ARRONDISSEMENT
VERY EXPENSIVE

Lasserre ✿✿✿ ★★★ MODERN & TRADITIONAL FRENCH   This elegant restaurant was a bistro before World War II and has since become a legend attracting world gourmets. The main salon stretches two stories high, with a mezzanine on each side. Tall silk-draped arched windows frame tables set with fine porcelain, gold-edged crystal glasses, and silver candelabras. The ceiling is painted with white clouds and a cerulean sky, but in good weather the staff slides back the roof to reveal the real sky. The food is a mix of Classicism and originality; count on high drama in the presentation. The appetizers are among Paris's finest, including truffle salad, three-meat terrine, and Chablis-flavored Belon oysters. The signature main course is poached sole filets *Club de la Casserole*, in puff pastry with asparagus tips and asparagus-flavored cream sauce; also wonderful are the veal kidneys flambé and pigeon André Malraux. Among the desserts are soufflé Grand Marnier and three fresh sorbets of the season. The wine cellar, with some 160,000 bottles, is among the city's most remarkable.

17 av. Franklin-D-Roosevelt, 8e. ✆ **01-43-59-53-43.** Fax 01-45-63-72-23. Reservations required far in advance. Main courses 27€–44€ ($24–$39); fixed-price menu 52€ ($46) at lunch, 122€ ($109) at dinner. AE, MC, V. Tues–Sat 12:15–2pm and 7:30–10:30pm. Closed Aug. Métro: F. D. Roosevelt.

L'Astor ✿✿✿ MODERN FRENCH   What happens to a great French chef when he retires? If he's lucky and respected enough, he takes on the title of "culinary consultant" and attaches himself to a restaurant where he can drop in several times a week to keep an eye on things. That's what happened when guru Joël Robuchon retired from his avenue Raymond-Poincaré citadel for a quieter life (his replacement was Alain Ducasse). The chef here is respected Eric Lecerf, who knows better than anyone else how to match his master's tours de force. The setting is a tawny-colored enclave beneath an etched-glass Art Deco ceiling, with luxurious touches inspired by the 1930s. Expect an almost religious devotion to Robuchon's specialties and less emphasis on newer dishes created by Lecerf. Examples of "classic Robuchon" are caramelized sea urchins in aspic with fennel-flavored cream sauce, eggplant-stuffed cannelloni with tuna filets and olive oil, and spit-roasted Bresse chicken with flap mushrooms. Items created by Lecerf include carpaccio of Breton lobster with olive oil and tomato confit, creamy cannelloni with eggplant, roasted and braised rack of lamb, and pigeon supreme with cabbage and foie gras. *Lievre la royale du Senateur Couteaux* is wild hare cooked in a mixture of red wine and its own blood, named for a famed 19th-century gastronome, Senator Couteaux. This is a classic in the Escoffier tradition.

In the Hôtel Astor, 11 rue d'Astorg, 8e. ⓒ **01-53-05-05-20.** Fax 01-53-05-05-30. Reservations required far in advance. Main courses 25€–49€ ($22–$44); fixed-price menus 49€ ($44) at lunch, 99€ ($88) at dinner. AE, DC, MC, V. Mon–Fri noon–2pm and 7:30–10pm. Closed Aug. Métro: St-Augustin or Madeleine.

Les Elysées du Vernet ★★★ PROVENÇAL   This darling of *tout Paris* is fast-rising as a gastronomic wonder. Capping the restaurant is one of the neighborhood's most panoramic glass ceilings, a gray and green translucent dome designed by Gustav Eiffel. That, plus the fact that the Montpellier-born chef, Alain Solivérès, has two Michelin stars, keeps the crowds lined up. Menu items are focused on Provençal models, and change every 2 months, based on whatever is fresh at the season of your arrival. During our midwinter visit, award-winning examples included scallops with truffles, *tournedos Rossini* (a slab of beef layered with foie gras), and a *cocotte* (small stew-pot) of lobster. There's also a melt-in-your-mouth version of apple charlotte, and even a newfangled take on black-truffle ice cream, a dish that traditionalists consider somewhat far-fetched. Candles help illuminate the place at night, and during the dinner hour there's a pianist.

In the Hotel Vernet, 25 rue Vernet, 8e. ⓒ **01-44-31-98-98.** Reservations required. Main courses 43€–56€ ($38–$50). Set lunch 52€–64€ ($46–$57); menu gastronomique 149€ ($133). AE, DC, MC, V. Mon–Fri 12:30–1:30pm and 7:30–9:30pm. Métro: George V.

Pierre Gagnaire ★★★ MODERN FRENCH   Though the PR here may be the worst in Paris, if you're able to make a reservation, it's worth the effort. The menus are seasonally adjusted to take advantage of France's rich bounty; Pierre Gagnaire, the famous owner, demands perfection, and the chef has a dazzling way of blending flavors and textures. One critic wrote, "Picasso stretched the limits of painting; Gagnaire does it with cooking." Try anything from a menu that changes every 2 months: Stellar examples are freshwater crayfish cooked tempura-style with thin-sliced flash-seared vegetables and sweet-and-sour sauce as well as turbot cooked in a bag and served with fennel and Provençal lemons. Chicken with truffles is part of a two-tiered service—first the breast in a wine-based aspic, second the thighs chopped into roughly textured pieces. For dessert, try the chocolate soufflé served with a frozen parfait and Sicilian pistachios.

6 rue Balzac, 8e. ⓒ **01-58-36-12-50.** Fax 01-58-36-12-51. Reservations are imperative and difficult to make. Main courses 53€–91€ ($48–$81); fixed-price menus 79€–99€ ($71–$88) at lunch, 190€ ($170) at dinner. AE, DC, MC, V. Mon–Fri noon–1:30pm and 7–10pm. Métro: George V.

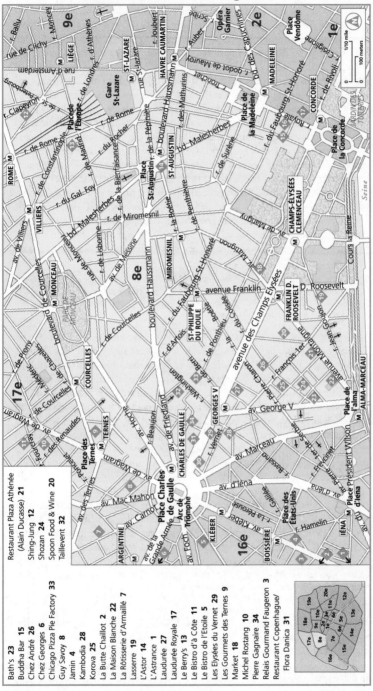

Bath's **23**
Buddha Bar **15**
Chez André **26**
Chez Georges **6**
Chicago Pizza Pie Factory **33**
Guy Savoy **8**
Jamin **4**
Kambodia **28**
Korova **25**
La Butte Chaillot **2**
La Maison Blanche **22**
La Rôtisserie d'Armaillé **7**
Lasserre **19**
L'Astor **14**
L'Astrance **1**
Ladurée **27**
Ladurée Royale **17**
Le Berry's **13**
Le Bistro d'à Côte **11**
Le Bistro de l'Etoile **5**
Les Elysées du Vernet **29**
Les Gourmets des Ternes **9**
Market **18**
Michel Rostang **10**
Pierre Gagnaire **34**
Relais Gourmand Faugeron **3**
Restaurant Copenhague/
Flora Danica **31**

Restaurant Plaza Athénée
(Alain Ducasse) **21**
Shing-Jung **12**
Shozan **24**
Spoon Food & Wine **20**
Taillevent **32**

Restaurant Plaza Athénée (Alain Ducasse) ★★★ MODERN & TRADI-
TIONAL FRENCH   Few other chefs in the history of French cuisine have
been catapulted to international fame as quickly as Alain Ducasse. The most
recent setting for his world-renowned cuisine is a world-renowned hotel, the
Plaza Athénée. There's a lot of marketing and glitter associated with this new
marriage de convenience, but what you'll find is a lobby-level hideaway that top-
notch decorator Patrick Jouin transformed with layers of pearl-gray paint and
many yards of translucent organdy. By anyone's standards, the cuisine is spectacular. This five-star Michelin chef seeds his dishes with produce from every
corner of France—rare local vegetables, fish from the coasts, and dishes incorporating cardoons, turnips, celery, turbot, cuttlefish, and Bresse fowl. His
French cuisine is contemporary and Mediterranean yet not new. Though many
dishes are light, Ducasse isn't afraid of lard, as he proves by his thick, oozing slabs
of pork grilled to a crisp. Among the dishes we've sampled and heartily recommend are line-caught filets of sole prepared in the style of a Viennese schnitzel;
crayfish with a thick, caviar-enhanced cream sauce; and duck wrapped in fig
leaves and seasoned with aged vinegar. The wine list is superb, with some selections deriving from the best vintages of France, Germany, Switzerland, Spain,
California, and Italy.

In the Hotel Plaza Athénée, 25 av. Montaigne, 8e. ✆ **01-53-67-65-00.** Fax 01-53-67-65-12. Reservations
required 6 weeks in advance. Main courses 67€–90€ ($60–$80); fixed-price menus 189€–249€
($168–$223). AE, DC, MC, V. Thurs–Fri noon–2pm; Mon–Fri 8–10:30pm. Closed mid-July to mid-Aug and Dec
21–31. Métro: F.D. Roosevelt or Alma-Marceau.

Taillevent ★★★ MODERN & TRADITIONAL FRENCH   This is the
Parisian *ne plus ultra* of gastronomy. Taillevent opened in 1946 and has climbed
steadily in excellence until today it ranks as Paris's most outstanding all-around
restaurant, challenged only by Lucas-Carton and Pierre Gagnaire. The restaurant,
named after 14th-century chef Guillaume Tirel Taillevent, who wrote one of the
oldest known books on French cookery, is in a grand 19th-century town house
off the Champs-Elysées, with paneled rooms and crystal chandeliers. The place is
small, as the owner wishes, so he can give personal attention to every facet of the
operation and maintain a discreet club atmosphere. You might begin with a
boudin (sausage) of Breton lobster à la Nage, cream of watercress soup with
Sevruga caviar, or duck liver with spice bread and ginger. Main courses include
red snapper with black olives, Scottish salmon cooked in sea salt with a sauce of
olive oil and lemons, and cassolette of crayfish from Brittany. Dessert might be a
nougatine glacé with pears. The wine list is among the best in Paris. Though
owner M. Vrinat likes Americans, it isn't always easy for visitors from the States
to book a table, because he prefers about 60 percent of his guests to be French.

15 rue Lamennais, 8e. ✆ **01-44-95-15-01.** Fax 01-42-25-95-18. Reservations required 4 to 6 weeks in
advance. Main courses 40€–94€ ($35–$84); menu dégustation 129€ ($115). AE, DC, MC, V. Mon–Fri
noon–2:30pm and 7–10pm. Closed Aug. Métro: George V.

EXPENSIVE

Bath's AUVERGNAT/TRADITIONAL FRENCH   The rocky and agrarian
region of central France known as L'Auvergne has never been considered particularly chic. This restaurant, however, more than any other Auvergnat restaurant
in Paris, manages to transform the region's provincial image into something
that's cozy but elegant. The setting is a well-upholstered, ocher-colored dining
room where menu items are equally divided between the pork-based culinary
specialties of the Auvergne and lighter dishes from the rest of France. The finest

examples include ravioli stuffed with a pungent Cantal cheese from the Auvergne; cream of lentil soup studded with foie gras "bonbons"; filet of beef from Salers (a part of the Auvergne) served with lentils; roasted veal served with morel-studded macaroni; and something that's absolutely not native to the Auvergne, a *cassoulet* (stewpot) of lobster. Jean-Yves Bath, the owner and chef, earned a Michelin star just a few months after the place opened in 1999.

9 rue de la Trémoille, 8e. © 01-40-70-01-09. Reservations required. Main courses 18€–33€ ($16–$30); set-price lunch 129€ ($26); set-price dinner 68€ ($61). AE, DC, MC, V. Mon–Fri noon–2:30pm and 7:30–10:30pm. Métro: Alma-Marceau.

Buddha Bar 👁👁 MODERN FRENCH/PACIFIC RIM   This place still remains Paris's "restaurant of the moment," even though it has been around a while. A location on a chic street near the Champs-Elysées and place de la Concorde and an allegiance to a fusion of French, Asian, and Californian cuisines guarantees trendy diners devoted to the whims of fashion. The vast dining room is presided over by a giant Buddha, and the cutting-edge culinary theme combines Japanese sashimi, Vietnamese spring rolls, lacquered duck, sautéed shrimp with black-bean sauce, grilled chicken skewers with orange sauce, sweet-and-sour spareribs, and crackling squab à l'orange. There are two sittings for dinner: 7 to 9pm and 10:30pm to 12:30am. Many come here just for a drink in the carefully lacquered and very hip bar, located upstairs from the street-level dining room.

8 rue Boissy d'Anglas, 8e. © 01-53-05-90-00. Reservations required far in advance. Main courses 18€–40€ ($16–$35). AE, MC, V. Mon–Fri noon–3pm; daily 7pm–12:30am. Métro: Concorde.

La Maison Blanche 👁 PROVENÇAL   Its setting is mostly white in contrast to the lush views of Paris that sweep out from its oversized windows. To reach it, you'll take one of two express elevators from the lobby of the Art Deco Théâtre des Champs-Elysées to the restaurant. It was established in 1990, but until its recent acquisition by twin brothers Jacques and Laurent Pourcel and their associate Olivier Château, it never carried much distinction. That is definitely not the case now, as the place is jammed at virtually every meal with stylish residents of the megaexpensive neighborhood that contains it. Menu items change with the seasons, but they're likely to include ravioli stuffed with black truffles and foie gras; deviled sea urchins whose flavors are enhanced with crabmeat and caviar; strips of grilled red mullet served with a shallot-based *tarte Tatin;* and lentil gazpacho flavored with peppermint. Main courses include pigeon roasted with cinnamon, suckling veal with orange-braised endives, and a wild duckling pie laced with foie gras. An absolutely fabulous dessert might include pears roasted with vanilla and served with vanilla-flavored cream.

On the 7th floor of the Théâtre des Champs-Elysées, 15 av. Montaigne, 8e. © 01-47-23-55-99. Reservations required 1 week in advance for lunch, 3 weeks for dinner. Main courses 27€–38€ ($24–$34); AE, DC, MC, V. Mon–Fri noon–2pm; daily 8–11pm. Métro: Alma-Marceau.

Market 👁 FUSION   One of the city's newest restaurants incorporates a sophisticated internationalism that has succeeded among jaded Paris gastronomes. The creative force derives from Alsatian Jean-Georges Vongerichten, whose restaurants in New York, Hong Kong, London, and Las Vegas are classified by local critics as both megahip and top tier. The newest gemstone in the Vongerichten empire holds 140 diners in a postmodern decor that's dotted with art objects on loan from the Paris branch of Christie's auction house. Menu items might remind you of the fare that might be popular in a superhip Los Angeles restaurant loaded with Hollywood types. Examples include a pizza with black truffles and fontina cheese; foie gras with a purée of quince, corn pancakes, and wild cranberries; or crabmeat salad with mango. Main courses might feature *daurade* (bream or porgy) baked in a salt crust; a faux-filet with exotic mushrooms; or a "black plate" for two diners, loaded high with shellfish and their garnishes. There's a lavish assortment of oysters, clams, and shellfish; and a wine list that most oenophiles consider extremely interesting in its own right.

15 av. Matignon, 8e. ℰ **01-56-43-40-90.** Reservations required. Set-price lunch 39€ ($35); pizzas 11€–17€ ($10–$15); main courses 23€–37€ ($20–$33). AE, MC, V. Daily noon–3pm and 7–11:30pm. Métro: Champs-Elysées–Clémenceau.

Restaurant Copenhague/Flora Danica ℱ DANISH   Danish specialties are served with flair at the "Maison du Danemark," in many ways the best restaurant on the Champs-Elysées, with an outdoor terrace for midsummer dining. There are two dining areas: the street-level Flora Danica and the somewhat more formal Restaurant Copenhague upstairs. To be thoroughly Danish, order an aperitif of aquavit and ignore the wine list in favor of Carlsberg. Menu items include reindeer terrine, foie gras, smoked salmon, fresh shrimp, and elegant open-faced sandwiches. The house specialty is a platter of Scandinavian delicacies drawn from the many seafood and dairy specialties the Danes prepare exceptionally well. Our preferred dish is grilled Norwegian salmon cooked on one side only.

142 av. des Champs-Elysées, 8e. ℰ **01-44-13-86-26.** Reservations recommended far in advance. Main courses in Copenhague 29€–44€ ($26–$39); fixed-price menu 44€ ($39). Main courses in Flora Danica 14€–30€ ($13–$27); fixed-price menu 29€ ($26). AE, DC, MC, V. Mon–Fri noon–2:30pm; Mon–Sat 7:15–11pm. Restaurant Copenhague closed Aug and Jan 1–7. Métro: George V.

Shozan ℱ MODERN FRENCH/JAPANESE   East and West form a perfect synthesis in this Franco-Japanese alliance. It's not for the traditionalist, but trendy young Paris enjoys the new flavors. For example, the classic foie gras appears as foie gras sushi with sansho pepper, and the roast lamb comes with a green-tea crust. The roast tuna with buckwheat seed and the scampi concoction are delectable. A chef's specialty is lobster with white-sesame sauce spiked with sweet sake. Famous interior designer Christian Liaigre created the stunning setting, dominated by wood and leather; you sit at wooden tables without cloths.

11 rue de la Trémoille, 8e. ℰ **01-47-23-37-32.** Reservations recommended far in advance. Main courses 25€–33€ ($22–$30); fixed-price menu 25€–30€ ($23–$27) at lunch, 60€ ($54) at dinner. AE, DC, MC, V. Mon–Fri noon–2:30pm and 7–10:30pm. Closed 3 weeks in Aug. Métro: Alma-Marceau.

Spoon, Food & Wine ℱ INTERNATIONAL   This modern venture of *wunderkind* chef Alain Ducasse is hailed as a "restaurant for the millennium" and condemned by some food critics as surreal and a bit absurd. Despite that, there can be a wait of 2 weeks for a dinner reservation, and the sense that this upscale but relatively affordable restaurant might be the least pretentious and most hip manifestation of any of Ducasse's ventures. The somewhat claustrophobic dining room evokes a stylish blend of Parisian and Californian references, and the cuisine—the menu changes every 2 months—roams the world for inspiration. Examples include roasted spareribs, grilled tuna steak with satay sauce, deliberately undercooked grilled squid (part of it will evoke a sushi dish) served with curry sauce, roasted pigeon with an Italian *dolce-forte* (sweet-and-sour) sauce, and grilled beefsteak with a tomato-flavored béarnaise. Vegetarians appreciate stir-fried dishes wherein you can mix and match up to 15 separate ingredients, including iceberg lettuce. Pastas come with a selection of three sauces, including a three-tomato marmalade. Desserts feature Parisian versions of such U.S.-inspired dishes as cheesecake and doughnuts drenched with bitter chocolate.

In the Hôtel Marignan-Elysée, 14 rue Marignan, 8e. ✆ 01-40-76-34-44. Reservations recommended 2 weeks in advance. Main courses with vegetable side dishes 23€–38€ ($20–$34). AE, DC, V. Mon–Fri noon–2pm and 7–11pm. Métro: F. D. Roosevelt.

MODERATE

Chez André TRADITIONAL FRENCH   Chez André is one of the neighborhood's favorite bistros with an ambience that evokes France of the 1950s with a clientele that mingles everyday folk with some of the most prosperous residents of this extremely upscale neighborhood. Outside, a discreet red awning stretches over an array of shellfish on ice; inside, an Art Nouveau decor includes etched glass and masses of flowers. This has been a landmark on rue Marbeuf since 3 years before the invasion of France in 1940. It remains the same as it was when it was founded (an agreement was made with the original owners). The old-style cuisine on the menu includes paté of thrush, Roquefort in puff pastry, grilled veal kidneys, roast rack of lamb, several kinds of omelets, calves' head vinaigrette, a potage du jour, fresh shellfish, and on Fridays, bouillabaisse. There are several reasonably priced wines offered as well. For variety, some locals opt for the plat du jour. The dessert choices may be rum baba, chocolate cake, or a daily pastry.

12 rue Marbeuf (at rue Clément-Marot), 8e. ✆ 01-47-20-59-57. Reservations recommended. Main courses 14€–23€ ($12–$21); fixed-price menu 27€ ($24). AE, DC, MC, V. Daily noon–1am. Métro: F. D. Roosevelt.

Korova ★ *Finds* INTERNATIONAL   Stylish, hip, and comfortable, this place offers a postmodern decor and a staff that creates the illusion that you've just stepped into a private club. You'll be ushered into one of four different "areas," each designed by architect Christian Biecher, and each small enough for a sense of intimacy. If the amphetamines or diet pills you swallowed earlier in the evening are beginning to make you jittery, consider the "chill-out room," wherein low seating, dim lights, and a Zen-inspired simplicity will calm you down to the point where you'll actually be able to eat. Menu items are flavorful and comforting, and in some cases, controversial—in keeping with co-owner Fréderick Grasser Hermé's reputation as an author of shocking (by French standards) cookbooks. Examples include chicken cooked with Coca-Cola, and top-of-the-line sardines served directly from the can, accompanied with fresh bread and creamy butter. Other choices include a tempura of king crab, fondue of Camembert with roasted potatoes, tuna *à la plancha* (grilled) with matchstick potatoes, and risotto with scallops. Dessert might include macaroons with rosewater and fresh raspberries.

33 rue Marbeuf, 8e. ✆ 01-53-89-93-93. Reservations recommended. Main courses 16€–30€ ($14–$26). AE, DC, MC, V. Mon–Fri noon–3pm; daily 7:30pm–midnight. Métro: F. D. Roosevelt.

Ladurée TRADITIONAL FRENCH   Ladurée, acclaimed since 1862 as one of Paris's grand cafes (located near La Madeleine), is now installed on the Champs-Elysées, adding a touch of class to this neighborhood of fast-food places. This offshoot expanded in 1999 and caters to an international set wearing everything from Givenchy to Gap. Expect a stylish, somewhat chaotic venue that changes from tearoom to full-fledged restaurant at least twice during the course of any day. The Belle Epoque setting is ideal for sampling Ladurée's celebrated macaroons—not the sticky coconut version familiar to Americans, but two almond meringue cookies, flavored with vanilla, coffee, strawberry, pistachio, or other flavor, stuck together with butter cream. The menu of talented chefs is constantly adjusted to take advantage of the freshest daily ingredients and may include a crisp and tender pork filet with potato-and-parsley purée and marinated red mullet filets on a salad of cold ratatouille. If you're looking for a midafternoon pick-me-up to accompany your tea and macaroons, consider a *plaisir sucré*, a chocolate confection artfully decorated with spun sugar. The service isn't always efficient.

75 av. des Champs-Elysées, 8e. ✆ **01-40-75-08-75.** Reservations required for the restaurant, not for the cafe. Main courses 24€–40€ ($22–$36); pastries from 5.30€ ($4.70). AE, DC, MC, V. Daily 7:30am–12:30am. Métro: Madeleine.

INEXPENSIVE

Le Berry's TRADITIONAL FRENCH   This inexpensive bistro, with a setting celebrating rugby, complements one of the area's grandest restaurants, Le Grenadin. Its platters emerge from the same kitchen and are infused with the same kind of zeal as those presented next door for three times the price. Don't expect cutting-edge fare, but look for honest dishes from France's agrarian heartland and a lack of pretension. The dishes listed on a chalkboard include fricassee of chicken with olives and mashed potatoes, thin-sliced smoked ham from Sancerre, veal filet with red-wine sauce, raw pike with cabbage, and a traditional pear tart.

46 rue de Naples, 8e. ✆ **01-40-75-01-56.** Reservations recommended. Main courses 8.50€–14€ ($7.55–$13); fixed-price menu 17€ ($15). MC, V. Mon–Fri noon–2:30pm; Tues–Sat 7pm–1am. Métro: Villiers.

Les Gourmets des Ternes *(Value)* TRADITIONAL FRENCH   Les Gourmets des Ternes caters to hordes who appreciate its affordable prices and lack of pretension. Despite the brusque service, diners have included the mayor of Atlanta, who wrote the bistro a thank-you letter, as well as hundreds of folks from this neighborhood. Thriving in this spot since 1892, the place retains an early-1900s paneled decor, with some additions from the 1950s, including Bordeaux-colored banquettes, mirrors, wooden panels, touches of brass, and paper tablecloths. During clement weather, there's an outdoor terrace as well. The finely grilled signature dishes include rib steak with marrow sauce and fries; country patés and sausages; sole, turbot, and monkfish; and satisfying desserts like peach Melba and *baba au Rhum* (rum cake with raisins).

87 bd. de Courcelles, 8e. ✆ **01-42-27-43-04.** Main courses 12€–20€ ($11–$18). AE, MC, V. Mon–Fri noon–2:30pm and 7–10pm. Métro: Ternes.

Shing-Jung KOREAN   Among the 30 or so Korean restaurants in Paris, Shing-Jung is the best known for low prices. Its sashimi is comparable to Japanese versions, though the portions of the fresh tuna, salmon, or daurade tend to be more generous. A specialty is the Korean barbecue called *bulgoogi,* which seems more authentic thanks to a clever decor juxtaposing Korean chests and paintings.

7 rue Clapeyron, 8e. ✆ **01-45-22-21-06.** Reservations recommended for dinner. Main courses 13€–17€ ($12–$15); fixed-price menus 11€–12€ ($10–$11) at lunch, 17€–32€ ($15–$29) at dinner. MC, V. Mon–Fri noon–2:30pm; daily 7–10:30pm. Métro: Rome.

16TH ARRONDISSEMENT
VERY EXPENSIVE

Jamin ✦✦✦ TRADITIONAL FRENCH   This is where Paris's great chef of the 1980s, Joël Robuchon, made his sensational mark. Now in charge is Robuchon's longtime second in command, Benoit Guichard, clearly inspired by his master but an imaginative chef in his own right. Guichard has chosen pale-green panels and pink banquettes (referred to as "Italo–New Yorkaise") for a backdrop to his brief but well-chosen menu. Lunches can be simple, though each dish, like a beautifully seasoned salmon tartare, is done to perfection. Classic technique and an homage to tradition characterize the cuisine—John Dory with celery and fresh ginger; pigeon sausage with foie gras, pistachios, and mâche lettuce; and beef shoulder so tender it had obviously been braising for hours. A particularly earthy dish celebrates various parts of the sow, blending the tail and cheeks on a platter with walnuts and fresh herbs. Finish with a *tarte tatin*.

32 rue de Longchamp, 16e. ℂ **01-45-53-00-07.** Fax 01-45-53-00-15. Reservations required far in advance. Main courses 35€–50€ ($31–$45); fixed-price menus 47€–75€ ($42–$67) at lunch, 79€ ($70) at dinner. AE, DC, MC, V. Mon–Fri 12:30–2pm and 7:45–10pm. Métro: Trocadéro.

Relais Gourmand Faugeron ★★★ TRADITIONAL FRENCH   Henri Faugeron is an inspired chef who opened this restaurant many years ago as an elegant yet unobtrusive backdrop for his superb cuisine, which he calls "revolutionary." The interior of this early-1900s building glitters with discreet touches of gilt and has a sun motif emblazoned on the ceiling. The food, which is inspired by the Corrèze region of France, outshines its surroundings. Much of the zesty cuisine depends on the season and market, because Faugeron chooses only the freshest ingredients. In winter your taste for truffles can be indulged by one of the many dishes expertly prepared, like the *brunoise* (shredded vegetable mixture, cooked slowly in butter) of truffles with asparagus and olive oil, and ravioli stuffed with truffles and foie gras. Roasted leg of milk-fed veal and lamb and crispy-skinned quail are also great choices. If you want something esoteric, consider the *vol-au-vent* (puff pastry shell with lid) of lobster, sweetbreads, and morels.

52 rue de Longchamp, 16e. ℂ **01-47-04-24-53.** Fax 01-55-73-11-27. Reservations required far in advance. Main courses 38€–61€ ($34–$54); fixed-price menus 53€–134€ ($47–$119) at lunch, 99€–137€ ($88–$122) at dinner. AE, MC, V. Mon–Fri noon–2pm and 7–10pm. Closed Aug. Métro: Trocadéro or Boissière.

EXPENSIVE

L'Astrance ★★★ MODERN FRENCH   It's small, it's charming, and shortly after its debut in 2000, it exploded into the Parisian consciousness with more fanfare and praise than anyone can remember. Its creative flair derives from the partnership of two former employees (some say "disciples") of megachef Alain Passard, scion of l'Arpège, an ultraglam restaurant in the 7th arrondissement. The perfectly mannered Christophe Rohat, supervising the dining room, is the more visible of the two; but Pascal Barbot, the chef creating the food that emerges from the kitchens, has emerged as a culinary force. Expect a crisply contemporary dining room. The menu, wherein flavors practically jump off the plates, might include an unusual form of "ravioli," wherein thin slices of avocado encase a filling of seasoned crabmeat, all of it accompanied with salted almonds and a splash of almond oil. A mussel salad is enriched with cumin, chervil, and carrots. And buckwheat blinis come layered with a confit of shallots and a cupful of oyster-based "cappuchino." The name of the place derives, incidentally, from a pale-blue flower (*l'astrance*) that grows wild in the hillsides of the Auvergne.

4 rue Beethoven, 16e. ℂ **01-40-50-84-40.** Reservations required 3 or 4 weeks in advance. Main courses 19€–32€ ($17–$29); fixed-price lunches 28€–57€ ($25–$51); fixed-price dinners 57€ ($51). Menu "surprise" available at lunch and dinner, including a "surprise" assortment of wines, 75€ ($67). AE, DC, MC, V. Wed–Sun 12:30–2:30pm; Tues–Sun 8–11:30pm. Closed 3 weeks in Aug. Métro: Trocadéro.

MODERATE

Kambodia ASIAN/CAMBODIAN   The waiters, all dressed in black cotton tunics, will welcome you to this excellent eatery that serves some of the best and most flavor-filled Asian dishes in Paris. The basement atmosphere has been called "Zen-like," but the service is welcoming and it's a good choice for a

(Kids) Family-Friendly Restaurants

Meals at Paris's grand restaurants are rarely suitable for young children. Nevertheless, many parents drag their kids along, often to the annoyance of other diners. You may have to make some compromises, such as dining earlier than most Parisians. **Hotel dining rooms** can be another good choice for family dining. They usually have children's menus or at least one or two *plats du jour* cooked for children, like spaghetti with meat sauce.

If you take your child to a **moderate** or an **inexpensive restaurant,** ask if they will serve a child's plate. If not, order a *plat du jour* or *plat garni,* which will be suitable for most children, particularly if a dessert is to follow. Most **cafes** welcome children during the day and early evening. At a cafe, children seem to like the sandwiches (try a *croque monsieur*), the omelets, and the *pommes frites* (french fries). Though this chapter lists a number of cafes (see "The Top Cafes" later in this chapter), one that appeals to children is **La Samaritaine,** 75 rue de Rivoli (© **01-40-41-20-20;** Métro: Pont Neuf). The snack bar below doesn't have a panoramic view, but the fifth-floor restaurant does. You can take children to the top and order ice cream at teatime daily from 3:30 to 6pm. The snack bar is open Friday to Wednesday from 9:30am to 7pm and Thursday from 9:30am to 10pm.

Les Drug Stores, 149 bd. St-Germain-des-Prés, 6e, and at Publicis Champs-Elysées, 133 av. des Champs-Elysées, 8e—like American drug stores but with sections for upscale gift items and food service—also welcome children, especially in the early evening, as do most **tearooms,** and you can tide the kids over with pastries and ice cream if dinner will be late. You could also try a **picnic** in the park or one of the many fast-food chains, like **Pizza Hut** and **McDonald's,** all over the city.

Androuët sur le Pouce (p. 124)   If your kids love cheese, they'll get the fill of a lifetime here, where cheese is part of all the dishes. Especially delectable is the ravioli stuffed with goat cheese.

Café la Parisienne (p. 132)   This is the ideal choice when visiting the Beaubourg, with a captivating view of the most playful fountain in Paris from its terrace.

Chicago Pizza Pie Factory, 5 rue Berri, 8e (© **01-45-62-50-23**). There are no frogs' legs or snails to gross out little minds and stomachs at the Chicago Pizza Pie Factory, just the City of Light's best pizza followed by a kid-pleasing cheesecake.

Crémerie-Restaurant Polidor (p. 158)   One of the most popular restaurants on the Left Bank, this reasonably priced dining room is so family-friendly it calls its food *cuisine familiale.* This might be the best place to introduce your child to bistro food.

Hard Rock Cafe (p. 133)   At the Paris branch of this chain, good old American burgers and more are served against a background of rock memorabilia and loud rock music.

Joe Allen (p. 125)   This American restaurant in Les Halles delivers everything from chili to chocolate-mousse pie to the best hamburgers in Paris.

romantic dinner not far from the Champs-Elysées. Fresh ingredients are used, the best from the Asian markets. Our favorite dish is a superb seafood pot-au-feu. One Cambodian dish that's a delight is ginger fish wrapped in a banana leaf.

15 rue de Bassano, 16e. ℂ **01-47-23-31-80.** Reservations required. Main courses 11€–19€ ($10–$17); fixed-price lunch 18€–23€ ($16–$20). AE, MC, V. Mon–Fri noon–2:30pm; Mon–Sat 7:30–11pm. Métro: George V.

La Butte Chaillot ★ *Value* TRADITIONAL FRENCH   This baby bistro showcases culinary high priest Guy Savoy and draws a crowd from the affluent neighborhood's many corporate headquarters. Diners congregate in posh but congested areas. Menu items change weekly (sometimes daily) and betray a sense of mass production not unlike that found in a luxury cruise line's dining room. Examples are a sophisticated medley of terrines; a "low-fat" version of chunky mushroom soup; a salad of snails and herbed potatoes; succulent rack of lamb; and roasted rabbit with sage and a compote of onions, bacon, and mushrooms. A starkly contemporary stainless-steel staircase leads to extra seating in the cellar.

110 bis av. Kléber, 16e. ℂ **01-47-27-88-88.** Reservations recommended. Main courses 15€–21€ ($14–$18); fixed-price menus 30€ ($26). AE, DC, MC, V. Sun–Fri noon–2:30pm; daily 7–11pm. Métro: Trocadéro.

INEXPENSIVE
Le Bistro de l'Etoile ★ *Value* TRADITIONAL FRENCH   This is the more interesting of the two baby bistros, both with the same name, clustered around place Charles de Gaulle-Etoile. They serve affordable versions of the grand cuisine featured in Guy Savoy's nearby three-star restaurant (see below). The setting is a warmly contemporary dining room in shades of butterscotch and caramel. Menu items include a *mijotée* (pork and sage cooked over low heat for hours, coming out extremely tender), codfish studded with lard and prepared with a coconut-lime sauce, and red-snapper filets with caramelized endive and exotic mushrooms. A particularly interesting sampler combines three of Savoy's creations on a platter—a cup of lentil cream soup, a fondant of celery, and a pan-fried slice of foie gras. Expect some odd terms on the dessert menu, which only a professional chef can fully describe: An example is spice bread baked in the fashion of *pain perdu* (lost bread) garnished with banana sorbet and pineapple sauce.

19 rue Lauriston, 16e. ℂ **01-40-67-11-16.** Reservations recommended. Main courses 16€–24€ ($14–$21); fixed-price lunch 25€ ($22). AE, DC, MC, V. Mon–Fri noon–2:30pm; Mon–Sat 7:30pm–midnight. Métro: Kléber.

17TH ARRONDISSEMENT
VERY EXPENSIVE
Guy Savoy ★★★ TRADITIONAL FRENCH   One of the hottest chefs in Europe, Guy Savoy serves the kind of food he likes to eat prepared with consummate skill. We think he has a slight edge over his nearest rival, Michel Rostang (see below), though Ducasse (p. 142) surpasses them both, at least in media coverage. Though the food is superb and meals comprise as many as nine courses, the portions are small; you won't necessarily be satiated at the end. The menu changes with the seasons but may include a light cream soup of lentils and crayfish, duckling foie gras with aspic and gray salt, and veal chops with truffle-studded mashed potatoes; or sea bass grilled in a salt shell and served with a sauce of sweet herbs. If you come in the right season, you may have a chance to order masterfully prepared game like mallard and venison. Savoy is fascinated with mushrooms and has been known to serve a dozen types, especially in autumn. An example includes a pan-fried combination of mussels and wild mushrooms.

18 rue Troyon, 17e. ℭ **01-43-80-40-61.** Fax 01-43-80-36-22. Reservations required 1 week in advance. Main courses 49€–91€ ($43–$81); menu dégustation (tasting menu) 175€–228€ ($156–$204). AE, DC, MC, V. Mon–Fri noon–2pm; Mon–Sat 7:30–10:30pm. Métro: Charles de Gaulle-Etoile or Ternes.

Michel Rostang ★★★ MODERN & TRADITIONAL FRENCH   Michel Rostang is one of Paris's most creative chefs, the fifth generation of a distinguished French "cooking family." His restaurant contains four dining rooms paneled in mahogany, cherry, or pearwood; some have frosted Lalique crystal panels. Changing every 2 months, the menu offers modern improvements on *cuisine bourgeoise*. Truffles are the dish of choice in midwinter, and you'll find racks of suckling lamb from the salt marshes of France's western seacoasts in spring; in game season, look for sophisticated preparations of pheasant and venison. Three year-round staples are quail eggs with a *coque* (shell) of sea urchins, fricassee of sole, and young Bresse chicken with crusty mushroom purée and a salad composed of the chicken's thighs.

20 rue Rennequin, 17e. ℭ **01-47-63-40-77.** Fax 01-47-63-82-75. Reservations required far in advance. Main courses 32€–61€ ($29–$54); fixed-price menus 59€–150€ ($53–$134) at lunch, 150€ ($134) at dinner. AE, DC, MC, V. Tues–Fri 12:30–2:30pm; Mon–Sat 8–10:30pm. Closed 3 weeks in Aug. Métro: Ternes.

EXPENSIVE

Le Bistro d'á Côté ★ *Value* MODERN & TRADITIONAL FRENCH   This is one of the four branches of Michel Rostang's baby bistro, each of which features a pared-down version of his *haute gastronomie* (see above). This branch is the most interesting because it's next door to the source. You'll enter a nostalgically decorated dining area ringed with unusual porcelain and antique copies of Michelin guides. The venue is breezy, stylishly informal, and chic, with a simple menu enhanced by daily specials written on a chalkboard. Tantalizing items include ravioli stuffed with lobster, an upscale version of macaroni with Serrano ham, and *rable de lievre* (rabbit stew) *en cocotte*.

10 rue Gustave Flaubert, 17e. ℭ **01-42-67-05-81.** Reservations recommended far in advance. Main courses 18€–24€ ($16–$21); fixed-price lunch 27€ ($24). AE, DC, MC, V. Daily 12:30–2:30pm and 7:30–11pm. Métro: Ternes.

MODERATE

Chez Georges TRADITIONAL FRENCH   Not to be confused with a bistro of the same name in the 2nd arrondissement, this is a worthy choice. It has flourished since 1926, despite an obscure location. The setting has changed little—cheerfully harassed waiters barge through a dining room sheathed with old-fashioned paneling and etched glass, and savory odors emerge from the hysterically busy kitchen. Two enduring specialties are leg of lamb with white kidney beans and standing rib roast with herbs (especially thyme) in its own juices and a gratin of potatoes. Preceding these might be Baltic herring in cream

---

⌒*Tips*   **Can You Dine Badly in Paris?**

The answer is an emphatic yes. Our mailbox fills with complaints from readers who've encountered haughty service and paid outrageous prices for swill. Often these complaints are about restaurants catering to tourists. Avoid them by following our suggestions or looking in non-touristy areas for new discoveries. If you ask Parisians for recommendations, specify that you're looking for restaurants where *they'd* dine, not where they think you, as a tourist, would dine.

sauce, cheese ravioli, cabbage soup, or a wide selection of sausages and pork products that taste best when eaten with bread, butter, and sour pickles. The adventurous French love the calf's head and the braised veal trotters, both served cold in vinaigrette.

273 bd. Pereire, 17e. © **01-45-74-31-00.** Reservations recommended. Main courses 15€–27€ ($13–$24). MC, V. Daily noon–2:30pm and 7pm–midnight. Métro: Porte Maillot.

La Rôtisserie d'Armaillé ⭑⭑ *Value* TRADITIONAL FRENCH   The impresario behind this attractive baby bistro is Jacques Cagna, who established his role as a gastronomic star long ago from his headquarters in the Latin Quarter (see below). The chic place is popular for business lunches and dinners, also drawing residents and shoppers from the grand neighborhood. It's ringed with light-colored wood paneling and banquettes with patterns of pink and green. At lunch, the menu includes a main course and a starter or dessert; the pricier dinner meal includes a starter, main course, and dessert. Either way, you'll have many choices in each category. Examples are wild-mushroom flan with red-wine sauce, a salad of sweetbreads and crayfish, and rack of lamb with parsley and sage, with apple beignets and champagne-drenched pineapple-and-mango soup for dessert. The artwork features bucolic cows, pigs, and lambs that are likely to figure among the grilled steaks and chops featured on the menu.

6 rue d'Armaillé, 17e. © **01-42-27-19-20.** Reservations recommended. Main courses 20€–26€ ($18–$23). Fixed-price menu 28€–38€ ($25–$34) at lunch, 38€ ($34) at dinner. AE, DC, MC, V. Mon–Fri noon–2:30pm; Mon–Sat 7:30–10pm. Métro: Charles de Gaulle-Etoile.

4 On the Left Bank

We'll begin with the most centrally located arrondissements on the Left Bank, then work our way through the more outlying neighborhoods and to the area near the Eiffel Tower.

5TH ARRONDISSEMENT
VERY EXPENSIVE

La Tour d'Argent ⭑⭑⭑ TRADITIONAL FRENCH   This penthouse restaurant, a national institution, serves up a panoramic view over the Seine and the apse of Notre-Dame. Although La Tour d'Argent's long-established reputation as "the best" in Paris has been eclipsed, dining here remains an unsurpassed event. A restaurant has stood on this site since at least 1582: Mme de Sévigné refers to a cafe here in her celebrated letters, and Dumas used it as a setting for one of his novels. The fame of La Tour d'Argent spread during its ownership by Frédéric Delair, who started the practice of issuing certificates to diners who ordered the house specialty—*caneton* (pressed duckling). The birds are numbered: The first was served to Edward VII in 1890, and now they're up over one million! Under the sharp eye of current owner Claude Terrail, the cooking is superb and the service impeccable. A good part of the menu is devoted to duck, but the kitchen does know how to prepare other dishes. We especially recommend you start with the pheasant consommé or the pike-perch quenelles André Terrail and follow with the ravioli with foie gras or the filet of sole Cardinal with shrimp sauce.

15-17 quai de la Tournelle, 5e. © **01-43-54-23-31.** Fax 01-44-07-12-04. Reservations required far in advance. Main courses 59€–91€ ($53–$81); fixed-price lunch 59€ ($53). AE, DC, MC, V. Tues–Sun noon–1:15pm and 7:30–9pm. Métro: St-Michel or Pont Marie.

Where to Dine on the Left Bank (5–6 & 13–14e)

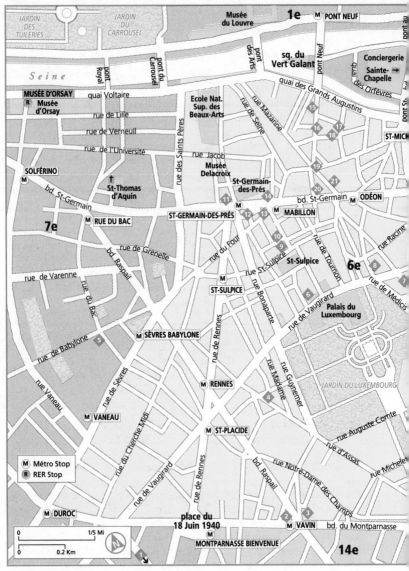

MODERATE

Brasserie Balzar ★★ TRADITIONAL FRENCH Opened in 1898, Brasserie Balzar is battered but cheerful, with some of Paris's most colorful waiters. The menu makes almost no concessions to modern cuisine and includes onion soup, pepper steak, sole meunière, sauerkraut with ham and sausage, pig's feet, and fried calf's liver served without garnish. Be warned that if you want just coffee or a drink, you probably won't get a table at meal hours. But, accustomed as they are to the odd hours of their patrons, the staff will be happy to serve you if you want a full dinner in the midafternoon. Former

Al Dar **24**
Alcazar Bar
   & Restaurant **20**
Allard **19**
Auberge Etchegorry **29**
Aux Charpentiers **10**
Bistro de la Grille **9**
Brasserie Balzar **23**
Brasserie Lipp **12**
Café Cosmos **5**
Café de Flore **11**
Chez Diane **6**
Chez Gramond **4**
Closerie des Lilas **28**
Coco de Mer **32**
Crémerie-Restaurant
   Polidor **7**
Jacques Cagna **17**
Keryado **25**
L'Assiette **1**
La Bastide Odéon **8**
La Cagouille **1**
La Coupole **3**
La Palette **15**
La Petite Hostellerie **22**
La Régalade **1**
La Rôtisserie d'en Face **18**
La Rotonde **2**
La Tour d'Argent **25**
Le Canton **13**
Le Petit Marguery **30**
Le Procope **21**
Lerch **26**
Les Deux Magots **14**
Marty **31**
Perraudin **27**
Restaurant Bleu **1**
Yugaraj **16**

patrons have included Sartre and Camus (who often got in arguments), James Thurber, countless professors from the nearby Sorbonne, and bevies of English and American journalists.

49 rue des Ecoles, 5e. ⓒ **01-43-54-13-67.** Reservations strongly recommended. Main courses 14€–20€ ($12–$18). AE, MC, V. Daily noon–11:45pm. Métro: Odéon or Cluny-La Sorbonne.

Marty ⭐ *Finds* MODERN FRENCH   This is one of the few brasseries in Paris that's not been gobbled up by a chain. Charming, with a stone-trimmed decor that's authentic to the era (1913) in which it was established, this restaurant has suddenly been "discovered" by new generations of restaurant-goers. Named after its founders, Etienne and Marthe Marty, its fame now extends way beyond the 5th arrondissement neighborhood that contains it. Service is attentive, and there are lots of Jazz Age murals highlighting the walls. Food is savory, satisfying, and appealingly unfussy. If someone opts to seat you on one of the hideaway tables positioned on the mezzanine, don't resist, since views from here sweep over the entire Human Comedy unfolding above and below you. Begin your meal with a tartare of sea bream flavored with anis and lime; lobster ravioli with sherry vinegar; or fresh oysters. Continue with a supreme of guinea fowl with a vegetable moussaka; a platter that combines grilled squid with grilled strips of red mullet; or perhaps a brochette of hake and salmon, served with a mustard-flavored olive tapenade. Dessert might include a soup of red fruits with orange-flavored liqueur. There's a bar on the street level of this place, where a succulent array of tapas and shellfish can be combined into savory accompaniments for your drinks.

20 av. des Gobelins, 5e. ℭ **01-43-31-39-51.** Tapas 5.30€–6.85€ ($4.70–$6.10); set menu 30€ ($27); main courses 14€–32€ ($13–$29). AE, DC, MC, V. Daily noon–midnight. Métro: Gobelins.

INEXPENSIVE

Al Dar LEBANESE   This well-respected restaurant works hard to popularize the savory cuisine of Lebanon. You'll dine on dishes like *taboulé*, a refreshing combination of finely chopped parsley, mint, milk, tomatoes, onions, lemon juice, olive oil, and salt; *baba ganoush*, pulverized and seasoned eggplant; and *hummus*, pulverized chickpeas with herbs. These can be followed with savory roasted chicken; tender minced lamb prepared with mint, cumin, and Mediterranean herbs; and any of several kinds of delectable tangines and couscous.

8 rue Frédéric-Sauton, 5e. ℭ **01-43-25-17-15.** Reservations recommended. Main courses 14€–17€ ($13–$15). AE, MC, V. Daily noon–midnight. Métro: Maubert-Mutualité.

Coco de Mer ⭐ *Finds* SEYCHELLE ISLANDS   The theme of this restaurant tugs at the emotions of the thousands of Parisians who have spent their holidays on the beaches of the Seychelles in the Indian Ocean. It contains at least three dining rooms, one of which is outfitted like a beach, with a sand-covered floor, replicas of palm trees, and conch shells. Menu items feature such exotic dishes as tartare of tuna flavored with ginger, olive oil, salt, and pepper; and smoked swordfish, served either as a carpaccio or in thin slices with mango mousse and a spicy sauce. Main courses focus on fish, including a species of delectable red snapper (*boirzoes*), which is imported from the Seychelles. Dessert might consist of a *crème de banana gratinée*.

354 bd. St-Marcel, 5e. ℭ **01-47-07-06-64.** Reservations recommended. Main courses 17€–21€ ($15–$19); set menus 21€–26€ ($18–$23). AE, DC, MC, V. Tues–Sat noon–3pm; Mon–Sat 7:30pm–midnight. Métro: Les Gobelins or St-Marcel.

La Petite Hostellerie ⭐ *Value* TRADITIONAL FRENCH   This 1902 restaurant offers a ground-floor dining room that's usually crowded and a larger one (seating 100) upstairs with attractive 18th-century woodwork. People come for the cozy ambience and decor, decent French country cooking, polite service, and excellent prices. The fixed-price dinner menu might feature favorites like coq au vin, duckling á l'orange, and steak with mustard sauce. Start with onion soup or stuffed mussels, and finish with cheese or salad and peach Melba or an apple tart.

35 rue de la Harpe (just east of bd. St-Michel), 5e. ℭ **01-43-54-47-12.** All main courses 8.95€ ($7.95); fixed-price menus 9.90€–14€ ($8.80–$12). MC, V. Wed–Sun noon–2pm; Tues–Sun 6:30–11pm. Closed 2 weeks in Feb and 3 weeks in Aug. Métro: St-Michel or Cluny-La Sorbonne.

> **Moments   Street Eats**
>
> You can find a large variety of street food sold everywhere from the Latin Quarter to outside the *grands magasins* on the Right Bank. Sandwiches, crêpes, *frites*, and (in cold weather) roasted chestnuts are just a few of the items available. The crêpes are especially good—freshly made and filled with your choice of ingredients: cheese, ham, egg (or a combination of these); chocolate and nuts; apricot jam; or some other treat.

Perraudin ★★ TRADITIONAL FRENCH   Everything about this place— decor, cuisine, price, and service—attempts to duplicate an early-1900s bistro. This one was built in 1870 as an outlet for coal and wine. Eventually it evolved into the wood-paneled bistro you see today, where little has changed since Zola was buried nearby in the Panthéon. The walls look like they've been marinated in tea; the marble-topped tables, old mirrors, and Parisian vaudeville posters have likely been here forever. Reservations aren't made in advance: Instead, diners usually drink a glass of kir at the zinc-topped bar as they wait. (Tables turn over quickly.) The menu includes roast leg of lamb with dauphinois potatoes, navarin of lamb, boeuf bourguignonne, and grilled salmon with sage sauce. An onion tart, pumpkin soup, or a terrine can precede the main course.

157 rue St-Jacques, 5e. ✆ 01-46-33-15-75. Main courses 12€–18€ ($11–$16); fixed-price menu 12€–30€ ($11–$26) at lunch, 30€ ($26) at dinner. No credit cards. Mon–Fri noon–2:15pm and 7:30–10:15pm. Closed 2 weeks in Aug. Métro: Cluny-La Sorbonne. RER: Luxembourg.

6TH ARRONDISSEMENT
VERY EXPENSIVE

Jacques Cagna ★★★ MODERN & TRADITIONAL FRENCH   St-Germain knows no finer dining than at Jacques Cagna, a sophisticated restaurant in a 17th-century town house with massive timbers, burnished paneling, and 17th-century Dutch paintings. Jacques Cagna is one of the best classically trained chefs in Paris, though he has become a half-apostle to *cuisine moderne*. This is evident in his delectable carpaccio of pearly sea bream with caviar-lavished *céleric rémoulade* (celery root in mayonnaise with capers, parsley, gherkins, spring onions, chervil, chopped tarragon, and anchovy essence). Also sublime are the rack of suckling veal with ginger-and-lime sauce, Challons duckling in burgundy sauce, and fried scallops with celery and potatoes in truffle sauce. The menu is forever changing according to the season and Cagna's inspirations, but if you're lucky, it will include his line-caught sea bass served with caviar in a potato shell.

14 rue des Grands-Augustins, 6e. ✆ 01-43-26-49-39. Fax 01-43-54-54-48. Reservations required far in advance. Main courses 27€–53€ ($24–$48); fixed-price menus 40€–79€ ($35–$71) at lunch, 79€ ($71) at dinner. AE, DC, MC, V. Tues–Fri noon–2pm; Mon–Sat 7:30–10:30pm. Closed 3 weeks in Aug. Métro: St-Michel or Odéon.

EXPENSIVE

Closerie des Lilas ★★ TRADITIONAL FRENCH   Opened in 1847, the Closerie was long a social and culinary magnet for the avant-garde. The famous people who have sat in the "Pleasure Garden of the Lilacs" are countless: Gertrude Stein and Alice B. Toklas, Ingrès, Henry James, Chateaubriand, Picasso, Hemingway, Apollinaire, Lenin and Trotsky (at the chess board), Whistler, and others. Today the crowd is likely to include both stars and the starstruck. The place resounds with the sometimes-loud sounds of a jazz pianist, making the interior seem more claustrophobic than it already is. It can be tough to get a seat in what's called the *bâteau* (boat) section, but you can make the wait more enjoyable by ordering the world's best champagne julep at the bar. It's possible to have coffee or a drink at the bar, though the food is better than ever. Try the veal kidneys with mustard, veal ribs in cider sauce, steak tartare, or pike-perch quenelles.

171 bd. du Montparnasse, 6e. 𝄞 **01-40-51-34-50.** Reservations recommended far in advance (restaurant only). Main courses 18€–33€ ($16–$30); brasserie main courses 14€–27€ ($12–$24). AE, DC, V. Restaurant daily noon–3pm and 7:30–11:30pm. Brasserie daily 11:30am–1am. Métro: Port Royal or Vavin.

MODERATE

Alcazar Bar & Restaurant ⚘ MODERN FRENCH Paris's most high-profile *brasserie de luxe* is this artfully high-tech place funded by British restaurateur/wunderkind Sir Terence Conran. (His chain of restaurants in London has succeeded in captivating a tough audience of jaded European foodies.) It features an all-white futuristic decor in a large street-level dining room and a busy bar a floor above. Menu examples are grilled entrecôte with béarnaise sauce and fried potatoes, Charolais duckling with honey and spices, sashimi and sushi with lime, monkfish filet with saffron in puff pastry, and a collection of shellfish and oysters from the waters of Brittany. The wines are as stylish and diverse as you'd expect, and the trendy crowd tends to wear a lot of black.

62 rue Mazarine, 6e. 𝄞 **01-53-10-19-99.** Reservations recommended. Main courses 14€–27€ ($13–$24); fixed-price lunch menus 21€–24€ ($19–$22). AE, DC, MC, V. Daily noon–3pm and 7pm–1am. Métro: Odéon.

Allard ⚘⚘ TRADITIONAL FRENCH Long missing from this guide, this old-time bistro, opened in 1931, is back and as good as ever following a long decline. Once it was the leading bistro, although today the competition is too great to reclaim that reputation. In the front room is a zinc bar, a haven preferred by many celebrities over the years, including Mme. Pompidou and movie actor Alain Delon. All the old Allard specialties are still offered, with quality ingredients deftly handled by the kitchen. Try the snails, foie gras, veal stew, or frogs' legs. We head here on Mondays for the *cassoulet Toulousian* and on Saturday for the coq au vin. The *cassoulet Toulousian* (casserole of white beans and goose and other meats) remains one of the Left Bank's best. For dessert, we vote for the tarte tatin.

41 rue St-André-des-Arts, 6e. 𝄞 **01-43-26-48-23.** Reservations required. Main courses 18€–35€ ($16–$31); fixed-price menus 23€–30€ ($20–$27) at lunch, 30€ ($27) at dinner. AE, DC, MC, V. Mon–Sat 12:30–2:30pm and 7:30–11pm. Métro: St-Michel or Odéon.

Chez Gramond ⚘ *Finds* TRADITIONAL FRENCH Aficionados of the way France used to be seek out this place, and if you're looking for the kind of cuisine that used to satisfy the *grands intellectuels* of the Latin Quarter in the 1960s, you might find it appealing. It seats only 20 people, each of whom is treated to the savoir-faire of Auvergne-born Jean-Claude Gramond and his charming wife, Jeannine. Listed in purple ink that's duplicated on an old-time mimeograph machine, the menu items may include a marinade of mushrooms with coriander; a *navarin* (rich stew) of lamb with scotch beans; roasted grouse with figs; scallops cooked with white wine, leeks, and shallots; partridge (this is increasingly rare and expensive) served with an *émincé* (shredded mixture) of cabbage; sautéed pheasant with a Calvados-flavored cream sauce; and two different preparations of rabbit, one of which is a *civet* (stew) served Alsatian-style, with noodles and a sauce made from a mixture of red wine and the rabbit's own blood.

Try the *soufflé Grand Marnier* for dessert. The wine list is carefully balanced and fairly priced.

5 rue de Fleurus, 6e. © **01-42-22-28-89.** Reservations recommended. Main courses 21€–27€ ($19–$24). MC, V. Mon–Sat noon–2:30pm and 7–10:30pm. Closed in Aug. Métro: Notre-Dame des Champs.

La Rôtisserie d'en Face ✦ *Value* TRADITIONAL FRENCH This is Paris's most frequented baby bistro, operated by Jacques Cagna, whose expensive restaurant (see above) is across the street. The informal place features a post-modern decor with high-tech lighting and black lacquer chairs, and the simply prepared food is very good and uses high-quality ingredients. It includes several types of ravioli, paté of duckling en croûte with foie gras, *friture d'éperlans* (tiny fried freshwater fish), and smoked Scottish salmon with spinach. Monsieur Cagna has added pork cheeks, based on an old family recipe. His Barbary duckling in red-wine sauce is incomparable.

2 rue Christine, 6e. © **01-43-26-40-98.** Reservations recommended. Fixed-price menus 23€–26€ ($20–$23) at lunch, 39€ ($35) at dinner. AE, DC, MC, V. Mon–Fri noon–2:30pm; Mon–Sat 7–11:30pm. Métro: Odéon.

Yugaraj INDIAN On two floors of an old Latin Quarter building, Yugaraj serves flavor-filled food based on the recipes of northern and (to a lesser degree) southern India. In recently renovated rooms done in vivid shades of ochre, with a formally dressed staff and lots of intricately carved Kashmiri panels and statues, you can sample the spicy, aromatic tandoori dishes that are all the rage in France. Seafood specialties are usually made with warm-water fish imported from the Seychelles, including thiof, capitaine, and bourgeois, prepared as they would be in Calcutta, with tomatoes, onions, cumin, coriander, ginger, and garlic. Curried lamb with coriander is a particular favorite.

14 rue Dauphine, 6e. © **01-43-26-44-91.** Reservations recommended. Main courses 16€–26€ ($14–$23); fixed-price menus 15€–44€ ($13–$39) at lunch, 27€–44€ ($24–$39) at dinner. AE, DC, MC, V. Tues–Sun noon–2:15pm; Tues–Sat 7–11pm. Métro: Pont-Neuf.

INEXPENSIVE

Aux Charpentiers TRADITIONAL FRENCH This battered veteran attracts those seeking the Left Bank Paris of yesteryear. The bistro, opened more than 130 years ago, was once the rendezvous of the carpenters whose guild was next door. Nowadays young men bring their dates here. Though the food isn't especially imaginative, it's well prepared in the tradition of *cuisine bourgeoise*— hearty but not effete. Appetizers include paté of duck and rabbit terrine. Especially recommended is the roast duck with olives. The plats du jour recall French home cooking: salt pork with lentils, pot-au-feu, and stuffed cabbage. The wine list has a large selection of Bordeaux, including Château Gaussens.

10 rue Mabillon, 6e. © **01-43-26-30-05.** Reservations required. Main courses 14€–20€ ($12–$18); fixed-price menu 19€ ($17) at lunch, 25€ ($22) at dinner. AE, DC, MC, V. Daily noon–3pm and 7–11:30pm. Métro: St-Germain-des-Prés.

Bistro de la Grille TRADITIONAL FRENCH Many of your fellow diners at this arts-conscious bistro are likely to own or work in nearby boutiques. If you're alone, you might opt to dine at the bar near the entrance, surrounded by photos of film stars from the early years of the French Pathé cinema. The tables upstairs are moderately more sedate than those on the bustling street level. Menu items arrive in generous portions but are rarely daring—platters of fresh shellfish, traditional bone marrow spread over roughly textured bread, sautéed salmon with wild mushrooms, and the ever-popular (at least in France) veal's head with capers and mayonnaise and mustard sauce. Desserts include traditional favorites like tarte tatin, mousse au chocolat, and gratin de fruit de saison.

14 rue Mabillon, 6e. ☎ 01-43-54-16-87. Reservations recommended. All main courses 11€ ($10); fixed-price menu 18€–21€ ($16–$19). MC, V. Tues–Sun noon–midnight. Métro: St-Germain-des Prés.

Chez Diane MODERN & TRADITIONAL FRENCH Come here for fashionable food at simple bistro prices. Designed to accommodate only 40 diners, this place is illuminated with Venetian glass chandeliers and paved with old-fashioned floor tiles. The deep ochres and terra-cottas are redolent of Provence's landscapes and villas. Chez Diane's offerings change with the seasons and the owners' inspirations. Recently we enjoyed sweetbreads in flap mushroom sauce, nuggets of wild boar in honey sauce, minced salmon terrine with green peppercorns, and a light-textured modern adaptation of *hachis Parmentier*, an elegant meat loaf lightened with parsley, chopped onions, and herbs. To finish with a sweet touch, we recommend the *charlotte au fromage blanc*, a tasty cheesecake with blueberry sauce.

25 rue Servandoni, 6e. ☎ 01-46-33-12-06. Reservations recommended for groups of 4 or more. Main courses 15€–21€ ($14–$19); fixed-price menu 25€ ($22). MC, V. Mon–Fri noon–2pm; Mon–Sat 8–11:30pm. Métro: St-Sulpice.

Crémerie-Restaurant Polidor ★★ (Kids) TRADITIONAL FRENCH Crémerie Polidor is the most traditional bistro in the Odéon area, serving *cuisine familiale*. Its name dates from the early 1900s, when it specialized in frosted cream desserts, but the restaurant itself can trace its history back to 1845. The Crémerie was André Gide's favorite, and Joyce, Hemingway, Valéry, Artaud, and Kerouac also dined here. The place is still frequented largely by students and artists, who head for the rear. Peer beyond the lace curtains and brass hat racks to see drawers where repeat customers lock up their cloth napkins. Overworked but smiling waitresses with frilly aprons and T-shirts bearing the likeness of old mère Polidor serve the 19th-century cuisine. Try the pumpkin soup followed by boeuf bourguignonne, Basque-style chicken, or blanquette de veau. For dessert, get a chocolate, raspberry, or lemon tart—the best in all Paris.

41 rue Monsieur-le-Prince, 6e. ☎ 01-43-26-95-34. Main courses 6.85€–13€ ($6.10–$12); fixed-price menu 8.95€ ($7.95). Mon–Fri only, 18€ ($16) fixed-price dinner. No credit cards. Daily noon–2:30pm; Mon–Sat 7pm–12:30am; Sun 7–11pm. Métro: Odéon.

La Bastide Odéon ★ (Finds) PROVENÇAL The sunny climes of Provence come through in the pale-yellow walls, oak tables, and artfully arranged bouquets of wheat and dried roses. Chef Gilles Ajuelos prepares a market-based cuisine. His simplest first courses are the most satisfying, like pumpkin soup with oysters and mussels, grilled eggplant with herbs and oil, and eggplant-stuffed roasted rabbit with olive toast and balsamic vinegar. Main courses include wild duckling with pepper sauce and exotica like lamb's feet and giblets. A winning dessert is the warm almond pie with prune and Armagnac ice cream.

7 rue Corneille, 6e. ☎ 01-43-26-03-65. Reservations recommended. Fixed-price menus 26€–32€ ($23–$29). AE, MC, V. Tues–Sat 12:30–2pm and 7:30–10:30pm. Métro: Odéon. RER: Luxembourg.

Le Canton (Finds) CHINESE/VIETNAMESE The cuisine is exotic, especially the Vietnamese dishes, and the setting relaxing and evocative of Asia. Best of all, the food is affordable and more savory than at the nearby fast-food joints. Begin with any of the versions of *nem* (Vietnamese ravioli) stuffed with shrimp and vegetables. Delicate dim sum are available, as well as main courses like salt-and-pepper shrimp, Szechuan-style chicken, and the best-selling Yorkson shrimp quick-fried with garlic, peppers, and onions. The soups are wonderful. The chefs amply use basil, the smell of which permeates the two dining rooms.

5 rue Gozlin, 6e. ℰ **01-43-26-51-86.** Reservations recommended. Main courses 7.15€–9.90€ ($6.35–$8.80); fixed-price menus 11€ ($10) at lunch, 12€–14€ ($11–$13) at dinner. MC, V. Mon–Sat noon–2:30pm and 7–11pm. Métro: St-Germain-des-Prés.

13TH ARRONDISSEMENT
MODERATE

Auberge Etchegorry BASQUE   Its windows overlook a verdant patch of lawn that's so green you might for a moment imagine you've entered a rustic countryside inn. Dark paneling, deep colors, hanging hams and pigtails of garlic, and lacy curtains emulate the Basque country, the corner of southwestern France adjacent to Spain. Victor Hugo and Chateaubriand ate here in centuries past. The cramped tables are a drawback, but not much of one in this rich atmosphere. The menu includes a roster of specialties like cassoulet, magret of duckling, beef filet with peppercorns, a peppery omelet known as *piperades,* cocottes of mussels, and terrines or pan-fried slices of foie gras. The comfortable three-star Hôtel du Vert Galant (p. 105) is associated with the restaurant.

41 rue Croulebarbe, 13e. ℰ **01-44-08-83-51.** Reservations recommended. Main courses 15€–19€ ($14–$17); fixed-price menus 24€–35€ ($21–$31) at lunch, 24€–35€ ($21–$31) at dinner. AE, DC, MC, V. Mon–Sat noon–2:30pm and 7:30–10:30pm. Métro: Gobelins or Corvisart.

Le Petit Marguery TRADITIONAL FRENCH/POITEVINE   The aura of this place is that of a turn-of-the-20th-century bistro, with antique floor tiles, banquettes, etched glass, vested waiters, and a color scheme of dark rose. Menu items are firmly based in old-fashioned French traditions, especially those from the Poitou region, with emphasis on game dishes in autumn and fresh produce in summer. The finest examples include slices of wild duck breast, dusted with white pepper and strewn over mounds of shredded cabbage; a sauté of wild mushrooms; a *petit sale* of duckling that's served with braised cabbage and garlic-flavored cream sauce; and an old-fashioned version of chitterling sausage (*andouillettes*) that many older French people remember from their childhoods.

9 bd. du Port-royal, 13e. ℰ **01-43-31-58-59.** Reservations recommended. 3-course lunch 25€–33€ ($22–$30); 3-course dinner 33€ ($30). AE, DC, MC, V. Tues–Sat noon–2pm and 7:30–10pm. Métro: Les Gobelins.

INEXPENSIVE

Keryado ⭐ *Finds* SEAFOOD   Since it was taken over by sophisticated management in 1992, this blue-and-white seafood bistro specializes in a dish only the most dedicated or arrogant chef would try at home: bouillabaisse. This fish stew has led to more lost reputations, crack-ups, and suicides than any other dish in the history of French cuisine. Fortunately, Keryado's version is as rich, savory, and satisfying as what you'd get in some of the best restaurants of Provence. And it's a relatively modest 21€ ($19) per person. If bouillabaisse isn't your cup of soup, consider other fish dishes like *chaudrée de poissons aïoli,* a stew pot of filets from six types of fish, laced with a rich garlicky broth. Slightly more experimental is a stingray with green cabbage and curry.

32 rue de Regnault, 13e. ℰ **01-45-83-87-58.** Reservations recommended. Main courses 12€–22€ ($11–$20); fixed-price menus 17€–23€ ($15–$20); fixed-price lunch 8.95€ ($7.95) Mon–Fri. MC, V. Mon–Sat noon–2:30pm; Tues–Sat 7:30–10:30pm. Métro: Porte d'Ivry or Bibliothèque de France.

14TH ARRONDISSEMENT
MODERATE

La Cagouille ★ *Finds* CENTRAL EUROPEAN/TRADITIONAL FRENCH/ SEAFOOD   Don't expect to find meat at this temple of seafood—burly and genteel owner Gérard Allamandou refuses to feature it on his menu. Everything about La Cagouille is a testimonial to a modern version of the culinary arts of La Charente, the flat sandy district hugging the Atlantic south of Bordeaux. In a trio of simple oak-sheathed dining rooms with marble-topped tables, you'll sample seafood prepared as simply and naturally as possible, with no fancy sauces or elaborate cooking techniques. Allamandou's preferred fish is red mullet, which might appear sautéed in a bland oil or baked in rock salt. The name of the place derives from the regional symbol of La Charente: the sea snail, whose preparation is elevated to a fine culinary art here. Look for a vast assemblage of all-French, mostly white wines and at least 150 cognacs. On place Constantine-Brancusi, during the summer there's a partially concealed terrace for outside dining.

10-12 place Constantine-Brancusi, 23 rue de l'Ouest, 14e. ℭ 01-43-22-09-01. Reservations recommended. Main courses 18€–32€ ($16–$29); fixed-price menus 23€–38€ ($20–$34). AE, V. Daily noon–2:30pm and 7:30–10:30pm. Métro: Gaité.

La Régalade SOUTHWESTERN FRENCH   The setting is a bistro with banquettes the color of aged Bordeaux wine, congenially harried service, and unexpectedly good food. The fixed-price menu presents a choice of at least 10 starters, 10 main courses, and about a dozen fresh desserts or selections from a cheese tray. The inspiration is Yves Camdeborde's, known for his training at the Hôtel de Crillon. The menu changes with the seasons but may include wild-boar filet with red-wine sauce, a savory mix of potatoes with blood sausage, and an always-popular platter of fried goose liver served on toasted slices of spice bread.

49 av. Jean-Moulin, 14e. ℭ 01-45-45-68-58. Reservations recommended. Fixed-price menu 30€ ($26). V. Tues–Fri noon–2pm; Tues–Sat 7pm–midnight. Closed mid-July to mid-Aug. Métro: Alésia.

L'Assiette SOUTHWESTERN FRENCH   Everything about this place appeals to a crowd seeking down-to-earth prices and flavorful food. You'll recognize it by the Bordeaux-colored facade and potted plants in the windows. The place was a *charcuterie* (pork butcher's shop) in the 1930s and today maintains some of its old accessories. Mitterrand used to drop in with his cronies for oysters, crayfish, sea urchins, and clams. The food is unashamedly inspired by Paris's long tradition of bistro cuisine, with a few twists. Examples are chanterelle mushroom salad; *rillettes* (a roughly textured paté) of mackerel; roasted guinea fowl; and desserts made on the premises, including a crumbly version of apple cake with fresh North African figs. Particularly delicious is a *petit salé* (stew with vegetables) of duckling with wine from the Poitou region of west-central France.

181 rue du Château, 14e. ℭ 01-43-22-64-86. Reservations recommended. Main courses 26€–53€ ($23–$48); fixed-price menu 35€ ($31). AE, MC, V. Wed–Sun noon–2:30pm and 8–10:30pm. Closed Aug. Métro: Gaité.

INEXPENSIVE

Restaurant Bleu AUVERGNAT   Why is this restaurant named blue? The answer is no secret—it's in honor of the eyes of chef/owner Simon Christian, who has been entertaining Paris diners for the last 6 years. The decor evokes a market town's inn, with dark paneling, farm implements, paintings of barnyard animals (especially sheep), and souvenirs of long ago. The English-speaking hostess recommends a house specialty (*truffade des bergers*) to anyone who doesn't know a *saucisson* from a *saucisse*. Made with potatoes, goose fat, Auvergnat cheese, and parsley, it's a worthy opener for main courses like grilled Charolais beefsteak with a sauce made from heady Cahors red wine, grilled blood sausage, braised pork shoulder, and cassoulet of fish. Prune tarts make a flavorful ending. There are only about 40 seats, so reservations are important.

46 rue Didot, 14e. ℭ **01-45-43-70-56.** Reservations required. Fixed-price menu 17€–28€ ($15–$25) at lunch, 21€–28€ ($19–$25) at dinner. MC, V. Tues–Fri noon–2:30pm; Tues–Sat 7:30–10:15pm. Closed Aug. Métro: Alésia.

7TH ARRONDISSEMENT
VERY EXPENSIVE

L'Arpège ✮✮✮ MODERN FRENCH   L'Arpège is best known for Alain Passard's adventurous specialties—no restaurant in the 7th serves better food. Across from the Musée Rodin in a residential neighborhood, L'Arpège has claimed the site of what for years was the world-famous L'Archestrate, where Passard worked in the kitchens. Amid a modern decor of etched glass, burnished steel, monochromatic oil paintings, and pearwood paneling, you can enjoy specialties like a light couscous of vegetables and shellfish, lobster braised in the yellow wine of the Jura, pigeon roasted with almonds and honey-flavored mead, medallions of lobster with a rosemary-flavored sweet-and-sour sauce, and carpaccio of crayfish with a caviar-flavored sauce. While Alan Passard is loathe to include red meat on his menus, it does appear from time to time, as in the examples of Japan-derived Kobe beef, and superb dishes of venison during late autumn and early winter. But more and more, he focuses on fish, shellfish, poultry, and—his current passion—vegetables. These he elevates to levels unequalled by any other chef in Paris. The signature dessert is a candied tomato stuffed with 12 kinds of dried and fresh fruit and served with anise-flavored ice cream.

84 rue de Varenne, 7e. ℭ **01-47-05-09-06.** Fax. 01-44-18-98-39. Reservations required far in advance. Main courses 64€–109€ ($57–$98); menu dégustation 213€–243€ ($190–$217). AE, DC, MC, V. Mon–Fri 12:30–2pm and 8–10pm. Métro: Varenne.

EXPENSIVE

Le Violon d'Ingres ✮✮✮ MODERN & TRADITIONAL FRENCH   This restaurant is Paris's pièce de résistance. Chef/owner Christian Constant is "the new Robuchon." Those who are fortunate enough to dine in the Violon's warm atmosphere always rave about the cleverly artistic dishes. They range from a starter of pan-fried foie gras with gingerbread and spinach salad to more elegant main courses like lobster ravioli with crushed vine-ripened tomatoes, roasted veal in a light and creamy milk sauce served with tender spring vegetables, and even a selection from the rotisserie, like spit-roasted leg of lamb rubbed with fresh garlic and thyme. Chef Constant keeps a well-chosen selection of wine to accompany his meals. The service is charming and discreet.

135 rue St-Dominique, 7e. ℭ **01-45-55-15-05.** Fax 01-45-55-48-42. Reservations required at least 3–4 days in advance. Main courses 38€–43€ ($34–$38); fixed-price dinner menu dégustation 100€ ($89); fixed-price lunch 65€ ($58). AE, MC, V. Mon–Sat 7–11pm. Métro: Ecole Militaire.

Paul Minchelli ✮ SEAFOOD   Much of the appeal of this restaurant comes from its deliberate earthiness and refusal to indulge in gratuitous rituals. The cuisine of Marseille-born Paul Minchelli is described even by his financial backers as "marginal," rejecting Paris's culinary conventions in favor of an old-fashioned Provençal technique. He's said to have reinvented fish (at least the way we cook it) by stripping away extra sauces and conflicting flavors to reveal the true "taste of the sea." The setting evokes the dining room on an expensive cruise ship, thanks to contemporary-looking wood paneling, a brass-trimmed bar in the room's center around which the tables are arranged, and a bubbling saltwater aquarium that holds an ample inventory of lobsters. Try the old-fashioned merlan Colbert, grilled John Dory, sea bass filet steamed in seaweed, lobster cooked with honey and spices, and one of the best herring salads in Paris. *Be warned:* There aren't many alternatives for those who dislike fish.

54 bd. de la Tour-Maubourg, 7e. ℂ 01-47-05-89-86. Reservations recommended. Main courses 44€–96€ ($39–$86); fixed-price lunch 53€ ($48). MC, V. Tues–Sat noon–3pm and 8–11pm. Closed Aug. Métro: La Tour Maubourg.

MODERATE

La Petite Chaise TRADITIONAL FRENCH   This is Paris's oldest restaurant, opened as an inn in 1680 by the baron de la Chaise at the edge of what was a large hunting preserve. (According to popular lore, the baron used the upstairs bedrooms for afternoon dalliances, between fox and pheasant hunts.) Very Parisian, the "Little Chair" invites you into a world of cramped but attractive tables, old wood paneling, and ornate wall sconces. A vigorous chef has brought renewed taste and flavor to this longtime favorite, and the four-course set menu offers a large choice of dishes in each category. Examples are a salad with duck breast strips on a bed of fresh lettuce, seafood-and-scallop ragout with saffron, beef filet with green peppercorns, and poached fish with steamed vegetables served in a sauce of fish and vegetable stock and cream.

36-38 rue de Grenelle, 7e. ℂ 01-42-22-13-35. Reservations recommended. Fixed-price menus 24€–30€ ($22–$26). AE, MC, V. Daily noon–2pm and 7–11pm. Métro: Sèvres-Babylone or Rue du Bac.

INEXPENSIVE

Au Pied de Fouet TRADITIONAL FRENCH   This is one of the neighborhood's oldest and most reasonably priced restaurants. In the 1700s it was a stopover for carriages en route to Paris, offering wine, food, and stables. Don't expect a leisurely or attentive meal: Food and drink will disappear quickly from your table, under the gaze of others waiting their turn. The dishes are solid and unpretentious and include blanquette de veau, *petit salé* (a savory family-style stew made from pork and vegetables), and filet of sea wolf or filet of codfish.

45 rue de Babylone, 7e. ℂ 01-47-05-12-27. Main courses 8.35€–9.90€ ($7.45–$8.80). No credit cards. Mon–Sat noon–2:30pm; Mon–Fri 7–9:30pm. Closed Aug. Métro: Vaneau.

Chez l'Ami Jean BASQUE/SOUTHWESTERN FRENCH   This restaurant was opened by a Basque nationalist in 1931, and fans claim its Basque cuisine and setting are the most authentic on the Left Bank. Decorative details include wood panels, memorabilia from *pelote* (a Basque game like jai alai) and soccer, and red-and-white woven tablecloths like the ones sold in Bayonne. Menu items include Bayonne ham; herb-laden Béarn-influenced vegetable soups; a succulent omelet with peppers, tomatoes, and onions; squid stewed in its own ink and served with tomatoes and herbs; and *poulet basquaise,* cooked with spicy sausage, onions, peppers, and strong red wine. In springtime, look for a specialty rarely available elsewhere: *saumon de l'Adour* (Adour salmon) with béarnaise sauce.

27 rue Malar, 7e. ℂ 01-47-05-86-89. Reservations recommended. Main courses 12€–15€ ($11–$13); 3-course Basque menu 14€ ($12). MC, V. Mon–Sat noon–3pm and 7–10:30pm. Métro: Invalides.

La Fontaine de Mars PYRENEE/SOUTHWESTERN FRENCH   The restaurant name derives not from its location near the Champ de Mars but from

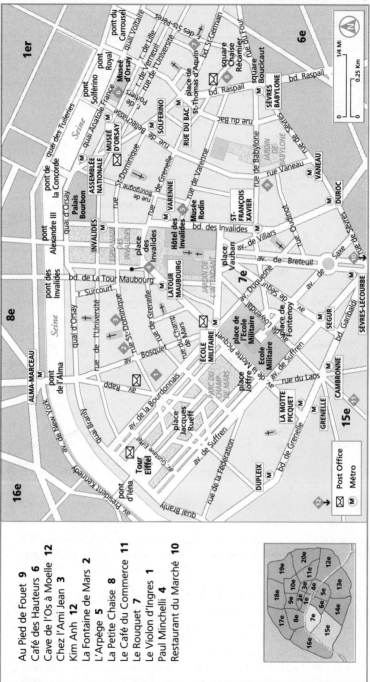

Au Pied de Fouet **9**
Café des Hauteurs **6**
Cave de l'Os à Moelle **12**
Chez l'Ami Jean **3**
Kim Anh **12**
La Fontaine de Mars **2**
L'Arpège **5**
La Petite Chaise **8**
Le Café du Commerce **11**
Le Rouquet **7**
Le Violon d'Ingres **1**
Paul Minchelli **4**
Restaurant du Marché **10**

In Pursuit of the Perfect Parisian Pastry

Could it be true, as rumor has it, that more eggs, sugar, cream, and butter per capita are consumed in Paris than in any other city? From a modern-day Proust sampling a madeleine to a child munching a *pain au chocolat* (chocolate-filled croissant), everyone in Paris seems to be looking for two things: the perfect lover and the perfect pastry, not necessarily in that order. As a Parisian food critic once said, "A day without a pastry is a day in hell!"

Who'd think of beginning a morning in Paris without a **croissant** or two—freshly baked, flaky and light and made with real butter, preferably from Norman cows. The Greeks may have invented pastry making, but the French perfected it. Some French pastries have made a greater impact than others. The croissant and the *brioche,* a yeasty sweet breakfast bread, are baked around the world today, as is the fabled *éclair au chocolat* (chocolate éclair), a pastry filled with whipped cream or pastry cream and topped with chocolate. Another pastry you should sample on its home turf is the **Napolitain**—layers of cake flour and almonds alternating with fruit purée. (Don't confuse this term with *Neapolitan,* meaning sweets and cakes made with layers of two or more colors, each layer flavored differently.) Very much in vogue is the *mille-feuille* ("thousand leaves"), made by arranging thin layers of flaky pastry on top of each other, along with layers of cream or fruit purée or jam; the American version is the napoleon.

Here are some of our favorite pâtisseries: **Stohrer,** 51 rue Montorgueil, 2e (✆ **01-42-33-38-20**; Métro: Sentier or Les Halles), has been going strong ever since it was opened by Louis XV's pastry chef in 1730. A pastry always associated with this place is *puits d'amour* (well of love), which consists of caramelized puff pastry filled with vanilla ice cream. Available at any time is one of the most luscious desserts in Paris, *baba au rhum,* or its even richer cousin, *un Ali Baba,* which also incorporates cream-based rum-and-raisin filling. Stohrer boasts an interior decor classified as a national historic treasure, with frescoes of damsels in 18th-century costume bearing flowers and (what else?) pastries.

the historic stone fountain on its tree-lined terrace. You'll find a sometimes-boisterous dining room on the street level, plus two cozier and calmer upstairs rooms whose round tables and wooden floors make you feel like you're in a private home. An additional 70 or so seats become available by the fountain whenever weather permits. Much of the cuisine derives from the Pyrénées and southwestern France, bearing rich, heady flavors that go well with robust red wines. Examples are duckling confit with parsley potatoes, a Toulouse-inspired cassoulet, veal chops with morels, and red mullet or monkfish filets with herb-flavored butter. Our favorite dessert is a thin tart filled with a sugared purée of apples, capped with more apples, and garnished with Calvados and prunes.

129 rue St-Dominique, 7e. ✆ **01-47-05-46-44.** Reservations recommended. Main courses 11€–25€ ($10–$22). AE, MC, V. Daily noon–2:30pm and 7:30–11pm. Métro: Ecole Militaire.

Opened in 1862, a few steps from La Madeleine, **Ladurée Royale,** 16 rue Royale, 8e (© **01-42-60-21-79;** Métro: Concorde or Madeleine), is Paris's dowager tearoom. Its pastry chefs are known for the **macaron,** a pastry for which this place is celebrated. Karl Lagerfeld comes here and raves about them, as did the late ambassador Pamela Harriman. This isn't the sticky coconut-version macaroon known to many, but two almond meringue cookies, flavored with chocolate, vanilla, pistachio, coffee, or other flavor, stuck together with butter cream. You may also want to try one of Hermé's latest creations—the **Le Faubourg,** a lusciously dense chocolate cake with layers of caramel and apricots.

In business since Napoleon was in power, **Dalloyau,** 101 rue du Faubourg St-Honoré, 8e (© **01-42-99-90-00;** Métro: St-Philippe du Roule), has a name instantly recognizable throughout Paris; it supplies pastries to the Elysée Palace (the French White House) and many Rothschild mansions nearby. Its specialties are Le Dalloyau, praline cake filled with almond meringue that's marvelously light-textured, and un Opéra, composed of an almond-flavored biscuit layered with butter cream, chocolate, coffee, and cashews. Unlike Stohrer, Dalloyau has a tearoom (open daily 8am–7pm) one floor above street level, where ladies who lunch can drop in for a slice of pastry that Dalloyau warns is "too fragile to transport, or to mail, over long distances."

The best way to end your pastry tour is to follow Proust's lead and sample a **madeleine,** a buttery teacake shaped like a scallop shell. We head for **Lerch,** 4 rue Cardinal-Lemoine, 5e (© **01-43-26-15-80;** Métro: Cardinal Lemoine), founded in 1971 by the Alsatian-born Lerch family. It sells goods to luminaries like Martha Stewart as well as the Proust fans who come hoping the madeleine will "invade their senses with exquisite pleasure," as it did for the narrator of *A la recherché du temps perdu.* Ideally, the madeleine is dipped into tea, preferably the slightly lime-flavored *tilleuil.*

15TH ARRONDISSEMENT
MODERATE

Kim Anh VIETNAMESE   This is one of the best addresses in Paris for the savory, spicy cuisine of its former colony. It's a bit lost down in the 15th, but many Parisian foodies journey here anyway. The success of this restaurant at a smaller location a short walk away prompted a recent move into bigger, more appealing premises early in 2001. The cuisine includes the sharp, spicy, sour, and succulent flavors of Vietnam, as prepared in pork, chicken, fish, and beef dishes, many of them excellent. Waiters are very patient in explaining various dishes to newcomers. We are especially fond of the caramelized langoustines and most definitely the stuffed crabs and steamed pork ravioli.

49 av. Emile Zola, 15e. © **01-45-79-40-96.** Reservations recommended. Main courses 15€–23€ ($13–$20); fixed-price menus 33€ ($30). AE, DC, MC, V. Tues–Sun 7–11pm. Métro: Charles-Michels.

Restaurant du Marché SOUTHWESTERN FRENCH Little about this place has changed since the 1930s; its wood panels are waxed constantly and the bouquets of fresh flowers frequently replenished. Menu items derive from dishes popular in and around Bordeaux and include a good roster of that region's wines to accompany the platters of foie gras, deboned hare stuffed with foie gras and braised in red wine and brandy, and hen stewed with vegetables and Armagnac. The restaurant's name derives from the fact that many of its fresh ingredients are supplied directly by producers in the Landes district, near Bordeaux.

57-59 rue de Dantzig, 15e. (*C*) **01-48-28-31-55.** Reservations recommended. Main courses 16€–39€ ($14–$35); fixed-price menu 26€ ($23). AE, DC, MC, V. Tues–Fri noon–2:30pm; Mon–Sat 7–10:30pm. Métro: Porte de Versailles.

INEXPENSIVE

Cave de l'Os à Moelle *Finds* TRADITIONAL FRENCH This restaurant features family-style dining. It contains three large tables, where guests are seated next to "potluck" strangers, who they often end up toasting with one or more glasses of wine before the end of the meal. There's only one option here: a 20€ ($18) "grand-mère" fixed-price menu with bowls of soup and platters of paté, rillettes, and cheese. Main-course and dessert selections are plunked down on a corner buffet, and guests serve themselves till their appetites are sated. Anticipate country-style beef stews, blood-sausage terrine, tiny shellfish with freshly made mayonnaise, and a vast array of desserts not unfamiliar to a Norman farmer's wife. Wines are numerous and cheap—the restaurant sells glasses and bottles of wine at rates substantially less than what's available at other competitors. Overall, the experience is satisfying and jolly. Management encourages guests to come either at 7:30 or 9:30pm, as part of a carefully controlled access.

181 rue de Lourmel. 15e. (*C*) **01-45-57-28-28.** Reservations recommended. Fixed-price menus 20€ ($18). MC, V. Tues–Sun noon–2:30pm; Tues–Sat 7:30–9:30pm. Métro: Lourmel.

Le Café du Commerce TRADITIONAL FRENCH Le Café is one of this area's best dining bargains. Opened in 1922, this trilevel brasserie was renovated in the late 1980s, its decor designed to hearken back to the glory days of the 1920s, with dozens of verdant plants and photos of the various writers who scribbled manuscripts on its premises. The tables are illuminated by an overhead atrium. The menu choices are old-fashioned, with no attempt at modernity or high style. Examples are warm goat cheese on a bed of lettuce, roasted chicken in its own juice, duck breast with green-pepper sauce, sole meunière, tuna steak braised in red wine, and escalope of salmon with Béarnaise sauce. Crème caramel or chocolate mousse makes for a satisfying dessert. This place is always crowded, but thanks to its three floors, there's usually an available table.

51 rue du Commerce, 15e. (*C*) **01-45-75-03-27.** Reservations recommended. Main courses 11€–13€ ($9.40–$11). Fixed-price lunch Mon–Fri 11€ ($10); fixed-price menu available anytime 20€ ($18). AE, DC, MC, V. Daily noon–midnight. Métro: Emile Zola, Grenelle, or La Motte-Picquet.

5 The Top Cafes

As surely everyone knows, the cafe is a Parisian institution. Parisians use them as combination club/tavern/snack bars, almost as extensions of their living rooms. They're spots where you can sit alone reading your newspaper, doing your homework, or writing your memoirs; meet a friend or lover; nibble at a hard-boiled egg; or drink yourself into oblivion. At cafes you meet your dates to go on to a show or to stay and talk. Above all, cafes are for people-watching.

Their single common denominator is the encouragement of leisurely sitting. Regardless of whether you have one small coffee or the house's most expensive cognac, nobody will badger, pressure, or hurry you. If you wish to sit there until the place closes, that's your affair. Cafes keep flexible hours depending on the season, the traffic, and the part of town they're in. Nearly all stay open until 1 or 2am, and a few are open all night.

Coffee, of course, is the chief drink. It comes black in a small cup, unless you specifically order it *au lait* (with milk). Tea (*thé*, pronounced *tay*) is also fairly popular but is generally not of a high quality. If you prefer beer, we advise you to pay a bit more for the imported German, Dutch, or Danish brands, which are much better than the local brew. If you insist on a French beer, at least order it *à pression* (draft), which is superior. There's also a vast variety of fruit drinks, as well as Coca-Cola, which can be rather expensive. French chocolate drinks—either hot or iced—are absolutely superb and on par with the finest Dutch brands. They're made from ground chocolate, not a chemical compound.

Now just a few words on cafe etiquette: You don't pay when you get your order—only when you intend to leave. Payment indicates you've had all you want. *Service compris* means the tip is included in your bill, so it isn't necessary to tip extra; still, most people leave an extra franc or so. You'll hear the locals call for the *"garçon,"* but as a foreigner it would be more polite to say *"monsieur."* All waitresses, on the other hand, are addressed as *"mademoiselle,"* regardless of age or marital status. In the smaller cafes, you may have to share your table. In that case, even if you haven't exchanged a word with your table companion, when you leave it's customary to bid him or her *au revoir.*

For the locations of these cafes, see the corresponding arrondissement maps earlier in this chapter.

EXPENSIVE

Brasserie Lipp   This is a Left Bank institution. On the day of Paris's liberation in 1944, late owner Roger Cazes welcomed Hemingway as the first man to drop in for a drink. Then, as now, famous people often drop by for beer, wine, and conversation. Cazes's nephew, Michel-Jacques Perrochon, runs this quintessential Parisian brasserie, where the food is secondary, yet good, providing you can get a seat (a 1½-hr. waiting time is customary if the management doesn't know you). The specialty is *choucroute garni*, Paris's best—you get not only sauerkraut but also a thick layer of ham and braised pork, which you can down with the house Riesling (an Alsatian white wine) or beer. Even if you don't go inside, you can sit at a sidewalk table to enjoy a cognac and people-watch.

151 bd. St-Germain, 6e. ✆ 01-45-48-53-91. Full meals average 46€ ($41); café au lait 2.75€ ($2.45). AE, DC, MC, V. Daily 9am–2am; restaurant service 11am–1am. Métro: St-Germain-des-Prés.

Café de Flore ★★   It's the most famous cafe in the world, still fighting to maintain the Left Bank aura in spite of hordes of visitors from around the world. Sartre—the granddaddy of existentialism, a key figure in the Resistance, and a renowned cafe-sitter—often came here during World War II. Wearing a leather jacket and beret, he sat at his table and wrote his trilogy, *Les Chemins de la Liberté* (The Roads to Freedom). Camus, Picasso, and Apollinaire also frequented the Flore. The cafe is still going strong, though the famous patrons have moved on and tourists have taken up all the tables. The menu offers omelets, salads, club sandwiches, and more. The place is especially popular on Sunday mornings.

172 bd. St-Germain, 6e. ✆ 01-45-48-55-26. Café espresso 3.95€ ($3.50); glass of beer 6.85€ ($6.10). AE, MC, V. Daily 7am–1:30am. Métro: St-Germain-des-Prés.

Fouquet's ★ For people-watching, this is definitely on the see-and-be-seen circuit. Fouquet's has been collecting anecdotes and a patina since it was founded in 1901. A celebrity favorite, it has attracted Chaplin, Chevalier, Dietrich, Churchill, Roosevelt, and Jackie Onassis. The premier cafe on the Champs-Elysées sits behind a barricade of potted flowers at the edge of the sidewalk. You can choose a table in the sunshine or retreat to the glassed-in elegance of the leather banquettes and rattan furniture of the grillroom. Though this is a full-fledged restaurant, with a beautiful formal dining room on the second floor, most visitors come by just for a glass of wine, coffee, or sandwich.

99 av. des Champs-Elysées, 8e. ℂ **01-47-23-50-00.** Glass of wine from 6.40€ ($5.70); sandwiches 8.35€–9.10€ ($7.45–$8.15); main courses 23€–53€ ($20–$48); fixed-price menu 50€ ($45). AE, MC, V. Daily 8am–2am. Restaurant daily noon–3pm and 7pm–midnight; bar 9–2am. Métro: George V.

Le Rouquet ★ *Finds* Despite its conventional food and high prices, Le Rouquet enjoys an enviable cachet and sense of chic, partly because it competes on a less flamboyant scale with the nearby Café de Flore and Les Deux Magots and partly because the decor hasn't changed since a 1954 remodeling. Less than 60 yards from St-Germain church, you can sit for as long as you want, watching a crowd of stylish Italians and Americans performing shopping and people-watching rituals barely altered since Le Rouquet's founding in 1922.

188 bd. St-Germain, 7e. ℂ **01-45-48-06-93.** Café au lait 2€ ($1.80) counter, 3.60€ ($3.20) at table; plats du jour 9.10€ ($8.10). MC, V. Mon–Sat 7am–9pm. Métro: St-Germain-des-Prés.

MODERATE

Café Beaubourg Next to the all-pedestrian plaza of the Centre Pompidou, this is a trendy cafe with soaring concrete columns and a minimalist decor. Many of the regulars work in the neighborhood's eclectic shops and galleries. You can order salads, omelets, grilled steak, chicken Cordon Bleu, pastries, and daily platters. In warm weather, tables are set up on the sprawling outdoor terrace, providing an appropriate niche for watching the young and the restless go by.

100 rue St-Martin, 4e. ℂ **01-48-87-63-96.** Glass of wine 3.80€–5.30€ ($3.40–$4.70); beer 4.85€–6.10€ ($4.35–$5.45); American breakfast 12€–21€ ($11–$19); sandwiches and platters 6.85€–27€ ($6.10–$24). AE, DC, MC, V. Sun–Thurs 8am–1am; Fri–Sat 8am–2am. Métro: Rambuteau or Hôtel de Ville.

Café Cosmos ★★ In days of yore, you might have seen literary masterpieces being scribbled by hand at some of the tables of this crowded cafe. Today, in an age where most novels are written at home with word processors, it's where the hip media crowd gathers to discuss the film scripts and modeling contracts they're cultivating at the time. The cafe features wooden tables, black leather chairs, and black clothing in winter—the perfect backdrop for smoked salmon with toast, rump steak with Roquefort sauce, or grilled tuna steak.

101 bd. du Montparnasse, 6e. ℂ **01-43-26-74-36.** Café espresso 3.95€ ($3.55); platters 6.85€–14€ ($6.10–$12); fixed-price lunch 11€ ($9.35). AE, DC, MC, V. Daily 8–2am. Métro: Vavin.

Café de la Musique This cafe's location in one of the grandest of Mitterrand's *grands travaux* guarantees a crowd passionately devoted to music; the recorded sounds that play in the background are likely to be more diverse and more eclectic than those in any other cafe in Paris. The red-and-green velour setting might remind you of a modern opera house, with windows overlooking nearby place de la Fontaine. On the menu you'll find pasta with shellfish, roast pork in cider sauce, and braised stingray in black butter sauce. Wednesday from 10pm to 1am brings a program of live jazz and Friday from 10pm to 1am brings live music; Saturday a DJ entertains with disco music.

In the Cité de la Musique, Place Fontaine Aux Lions, 212 av. Jean-Jaurès, 19e. ℰ **01-48-03-15-91**. Plats du jour 12€ ($11). AE, DC, MC, V. Daily 7:30am–2pm (full menu daily 11am–midnight). Métro: Porte de Pantin.

Café des Hauteurs   The designers of the Musée d'Orsay recognize the fatigue that can sometimes come with a museum visit. That's why this fifth-floor cafe is midway between a bar and a short-term rest home, where you can recuperate in front of a sweeping view stretching as far as Notre-Dame and Sacré-Coeur and looking over the glass-encased mechanism of a huge clock. In addition to the usual doses of caffeine and alcohol, you can order platters more substantial than a snack but less filling than the main course of a conventional meal. Examples are smoked salmon with shrimp salad and rye bread, and a platter of assorted cheeses.

In the Musée d'Orsay, 1 rue de Bellechasse, (5th floor), 7e. ℰ **01-45-49-47-03**. Salads and light platters 6.85€–12€ ($6.10–$11). AE, MC, V. Tues–Wed and Fri–Sun 10am–5pm; Thurs 10am–9pm. Métro: Solférino. RER: Musée d'Orsay.

La Coupole ⭐   Born in 1927 and once a leading center of artistic life, La Coupole is now the epitome of the grand Paris brasserie in Montparnasse. Former patrons included Josephine Baker, Henry Miller, Dalí, Calder, Hemingway, Fitzgerald, and Picasso. At one of its sidewalk tables, you can sit and watch the passing scene and order a coffee or a cognac VSOP. The food is quite good, despite the fact that the dining room resembles an enormous rail-station waiting room. Try main dishes like sole meunière, cassoulet, fresh oysters, shellfish, and some of the best pepper steak in Paris. The waiters are as rude and inattentive as ever, and aficionados of the place wouldn't have it any other way.

102 bd. du Montparnasse, 14e. ℰ **01-43-20-14-20**. Breakfast buffet 12€ ($11); main courses 14€–31€ ($13–$27); fixed-price menus 21€–30€ ($19–$27) at lunch, 30€ ($27) at dinner. AE, DC, MC, V. Daily 8:30am–1am (breakfast buffet Mon–Fri 8:30–10:30pm). Métro: Vavin.

La Palette ⭐⭐   The staff here defiantly maintains old-fashioned Parisian traditions that haven't changed much since the days of Picasso and Braque—the same drinks (Ricard and Pernod, among others) are still popular. A bustle of comings and goings makes La Palette an insider's version of a battered, artistically evocative Quartier Latin cafe. The decor, inhabited by amiably crotchety waiters, consists of tiled murals, installed around 1935, advertising the virtues of a brand of liqueur that's no longer manufactured. If you happen to drop in during mealtime, you'll have a limited selection of salads and *croque monsieur,* plus one plat de jour per day, always priced at 11€ ($10), which may include roast beef, lamb stew, fish, and gigot of lamb. The food is well-prepared, and the dish of the day is usually announced as a kind of surprise to the joint's many devoted fans.

43 rue de Seine, 6e. ℰ **01-43-26-68-15**. Sandwiches, omelets, and plats de jour 5.30€–11€ ($4.75–$10). MC, V. Cafe and bar Mon–Sat 8am–2am; restaurant Mon–Sat 11:30am–3pm. Métro: Mabillon or St-Germain-des-Prés.

La Rotonde   Once patronized by Hemingway, the original Rotonde faded into history but is immortalized in the pages of *The Sun Also Rises,* in which Papa wrote, "No matter what cafe in Montparnasse you ask a taxi driver to bring you

---

⟨ **Value** **Did You Know?**

You'll pay substantially less in a cafe if you stand at the counter rather than sit at a table, because there's no service charge.

to from the right bank of the river, they always take you to the Rotonde." Lavishly upgraded, its reincarnation has a paneled Art Deco elegance and shares the site with a cinema. The menu includes hearty fare like pepper steak with *pommes frites,* shellfish in season, and sea-bass filets with herb-flavored lemon sauce.

105 bd. du Montparnasse, 6e. ☎ **01-43-26-48-26.** Glass of wine 3.50€ ($3.10); fixed-price menu 18€–25€ ($16–$22). AE, MC, V. Cafe daily 7am–1am; food service daily noon–2am. Métro: Vavin.

Le Procope ★★ To fans of French history, this is the holy grail of Parisian cafes. Opened in 1686, it occupies a three-story town house whose architectural details are categorized as a historic monument. Inside, nine salons and dining rooms, each of whose 300-year-old walls have been carefully preserved and painted a deep red, are available for languorous afternoon coffee breaks or well-presented meals. Menu items include platters of shellfish, onion soup au gratin, coq au vin, duck breast in honey sauce, and grilled versions of various meats and fish. Every day between 3 and 7pm, the place makes itself available to sightseers who come to look but not necessarily eat and drink at the site that welcomed such movers and shakers as Diderot, Voltaire, Georges Sand, Victor Hugo, and Oscar Wilde. Of special charm is the ground-floor room outfitted like an antique library.

13 rue de l'Ancienne-Comédie, 6e. ☎ **01-40-46-79-00.** Reservations recommended. Main courses 15€–27€ ($14–$24). AE, DC, MC, V. Daily noon–midnight. Métro: Odéon.

Les Deux Magots ★★ This legendary hangout for the sophisticated residents of St-Germain-des-Prés becomes a tourist favorite in summer. Visitors monopolize the few sidewalk tables as the waiters rush about, seemingly oblivious to anyone's needs. Regulars from around the neighborhood reclaim it in the off-season. Les Deux Magots was once a gathering place of the intellectual elite, like Sartre and de Beauvoir and Giraudoux. Inside are the two large statues of Confucian wise men (*magots*) that give the cafe its name. The crystal chandeliers are too brightly lit, but the regulars seem to be accustomed to the glare. After all, some of them even read their daily newspapers here. You can order salads, pastries, ice cream, or one of the daily specials; the fresh fish is usually a good bet.

6 place St-Germain-des-Prés, 6e. ☎ **01-45-48-55-25.** Café au lait 4.25€ ($3.80); whiskey soda 11€–13€ ($10–$12); plats du jour 14€–23€ ($12–$20). AE, DC, V. Daily 7:30am–1:30am. Métro: St-Germain-des-Prés.

Restaurant/Salon de Thé Bernardaud ★★ Few other Paris cafes/tearooms mingle salesmanship with culinary pizzazz as effectively as this one. The Limoges-based manufacturer of porcelain Bernardaud opened it in 1995, and the beautiful stuff is on display everywhere. Occupying some of Europe's most expensive commercial real estate, the medium-green space is upscale Art Deco in style. Lunchtime is flooded with employees of the nearby offices and shoppers. You can opt for just a salad or something more substantial, like a medley of fresh fish in herb sauce with vegetables. Afternoon tea adds a new twist: A staff member will present a choice of five porcelain patterns in which your tea will be served, and if you finish your Earl Grey with a fixation on the pattern you've chosen, you'll be directed into the adjacent showroom to place your order.

9 rue Royale, 8e. ☎ **01-42-66-22-55.** Reservations recommended at lunch. Continental breakfast 12€–20€ ($11–$18); lunch main courses 14€–24€ ($12–$22); afternoon tea with pastry 11€ ($10). MC, V. Mon–Fri 8am–7pm; Sat 9am–7pm. Métro: Concorde.

INEXPENSIVE

Café de l'Industrie This place is so old it's new again. Founded pre–World War II, this cafe received a vital new lease on life after the opening of the nearby

Opéra Bastille. Today its three dining rooms boast a decor evoking aspects of both the tropics and faux-baroque Europe, with green plants and lots of original oil paintings by long-term patrons. Known for decanting obscure vintages from the Touraine and the region around Beaujolais and Bordeaux, it appeals to photographers and lesser-known characters in French-speaking showbiz. If you're hungry, consider any of the generous plats du jour. Examples are leeks steeped in vinaigrette, minced chicken with tarragon, boeuf bourguignonne, fried haddock, and tagliatelle with salmon, chives, and cream sauce.

16 rue St-Sabin, 11e. ✆ **01-47-00-13-53.** Glass of wine 2.90€–3.95€ ($2.60–$3.55); main courses 7.30€–14€ ($6.50–$13). MC, V. Daily 10am–2am. Métro: Bastille or Breguier-Sabin.

Le Gutenberg   Behind the largest post office in France and named in honor of the printing presses that used to operate nearby, this is the most evocative and authentic of the cafes close to the Louvre. There's a zinc-top bar and two rooms are on each of two floors loaded with antique mirrors and uniformed staff members. No one can agree on whether the place is 150 or 225 years old. The food runs the gamut from light broths and simple salads to roasted duck breast with orange sauce and pork tenderloin with red wine and apples.

64 rue Jean-Jacques Rousseau, 1er. ✆ **01-42-36-14-90.** Café au lait 1.65€ ($1.50); sandwiches 2.75€ ($2.45); plats du jour 6.10€–7.60€ ($5.45–$6.80). MC, V. Mon–Fri 7am–9pm; Sat noon–9pm. Métro: Châtelet-Les Halles.

6 Gay-Friendly Restaurants

Though any restaurant recommended in this guide is tolerant of same-sex couples, this one is especially welcoming. For the location, see the corresponding arrondissement maps earlier in this chapter. For full coverage of Paris's gay/gay-friendly hotels and restaurants, see *Frommer's Gay & Lesbian Europe.*

INEXPENSIVE

L'Amazonial   MODERN FRENCH/INTERNATIONAL   One of Paris's most popular gay restaurants is in the heart of the Marais, occupying a 19th-century building with a flowered terrace extending onto the pavement. The dining room incorporates decorative elements from ancient Greece and Egypt and the Amazon basin. The menu is sometimes startling, featuring items like ostrich steak with exotic mushrooms; more conservative dishes include Barbados-style grilled prawns, *feijoada* (a Brazilian stew with beans and meat, usually pork), and plats du jour like flank steak with béarnaise sauce. Beware the standoffish waiters.

3 rue Ste-Opportune, 1er. ✆ **01-42-33-53-13.** Reservations recommended. Main courses 11€–19€ ($10–$17); fixed-price menus 13€–24€ ($12–$22). AE, DC, MC, V. Daily noon–3pm and 7pm–1:30am. Métro: Châtelet.

7

Exploring Paris

Paris is a city where taking in the street life—shopping, strolling, and hanging out—should claim as much of your time as sightseeing in churches or museums. Having a picnic in the Bois de Boulogne, taking a sunrise amble along the Seine, spending an afternoon at a flea market—Paris bewitches you with these kinds of experiences. For all the Louvre's beauty, you'll probably remember the Latin Quarter's crooked alleyways better than the 370th oil painting of your visit.

1 Sightseeing Suggestions for the First-Timer

IF YOU HAVE 1 DAY   Get up early and begin your day with some live theater by walking the streets around your hotel. Find a cafe and order a Parisian breakfast of coffee and croissants. If you're a museum and monument junkie and don't dare return home without seeing the "musts," the top two museums are the **Musée du Louvre** and **Musée d'Orsay,** and the top three monuments are the **Tour Eiffel, Arc de Triomphe,** and **Notre-Dame** (which you can see later in the day). If it's a toss-up between the Louvre and the d'Orsay, we'd choose the Louvre because it holds a greater variety of works. Among the monuments, we'd make it the Tour Eiffel for the panoramic view of the city.

If your day is too short to visit museums or wait in line for the tower, we suggest you spend your time strolling the streets. **Ile St-Louis** is the most elegant place for a walk. After exploring this island and its mansions, wander through such Left Bank districts as **St-Germain-des-Prés** and the area around **place St-Michel,** the heart of the student quarter. As the sun sets, head for **Notre-Dame,** standing along the banks of the Seine. This is a good place to watch the shadows fall over Paris as the lights come on for the night. Afterward, walk along the Seine, where vendors sell books and souvenir prints. Promise yourself a return visit and have dinner in the Left Bank bistro of your choice.

IF YOU HAVE 2 DAYS   Follow the above for day 1, except now you can fit in on day 2 more of the top five sights. Day 1 covered a lot of the Left Bank, so if you want to explore the Right Bank, begin at the **Arc de Triomphe** and stroll down the **Champs-Elysées,** Paris's main boulevard, until you reach the Egyptian obelisk at **place de la Concorde,** where some of France's most notable figures lost their heads on the guillotine. Place de la Concorde affords terrific views of **La Madeleine,** the **Palais Bourbon,** the **Arc de Triomphe,** and the **Musée du Louvre.** Nearby **place Vendôme** is worth a visit, as it represents the Right Bank at its most elegant, with the Hôtel Ritz and Paris's top jewelry stores. Now we suggest a rest stop in the **Jardin de Tuileries,** west and adjacent to the Louvre. After a bistro lunch, walk in the **Marais** for a contrast to monumental Paris. Our favorite stroll is along **rue des Rosiers,** the heart of the Jewish community.

Don't miss **place des Vosges.** After a rest, select a restaurant in **Montparnasse,** following in Hemingway's footsteps. This area is far livelier at night.

IF YOU HAVE 3 DAYS   Spend days 1 and 2 as above. As you've already gotten a look at the Left Bank and the Right Bank, this day should be about following your special interests. You might target the **Centre Pompidou** and the **Musée Carnavalet,** Paris's history museum. If you're a Monet fan, you might head for the **Musée Marmottan-Claude Monet.** Or perhaps you'd rather wander the sculpture garden of the **Musée Rodin.** If you select the **Musée Picasso,** you can use part of the morning to explore a few of the Marais's art galleries. After lunch, spend the afternoon on **Ile de la Cité,** where you'll get not only to see Notre-Dame again but also to visit the **Conciergerie,** where Marie Antoinette and others were held captive before they were beheaded. And you certainly can't miss the stunning stained glass of **Sainte-Chapelle** in the Palais de Justice. After dinner, if your energy holds, you can sample Paris's nightlife— whatever you fancy: the dancers at the **Lido** or the **Folies-Bergère** or a smoky Left Bank jazz club or a frenzied disco. If you'd like to just sit and have a drink, Paris has some of the most elegant hotel bars in the world—try the **Crillon** or the **Plaza Athénée.**

IF YOU HAVE 4 DAYS   For your first 3 days, follow the above. On day 4, head to **Versailles,** 21km (13 miles) south of Paris, the greatest attraction in the Ile de France. When Louis XIV decided to move to the suburbs, he created a spectacle unlike anything the world had ever seen. Most of the palace remains intact, in all its opulence and glitter. A full day here almost feels like too little time. After you return to Paris for the night, take a good rest and spend the evening wandering around the Left Bank's **Latin Quarter,** enjoying the student cafes and bars and selecting your bistro of choice for the evening. Two of the livelier streets for wandering are rue de la Huchette and rue Monsieur-le-Prince.

IF YOU HAVE 5 DAYS   Spend days 1 to 4 as above. On day 5, devote at least a morning to **Montmartre,** the community formerly known for its artists atop the highest of Paris's seven hills. Though the starving artists who made it the embodiment of *la vie de bohème* have long departed, there's much to enchant, especially if you wander the back streets and avoid place du Tertre. Away from the tacky shops and sleazy clubs, you'll see the picture-postcard lanes and stair-cases known to Picasso, Toulouse-Lautrec, and Utrillo. It's virtually mandatory to visit **Sacré-Coeur,** for the view if nothing else. Because it's your last night in Paris, let your own interests take over. Lovers traditionally spend it clasping hands in a walk along the Seine; less goo-goo–eyed visitors can still find a full agenda. We suggest an evening at **Willi's Wine Bar** (see p. 284), with more than 250 vintages and good food. For a nightcap, we always head for the **Hemingway Bar** at the Ritz, where Garbo, Coward, and Fitzgerald once lifted their glasses. If that's too elegant, head for **Closerie des Lilas** in the 6th arrondissement, where you can rub shoulders with the movers and shakers of the film and fashion industries.

2 Attractions by Arrondissement

For the locations of these sights, see the **"Top Paris Attractions"** map on p. 176 and the individual **arrondissement maps** that follow.

Top Paris Attractions

Arc de Triomphe **1**	Les Halles **9**
Cathédrale de Notre-Dame **7**	Musée du Louvre **5**
Centre Pompidou **10**	Musée Picasso **11**
Eiffel Tower **2**	Musée Rodin **4**
Hôtel des Invalides (Napoléon's Tomb) **3**	Panthéon **8**
	Sainte-Chapelle **6**
	Place de la Bastille **12**

Top attractions are listed here; for more attractions in each neighborhood, please see neighborhood maps.

Attractions in the 1st Arrondissement

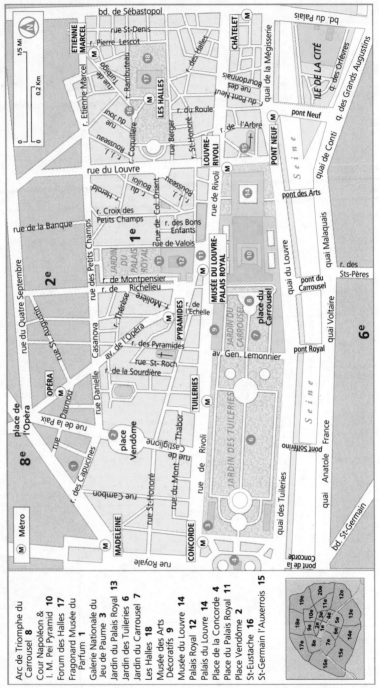

Arc de Triomphe du Carrousel 8
Cour Napoléon & I. M. Pei Pyramid 10
Forum des Halles 17
Fragonard Musée du Parfum 1
Galerie Nationale du Jeu de Paume 3
Jardin du Palais Royal 13
Jardin des Tuileries 6
Jardin du Carrousel 7
Les Halles 18
Musée des Arts Décoratifs 9
Musée du Louvre 14
Palais Royal 12
Palais du Louvre 14
Place de la Concorde 4
Place du Palais Royal 11
Place Vendôme 2
St-Eustache 16
St-Germain l'Auxerrois 15

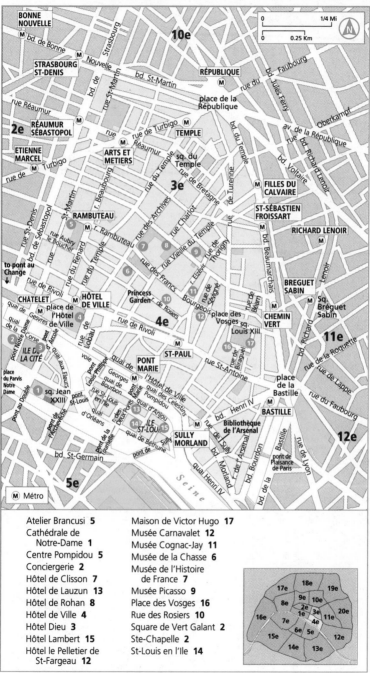

Atelier Brancusi **5**
Cathédrale de
   Notre-Dame **1**
Centre Pompidou **5**
Conciergerie **2**
Hôtel de Clisson **7**
Hôtel de Lauzun **13**
Hôtel de Rohan **8**
Hôtel de Ville **4**
Hôtel Dieu **3**
Hôtel Lambert **15**
Hôtel le Pelletier de
   St-Fargeau **12**

Maison de Victor Hugo **17**
Musée Carnavalet **12**
Musée Cognac-Jay **11**
Musée de la Chasse **6**
Musée de l'Histoire
   de France **7**
Musée Picasso **9**
Place des Vosges **16**
Rue des Rosiers **10**
Square de Vert Galant **2**
Ste-Chapelle **2**
St-Louis en l'Ile **14**

Attractions in the 5th–6th Arrondissements

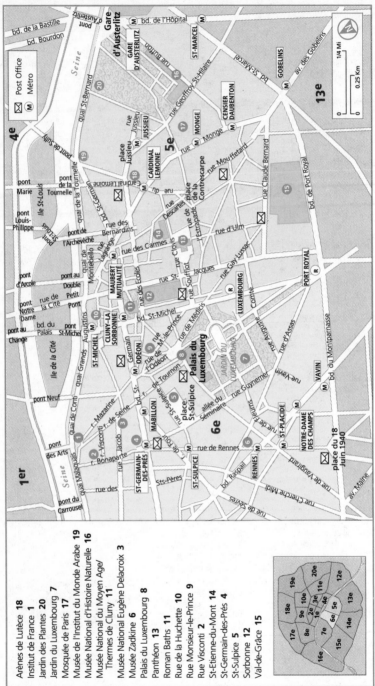

Arènes de Lutèce **18**
Institut de France **1**
Jardin des Plantes **20**
Jardin du Luxembourg **7**
Mosquée de Paris **17**
Musée de l'Institut du Monde Arabe **19**
Musée National d'Histoire Naturelle **16**
Musée National du Moyen Age/
Thermes de Cluny **11**
Musée National Eugène Delacroix **3**
Musée Zadkine **6**
Palais du Luxembourg **8**
Panthéon **13**
Roman Baths **11**
Rue de la Huchette **10**
Rue Monsieur-le-Prince **9**
Rue Visconti **2**
St-Etienne-du-Mont **14**
St-Germain-des-Prés **4**
St-Sulpice **5**
Sorbonne **12**
Val-de-Grâce **15**

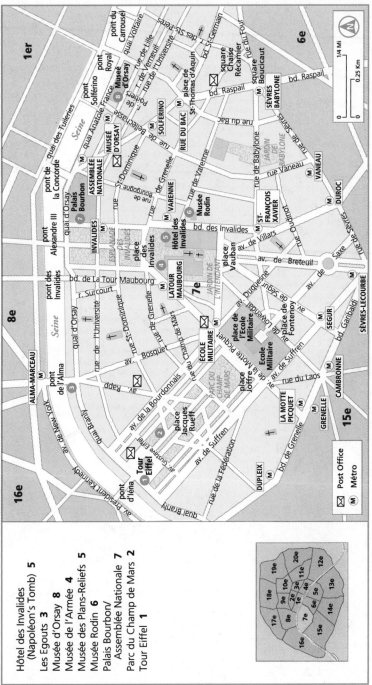

Hôtel des Invalides
  (Napoléon's Tomb) **5**
Les Egouts **3**
Musée d'Orsay **8**
Musée de l'Armée **4**
Musée des Plans-Reliefs **5**
Musée Rodin **6**
Palais Bourbon/
  Assemblée Nationale **7**
Parc du Champ de Mars **2**
Tour Eiffel **1**

⊠ Post Office
Ⓜ Métro

Attractions in the 8th Arrondissement

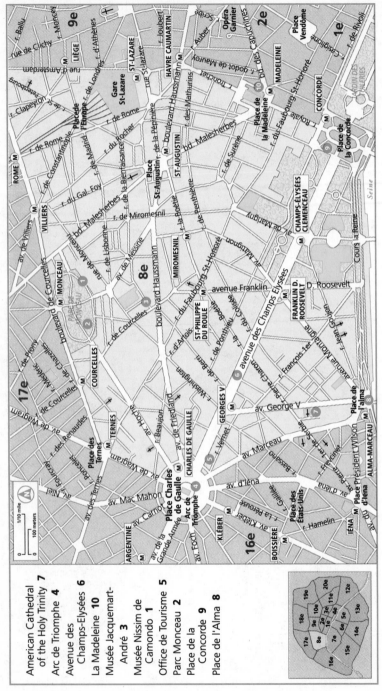

American Cathedral
  of the Holy Trinity **7**
Arc de Triomphe **4**
Avenue des
  Champs-Elysées **6**
La Madeleine **10**
Musée Jacquemart-
  André **3**
Musée Nissim de
  Camondo **1**
Office de Tourisme **5**
Parc Monceau **2**
Place de la
  Concorde **9**
Place de l'Alma **8**

182

Attractions in the 16th Arrondissement

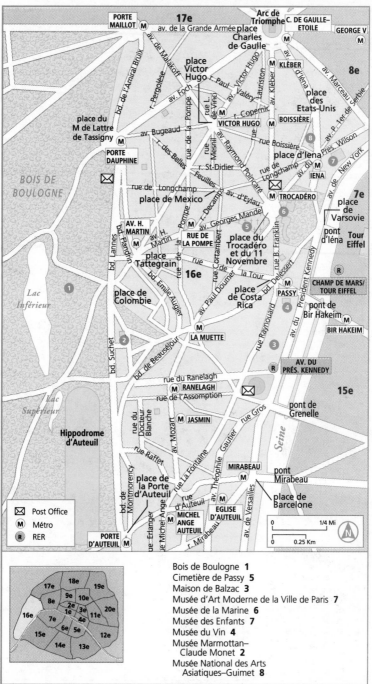

Post Office ✉
Métro Ⓜ
RER Ⓡ

Bois de Boulogne **1**
Cimetière de Passy **5**
Maison de Balzac **3**
Musée d'Art Moderne de la Ville de Paris **7**
Musée de la Marine **6**
Musée des Enfants **7**
Musée du Vin **4**
Musée Marmottan–Claude Monet **2**
Musée National des Arts Asiatiques–Guimet **8**

Attractions in the 18th Arrondissement

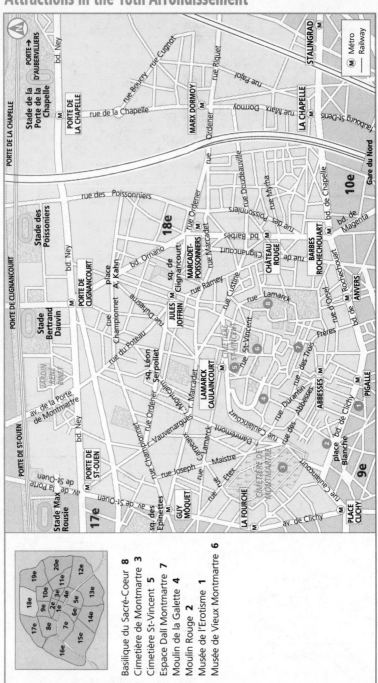

Basilique du Sacré-Coeur **8**
Cimetière de Montmartre **3**
Cimetière St-Vincent **5**
Espace Dalí Montmartre **7**
Moulin de la Galette **4**
Moulin Rouge **2**
Musée de l'Erotisme **1**
Musée de Vieux Montmartre **6**

3 The Top Attractions: From the Arc de Triomphe to the Tour Eiffel

Arc de Triomphe ★★★   At the western end of the Champs-Elysées, the Arc de Triomphe suggests one of those ancient Roman arches, only it's larger. Actually, it's the biggest triumphal arch in the world, about 49m (163 ft.) high and 44m (147 ft.) wide. To reach it, *don't try to cross the square,* Paris's busiest traffic hub. With a dozen streets radiating from the "Star," the roundabout has been called by one writer "vehicular roulette with more balls than numbers" (death is certain!). Take the underground passage and live a little longer.

Commissioned by Napoleon in 1806 to commemorate the victories of his Grand Armée, the arch wasn't ready for the entrance of his empress, Marie-Louise, in 1810 (he'd divorced Joséphine because she couldn't provide him an heir). It wasn't completed until 1836, under the reign of Louis-Philippe. Four years later, Napoleon's remains, brought from St. Helena, passed under the arch on their journey to his tomb at the Hôtel des Invalides. Since that time it has become the focal point for state funerals. It's also the site of the tomb of the Unknown Soldier, in whose honor an eternal flame is kept burning.

The greatest state funeral was Victor Hugo's in 1885; his coffin was placed under the arch, and much of Paris turned out to pay tribute. Another notable funeral was in 1929 for Ferdinand Foch, commander of the Allied forces in World War I. The arch has been the centerpiece of some of France's proudest moments and some of its most humiliating defeats, notably in 1871 and 1940. The memory of German troops marching under the arch is still painful to the French. Who can forget the 1940 newsreel of the Frenchman standing on the Champs-Elysées weeping as the Nazi storm troopers goose-stepped through Paris? The arch's happiest moment occurred in 1944, when the liberation-of-Paris parade passed beneath it. That same year, Eisenhower paid a visit to the tomb of the Unknown Soldier, a new tradition among leaders of state and important figures. After Charles de Gaulle's death, the French government (despite protests from anti-Gaullists) voted to change the name of this site from place de l'Etoile to place Charles de Gaulle. Nowadays it's often known as place Charles de Gaulle-Etoile.

Of the sculptures on the monument, the best known is Rude's *Marseillaise,* or *The Departure of the Volunteers.* J. P. Cortot's *Triumph of Napoléon in 1810* and Etex's *Resistance of 1814* and *Peace of 1815* also adorn the facade. The monument is engraved with the names of hundreds of generals (those underlined died in battle) who commanded French troops in Napoleonic victories.

You can take an elevator or climb the stairway to the top, where there's an exhibition hall with lithographs and photos depicting the arch throughout its history, as well as an observation deck with a fantastic view.

Tips Best City View

From the observation deck of the Arc de Triomphe, you can see up the Champs-Elysées and such landmarks as the Louvre, the Eiffel Tower, Sacré-Coeur, and La Défense. Although we don't want to get into any arguments about this, we think the view of Paris from this perspective is the grandest in the entire city.

Place Charles de Gaulle-Etoile, 8e. ☎ **01-55-37-73-77**. www.monuments.fr. Admission 7€ ($6.25) adults, 4.50€ ($4) ages 18–25, free for children 17 and under. Apr–Sept daily 9:30am–11pm; Oct–Mar daily 10am–10:30pm. Métro: Charles de Gaulle-Etoile. Bus: 22, 30, 31, 52, 73, or 92.

Basilique du Sacré-Coeur ★★   Sacré-Coeur is one of Paris's most characteristic landmarks and has been the subject of much controversy. One Parisian called it "a lunatic's confectionery dream." An offended Zola declared it "the basilica of the ridiculous." Sacré-Coeur has had warm supporters as well, including poet Max Jacob and artist Maurice Utrillo. Utrillo never tired of drawing and painting it, and he and Jacob came here regularly to pray. Atop the *butte* (hill) in Montmartre, its multiple gleaming white domes and *campanile* (bell tower) tower over Paris like a 12th-century Byzantine church. But it's not that old. After France's 1870 defeat by the Prussians, the basilica was planned as a votive offering to cure France's misfortunes. Rich and poor alike contributed money to build it. Construction began in 1876, and though the church wasn't consecrated until 1919, perpetual prayers of adoration have been made here day and night since 1885. The interior is brilliantly decorated with mosaics: Look for the striking Christ on the ceiling and the mural of his Passion at the back of the altar. The stained-glass windows were shattered during the struggle for Paris in 1944 but have been well replaced. The crypt contains what some of the devout believe is Christ's sacred heart—hence, the name of the church.

Insider's tip: Although the view from the Arc de Triomphe is the greatest panorama of Paris, we also want to endorse this view from the gallery around the inner dome of Sacré-Coeur. On a clear day your eyes take in a sweep of Paris extending for 48km (30 miles) into the Ile de France. You can also walk around the inner dome, an attraction even better than the interior of Sacré-Coeur itself.

Place St-Pierre, 18e. ☎ **01-53-41-89-00**. Free admission to basilica; joint ticket to dome and crypt 4.55€ ($4.05) adults, 2.45€ ($2.15) students/children. Basilica daily 7am–11pm. Dome and crypt daily 9am–7pm. Métro: Abbesses; then take the elevator to the surface and follow the signs to the funiculaire, which goes up to the church for the price of a Métro ticket.

Cathédrale de Notre-Dame ★★★   Notre-Dame is the heart of Paris and even of the country itself: Distances from the city to all parts of France are calculated from a spot at the far end of place du Parvis, in front of the cathedral, where a circular bronze plaque marks **Kilomètre Zéro.**

The cathedral's setting on the banks of the Seine has always been memorable. Founded in the 12th century by Maurice de Sully, bishop of Paris, Notre-Dame has grown over the years, changing as Paris has changed, often falling victim to whims of decorative taste. Its flying buttresses (the external side supports, giving the massive interior a sense of weightlessness) were rebuilt in 1330. Though many disagree, we feel Notre-Dame is more interesting outside than in, and you'll want to walk all around it to fully appreciate this "vast symphony of stone." Better yet, cross over the pont au Double to the Left Bank and view it from the quay.

The histories of Paris and Notre-Dame are inseparable. Many prayed here before going off to fight in the Crusades. The revolutionaries who destroyed the Galerie des Rois and converted the building into a secular temple didn't spare "Our Lady of Paris." Later, Napoleon crowned himself emperor here, yanking the crown out of Pius VII's hands and placing it on his own head before crowning his Joséphine empress (see David's *Coronation of Napoléon* in the Louvre). But carelessness, vandalism, embellishments, and wars of religion had already demolished much of the previously existing structure.

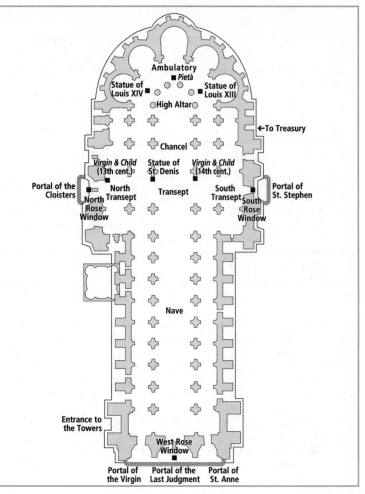

The cathedral was once scheduled for demolition, but, because of the popularity of Victor Hugo's *Hunchback of Notre-Dame* and the revival of interest in the Gothic period, a movement mushroomed to restore the cathedral to its original glory. The task was completed under Viollet-le-Duc, an architectural genius. The houses of old Paris used to crowd in on Notre-Dame, but during his redesigning of the city, Baron Haussmann ordered them torn down to show the cathedral to its best advantage from the parvis. This is the best vantage for seeing the three sculpted 13th-century portals.

On the left, the **Portal of the Virgin** depicts the signs of the zodiac and the coronation of the Virgin, an association found in dozens of medieval churches. The restored central **Portal of the Last Judgment** depicts three levels: The first shows Vices and Virtues; the second, Christ and his Apostles; and above that, Christ in triumph after the Resurrection. The portal is a close illustration of the Gospel according to Matthew. Over it is the remarkable **west rose window** ★★, 9.5m (31 ft.) wide, forming a showcase for a statue of the Virgin and Child. On

---

Moments   A Nighttime Walk & an "Abomination"

When Viollet-le-Duc designed the flying buttresses of the cathedral of Notre-Dame, they were denounced as "horrendous," "a blight of Paris," and an "abomination." Now they're a reason to go walking at night after a meal in a bistro. On the Ile de la Cité, wander through the garden in the rear of the cathedral. Near the Square Jean XXIII, cross the pont de l'Archevêche and walk along quai de Montebello along the Left Bank of the Seine for a wonderful perspective, especially when the *bateaux-mouches* light up the buttresses as they pass along.

---

the far right is the **Portal of St. Anne,** depicting scenes like the Virgin enthroned with Child; it's Notre-Dame's best-preserved and most perfect piece of sculpture. Equally interesting (though often missed) is the **Portal of the Cloisters** (around on the left), with its dour-faced 13th-century Virgin, a survivor among the figures that originally adorned the facade. (Alas, the Child she's holding has been decapitated.) Finally, on the Seine side of Notre-Dame, the **Portal of St. Stephen** traces that saint's martyrdom.

If possible, come to see Notre-Dame at sunset. Inside, of the three giant medallions warming the austere cathedral, the **north rose window** ✧✧ in the transept, from the mid-13th century, is best. The main body of the church is typically Gothic, with slender, graceful columns. In the **choir,** a stone-carved screen from the early 14th century depicts such biblical scenes as the Last Supper. Near the altar stands the 14th-century *Virgin and Child* ✧, highly venerated among Paris's faithful. In the **treasury** are displayed vestments and gold objects, including crowns. Exhibited are a cross presented to Haile Selassie, former emperor of Ethiopia, and a reliquary given by Napoleon. Notre-Dame is especially proud of its relic of the True Cross and the Crown of Thorns.

To visit those **gargoyles** ✧✧ immortalized by Hugo, you have to scale steps leading to the twin **towers** rising to a height of 68m (225 ft.). Once there, you can inspect the devils (some giving you the raspberry), hobgoblins, and birds of prey. Look carefully and you may see hunchback Quasimodo with Esmerelda.

Approached through a garden behind Notre-Dame is the **Mémorial des Martyrs Français de la Déportation de 1945 (Deportation Memorial),** out on the tip of Ile de la Cité. Here, birds chirp and the Seine flows gently by, but the memories are far from pleasant. The memorial commemorates the French citizens who were deported to concentration camps like Auschwitz and Buchenwald during World War II. Carved into stone are these blood-red words (in French): "Forgive, but don't forget." The memorial is open Monday to Friday from 8:30am to 9:45pm and Saturday and Sunday from 9am to 9:45pm. Admission is free.

6 place du Parvis Notre-Dame, 4e. ✆ **01-42-34-56-10.** www.paris.org/Monuments/NDame. Free admission to cathedral; towers 5.45€ ($4.90) adults, 3.95€ ($3.55) ages 18–25/over 60, free for children under 18; treasury 2.30€ ($2.05) adults, 1.50€ ($1.35) ages 12–25/over 60, .90€ (80¢) children 6–11, free for children 5 and under. Cathedral daily 8am–6:45pm year-round. Towers and crypt Apr–Sept daily 9:30am–7:30pm; Oct–Mar daily 10am–5:30pm. Museum Wed and Sat–Sun 2:30–5pm. Treasury Mon–Sat 9:30–11:30am and 1–5:45pm. Métro: Cité or St-Michel. RER: St-Michel.

Hôtel des Invalides/Napoleon's Tomb ✧✧✧   In 1670, the Sun King decided to build this "hotel" to house disabled soldiers. It wasn't an entirely benevolent gesture, because the men had been injured, crippled, or blinded while fighting his battles. When the building was finally completed (Louis XIV had long been dead), a gilded dome by Jules Hardouin-Mansart crowned it and its corridors stretched for miles. The best way to approach the Invalides is by crossing over the Right Bank via the early-1900s pont Alexander-III and entering the cobblestone forecourt, where a display of massive cannons makes a formidable welcome.

Before rushing on to Napoleon's Tomb, you may want to visit the world's greatest military museum, the **Musée de l'Armée.** In 1794, a French inspector started collecting weapons, uniforms, and equipment, and with the accumulation of war material over time, the museum has become a documentary of man's self-destruction. Viking swords, Burgundian battle axes, 14th-century blunderbusses, Balkan khandjars, American Browning machine guns, war pitchforks, salamander-engraved Renaissance serpentines, a 1528 Griffon, musketoons, grenadiers . . . if it can kill, it's enshrined here. As a sardonic touch, there's even the wooden leg of General Daumesnil, the governor of Vincennes who lost his leg in the battle of Wagram. Oblivious to the irony of committing a crime against a place that documents man's evil nature, the Nazis looted the museum in 1940.

Among the outstanding acquisitions are suits of armor worn by the kings and dignitaries of France, including Louis XIV, the best of which are in the new Arsenal. The most famous one, the "armor suit of the lion," was made for François I. Henri II ordered his suit engraved with the monogram of his mistress, Diane de Poitiers, and (perhaps reluctantly) that of his wife, Catherine de Médicis. Particularly fine are the showcases of swords and the World War I mementos, including those of American and Canadian soldiers—seek out the Armistice Bugle, which sounded the cease-fire on November 7, 1918, before the general cease-fire on November 11, 1918. The west wing's Salle Orientale shows arms of the Eastern world, including Asia and the Mideast Muslim countries, from the 16th century to the 19th century. Turkish armor (look for Bajazet's helmet) and weaponry and Chinese and Japanese armor and swords are on display.

Then there's that little Corsican who became France's greatest soldier. Here you can see the death mask Antommarchi made of him, as well as an oil by Delaroche, painted at the time of Napoleon's first banishment (April 1814) and depicting him as he probably looked, paunch and all. The First Empire exhibit displays Napoleon's field bed with his tent; in the room devoted to the Restoration, the 100 Days, and Waterloo, you can see his bedroom as it was at the time of his death on St. Helena. The Turenne Salon contains other souvenirs, like the hat Napoleon wore at Eylau, the sword from his Austerlitz victory, and his "Flag of Farewell," which he kissed before departing for Elba.

You can gain access to the **Musée des Plans-Reliefs** through the west wing. This collection shows French towns and monuments done in scale models (the model of Strasbourg fills an entire room) as well as models of military fortifications since the days of the great Vauban.

A walk across the Cour d'Honneur (Court of Honor) delivers you to the **Eglise du Dôme,** designed by Hardouin-Mansart for Louis XIV. The architect began work on the church in 1677, though he died before its completion. The dome is the second-tallest monument in Paris (the Tour Eiffel is the tallest, of course). The hearse used at the emperor's funeral on May 9, 1821, is in the Napoleon Chapel.

To accommodate **Napoleon's Tomb** ✹✹✹, the architect Visconti had to redesign the church's high altar in 1842. First buried on St. Helena, Napoleon's remains were exhumed and brought to Paris in 1840 on the orders of Louis-Philippe, who demanded the English return the emperor to French soil. The remains were locked inside six coffins in this tomb made of red Finnish porphyry, with a green granite base. Surrounding it are a dozen Amazon-like figures representing Napoleon's victories. Almost lampooning the smallness of the man, everything is done on a gargantuan scale. In his coronation robes, the statue of Napoleon stands 2.5m (8½ ft.) high. The grave of the "King of Rome," his son by second wife Marie-Louise, lies at his feet. Napoleon's Tomb is surrounded by those of his brother Joseph Bonaparte; the great Vauban, who built many of France's fortifications; World War I Allied commander Foch; and the vicomte de Turenne, the republic's first grenadier (actually, only his heart is entombed here).

Place des Invalides, 7e. ✆ **01-44-42-37-72.** Admission to Musée de l'Armée, Napoleon's Tomb, and Musée des Plans-Reliefs 6.10€ ($5.45) adults, 4.55€ ($4.05) ages 12–17, free for children 11 and under. Oct–Mar daily 10am–5pm; Apr–May and Sept daily 10am–6pm; June–Aug daily 10am–7pm. Closed Jan 1, May 1, Nov 1, and Dec 25. Métro: Latour-Maubourg, Varenne, or Invalides.

Musée du Louvre ✹✹✹   The Louvre is the world's largest palace and museum. As a palace, it leaves us cold, except for the **Cour Carrée.** As a museum, it's one of the greatest art collections ever. To enter, you pass through I. M. Pei's controversial 21m (71-ft.) **glass pyramid** ✹—a startling though effective contrast of ultramodern against the palace's classical lines. Commissioned by the late president François Mitterrand and completed in 1989, it allows sunlight to shine on an underground reception area with a complex of shops and restaurants. Ticket machines relieve the long lines of yesteryear.

People on one of those "Paris-in-a-day" tours try to break track records to get a glimpse of the Louvre's two most famous ladies: the beguiling *Mona Lisa* and the armless *Venus de Milo* ✹✹✹. The herd then dashes on a 5-minute stampede in pursuit of *Winged Victory* ✹✹✹, the headless statue discovered at Samothrace and dating from about 200 B.C. In defiance of the assembly-line theory of art, we head instead for David's *Coronation of Napoleon,* showing Napoleon poised with the crown aloft as Joséphine kneels before him, just across from his *Portrait of Madame Récamier* ✹, depicting Napoleon's opponent at age 23; she reclines on her sofa agelessly in the style of classical antiquity.

Tips **Some Louvre Tips**

Long waiting lines outside the Louvre's pyramid entrance are notorious, but there are some tricks for avoiding them:

- Order tickets by phone at ✆ **08-03-80-88-03,** paying with a credit card, then pick them up at any FNAC store (see chapter 9). This gives you direct entry through the Passage Richelieu, 93 rue de Rivoli.
- Enter via the underground shopping mall, the Carrousel du Louvre, at 99 rue de Rivoli.
- Enter directly from the Palais Royal-Musée du Louvre Métro station.
- Buy Le Carte Musées et Monuments (Museums and Monuments Pass), allowing direct entry through the priority entrance at the Passage Richelieu, 93 rue de Rivoli. For details on the pass, see "The Major Museums" later in this chapter.

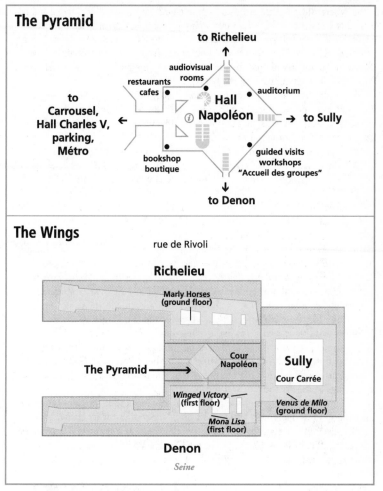

Then a big question looms: Which of the rest of the 30,000 works on display would you like to see?

Between the Seine and rue de Rivoli, the Palais du Louvre suffers from an embarrassment of riches, stretching for almost a kilometer (half a mile). In the days of Charles V, it was a fortress, but François I, a patron of Leonardo da Vinci, had it torn down and rebuilt as a royal residence. Less than a month after Marie Antoinette's head and body parted company, the Revolutionary Committee decided the king's collection of paintings and sculpture should be opened to the public. At the lowest point in its history, in the 18th century, the Louvre was home for anybody who wanted to set up housekeeping there. Laundry hung out the windows, corners were pigpens, and families built fires to cook their meals during the long winters. Napoleon ended all that, chasing out the squatters and restoring the palace. In fact, he chose the Louvre as the site of his wedding to Marie-Louise.

So where did all these paintings come from? The kings of France, notably François I and Louis XIV, acquired many of them, and others were willed to or purchased by the state. Many contributed by Napoleon were taken from reluctant donors: The church was one especially heavy and unwilling giver. Much of Napoleon's plunder had to be returned, though France hasn't yet seen its way clear to giving back all the booty.

The collections are divided into seven departments: Egyptian Antiquities; Oriental Antiquities; Greek, Etruscan, and Roman Antiquities; Sculpture; Painting; Decorative Arts; and Graphic Arts. A number of galleries, devoted to Italian paintings, Roman glass and bronzes, Oriental antiquities, and Egyptian antiquities, were opened in 1997 and 1998. If you don't have to do Paris in a day, perhaps you can visit several times, concentrating on different collections or schools of painting. Those with little time should go on a guided tour in English.

Acquired by François I to hang above his bathtub, Leonardo's *La Gioconda* (*Mona Lisa*) ★★★ has been the source of legend for centuries. Note the guard and bulletproof glass: The world's most famous painting was stolen in 1911 and found in Florence in 1913. At first, both the poet Guillaume Apollinaire and Picasso were suspected, but it was discovered in the possession of a former Louvre employee, who'd apparently carried it out under his overcoat. Two centuries after its arrival at the Louvre, the *Mona Lisa* in 2003 was assigned a new gallery of her own. Less well known (but to us even more enchanting) are Leonardo's *Virgin and Child with St. Anne* ★ and the *Virgin of the Rocks.*

After paying your respects to the "smiling one," allow time to see some French works stretching from the Richelieu wing through the entire **Sully wing** and even overflowing into the **Denon wing.** It's all here: Watteau's *Gilles* with the mysterious boy in a clown suit staring at you; Fragonard's and Boucher's rococo renderings of the aristocracy; and the greatest masterpieces of David, including his stellar 1785 *The Oath of the Horatii* and the vast and vivid *Coronation of Napoleon.* Only Florence's Uffizi rivals the Denon wing for its Italian Renaissance collection—everything from Raphael's *Portrait of Balthazar Castiglione* to Titian's *Man with a Glove.* Veronese's gigantic *Wedding Feast at Cana* ★, a romp of Viennese high society in the 1500s, occupies an entire wall (that's Paolo himself playing the cello).

Of the Greek and Roman antiquities, the most notable collections, aside from the *Venus de Milo* and *Winged Victory,* are fragments of a **Parthenon frieze** (in the Denon wing). In Renaissance sculpture, you'll see Michelangelo's *Esclaves* (*Slaves*), originally intended for the tomb of Julius II but sold into other bondage. The Denon wing houses masterpieces like Ingres's *The Turkish Bath;* the **Botticelli frescoes** from the Villa Lemmi; Raphael's *La Belle Jardinière;* and Titian's *Open Air Concert.* The Sully wing is also filled with old masters, like Boucher's *Diana Resting After Her Bath* and Fragonard's *Bathers.*

The **Richelieu wing** ★★★, reopened in 1993 after lying empty for years, was expanded to add some 69,000m² (230,000 sq. ft.) of exhibition space. It houses northern European and French paintings, along with decorative arts, sculpture, Oriental antiquities (a rich collection of Islamic art), and the Napoleon III salons. One of its galleries displays 21 works Rubens painted in a space of only 2 years for Marie de Médicis's Palais de Luxembourg. The masterpieces here include Dürer's *Self-Portrait,* Van Dyck's *Portrait of Charles I of England,* and Holbein the Younger's *Portrait of Erasmus of Rotterdam.*

When you get tired, consider a pick-me-up at **Café Marly** in the Cour Napoléon. This cafe overlooks the glass pyramid and offers coffees, pastries (by Paris's legendary pastry-maker, Lenôtre), salads, sandwiches, and simple platters.

34-36 quai du Louvre, 1er. Main entrance in the glass pyramid, Cour Napoléon. ℭ **01-40-20-53-17** (01-40-20-51-51 recorded message, 08-03-80-88-03 advance credit-card sales). www.louvre.fr. Admission 7€ ($6.25) before 3pm, 4.55€ ($4.05) after 3pm and on Sun, free for ages 17 and under, free 1st Sun of every month. Mon and Wed 9am–9:45pm (Mon short tour only); Thurs–Sun 9am–6pm. (Parts of the museum close at 5:30pm.) 1½-hr. English-language tours leave Mon and Wed–Sat various times of the day for 2.75€ ($2.45), free for children 12 and under with museum ticket. Métro: Palais Royal–Musée du Louvre.

Musée d'Orsay ★★★ Architects created one of the world's great museums from an old rail station, the neoclassical Gare d'Orsay, across the Seine from the Louvre and the Tuileries. Don't skip the Louvre, of course, but come here even if you have to miss all the other art museums in town. The Orsay boasts an astounding collection devoted to the watershed years 1848 to 1914, with a treasure trove by the big names plus all the lesser-known groups (the symbolists, pointillists, nabis, realists, and late Romantics). The 80 galleries also include Belle Epoque furniture, photographs, objets d'art, and architectural models. There's even a cinema showing classic films.

A monument to the Industrial Revolution, the Orsay is covered by an arching glass roof allowing in floods of light. It displays works ranging from the creations of academic and historic painters like Ingres to Romanticists like Delacroix, to neo-realists like Courbet and Daumier. The Impressionists and Post-Impressionists, including Manet, Monet, Cézanne, van Gogh, and Renoir, share space with the fauves, Matisse, the cubists, and the expressionists in a setting once used by Orson Welles to film a nightmarish scene in *The Trial,* based on Kafka's unfinished novel. You'll find Millet's sunny wheat fields, Barbizon landscapes, Corot's mists, and parti-colored Tahitian Gauguins all in the same hall.

But it's the Impressionists who draw the crowds. When the nose-in-the-air Louvre chose not to display their works, a great rival was born. Led by Manet, Renoir, and Monet, the Impressionists shunned ecclesiastical and mythological set pieces for a light-bathed Seine, faint figures strolling in the Tuileries, pale-faced women in hazy bars, and even vulgar rail stations like the Gare St-Lazare. And the Impressionists were the first to paint that most characteristic feature of Parisian life: the sidewalk cafe, especially in the artists' quarter of Montmar

The most famous painting from this era is Manet's 1863 *Déjeu l'herbe* (*Picnic on the Grass*), whose forest setting with a nude wom fully clothed men sent shock waves through respectable society w' exhibited. Two years later, Manet's *Olympia* created another ing a woman lounging on her bed and wearing nothing b and high-heeled shoes; she's attended by an African Zola called Manet "a man among eunuchs."

One of Renoir's most joyous paintings is b (1876). Degas is represented by his paintings cafe scene, *Absinthe,* remains one of b' Monet was fascinated by the effect c' and its stone bubbles to life in a series *Cathédrale: Full Sunlight.* Another c Whistler's *Arrangement in Grey and Black* better known as *Whistler's Mother.* It's said th though many critics denounced it at the time be Whistler was content to claim he'd made "Mummy

1 rue de Bellechasse or 62 rue de Lille, 7e. © **01-40-49-48-14**. www.musee-orsay.fr. Admission 6.85€ ($6.10) adults, 5.30€ ($4.75) ages 18–24/seniors, free for children 17 and under. Tues–Wed and Fri–Sat 10am–6pm; Thurs 10am–9:45pm; Sun 9am–6pm (June 20–Sept 20 opens 9am). Métro: Solférino. RER: Musée d'Orsay.

Sainte-Chapelle ★★★   Countless writers have called this tiny chapel a jewel box. Yet that hardly suffices. Nor will it do to call it "a light show." Go when the sun is shining and you'll need no one else's words to describe the remarkable effects of natural light on Sainte-Chapelle. You approach the church through the Cour de la Sainte-Chapelle of the Palais de Justice. If it weren't for the chapel's 74m (247-ft.) spire, the law courts here would almost swallow it up.

Begun in 1246, the bilevel chapel was built to house relics of the True Cross, including the Crown of Thorns acquired by St. Louis (the Crusader king, Louis IX) from the emperor of Constantinople. (In those days, cathedrals throughout Europe were busy acquiring relics for their treasuries, regardless of their authenticity. It was a seller's, perhaps a sucker's, market.) Louis IX is said to have paid heavily for his relics, raising the money through unscrupulous means. He died of the plague on a crusade and was canonized in 1297.

You enter through the *chapelle basse* (**lower chapel**), used by the palace servants; it's supported by flying buttresses and ornamented with fleur-de-lis designs. The king and his courtiers used the *chapelle haute* (**upper chapel**), one of the greatest achievements of Gothic art; you reach it by ascending a narrow spiral staircase. Viewed on a bright day, the 15 stained-glass windows up there seem to glow with Chartres blue and with reds that have inspired the saying "wine the color of Sainte-Chapelle's windows." The walls consist almost entirely of the glass, 612m^2 (2,038 sq. ft.) of it, which had to be removed for safekeeping during the Revolution and again during both world wars. In their Old and New Testament designs are embodied the hopes and dreams (and the pretensions) of the kings who ordered their construction. The 1,134 scenes depict the Christian story from the Garden of Eden through the Apocalypse, and you read them from bottom to top and from left to right. The great rose window depicts the Apocalypse.

Sainte-Chapelle stages **concerts** most nights in summer, with tickets from 18€ to 23€ ($16–$20). Call © **01-42-77-65-65** for more details (daily 11am–6pm).

Palais de Justice, 4 bd. du Palais, 1er. © **01-53-73-78-50**. www.monuments.fr. Admission 6.10€ ($5.45) adults, 3.80€ ($3.40) students/ages 18–25, free for ages 17 and under. Apr–Sept daily 9:30am–6:30pm; Oct–Mar daily 10am–5pm. Métro: Cité, St-Michel, or Châtelet-Les Halles. RER: St-Michel.

Tour Eiffel ★★★   This is without doubt the most recognizable structure in the world. Weighing 7,000 tons but exerting about the same pressure on the ground as an average-size person sitting in a chair, the wrought-iron tower n't meant to be permanent. Gustave-Alexandre Eiffel, the French engineer

ue Tour Eiffel Bargain

st expensive way to see the Tour Eiffel is to walk up the first two a cost of 3.05€ ($2.70). That way you also avoid the long lines r the elevator. If you dine at the tower's own **Altitude 95** (© **01-**), an Eiffel restaurant on the first floor, management allows t to the head of the line.

> **Tips   Time Out at the Tower**
>
> To see Tour Eiffel best, don't sprint—approach it gradually. We suggest taking the Métro to the Trocadéro stop and walking from the Palais de Chaillot to the Seine to get the full effect of the tower and its surroundings; then cross the pont d'Iéna and head for the base, where you'll find elevators in two of the pillars—expect long lines. (When the tower is open, you can see the 1889 lift machinery in the eastern and western pillars.) You visit the tower in three stages: The first landing provides a view over the rooftops as well as a cinema museum showing films, restaurants and a bar. The second landing offers a panoramic look at the city. The third landing gives the most spectacular view; Eiffel's office has been re-created on this level, with wax figures depicting the engineer receiving Thomas Edison.
>
> Of course, it's the view most people come for, and this extends for 64km (40 miles), theoretically (weather conditions tend to limit it). Nevertheless, it's fabulous, and the best time for visibility is about an hour before sunset.

whose fame rested mainly on his iron bridges, built it for the 1889 Universal Exhibition. (Eiffel also designed the framework for the Statue of Liberty.) Praised by some and denounced by others (some called it a "giraffe," the "world's greatest lamppost," or the "iron monster"), the tower created as much controversy in the 1880s as I. M. Pei's glass pyramid at the Louvre did in the 1980s. What saved it from demolition in the early 1890s was the advent of radio—as the tallest structure in Europe, it made a perfect spot to place a radio antenna (now a TV antenna).

The tower, including its TV antenna, is 317m (1,056 ft.) high. On a clear day you can see it from 64km (40 miles) away. An open-framework construction, the tower unlocked the almost unlimited possibilities of steel construction, paving the way for skyscrapers. Skeptics said it couldn't be built, and Eiffel actually wanted to make it soar higher. For years it remained the tallest man-made structure on earth, until skyscrapers like the Empire State Building surpassed it.

We could fill an entire page with tower statistics. (Its plans spanned 6,000 square yards of paper, and it contains 2½ million rivets.) But forget the numbers. Just stand beneath the tower and look straight up. It's like a rocket of steel lacework shooting into the sky.

Champ de Mars, 7e. ℂ 01-44-11-23-23. www.tour-eiffel.fr. Admission to 1st landing 3.65€ ($3.25), 2nd landing 6.85€ ($6.10), 3rd landing 9.90€ ($8.80). Stairs to 2nd floor 3.05€ ($2.70). Sept–May daily 9:30am–11pm; June–Aug daily 9am–midnight. Fall and winter, stairs open only to 6:30pm. Métro: Trocadéro, Ecole Militaire, or Bir-Hakeim. RER: Champ de Mars-Tour Eiffel.

4 The Major Museums

Turn to "The Top Attractions" above, for a comprehensive look at the **Musée du Louvre** and the **Musée d'Orsay.**

You can buy **La Carte Musées et Monuments (Museum and Monuments Pass)** at any of the 70 museums and monuments honoring it or at any branch of the Paris Tourist Office (see p. 25). It offers entrance to the permanent collections of monuments and museums in Paris and the Ile de France. A 1-day pass costs 17€ ($15), a 3-day pass 34€ ($30), and a 5-day pass 50€ ($45). See p. 66 for details on the **Paris Visite** pass, valid for 1 to 5 days on the public transport system, including the Métro, the city buses, the RER (regional express) trains within Paris city limits, and even the funicular to the top of Montmartre.

Centre Pompidou ★★★   Reopened in January 2000 in what was called in the 1970s "the most avant-garde building in the world," the restored Centre Pompidou is packing in the art-loving crowds again. The dream of former president Georges Pompidou, this center for 20th- and 21st-century art, designed by Richard Rogers and Renzo Piano, opened in 1977 and quickly became the focus of controversy. Its bold exoskeletal architecture and the brightly painted pipes and ducts crisscrossing its transparent facade (green for water, red for heat, blue for air, yellow for electricity) were jarring in the old Beaubourg neighborhood. Perhaps the detractors were right all along—within 20 years the building began to deteriorate so badly a major restoration was called for. The renovation added 450m² (5,000 sq. ft.) of exhibit space and a rooftop restaurant, a cafe, and a boutique; in addition, a series of auditoriums was created for film screenings and dance, theater, and musical performances. Access for visitors with disabilities has also been improved.

The Centre Pompidou encompasses five attractions:

Musée National d'Art Moderne (National Museum of Modern Art) ★★★ offers a large collection of 20th- and 21st-century art. With some 40,000 works, this is the big attraction, though only some 850 works can be displayed at one time. If you want to view some real charmers, seek out Calder's 1926 *Josephine Baker*, one of his earlier versions of the mobile, an art form he invented. You'll also find two examples of Duchamps' series of dada-style sculptures he invented in 1936: *Boîte en Valise* (1941) and *Boîte en Valise* (1968). And every time we visit we have to see Dalí's *Hallucination partielle: Six images de Lénine sur un piano* (1931), with Lenin dancing on a piano.

In the **Bibliothèque Information Publique (Public Information Library)**, people have free access to a million French and foreign books, periodicals, films, records, slides, and microfilms in nearly every area of knowledge. The **Centre de Création Industriel (Center for Industrial Design)** emphasizes the contributions made in the fields of architecture, visual communications, publishing, and community planning; and the **Institut de Recherche et de Coordination Acoustique-Musique (Institute for Research and Coordination of Acoustics/ Music)** brings together musicians and composers interested in furthering the cause of contemporary and traditional music. Finally, you can visit a re-creation of the Jazz Age studio of Romanian sculptor Brancusi, the **Atelier Brancusi** ★, a minimuseum slightly separate from the rest of the action.

Tips **A Time-Saving Tip**

Museums require you to check shopping bags and book bags, and sometimes lines for these can be longer than the ticket lines. If you value your time, leave your bags in your hotel room or don't go shopping before hitting the museums: Some lines can take 30 minutes. Ask if a museum has more than one check line, and, if so, go to the less-frequented ones.

The museum's **forecourt** is a free "entertainment center" featuring mimes, fire-eaters, circus performers, and sometimes musicians. Don't miss the nearby **Stravinsky fountain,** containing mobile sculptures by Tinguely and Saint Phalle.

Place Georges-Pompidou, 4e. ✆ **01-44-78-12-33.** www.centrepompidou.fr. Admission 5.50€ ($4.90) adults, 3.50€ ($3.15) students, free for children under 18. Special exhibits 6.50€ ($5.80) adults, 4.50€ ($4) students, free for children under 13. Wed–Mon 11am–9pm. Métro: Rambuteau or Hôtel de Ville. RER: Châtelet-Les Halles.

Galerie Nationale du Jeu de Paume ⊛   For years, the Jeu de Paume was one of Paris's treasures, displaying some of the finest works of the Impressionists. To the regret of many, that collection was hauled off to the Musée d'Orsay in 1986. After a $12.6-million face-lift, the Second Empire building was transformed into a state-of-the-art gallery with a video screening room. There's no permanent collection—a new show is mounted every 2 or 3 months. Sometimes the works of little-known contemporary artists are displayed; other times exhibits feature unexplored aspects of established artists. Originally, Napoleon III built in this part of the gardens a ball court on which *jeu de paume,* an antecedent of tennis, was played—hence, the museum's name. The most infamous period in the gallery's history came during the Nazi occupation, when it served as an "evaluation center" for modern artworks: Paintings from all over France were shipped to the Jeu de Paume, and any condemned by the Nazis as "degenerate" were burned.

In the northeast corner of the Jardin des Tuileries/1 place de la Concorde, 1er. ✆ **01-47-03-12-50.** Admission 5.80€ ($5.15) adults, 4.25€ ($3.80) students, free for children 13 and under. Tues noon–9:30pm; Wed–Fri noon–7pm; Sat–Sun 10am–7pm. Métro: Concorde.

Musée Carnavalet-Histoire de Paris ⊛⊛ *Kids*   If you enjoy history, but history tomes bore you, spend some time here for some insight into Paris's past, which comes alive in detail, right down to the chessmen Louis XVI used to distract himself while waiting to go to the guillotine. The comprehensive and lifelike exhibits are great for kids. The building, a Renaissance palace, was built in 1544 by Pierre Lescot and Jean Goujon and later acquired by Mme de Carnavalet. The great François Mansart transformed it between 1655 and 1661.

The palace is best known because one of history's most famous letter writers, Mme de Sévigné, moved here in 1677. Fanatically devoted to her daughter (she ended up moving in with her because she couldn't bear their separation), she poured out nearly every detail of her life in her letters, virtually ignoring her son. A native of the Marais district, she died at her daughter's château in 1696. In 1866, the city of Paris acquired the mansion and turned it into a museum. Several salons cover the Revolution, with a bust of Marat, a portrait of Danton, and a model of the Bastille (one painting shows its demolition). Another salon tells the story of the captivity of the royal family at the Conciergerie, including the bed in which Mme Elisabeth (the sister of Louis XVI) slept and the dauphin's exercise book.

Exhibits continue at the **Hôtel le Pelletier de St-Fargeau,** across the courtyard. On display is furniture from the Louis XIV period to the early 20th century, including a replica of Marcel Proust's cork-lined bedroom with his actual furniture, including his brass bed. This section also exhibits artifacts from the museum's archaeological collection, including some Neolithic pirogues, shallow oak boats used for fishing and transport from about 4400 to 2200 B.C.

23 rue de Sévigné, 3e. ✆ **01-44-59-58-58.** Admission 5.30€ ($4.75) adults, 3.05€ ($2.70) ages 7–26, free for children under 7. Tues–Sun 10am–5:40pm. Métro: St-Paul or Chemin-Vert.

Musée Jacquemart-André ★★   This is the finest museum of its type in Paris, the treasure trove of a couple devoted to 18th-century French paintings and furnishings, 17th-century Dutch and Flemish paintings, and Italian Renaissance works. Edouard André, the last scion of a family that made a fortune in banking and industry in the 19th century, spent most of his life as an army officer stationed abroad; he eventually returned to marry a well-known portraitist of government figures and the aristocracy, Nélie Jacquemart, and they went on to compile a collection of rare decorative art and paintings in this 1850s town house.

In 1912, Mme Jacquemart willed the house and its contents to the Institut de France, which paid for an extensive renovation and enlargement. The salons drip with gilt and the ultimate in fin-de-siècle style. Works by Bellini, Carpaccio, Uccelo, Van Dyck, Rembrandt (*The Pilgrim of Emmaus*), Tiepolo, Rubens, Watteau, Boucher, Fragonard, and Mantegna are complemented by Houdon busts, Savonnerie carpets, Gobelin tapestries, della Robbia terra-cottas, and an awesome collection of antiques. Outstanding are the three 18th-century Tiepolo frescoes depicting spectators on balconies viewing Henri III's 1574 arrival in Venice.

Take a break with a cup of tea in Mme Jacquemart's high-ceilinged dining room, adorned with 18th-century tapestries. Salads, tarts, *tourtes* (pastries filled with meat or fruit), and Viennese pastries are served during museum hours.

158 bd. Haussmann, 8e. ℂ 01-42-89-04-91. www.musee-jacquemart-andre.com. Admission 8€ ($7.15) adults, 6€ ($5.35) ages 7–17, free for children 6 and under. Daily 10am–6pm. Métro: Miromesnil or St-Philippe-du-Roule.

Musée Marmottan-Claude Monet ★★   In the past, an art historian or two would sometimes venture here to the edge of the Bois de Boulogne to see what Paul Marmottan had donated to the Académie des Beaux-Arts. Hardly anyone else did until 1966, when Claude Monet's son Michel died in a car crash, leaving a then-$10-million bequest of his father's art to the little museum. The Académie suddenly found itself with 130-plus paintings, watercolors, pastels, and drawings . . . and a passel of Monet lovers, who can now trace the evolution of the great man's work in a single museum. The collection includes more than 30 paintings of Monet's house at Giverny and many of water lilies, his everlasting fancy, plus **Willow** (1918), **House of Parliament** (1905), and a **Renoir portrait** of the 32-year-old Monet. The museum had always owned Monet's **Impression: Sunrise** (1872), from which the Impressionist movement got its name. Paul Marmottan's original collection includes fig-leafed nudes, First Empire antiques, assorted objets d'art, Renaissance tapestries, bucolic paintings, and crystal chandeliers. You can also see countless miniatures donated by Daniel Waldenstein.

2 rue Louis-Boilly, 16e. ℂ 01-42-24-07-02. Admission 6.50€ ($5.80) adults, 4€ ($3.55) ages 8–24, free for children 7 and under. Tues–Sun 10am–5pm. Métro: La Muette.

Musée National du Moyen Age/Thermes de Cluny (Musée de Cluny) ★★   Along with the Hôtel de Sens in the Marais, the Hôtel de Cluny is all that remains of domestic medieval architecture in Paris. Enter through the cobble-stoned **Cour d'Honneur** (Court of Honor), where you can admire the Flamboyant Gothic building with its vines, turreted walls, gargoyles, and dormers with seashell motifs. First the Cluny was the mansion of a rich 15th-century abbot, built on top of/next to the ruins of a Roman bath (see below). By 1515, it was the residence of Mary Tudor, widow of Louis XII and daughter

---

Finds **Museum Oasis**

Inaugurated at the Musée de Cluny is a garden that's a return to the Middle Ages. The garden was inspired by the detail of the museum's most fabled treasure, the tapestry *"The Lady of the Unicorn."* The garden is small but richly planted and rests under chestnuts and sycamores.

---

of Henry VII and Elizabeth of York. Seized during the Revolution, the Cluny was rented in 1833 to Alexandre du Sommerard, who adorned it with medieval artworks. After his death in 1842, the building and the collection were bought by the government.

This collection of medieval arts and crafts is superb. Most people come to see the *Unicorn Tapestries*, the most acclaimed tapestries of their kind. A beautiful princess and her handmaiden, beasts of prey, and just plain pets—all the romance of the age of chivalry lives on in these remarkable yet mysterious tapestries discovered only a century ago in Limousin's Château de Boussac. Five seem to deal with the senses (one, for example, depicts a unicorn looking into a mirror held by a dour-faced maiden). The sixth shows a woman under an elaborate tent with jewels, her pet dog resting on an embroidered cushion beside her, with the lovable unicorn and his friendly companion, a lion, holding back the flaps. The background in red and green forms a rich carpet of spring flowers, fruit-laden trees, birds, rabbits, donkeys, dogs, goats, lambs, and monkeys.

The other exhibits range widely: Flemish retables; a 14th-century Sienese John the Baptist and other sculptures; statues from Sainte-Chapelle (1243–48); 12th- and 13th-century crosses; chalices, manuscripts, carvings, vestments, leatherwork, jewelry, coins; a 13th-century Adam; and recently discovered heads and fragments of statues from Notre-Dame de Paris. In the fan-vaulted medieval chapel hang tapestries depicting scenes from the life of St. Stephen.

Downstairs are the ruins of the **Roman baths,** from around A.D. 200. The best-preserved section is seen in room X, the frigidarium (where one bathed in cold water). Once it measured 21m x 11m (70 by 36 ft.), rising to a height of 15m (50 ft.), with stone walls nearly 1.5m (5 ft.) thick. The ribbed vaulting here rests on consoles evoking ships' prows. Credit for this unusual motif goes to the builders of the baths, Paris's boatmen. During Tiberius's reign, a column to Jupiter was found beneath Notre-Dame's chancel and is now on view in the court—called the "Column of the Boatmen," it's believed to be the oldest sculpture created in Paris.

In the Hôtel de Cluny, 6 place Paul-Painlevé, 5e. ✆ **01-53-73-78-15.** www.musee-moyenage.fr. Admission 5.50€ ($4.90) adults, 4€ ($3.55) ages 18–25, free for children 17 and under. Wed–Mon 9:15am–5:45pm. Métro: Cluny-La Sorbonne.

Musée National Eugène Delacroix This museum is for Delacroix groupies, among whom we include ourselves. If you want to see where he lived, worked, and died, this is worth at least an hour. Delacroix (1798–1863) is something of an enigma to art historians. Even his parentage is a mystery. Many believe Talleyrand had the privilege of fathering him. One biographer saw him "as an isolated and atypical individualist—one who respected traditional values, yet emerged as the embodiment of Romantic revolt." Baudelaire called him "a volcanic crater artistically concealed beneath bouquets of flowers." The museum is on one of the Left Bank's most charming squares, with a romantic garden. A large arch on a courtyard leads to Delacroix's studio—no poor artist's studio, but the creation of a solidly established man. Sketches, lithographs, watercolors, and oils are hung throughout. If you want to see more of Delacroix's work, head to the Chapelle des Anges in St-Sulpice (see p. 209).

6 place de Furstenberg, 6e. ℂ 01-44-41-86-50. Admission 3.80€ ($3.40) adults, 2.55€ ($2.30) ages 18–25, free for children 17 and under. Wed–Mon 9:30am–5pm. Métro: St-Germain-des-Prés.

Musée Picasso ✦✦ When it opened at the beautifully restored Hôtel Salé (Salt Mansion, built by a man who made his fortune by controlling the salt distribution in 17th-century France) in the Marais, the press hailed it as a "museum for Picasso's Picassos." And that's what it is. The state acquired the world's greatest Picasso collection in lieu of $50 million in inheritance taxes: 203 paintings, 158 sculptures, 16 collages, 19 bas-reliefs, 88 ceramics, and more than 1,500 sketches and 1,600 engravings, along with 30 notebooks. These works span some 75 years of the artist's life and ever-changing style.

The range of paintings includes a remarkable 1901 self-portrait; *The Crucifixion* and *Nude in a Red Armchair;* and *Le Baiser* (*The Kiss*), *Reclining Nude,* and *Man with a Guitar,* all painted at Mougins on the Riviera in 1969 and 1970. Stroll through the handsome museum seeking your own favorite— perhaps a wicked one: *Jeune garçon à la langouste* (*Young Man with a Lobster*), painted in Paris in 1941. There are also several intriguing studies for *Les Demoiselles d'Avignon,* which shocked the establishment and launched cubism in 1907. Because the collection is so vast, temporary exhibits featuring items like his **studies of the Minotaur** are held twice per year. Also here is Picasso's own treasure trove of art, with works by Cézanne, Rousseau, Braque, Derain, and Miró. Picasso was fascinated with African masks, many of which are on view.

In the Hôtel Salé, 5 rue de Thorigny, 3e. ℂ 01-42-71-25-21. www.paris.org/Musees/Picasso. Admission 4.55€ ($4.05) adults, 3.05€ ($2.70) ages 18–25, free for children 17 and under. Apr–Sept Wed–Mon 9:30am–6pm; Oct–Mar Wed–Mon 9:30am–5:30pm. Métro: St-Paul, Filles du Calvaire, or Chemin Vert.

Musée Rodin ✦✦ Today Rodin is acclaimed as the father of modern sculpture, but in a different era his work was labeled obscene. The world's artistic taste changed, and in due course in 1911 the French government purchased Rodin's studio in this gray-stone 18th-century mansion in the faubourg St-Germain. The government restored the rose gardens to their 18th-century splendor, making them a perfect setting for Rodin's most memorable works.

In the courtyard are three world-famous creations. Rodin's first major public commission, *The Burghers of Calais* commemorated the heroism of six citizens of Calais who in 1347 offered themselves as a ransom to Edward III in return for ending his siege of their port. Perhaps the single best-known work, *The Thinker,* in Rodin's own words, "thinks with every muscle of his arms, back, and legs, with his clenched fist and gripping toes." Not completed when Rodin died, *The Gate of Hell,* as he put it, is "where I lived for a whole year in Dante's *Inferno.*"

⌒ **Finds** **Looking for a Quick Escape?**

The little alley behind the Musée Rodin winds its way down to a pond with fountains and flower beds and even sand pits for children. It's one of the most idyllic hidden spots in Paris.

Inside, the sculpture, plaster casts, reproductions, originals, and sketches reveal the freshness and vitality of a remarkable artist. You can practically see many of his works emerging from marble into life. Everybody is attracted to *Le Baiser* (*The Kiss*), of which one critic wrote, "the passion is timeless." Upstairs are two versions of the celebrated and condemned **nude of Balzac,** his bulky torso rising from a tree trunk (Albert E. Elsen commented on the "glorious bulging" stomach). Included are many versions of his *Monument to Balzac* (a large one stands in the garden), Rodin's last major work. Other significant sculptures are the soaring *Prodigal Son, The Crouching Woman* (the "embodiment of despair"), and *The Age of Bronze,* an 1876 study of a nude man modeled after a Belgian soldier. (Rodin was falsely accused of making a cast from a living model.) Generally overlooked is a room devoted to Rodin's mistress, Camille Claudel, a towering artist in her own right. She was his pupil, model, and lover, and created such works as *Maturity, Clotho,* and the recently donated *The Waltz* and *The Gossips.*

In the Hôtel Biron, 77 rue de Varenne, 7e. © **01-44-18-61-10.** www.musee-rodin.fr. Admission 4.25€ ($3.80) adults, 2.75€ ($2.45) ages 18–25, free for 17 and under. Apr–Sept Tues–Sun 9:30am–5:45pm; Oct–Mar Tues–Sun 9:30am–4:45pm. Métro: Varenne.

5 Specialty Museums

Be sure to turn to "The Top Attractions" and "The Major Museums" for the cream of the crop. "Especially for Kids" includes museums parents and kids alike will love. The museums below represent the curious, fascinating, and sometimes arcane balance of Paris's offerings.

ART & MUSIC MUSEUMS

Musée Bourdelle ★ Here you can see works by the star pupil of Rodin, Antoine Bourdelle (1861–1929), who became a celebrated artist in his own right. Along with changed exhibits, the museum displays the artist's drawings, paintings, and sculptures, and lets you wander through his studio, garden, and house. The original plaster casts of some of his greatest works are on display, but the most notable works are his 21 studies of Beethoven. Though some of the exhibits are badly captioned, you'll still feel the impact of Bourdelle's genius.

18 rue Antoine-Bourdelle, 15e. © **01-49-54-73-73.** Admission 3.35€ ($3) adults. Free for ages 26 and under. Tues–Sun 10am–5:40pm. Métro: Montparnasse-Bienvenue.

Musée Cognacq-Jay ★ The founders of La Samaritaine department store, Ernest Cognacq and his wife, Louise Jay, were fabled for their exquisite taste. To see what they accumulated from around the world, head for this museum in the 16th-century Hôtel Denon, with its Louis XV and Louis XVI paneled rooms. Some of the 18th century's most valuable decorative works are exhibited, ranging from ceramics and porcelain to delicate cabinets and paintings by Canaletto, Fragonard, Greuze, Chardin, Boucher, Watteau, and Tiepolo.

In the Hôtel Donon, 8 rue Elzévir, 3e. © **01-40-27-07-21.** Admission 4.55€ ($4.05) adults, 2.30€ ($2.05) ages 18–26, free for children 17 and under. Tues–Sun 10am–5:40pm. Métro: St-Paul or Rambuteau.

Musée d'Art Moderne de la Ville de Paris & Musée des Enfants This museum bordering the Seine has a permanent collection of paintings and sculpture owned by the city, but come here only if visits to the d'Orsay and Louvre haven't satiated you. It presents ever-changing exhibits on individual artists from all over the world or on trends in international art. You'll find works by Chagall, Matisse, Léger, Rothko, Braque, Dufy, Picasso, Utrillo, and Modigliani. Seek out Pierre Tal Coat's *Portrait of Gertrude Stein* and keep Picasso's version of this difficult subject in mind. The Musée des Enfants has exhibits and shows for children.

11 av. du Président-Wilson, 16e. ℭ **01-53-67-40-00.** Admission 4.55€ ($4.05) adults, free for ages 26 and under. Tues–Fri 10am–5:30pm; Sat–Sun 10am–6:45pm. Métro: Iéna or Alma-Marceau.

Musée de la Musique In the $120-million stone-and-glass Cité de la Musique, this museum serves as a tribute and testament to music. You can view 4,500 instruments from the 16th century to the present as well as paintings, engravings, and sculptures that relate to musical history. It's all here: cornets disguised as snakes, mandolins, lutes, zithers, music boxes, even a postwar electric guitar. Models of the world's great concert halls and interactive display areas give you a chance to hear and better understand musical art and technology.

In the Cité de la Musique, 221 av. Jean-Jaurès, 19e. ℭ **01-44-84-46-11.** www.cite-musique.fr. Admission 6.10€ ($5.45) adults, 4.55€ ($4.05) students, 2.30€ ($2.05) ages 6–18, free for children 5 and under. Visits with commentary, 9.10€ ($8.15) adults, 6.85€ ($6.10) students, 3.05€ ($2.70) ages 6–18. Tues–Thurs noon–6pm; Fri–Sat noon–7:30pm; Sun 10am–6pm. Métro: Porte de Pantin.

Musée des Arts d'Afrique et d'Océanie In this Art Deco building built for the 1931 French Colonial exhibition, you'll find an extensive collection of central African art that's especially rich in carved masks, carved statues, and Aboriginal bark paintings, as well as some magnificent bronzes from Benin. There are also some art objects from the Pacific islands and a limited collection of woven carpets and gold jewelry from the Magreb region of Arab-speaking North Africa. In the cellars are aquariums and terrariums containing crocodiles, iguanas, and tortoises.

293 av. Daumesnil, 12e. ℭ **01-43-46-51-61.** Admission 4.55€ ($4.05) adults, free for children under 18. Fri–Wed 10am–5:30pm. Métro: Porte Dorée.

Musée des Arts Décoratifs ✿ In the northwest wing of the Louvre's Pavillon de Marsan, this museum boasts furnishings, fabrics, wallpaper, and objets d'art from the Middle Ages to the present—but it's recommended only if you have an abiding interest in the subject. Notable on the first floor are the 1920s Art Deco boudoir, bath, and bedroom of couturier Jeanne Lanvin by Rateau. Decorative art from the Middle Ages to the Renaissance is on the second floor; collections from the 17th, 18th, and 19th centuries occupy the third and fourth floors. The fifth has centers on wallpaper and drawings and documentary centers detailing fashion, textiles, toys, crafts, and glass trends. The newest addition is a **Musée de la Publicité** (**Museum of Advertising**), with posters from the 18th century, and film, TV, and radio commercials from the 1930s to today. Architect Jean Nouvel designed a cutting-edge interior that also displays avant-garde video techniques.

In the Union Centrale des Décoratifs, 107 rue de Rivoli, 1er. ℭ **01-44-55-57-50.** Admission 5.30€ ($4.75) adults, 3.80€ ($3.40) ages 18–25, free for 17 and under. Tues and Thurs–Fri 11am–6pm; Wed 11am–9pm; Sat–Sun 10am–6pm. Métro: Palais Royal or Tuileries.

Musée Edith Piaf This privately run museum is filled with Piaf memorabilia, like photos, costumes, and personal possessions. The daughter of an acrobat, Giovanna Gassion grew up in this neighborhood and assumed the name of Piaf ("little sparrow"); her songs, like "La Vie en Rose" and "Non, je ne regrette rien," eventually were heard around the world. You must phone in advance to get the security code you'll need to buzz your way in. Nearby is the **Villa Calte,** a beautiful example of the fine architecture many locals are

---

Finds Spying on Paris as a Shopper

Everyone knows about the views from the Eiffel Tower and Sacré-Coeur. Here's another. Shoppers can take the elevator and some stairs to the 11th floor at the top of the **La Samaritaine** department store (No. 2) at 19 rue de la Monnaie, 1er (🕿 **01-40-41-23-16**; Métro: Pont Neuf or Châtelet-Les Halles). At 74m (245 ft.), a 360-degree panorama sweeps across Paris, including the bridge Pont Neuf, the dome of Invalides where Napoleon rests, and the cathedral at Notre-Dame. An enamel frieze on the store's roof identifies the landmarks for you. The platform is open Monday to Saturday from 9:30am to 7pm (until 10pm Thurs).

---

trying to save (ask for directions at the Piaf museum). Fronted by an intricate wrought-iron fence, the house has a pleasant garden where parts of Truffaut's *Jules et Jim* were filmed.

5 rue Crespin-du-Gast, 11e. 🕿 01-43-55-52-72. Free admission but donations appreciated. Mon–Thurs 1–6pm by appointment only. Métro: Ménilmontant.

Musée National des Arts Asiatiques-Guimet ★★   This vastly expanded museum and one of the most beautiful Asian museums in the world is filled with treasures from the East. It is, in fact, one of the world's finest collections of Asian art, and some 3,000 pieces of the museum's 45,000 works are on display. The museum was named for its founder, research chemist/industrialist Emile Guimet. The Guimet, opened in Lyon but transferred to Paris in 1889, received the Musée Indochinois du Trocadéro's collections in 1931 and the Louvre's Asian collections after World War II. The most interesting exhibits are Buddhas, serpentine monster heads, funereal figurines, and antiquities from the temple of Angkor Wat. Some galleries are devoted to Tibetan art, including fascinating scenes of the Grand Lamas entwined with serpents and demons.

6 place d'Iéna, 16e. 🕿 01-56-52-53-00. Admission 5.45€ ($4.90) adults, 3.95€ ($3.55) ages 18–25, free for 17 and under. Wed–Mon 10am–6pm. Métro: Iéna or Alma-Marceau.

Musée Nissim de Camondo ★   Visit this museum for a keen insight into the decorative arts of the 18th century. The pre–World War I town house was donated to the Musée des Arts Décoratif by Comte Moïse de Camondo in memory of his son, Nissim, a French aviator killed in combat during World War I. The museum is like the home of an aristocrat—rich with needlepoint chairs, tapestries (many from Beauvais or Aubusson), antiques, paintings, bas-reliefs, silver, Chinese vases, crystal chandeliers, Sèvres porcelain, Savonnerie carpets, and even a Houdon bust. The Blue Salon, overlooking Parc Monceau, is most impressive. The kitchen of the original mansion has been reopened in its original format, capable of serving hundreds of dinner guests at one time, with few alterations from its original Belle Epoque origins. Fittings and many of the cooking vessels are in brass or copper, and the walls are tiled.

63 rue de Monceau, 8e. 🕿 01-53-89-06-40. Admission 4.55€ ($4.05) adults, 3.05€ ($2.70) ages 18–25, free for children 17 and under. Wed–Sun 10am–5pm. Closed Jan 1, May 1, Bastille Day (July 14), and Dec 25. Métro: Villiers.

Musée Zadkine   This museum near the Jardin du Luxembourg was once the home of sculptor Ossip Zadkine (1890–1967), and his collection has been turned over to the city for public viewing. Included are some 300 pieces of sculpture, displayed in the museum and the garden. Some drawings and tapestries are also exhibited. At these headquarters where he worked from 1928 until his death, you can see how he moved from "left wing" cubist extremism to a renewed appreciation of the classic era. You can visit his garden for free even if you don't want to go into the museum—in fact it's one of the finest places to relax in Paris on a sunny day, sitting on a bench taking in the two-faced *Woman with the Bird.*

100 bis rue d'Assas, 6e. ℭ 01-43-26-91-90. www.paris-france.org/musees. Admission 3.35€ ($3) adults, free for ages 26 and under. Tues–Sun 10am–5:30pm. Métro: Notre-Dame des Champs or Vavin.

CRAFT & INDUSTRY MUSEUMS

Manufacture Nationale des Gobelins ⭐ Did you know a single tapestry can take 4 years to complete, employing as many as three to five full-time weavers? The founder of this dynasty, Jehan Gobelin, came from a family of dyers and clothmakers and in the 15th century discovered a scarlet dye that made him famous. By 1601, Henry IV imported 200 weavers from Flanders to make tapestries full-time. Until this endeavor, the Gobelin family hadn't made any tapestries. Colbert, Louis XIV's minister, bought the works, and under royal patronage the craftsmen set about executing designs by Le Brun. After the Revolution, the industry was reactivated by Napoleon. Les Gobelins is still going strong, and some of the antique high-warp looms are still in use. You can visit the *ateliers* (studios) of the weavers, who sit behind huge screens of thread, patiently inserting stitch after stitch.

42 av. des Gobelins, 13e. ℭ 01-44-54-19-33. Tours in French (with English pamphlets) 7.60€ ($6.80) adults, 6.10€ ($5.45) ages 7–24, free for children under 7. Tues–Thurs 2 and 2:45pm. Métro: Les Gobelins.

Musée de Baccarat In a Directoire building that houses Baccarat's headquarters, this museum resembles an ice palace filled with crystal of all shapes and sizes, with some of the most impressive pieces produced by the company through the years. Czars, royalty, and oil-rich sheiks have numbered among the best patrons of the prestigious company, established in 1764. At the museum entrance stands "Lady Baccarat," a chandelier in the form and size of a woman.

30 bis rue de Paradis, 10e. ℭ 01-47-70-64-30. Admission 2.30€ ($2.05) adults, 1.50€ ($1.35) students, 1.15€ ($1) under age 17/over 60. Mon–Sat 9am–6pm. Métro: Poissonnière or Château d'Eau.

Musée National de Céramique de Sèvres ⭐⭐ Next door to the Manufacture Nationale de Sèvres (see p. 252), this museum boasts one of the world's finest collections of faïence and porcelain, some of which belonged to Mme du Barry, Mme de Pompadour's successor as Louis XV's mistress (Mme de Pompadour *loved* Sèvres porcelain). On view is the Pompadour rose (which the English called the rose du Barry), a style much in vogue in the 1750s and 1760s. The painter Boucher made some of the designs used by the factory, as did the sculptor Pajou (he created the bas-reliefs for the Opéra at Versailles). The factory pioneered what became known as the Louis Seize (Louis XVI) style—it's all here, plus lots more, including works from Sèvres's arch rival, Meissen.

Place de la Manufacture, Sèvres, 15e. ℭ 01-41-14-04-20. Admission 3.35€ ($3) adults, 2.30€ ($2.05) ages 18–25, free for children 17 and under. Wed–Mon 10am–5pm. Métro: Pont de Sèvres, then walk across the Seine to the Left Bank.

HISTORY MUSEUMS

Musée de l'Histoire de France (Musée des Archives Nationales) ⭐ The official home of the archives that reflect the convoluted history of France, this small but noteworthy palace was first built in 1371 as the Hôtel de Clisson, and later acquired by the ducs de Guise, who figured prominently in France's bloody wars of religion. In 1705, most of it was demolished by the Prince and Princesse de Soubise, through their architect, the much-underrated Delamair, and rebuilt with a baroque facade. The princesse de Soubise was once the mistress of Louis XIV, and apparently, the Sun King was very generous, giving her the funds to remodel and redesign the palace into one of the most beautiful buildings in the Marais. *Tip:* Before entering through the building's main entrance, the gracefully colonnaded Cour d'Honneur (Court of Honor), walk around the corner to 58 rue des Archives, where you'll see the few remaining vestiges—a turreted medieval gateway—of the original Hôtel de Clisson.

In the early 1800s, the site was designated by Napoleon as the repository for his archives, and it has served in that function ever since. The archives contain documents that predate Charlemagne. But depending on the policies of the curator, only some of them are ever on display at any given moment, and usually as part of an ongoing series of temporary exhibitions that sometimes spill out into the **Hôtel de Rohan,** just around the corner on the rue Vieille du Temple.

Within these exhibitions, you're likely to see the penmanship of Marie Antoinette, in the form of a farewell letter she composed just before her execution; Louis XVI's last will and testament; and documents from Danton, Robespierre, Napoleon I, and Joan of Arc. The Archives have the only known sketch of the Maid of Orléans that was completed during her lifetime. Even the jailers' keys from the long-since-demolished Bastille are here. Despite the undeniable appeal of the documents it shelters, one of the most appealing aspects of this museum involves the layout and decor of rooms that have changed very little since the 18th century. One of the finest is the **Salon de la Princesse (a.k.a., the Salon Ovale)**, an oval-shaped room with sweeping expanses of gilt and crystal and a series of artfully executed ceiling frescoes by Van Loo, Boucher, and Natoire.

In the Hotel de Soubise, 60 rue des Francs-Bourgeois, 3e. ℂ **01-40-27-60-96.** Admission 3.50€ ($3.10) adults, 2.50€ ($2.25) for persons 18–25, free for children under 18. Mon and Wed–Fri 10am–5:45pm; Sat–Sun 1:45–5:45pm. Métro: Hôtel de Ville or Rambuteau.

Paris-Story *(Kids)*   This very touristy 45-minute multimedia show retraces the city's history in a state-of-the-art theater. The 2,000 years since Paris's birth unroll to the music of such varied musicians as Wagner and Piaf. Maps, portraits, and scenes from dramatic times are projected on the large screen as a running commentary (heard through headphones in 1 of 12 languages) gives details about art, architecture, and events. Many visitors come here for a preview of what they want to see; others stop for an in-depth look at what they've already visited.

11 bis rue Scribe, 9e. ℂ **01-42-66-62-06.** www.paris-story.com. Admission 8€ ($7.15) adults, 5€ ($4.45) students/under age 18. Daily 9am–7pm. Shows begin every hr. on the hr. Métro: Opéra. RER: Auber.

THE OFFBEAT

Musée de la Chasse (Hunting Museum)   Near the Musée Carnavalet, this mansion was also designed by Mansart, and its museum is for the specialist who, like Hemingway, hunts for sport. Mounted heads are plentiful, from the antelope to the elephant, from the bushbuck to the waterbuck to the bush pig. You'll find a Rembrandt sketch of a lion, a number of Desportes wild-animal portraits, and rifles (many from the 17th century) inlaid with pearls or engraved with ivory. The outstanding hunt tapestries are often perversely amusing—one a cannibalistic romp, another showing a helmeted man standing eye to eye with a bear he's stabbing to death. The collection of paintings includes works by Rubens, Breughel, Oudry, Chardin, and Corot.

In the Hôtel Guénégaud, 60 rue des Archives, 3e. ℂ **01-53-01-92-40.** Admission 4.55€ ($4.05) adults, 2.30€ ($2.05) students/seniors, .75€ (70¢) ages 5–16, free for children 4 and under. Tues–Sun 11am–6pm. Métro: Rambuteau or Hôtel de Ville.

Musée de l'Erotisme   A tribute to the primal appeal of human sexuality, this art gallery/museum opened in 1997 in a 19th-century town house that had been a raunchy cabaret. It presents a tasteful but risqué collection of art and artifacts, with six floors boasting an array of exhibits like erotic sculptures and drawings. The oldest object is a palm-size Roman *tintinabulum* (bell), a phallus-shaped animal with the likeness of a nude woman riding astride it. Modern objects include resin, wood, and plaster sculptures by French artist Alain Rose and works by American, Dutch, German, and French artists, including the free-form works of Robert Combas. Also look for everyday items with erotic themes from South America (terra-cotta pipes shaped like phalluses) and the States (a 1920s belt buckle that resembles a praying nun when it's fastened and a nude woman when it's open). The gift shop sells Asian amulets, African bronzes, and terra-cotta figurines from South America. There's also a gallery where serious works of art are sold.

72 bd. de Clichy, 18e. ℂ **01-42-58-28-73.** Admission 6.10€ ($5.45) adults, children under 17 not permitted. Daily 10am–2am. Métro: Blanche.

Fragonard Musée du Parfum (Perfume Museum)   This museum is in a 19th-century theater on one of Paris's busiest thoroughfares. As you enter the lobby through a courtyard, the lightly scented air will remind you why you're there—to appreciate perfume enough to buy a bottle in the ground-floor shop. But first, a short visit upstairs introduces you to the rudiments of perfume history. The copper containers with spouts and tubes were used in the distillation of perfume oils, and the exquisite collection of perfume bottles from the 17th century to the 20th century is impressive. Even if perfume bores you, the air-conditioning is a welcome relief in summer, and the restrooms are spotless and free.

39 bd. des Capucines, 1er. ℂ **01-47-42-04-55.** Free admission. Mon–Sat 9am–5:20pm. Métro: Opéra.

Musée de l'Institut du Monde Arabe (Arab Institute)   Many factors have contributed to France's preoccupation with the Arab world, but three of the most important include trade links that developed during the Crusades, a large Arab population living today in France, and the still-painful memories of France's lost colonies and *départements* in North Africa. For insights into the way France has handled its relations with the Arab world, consider making a trek to this bastion of Arab intellect and aesthetics. Designed in 1987 by architect Jean Nouvel, it includes expositions on calligraphy, decorative arts, architecture, and photography produced by the Arab/Islamic world, and insights into its religion, philosophy, and politics. There's a gift shop and bookshop on-site, and archival resources that are usually open only to bona-fide scholars. Views from the windows of the on-site Moroccan restaurant encompass Notre-Dame l'Ile de la Cité, and Sacré-Coeur.

1 rue des Fossés St-Bernard, 5e. ℂ **01-40-51-38-38.** Entrance to permanent exhibitions 3.80€ ($3.40) adults, 3.05€ ($2.70) students, free for children under 12. Entrance to temporary exhibits 5.30€–7.60€ ($4.75–$6.80) adults, 3.80€–6.10€ ($3.40–$5.45) students, free for children under 12. Tues–Sun 10am–6pm. Métro: Jussieu.

Musée du Vin (Wine Museum)   This museum is in an ancient stone-and-clay quarry used by 15th-century monks as a wine cellar. It provides an introduction to the art of wine making, displaying various tools, beakers, cauldrons, and bottles in a series of exhibits. The quarry is right below Balzac's house (p. 214), and the ceiling contains a trap door he used to escape from his creditors.

5 rue des Eaux, 16e. ✆ 01-45-25-63-26. Admission 6€ ($5.35) adults, 5.25€ ($4.70) students. Tues–Sun 10am–6pm. Métro: Passy.

6 The Important Churches

Turn to "The Top Attractions" earlier in this chapter, for a full look at the **Cathédrale de Notre-Dame, Basilique du Sacré-Coeur,** and **Sainte-Chapelle.**

American Cathedral of the Holy Trinity   This cathedral is one of Europe's finest examples of Gothic Revival architecture and a center for the presentation of music and art. Consecrated in 1886, George Edmund Street, best known for the London Law Courts, created it. Aside from the architecture, you'll find remarkable pre-Raphaelite stained-glass windows illustrating the *Te Deum,* an early-15th-century triptych by the Roussillon Master, an anonymous painter, probably a monk; a needlepoint collection including kneelers depicting the 50 state flowers; and the 50 state flags in the nave. A **Memorial Cloister** commemorates Americans who died in Europe in World War I and all the victims of World War II. Documentation in several languages explains these and other highlights. The cathedral is also a center of worship and community outreach, with a schedule of Sunday and weekday services in English. Les Arts George V, a cultural organization, presents reasonably priced choral concerts, lectures, and art shows.

23 av. George V, 8e. ✆ 01-53-23-84-00. Free admission. Mon–Fri 9am–5pm. Sun Holy Eucharist 9am and 11am. Métro: Alma-Marceau or George V.

Basilique St-Denis ★★   In the 12th century, Abbot Suger placed an inscription on the bronze doors here: "Marvel not at the gold and expense, but at the craftsmanship of the work." France's first Gothic building that can be dated precisely, St-Denis was the "spiritual defender of the State" during the reign of Louis VI ("The Fat"). The facade has a rose window and a crenellated parapet on the top similar to the fortifications of a castle. The stained-glass windows—in stunning mauve, purple, blue, and rose—were restored in the 19th century.

The first bishop of Paris, St. Denis became the patron saint of the monarchy, and royal burials began in the 6th century and continued until the Revolution. The sculpture designed for the **tombs**—some two stories high—span French artistic development from the Middle Ages to the Renaissance. (There are guided tours in French of the Carolingean era crypt.) François I was entombed at St-Denis, and his funeral statue is nude, though he demurely covers himself with his hand. Other kings and queens here include Louis XII and Anne de Bretagne, as well as Henri II and Catherine de Médicis. Revolutionaries stormed through the basilica during the Terror, smashing many marble faces and dumping royal remains in a lime-filled ditch in the garden. (These remains were reburied under the main altar during the 19th century.) Free organ concerts are given Sundays at 11:15am.

Place de l'Hôtel-de-Ville, 2 rue de Strasbourg, St-Denis. ✆ 01-48-09-83-54. Admission 5.45€ ($4.90) adults, 3.50€ ($3.10) seniors/students, 11 and under free. Apr–Sept Mon–Sat 10am–7:30pm; Sun noon–6:30pm; Oct–Mar Mon–Sat 10am–5pm; Sun noon–5pm. Métro: St-Denis.

La Madeleine ★★   La Madeleine is one of Paris's minor landmarks, dominating rue Royale, which culminates in place de la Concorde. Though construction began in 1806, it wasn't consecrated until 1842. Resembling a Roman temple, the building was intended as a monument to the glory of the Grande Armée (Napoleon's idea, of course). Later, several alternative uses were considered: the National Assembly, the Bourse, and the National Library. Climb the 28 steps to the facade and look back: You'll be able to see rue Royale, place de la Concorde and its obelisk, and (across the Seine) the dome of the Hôtel des Invalides. Don't miss Rude's *Le Baptême du Christ,* to the left as you enter.

Place de la Madeleine, 8e. ✆ 01-40-07-03-91. Free admission. Daily 7:30am–7pm. Métro: Madeleine.

Mosquée de Paris ★   This beautiful pink marble mosque was built in 1922 to honor the North African countries that had given aid to France during World War I. Today, North Africans living in Paris gather on Friday, the Muslim holy day, and during Ramadan to pray to Allah. Short tours are given of the building, its central courtyard, and its Moorish garden; guides present a brief history of the Islamic faith. However, you may want just to wander around on your own, then join the students from nearby universities for couscous and sweet mint tea at the Muslim **Restaurant de la Mosquée de Paris** (✆ 01-43-31-18-14), adjoining the grounds, open daily from noon to 3pm and 7 to 10:30pm.

Place du Puits-de-l'Ermite, 5e. ✆ 01-45-35-97-33. Admission 2.30€ ($2.05) adults, 1.50€ ($1.35) students/children. Sat–Thurs 9:30am–5pm. Métro: Monge.

St-Germain-des-Prés ★★   Outside, it's a handsome early-17th-century town house. Inside, it's one of Paris's oldest churches, from the 6th century, when a Benedictine abbey was founded here by Childebert, son of Clovis. Alas, the marble columns in the triforium are all that remain from then. The Normans nearly destroyed the abbey at least four times. The present building has a Romanesque nave and a Gothic choir with fine capitals. At one time, the abbey was a pantheon for Merovingian kings. Restoration of the site of their tombs, **Chapelle de St-Symphorien,** began in 1981, and unknown Romanesque paintings were discovered on the triumphal arch. Among the others interred here are Descartes (his heart at least) and Jean-Casimir, the king of Poland who abdicated his throne. The Romanesque tower, topped by a 19th-century spire, is the most enduring landmark in St-Germain-des-Prés. Its church bells, however, are hardly noticed by the patrons of Les Deux Magots across the way.

When you leave the church, turn right on rue de l'Abbaye and have a look at the 17th-century pink **Palais Abbatial.**

3 place St-Germain-des-Prés, 6e. ✆ 01-43-25-41-71. Free admission. Daily 8am–7:45pm. Métro: St-Germain-des-Prés.

⟨**Moments** Gregorians Unplugged

St-Germain-des-Prés stages wonderful concerts on the Left Bank; it boasts fantastic acoustics and a marvelous medieval atmosphere. The church was built to accommodate an age without microphones, and the sound effects will thrill you. For more information, call ✆ 01-43-25-41-71. Arrive about 45 minutes before the performance if you'd like a front-row seat. Tickets are 18€ to 38€ ($16–$34).

St-Sulpice ★★ Pause first outside St-Sulpice. The 1844 fountain by Visconti displays the sculpted likenesses of four bishops of the Louis XIV era: Fenelon, Massillon, Bossuet, and Flechier. Work on the church, at one time Paris's largest, began in 1646. Though laborers built the body by 1745, work on the bell towers continued until 1780, when one was finished and the other incomplete. One of the priceless treasures inside is Servandoni's rococo **Chapelle de la Madone (Chapel of the Madonna)**, with a Pigalle statue of the Virgin. The church has one of the world's largest organs, comprising 6,700 pipes; it has been played by musicians like Charles-Mari Widor and Marcel Dupré.

The real reason to come here is to see the Delacroix frescoes in the **Chapelle des Anges (Chapel of the Angels)**, the first on your right as you enter. Seek out his muscular Jacob wrestling (or dancing?) with an effete angel. On the ceiling, St. Michael is having some troubles with the Devil, and yet another mural depicts Heliodorus being driven from the temple. Painted in Delacroix's final years, the frescoes were a high point in his baffling career. If these impress you, pay the painter tribute by visiting the Musée Delacroix (see "The Major Museums").

Rue St-Sulpice, 6e. ℂ 01-46-33-21-78. Free admission. Daily 7:30am–7:30pm. Métro: St-Sulpice.

St-Etienne-du-Mont ★★ Once there was an abbey here, founded by Clovis and later dedicated to St. Geneviève, the patroness of Paris. Such was the fame of this popular saint that the abbey proved too small to accommodate the pilgrimage crowds. Now part of the Lycée Henri IV, the Tour de Clovis (Tower of Clovis) is all that remains of the ancient abbey—you can see the tower from rue Clovis. Today the task of keeping St. Geneviève's cult alive has fallen on this church, practically adjoining the Panthéon. The interior is Gothic, an unusual style for a 16th-century church. Building began in 1492 and was plagued by delays until the church was finally finished in 1626.

Besides the patroness of Paris, such men as Pascal and Racine were entombed here. St. Geneviève's tomb was destroyed during the Revolution, but the stone on which her coffin rested was discovered later, and her relics were gathered for a place of honor at St-Etienne. The church possesses a remarkable early-16th century **rood screen:** Crossing the nave, it's unique in Paris—called spurious by some and a masterpiece by others. Another treasure is a wood **pulpit,** held up by Samson, clutching a bone in one hand, with a slain lion at his feet. The fourth chapel on the right when you enter contains impressive 16th-century stained glass.

1 Place Ste-Geneviève, 5e. ℂ 01-43-54-11-79. Free admission. Sept–June Mon–Sat 8:30am–noon and 2–7pm; Sun 8:30am–noon and 3–7:30pm. July–Aug Tues–Sun 10am–noon and 4–7pm. Métro: Cardinal Lemoine or Luxembourg.

St-Eustache ★★ This Gothic and Renaissance church completed in 1637 is rivaled only by Notre-Dame. Madame de Pompadour and Richelieu were baptized here, and Molière's funeral was held here in 1673. The church has been known for organ recitals ever since Liszt played in 1866. Inside rests the **black-marble tomb** of Jean-Baptiste Colbert, the minister of state under Louis XIV; atop the tomb is his marble effigy flanked by statues of *Abundance* by Coysevox and *Fidelity* by Tuby. The church's most famous painting is Rembrandt's *The Pilgrimage to Emmaus.* There's a side entrance on rue Rambuteau.

2 rue du Jour, 1er. ℂ 01-42-36-31-05. www.st-eustache.org. Free admission. Daily 9:30am–7:30pm. Sun mass 9:30am, 11am, and 6pm; Sun organ recitals 5:30pm. Métro: Les Halles.

St-Germain l'Auxerrois ★★ Once it was the church for the Palais du Louvre, drawing an assortment of royalty, courtesans, men of art and law, and local artisans. Sharing place du Louvre with Perrault's colonnade, the church contains only the foundation stones of its original 11th-century belfry. The chapel that had stood here was greatly enlarged in the 14th century by the addition of side aisles and became a beautiful church, with 78m (260 ft.) of stained glass, including some rose windows from the Renaissance. The intricately carved **church-wardens' pews** are outstanding, based on 17th-century Le Brun designs. Behind them is a **15th-century triptych** and **Flemish retable,** so badly lit you can hardly appreciate it. The organ was ordered by Louis XVI for Sainte-Chapelle. Many famous men were entombed here, including the sculptor Coysevox and the architect Le Vau. Around the chancel is an intricate **18th-century grille.**

The saddest moment in the church's history was on August 24, 1572, the evening of the St. Bartholomew Massacre. The tower bells rang, signaling the supporters of Catherine de Médicis, Marguerite de Guise, Charles IX, and the future Henri III to launch a slaughter of thousands of Huguenots, who'd been invited to celebrate the marriage of Henri de Navarre to Marguerite de Valois.

2 place du Louvre, 1er. ✆ 01-42-60-13-96. Free admission. Daily 8am–7:30pm. Métro: Louvre-Rivoli.

Val-de-Grâce ★★ According to an old proverb, to understand the French you must like Camembert cheese, the pont Neuf, and the dome of Val-de-Grâce. Its origins go back to 1050, when a Benedictine monastery was built here. In 1619, Louis XIII appointed as abbess Marguerite Veni d'Arbouze, who asked Louis's wife, Anne of Austria, for a new monastery. After 23 years of a childless marriage, Anne gave birth to a boy who went on to be known as the Sun King. To express his gratitude, Louis XIII approved the rebuilding of the church, and at the age of 7, on April 1, 1645, the future Louis XIV laid Val-de-Grâce's first stone. Mansart was the main architect, and to him we owe the facade in the Jesuit style. Le Duc, however, designed the dome, and Mignard added the frescoes. Le Mercier and Le Muet also had a hand in the church's fashioning. The church was turned into a military hospital in 1793 and an army school in 1850.

1 place Alphonse-Laveran, 5e. ✆ 01-40-51-51-92. Admission 4.55€ ($4.05) adults, under 6 free. Tues–Wed noon–5pm, Sat 1–5pm, Sun 1–5pm (5pm is last entrance). Métro: Port Royal.

7 Architectural & Historic Highlights

Arènes de Lutèce Discovered and partially destroyed in 1869, this amphitheater is Paris's second most important Roman ruin after the baths in the Musée de Cluny (p. 198). Today the site is home to a small arena, not as grand as the original, and gardens. You may feel as if you've discovered a private spot in the heart of the city, but don't be fooled. Your solitude is sure to be interrupted, if not by groups of students playing soccer then by parents pushing strollers down the paths. This is an ideal spot for a picnic—bring a bottle of wine and baguettes to enjoy in this vestige of the ancient city of Lutétia.

At rues Monge and Navarre, 5e. No phone. Free admission. May–Sept daily 10am–10pm; Oct–Apr daily 10am–5:30pm. Métro: Jussieu.

Bibliothèque Nationale de France, Site Tolbiac/François Mitterrand (French National Library) Opened in 1996 with a futuristic design by Dominique Perrault (a quartet of 24-story towers evoking the look of open books), this is the last of the *grand projets* of the late François Mitterrand. It boasts the same grandiose scale as the Cité de la Musique (p. 271) and houses the nation's literary and historic archives; it's regarded as a repository of the French soul, replacing outmoded facilities on rue des Archives. The library incorporates space for 1,600 readers at a time, many of whom enjoy views over two levels of a garden-style courtyard that seems far removed from the urban congestion of Paris.

This is one of Europe's most user-friendly academic facilities, emphasizing computerized documentation and microfiche—a role model that'll set academic and literary priorities well into the future. The public has access to as many as 180,000 books plus thousands of periodicals, with an additional 10 million historic (including medieval) documents shown to qualified experts. Though the appeal of this place extends mainly to serious scholars, there's a handful of special exhibits that might interest you, as well as concerts and lectures. Concert tickets rarely exceed 15€ ($13) for adults and 10€ ($9) for students, seniors, and children; a schedule is available at the library.

Quai François-Mauriac, 13e. ℭ **01-53-79-49-49**. www.bnf.fr. Admission 3.05€ ($2.70). No one under 16 admitted. Tues–Sat 10am–8pm; Sun noon–7pm. Métro: Bibliothèque François-Mitterrand.

Conciergerie ★★ London has its Bloody Tower and Paris has its Conciergerie. Even though the Conciergerie had a long regal history before the Revolution, it was forever stained by the Reign of Terror and lives as an infamous symbol of the time when carts pulled up constantly to haul off fresh supplies of victims for Dr. Guillotin's wonderful little invention.

Much of the Conciergerie was built in the 14th century as an extension of the Capetian royal Palais de la Cité. You approach through its landmark twin towers, the **Tour d'Argent** (where the crown jewels were stored at one time) and **Tour de César,** but the **Salle des Gardes (Guard Room)** is the actual entrance. Even more interesting is the dark and foreboding Gothic **Salle des Gens d'Armes (Room of People at Arms),** utterly changed from the days when the king used it as a banquet hall. However, architecture plays a secondary role to the list of prisoners who spent their last days here. Few in its history endured tortures as severe as those imposed on Ravaillac, who assassinated Henry IV in 1610. In the Tour de César, he received pincers in the flesh and had hot lead and boiling oil poured on him like bath water before being executed (see the Hôtel de Ville entry below). During the Revolution, the Conciergerie became a symbol of terror to the nobility and enemies of the State. A short walk away, the Revolutionary Tribunal dispensed a skewed, hurried justice—if it's any consolation, the jurists didn't believe in torturing their victims, only in decapitating them.

After being seized by a crowd of peasants who stormed Versailles, Louis XVI and Marie Antoinette were brought here to await their trials. In failing health and shocked beyond grief, *l'Autrichienne* ("the Austrian," as she was called with malice) had only a small screen (sometimes not even that) to protect her modesty from the gaze of guards stationed in her cell. By accounts of the day, she was shy and stupid, though the evidence is that on her death she displayed the nobility of a true queen. (What's more, the famous "Let them eat cake" she supposedly uttered when told the peasants had no bread, is probably apocryphal—besides, at the time, cake flour was less expensive than bread flour, so even if she said this, it wasn't meant cold-heartedly.) It was shortly before noon on the morning of October 16, 1793, when her executioners came for her, grabbing her and cutting her hair, as was the custom for victims marked for the guillotine.

Later, the Conciergerie housed other prisoners, including Mme Elisabeth; Mme du Barry, mistress of Louis XV; Mme Roland ("O Liberty! Liberty! What crimes are committed in thy name!"); and Charlotte Corday, who killed Marat while he was taking a sulphur bath. In time, the Revolution consumed its own leaders, such as Danton and Robespierre. Finally, even one of Paris's most hated men, public prosecutor Fouquier-Tinville, faced the guillotine to which he'd sent so many others. Among the few interned here who lived to tell the tale was America's Thomas Paine, who reminisced about his chats in English with Danton.

1 quai de l'Horloge, 4e. ✆ 01-53-73-78-50. www.paris.org/Monuments/Conciergerie. Admission 5.45€ ($4.90) adults, 3.50€ ($3.10) ages 18–25, free for 17 and under. Apr–Sept daily 9:30am–6:30pm; Oct–Mar daily 10am–5pm. Métro: Cité, Châtelet, or St-Michel. RER: St-Michel.

Hôtel de Ville ✯ On a large square with fountains and early-1900s lamp-posts, the 19th-century Hôtel de Ville isn't a hotel but Paris's grandiose City Hall. The medieval structure it replaced had witnessed countless municipally ordered executions. Henry IV's assassin, Ravaillac, was quartered alive on the square in 1610, his body tied to four horses that bolted in opposite directions. On May 24, 1871, the communards doused the City Hall with petrol, creating a blaze that lasted for 8 days. The Third Republic ordered the structure rebuilt, with many changes, even creating a Hall of Mirrors evocative of that at Versailles. For security reasons, the major splendor of this building is closed to the public. However, the information center sponsors exhibits on Paris in the main lobby.

29 rue de Rivoli, 4e. ✆ 01-42-76-43-43. Free admission. Information center Mon–Sat 9am–6:30pm. Métro: Hôtel de Ville.

Institut de France ✯ Designed by Louis Le Vau, this dramatic baroque building with an enormous cupola is the seat of all five Academies that domi-nate France's intellectual life—Française, Sciences, Inscriptions et Belles Lettres, Beaux-Arts, and Sciences Morales et Politiques. The members of the Academie Française (limited to 40), guardians of the French language referred to as "the immortals," gather here. Many are unfamiliar figures (though Jacques Cousteau and Marshall Pétain were members), and the Academy is remarkable for the great writers and philosophers who have *not* been invited to join—Balzac, Baudelaire, Diderot, Flaubert, Descartes, Proust, Molière, Pascal, Rousseau, and Zola, to name only a few. The cenotaph was designed by Coysevox for Mazarin.

23 quai de Conti, 6e. ✆ 01-44-41-44-41. Free admission (guests can walk into courtyard only). Métro: Pont Neuf or Odéon.

La Grande Arche de La Défense ✯ Designed as the architectural center-piece of the sprawling satellite suburb of La Défense, this massive steel-and-masonry arch rises 35 stories. It was built with the blessing of the late François Mitterrand and extends the magnificently engineered straight line linking the Louvre, Arc de Triomphe du Carrousel, Champs-Elysées, Arc de Triomphe, avenue de la Grande Armée, and place du Porte Maillot. The arch is ringed with a circular avenue patterned after the one winding around the Arc de Triomphe. The monument is tall enough to shelter Notre-Dame beneath its heavily trussed canopy. An elevator carries you up to an observation platform, where you get a view of the carefully planned geometry of the surrounding streets.

You'll notice nets rigged along the Grande Arche. When pieces of Mitterrand's *grand projet* started falling to the ground, they were erected to catch the falling fragments. If only such protection existed from all politicians' follies!

1 place du parvis de La Défense, Puteaux, 15e. ✆ 01-49-07-27-57. Admission 7€ ($6.25) adults, 5.30€ ($4.75) ages 15–17, 4.55€ ($4.05) ages 6–14, free for children 5 and under. Daily Apr–Oct 10am–7pm; off-season 10am–8pm. RER: La Défense.

Palais Bourbon/Assemblée Nationale ✸

The French parliament's lower house, the Chamber of Deputies, meets at this 1722 mansion built by the duchesse de Bourbon, a daughter of Louis XIV. You can make reservations for one of two types of visits as early as 6 months in advance. Tours on art, architecture, and basic French government processes are given Monday, Friday, and Saturday. They're in French (in English with advance booking). You may also observe sessions of the National Assembly, held Tuesday afternoon and all day Wednesday and Thursday beginning at 9:30am. Do remember this is a working government building, and all visitors are subject to rigorous security checks.

33 quai d'Orsay, 7e. ✆ 01-40-63-64-08. Free admission. Hours vary, so call ahead. Métro: Assemblée Nationale.

Palais Royal ✸✸

The Palais Royal was originally known as the Palais Cardinal, for it was the residence of Cardinal Richelieu, Louis XIII's prime minister. Richelieu had it built, and after his death it was inherited by the king, who died soon after. Louis XIV spent part of his childhood here with his mother, Anne of Austria, but later resided at the Louvre and Versailles. The palace was later owned by the duc de Chartres et Orléans (see the entry for Parc Monceau under "Parks & Gardens"), who encouraged the opening of cafes, gambling dens, and other public entertainments. Though government offices occupy the Palais Royal and are not open to the public, do visit the **Jardin du Palais Royal,** an enclosure bordered by arcades. Don't miss the main courtyard, with the controversial 1986 Buren sculpture—280 prison-striped columns, oddly placed.

Rue St-Honoré, 1er. No phone. Free admission. Daily 8am–7pm. Métro: Palais Royal–Musée du Louvre.

Panthéon ✸✸

Some of the most famous men in French history (Victor Hugo, for one) are buried here on the crest of the mount of St. Geneviève. In 1744, Louis XV vowed that if he recovered from a mysterious illness, he'd build a church to replace the Abbaye de Ste-Geneviève. He recovered but took his time fulfilling his promise. It wasn't until 1764 that Mme de Pompadour's brother hired Soufflot to design a church in the form of a Greek cross with a dome reminiscent of St. Paul's in London. When Soufflot died, his pupil Rondelet carried out the work, completing the structure 9 years after his master's death.

After the Revolution, the church was converted into a "Temple of Fame" and became a pantheon for the great men of France. Mirabeau was buried here, though his remains were later removed. Likewise, Marat was only a temporary tenant. Voltaire's body was exhumed and placed here—and allowed to remain. In the 19th century, the building changed roles so many times—a church, a pantheon, a church—that it was hard to keep its function straight. After Hugo was buried here, it became a pantheon once again. Other notable men entombed within are Rousseau, Soufflot, Zola, and Braille. Only one woman has so far been deemed worthy of placement here, Marie Curie, who joined her husband, Pierre. Most recently, the ashes of André Malraux were transferred to the Panthéon because, according to President Jacques Chirac, he "lived [his] dreams and made them live in us." As Charles de Gaulle's culture minister, Malraux decreed the arts should be part of the lives of all French people, not just Paris's elite.

Before entering the crypt, note the striking frescoes: On the right wall are scenes from Geneviève's life, and on the left are the saint with a white-draped head looking out over medieval Paris, the city whose patron she became, as well as Geneviève relieving victims of famine with supplies.

Place du Panthéon, 5e. ✆ **01-44-32-18-00.** Admission 7€ ($6.25) adults, 4.15€ ($3.70) ages 18–25, free for 18 and under. Apr–Sept daily 9:30am–6:30pm; Oct–Mar daily 10am–6:15pm (last entrance 45 min. before closing). Métro: Cardinal Lemoine or Maubert-Mutualité.

8 Literary Landmarks

If there's a literary bone in your body, you'll feel a vicarious thrill on discovering the haunts of the writers and artists who've lived, worked, and played in Paris.

Take the Métro to place St-Michel to begin your tour. As you wander away from the Seine, you'll encounter **rue de la Huchette,** one of the Left Bank's most famous streets. Its inhabitants were immortalized in Eliot Paul's *The Last Time I Saw Paris.* Continuing on, you'll enter the territory of the Beat Generation, home to the **Café Gentilhomme** (no longer there) described by Jack Kerouac in *Satori in Paris.* Allen Ginsberg's favorite, the **Hôtel du Vieux-Paris,** 9 rue Gît-le-Coeur, still attracts those in search of the Beats.

Stroll down **rue Monsieur-le-Prince,** the "Yankee alleyway," where Richard Wright, James McNeill Whistler, Henry Wadsworth Longfellow, and Oliver Wendell Holmes lived at one time or another. During a visit in 1959, Martin Luther King Jr. came to call on Richard Wright, the Mississippi-born African-American novelist famous for *Native Son.* King climbed to the third-floor apartment at **no. 14,** to find that Wright's opinions on the civil rights movement conflicted with his own. Whistler rented a studio at **no. 22,** and, in 1826, Longfellow lived at **no. 49.** Oliver Wendell Holmes Sr. lived at **no. 55.** After strolling along this street, you can dine at the haunts of Kerouac and Hemingway. (See our recommendation of **Crémerie-Restaurant Polidor,** 41 rue Monsieur-le-Prince, 6e, on p. 158.) Or cross back over to the Right Bank for a drink at the famed **Hôtel de Crillon,** 10 place de la Concorde, 8e (p. 88), where heroine Brett Ashley broke her promise to rendezvous with Jake Barnes in Hemingway's *The Sun Also Rises.* Zelda and F. Scott Fitzgerald lifted their glasses here as well.

For details on **Harry's New York Bar,** 5 rue Daunou, 2e, see "Literary Haunts" in chapter 10, "Paris After Dark." For a description of **Les Deux Magots, Le Procope,** and **La Rotonde,** see "The Top Cafes" in chapter 6. And for coverage of the bookstore **Shakespeare and Company,** see p. 251.

Here are two great museums for hard-core literary fans:

Maison de Balzac   In the residential district of Passy, near the Bois de Boulogne, sits this modest house with a courtyard and garden. Honoré de Balzac fled to this house in 1840 after his possessions and furnishings were seized, and lived here for 7 years (to see him, you had to know a password). If a creditor knocked on the rue Raynouard door, Balzac was able to escape through the rue Berton exit. The museum's most notable memento is Balzac's "screech-owl" (his nickname for his tea kettle), which he kept hot throughout the night as he wrote *La Comédie humaine.* Also enshrined are Balzac's writing desk and chair and a library of special interest to scholars. The little house is filled with caricatures of Balzac. A biographer once wrote: "With his bulky baboon silhouette, his blue suit with gold buttons, his famous cane like a golden crowbar, and his abundant, disheveled hair, Balzac was a sight for caricature."

47 rue Raynouard, 16e. © 01-55-74-41-80. www.paris-france.org/musees. Admission 4.55€ ($4.05) adults, 3.05€ ($2.70) 26 and under. Tues–Sun 10am–5:40pm. Métro: Passy or La Muette.

Maison de Victor Hugo ★   Today, theatergoers who've seen *Les Misérables,* even those who haven't read anything by Paris's 19th-century novelist, come to place des Vosges to see where Hugo lived and wrote. Some thought him a genius, but Cocteau called him a madman, and an American composer discovered that in his old age he was carving furniture with his teeth! From 1832 to 1848, the novelist/poet lived on the second floor of the Hôtel Rohan Guéménée, built in 1610 on what was then place Royale. The museum owns some of Hugo's furniture as well as pieces that once belonged to Juliette Drouet, the mistress with whom he lived in exile on Guernsey, one of the Channel Islands.

Worth the visit are Hugo's drawings, more than 450, illustrating scenes from his own works. Mementos of the great writer abound, including samples of his handwriting, his inkwell, and first editions of his works. A painting of Hugo's 1885 funeral procession at the Arc de Triomphe is on display, as are plentiful portraits and souvenirs of his family. Of the furnishings, a chinoiserie salon stands out. The collection even contains Daumier caricatures and a bust of Hugo by David d'Angers, which, compared to Rodin's, looks saccharine.

6 place des Vosges, 4e. © 01-42-72-10-16. Admission 3.35€ ($3) adults, free for 26 and under. Tues–Sun 10am–5:40pm. Closed national holidays. Métro: St-Paul, Bastille, or Chemin-Vert.

9 Parks & Gardens
JARDIN DES TUILERIES
The spectacular statue-studded **Jardin des Tuileries** ★★, bordering place de la Concorde, 1st arrondissement (© 01-44-50-75-01; Métro: Tuileries or Concorde), are as much a part of Paris as the Seine. Le Nôtre, Louis XIV's gardener and planner of the Versailles grounds, designed them. Some of the gardens' most distinctive statues are the 18 enormous bronzes by Maillol, installed within the Jardin du Carroussel, a subdivision of the Jardins des Tuileries, between 1964 and 1965, under the direction of then-Culture Minister André Malraux.

About 100 years before that, Catherine de Médicis ordered a palace built here, the **Palais des Tuileries;** other occupants have included Louis XVI (after he left Versailles) and Napoleon. Twice attacked by Parisians, it was burned to the ground in 1871 and never rebuilt. The gardens, however, remain. In orderly French manner, the trees are arranged according to designs and even the

---

Fun Fact Did You Know?

The odd name of the Jardins des Tuileries comes from the clay earth of the land here, once used to make roof tiles called *tuiles.*

Half of Paris can be found in the Tuileries on a warm spring day, listening to the birds and admiring the daffodils and tulips. As you walk toward the Louvre, you'll enter the **Jardin du Carroussel,** dominated by the **Arc de Triomphe du Carroussel,** at the Cour du Carroussel. Pierced with three walkways and supported by marble columns, the monument honors Napoleon's Grande Armée, celebrating its victory at Austerlitz. The arch is surmounted by statuary, a chariot, and four bronze horses.

paths are arrow-straight. Breaking the sense of order and formality are bubbling fountains.

JARDIN DU LUXEMBOURG

Hemingway once told a friend that the **Jardin du Luxembourg** ✹✹ in the 6th arrondissement (Métro: Odéon; RER: Luxembourg) "kept us from starvation." He related that in his poverty-stricken days in Paris, he wheeled a baby carriage (the vehicle was considered luxurious) through the garden because it was known "for the classiness of its pigeons." When the gendarme went across the street for a glass of wine, the writer would eye his victim, preferably a plump one, then lure him with corn and "snatch him, wring his neck," and hide him under the blanket. "We got a little tired of pigeon that year," he confessed, "but they filled many a void."

The Luxembourg has always been associated with artists, though children, students, and tourists predominate nowadays. Watteau came this way, as did Verlaine. Balzac didn't like the gardens at all. In 1905, Gertrude Stein would cross them to catch the Batignolles/Clichy/Odéon omnibus, pulled by three gray mares, to meet Picasso in his studio at Montmartre, where he painted her portrait.

Marie de Médicis, the wife of Henri IV, ordered the **Palais du Luxembourg** built on this site in 1612, shortly after she was widowed. A Florentine by birth, the regent wanted to create another Pitti Palace, where she could live with her "witch" friend, Leonora Galigal. Architect Salomon de Brossee wasn't entirely successful, though the overall effect is Italianate. Alas, the queen didn't get to enjoy the palace, as her son, Louis XIII, forced her into exile when he discovered she was plotting to overthrow him. She died in poverty in Cologne. For her palace, she'd commissioned from Rubens 21 paintings that glorified her life, but they're now in the Louvre. You can visit the palace only the first Sunday of each month at 10:30am, for 7.60€ ($6.80) for adults or 6.10€ ($5.45) for those 25 years old or under. However, you must call ✆ **01-44-61-21-66** to make a reservation.

You don't really come to the Luxembourg to visit the palace; the gardens are the attraction. For the most part, they're in the classic French tradition: well groomed and formally laid out, the trees planted in patterns. Urns and statuary on pedestals, one honoring Paris's patroness, St. Geneviève, with pigtails reaching to her thighs, encircle a central water basin. Another memorial is dedicated to Stendhal. Kids can sail a toy boat, ride a pony, or attend an occasional Grand Guignol puppet show. And you can play *boules* with a group of elderly men who wear black berets and have Gauloises dangling from their mouths.

BOIS DE BOULOGNE

One of the most spectacular parks in Europe is the **Bois de Boulogne** ✹✹, Porte Dauphine, 16th arrondissement (✆ **01-40-67-90-82;** Métro: Les Sablons, Porte Maillot, or Porte Dauphine), often called the "main lung" of Paris. Horse-drawn carriages traverse it, but you can also drive through. Its hidden pathways, however, can be discovered only by walking. You could spend days in the Bois de Boulogne and still not see everything.

Porte Dauphine is the main entrance, though you can take the Métro to Porte Maillot as well. West of Paris, the park was once a forest kept for royal hunts. It was in vogue in the late 19th century: Along avenue Foch, carriages with elegantly attired and coiffured Parisian damsels would rumble along with their foppish escorts. Nowadays, it's more likely to attract run-of-the-mill picnickers. (And at night, hookers and muggers are prominent, so be duly warned.)

When Napoleon III gave the grounds to the city in 1852, they were developed by Baron Haussmann. Separating Lac Inférieur from Lac Supérieur is the **Carrefour des Cascades** ✿ (you can stroll under its waterfall). The Lower Lake contains two islands connected by a footbridge. From the east bank, you can take a boat to these idyllically situated grounds, perhaps stopping off at the cafe/restaurant on one of them.

Restaurants in the bois are numerous, elegant, and expensive. The **Pré Catelan** ✿ contains a deluxe restaurant of the same name (✆ **01-44-14-41-14**) occupying a gem of a Napoleon III–style château and a Shakespearean theater in a garden planted with trees mentioned in the bard's plays. Nearby is **La Grande Cascade** (✆ **01-45-27-33-51**), once a hunting lodge for Napoleon III.

Jardin d'Acclimatation, at the northern edge of the park, is for children, with a zoo, an amusement park, and a narrow-gauge railway (see "Especially for Kids" for more details). Two racetracks, the **Hippodrome de Longchamp** ✿✿✿ and the **Hippodrome d'Auteuil,** are in the park (see "A Day at the Races"). The Grand Prix is run in June at Longchamp (the site of a medieval abbey). Fashionable Parisians always turn out for this, the women in their finest haute couture. To the north of Longchamp is the **Grand Cascade,** an artificial waterfall.

In the western section of the bois, the 60-acre **Parc de Bagatelle** ✿ (✆ **01-40-67-97-00**) owes its existence to a bet between the comte d'Artois (later Charles X) and Marie Antoinette, his sister-in-law. The comte wagered he could erect a small palace in less than 3 months, so he hired nearly 1,000 craftsmen (cabinetmakers, painters, Scottish landscape architect Thomas Blaikie, and others) and irritated the locals by requisitioning all shipments of stone and plaster arriving through Paris's west gates. He won his bet. If you're here in late April, it's worth visiting the Bagatelle just for the tulips. In late May, one of the finest rose collections in Europe is in full bloom. For some reason, as the head gardener confides to us, "This is the major rendezvous point in Paris for illicit couples." In September, the light is less harsh than in summer or even in February; when stripped of much of its greenery, the park's true shape can be seen.

Parc de Bagatelle is open daily from 9am to dusk, charging adults 1.50€ ($1.35) and ages 7 to 26 .75€ (70¢); it's free for children 6 and under.

PARC MONCEAU

Much of **Parc Monceau** ✿, 8th arrondissement (✆ **01-42-27-08-64;** Métro: Monceau or Villiers), is ringed with 18th- and 19th-century mansions, some evoking Proust's *Remembrance of Things Past.* Carmontelle designed it in 1778 as a private hideaway for the duc d'Orléans (who came to be known as Philippe-Egalité), at the time the richest man in France. The duke was noted for his debauchery and pursuit of pleasure, so no ordinary park would do. It was opened to the public in the days of Napoleon III's Second Empire.

Monceau was laid out with an Egyptian-style obelisk, a medieval dungeon, a thatched farmhouse, a Chinese pagoda, a Roman temple, an enchanted grotto, various chinoiseries, and a waterfall. These fairy-tale touches have largely disappeared, except for a pyramid and an oval naumachia fringed by a colonnade. Now the park is filled with solid statuary and monuments, one honoring Chopin. In spring, the red tulips and magnolias are worth the air ticket to Paris.

10 Cemeteries

Sightseers often view Paris's cemeteries as being somewhat like parks, suitable places for strolling. The graves of celebrities are also a major lure. Père-Lachaise, for example, is a major sightseeing goal; the other cemeteries are of lesser interest.

Cimetière de Montmartre ✿ This cemetery, from 1795, lies west of Montmartre and north of boulevard de Clichy. Russian dancer **Vaslav Nijinsky,** novelist **Alexandre Dumas** *fils,* impressionist **Edgar Degas,** and composers **Hector Berlioz** and **Jacques Offenbach** are interred here, along with **Stendhal** and lesser literary lights like **Edmond** and **Jules de Goncourt** and **Heinrich Heine.** A more recent tombstone honors **François Truffaut,** film director of the *nouvelle vague.* We like to pay our respects at the tomb of **Alphonsine Plessis,** heroine of *La Dame aux camélias,* and **Mme Récamier,** who taught the world how to lounge. **Emile Zola** was buried here, but his corpse was exhumed and promoted to the Panthéon in 1908. In tragic 1871, the cemetery was used for mass burials of victims of the Siege and the Commune.

20 av. Rachel, 18e. ✆ **01-43-87-64-24.** Free admission. Mon–Fri 8am–6pm; Sat 8:30am–6pm; Sun 9am–6pm (to 5:30pm in winter). Métro: Blanche or Place Clichy.

Cimetière de Passy This cemetery runs along Paris's old northern walls, south and southwest of Trocadéro. It's a small graveyard sheltered by chestnut trees, but it contains many gravesites of the famous—a concierge at the gate can guide you. Painters **Edouard Manet** and **Romaine Brooks** and composer **Claude Debussy** are tenants. Many great literary figures since 1850 were interred here, including **Tristan Bernard, Jean Giraudoux,** and **François de Croisset.** Also present are composer **Gabriel Fauré,** aviator **Henry Farman,** actor **Fernandel,** and high priestess of the city's most famous literary salon, **Natalie Barney,** along with **Renée Vivien,** one of her many lovers.

2 rue du Comandant-Schloesing, 16e. ✆ **01-47-27-51-42.** Free admission. Mar–Nov daily 8:30am–5:45pm; Dec–Feb daily 8:30am–5:15pm. Métro: Trocadéro.

Cimetière du Montparnasse ✿ In the shadow of the Tour Montparnasse, this debris-littered cemetery is a burial ground of yesterday's celebrities. A map available to the left of the main gateway will direct you to the gravesite of its most famous couple, **Simone de Beauvoir** and **Jean-Paul Sartre.** Others resting here include **Samuel Beckett, Guy de Maupassant, Pierre Larousse** (famous for his dictionary), **Capt. Alfred Dreyfus,** auto tycoon **André Citroën,** sculptors **Ossip Zadkine** and **Constantin Brancusi,** actress **Jean Seberg,** composer **Camille Saint-Saëns,** photographer **Man Ray,** and **Charles Baudelaire,** who'd already written about "plunging into the abyss, Heaven or Hell."

3 bd. Edgar-Quinet, 14e. ✆ **01-44-10-86-50.** Free admission. Mon–Fri 8am–6pm; Sat 8:30am–6pm; Sun 9am–6pm (to 5:15pm Nov–Mar). Métro: Edgar Quinet.

Cimetière du Père-Lachaise ✿✿✿ When it comes to name-dropping, this cemetery knows no peer; it has been called the "grandest address in Paris." A free map of Père-Lachaise is available at the newsstand across from the main entrance (also see the map on p. 220).

Everybody from Sarah Bernhardt to Oscar Wilde to Richard Wright is here, along with Honoré de Balzac, Jacques-Louis David, Eugène Delacroix, Maria Callas, Max Ernst, and Georges Bizet. Colette was taken here in 1954; her black granite slab always sports flowers, and legend has it that cats replenish the roses. In time, the little sparrow, Edith Piaf, followed. The lover of George Sand, poet Alfred de Musset, was buried under a weeping willow. Napoleon's marshals, Ney and Masséna, lie here, as do Frédéric Chopin and Molière. Marcel Proust's black tombstone rarely lacks a tiny bunch of violets (he wanted to be buried beside his friend/lover, composer Maurice Ravel, but their families wouldn't allow it).

Some tombs are sentimental favorites: Love-torn graffiti radiates 1km (half a mile) from the tomb of Doors singer **Jim Morrison.** The great dancer **Isadora Duncan** came to rest in the Columbarium, where bodies have been cremated and "filed" away. If you search hard enough, you can find the tombs of that star-crossed pair **Abélard** and **Héloïse,** the ill-fated lovers of the 12th century—at Père-Lachaise they've found peace at last. Other famous lovers also rest here: A stone is marked **"Alice B. Toklas"** on one side and **"Gertrude Stein"** on the other, and eventually France's First Couple of film were reunited when **Yves Montand** joined his wife, **Simone Signoret.** (Montand's gravesite attracted much attention in 1998: His corpse was exhumed in the middle of the night for DNA testing in a paternity lawsuit— he wasn't the father.)

Covering more than 110 acres, Père-Lachaise was acquired by the city in 1804. Nineteenth-century sculpture abounds, as each family tried to outdo the other in ostentation. Monuments also honor Frenchmen who died in the Resistance or in Nazi concentration camps. Some French Socialists still pay tribute at the **Mur des Fédérés,** the anonymous gravesite of the Communards who were executed in the cemetery on May 28, 1871. When these last-ditch fighters of the Commune, the world's first anarchist republic, made their final desperate stand against the troops of the French government, they were overwhelmed, lined up against the wall, and shot in groups. A handful survived and lived hidden in the cemetery for years like wild animals, venturing into Paris at night to forage for food.

16 rue du Repos, 20e. (℃) **01-55-25-82-10.** Free admission. Mon–Fri 8am–6pm; Sat 8:30am–6pm; Sun 9am–6pm (to 5:30pm early Nov to early Mar). Métro: Père-Lachaise.

Cimetière St-Vincent Because of the artists and writers who have their resting places in the modest burial ground of St-Vincent, with a view of Sacré-Coeur on the hill, it's sometimes called "the most intellectual cemetery in Paris"—but that epithet seems more apt for other graveyards. Artists **Maurice Utrillo** and **Théopile-Alexandre Steinien** were buried here, as was musician **Arthur Honegger** and writer **Marcel Aymé.** In theory, the cemetery is open all day, but if you disturb the caretaker's lunch—any time from noon to 2pm— you'll regret it.

6 rue Lucien-Gaulard, 18e. (℃) **01-46-06-29-78.** Free admission. Mar 16–Nov 5 Mon–Sat 8:30am–6pm; Sun 9am–6pm. Nov 6–Mar 15 Mon–Fri 8am–5:30pm; Sat 8:30am–5:15pm; Sun 9am–5:15pm. Métro: Lamarck-Caulaincourt.

Père-Lachaise Cemetery

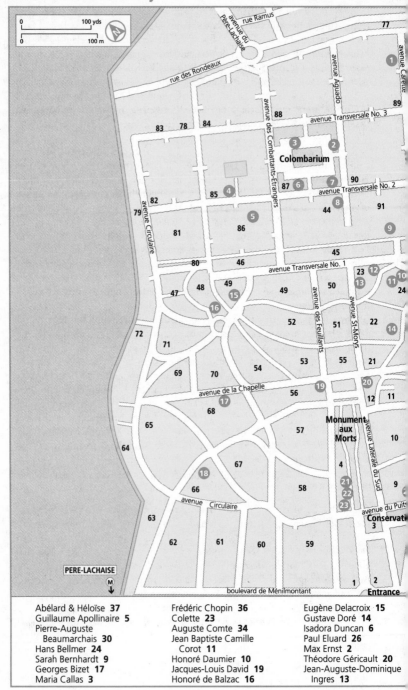

Abélard & Héloïse **37**
Guillaume Apollinaire **5**
Pierre-Auguste
  Beaumarchais **30**
Hans Bellmer **24**
Sarah Bernhardt **9**
Georges Bizet **17**
Maria Callas **3**

Frédéric Chopin **36**
Colette **23**
Auguste Comte **34**
Jean Baptiste Camille
  Corot **11**
Honoré Daumier **10**
Jacques-Louis David **19**
Honoré de Balzac **16**

Eugène Delacroix **15**
Gustave Doré **14**
Isadora Duncan **6**
Paul Eluard **26**
Max Ernst **2**
Théodore Géricault **20**
Jean-Auguste-Dominique
  Ingres **13**

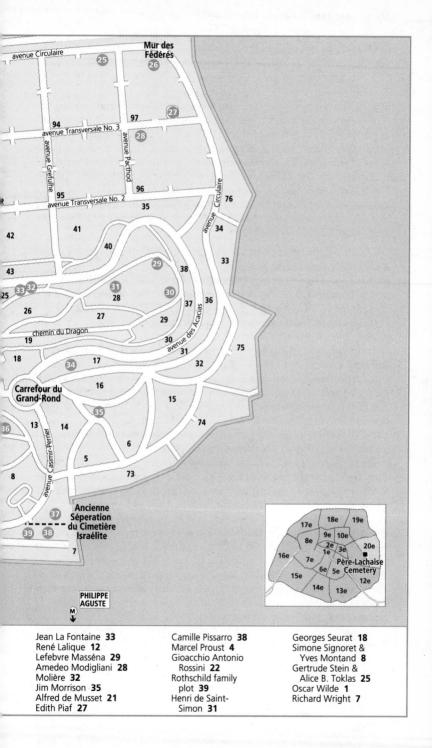

avenue Circulaire

Mur des Fédérés

(25)
(26)

94
97
(27)
(28)

avenue Transversale No. 3

avenue Greffulhe

avenue Pacthod

95
96
76

avenue Transversale No. 2

35

42
41

34

43
40

33

(29)
38

25
(33)(32)

(31)
28

(30)

36

26
27

37

avenue des Acacias

avenue Circulaire

chemin du Dragon

29

19
30

31

75

18
(34)
17

32

Carrefour du Grand-Rond

16

35

15

74

36
13
14

avenue Casimir-Perrier

6

8
5

73

Ancienne Séperation du Cimetière Israélite

37

(39)(38)

7

PHILIPPE AUGUSTE
M

Jean La Fontaine **33**
René Lalique **12**
Lefebvre Masséna **29**
Amedeo Modigliani **28**
Molière **32**
Jim Morrison **35**
Alfred de Musset **21**
Edith Piaf **27**

Camille Pissarro **38**
Marcel Proust **4**
Gioacchio Antonio
  Rossini **22**
Rothschild family
  plot **39**
Henri de Saint-
  Simon **31**

Georges Seurat **18**
Simone Signoret &
  Yves Montand **8**
Gertrude Stein &
  Alice B. Toklas **25**
Oscar Wilde **1**
Richard Wright **7**

17e
18e
19e
9e
10e
8e
2e
3e
20e
16e
1e
Père-Lachaise Cemetery
7e
6e
5e
15e
12e
14e
13e

221

11 Paris Underground

Les Catacombes ⚡ Every year an estimated 50,000 visitors explore some 910m (1,000 yards) of tunnel in these dank catacombs to look at 6 million ghoulishly arranged skull-and-crossbones skeletons. First opened to the public in 1810, this "empire of the dead" is now illuminated with electric lights over its entire length. In the Middle Ages, the catacombs were quarries, but by the end of the 18th century, overcrowded cemeteries were becoming a menace to public health. City officials decided to use the catacombs as a burial ground, and the bones of several million persons were transferred here. In 1830, the prefect of Paris closed the catacombs, considering them obscene and indecent. During World War II, the catacombs were the headquarters of the French Resistance.

1 place Denfert-Rochereau, 14e. ⓒ 01-43-22-47-63. www.multimania.com/houze. Admission 5€ ($4.50) adults, 3.50€ ($3.10) seniors, 2.60€ ($2.30) ages 7–25/students, free for children 6 and under. Tues–Sun 2–4pm; Sat–Sun 9–11am. Métro: Denfert-Rochereau.

Les Egouts (Sewers of Paris) ⚡ Some sociologists assert that the sophistication of a society can be judged by the way it disposes of waste. If so, Paris receives good marks for its mostly invisible sewer network. Victor Hugo is credited with making them famous in *Les Misérables:* Jean Valjean takes flight through them, "all dripping with slime, his soul filled with a strange light." Hugo also wrote, "Paris has beneath it another Paris, a Paris of sewers, which has its own streets, squares, lanes, arteries, and circulation."

In the early Middle Ages, drinking water was taken directly from the Seine and wastewater poured onto fields or thrown onto the then-unpaved streets, transforming the urban landscape into a sea of rather smelly mud. Around 1200, the streets were paved with cobblestones, and open sewers ran down the center of each. These open sewers helped spread the Black Death, which devastated the city. In 1370, a vaulted sewer was built on rue Montmartre, draining effluents into a Seine tributary. During Louis XIV's reign, improvements were made, but the state of waste disposal in Paris remained deplorable.

During Napoleon's reign, 31km (19 miles) of sewer were constructed beneath Paris. By 1850, as the Industrial Revolution made the manufacture of iron pipe and steam-digging equipment more practical, Baron Haussmann developed a system that used separate channels for drinking water and sewage. By 1878, it was 580km (360 miles) long. Beginning in 1894, the network was enlarged, and laws required that discharge of all waste and storm-water runoff be funneled into the sewers. Between 1914 and 1977, an additional 966km (600 miles) were added. Today, the network of sewers is 2,093km (1,300 miles) long. It contains freshwater mains, compressed air pipes, telephone cables, and pneumatic tubes. Every day, 1.2 million cubic meters of wastewater are collected and processed by a plant in the suburb of Achères. One of the largest in Europe, it's capable of treating more than 2 million cubic meters of sewage per day.

The city's *égouts* are constructed around four principal tunnels, one 5.5m (18 ft.) wide and 4.5m (15 ft.) high. It's like an underground city, with the street names clearly labeled. Each branch pipe bears the number of the building to which it's connected. These underground passages are truly mammoth. Sewer tours begin at pont de l'Alma on the Left Bank, where a stairway leads into the city's bowels. However, you often have to wait in line as much as half an hour. Visiting times might change during bad weather, as a storm can make the sewers dangerous. The tour consists of a film, a small museum visit, and then a short trip through the maze. *Be warned:* The smell is pretty bad, especially in summer.

Pont de l'Alma, 7e. ⓒ **01-53-68-27-82.** Admission 3.80€ ($3.40) adults, 3.05€ ($2.70) students/seniors/children 5–12, free for children under 5. May–Oct Sat–Wed 11am–5pm; Nov–Apr Sat–Wed 11am–4pm. Closed 3 weeks in Jan. Métro: Alma-Marceau. RER: Pont de l'Alma.

12 A Day at the Races

Paris boasts an army of avid horse-racing fans who get to the city's eight race-tracks whenever possible. Information on current races is available in newspapers and magazines like *Tierce, Paris-Turf, France-Soir,* and *L'Equipe,* all sold at kiosks throughout the city.

The epicenter of Paris horse racing is the **Hippodrome de Longchamp** ★★★, in the Bois de Boulogne (ⓒ **01-44-30-75-00;** RER or Métro: Porte Maillot, then a shuttle bus). Established in 1855, during the autocratic but pleasure-loving reign of Napoleon III, it's the most prestigious, boasts the greatest number of promising thoroughbreds, and awards the largest purse in France. The most important events at Longchamp are the **Grand Prix de Paris** in late June and the **Prix de l'Arc de Triomphe** in early October.

Another racing venue is the **Hippodrome d'Auteuil,** in the Bois de Boulogne (ⓒ **01-40-71-47-47;** Métro: Porte Auteuil, and then walk). Known for its steeplechases and obstacle courses, it sometimes attracts more than 50,000 Parisians at a time. Spectators appreciate the park's promenades as much as they do the equestrian events. Races are conducted early March to late December.

13 Neighborhood Highlights

Paris's neighborhoods can be attractions unto themselves. The 1st arrondissement, probably has a higher concentration of attractions per block than anywhere else. Though all Paris's neighborhoods are worth wandering, some are more interesting than others. This is especially true of Montmartre, the Latin Quarter, and the Marais, so we've featured them as walking tours in chapter 8.

ISLANDS IN THE STREAM: ILE DE LA CITE & ILE ST-LOUIS
ILE DE LA CITE: WHERE PARIS WAS BORN ★★★   Medieval Paris, that blend of grotesquerie and Gothic beauty, bloomed on this island in the Seine (Métro: Cité). Ile de la Cité, which the Seine protects like a surrounding moat, has been known as "the cradle" of Paris ever since. As Sauval once observed, "The Island of the City is shaped like a great ship, sunk in the mud, lengthwise in the stream, in about the middle of the Seine."

Few have written more movingly about its heyday than Victor Hugo, who invited the reader "to observe the fantastic display of lights against the darkness of that gloomy labyrinth of buildings; cast upon it a ray of moonlight, showing the city in glimmering vagueness, with its towers lifting their great heads from that foggy sea." Medieval Paris was a city not only of legends and lovers but of blood-curdling tortures and brutalities. No story illustrates this better than the affair of Abélard and his charge Héloïse, whose jealous uncle hired ruffians to castrate her lover. (The attack predictably quelled their ardor, and he became a monk, she an abbess.) You can see their graves at Père-Lachaise (see "Cemeteries").

Because you'll want to see all the attractions on Ile de la Cité, begin at the cathedral of Notre-Dame. Proceed next to the Ste-Chapelle moving west. After a visit there, you can head northeast to the Conciergerie. To cap your visit, and for the best scenic view, walk to the northwestern end of the island for a view of the bridge, pont Neuf, seen from Square du Vert Galant.

The island's stars, as mentioned, are **Notre-Dame, Sainte-Chapelle,** and the **Conciergerie**—all described earlier. Across from Notre-Dame is the **Hôtel Dieu,** built from 1866 to 1878 in neo-Florentine style. This is central Paris's main hospital, replacing the 12th-century hospital that ran the island's entire width. Go in the main entrance and take a break in the spacious neoclassical courtyard whose small garden and fountain make a quiet oasis.

Don't miss the ironically named **pont Neuf** ("New Bridge") at the tip of the island opposite from Notre-Dame. The span isn't new—it's Paris's oldest bridge, begun in 1578 and finished in 1604. In its day it had two unique features: It was paved and it wasn't flanked with houses and shops. Actually, with 12 arches, it's not one bridge but two (they don't quite line up)—one from the Right Bank to the island and the other from the Left Bank to the island. At the **Musée Carnavalet** (p. 197), a painting called *The Spectacle of Buffoons* shows what the bridge was like between 1665 and 1669. Duels were fought on it, the nobility's great coaches crossed it, peddlers sold their wares, and entertainers like Tabarin went there to seek a few coins from the gawkers. As public facilities were lacking, the bridge also served as a de facto outhouse.

Just past pont Neuf is the "prow" of the island, the **square du Vert Galant.** Pause to look at the equestrian statue of the beloved Henri IV, who was assassinated by Ravaillac (see the entry for the Conciergerie). A true king of his people, Henri was also (to judge from accounts) regal in the boudoir—hence the nickname "Vert Galant" (Old Spark). Gabrielle d'Estrées and Henriette d'Entragues were his best-known mistresses, but they had to share him with countless others, some of whom would casually catch his eye as he was riding along the streets. In fond memory of the king, the little triangular park continues to attract lovers. If at first it appears to be a sunken garden, that's because it remains at its natural level; the rest of the Cité has been built up during the centuries.

ILE ST-LOUIS ★★   Cross pont St-Louis, the footbridge behind Notre-Dame, to Ile St-Louis, and you'll find a world of tree-shaded quays, town houses with courtyards, restaurants, and antiques shops. (You can also take the Métro to Sully-Morland or Pont Marie and cross the bridge.) The fraternal twin of Ile de la Cité, Ile St-Louis is primarily residential; nearly all the houses were built from 1618 to 1660, lending the island a remarkable architectural unity. Plaques on the facades identify the former residences of the famous. **Marie Curie** lived at 36 quai de Béthune, near pont de la Tournelle, and sculptor **Camille Claudel** (Rodin's mistress) lived and worked in the Hôtel de Jassaud, 19 quai de Bourbon.

The most exciting mansion—though perhaps with the saddest history—is the 1656–57 **Hôtel de Lauzun,** 17 quai d'Anjou, built for Charles Gruyn des Bordes. He married Geneviève de Mouy and had her initials engraved on much of the interior decor; their happiness was short-lived, because he was convicted of embezzlement and sent to prison in 1662. The next occupant was the duc de Lauzun, who resided there for only 3 years. He had been a favorite of Louis XIV until he asked for the hand of the king's cousin, the duchesse de Montpensier. Louis refused and had Lauzun tossed into the Bastille. Eventually the duchesse pestered Louis into releasing him, and they married secretly and moved here in 1682, but domestic bliss eluded them—they fought often and separated in 1684. Lauzun sold the house to the grand-nephew of Cardinal Richelieu and his wife, who had such a grand time throwing parties, they went bankrupt. Baron Pichon bought it in 1842 and rented it out to a hashish club. Tenants

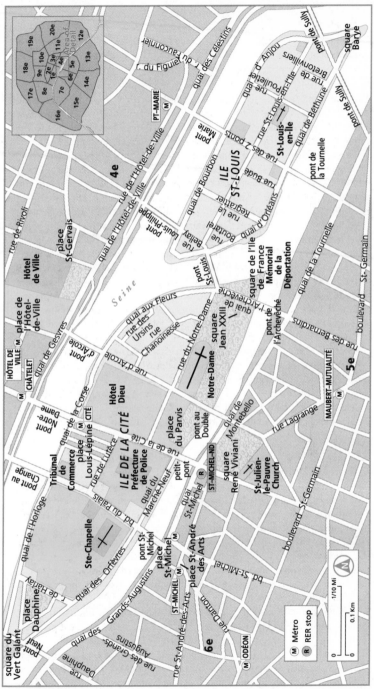

square Barye

pont de Sully

quai de Béthune

rue de Bretonvillers

rue d'Anjou

rue St-Louis-en-l'Ile

quai d'Anjou

St-Louis-en-l'Ile

pont de Sully

r. du Figuier

quai des Célestins

r. du Fauconnier

PT-MARIE Ⓜ

pont Marie

ILE ST-LOUIS

rue des 2 ponts

rue Budé

pont de la Tournelle

quai de Bourbon

quai d'Orléans

rue Le Regrattier

rue Le Regrattier

4e

rue de l'Hôtel-de-Ville

pont Louis-Philippe

rue Boutarel

rue Le Bellay

Hôtel de Ville

place St-Gervais

St-Germain

rue de Rivoli

Seine

quai de Gesvres

pont St-Louis

square de l'Ile de France

Mémorial de la Déportation

quai de la Tournelle

place de l'Hôtel-de-Ville

place de l'Hôtel-de-Ville

HÔTEL DE VILLE Ⓜ

CHÂTELET Ⓜ

pont d'Arcole

rue d'Arcole

quai aux Fleurs

rue des Ursins

rue Chanoinesse

rue du Notre-Dame

quai de la Corse

Hôtel Dieu

square Jean XXIII

Notre-Dame ✝

quai de l'Archevêché

pont de l'Archevêché

rue des Bernardins

boulevard St-Germain

5e

MAUBERT-MUTUALITÉ Ⓜ

pont Notre-Dame

place Louis-Lépine

CITÉ Ⓜ

rue de la Cité

place du Parvis

pont au Double

quai de Montebello

rue Lagrange

pont au Change

Tribunal de Commerce

ILE DE LA CITÉ

Préfecture de Police

quai du Marché-Neuf

petit pont

ST-MICHEL-ND Ⓡ

square René Viviani

St-Julien-le-Pauvre Church ✝

bd. du Palais

rue de Lutèce

quai St-Michel

quai de l'Horloge

Ste-Chapelle ✝

quai des Orfèvres

pont St-Michel

place St-Michel

ST-MICHEL Ⓜ

ST-MICHEL Ⓜ

place St-André des Arts

bd. St-Michel

boulevard St-Germain

place Dauphine

r. de Harlay

pont Neuf

rue St-André-des-Arts

rue Danton

ODÉON Ⓜ

6e

square du Vert Galant

rue Dauphine

quai des Grands-Augustins

rue des Grands-Augustins

Ⓜ Métro
Ⓡ RER stop

0   1/10 Mi
0   0.1 Km

Tips Ice Cream

If you need a refreshment break on Ile St-Louis, head for ice cream at **Berthillon,** 31 rue St-Louis-en-l'Ile.

Baudelaire and Gaultier regularly held hashish soirées in which Baudelaire did research for his *Les Paradis artificiels* and Gaultier for his *Le Club hes hachichins.* Now the mansion belongs to the city and is used to house official guests. The interior is sometimes open for temporary exhibits, so call the tourist office.

Hôtel Lambert, 2 quai d'Anjou, was built in 1645 for Nicholas Lambert de Thorigny. The portal on rue St-Louis-en-l'Ile gives some idea of the splendor within, but the house's most startling element is the oval gallery extending into the garden. Designed to feature a library or art collection, it's best viewed from the beginning of quai d'Anjou. Voltaire and his mistress, Emilie de Breteuil, lived here—their quarrels were legendary. The mansion also housed the Polish royal family for over a century, before becoming the residence of actress Michèle Morgan. It now belongs to the Rothschild family and isn't open to the public.

Nos. 9, 11, 13, and 15 quai d'Anjou also belonged to the Lamberts. At **no. 9** is the house where painter/sculptor/lithographer Honoré Daumier lived from 1846 to 1863, producing hundreds of caricatures satirizing the bourgeoisie and attacking government corruption. He was imprisoned because of his 1832 cartoon of Louis-Philippe swallowing bags of gold that had been extracted from the people.

Near the Hôtel de Lauzun is the church of **St-Louis-en-l'Ile,** no. 19 bis rue St-Louis-en-l'Ile. Despite a dour exterior, the ornate interior is one of the finest examples of Jesuit baroque. Built between 1664 and 1726, this church is still the site of many weddings—with all the white stone and gilt, you'll feel as if you're inside a wedding cake. Look for the 1926 plaque reading "In grateful memory of St. Louis in whose honor the city of St. Louis, Missouri, USA, is named."

RIGHT BANK HIGHLIGHTS

LES HALLES 🐸 For 8 centuries, **Les Halles** (Métro: Les Halles; RER: Châtelet-Les Halles) was the city's major wholesale fruit, meat, and vegetable market. In the 19th century, Zola called it "the underbelly of Paris." The smock-clad vendors, beef carcasses, and baskets of vegetables all belong to the past, for the original market, with zinc-roofed Second Empire "iron umbrellas," has been torn down. Today the action has moved to a steel-and-glass edifice at Rungis, a suburb near Orly. In 1979, the area saw the opening of the **Forum des Halles,** 1-7 rue Pierre-Lescot, 1er. This large complex, much of it underground, contains shops, restaurants, and movie theaters. Many of the shops are unattractive, but others contain a wide display of merchandise that has made the mall popular with both residents and visitors.

For many visitors, a night on the town still ends in the wee hours with a bowl of onion soup at Les Halles, usually at **Au Pied de Cochon (The Pig's Foot),** 6 rue Coquillière, 1er (p. 122), or at **Au Chien Qui Fume (The Smoking Dog),** 33 rue du Pont-Neuf, 1er (✆ **01-42-36-07-42**). One of the classic scenes of old Paris was elegantly dressed Parisians (many fresh from Maxim's) standing at a bar drinking cognac with blood-smeared butchers. Some writers have suggested that 19th-century poet Gérard de Nerval introduced the custom of frequenting Les Halles at such an unearthly hour.

A newspaper correspondent described today's scene: "Les Halles is trying to stay alive as one of the few places where one can eat at any hour of the night."

LEFT BANK HIGHLIGHTS

ST-GERMAIN-DES-PRES ✦✦ This neighborhood in the 6th arrondissement (Métro: St-Germain-des-Prés) was the postwar home of existentialism, associated with Sartre, de Beauvoir, Camus, and an intellectual bohemian crowd that gathered at **Café de Flore, Brasserie Lipp,** and **Les Deux Magots** (see chapter 6). Among them, black-clad poet and singer Juliette Greco was known as *la muse de St-Germain-des-Prés,* and to Sartre she was the woman who had "millions of poems in her throat." Her long hair, black slacks, black sweater, and black sandals launched a fashion trend adopted by young women everywhere. In the 1950s, new names appeared, like Françoise Sagan, Gore Vidal, and James Baldwin, but by the 1960s, tourists became firmly entrenched.

St-Germain-des-Prés still retains an intellectually stimulating bohemian street life, full of many interesting bookshops, art galleries, *cave* (basement) clubs, bistros, and coffeehouses. But the stars of the area are two churches, **St-Germain-des-Prés,** 3 place St-Germain-des-Prés, 6e, and **St-Sulpice,** rue St-Sulpice, 6e (for both, see "The Important Churches" earlier in this chapter), and the **Musée National Eugène Delacroix,** 6 place de Furstemburg, 6e (p. 199). Nearby, **rue Visconti** was designed for pushcarts and is worth visiting today. At **nos. 20-24** is the residence where dramatist Jean-Baptiste Racine died in 1699. And at **no. 17** is the house where Balzac established his printing press in 1825. (The venture ended in bankruptcy, forcing the author back to his writing desk.) Such celebrated actresses as Champmeslé and Clairon also lived here.

MONTPARNASSE ✦✦ For the "lost generation," life centered around the cafes of Montparnasse, at the border of the 6th and 14th arrondissements (Métro: Montparnasse-Bienvenue). Hangouts like the **Dôme, Coupole, Rotonde,** and **Sélect** became legendary, as artists—especially American expatriates—turned their backs on Montmartre as too touristy. Picasso, Modigliani, and Man Ray came this way, and Hemingway was also a popular figure. So was Fitzgerald when he was poor (when he wasn't, you'd find him at the Ritz). Faulkner, MacLeish, Duncan, Miró, Joyce, Ford Madox Ford, and even Trotsky spent time here.

The most notable exception was Gertrude Stein, who never frequented the cafes. To see her, you had to wait for an invitation to her salon at **27 rue de Fleurus.** She bestowed this favor on Sherwood Anderson, Elliot Paul, Ezra Pound, and, for a time, Hemingway. When Pound launched himself into a beloved chair and broke it, he incurred Stein's wrath, and Hemingway decided there wasn't "much future in men being friends with great women" (for more on Gertrude, see the box "The Mother of the Lost Generation" below).

American expatriate writer Natalie Barney, who moved to Paris as a student in 1909 and stayed for over 60 years, held her grand salons at **20 rue Jacob** (actually in St-Germain-des-Prés). Every Friday, her salon attracted the literati of her day, like Gertrude Stein, Djuna Barnes, Colette, Sherwood Anderson, T. S. Eliot, Janet Flanner, James Joyce, Sylvia Beach, Marcel Proust, and William Carlos Williams. The group met on and off for half a century, interrupted only by two world wars. Near place de Furstemburg, Barney's former residence is landmarked but not open to the public. In the garden you can see a small Doric temple bearing the inscription *A l'Amitié,* "to friendship."

The Mother of the Lost Generation

"So Paris was the place that suited those of us that were to create the twentieth century art and literature, naturally enough." Gertrude Stein, who made this pronouncement, wasn't known for her modesty.

In the 1920s, she and her lover, Alice B. Toklas, became the most famous expats in Paris. To get an invitation to call on Lovey and Pussy (nicknames for Gertrude and Alice) at **27 rue de Fleurus,** in the heart of Montparnasse, was to be invited into the innermost circle of expatriate Paris. Though their former residence is in private hands and you can't go inside, literary fans flock to this fabled address to stare at the facade.

Though Gertrude didn't achieve popular success until the 1933 publication of her *Autobiography of Alice B. Toklas,* she was adored by many members of the Lost Generation—all except Ernest Hemingway, who tarred her in his posthumous memoir, *A Moveable Feast.* But to many sensitive young men (often gay) arriving from America in the 1920s, La Stein was "The Mother of Us All." These young fans hung on to her every word, while Alice baked her notorious hash brownies in the kitchen.

At rue de Fleurus, Gertrude and Alice surrounded themselves with modern paintings, including pieces by Vallotton, Toulouse-Lautrec, Picasso, Gauguin, and Matisse. Gertrude paid $1,000 for her first Matisse and $30 for her first Picasso. The Saturday-night soirées became legendary, and one writer said her salon was an international conspiracy to promote modern art. Many denounced Gertrude, however, including avant-garde magazines of the time, which called her a "fraud, egomaniac, and publicity seeking." Braque called her claim to influence art in Paris "nonsense."

In spite of the attacks, jokes, and speculation, Stein, at least in public, kept her ego intact. Bernard Fay once told her he'd met three people in his life who ranked as geniuses: Gide, Picasso, and herself. "Why include Gide?" Stein asked.

Aside from the literary legends, one of the most notable characters was **Kiki de Montparnasse** (actually named Alice Prin). She was raised by her grandmother in Burgundy until her mother called her to Paris to work. When a sculptor discovered her, she became an artist's model and adopted her new name; soon she became a prostitute, and would bare her breasts to anyone who'd pay her three francs. She sang at **Le Jockey,** 127 bd. du Montparnasse, which no longer exists: In her black hose and garters, she captivated dozens of men, among them Frederick Kohner, who went so far as to entitle his memoirs *Kiki of Montparnasse.* Kiki later wrote her own memoirs, with an introduction by Hemingway. Papa called her "a Queen," noting that was "very different from being a lady."

Completed in 1973 and rising 206m (688 ft.) above the skyline, the **Tour Montparnasse** (© **01-45-38-52-56**) was denounced by some as "bringing Manhattan to Paris." The city soon passed an ordinance outlawing any further structures of this size in the heart of Paris. Today, the modern tower houses an underground shopping mall as well as much of the infrastructure for the Gare de Montparnasse rail station. You can ride an elevator up to the 56th floor (where you'll find a bar and restaurant), and then climb three flights to the roof terrace. The view includes virtually every important Paris monument, including Sacré-Coeur, Notre-Dame, and La Défense. Admission to the tower costs 7€ ($6.25) for adults, 5.80€ ($5.15) for seniors, 5.30€ ($4.75) for students, and 4.55€ ($4.05) for children 5 to 14 (children 4 and under enter free). April to September, it's open daily from 9:30am to 11:30pm; October to March, hours are Sunday to Thursday from 9:30am to 10:30pm and Friday to Saturday from 9:20am to 11pm.

The life of Montparnasse still centers around its cafes and exotic nightclubs, many only a shadow of what they used to be. Its heart is at the crossroads of **boulevard Raspail** and **boulevard du Montparnasse,** one of the settings of *The Sun Also Rises.* Hemingway wrote that "boulevard Raspail always made dull riding." Rodin's controversial statue of Balzac swathed in a large cape stands guard over the prostitutes who cluster around the pedestal. Balzac seems to be the only one in Montparnasse who doesn't feel the weight of time.

14 Especially for Kids

If you're staying on the Right Bank, take the children for a stroll through the **Jardin des Tuileries** (p. 215), where there are donkey rides, ice-cream stands, and a marionette show; at the circular pond, you can rent a toy boat. On the Left Bank, similar delights exist in the **Jardin du Luxembourg** (p. 216). After a visit to the Eiffel Tower, you can take the kids for a donkey ride in the **Champ de Mars** (see the "Time Out at the Tower" box, earlier in this chapter).

A Paris tradition, **puppet shows** are worth seeing for their colorful productions—they're a genuine French child's experience. At the Jardin du Luxembourg, puppets reenact plots set in Gothic castles and Oriental palaces; many young critics say the best puppet shows are held in the Champ de Mars.

On Sunday afternoon, French families head to the **Butte Montmartre** to bask in the fiesta atmosphere. You can join in: Take the Métro to Anvers and walk to the *funiculaire* (the cable car that carries you up to Sacré-Coeur). Once up top, follow the crowds to place du Tertre, where a Sergeant Pepper–style band will usually be blasting off-key and you can have the kids' pictures sketched by local artists. You can take in the views of Paris from the various vantage points and treat your children to ice cream. For a walking tour of Montmartre, see chapter 8.

Your kids will likely want to check out the Gallic versions of Mickey Mouse and his pals, so see chapter 11, "Side Trips from Paris" for **Disneyland Paris.**

MUSEUMS

Cité des Sciences et de l'Industrie ★★   A city of science and industry has risen here from the most unlikely ashes. When a slaughterhouse was built on the site in the 1960s, it was touted as the most modern of its kind. It was abandoned in 1974, and the location on the city's northern edge presented the government with a problem. What could be built in such an unlikely place? In 1986, the converted premises opened as the world's most expensive ($642 million) science complex, designed to "modernize mentalities" in the service of modernizing society.

The place is so vast, with so many exhibits, that a single visit gives only an idea of the scope of the Cité. Busts of Plato, Hippocrates, and a double-faced Janus gaze silently at a tube-filled riot of high-tech girders, glass, and lights. The sheer dimensions pose a challenge to the curators of its constantly changing exhibits. Some exhibits are couched in Gallic humor—imagine using the comic-strip adventures of a jungle explorer to explain seismographic activity. **Explora,** a permanent exhibit, occupies the three upper levels of the building and examines four themes: the universe, life, matter, and communication. The Cité also has a **multimedia library,** a **planetarium,** and an **"inventorium"** for kids. The silver-skinned geodesic dome called **La Géode**—a 34m (112 ft.) high sphere with a 370-seat theater—projects the closest thing to a 3-D cinema in Europe and has several surprising additions, including a real submarine.

The Cité is in the **Parc de La Villette,** an ultramodern science park surrounding some of Paris's newest housing developments. This is Paris's largest park—twice the size of the Tuileries. The playgrounds, fountains, and sculptures are all innovative creations. Here you'll find a belvedere, a video workshop for children, and information about exhibits and events, along with a cafe and restaurant.

In the Parc de La Villette, 30 av. Corentine-Cariou, La Villette, 19e. ✆ **01-40-05-80-00.** www.cite-sciences.fr. Cité Pass (entrance to all exhibits) 7.60€ ($6.80) adults, free for children 7 and under. Géode 8.65€ ($7.75). Tues–Sat 10am–6pm; Sun 10am–7pm. Métro: Porte de La Villette.

Musée de la Marine 🐸🐸 If your children have salt water in their veins, you may want to take them to this museum. Old ship models abound, like the galley *La Réale,* the *Royal-Louis,* the ivory *Ville de Dieppe,* the gorgeous *Valmy,* and a **barge** built in 1811 for Napoleon I, used to carry Napoleon III and Empress Eugénie on their visit to Brest in 1858. You'll find some souvenirs of explorer Laperouse's wreck on Vanikoro Island in 1788 as well as many documents and artifacts concerning merchant fishing and pleasure fleets, oceanography, and hydrography, with films illustrating the subjects. Thematic exhibits explain ancient wooden shipbuilding and the development of scientific instruments.

In the Palais de Chaillot, place du Trocadéro, 16e. ✆ **01-53-65-69-69.** Admission 5.95€ ($5.30) adults, 3.95€ ($3.55) ages 8–25/over 65, free for children 7 and under. Wed–Mon 10am–5:30pm. Métro: Trocadéro.

Musée Grévin 🐸 The Grévin is Paris's No. 1 waxworks. Comparisons to Madame Tussaud's are almost irresistible, but it isn't all blood and gore and doesn't shock as much as Tussaud's. It presents French history in a series of tableaux. Depicted are the 1429 consecration of Charles VII in the Cathédrale de Reims (armored Joan of Arc, carrying her standard, stands behind the king); Marguerite de Valois, first wife of Henri IV, meeting on a secret stairway with La Molle, who was soon to be decapitated; Catherine de Médicis with Florentine alchemist David Ruggieri; Louis XV and Mozart at the home of the marquise de Pompadour; and Napoleon on a rock at St. Helena, reviewing his victories and defeats. There are also displays of contemporary sports and political figures, as well as 50 of the world's best-loved film stars.

Two shows are staged frequently throughout the day. The first, called the **"Palais des Mirages,"** starts off as a sort of Temple of Brahma and, through magically distorting mirrors, changes into an enchanted forest, then a fête at the Alhambra in Granada. A magician is the star of the second show, **"Le Cabinet Fantastique";** he entertains children of all ages.

10 bd. Montmartre, 9e. ℭ 01-47-70-85-05. Admission 15€ ($13) adults, 9€ ($8.05) children 14 and under. Daily 10am–7pm. Ticket office closes 1 hr. before museum. Métro: Grands Boulevards.

Musée National d'Histoire Naturelle (Museum of Natural History) ⚐ This museum in the Jardin des Plantes, founded in 1635 as a research center by Guy de la Brosse, physician to Louis XIII, has a range of science and nature exhibits. The museum's **Grande Gallery of Evolution** recently received a $90 million restoration. At the entrance, an 26m (85-ft.) skeleton of a whale greets you. One display containing the skeletons of dinosaurs and mastodons is dedicated to endangered and vanished species, and there are galleries specializing in paleontology, anatomy, mineralogy, and botany. Within the museum's grounds are **tropical hothouses** containing thousands of species of unusual plant life and a **menagerie** with small animal life in simulated natural habitats.

57 rue Cuvier, 5e. ℭ 01-40-79-30-00. www.mnhn.fr. Admission 6.10€ ($5.45) adults, 4.55€ ($4.05) students, seniors (over 60), and kids 4–16. Apr–Sept Wed–Mon 10am–6pm; Oct–Mar Wed–Mon 10am–5pm. Métro: Jussieu or Gare d'Austerlitz.

AN AMUSEMENT PARK

Jardin d'Acclimatation ⚐ Paris's definitive children's park is the 25-acre Jardin d'Acclimation in the northern part of the Bois de Boulogne. This is the kind of place that satisfies tykes and adults, but not teenagers. The visit starts with a ride on a green-and-yellow narrow-gauge train from Porte Maillot to the Jardin entrance, through a stretch of wooded park. The train operates at 30-minute intervals Wednesday, Saturday, and Sunday from 10:30am until the park closes; one-way fare costs 1.15€ ($1). En route you'll find a **house of mirrors,** an **archery range,** a **miniature-golf course, zoo animals,** a **bowling alley,** a **puppet theater** (performances Thurs, Sat, Sun, and holidays), a **playground,** a **hurdle-racing course, junior-scale rides, shooting galleries,** and **waffle stalls.** You can trot the kids off on a **pony** or join them in a **boat** on a mill-stirred lagoon. **La Prévention Routière** is a miniature roadway operated by the Paris police: Youngsters drive through in small cars equipped to start and stop, and are required by two genuine gendarmes to obey street signs and light changes. Inside the gate is an easy-to-follow map. The park is circular—follow the road in either direction, and it'll take you all the way around and bring you back to the train at the end.

In the Bois de Boulogne, 16e. ℭ 01-40-67-90-82. Admission 2.30€ ($2.05), free for children 3 and under. June–Sept daily 10am–7pm; Oct–May daily 10am–6pm. Métro: Sablons.

A ZOO

Parc Zoologique de Paris There's a modest zoo in the Jardin des Plantes, but without a doubt, the best zoo is here on the southeastern outskirts of Paris, quickly reachable by Métro. Many of this modern zoo's animals, which seem happy and are playful, live in settings similar to their natural habitats, hemmed in by rock barriers, not bars or cages. You'll never see an animal in a cage too small for it. The lion has an entire veldt to himself, and you can lock eyes comfortably across a deep protective moat. On a cement mountain like Disneyland's Matterhorn, exotic breeds of mountain goats and sheep leap from ledge to ledge or pose gracefully for hours watching the penguins in their pools at the mountain's foot. Keep well back from the bear pools or you might get wet.

In the Bois de Vincennes, 53 av. de St-Maurice, 12e. ⓒ **01-44-75-20-10.** Admission 7.60€ ($6.80) adults, 4.55€ ($4.05) children 4–15/students and 16–25/over 60, free for children 3 and under. Daily 9am–6pm (to 5pm Dec–Mar). Métro: Porte Dorée.

15 Organized Tours

BY BUS

Tours are offered by **Cityrama,** 149 rue St-Honoré, 1er (ⓒ **01-44-55-61-00;** Métro: Palais Royal or Musée du Louvre), which operates double-decker red-and-yellow buses with oversize windows and multilingual recorded commentaries giving an overview of Paris's history and monuments.

By far the most popular is a 2-hour bus ride, with recorded commentary in your choice of 13 languages, through Paris's monumental heart. Departing from place des Pyramides, adjacent to rue de Rivoli, it's offered eight times a day between May and October, and four times a day between November and April. Cost for this is 24€ ($21) per person; free for children under 12. Other, more specialized (and detailed) tours include a 3½-hour "Artistic Tour" that encompasses the interiors of Notre-Dame and the Louvre (Mon and Wed–Sat, departing at 9:45am), priced at 49€ ($44). Guided tours to the mammoth royal palace at Versailles depart twice a day (at 9:30am and 2:45pm) year-round for a price of 52€ ($46) per person. And 5-hour jaunts to the majestic gothic cathedral at Chartres depart every Tuesday, Thursday, and Saturday April to October at 1:45pm for a per person price of 47€ ($42). Tours of Paris by night depart at 10pm April to October for a price of 24€ ($21) per person. Any of these night tours can be supplemented—for an additional fee—with optional add-ons that include river cruises on the Seine and attendance at selected cabaret shows.

CRUISES ON THE SEINE

A Seine boat tour provides sweeping vistas of the riverbanks and some of the best views of Notre-Dame. Many of the boats have open sun decks, bars, and restaurants. **Bateaux-Mouche** cruises (ⓒ **01-40-76-99-99;** Métro: Alma-Marceau) depart from the Right Bank, next to pont de l'Alma, and last about 75 minutes, costing 6.85€ ($6.10) for adults and 3.05€ ($2.70) for children 4 to 12. May to October, tours leave daily at 30-minute intervals, beginning at 11am and ending at 11pm; November to April, there are at least nine departures daily from 11am to 9pm, with a schedule that changes according to demand and the weather. Three-hour dinner cruises depart daily at 8:30pm and cost 76€ to 122€ ($68–$109), depending on which fixed-price menu you order; jackets and ties are required for men. Less formal lunch cruises, departing every day at 1pm and returning about 2 hours later, cost 46€ ($41) per person.

Some people prefer longer excursions on the Seine and its canals. The 3-hour **Seine et le Canal St-Martin** tour, offered by **Paris Canal** (ⓒ **01-42-40-96-97**), requires reservations. The tour begins at 9:30am on the quays in front of the Musée d'Orsay (Métro: Solférino) and at 2:30pm in front of the Cité des Sciences et de l'Industrie at Parc de La Villette (Métro: Porte de La Villette). Excursions negotiate the waterways of Paris, including the Seine, an underground tunnel below place de la Bastille, and the Canal St-Martin. Tours are offered twice daily from mid-March to mid-November; the rest of the year, on Sunday only. The cost is 15€ ($13) for adults; free for children under 4. With the exception of trips on Sundays and holidays, prices are usually reduced to 11€ ($10) for students and seniors, and to 8.35€ ($7.45) for children 4 to 11.

BIKE TOURS

The best are offered by **Bullfrog Bike Tours** (© **06-09-98-08-60**), departing from avenue Gustave-Eiffel near the tower (look for a large green flag advertising the tours). From May to August 15, tours leave daily at 11am and 3:30pm, costing 23€ ($21). At other times of the year, departures are only at 11am. Night tours are at 7pm Sunday and Friday. You get an English-speaking look at Paris almost entirely on sidewalks, in parks, and along the Seine, taking in the most famous landmarks, like the Louvre and Notre-Dame.

8

Strolling Around Paris

The best way to discover Paris is on foot. Our favorite walks are along the Seine and down the Champs-Elysées from the Arc de Triomphe to the Louvre. In this chapter we highlight the attractions of Montmartre, the Latin Quarter, and the Marais.

For more walking tours in the City of Light, see *Frommer's Memorable Walks in Paris*.

WALKING TOUR 1   MONTMARTRE

Start	Place Pigalle (Métro: Pigalle).
Finish:	Place Pigalle.
Time:	5 hours, more if you break for lunch. It's a 4km (2½-mile) trek.
Best Time:	Any day it isn't raining. Set out by 10am at the latest.
Worst Time:	After dark.

There are soft white three-story houses and slender barren trees sticking up from the ground like giant toothpicks—that's how Utrillo, befogged by absinthe, saw Montmartre. Toulouse-Lautrec painted it into a district of cabarets, circus freaks, and prostitutes. Today Montmartre remains truer to the dwarfish Toulouse-Lautrec's conception than it does to Utrillo's.

Before all this, Montmartre was a sleepy farm community with windmills dotting the landscape. The name has always been the subject of disagreement, some arguing it originated from the "mount of Mars," a Roman temple at the top of the hill, others asserting it's "mount of martyrs," a reference to the martyrdom of St. Denis, who was beheaded here with fellow saints Rusticus and Eleutherius.

Turn right after leaving the Métro station and go down boulevard de Clichy, turn left at the Cirque Medrano, and begin the climb up rue des Martyrs. On reaching rue des Abbesses, turn left and walk along this street, crossing place des Abbesses. Go uphill along rue Ravignan, which leads to tree-studded place Emile-Goudeau, in the middle of rue Ravignan. At no. 13, across from the Timhôtel, is the:

❶ Bateau-Lavoir (Boat Washhouse)
Though gutted by fire in 1970, this building, known as the cradle of cubism, has been reconstructed by the city. While Picasso lived here (1904–12), he painted one of the world's most famous portraits, *The Third Rose* (of Gertrude Stein), as well as *Les Demoiselles d'Avignon*. Other residents were van Dongen, Jacob, Gris, and Modigliani, Rousseau, and Braque had studios nearby.

Rue Ravignan ends at place Jean-Baptiste-Clément. Go to the end of the street and cross onto rue Norvins (on your right). Here rues Norvins, St-Rustique, and des Saules collide a few steps from rue Poulbot, a scene captured in a famous Utrillo painting. Turn right and go down rue Poulbot. At no. 11 you come to:

Walking Tour 1: Montmartre

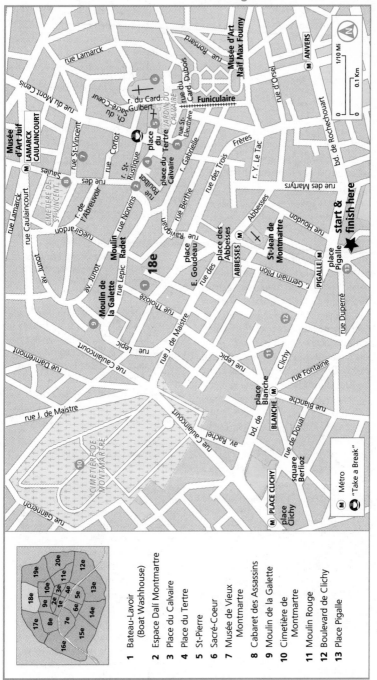

1   Bateau-Lavoir
    (Boat Washhouse)
2   Espace Dalí Montmartre
3   Place du Calvaire
4   Place du Tertre
5   St-Pierre
6   Sacré-Coeur
7   Musée de Vieux
    Montmartre
8   Cabaret des Assassins
9   Moulin de la Galette
10 Cimetière de
    Montmartre
11 Moulin Rouge
12 Boulevard de Clichy
13 Place Pigalle

② Espace Dalí Montmartre

This phantasmagorical world of Espace Montmartre Dalí (℃ 01-42-64-40-10) features 300 original Dalí works, including his famous 1956 lithograph of Don Quixote.

Rue Poulbot crosses tiny:

③ Place du Calvaire

Here you find a panoramic view of Paris. On this square once lived artist/painter/lithographer Maurice Neumont (a plaque marks the house).

From place du Calvaire, head east along rue Gabrielle, taking the first left north along the tiny street rue du Calvaire, which leads to:

④ Place du Tertre

This old town square is tourist central. All around the square are terrace restaurants with dance floors and colored lights, while Sacré-Coeur gleams through the trees. The cafes overflow with people, as do the indoor and outdoor art galleries. Some of the "artists" still wear berets (you'll be asked countless times if you want your portrait sketched). So loaded with local color, applied as heavily as bad makeup, the square can seem gaudy and inauthentic.

TAKE A BREAK Many restaurants in Montmartre, especially those around place du Tertre, are unabashed tourist traps. An exception is **La Crémaillère 1900**, 15 place du Tertre, 18e. (℃ 01-46-06-58-59). As its name suggests, this is a Belle Epoque dining room, retaining much of its original look, including many paintings. You can sit on the terrace opening onto the square or retreat to the courtyard garden. A full menu is served throughout the day, including a standard array of French classics. Go any time daily from noon to 12:30am.

Right off the square fronting rue du Mont-Cenis is:

⑤ St-Pierre

Originally a Benedictine abbey, this church has played many roles: a Temple of Reason during the Revolution, a food depot, a clothing store, and even a munitions factory. These days, one of Paris's oldest churches is back to being a church.

Facing St-Pierre, turn right and follow rue Azaïs to:

⑥ Sacré-Coeur

The basilica's Byzantine domes and bell tower loom above Paris and present a wide vista (see "The Top Attractions" in chapter 7). Behind the church clinging to the hillside are steep, crooked little streets that have survived the march of progress.

Facing the basilica, take the street on the left (rue du Cardinal-Guibert), then go left onto rue du Chevalier-de-la-Barre and right onto rue du Mont-Cenis. Continue on this street to rue Cortot, then turn left. At no. 12 is the:

⑦ Musée de Vieux Montmartre

Musée de Vieux Montmartre (℃ 01-46-06-61-11) presents a collection of mementos of the neighborhood. Luminaries like Dufy, van Gogh, Renoir, and Suzanne Valadon and her son, Utrillo, occupied this 17th-century house, and it was here that Renoir put the final touches on his *Moulin de la Galette* (see below).

From the museum, turn right, heading up rue des Saules past a winery, a reminder of the days when Montmartre was a farming village on the outskirts of Paris. A grape-harvesting festival is held here every October. The intersection of rue des Saules and rue St-Vincent is one of the most visited and photographed corners of the Butte. Here, on one corner, sits what was the famous old:

⑧ Cabaret des Assassins

This was long ago renamed **Au Lapin Agile** (see "Chansonniers" in chapter 10). Picasso and Utrillo frequented this little cottage, which numerous artists have patronized and painted. On any given afternoon, French folk tunes, love ballads, army songs, sea chanteys, and music hall ditties stream out of the cafe and onto the street.

Turn left on rue St-Vincent, passing the Cimetière St-Vincent on your right (see

"Cemeteries" in chapter 7). Take a left onto rue Girardon and climb the stairs. In a minute or two, you'll spot on your right two of the windmills (moulins) that used to dot the Butte. One of these, at no. 75, is the:

⑨ Moulin de la Galette

This windmill (entrance at 1 av. Junot) was built in 1622 and was immortalized in oil by Renoir (see the painting in the Musée d'Orsay). When it was turned into a dance hall in the 1860s, it was named for the galettes (cakes made with flour ground inside the mills) that were sold here. Later, Toulouse-Lautrec, van Gogh, and Utrillo visited the dance hall. A few steps away at the angle of rue Lepic and rue Girardon is the Moulin Radet, now part of a restaurant.

Turn right onto rue Lepic and walk past no. 54. In 1886, van Gogh lived here with his brother Guillaumin. Take a right turn onto rue Joseph-de-Maistre, then left again on rue Caulaincourt until you reach the:

⑩ Cimetière de Montmartre

This final resting place is second in fame only to Père-Lachaise and is the haunt of Nijinsky, Dumas fils, Stendhal, Degas, and Truffaut, among others (see "Cemeteries" in chapter 7).

From the cemetery, take avenue Rachel, turn left onto boulevard de Clichy, and go to place Blanche, where stands a windmill even better known than the one in Renoir's painting, the:

⑪ Moulin Rouge

One of the world's most talked about nightclubs, Toulouse-Lautrec immortalized the Moulin Rouge. The windmill is still here, so is the cancan, but the rest has become an expensive, slick variety show with an emphasis on undraped females (see "Nightclubs & Cabarets" in chapter 10).

From place Blanche, you can begin a descent on:

⑫ Boulevard de Clichy

En route, you'll have to fight off the pornographers and hustlers trying to lure you into sex joints. With some rare exceptions, notably the citadels of the *chansonniers* (songwriters), boulevard de Clichy is one gigantic tourist trap. But everyone who comes to Paris invariably winds up here.

The boulevard strips and peels its way down to where you started:

⑬ Place Pigalle

The center of nudity in Paris was named after a French sculptor, Pigalle, whose closest brush with nudity was a depiction of Voltaire in the buff. Toulouse-Lautrec had his studio right off the square at 5 av. Frochot. Of course, place Pigalle was the notorious "Pig Alley" of World War II. When Edith Piaf was lonely and hungry, she sang in the alleyways, hoping to earn a few francs for the night.

WALKING TOUR 2   **THE LATIN QUARTER**

Start:	Place St-Michel (Métro: St-Michel).
Finish:	The Panthéon.
Time:	3 hours, not counting stops.
Best Time:	Any weekday, Monday to Friday from 9am to 4pm.
Worst Time:	Sunday morning, when everybody is asleep.

This is the precinct of the Université de Paris (known for its most famous branch, the Sorbonne), where students meet and fall in love over café crème and croissants. Rabelais named it the Quartier Latin after the students and the professors who spoke Latin in the classroom and on the streets. The sector teems with belly dancers, restaurants, cafes, bookstalls, *caveaux* (basement nightclubs), *clochards* (bums), *chiffonniers* (ragpickers), and *gamins* (boys and girls).

A good starting point for your tour is:

❶ Place St-Michel

Balzac used to draw water from the fountain (Davioud's 1860 sculpture of St. Michel slaying the dragon) when he was a youth. This was the scene of frequent skirmishes between the Germans and the Resistance in the summer of 1944, and the names of those who died here are engraved on plaques around the square.

>
> **TAKE A BREAK**
> Open 24 hours, **Café le Départ St-Michel**, 1 place St-Michel (℡ **01-43-54-24-55**), lies on the banks of the Seine. The decor is warmly modern, with etched mirrors reflecting the faces of a diversified crowd. If you want to fortify yourself for your walk, opt for one of the warm or cold snacks, including sandwiches.

To the south, you find:

❷ Boulevard St-Michel

Also called by locals. Boul' Mich, this is the main street of the Latin Quarter as it heads south. This is a major tourist artery and won't give you a great insight into local life. For that, you can branch off onto any of the streets that feed into the boulevard, and find cafes, bars, gyro counters, ice-cream stands, crêpe stands, and bistros like those pictured in movies set in Paris in the 1950s. The Paris Commune began here in 1871, as did the student uprisings of 1968.

From place St-Michel, with your back to the Seine, turn left down:

❸ Rue de la Huchette

This typical street was the setting of Elliot Paul's *The Last Time I Saw Paris* (1942). Paul first wandered here "on a soft summer evening, and entirely by chance," in 1923 and then moved into no. 28, the Hôtel Mont-Blanc. Though much has changed, some of the buildings are so old they have to be propped up by timbers. Paul captured the spirit of the street more evocatively than anyone, writing of "the delivery wagons, makeshift vehicles propelled by pedaling boys, pushcarts of itinerant vendors, knife-grinders, umbrella menders, a herd of milk goats, and the neighborhood pedestrians." (The local bordello has closed, however.) Today you see lots of Greek restaurants.

Branching off from this street to your left is:

❹ Rue du Chat-qui-Pêche

This is said to be the shortest, narrowest street in the world, containing not one door and only a handful of windows. It's usually filled with garbage or lovers or both. Before the quay was built, the Seine sometimes flooded the cellars of the houses, and legend has it that an enterprising cat took advantage of its good fortune and went fishing in the confines of the cellars—hence the street's name, which means "Street of the Cat Who Fishes."

Now retrace your steps toward place St-Michel and turn left at the intersection with rue de la Harpe, which leads to rue St-Séverin. At the intersection, take a left to see:

❺ St-Séverin

A flamboyant Gothic church named for a 6th-century recluse, St-Séverin was built from 1210 to 1230 and was reconstructed in 1458, over the years adopting many of the features of Notre-Dame, across the river. The tower was completed in 1487 and the chapels from 1498 to 1520; Hardouin-Mansart designed the Chapelle de la Communion in 1673 when he was 27, and it contains some beautiful Roualt etchings from the 1920s. Before entering, walk around the church to examine the gargoyles, birds of prey, and reptilian monsters projecting from its roof. To the right, facing the church is the 15th-century "garden of ossuaries." The stained glass inside St-Séverin, behind the altar, is a stunning adornment using great swaths of color to depict the Seven Sacraments.

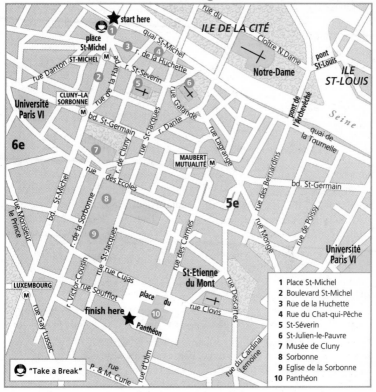

start here

place St-Michel

ST-MICHEL Ⓜ

rue Danton

rue du

quai St-Michel

r. de la Huchette

r. St-Séverin

CLUNY–LA SORBONNE Ⓜ

Université Paris VI

6e

rue de la Harp

bd. St-Germain

rue Galande

r. Dante

r. St-Jacques

ILE DE LA CITÉ

Cloître N.Dame

Notre-Dame

pont St-Louis

ILE ST-LOUIS

pont de l'Archevêché

Seine

quai de la Tournelle

rue Lagrange

MAUBERT MUTUALITÉ Ⓜ

rue des Bernardins

bd. St-Germain

5e

rue Monge

rue de Poissy

Université Paris VI

rue des Ecoles

r. de Cluny

bd. St-Michel

r. de la Sorbonne

r. St-Jacques

rue des Carmes

rue Cujas

LUXEMBOURG Ⓜ

r. Victor-Cousin

rue Soufflot

rue Gay Lussac

place du Panthéon

finish here

Panthéon

St-Etienne du Mont

rue Clovis

rue Descartes

rue du Cardinal Lemoine

rue P. & M. Curie

rue d'Ulm

rue Monsieur le Prince

1 Place St-Michel
2 Boulevard St-Michel
3 Rue de la Huchette
4 Rue du Chat-qui-Pêche
5 St-Séverin
6 St-Julien-le-Pauvre
7 Musée de Cluny
8 Sorbonne
9 Eglise de la Sorbonne
10 Panthéon

☕ "Take a Break"

After visiting the church, go back to rue St-Séverin and follow it to rue Galande, then continue on until you reach:

⑥ St-Julien-le-Pauvre

This church is located on the south side of square René-Viviani. First stand at the gateway and look at the beginning of rue Galande, especially the old houses with the steeples of St-Séverin rising across the way; it's one of the most frequently painted scenes on the Left Bank. Enter the courtyard and you'll be in medieval Paris. The garden to the left offers the best view of Notre-Dame. Everyone from Rabelais to Thomas Aquinas has passed through the doors of this church. Before the 6th century, a chapel stood on this spot. The present church goes back to the Longpont monks, who began work on it in 1170 (making it the oldest church in Paris).

In 1655, it was given to the Hôtel Dieu and in time became a small warehouse for salt. In 1889, it was presented to the followers of the Melchite Greek rite, a branch of the Byzantine church.

Return to rue Galande and turn left at the intersection with rue St-Séverin. Continue until you reach rue St-Jacques, turn left, and turn right when you reach boulevard St-Germain. Follow this boulevard to rue de Cluny, turn left, and head toward the entrance to the:

⑦ Musée de Cluny

Even if you're rushed, see *The Lady and the Unicorn* tapestry and the remains of the Roman baths. (See "The Major Museums" in chapter 7.)

After your visit to the Cluny, exit onto boulevard St-Michel, but instead of heading back to place St-Michel, turn left and walk to place de la Sorbonne and the:

⑧ Sorbonne

One of the most famous academic institutions in the world, the Sorbonne was founded in the 13th century by Robert de Sorbon, St. Louis's confessor, for poor students who wished to pursue theological studies. By the next century it had become the most prestigious university in the West, attracting such professors as Thomas Aquinas and Roger Bacon and such students as Dante, Calvin, and Longfellow. Napoleon reorganized it in 1806. The courtyard and galleries are open to the public when the university is in session. In the Cour d'Honneur are statues of Hugo and Pasteur.

At first glance from place de la Sorbonne, the Sorbonne seems architecturally undistinguished. In truth, it was rather indiscriminately reconstructed in the early 1900s. A better fate lay in store for the:

⑨ Eglise de la Sorbonne

Built in 1635 by Le Mercier, this church contains the marble tomb of Cardinal Richelieu, a work by Girardon based on a design by Le Brun. At his feet is the remarkable statue *Learning in Tears*.

From the church, go south on rue Victor-Cousin and turn left at rue Soufflot. At street's end lies place du Panthéon and the:

⑩ Panthéon

Sitting atop Mont Ste-Geneviève, this nonreligious temple is the final resting place of such distinguished figures as Hugo, Zola, Rousseau, Voltaire, and Curie. (See "Architectural & Historic Highlights" in chapter 7.)

WALKING TOUR 3 THE MARAIS

Start:	Place de la Bastille (Métro: Bastille).
Finish:	Place de la Bastille.
Time:	4½ hours, with only cursory stops en route. The distance is about 4.5km (2¾ miles).
Best Time:	Monday to Saturday, when more buildings and shops are open. If interiors are open, often you can walk into courtyards.
Worst Time:	Toward dusk, when shops and museums are closed, and it's too dark to admire the architectural details.

When Paris began to overflow the confines of Ile de la Cité in the 13th century, the citizenry began to settle in Le Marais, a marsh that used to be flooded by the Seine. By the 17th century, the Marais had become the center of aristocratic Paris and some of its great mansions (*hôtels particuliers*), many now restored or still being spruced up, were built by the finest craftsmen in France. In the 18th and 19th centuries, fashion deserted the Marais for the expanding Faubourg St-Germain and Faubourg St-Honoré. Industry took over, and once-elegant hotels deteriorated into tenements. There was talk of demolishing the neighborhood, but in 1962 the community banded together and saved the historic district.

Today, the 17th-century mansions are fashionable once again. The *International Herald Tribune* called this area the latest refuge for the Paris artisan fleeing the tourist-trampled St-Germain-des-Prés. (However, that doesn't mean the area doesn't get its share of tourist traffic; quite the contrary.) The "marsh" sprawls across the 3rd and 4th arrondissements bounded by the Grands Boulevards, rue du Temple, place des Vosges, and the Seine. It has become Paris's center of gay/lesbian life, particularly on rues St-Croix-de-la-Bretonnerie, des Archives, and Vieille-du-Temple, and is a great place for window-shopping in trendy boutiques, up-and-coming galleries, and more.

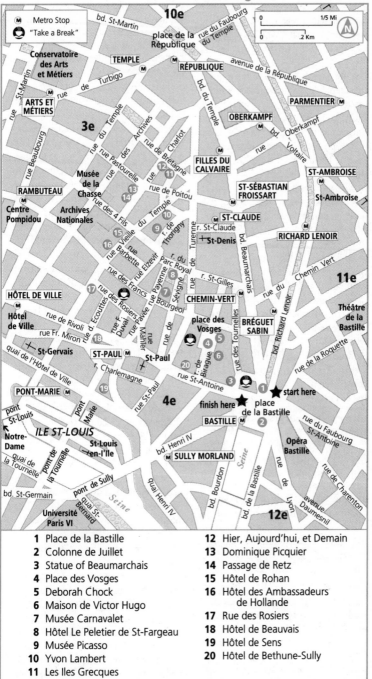

Legend:
- M Metro Stop
- "Take a Break"

1 Place de la Bastille
2 Colonne de Juillet
3 Statue of Beaumarchais
4 Place des Vosges
5 Deborah Chock
6 Maison de Victor Hugo
7 Musée Carnavalet
8 Hôtel Le Peletier de St-Fargeau
9 Musée Picasso
10 Yvon Lambert
11 Les Iles Grecques

12 Hier, Aujourd'hui, et Demain
13 Dominique Picquier
14 Passage de Retz
15 Hôtel de Rohan
16 Hôtel des Ambassadeurs
   de Hollande
17 Rue des Rosiers
18 Hôtel de Beauvais
19 Hôtel de Sens
20 Hôtel de Bethune-Sully

Begin your tour at the site that spawned one of the most celebrated and abhorred revolutions in human history:

➊ Place de la Bastille

On July 14, 1789, a mob attacked the Bastille prison located here, igniting the French Revolution. Now nothing of this symbol of despotism remains. Built in 1369, its eight huge towers once loomed over Paris. Within them, many prisoners, some sentenced by Louis XIV for "witchcraft," were kept, the best known being the "Man in the Iron Mask." And yet when the revolutionary mob stormed the fortress, only seven prisoners were discovered. (The Marquis de Sade had been shipped to the madhouse 10 days earlier.) The authorities had discussed razing it, so the attack meant little. But what it symbolized and what it unleashed can never be undone, and each July 14 the country celebrates Bastille Day with great festivity. Since the late 1980s, what had been scorned as a grimy-looking traffic circle has become an artistic focal point, thanks to the construction of the Opéra Bastille (p. 271) on its eastern edge.

It was probably easier to storm the Bastille in 1789 than it is now to cross over to the center of the square for a close-up view of the:

➋ Colonne de Juillet

The July Column doesn't commemorate the Revolution but honors the victims of the July Revolution of 1830, which put Louis-Philippe on the throne after the heady but wrenching victories and defeats of Napoleon Bonaparte. The winged God of Liberty, whose forehead bears an emerging star, crowns the tower.

From place de la Bastille, walk west along rue St-Antoine for about a block. Turn right and walk north along rue des Tournelles, noting the:

➌ Statue of Beaumarchais

Erected in 1895, it honors the 18th-century author of *The Barber of Seville* and *The Marriage of Figaro*, set to music by Rossini and Mozart

Continue north for a long block along rue des Tournelles, then turn left at medieval-looking rue Pas-de-la-Mule (Footsteps of the Mule), which will open suddenly onto the northeastern corner of enchanting:

➍ Place des Vosges

This is Paris's oldest square and once its most fashionable, boasting 36 brick-and-stone pavilions rising from covered arcades that allowed people to shop no matter what the weather. The buildings were constructed according to a strict plan: The height of the facades is equal to their width and the height of the triangular roofs is half the height of the facades. It was begun on Henri IV's orders and called place Royal; the king intended the square to be the scene of businesses and social festivities and even planned to live there, but Ravaillac had other plans and assassinated Henri 2 years before its completion. In 1559, Henri II was killed while jousting on the square, near the Hôtel des Tournelles; his widow, Catherine de Médicis, had the place torn down. By the 17th century, the square was the home of many aristocrats. During the Revolution, it was renamed place de l'Invisibilité, and its statue of Louis XIII was stolen (probably melted down). A replacement now stands in its place.

In 1800, the square was renamed place des Vosges because the Vosges département was the first in France to pay its taxes to Napoleon. The addition of chestnut trees sparked a controversy; critics say they spoil the perspective. Even though its fortunes waned when the Marais went out of fashion, place des Vosges is back big time. Over the years, the famous often took up residence: Descartes, Pascal, Cardinal Richelieu, courtesan Marion Delorme, Gautier, Daudet, and Mme de Sévigné all lived here. But its best-known occupant was Victor Hugo (his home, now a museum, is the only house open to the public).

Place des Vosges is the centerpiece of many unusual, charming, and/or funky shops. At 20 place des Vosges is one of the best of these:

⑤ Deborah Chock

This shop (© **01-48-04-86-86**) sells reproductions of the colorful and contemporary paintings of Deborah Chock, who is noted for the pithy phrases on the background of her paintings, these phrases reflecting insights from the worlds of poetry, philosophy, and psychoanalysis. Use it as a debut before you explore the many other art galleries in the neighborhood. The staff is English-speaking and well versed in the currents of the Paris art scene.

TAKE A BREAK
Two cafes hold court from opposite sides of place des Vosges, both serving café au lait, wine, and *eaux de vie*, sandwiches, pastries, and tea: **Ma Bourgogne** at no. 19 (© **01-42-78-44-64**), on the western edge, and **La Chope des Vosges** at no. 22 (© **01-42-72-64-04**).

Near the square's southeastern corner at 6 place des Vosges, commemorating the life and times of a writer whose works were read with passion in the 19th century, is the:

⑥ Maison de Victor Hugo

Hugo's former home is now a museum (© **01-42-72-10-16**) and literary shrine you can visit (see "Literary Landmarks" in chapter 7). Hugo lived there from 1832 to 1848, when he went into voluntary exile on the Channel Islands after the rise of the despotic Napoleon III.

Exit from place des Vosges from its northwestern corner (opposite the Maison de Victor Hugo) and walk west along rue des Francs-Bourgeois until you reach the intersection with rue de Sévigné, then make a right. At no. 23 is the:

⑦ Musée Carnavalet

This 16th-century mansion is now a museum (© **01-42-72-21-13**) devoted

to the history of Paris and the French Revolution (see "The Major Museums" in chapter 7).

Continue to a point near the northern terminus of rue de Sévigné, noting no. 29 (now part of the Carnavalet). This is the:

⑧ Hôtel le Peletier de St-Fargeau

The structure bears the name of its former occupant, who was considered responsible for the death sentence of Louis XVI. It's used as offices and can't be visited.

At the end of the street, make a left onto lovely rue du Parc-Royal, lined with 17th-century mansions. It leads to place de Thorigny, where at no. 5 you'll find the:

⑨ Musée Picasso

The museum occupies the **Hôtel Salé**, built by a salt-tax collector (see "The Major Museums" in chapter 7). You can visit the museum either now or come back at the end of the tour.

Walk northeast along rue Thorigny and turn left onto rue Debelleyme. After a block, near the corner of rue Vieille-du-Temple, at 108 rue Vieille-du-Temple, is a worthwhile art gallery among the dozens in this neighborhood:

⑩ Yvon Lambert

This gallery (© **01-42-71-09-33**) specializes in contemporary and sometimes radically avant-garde art from international artists. The art is displayed in a cavernous main showroom, spilling over into an "annex" room. An excellent primer for the local arts scene, it provides an agreeable contrast to the 17th-century trappings all around you.

Continue north for 2 short blocks along rue Debelleyme until you reach rue de Bretagne. Anyone who appreciates a really good deli will want to stop at 14 rue de Bretagne:

⑪ Les Iles Grecques

This deli (© **01-42-71-00-56**) is the most popular of the area's ethnic takeout restaurants, a perfect place to buy picnic supplies before heading to square du Temple (up rue de Bretagne) or place des Vosges. You'll find moussaka, stuffed eggplant, stuffed grape leaves, olives, tarama (a savory paste made from fish roe), and both meatballs and vegetarian balls. It's open Monday from 3:30 to 8pm and Tuesday to Sunday from 10am to 2pm and 3:30 to 8pm.

After you fill up on great food, note that at the same address is:

⑫ Hier, Aujourd'hui, et Demain

At this shop (✆ **01-42-77-69-02**) you can appreciate France's love affair with 1930s Art Deco. Michel, the owner, provides an array of bibelots and art objects, with one of the widest selections of colored glass in town. Works by late-19th-century glassmakers such as Daum, Gallé, and Legras are shown. Some items require special packing and great care in transport; others (many amusing) can be carted home as souvenirs.

Now walk southeast along rue Charlot to no. 10 at the corner of rue Pastourelle, where you'll be tempted by the fabrics of:

⑬ Dominique Picquier

Looking to redo your settee? This stylish shop (✆ **01-42-72-39-14**) sells a wide roster of fabric (50% cotton, 50% linen) that stands up to rugged use. Most patterns are based on some botanical inspiration, like ginkgo leaves, vanilla pods and vines, and magnolia branches. Most cost 65€ ($58) per meter (3¼ ft.), although some particularly plush velvets can go as high as 95€ ($85) per meter.

Nearby, at 9 rue Charlot, adjacent to the corner of rue Charlot and rue du Perche, is the Marais's large experimental art gallery, the:

⑭ Passage de Retz

Opened in 1994, this avant-garde gallery (✆ **01-48-04-37-99**) has about 630m² (2,100 sq. ft.) of space to show off its highly amusing exhibits. It has shown Japanese textiles, American abstract expressionist paintings, modern Venetian glass, contemporary Haitian paintings, and selections from affiliated art galleries in Québec.

Walk 1 block farther along rue Charlot, turn left for a block onto rue des 4 Fils, then go right on rue Vieille-du-Temple to no. 87, where you'll come across Delamair's:

⑮ Hôtel de Rohan

The fourth Cardinal Rohan, the larcenous cardinal of the "diamond necklace scandal" that led to a flood of destructive publicity for Marie Antoinette, once lived here. The first occupant of the hotel was reputed to be the son of Louis XVI. The interior is usually closed to the public, except during an occasional exhibit. If it's open, check out the amusing **Salon des Singes (Monkey Room)**. Sometimes you can visit the courtyard, which boasts one of the finest sculptures of 18th-century France, *The Watering of the Horses of the Sun,* with a nude Apollo and four horses against a background of exploding sunbursts. (If you want to see another Delamair work, detour to 60 rue des Francs-Bourgeois to see the extraordinary *Hôtel de Soubise,* now housing the **Musée de l'Histoire de France** [p. 204].)

Along the same street at no. 47 is the:

⑯ Hôtel des Ambassadeurs de Hollande

Here, Beaumarchais wrote *The Marriage of Figaro.* It's one of the most splendid mansions in the Marais and despite its name was never occupied by the Dutch embassy.

Continue walking south along rue Vieille-du-Temple until you reach:

⑰ Rue des Rosiers

Rue des Rosiers (Street of the Rosebushes) is one of the most colorful and typical streets remaining from Paris's old Jewish quarter, and you'll find an intriguing blend of living memorials to Ashkenazi and Sephardic traditions. The Star of David shines from some of the shop windows; Hebrew letters appear, sometimes in neon; couscous is sold from shops run by Moroccan, Tunisian, or Algerian Jews; restaurants serve kosher food; and signs appeal for Jewish liberation. You'll come across many delicacies you might've read about but never seen, such as sausage stuffed in a gooseneck, roots of black horseradish, and pickled lemons.

☕ **TAKE A BREAK**
The street offers a cornucopia of ethnic eateries that remain steadfast to their central European, Ashkenazi origins. **Chez Jo Goldenberg**, 7 rue des Rosiers (ⓒ 01-48-87-20-16), has plenty of room to sit down and eat (see p. 132 for more details).

Take a left onto rue des Rosiers and head down to rue Pavée, which gets its name because it was the first street in Paris, sometime during the 1300s, to have cobblestones placed over its open sewer. At this "Paved Street," turn right and walk south until you reach the St-Paul Métro stop. Make a right along rue François-Miron and check out no. 68, the 17th-century:

⑱ Hôtel de Beauvais

Though the facade was damaged in the Revolution, it remains one of Paris's most charming hôtels. A plaque announces that Mozart lived there in 1763 and played at the court of Versailles. (He was 7 at the time.) Louis XIV presented the mansion to Catherine Bellier, wife of Pierre de Beauvais and lady-in-waiting to Anne of Austria; she reportedly had the honor of introducing Louis, then 16, to the facts of life. To visit the interior, apply to the **Association du Paris Historique** on the ground floor.

Continue your walk along rue François-Miron until you come to a crossroads, where you take a sharp left along rue de Jouy, cross rue Fourcy, and turn onto rue du Figuier, where at no. 1 you'll see the:

⑲ Hôtel de Sens

The structure was built between the 1470s and 1519 for the archbishops of Sens. Along with the Cluny on the Left Bank, it's the only domestic architecture remaining from the 15th century. Long after the archbishops had departed in 1605, the wife of Henri IV, Queen Margot, lived here. Her new lover, "younger and more virile," slew her old lover as she looked on in amusement. Today, the hotel houses the **Bibliothèque Forney** (ⓒ 01-42-78-14-60). Leaded windows and turrets characterize the facade; you can go into the courtyard to see more ornate stone decoration—the gate is open Tuesday to Friday from 1:30 to 8:30pm and Saturday from 10am to 8:30pm.

Retrace your steps to rue de Fourcy, turn right, and walk up the street until you reach the St-Paul Métro stop again. Turn right onto rue St-Antoine and continue to no. 62:

⑳ Hôtel de Bethune-Sully

Work began on this mansion in 1625, on the order of Jean Androuet de Cerceau. In 1634, it was acquired by the duc de Sully, once Henri IV's minister of finance. After a straitlaced life as the "accountant of France," Sully broke loose in his declining years, adorning himself with diamonds and garish rings and a young bride, who's said to have had a thing for very young men. The hotel was acquired by the government just after World War II and is now the seat of the National Office of Historical Monuments and Sites, with an information center and a bookshop inside. Recently restored, the relief-studded facade is especially appealing. You can visit the interior with a guide on Saturday or Sunday at 3pm and can visit the courtyard and the garden any day; chamber music concerts are frequently staged here.

9

Shopping

Shopping is a favorite pastime of Parisians; some would even say it reflects the City of Light's soul. This is one of the rare places in the world where you don't have to go to any special area to shop—shopping opportunities surround you wherever you may be. Each walk you take will immerse you in uniquely French styles. The windows, stores, and people (even their dogs) brim with energy, creativity, and a sense of visual expression found in few other cities.

You don't have to buy anything to appreciate shopping in Paris—just soak up the art form the French have made of rampant consumerism. Peer in the *vitrines* (display windows), absorb cutting-edge ideas, witness new trends, and take home with you a whole new education in style.

1 The Shopping Scene

BEST BUYS

PERFUMES, MAKEUP & BEAUTY TREATMENTS A discount of 20% to 30% makes these items a great buy; qualify for a VAT refund (see below) and you'll save 40% to 45% off the Paris retail price, allowing you to bring home goods at half the U.S. price. Duty-free shops abound in Paris and are always less expensive than the ones at the airports.

For bargain cosmetics, try out French dime-store and drugstore brands like **Bourjois** (made in the Chanel factories), **Lierac,** and **Galenic. Vichy,** famous for its water, has a skin-care and makeup line. The newest retail trend in Paris is the *parapharmacie,* a type of discount drugstore loaded with inexpensive brands, health cures, beauty regimes, and diet plans. These usually offer a 20% discount.

FOODSTUFFS Nothing makes a better souvenir than a product of France brought home to savor later. Supermarkets are located in tourist neighborhoods; stock up on coffee, designer chocolates, mustards (try Maille or Meaux brand), and perhaps American products in French packages for the kids. However, to be sure you don't try to bring home a prohibited foodstuff, see "Entry Requirements & Customs Regulations" in chapter 3, "Planning Your Trip to Paris."

FUN FASHION Sure you can spend on couture or *prêt-à-porter,* but French teens and trendsetters have their own stores where the latest looks are affordable. Even the dime stores in Paris sell designer copies and hotshot styles. In the stalls in front of the department stores on boulevard Haussmann, you'll find some of the latest accessories, guaranteed for a week's worth of small talk once you get home.

GETTING A VAT REFUND

The French **value-added tax** (**VAT—TVA** in French) is 19.6%, but you can get most of that back if you spend 182€ ($163) or more in any store that participates in the VAT refund program. Most stores participate.

Tips **Shopping Etiquette**

When you walk into a French store, it's traditional to greet the owner or sales clerk with a direct address, not a fey smile or even a weak *bonjour*. Only a clear and pleasant *"Bonjour, madame/monsieur"* will do.

And if you plan to enter the rarefied atmospheres of the top designer boutiques (to check out the pricey merchandise if not to buy anything), be sure to dress the part. You don't need to wear couture, but do leave the sneakers and sweat suit back at your hotel. The sales staff will be much more accommodating if you look as if you belong there.

Once you meet your required minimum purchase amount, you qualify for a tax refund. The amount of the refund varies with the way the refund is handled and the fee some stores charge you for processing it. So the refund at a department store may be 13%, whereas at a small shop it may be 15% or even 18%.

You'll receive **VAT refund papers** in the shop; some stores, like Hermès, have their own; others provide a government form. Fill in the forms before you arrive at the airport and expect to stand in line at the Customs desk for as long as half an hour. You're required to show the goods at the airport, so have them on you or visit the Customs office before you check your luggage. Once the papers have been mailed, a credit will appear, often months later, on your credit-card bill. All refunds are processed at the point of departure from the **European Union (EU),** so if you're going to another EU country, don't apply for the refund in France.

Be sure to mark the paperwork to request that your refund be applied to your credit card so you aren't stuck with a check in euros that's hard to cash. This also ensures the best rate of exchange. In some airports, you're offered the opportunity to get your refund back in cash, which is tempting. But if you accept cash in any currency other than euros, you'll be losing money on the conversion rate.

To avoid VAT refund hassles, ask for a Global Refund form ("Shopping Checque") at a store where you make a purchase. When leaving an EU country, have it stamped by Customs, after which you take it to a Global Refund counter at one of more than 700 airports and border crossings in Europe. Your money is refunded on the spot. For information, contact **Global Refund,** 707 Summer St., Stamford, CT 06901 (© **800/566-9828;** www.globalrefund.com).

DUTY-FREE BOUTIQUES

The advantage of duty-free shops is that you don't have to pay the VAT, so you avoid the red tape of getting a refund. Both Charles de Gaulle and Orly airports have shopping galore (de Gaulle has a virtual mall with crystal, cutlery, chocolates, luggage, wine, pipes and lighters, lingerie, silk scarves, perfume, knitwear, jewelry, cameras, cheeses, even antiques). You'll find duty-free shops on the avenues branching out from the Opéra Garnier, in the 1st arrondissement. Sometimes there are bargains, but most often not. Usually these stores jack prices up, so even though there's no duty, most goods are not a bargain. In general, these duty-free shops are best for last-minute buys or the impulse shopper who feels he or she is leaving Paris without having bought enough.

BUSINESS HOURS

Usual shop hours are Monday to Saturday from 10am to 7pm, but hours vary, and Monday mornings don't run at full throttle. Small shops sometimes close for a 2-hour lunch break and may not open at all until after lunch on Monday. Thursday is the best day for late-night shopping, with stores open to 9 or 10pm.

Sunday shopping is limited to tourist areas and flea markets, though there's growing demand for full-scale Sunday hours. The department stores are now open on the five Sundays before Christmas. The **Carrousel du Louvre,** a mall adjacent to the Louvre, is hopping on Sunday, but closed on Monday. The tourist shops lining rue de Rivoli across from the Louvre are open on Sunday, as are the antiques villages, flea markets, and specialty events. There are several food markets in the streets on Sunday. For our favorites, see the box "Food Markets" (p. 259). The **Virgin Megastore** on the Champs-Elysées, a big teen hangout, pays a fine to stay open on Sunday.

SHIPPING IT HOME

Shipping charges will possibly double your cost, and you may have to pay duties on the items (see above). The good news: The VAT refund is automatically applied to all shipped items, so there's no need to worry about the 182€ ($163) minimum. Some stores have a $100 minimum for shipping. You can also walk into any post office and mail home a jiffy bag or box of goodies. French do-it-yourself boxes can't be reopened once closed, so pack carefully. The clerk at the post office will help you assemble the box (it's tricky), seal it, and send it off.

GREAT SHOPPING NEIGHBORHOODS

Here are the best of the shopping arrondissements:

1ST & 8TH ARRONDISSEMENTS These two quartiers adjoin each other and form the heart of Paris's best Right Bank shopping strip—they're one big hunting ground. This area includes the **rue du Faubourg St-Honoré,** where the big designer houses are, and the **Champs-Elysées,** where the mass-market and teen scene are hot. At one end of the 1st is the **Palais Royal,** one of the best shopping secrets in Paris, where an arcade of boutiques flanks each side of the garden of the former palace.

Also here is **avenue Montaigne,** Paris's most glamorous shopping street, boasting 2 blocks of ultrafancy shops, where you float from big name to big name and in a few hours can see everything from Dior to Caron. Avenue Montaigne is also the address of **Joseph,** a British design firm, and **Porthault,** makers of the poshest sheets in the world.

2ND ARRONDISSEMENT Right behind the Palais Royal is the **Garment District (Sentier),** as well as a few sophisticated shopping secrets, such as **place des Victoires.**

In the 19th century, this area became known for its *passages,* glass-enclosed shopping streets—in fact, the world's first shopping malls. They were also the city's first buildings to be illuminated by gaslight. Many have been torn down, but a dozen or so have survived. Of them all, we prefer *Passage du Grand Cerf,* between 145 rue St-Denis and 10 rue Dussoubs, 2e (Métro: Bourse), lying a few blocks from the Beaubourg. It's a place of wonder, filled with everything from retro-chic boutiques and (increasingly) Asian-themed shops. What's exciting is to come upon a discovery, perhaps a postage-stamp shop with some special jeweler who creates unique products such as jewel-toned safety pins.

3RD & 4TH ARRONDISSEMENTS The border between these two arrondissements gets fuzzy, especially around **place des Vosges,** center stage of the Marais. The districts offer several dramatically different shopping experiences.

On the surface, the shopping includes the "real people stretch" (where all the non-millionaires shop) of **rue de Rivoli** and **rue St-Antoine,** featuring everything from Gap and a branch of Marks & Spencer to local discount stores and mass merchants. Two "real people" department stores are in this area, **Samaritaine** and **BHV;** there's also **Les Halles** and the **Beaubourg** neighborhood, which is anchored by the Centre Pompidou.

Hidden in the Marais is a medieval warren of twisting streets chockablock with cutting-edge designers and up-to-the-minute fashions and trends. Start by walking around place des Vosges for galleries, designer shops, and special finds, then dive in and lose yourself in the area leading to the Musée Picasso.

Finally, the 4th is the home of the **Bastille,** an up-and-coming area for artists and galleries where you'll find the newest entry on the retail scene, the **Viaduc des Arts** (which actually stretches into the 12th). It's a collection of about 30 stores occupying a series of narrow vaulted niches under what used to be railroad tracks. They run parallel to avenue Daumesnil, centered around boulevard Diderot.

6TH & 7TH ARRONDISSEMENTS   Though the 6th is one of the most famous shopping districts in Paris—it's the soul of the Left Bank—a lot of the good stuff is hidden in the zone that turns into the residential district of the 7th. **Rue du Bac,** stretching from the 6th to the 7th in a few blocks, stands for all that wealth and glamour can buy.

9TH ARRONDISSEMENT   To add to the fun of shopping the Right Bank, the 9th sneaks in behind the 1st, so if you choose not to walk toward the Champs-Elysées and the 8th, you can head to the city's big department stores, all built in a row along **boulevard Haussmann** in the 9th. Department stores include not only the two big French icons, **Au Printemps** and **Galeries Lafayette,** but also a large branch of Britain's **Marks & Spencer** and a branch of the Dutch answer to Kmart, low-priced **C&A.**

2 Shopping A to Z

ANTIQUES

Argenterie de Turenne *Finds*   Inside, you'll find old-fashioned gentility and masses of silver, both secondhand sterling and plated, much made in France during the 19th and early 20th centuries. The array of trays, water pitchers, cutlery, napkin rings, tumblers, and punchbowls is staggering, but what many visitors find amazing is that congenially battered silver-plated forks and spoons are sold by weight, at the rate of 61€ ($54) per kilo. The store lies within the Marais, a short walk from place des Vosges, on a block that's lined with purveyors of other old-fashioned grace notes that include antique glassware and porcelain. 19 rue de Turenne, 4e. ℂ **01-42-72-04-00.** Tues–Sat 10:30am–7pm. Métro: St-Paul.

Le Louvre des Antiquaires   Across from the Louvre, this store offers three levels of fancy knickknacks and 250 vendors. It's just the place if you're looking for 30 matching Baccarat crystal champagne flutes from the 1930s, a Sèvres tea service from 1773, or a signed Jean Fouquet gold-and-diamond pin. Too stuffy? No problem. There's always the 1940 Rolex with the aubergine crocodile strap. Prices can be high, but a few reasonable items are hidden here. What's more, the Sunday scene is fabulous, and there's a cafe with a variety of lunch menus beginning around 15€ ($13). Pick up a free map and brochure of the premises from the information desk. 2 place du Palais-Royal, 1er. ℂ **01-42-97-27-00.** Tues–Sun 11am–7pm. Closed Sun July–Aug. Métro: Palais Royal.

Mlinaric, Henry, and Zervudachi　David Mlinaric is the British interior designer who redecorated Spencer House (Princess Diana's ancestral home in London) as well as all of Lord Rothschild's private residences. Tino Zervudachi is one of the hot Young Turks of Paris design. Hugh Henry, like Mlinaric, is English. Together, these three musketeers are the chicest antiques dealers on the Right Bank, specializing in museum-quality 18th-century items. 54 Galerie de Montpensier, Palais-Royal, 1er. ✆ **01-42-96-08-62.** Mon–Fri 9:30am–1pm and 2–6:30pm (Fri to 5:30pm). Métro: Palais Royal.

Village St-Paul　This isn't an antiques center but a cluster of dealers in their own hole-in-the-wall hideout. It really hops on Sunday. Bring your camera, because inside the courtyards and alleys is a dream vision of hidden Paris: dealers in a courtyard selling furniture and other decorative items in French-country and formal styles. The rest of the street, stretching from the river to the Marais, is also lined with dealers. 23-27 rue St-Paul, 4e. No phone. Thurs–Mon 11am–7pm. Métro: St-Paul.

ART

Artcurial　This is the best, most famous, and most prestigious place in Paris for contemporary art. Many art forms are displayed here, from jewelry and design to sculpture and tapestries. Centre d'Art Contemporain, 61 av. Montaigne, 8e. ✆ **01-42-99-16-16.** Métro: F. D. Roosevelt.

Galerie Adrien Maeght　This art house is among the most famous names, selling contemporary art on a fancy Left Bank street that's far more fashionable than the bohemian Left Bank Picasso knew. 42 rue du Bac, 7e. ✆ **01-45-48-45-15.** Mon 10am–6pm; Tues–Sat 9:30am–7pm. Métro: Rue du Bac.

Galerie 27　This tiny closet sells lithographs by famous artists of the early 20th century, including Picasso, Miró, and Léger. Contemporary artists are also represented. 27 rue de Seine, 6e. ✆ **01-43-54-78-54.** Tues–Sat 10am–1pm and 2:30–7pm. Métro: St-Germain-des-Prés or Odéon.

Librairie Elbe　The souvenir stands are filled with copies of Toulouse-Lautrec posters, but if you want something original, this shop sells early-1900s advertising and railroad posters, as well as etchings and cartoons, at very reasonable prices. 213 bis bd. St-Germain, 7e. ✆ **01-45-48-77-97.** Tues–Sat 10am–1pm and 2–6:30pm. Closed Aug. Métro: Rue du Bac.

Viaduc des Arts　This complex of boutiques and crafts workshops occupies the vaulted spaces beneath one of the 19th-century railway access routes into the Gare de Lyon. Around 1990, crafts artists, including furniture makers, potters, glassblowers, and weavers, began renting the then-empty niches beneath the viaduct, selling their wares to homeowners and members of Paris's decorating trades. Additional spaces have since then been rented by several trend-setting home-furnishing outfits. Stretching for more than 2 blocks between the Opéra Bastille and the Gare de Lyon, it offers the possibility of seeing what Parisians consider chic in terms of home decorating. 9-147 av. Daumesnil, 12e. ✆ **01-44-75-80-66.** Mon–Sat 11am–7pm. Métro: Bastille or Gare de Lyon.

BOOKS

If you like the rare and unusual in books, patronize one of the *bouquinistes,* the owners of those army-green stalls that line the Seine. Perhaps you'll get lucky and find an original edition of Henry Miller's *Tropic of Cancer,* banned for decades in the United States. This is where tourists in the 1920s and 1930s went to buy "dirty" French postcards. Occasionally you'll come across some treasured book. We like to start with the guy who sells travel posters, perhaps of old Pan

---

(Finds   An Open-Air Canvas Gallery

The **Paris Art Market** is "the place to go" on a Sunday. At the foot of
Montparnasse Tower, this market is like an open-air gallery and has done
much to restore the reputation of Montparnasse (14e) as a *quartier* for
artists. Some 100 artists participate, including painters, sculptors, and photographers, even jewelers and hat makers. Head for the mall along the
boulevard Edgar Quinet for the best work. Go any time on Sunday
between 10am and 7:30pm (Métro: Montparnasse).

Am jets, lying right off the pont des Arts, and work our way toward all the rest.
Some of the banquinistes are noted for giving the Parisians a reputation for
rudeness. But don't let them intimidate you, although they'll often try.

See also the **Marché aux Livres** under "Markets" and **FNAC** and **Virgin
Megastore** under "Music."

Brentano's   A block from the Opéra Garnier, Brentano's is a large English-language bookstore selling guides, maps, novels, and nonfiction as well as greeting
cards, postcards, holiday items, and gifts. 37 av. de l'Opéra, 2e. ✆ **01-42-61-52-50.**
Mon–Sat 10am–7:30pm. Métro: Opéra or Pyramide.

Galignani   Sprawling over a large street level and supplemented by a mezzanine, this venerable wood-paneled bookstore has thrived since 1810. Enormous
numbers of books are available in French and English, with a special emphasis
on French classics, modern fiction, sociology, and fine arts. Looking for English-
language translations of works by Balzac, Flaubert, Zola, or Colette? Most of
them are here; if not, they can be ordered. 224 rue de Rivoli, 1er. ✆ **01-42-60-76-07.**
Mon–Sat 10am–7pm. Métro: Tuileries.

Les Mots à la Bouche   This is Paris's largest, best-stocked gay bookstore. You
can find French- and English-language books as well as gay info magazines like
Illico, e.m@le, and *Lesbia.* You'll also find lots of free pamphlets advertising
gay/lesbian venues and events. 6 rue Ste-Croix-la-Bretonnerie, 4e. ✆ **01-42-78-88-30.**
Mon–Sat 11am–11pm; Sun 2–8pm. Métro: Hôtel de Ville.

Librairie la Bail-Weissert   Paris is filled with rare-book shops, but this one has
the best collection of atlases, rare maps, and engravings from the 15th century to
the 19th century. The shop sells original topographical maps of European and
world cities, along with various regions of Europe. There's also a superb collection
of architectural engravings. 5 rue Lagrange, 5e. ✆ **01-43-29-72-59.** Mon–Fri 10am–12:30pm
and 2–7pm. Sat only by appointment. Métro: Maubert-Mutualité or St-Michel.

Shakespeare and Company   The most famous bookstore on the Left Bank
was Shakespeare and Company, on rue de l'Odéon, home to Sylvia Beach,
"mother confessor to the Lost Generation." Hemingway, Fitzgerald, and Stein
were frequent patrons, as was Anaïs Nin, the diarist noted for her description of
struggling American artists in 1930s Paris. Nin helped her companion, Henry
Miller, publish *Tropic of Cancer,* a book so notorious in its day that returning
Americans trying to slip copies through Customs often had them confiscated as
pornography. (When times were hard, Nin herself wrote pornography for a dollar a page.) Long ago, the shop moved to rue de la Bûcherie, a musty old place
where expatriates still swap books and literary gossip and foreign students work
in exchange for modest lodgings. Check out the lending library upstairs. 37 rue
de la Bûcherie, 5e. No phone. Daily 11am–midnight. Métro: St-Michel.

Tea and Tattered Pages   At this largely English-language paperback book-shop, you can take a break from browsing to have tea. Though it's out of the way, an extra dose of charm makes it worth the trip. 24 rue Mayet, 6e. *C* 01-40-65-94-35. Mon–Sat 11am–7pm; Sun noon–6pm. Métro: Duroc.

Village Voice Bookshop   This favorite of expatriate Yankees is on a side street in the heart of the best Left Bank shopping district, near some of the gathering places described in Gertrude Stein's *The Autobiography of Alice B. Toklas.* Opened in 1981, the shop is a hangout for literati. Its name has nothing to do with the New York weekly. 6 rue Princesse, 6e. *C* 01-46-33-36-47. Mon 2–8pm; Tues–Sat 10am–8pm; Sun 2–7pm. Métro: Mabillon.

W. H. Smith   This store provides books, magazines, and newspapers published in English (most titles are from Britain). You can get the *Times* of London, of course, and the Sunday *New York Times* is available every Monday. There's a fine selection of maps and travel guides, plus a special children's section that includes comics. 248 rue de Rivoli, 1er. *C* 01-44-77-88-99. Mon–Sat 9am–7:30pm; Sun 1–7:30pm. Métro: Concorde.

CERAMICS, CHINA & PORCELAIN

La Maison Ivre   This charming shop is perfect for country-style ceramics that add authenticity to French-country decor. It carries an excellent selection of handmade pottery from all over France, with an emphasis on Provençal and southern French ceramics, including ovenware, bowls, platters, plates, pitchers, mugs, and vases. 38 rue Jacob, 6e. *C* 01-42-60-01-85. Mon 2–7pm; Tues–Sat 10:30am–7pm. Métro: St-Germain-des-Prés.

Limoges-Unic/Madronet   Housed in two shops on the same street, this store is crammed with crystals like Daum, Baccarat, Lalique, Haviland, and Bernar-daud. You'll also find other table items: glass and crystal, silver, whatever your heart desires. They'll ship your purchases, and English is widely spoken. 34 and 58 rue de Paradis, 10e. *C* 01-47-70-54-49 or 01-47-70-34-59. Mon–Sat 10am–6:30pm. Métro: Gare de l'Est.

Manufacture Nationale de Sèvres   Once endorsed and promoted by the mistresses to the French kings, Sèvres today manufactures only 4,000 to 5,000 pieces of porcelain every year, and of these, many are reserved in advance as replacements for government and historical entities. 4 place André-Malraux, 1er. *C* 01-47-03-40-20. Mon–Fri 11am–6pm. Métro: Palais Royal.

CHILDREN: FASHION & TOYS

Au Nain Bleu   This is the largest, oldest, and most centrally located toy store in Paris. More important, it's probably the fanciest toy store in the world. But don't panic—in addition to the expensive stuff, you'll find rows of cheaper items (like penny candy) in jars on the first floor. 406 rue St-Honoré, 8e. *C* 01-42-60-39-01. Mon–Sat 10am–6:30pm. Métro: Concorde or Madeleine.

Bonpoint   Grandparent alert! Bonpoint is part of a well-known almost-haute-couture chain specializing in clothing for children and adolescents ages 1 week to 16 years. The clothing is well tailored, traditional, and expensive. Drool over formal party and confirmation dresses and baptismal robes, embroidered in France and edged in lace. 15 rue Royale, 8e. *C* 01-47-42-52-63. Mon–Sat 10am–7pm. Métro: Concorde.

Dipaki *(Finds*   If you prefer clothes that have hip, hot style and color but are wearable, washable, and affordable, forget Bonpoint and try this small shop—it's a representative of a truly sensational French line of clothes for toddlers. And it's only a block from place de la Madeleine. 18 rue Vignon, 9e. ℂ **01-42-66-24-74.** Mon–Sat 10am–7pm. Métro: Madeleine.

Natalys Part of a French chain with a dozen stores in Paris and many elsewhere, Natalys sells upscale versions of children's (6 and under) and maternity wear. It has just enough French panache without going over the top in design or price. 92 av. des Champs-Elysées, 8e. ℂ **01-43-59-17-65.** Mon–Sat 10am–7:45pm. Métro: F. D. Roosevelt.

CRYSTAL

Baccarat Opened in 1764, Baccarat is one of Europe's leading purveyors of full-lead crystal. You won't be able to comparison-shop Baccarat crystal at its various branches—a central organization sets rigid prices. But if you're hunting for bargains, head for the rue de Paradis outlet and check out special sales or promotions on discontinued items. These sales are the biggest during 2 weeks in mid-January. Baccarat's more prestigious outlet is on place de la Madeleine, but the rue de Paradis one is larger and contains the **Musée de Baccarat** (p. 204). 11 place de la Madeleine, 8e. ℂ **01-42-65-36-26.** Tues–Fri 10am–7pm; Mon and Sat 10am–7:30pm. Métro: Madeleine. Also: 30 bis rue de Paradis, 10e. ℂ **01-47-70-64-30.** Mon–Fri 10am–6:30pm; Sat 10am–noon and 2–5:30pm. Métro: Gare de l'Est.

Lalique Lalique is known for its smoky frosted glass sculpture, Art Deco crystal, and unique perfume bottles. The shop sells a wide range of merchandise, including leather belts with Lalique buckles and silk scarves at about 213€ ($190), designed to compete directly with those sold by Hermès. 11 rue Royale, 8e. ℂ **01-53-05-12-12.** Mon–Wed 10am–6:30pm; Thurs–Fri 9:30am–6:30pm; Sat 9:30am–7pm. Métro: Concorde or Madeleine.

DEPARTMENT STORES

In addition to the stores below, **La Samaritaine,** 19 rue de la Monnaie, 1er (ℂ **01-40-41-20-20;** Métro: Pont Neuf or Châtelet-Les Halles), and **BHV,** 52 rue de Rivoli, 4e (ℂ **01-42-74-90-00;** Métro: Hôtel de Ville), offer the department-store experience at slightly lower prices. La Samaritaine has a fine inexpensive restaurant with a panoramic view on the top floor.

Au Bon Marché Don't be fooled by the name ("low-budget" or "cheap") of this two-part Left Bank department store—for about 20 years, it has worked hard to position itself in the luxury market, selling fashion for men, women, and children; furniture; upscale gifts; and housewares. Some visitors compare it to Bloomingdale's with a French accent. This is the oldest department store in Paris, dating from 1852. Of course, it can't compete with the grand *magasins* like Galeries Lafayette (see below), except in one category: Au Bon Marché has a superior rug department, which it has fine-tuned as its specialty since 1871. It also has one of the largest food halls in Paris. 24 rue de Sèvres, 7e. ℂ **01-44-39-80-00.** Mon–Wed and Fri 9:30am–7pm; Thurs 10am–9pm; Sat 9:30am–8pm. Métro: Sèvres-Babylone.

Au Printemps Take a look at the facade of this store for a reminder of the Gilded Age. Inside, the merchandise is divided into housewares (**Printemps Maison**), women's fashion (**Printemps de la Mode**), and men's clothes (**Le Printemps de l'Homme**). This is better for women's and children's fashion than Galeries Lafayette. As for perfume, it's in a dead-heat race with Galeries Lafayette, with all the top names. Although visitors feel more pampered in Galeries Lafayette, Au Printemps also dazzles with its customer services, putting all major department stores in London to shame. Check out the magnificent stained-glass dome, through which turquoise light cascades into the sixth-floor

Café Flo, where you can have a coffee or a full meal. Interpreters at the Welcome Service in Printemps de la Mode will help you find what you're looking for, claim your VAT refund, and so on. Au Printemps also has a tourist discount card, offering a flat 10% discount. Immediately adjacent to the store and under the same management, but with its own phone and storefront, is **Citadium,** 56 rue Caumartin, 9e (© **01-55-31-74-00**), which specializes in sporting equipment and sports clothes for men, women, and children. 64 bd. Haussmann, 9e. © **01-42-82-50-00.** Mon–Wed and Fri–Sat 9:35am–7pm; Thurs 9:35am–10pm. Métro: Havre-Caumartin. RER: Auber or Haussmann St-Lazare.

Colette Named after the great French writer, Colette is a swank citadel for *à la mode* fashion. It buzzes with excitement, displaying fashions by some of the city's most promising young talents, including Marni and Lucien Pellat-Finet. This is for the sophisticated shopper who'd never be caught dead shopping the Galeries Lafayette and the like. Not to be overlooked are home furnishings by designers like Tom Dixon and even zany Japanese accessories. Even if you don't plan to buy anything, patronize the tea salon, with its fresh quiches, salads, and cakes, plus 3 dozen brands of bottled water. 213 rue St-Honoré, 1er. © **01-55-35-33-90.** Mon–Sat 10:30am–7:30pm. Métro: Tuileries or Pyramide.

Galeries Lafayette Opened in 1896, with a lobby capped by an early-1900s stained glass cupola classified as a historic monument, Galeries Lafayette is Europe's largest department store. If you have time for only one department store, make it this one. This store could provision a small city with everything from perfume to fashion. It is more user-friendly than even Au Printemps, and in fashion it places more emphasis on upcoming designers. It also concentrates on an upscale roster of everything you'd need to furnish and maintain a home; thousands of racks of clothing for men, women, and children; and a staggering array of cosmetics, makeup products, and perfumes. Menswear is concentrated in a section called **Lafayette Hommes;** also in the complex is **Lafayette Gourmet,** one of the fanciest grocery stores in Paris, selling culinary exotica at prices usually lower than those at Fauchon (see "Food: Chocolate, Honey, Patés & More" below). A floor above street level is a concentration of high-end semi-independent boutiques, including Cartier, Vuitton, and Prada Sport. A fashion show is held at least once daily, usually in the **Salon Opéra.** At the street-level **Welcome Desk,** you can be told in many languages where you can find this or that in the store, where you can get a taxi back to your hotel, and so on. 40 bd. Haussmann, 9e. © **01-42-82-34-56.** Mon–Wed and Fri–Sat 9:30am–6:45pm; Thurs 9:30am–9pm. Métro: Chaussée d'Antin. RER: Auber.

FABRICS

Souleiado This is the only Paris branch of one of Provence's most successful purveyors of the bright fabrics and thick pottery of France's southern tier. Fabrics are measured out here by scissors-wielding saleswomen, then sold by the meter for seamstresses to whip into curtains, tablecloths, or whatever. There's also rack after rack of *prêt-à-poser* ("ready-to-hang") curtains, tablecloths, and bedcovers, each based on historically accurate reproductions of 18th-century prints as discovered in such cities as Avignon, Arles, and Marseille. In a separate shop just around the corner, at 78 rue de Seine (same phone), there are displays of table settings, housewares, and gift items, each reflecting the bright sunshine and colors (usually ochre, cerulean blue, and a strong medium green) of the Midi. 3 rue Lobineau, 6e. © **01-43-54-62-25.** Mon–Sat 10:30am–7pm. Métro: Odéon or Mabillon.

FASHION
CUTTING-EDGE CHIC

Azzedine Alaïa   Alaïa, who became the darling of French fashion in the 1970s, is the man who put body consciousness back into Paris chic. If you can't afford the current collection, try the **stock shop** around the corner at 18 rue de Verrerie, 4e (☎ **01-42-72-19-19**), where last year's leftovers are sold at serious discounts. Both outlets sell leather trench coats, knit dresses, pleated skirts, cigarette pants, belts, purses, and fashion accessories. 7 rue de Moussy, 4e. ☎ 01-42-72-19-19. Mon–Sat 10am–7pm. Métro: Hôtel de Ville.

Courrèges   Don't look now: André Courrèges is hot again. Even those little white vinyl go-go boots and disco purses in silver metallic cloth are back. Courrèges's brings a humorous touch to 1970s retro, with bold color, plastic, and fun. 40 rue François-Ier, 8e. ☎ 01-53-67-30-00. Mon–Sat 10am–7pm. Métro: F. D. Roosevelt.

Hervé Leger   This creator of the Band Aid Dress (*La Robe à bandes*), a tightly wrapped concoction of stretch materials and color, has opened his own shop for those with curves to flaunt and cash to burn. 29 rue du Faubourg St-Honoré, 8e. ☎ 01-40-20-16-50. Mon–Sat 11am–7pm. Métro: Concorde or Madeleine.

Jean-Charles de Castelbajac   Every year the design collection of this iconoclastic internationalist changes its theme and colors. Years past have focused on brightly colored clothing in primary colors with poetic inscriptions by Proust and French Impressionist poet Mallarmé. For the 2001-2002 season, colors reverted to blacks, whites, and khakis, sometimes with references to the Dracula craze (spider-web veils and the like) currently in vogue within Paris. Come here to be entertained and amused by whatever new bag of vogue-ish tricks this designer might pull out of his hat in collections to come. 31 place du Marché St-Honoré, 1er. ☎ 01-42-60-41-55. Mon–Sat 10am–7pm. Métro: Pyramide.

Jean Paul Gaultier   Supporters of this high-camp, high-fashion mogul describe him as an avant-garde classicist without allegiance to any of the aesthetic restrictions of the bourgeoisie. Detractors call him a glorified punk rocker with a gimmicky allegiance to futurist models as interpreted by "Star Trek." Whatever your opinion, it's always refreshing and insightful, especially for fashion buffs, to check out France's most iconoclastic designer. There's a franchise branch of his store at 6 rue Vivienne, 2e (☎ **01-42-86-05-05;** Métro: Bourse), but the company's main branch, and site of its biggest inventories, is at 30 rue du Faubourg St-Antoine, 12e. ☎ 01-44-68-84-84. Both branches Mon and Sat 10:30am–7pm; Tues–Fri 10am–7pm. Métro: Bastille.

Lolita Lempicka   Her name and reputation as a fashion designer originated in the underground arts scene of the Marais. Since then, she's gone mainstream with a pair of shops, each highly visible and stacked with the kind of long and short dresses a woman can wear at a formal or relaxed-chic cocktail or dinner party. Clothes are inventive and usually very sexy, usually in colors that include soft black, varying shades of pink, turquoise, and brownish-maroon. They also stock women's shoes. 18 rue du Faubourg St-Honoré, 8e. ☎ 01-49-24-94-01. Métro: Madeleine. Also 46 av. Victor Hugo, 16e. ☎ 01-45-02-14-46. All open Mon–Sat 10:30am–7pm. Métro: Etoile.

DESIGNER BOUTIQUES & FASHION FLAGSHIPS

There are two primary fields of dreams in Paris when it comes to showcasing the international big names: rue du Faubourg St-Honoré and avenue Montaigne. Though the Left Bank is gaining in status with recent additions like Dior,

Armani, and Vuitton, the heart of the international designer parade is on the Right Bank.

Rue du Faubourg St-Honoré is so famously fancy it's simply known as "the Faubourg." It was the traditional miracle mile until recent years, when the really exclusive shops shunned it for the wider and even more deluxe avenue Montaigne at the other end of the arrondissement. (It's a long but pleasant walk from one fashion strip to the other.) **Avenue Montaigne** is filled with almost unspeakably fancy shops, but a few of them have affordable cafes (try Joseph at no. 14) and all have sales help that's almost always cordial to the well dressed.

The mix is quite international—from British (**Joseph**), to German (**Jil Sander**), to Italian (**Krizia**). **Chanel, Lacroix, Porthault, Ricci, Dior,** and **Ungaro** are a few of the big French names. Also check out some of the lesser-known creative powers that be. And don't miss a visit to **Caron.** Most of the designer shops sell men's and women's clothing. The Faubourg hosts other traditional favorites: **Hermès, Lanvin, Jaeger, Rykiel,** and the upstart **Façonnable,** which sells preppy men's clothing in the United States through a business deal with Nordstroms. Note that Lanvin has its own men's shop (**Lanvin Homme**), which has a cafe that's perfect for a light (and affordable) lunch.

Alain Figaret   Alain Figaret is one of France's foremost designers of men's shirts and women's blouses. Though this store has a broad range of fabrics, 100% cotton is its specialty. Also check out the silk neckties in distinctively designed prints and the silk scarves for women. If you're comparison shopping, Figaret and Charvet (see below) are half a block apart. 21 rue de la Paix, 2e. ℂ **01-42-65-04-99.** Mon–Sat 10am–7:30pm. Métro: Opéra.

Chanel   If you can't have the sun, the moon, and the stars, at least buy something with Coco Chanel's initials on it, either a serious fashion statement (drop-dead chic) or something fun and playful (tongue in chic). Karl Lagerfeld's designs come in all flavors and have added a subtle twist to Chanel's classicism. This store is adjacent to the Chanel couture house and behind the Ritz, where Mlle Chanel once lived. Check out the beautiful staircase of the maison before you shop the two-floor boutique—it's well worth a peek. 31 rue Cambon, 1er. ℂ **01-42-86-28-00.** Mon–Sat 10am–7pm. Métro: Concorde or Madeleine.

Charvet   The duke of Windsor made Charvet famous, but Frenchmen of distinction have been buying their shirts here for years. The store offers ties, pocket squares, underwear, and pajamas as well, plus women's shirts, all custom-tailored or straight off the peg. 28 place Vendôme, 1er. ℂ **01-42-60-30-70.** Mon–Sat 10am–6:45pm. Métro: Opéra.

Christian Dior   This fashion house is set up like a small department store, selling men's, women's, and children's clothing, as well as affordable gift items, makeup, and perfume on the street level. For several years, cutting-edge Brit designer John Galliano has been in charge of the collections. Unlike some of the other big-name fashion houses, Dior is very approachable. 30-32 av. Montaigne, 8e. ℂ **01-40-73-54-44.** Mon–Sat 10am–7pm. Métro: F. D. Roosevelt.

Givenchy   This deluxe outlet opened in 1962 and is noted for high-profile good taste often mentioned in annual lists of best-dressed women. All three of the branches listed below sell very high-quality ready-to-wear clothing for both men and women, but if you're a woman who's looking for examples of an increasingly rarified art form, head for the branch on the avenue George V, and proceed one floor above street level. 3 av. George V, 8e. ℂ **01-44-31-50-00.** Métro: Alma-Marceau. Also:

28 rue du Faubourg St-Honoré, 8e. ✆ **01-42-65-54-54**. Métro: F. D. Roosevelt. 6 rue du Cherche-Midi, 6e. ✆ **01-42-65-03-37**. Métro: Odéon. All three locations open Mon–Sat 10am–7pm.

Hermès France's single most important status item is a scarf or tie from Hermès. Patterns on these illustrious scarves, retailing for about 228€ ($204), have recently included the galaxies, Africa, the sea, the sun, and horse racing and breeding. But the choices don't stop there—this large flagship store has beach towels and accessories, dinner plates, clothing for men and women, a large collection of Hermès fragrances, and even a saddle shop; a package of postcards is the least expensive item sold. Ask to see the private museum upstairs. Outside, note the horseman on the roof with his scarf-flag flying. 24 rue du Faubourg St-Honoré, 8e. ✆ **01-40-17-47-17**. Tues–Sat 10:15am–6:30pm; Mon 10:15am–1pm and 2:30–6:30pm. Métro: Concorde.

Louis Vuitton Its luggage is among the most famous and prestigious in the world, a standard accessory aboard the first-class cabins of aircraft flying transatlantic and transpacific. Not content to cover the world's luggage with his initials, Vuitton has branched into leather goods, writing instruments, travel products, and publishing. Look for the traditional collection of leather, including Vuitton's monogrammed brown-on-brown bags in printed canvas, on the street level. The mezzanine showcases upscale pens, writing supplies, and stationery. And the top floor carries the company's newest line of goods—women's shoes and bags. 101 av. des Champs-Elysées, 8e. ✆ 01-53-57-24-00. Mon–Sat 10am–8pm. Métro: Georges V. Also: 6 place St-Germain-des-Prés, 6e. ✆ 01-45-49-62-32. Mon–Sat 10am–7pm. Métro: St-Germain-des-Prés.

Yves Saint Laurent One of France's most creative and interesting designers burst into world fame in the 1970s with his use of rich patterns and textures in women's evening wear, and has been going strong ever since. If you're looking to acquire clothing designed (or inspired) by his precedents, there are several branches. Women's clothing, of all degrees of formality, is sold at 38 rue du Faubourg St-Honoré, 16e (✆ **01-44-31-64-00;** Métro: Concorde), and 19-21 av. Victor-Hugo, 16e (✆ **01-45-00-64-64;** Métro: Victor-Hugo). The only outlet in Paris with clothing for men (in addition to clothing for women) is at 9 place St-Sulpice, 6e (✆ **01-43-26-84-40** for the menswear department; **01-43-29-43-00** for women's wear). If you're looking for custom-tailored haute couture, and a fabulously expensive garment that might end up on the society pages of your local newspaper or in a museum in 20 years, head for Yves Saint Laurent Haute Couture. 5 av. Marceau, 16e. ✆ 01-44-31-64-00. Métro: Alma-Marceau. All stores open Mon 11am–7pm; Tues–Sat 10:30am–7pm.

VINTAGE COUTURE

Didier Ludot Fashion historians salivate when they're confronted with an inventory of the haute couture of yesteryear. In this frenetically stylish shop, albeit at prices that rival what you'd expect to pay for a serious antique, you'll find a selection of gowns and dresses created between 1900 and 1980 for designing women who looked *faaabulous* at Maxim's, at chic cocktail parties on the avenue Foch, in Deauville, or wherever. Maintaining the same hours, and just across the courtyard enclosed by the Palais-Royal, is **Didier Ludot's Little Black Dress Shop,** where only new cocktail dresses (specifically, prêt-à-porter black dresses, with their accessories) provide the kind of garment that might make any woman feel like Catherine Deneuve at her most alluring. Didier Ludot, 24 Galerie de Montpensier, in the arcades surrounding the courtyard of the Palais-Royal, 1er. ✆ **01-42-96-06-56**. Didier Ludot's Little Black Dress Shop, 125 Galerie de Valois, across the courtyard. ✆ **01-40-15-01-04**. Hours at both stores: Mon–Sat 11am–7pm. Métro: Palais-Royal.

DISCOUNT & RESALE

Anna Lowe   Positioned adjacent to the Bristol Hotel, one of the most expensive addresses in Paris, this is one of the city's premier boutiques for women who want to purchase heavily discounted clothing (new, with labels intact) from some of the world's best-known fashion designers. Expect discounts of up to 50% on last year's collections from such artists as Valentino, Thierry Mugler, John Galliano, Chanel, Versace, and many more. Your find might be what a model wore down the runway at last year's fashion show, excess inventories from factories that—for whatever reason—never got paid, or overstock from boutiques looking to make room for new inventories. Prices are reasonable and the labels, in many cases, still retain their old magic and sense of chic. 104 rue du Faubourg St-Honoré, 8e. ☎ 01-42-66-11-32. Mon–Sat 10am–7pm Métro: Miromesnil.

Annexe des Créateurs   At this discount outlet, you can sometimes—most often—pick up new designer merchandise at 40% to 60% reductions. Women interested in the classic look go here perhaps for Sonia Rykiel skirts and the like. 19 rue Godor de Mauroy, 9e. ☎ 01-42-65-46-40. Tues–Sat 10am–7pm. Métro: Madeleine.

Au Gre du Vent   First you should stroll along such fashionable shopping meccas as avenue Montaigne, 8th arrondissement, to learn what outrageous prices luxury goods cost off the Champs-Elysées. Then go over to the 6th arrondissement and browse through this amazing assortment of fashion, often at incredible markdowns. It's entirely possible, say, to purchase a $2,000 Hermès jacket for less than $100. Burberry raincoats, Chanel wallets, Stephane Kélian shoes—the merchandise changes almost every day. 10 rue des Quatre Vents, 6e. ☎ 01-44-07-28-73. Tues–Sat 10am–7pm. Métro: Mabillon.

Défilé des Marques   French TV stars often shop here, picking up St. Laurent, Dior, Lacroix, Prada, Chanel, Versace, Hermès, and others at a fraction of the price. Yes, they sell discounted Hermès scarves as well. Low prices here derive from the skill of the owners at picking up used clothing in good condition from last year's collections, and in some cases, retro-chic clothing from collections of many years ago, sometimes from estate sales. 171 rue de Grenelles, 7e. ☎ 01-45-55-63-47. Tues–Sat 10am–7:30pm. Métro: Latour-Maubourg.

Le Depot-Vente de Buci-Bourbon   This is one of the best consignment shops in the 6th arrondissement, with a wide array of merchandise for both men and women. Who knows what you'll turn up with? Perhaps marked-down Hermès scarves, Valentino skirts, Chanel shoes, and Givenchy blouses. 4-6 rue de Bourbon-de-Château, 6e. ☎ 01-46-34-45-07. Tues–Sat 10am–7pm. Métro: Mabillon.

L'Une et L'Autre *(Finds*   Hidden away in an apartment on the second floor of a building, this shop offers luxurious clothing. You get amazing discounts on the big brand names that sell in expensive 16th arrondissement boutiques. An item that might sell for 532€ ($475) in a boutique is sold here for 228€ ($204). We first accompanied a chic Parisian woman who purchased a cashmere coat at half its retail price here. 24 rue Feydeau, 2e. ☎ 01-44-76-03-03. Mon–Fri and 1st Sat of the month 11am–6pm. Métro: Bourse–Grands Boulevards.

Réciproque   Forget about serious bargains, but celebrate what could be your only opportunity to own designer clothing of this caliber. Within a series of seven storefronts side by side along the same avenue, you'll find used clothing from every major name in fashion, along with shoes, accessories, menswear, and wedding gifts. Everything has been worn, but some items only on fashion runways or during photo shoots. 88-123 rue de la Pompe, 16e. ☎ 01-47-04-30-28. Tues–Fri 11am–7:30pm; Sat 10:30am–7:30pm. Métro: Rue de la Pompe.

SR Store   This is where great designer Sonia Rykiel dumps all that good stuff she didn't move in main-line boutiques. Everything is half-price. You get some really good deals here. 64 rue d'Alésia, 14e. ✆ **01-43-95-06-13.** Tues 11am–7pm; Wed–Sat 10am–7pm. Métro: Alésia.

Tati   Some of its fans define this place as a low-end version of Galeries Lafayette (see above), with lower prices and a lot less class. What you'll find is crowded display racks, relatively indifferent service, and absolutely no emphasis on architectural finesse. Despite that, the place does a roaring business in, among others, sales of wedding dresses that range from bouffant to sleek. The displays sprawl over several floors of jumbled-up housewares, clothing, sportswear and sporting-goods equipment, and kitchenware. Genuine bargains can sometimes be culled from the maze. Tati Galerie Gaité, 68 rue du Maine, 14e. ✆ **01-56-80-06-80.** Métro: Gaité. Also: 13 place de la République, 3e. ✆ **01-48-87-72-81.** Métro: République. 4 bd. Rochechouart, 18e. ✆ **01-55-29-50-00.** Métro: Barbés. Hours for all stores Mon–Sat 10am–7:15pm.

FOOD: CHOCOLATE, HONEY, PATES & MORE

Albert Ménès   One of Paris's most prestigious small-scale purveyors of foodstuffs prides itself on selling only goods that have been picked, processed, and packaged by hand. The 45 producers represented offer sugared almonds, Breton sardines, exotic honeys, terrines, jams, and patés, baked goods, and more. It's all esoteric, even by French standards. Ménès prides itself, strangely enough, on being the first food store in France to import both Heinz Ketchup and Kellogg's Corn Flakes, both of which appeared on shelves for the first time here in the 1920s. 41 bd. Malesherbes, 8e. ✆ **01-42-66-95-63.** Mon 2–7pm; Tues–Fri 11am–7pm. Métro: St-Augustin or Madeleine.

Christian Constant   Opened in 1970, Christian Constant sells some of Paris's most delectable chocolates at 85€ ($76) per kilo. Each is a blend of ingredients from Ecuador, Colombia, or Venezuela, usually mingled with scents of spices and flowers like orange blossoms, jasmine, the Asian blossom *ylang*, and

---

✐ Food Markets

Outdoor markets are plentiful in Paris. Some of the better-known are the **Marché Buci** (see "Markets" below); the **rue Mouffetard market,** open Tuesday to Sunday from 9:30am to 1pm and Tuesday to Saturday from 4 to 7pm (6th arrondissement; Métro: Monge or Censier-Daubenton); and the **rue Montorgueil market,** behind the St-Eustache church, open Monday to Saturday from 9am to 7pm (1st arrondissement; Métro: Les Halles). The trendiest market is **Marché Biologique,** along boulevard Raspail, a tree-lined stretch lying between rue de Rennes and rue du Cherche-Midi, 6th arrondissement (Métro: Montparnasse). Even Parisian celebrities can be spotted shopping under brightly colored awnings among the stacks of organic dairy products, fish, seafood, and fresh fruits and vegetables. You can also eat here, perhaps lured to a vendor from Brittany making whole-grain crêpes or one selling algae bread. Nonfood items are also for sale. Do you own a doormat made from recycled tires? You could if you shop here.

vetiver and *verveine* (herbs usually used to brew tea). 37 rue d'Assas, 6e. ℂ 01-53-63-15-15. Mon–Fri 8:30am–9pm; Sat–Sun 8am–8:30pm. Métro: St-Placide or Rennes.

Fauchon   At place de la Madeleine stands one of the city's most popular sights—not the church, but Fauchon, a hyper-upscale mega-delicatessen that thrives within a city famous for its finicky eaters. It's divided into three divisions that include an *épicerie* (for jams, crackers, pastas, and exotic canned goods); a *pâtissier* (for breads, pastries, and chocolates); and a *traiteur* (for cheeses, terrines, patés, caviar, and fruits). Prices are steep, but the inventories—at least to serious foodies—are fascinating. At some (but not all) of the counters, you'll indicate to attendants what you want from behind glass display cases, and get an electronic ticket, which you'll carry to a *caisse* (cash register). Surrender your tickets, pay the tally, then return to the counter to pick up your groceries. In other cases, simply load up your shopping basket with whatever you want, and pay for your purchases at a cash register the way you would at any conventional grocery store.

On the same premises, Fauchon also offers a restaurant, **Brasserie Fauchon,** and a tea salon, which showcases the pastry-making talents of its chefs. Among the many offerings is a *Paris-Brest*, a ring in the shape of a bicycle wheel that's loaded with pastry cream, almond praline, buttercream, and hazelnut paste capped with almonds. 26-30 place de la Madeleine, 8e. ℂ 01-47-42-60-11. Mon–Sat 9:30am–7pm. Métro: Madeleine or Auber.

Hédiard   This 1850 temple of *haute gastronomie* has recently been renovated, perhaps to woo tourists away from Fauchon. The decor is a series of salons filled with almost Disneyesque displays meant to give the store the look of an early-1900s spice emporium. Hédiard is rich in coffees, teas, jams, and spices. The decor changes with whatever holiday (Halloween, Easter, Bastille Day) or special promotion (the coffees of Brazil, the teas of Ceylon) are in effect at the time. Upstairs, you can eat at the Restaurant de l'Epicerie. 21 place de la Madeleine, 8e. ℂ 01-43-12-88-77. Mon–Sat 9am–11pm. Métro: Madeleine or Auber.

Jadis et Gourmande   This chain of chocolatiers has a less lofty rep than Christian Constant and more reasonable prices. They're best known for their alphabetical chocolate blocks, which allow you to spell out any message (well . . . almost), in any language. *"Merci"* comes prepackaged. 27 rue Boissy d'Anglas, 8e. ℂ 01-42-65-23-23. Mon 1–7pm; Tues–Fri 9:30am–2:30pm and 3:30–7pm; Sat 10:30am–2:30pm and 3:30–7pm. Métro: Madeleine.

Les Abeilles *Finds*   This store inventories a greater supply of French honey than we've ever seen in one place. Test your understanding of France's geography by asking for honey that's culled from flowers in whatever region of the country you specify. And for a scented reminder of your trip to the City of Light, ask for "urban honey" from beehives within Paris and its suburbs. Because of the wide variety of flowers and shrubs from which urban bees gather their nectar, this honey may be among the most desirable of all. Jean-Jacques Schakmundes is the store owner and beekeeper. 21 rue de la Butte-aux-Cailles, 13e. ℂ 01-45-81-43-48. Tues–Sat 11am–7pm. Métro: Porte d'Italie or Corvisart.

Maison de la Truffe   Cramped and convivial, the layout of this shop was modeled after a Parisian's fantasy of an affable, cluttered, old-fashioned butcher shop in Lyon. It's an excellent source for foie gras, caviar, black and white truffles, and other high-end foodstuffs. Artfully assembled gift baskets are a house specialty. A corner of the site is devoted to a restaurant where many (but not all) of the dishes contain the costly items (especially truffles) sold in the shop. Examples include noodles or risottos with truffles, and caviar with all the fixings. A set-price menu costs 18€ ($16) without truffles, 57€ ($51) with truffles. Most main courses cost 23€ to 53€ ($20–$48), except for caviar, which begins at 137€ ($122) per person. The restaurant corner is open during the open hours of the shop, although the last food order is accepted 45 minutes prior to closing. 19 place de la Madeleine, 8e. ✆ 01-42-65-53-22. Mon 9am–8pm; Tues–Sat 9am–9pm. Métro: Madeleine or Auber.

Maison du Chocolat   At its five Paris locations, this shop offers racks of marvelous chocolates priced individually or by the kilo, at near or over 76€ ($68) per kilo. These stores offer a variety of chocolate-based products, including chocolate pastries, usually more affordable than the candy, and even chocolate milk! 225 rue du Faubourg St-Honoré, 8e. ✆ 01-42-27-39-44. Métro: Ternes. Also: 52 rue François-Ier, 8e. ✆ 01-47-23-38-25. Métro: Alma-Marceau. 8 bd. de la Madeleine, 8e. ✆ 01-47-42-86-52. Métro: Madeleine. 19 rue de Sèvres, 6e. ✆ 01-45-44-20-40. Métro: Rue de Sèvres. 89 av. Raymond-Poincaré, 16e. ✆ 01-40-67-77-83. Métro: Victor Hugo. All locations open Mon–Sat, May–Oct 10am–7pm; Nov–Apr 10am–7:30pm.

Maison du Miel   "The House of Honey" has been a family tradition since before World War I. The entire store is devoted to products made from honey: honey oil, honey soap, and various honeys to eat, including one made from heather. This store owes a tremendous debt to the busy bee. 24 rue Vignon, 9e. ✆ 01-47-42-26-70. Mon–Sat 9:15am–7pm. Métro: Madeleine.

Marks & Spencer   Okay, so it's a British department store specializing in clothing for men, women, and children. But the entire ground floor is a giant supermarket devoted to the St. Michael's brand of English foodstuff and includes prepared foods for picnics. 35 bd. Haussmann, 9e. ✆ 01-47-42-42-91. Mon, Wed, and Fri–Sat 9am–8pm; Tues 9:30am–8pm; Thurs 9am–9pm. Métro: Chausée d'Antin. Also: 88 rue de Rivoli, 4e. ✆ 01-44-61-08-00. Mon–Sat 10am–8pm. Métro: Hôtel de Ville.

Poilâne   One of Paris's best-loved bakeries, Poilâne hasn't changed much since it opened in 1932. Come here to taste and admire the beautiful loaves of bread decorated with simple designs of leaves and flowers that'll make you yearn for an all-but-disappeared Paris. Specialties include apple tarts, butter cookies, and a chewy sourdough loaf cooked in a wood-burning oven. Breads can be specially wrapped to stay fresh during your journey home. Cash only. *Note:* The branch on boulevard de Grenelle is closed Monday and the branch on rue du Cherche-Midi shuts down on Sunday. 8 rue du Cherche-Midi, 6e. ✆ 01-45-48-42-59. Mon–Sat 7:15am–8:15pm. Métro: St-Sulpice. Also: 49 bd. de Grenelle, 15e. ✆ 01-45-79-11-49. Tues–Sun 7:15am–8:15pm. Métro: Dupleix.

JEWELRY

Bijoux Burma   If you're crestfallen because you can't afford any of the spectacular and expensive bijoux at the city's world-famous jewelers, come here to console yourself with some of the best fakes anywhere. This quality costume jewelry is the secret weapon of many a Parisian woman. 50 rue François-Ier, 8e. ✆ 01-47-23-70-93. Mon–Sat 10am–6:30pm. Métro: F. D. Roosevelt.

Cartier   One of the most famous jewelers in the world, Cartier has prohibitive prices to match its glamorous image. Go to gawk, and if your pockets are deep enough, pick up an expensive trinket. 7 place Vendôme, 1er. ✆ 01-44-55-32-50. Mon–Sat 10:30am–7pm. Métro: Opéra or Tuileries.

Van Cleef & Arpels   Years ago, Van Cleef's designers came up with an intricate technique that remains a vital part of its allure—the invisible setting,

The City's Most Historic Shopping Arcade

When one of history's greatest shoppers, Thomas Jefferson, wanted, say, an ivory-handled knife or a timepiece, he headed for the **Palais Royal**, 1st arrondissement (Métro: Louvre-Palais Royal), just across rue de Rivoli from the Louvre. Even before the Revolution, the arcades of the Palais Royal were known for their sheltered shops and cafes.

Paris is rich in iron-and-glass galleries, the first "shopping malls" of the Western world, and some are a bit seedy. In our view, none has the charm of the Palais Royal. You can enter, among other choices, the arcades from the **rue de Montpensier** behind the Comédie-Française.

Following in the footsteps of Colette or Jean Cocteau, former residents, you can spend a lovely afternoon. The merchandise? Almost anything. As you wander, here's a sampling of what might await you: military medals, traditional lead-made French toy soldiers, vintage clothes from any number of fashionistas (perhaps creations of Patou or Balenciaga), silk vests, wooden toys, music boxes, accessories for women, bronze sculptures, china, cobalt glass, perfumes, antiques (mainly neoclassical), autographs of famous French celebrities, handcrafted shoes—you name it.

Le Grand Véfour, one of the greatest restaurants of Paris, is recommended in chapter 6. It's very expensive. You can dine much more modestly at **restaurant du Palais Royal**, 110 galerie de Valois (✆ **01-40-20-00-27**), which is closed Sunday. In summer the restaurant's tables spread out into the garden. Or you can order tea at **La Muscade**, 67 galerie de Montpensier (✆ **01-42-97-51-36**), with its restored garden. Treat yourself to the orange-and-chocolate tart. Closed Monday.

wherein a band of sparkling gemstones, each cut to interlock with its neighbor, creates an uninterrupted flash of brilliance. Come browse with the rich and famous. 22 place Vendôme, 1er. ✆ **01-53-45-45-45.** Mon–Sat 10am–7pm. Métro: Opéra or Tuileries.

KITCHENWARE

A. Simon   Established in 1884, this large kitchenware shop supplies restaurants and professional kitchens. But it will also cover your table with everything from menu cards and wine tags to knives, copper pots, and pans—not to mention white paper doilies and those funny little paper things they put on top of the tablecloth at bistros. 48 rue Montmartre, 2e. ✆ **01-42-33-71-65.** Mon 1:30–6:30pm; Tues–Sat 9am–6:30pm. Métro: Les Halles.

Dehillerin   Dehillerin is Paris's most famous cookware shop, in the "kitchen corridor," alongside A. Simon (see above) and several other kitchenware stores. The shop has more of a professional feel to it than beginner-friendly A. Simon, but don't be intimidated. Equipped with the right tools from Dehillerin, you, too, can learn to cook like a master chef. 18 rue Coquillière, 1er. ✆ **01-42-36-53-13.** Mon 9am–12:30pm and 2–6pm; Tues–Sat 9am–6pm. Métro: Les Halles.

LEATHER GOODS

Morabito This glamorous leather purveyor was originally established by an Italian entrepreneur on the place Vendôme in 1905. In the 1990s, it was partially acquired by an organization in Tokyo. Today, from a site on the very glamorous rue François 1er, it sells chicer-than-thou handbags that begin at a bare minimum of 304€ ($271) and quickly climb to 9,120€ ($8,144) and more. There are also suitcases—some of the best in Paris—for men and women. 55 rue François 1er, 8e. ✆ 01-53-23-90-40. Mon–Fri 10am–6:45pm; Sat 11am–6:30pm. Métro: F.D. Roosevelt or George V.

LINGERIE

Cadolle Herminie Cadolle invented the brassiere in 1889. Today the store she founded is managed by her family, and they still make the specialty brassieres for the Crazy Horse Saloon. This is the place to go if you want made-to-order items or are hard to fit. 14 rue Cambon, 1er. ✆ 01-42-60-38-37. Mon–Sat 9:30am–1pm and 2–6:30pm. Métro: Concorde.

Marie-Claude Fremau The French are big on shops that sell towels and bathrobes as well as underwear. Naturally, French bathroom wear has flair and style—we're talking about a yellow silk bathrobe with a ruffled collar for about 319€ ($285). 104 rue de Rennes, 6e. ✆ 01-45-48-82-76. Mon–Fri 10am–7pm; Sat 10:30am–7:30pm. Métro: Rennes.

Nikita This is the discount sales outlet for all the big names in lingerie, including Bolero, Lise Charmel, Lejaby, Simone Pérèle, and Aubade. Most of the lingerie sold here is half the price of its counterparts in Right Bank boutiques. 22 rue Levis, 7e. ✆ 01-42-12-01-30. Mon–Sat 9:30am–7pm. Métro: Villiers.

Sabbia Rosa Everything here is filmy, silky, and sexy. Look for undergarments (slips, brassieres, and panties) and the kind of negligees that might've been favored by Brigitte Bardot in *And God Created Woman*. Madonna has been spotted shopping for panties that can go as high as 506€ ($450). 73 rue des Sts-Pères, 6e. ✆ 01-45-48-88-37. Mon–Sat 10am–7pm. Métro: Sèvres-Babylone or St-Germain.

MALLS

Carrousel du Louvre If you want to combine an accessible location, a fun food court, boutiques, and plenty of museum gift shops with a touch of culture, don't miss the Carrousel. Always mobbed, this is one of the few venues allowed to open on Sunday. There's a Virgin Megastore, a branch of The Body Shop, and several other emporiums for conspicuous consumption. Check out Diane Claire for the fanciest souvenirs of Paris you've ever seen. 99 rue de Rivoli, 1er. No phone. Tues–Sun 10am–8pm. Métro: Palais Royal or Musée du Louvre.

Forum des Halles Once the site of Paris's great produce market, Les Halles is now a vast crater of modern metal with layers of boutiques built around a courtyard. There's one of everything here, but the feel is very sterile, without a hint of the famous French *joie de vivre*. 1-7 rue Pierre-Lescot, 1er. No phone. Mon–Sat 10am–7:30pm. Métro: Etienne-Marcel or Châtelet-Les Halles.

Les Trois Quartiers Named after the junction of the three neighborhoods (Madeleine, Opéra, and Concorde) where it sits, this is a mall of at least 19 upscale boutiques specializing in clothing, perfume, and cosmetics for men and women. The largest is Madelios, a menswear store that stocks Yves Saint Laurent, Ralph Lauren, and Hugo Boss, among others. 23 bd. de la Madeleine, 1er. ✆ 01-42-97-80-06. Mon–Sat 9am–8pm. Métro: Madeleine.

Marché St-Germain The Marché St-Germain used to be an open-air food market until it was transformed into a modern shopping mall. Now only a few food and vegetable stalls remain in one corner; low ceilings, neon lights, and mostly American and British chain stores like Kitchen Bazaar and Kenzo dominate the rest of the market. 14 rue Lobineau, 6e. © 01-43-26-01-44. Mon–Sat 10am–8pm. Métro: Mabillon.

Montparnasse Shopping Centre This shopping center is sort of a quick-fix minimall in a business center and hotel (Le Meredien) complex, with a small branch of Galeries Lafayette and some inexpensive boutiques. Visiting it is really worthwhile only if you also take a trip across the street to Inno, with its deluxe supermarket in the basement. Between rue de l'Arrivée and 22 rue du Départ, 14e. No phone. Mon–Sat 8:30am–10pm. Métro: Montparnasse-Bienvenue.

Palais des Congrès de Paris Boutiques A shopping center for convention-goers inside the Palais des Congrès, this mall offers some 50 shops, including branch stores of many French big names. You'll also find a Japanese department store and hairdresser. Its anonymity and distance from most of touristy Paris has taken its toll on some of the shops, but if you happen to be in the neighborhood, it might be useful. 2 place de la Porte-Maillot, 17e. No phone. Mon–Sat 10am–7pm. Métro: Porte Maillot.

MARKETS

Marché aux Fleurs Artists and photographers love to capture the Flower Market on canvas or film. The stalls are ablaze with color, and each is a showcase of flowers, most of which escaped the perfume factories of Grasse on the French Riviera. The Flower Market is along the Seine, behind the Tribunal de Commerce. On Sunday it becomes the **Marché aux Oiseaux** (**Bird Market**). Place Louis-Lépine, Ile de la Cité, 4e. No phone. Daily 8:30am–4pm. Métro: Cité.

Marché aux Livres Ancien et d'Occasion This charming two-building market for used books, old books, rare books, and ephemera is in the middle of nowhere but thronged by serious collectors. The market is covered but open, and doesn't close on a rainy day—the valuable texts are draped in plastic. (For more books, don't forget the **bouquinistes** along the left bank of the Seine, on quai de Montebello.) Parc Georges-Brassens, rue Brancion, 15e. © 01-45-32-12-17. Sun 10am–4pm in winter; 10am–6pm in summer. Métro: Porte de Vanves.

Marché aux Puces de la Porte de Vanves This weekend event sprawls along two streets and is the best flea market in Paris—dealers swear by it. There's little in terms of formal antiques and few pieces of furniture. It's better for old linens, used Hermès scarves, toys, ephemera, costume jewelry, perfume bottles, and bad art. Asking prices tend to be high, as dealers prefer to sell to nontourists. On Sunday there's a food market one street over. Av. Georges-Lafenestre, 14e. No phone. Sat–Mon 6:30am–4:30pm. Métro: Porte de Vanves.

Marché aux Puces St-Ouen de Clignancourt Paris's most famous flea market is a grouping of more than a dozen flea markets—a complex of 2,500 to 3,000 open stalls and shops on the northern fringe of the city, selling everything from antiques to junk, from new to vintage clothing. The market begins with stalls of cheap clothing along avenue de la Porte de Clignancourt. As you proceed, various streets will tempt you. Hold on until you get to rue des Rosiers, then turn left. Vendors start bringing out their offerings around 9am and start taking them in around 6pm. Hours are flexible depending on weather and crowds. Monday is traditionally the best day for bargain seekers, because the market is more sparsely attended and the merchants are more eager to sell.

First-timers always want to know two things: "Will I get any real bargains?" and "Will I get fleeced?" Actually, it's all relative. Obviously, the best buys have already been skimmed by dealers (who often have a prearrangement to have items held for them). And it's true that the same merchandise displayed here will sell for less in the provinces. But for the visitor who has only a few days to spend in Paris—and only half a day for shopping—the flea market is worth the experience. Vintage French postcards, old buttons, and bistro ware are affordable; each market has its own personality and an aura of Parisian glamour you can't find elsewhere.

Dress casually and show your knowledge if you're a collector. Most dealers are serious and get into the spirit of things only if you speak French or make it clear you know what you're doing. The longer you stay, the more you chat, the more you show your respect for the goods, the more room you'll have for negotiating. Most of the markets have restroom facilities; some have central offices to arrange shipping. Cafes, pizza joints, and even a few restaurants are scattered around. Almost without exception, they are bad. The exception is **Le Soleil,** 109 av. Michelet, St-Ouen (*©* **01-40-10-08-08**), which was converted from a cafe into a family-run restaurant by Louis-Jacques Vannucci. Catering to flea market shoppers, the restaurant looks like it was flea-market–decorated as well. The French food is excellent, especially the sautéed chicken in a light cream sauce, or the green-bean salad tossed with tomato cubes, or the fresh Norman cod and the tiny mussels cooked in a rich broth. Open daily for lunch and Thursday to Saturday for dinner. *Note:* Beware of pickpockets and teenage troublemakers while shopping the market. Av. de la Porte de Clignancourt, 18e. No phone. Sat–Mon 9am–7pm. Métro: Porte de Clignancourt (turn left and cross bd. Ney, then walk north on av. de la Porte Montmartre). Bus: 56, 85, 155, or 166.

Marché aux Timbres   This is where Audrey Hepburn figured it out in *Charade,* remember? At this stamp collector's paradise, nearly 2 dozen stalls are set up on a permanent basis under shady trees on the eastern edge of the Rond-Point. The variety of stamps is almost unlimited—some common, some quite rare. Av. Matignon, off the Champs-Elysées at Rond-Point, 8e. No phone. Generally Thurs–Sun 10am–7pm. Métro: F. D. Roosevelt or Champs-Elysées–Clémenceau.

Marché Buci   This traditional French food market is held at the intersection of two streets and is only a block long, but what a block it is! Seasonal fruits and vegetables dance across tabletops as chickens spin on the rotisserie. One stall is entirely devoted to big bouquets of fresh flowers. Monday mornings are light. Rue de Buci, 6e. No phone. Daily 9am–7pm. Métro: St-Germain-des-Prés.

MUSEUM SHOPS

Boutiques des Musées de France (Réunion des Musées Nationaux/RMN)
This shop contains a selection of reproductions of originals contained in France's 20 Musées Nationaux, including the Louvre, the Musée d'Orsay, the Grand Palais, and the Musée Picasso. Prices range from 15€ ($13) for a pair of ear clips to as much as 456€ ($407) for a reproduction of an object from Greek, Assyrian, or Roman antiquity. There are two branches of this organization, one beneath the glass pyramid of the Louvre. 99 rue de Rivoli, 1er. *©* **01-40-20-50-50.** Wed–Mon 9:30am–8pm. Métro: Louvre. Also: Level 2 of the Forum des Halles, Porte-Berger Niveau, 2e. *©* **01-40-39-92-21.** Mon–Sat 10:30am–7:30pm. Métro: Halles.

La Boutique de la Comédie Française This is the official gift/souvenir shop of France's most historic and prestigious theater. The plays commemorated inside have elicited in the French as much emotion and loyalty as Shakespeare has in the British. Look for plates and cups depicting 18th-century misers, maidens, and faithful servants, as well as scarves, pens, drinking glasses, and napkins honoring the French theater. You might appreciate the beer mugs (*les chopes*) emblazoned with the frontispiece of Molière's original folio for *Le Bourgeois Gentilhomme.* The gift shop remains open in August, when the theater is closed. 2 rue de Richelieu, 1er. ☎ **01-44-58-14-30.** Mon–Sat 11am–8:30pm; Sun 1–8:30pm. Métro: Palais Royal.

La Boutique du Musée de la Monnaie Jewelry made from coins and/or semiprecious stones, reproductions of antique coins, and medallions of every imaginable sort are sold here. If your tastes and interests involve small, cunning, and valuable objects, this might be the place for you. 11 quai de Conti (entrance at 2 rue Guénégaud), 6e. ☎ **01-40-46-55-35.** Tues–Fri 11am–5:30pm; Sat–Sun noon–5:30pm. Métro: Pont Neuf or Odéon.

La Boutique du Musée des Arts Décoratifs This two-part boutique is divided by the entryway to the museum. On the right as you enter is a fabulous bookstore. On the left is a boutique selling reproductions of museum items: gifts, knickknacks, and even a custom-made Hermès scarf. In the Palais du Louvre, 105 rue de Rivoli, 1er. ☎ **01-42-61-04-02.** Thurs–Tues 10am–7pm; Wed 10am–9pm. Métro: Palais Royal or Tuileries.

Printemps Design This shop's designers liken its merchandise to what's in the MOMA gift shop in New York City. Loosely associated with Le Printemps department store (but without the clothing), it features a frequently changing roster of stylish art objects and gift items. Many of the pieces are the work of well-known masters of their craft, like Phillippe Starck, Ron Arad, and the four-woman French design team known as Tse-Tse. Centre Pompidou, 19 rue Beaubourg, 4e. ☎ **01-44-78-15-78.** Wed–Mon 11am–9pm. Métro: Hôtel de Ville.

MUSIC

FNAC This is a large chain of music and bookstores known for its wide selection and discounted prices. There are eight branches in Paris, with the largest being at 136 rue de Rennes, Montparnasse. 136 rue de Rennes, 6e. ☎ **01-49-54-30-00.** Mon–Sat 10am–7:30pm. Métro: St-Placide. Also: 109 rue St-Lazare, 9e. ☎ **01-55-31-20-00.** Same hours as first location. Métro: St-Lazare. 74 av. des Champs-Elysées, 8e. ☎ **01-53-53-64-64.** Daily noon–midnight. Métro: Champs-Elysées–Clémenceau. Forum des Halles, 1-7 rue Pierre-Lescot, 1er. ☎ **01-40-41-40-00.** Mon–Sat 10am–7:30pm. Métro: Châtelet Les Halles. 26-30 av. des Ternes, 17e. ☎ **01-44-09-18-00.** Mon–Sat 10am–7:30pm. Métro: Ternes. 30 av. d'Italie, 13e. ☎ **01-58-10-30-00.** Mon–Sat 10am–8pm. Métro: Place d'Italie.

Virgin Megastore Paris has three branches of Europe's biggest, most widely publicized tape, CD, and record store. The Champs-Elysées branch is the city's largest music store; a bookstore and cafe are downstairs. The store's opening in a landmark building helped rejuvenate the avenue. You'll find a Virgin Megastore at each airport. 52-60 av. des Champs-Elysées, 8e. ☎ **01-49-53-50-00.** Mon–Sat 10am–midnight; Sun noon–midnight. Métro: F. D. Roosevelt. Also: Carrousel du Louvre, 99 rue de Rivoli, 1er. ☎ **01-44-50-03-10.** Sun–Tues 11am–8pm; Wed–Sun 11am–10pm. Métro: Palais Royal or Musée du Louvre. Gare Montparnasse, Level A, bd. de la Montparnasse, 15e. ☎ **01-45-38-06-06.** Mon–Thurs 7am–8pm; Fri 7am–9pm; Sat 7am–8pm. Métro: Montparnasse.

The Scent of a Parisian

If there's one reason international shoppers come to Paris, it's cosmetics—after all, the City of Light is the world capital of fragrances and beauty supplies. These are a few of our favorite perfume and makeup shops:

While you can buy **Parfums Caron** scents in any duty-free or discount parfumerie, it's worth visiting the source of some of the world's most famous perfumes. The tiny shop is at 34 av. Montaigne, 8e (© **01-47-23-40-82**; Métro: F. D. Roosevelt), boasting old-fashioned glass beakers filled with fragrances and a hint of yesteryear. Fleur de Rocaille, a Caron scent, was the featured perfume in the movie *Scent of a Woman.* Store hours are Monday to Saturday from 10am to 6:30pm.

While there are other branches and you can test Goutal bathroom amenities at many upscale hotels, the sidewalk mosaic tile and the unique scents make the **Annick Goutal,** at 14 rue Castiglione, 1er (© **01-42-60-52-82**; Métro: Concorde), worth stopping by. Try Eau d'Hadrien for a unisex splash of citrus and summer. Store hours are Monday to Saturday from 10am to 7pm.

Off a courtyard halfway between place de la Madeleine and the Champs-Elysées, **Makeup Forever,** 5 rue de la Boetie, 8e (© **01-42-66-01-60**; Métro: St-Augustin), is where models and actors go for their makeup. They also have sunglasses at reasonable prices. The outlet was created by French stylist/entrepreneur Dany Sanz in 1984 and maintains branches in New York and throughout the world. Check out the accessories, like suitcases, purses, and travel kits ranging from 11€ to 181€ ($10–$162). Store hours are Monday to Saturday from 10:30am to 7pm.

Shiseido, the world's fourth-largest maker of cosmetics and skin-care goods, has become more prominent thanks to the efforts of the **Salons du Palais Royal Shiseido,** 142 Galerie de Valois, Palais Royal, 1er (© **01-49-27-09-09**; Métro: Palais Royal). In addition to an awesome array of skin-care products and makeup, it stocks 18 exclusive fragrances created by the company's artistic director, Serge Lutens. Don't be afraid to wander in and ask for some scent strips. Open Monday to Saturday from 10am to 7pm.

PERFUME & MAKEUP (DISCOUNT)

Catherine *Finds* This family-owned shop sells an impressive stock of all the big-name perfumes and cosmetics at discounts of 20% to 25%. In addition, its paperwork is usually extremely well organized, allowing refunds of the value-added tax (VAT) to be cleared quickly through Customs. Many on the staff speak English. 7 rue Castiglione, 1er. © **01-42-61-02-89**. Tues–Sat 9am–7pm; Mon 10:30am–7pm. Métro: Concorde or Tuileries.

Freddy Parfums The discounts here are fabulous: up to 40% on perfumes, handbags, cosmetics, silk scarves, and neckties. Freddy of Paris is near American Express and the Opéra. 3 rue Scribe, 9e. © **01-47-42-63-41**. Mon–Fri 9am–7pm; Sat 9:30am–6:30pm. Métro: Opéra.

Finds   **Sign of the Times**

A shop like **Manufacture Plaques Emaillées** stands in sharp contrast to the mass-merchandise in most department stores. Established in 1908 when the Art Nouveau craze swept Paris, they have done a respectable business, promoting turn-of-the-20th-century Parisian charm, ever since. Their specialty is the custom manufacture of cast-iron plaques, enameled and baked, commemorating virtually any event, person (including yourself), or piece of real estate that appeals to you. Charles and Denis, the longtime owners, offer a variety of shapes, sizes, and colors for the finished product. The most endearing, in our opinion, are the street signs, *"style ville de Paris,"* that can bear the name of your home, your child, the street you live on (or would like to live on), or the fictitious boulevard of your choice: *"Avenue John Wayne, Las Vegas,"* for example. Colors run the spectrum of the rainbow, although Charles warns in advance that gilding or silver-plating is not an option. Expect to pay from around 100€ ($89) for a street-sign–size plaque, and much more for plaques that can measure up to about 2m (6 ft.) wide, suitable perhaps for a storefront. It will take 3 to 4 weeks for your plaque to be manufactured, after which it can be shipped. Shipping can be expensive, and in our opinion (because of the cast-iron nature of what's in the package), complicated. Much smaller plaques, some ready-made, are also available. It's located at 16 bd. des Filles-du-Calvaire, 11e (© **01-47-00-50-95;** Métro: St-Sébastien). Credit cards are not accepted.

Maki   You get some of the best deals in cosmetics and makeup here. In fact, it's the place where French actors and many models come for quality makeup products at discounted prices. The shop lies in the middle of a theater area. The staff will often give you advice about makeup. 9 rue Mansart, 9e. © **01-42-81-33-76.** Tues–Sat 11am–1pm and 2:30–6:30pm. Métro: Blanche.

Parfumerie du Havre   This shop offers good discounts, usually 20% to 45% depending on the brand. There are tons of fragrances and a few designer accessories in this bright, modern, chic shop. Discounts are included in the prices as marked. 15 place du Havre, 8e. © **01-43-87-35-15.** Mon–Sat 10:30am–7:30pm. Métro: St-Lazare.

SOUVENIRS & GIFTS

Au Nom de la Rose   Tasteful and frilly, this shop is divided into two distinct parts, one selling flowers, the other gift items. The flower shop, from which derive many of the arrangements that decorate local hotels and restaurants, is open Monday to Saturday from 9am to 9pm, Sunday from 9am to 2pm. The gift shop, open Monday to Saturday from 9am to 7:30pm, specializes in anything that's scented, emblazoned, or permeated with "the spirit or scent of the rose." Expect to find rose-hip jams and marmalades, scented soaps and candles, rose-water–based perfumes, decorative items for the home and kitchen, and handbags, makeup kits, and scarves, each decorated in a floral (usually rose-patterned) motif. 46 rue du Bac, 7e. © **01-42-22-22-12.** Métro: Rue du Bac.

Galerie Architecture Miniature Gault   This store features Lilliputian town models complete with houses, stores, and fountains—miniature versions of French villages and Parisian neighborhoods, all built to scale. A hand-painted ceramic depiction of a house or national monument ranges from 13€ to 608€

($12–$543), depending on its size and intricacy. 206 rue de Rivoli, 1er. ℂ **01-42-60-51-17**. Mon–Sat 10am–7pm; Sun 11am–7pm. Métro: Tuileries.

La Tuile à Loup   This emporium has been selling authentic examples of all-French handcrafts since around 1975, making a name through its concentration of hand-produced woven baskets, cutlery, and wood-carvings. Especially appealing are the hand-painted crockery and charming stoneware from traditional manufacturers like Quimper and Malicorne and from small-scale producers in the Savoie Alps and Alsace. 35 rue Daubenton, 5e. ℂ **01-47-07-28-90**. Mon 1–7pm; Tues–Sat 10:30am–7:30pm. Métro: Censier-Daubenton.

STATIONERY

Cassegrain   Nothing says elegance more than thick French stationery and note cards. Cassegrain offers beautifully engraved stationery, most often in traditional patterns, and business cards engraved to order. Several other items for the desk, many suitable for gifts, are for sale as well; there are even affordable pencils and small desktop accessories. 422 rue St-Honoré, 8e. ℂ **01-42-60-20-08**. Mon–Sat 10am–7pm. Métro: Concorde.

TABLEWARE

Conran Shop   This shop might remind you of an outpost of the British Empire, valiantly imposing Brit aesthetics and standards on the French-speaking world. Inside, you'll find articles for the kitchen and dining room, glass and crystal vases, fountain pens and stationery, reading material and postcards, and even a selection of chocolates, teas, and coffees to help warm up a foggy English day. 117 rue du Bac, 7e. ℂ **01-42-84-10-01**. Mon–Fri 10am–7pm; Sat 10am–7:30pm. Métro: Sèvres-Babylone. Also: 30 bd. des Capucines, 9e. ℂ **01-53-43-29-00**. Mon–Sat 10am–7:30pm. Métro: Madeleine.

Geneviève Lethu   This Provençal designer has shops all over France, with 19 others in and around Paris, all selling her clever and colorful Pottery-Barn-meets-French-Mediterranean tableware. The rue de Rennes branch is the largest, with the rue de Vaugirard branch runner-up. Newer designs stress influences from India, South America, and Africa as well. Energy, style, and verve are rampant here. The prices are moderate. 95 rue de Rennes, 6e. ℂ **01-45-44-40-35**. Mon–Sat 10:15am–7pm. Métro: St-Sulpice. Also: 317 rue de Vaugirard, 15e. ℂ **01-45-31-77-84**. Mon–Sat 10:15am–7pm. Métro: Convention.

WINES

Les Caves Taillevent   This is a temple to the art of making fine French wine. Associated with one of Paris's grandest restaurants, Taillevent, it occupies the street level and cellar of an antique building. Stored here are more than 25,000 bottles of wine, with easy access in nearby warehouses to almost a million more. 199 rue du Faubourg St-Honoré, 8e. ℂ **01-45-61-14-09**. Mon 2–8pm; Tues–Fri 9am–8pm; Sat 9am–7:30pm. Métro: Charles de Gaulle-Etoile or Ternes.

Nicholas *Finds*   The flagship store of this boutique chain, with more than 110 branches around Paris plus another 380 branches in France, offers fair prices for bottles you might not be able to find in the States. Aside from the usual Bordeaux and Burgundies, look at some of the rarer regional wines, like Gewürztraminer from Alsace, Collioure from Languedoc-Rousillon, and the pricey but sublime Côte Rotie from the Côtes du Rhône outside Lyon. 31 place de la Madeleine, 8e. ℂ **01-42-68-00-16**. Mon–Sat 9:30am–8pm. Métro: Madeleine.

10

Paris After Dark

When darkness falls, the City of Light lives up to its name—the monuments and bridges are illuminated, and the glow of old-fashioned and modern street lamps, the blaze of sidewalk-cafe windows, and the glare of neon signs flood the avenues and boulevards. Parisians start the serious part of their evenings as Anglos stretch, yawn, and announce it's time for bed. Once the workday is over, most people go to a cafe to meet with friends over a drink and perhaps a meal (see "The Top Cafes" in chapter 6); then they may head home or proceed to a restaurant or the theater; and much later they may grace a club, a bar, or a disco.

In this chapter, we describe Paris's after-dark diversions—from attending a Molière play at the Comédie-Française to catching a cancan show at the Moulin Rouge to sipping a sidecar at Harry's New York Bar to partying at Le Queen with all the boys.

1 The Performing Arts

LISTINGS   Announcements of shows, concerts, and operas are plastered on kiosks all over town. You'll find listings in the weekly *Pariscope,* an entertainment guide with a section in English, or the English-language bimonthly *Boulevard.* Performances start later in Paris than in London or New York—from 8 to 9pm—and Parisians tend to dine after the theater. You may not want to do the same, because many of the less-expensive restaurants close as early as 9pm.

TICKETS   There are many ticket agencies in Paris, most near the Right Bank hotels. *Avoid them if possible.* You can buy the cheapest tickets at the box office of the theater or at discount agencies that sell tickets at discounts of up to 50%. One is the **Kiosque Théâtre,** 15 place de la Madeleine, 8e (no phone; Métro: Madeleine), offering leftover tickets for about half price on the performance day. Tickets for evening shows are sold Tuesday to Friday from 12:30 to 8pm and Saturday from 2 to 8pm. Tickets for matinees are sold Saturday from 12:30 to 2pm and Sunday from 12:30 to 4pm. Other branches are in the basement of the Châtelet–Les Halles Métro station and in front of Gare Montparnasse.

Students with ID can often get last-minute tickets by applying at the box office an hour before curtain time.

The most effortless way to get tickets, especially if you're staying in a first-class or deluxe hotel, is to ask your concierge to arrange for them. This is also the most expensive way and a service fee is added, but it's a lot easier if you don't want to waste precious hours in Paris trying to secure tickets, often hard-to-get ones.

For easy availability of tickets for festivals, concerts, and the theater, try one of these locations of the **FNAC** record store chain: 136 rue de Rennes, 6e (© **01-49-54-30-00;** Métro: Montparnasse-Bienvenue), or in the Forum des Halles, 1-7 rue Pierre-Lescot, 1er (© **01-40-41-40-00;** Métro: Châtelet-Les Halles).

THEATER

Comédie-Française   Those with even a modest understanding of French can delight in a sparkling production of Molière at this national theater, established to keep the classics alive and promote important contemporary authors. Nowhere else will you see the works of Molière and Racine so beautifully staged. The box office is open daily from 11am to 6pm, but the hall is dark from mid-July to early September. In 1993 a Left Bank annex was launched, the **Comédie Française-Théâtre du Vieux-Colombier,** 21 rue du Vieux-Colombier, 4e (© **01-44-39-87-00**). Though its repertoire varies, it's known for presenting serious French dramas. Every ticket in the house costs 25€ ($22) for adults, 13€ ($12) for ages 26 and under. Discounts are available if you reserve in advance. 2 rue de Richelieu, 1er. © **01-44-58-15-15.** Tickets 12€–32€ ($11–$29). Métro: Palais Royal or Musée du Louvre.

OPERA, DANCE & CLASSICAL CONCERTS

Cité de la Musique   This testimony to the power of music has been the most widely applauded, the least criticized, and the most innovative of the late François Mitterrand's *grands projets*. At the city's northeastern edge in what used to be a run-down and depressing neighborhood, this $120-million stone-and-glass structure incorporates a network of concert halls, a library and research center for the study of all kinds of music, and a museum (see "Specialty Museums" in chapter 7). The complex hosts a rich variety of concerts, ranging from Renaissance music through 19th- and 20th-century works, including jazz and traditional music from nations around the world. 221 av. Jean-Jaurès, 19e. © **01-44-84-45-00,** or 01-44-84-44-84 for tickets. Tickets 12€–30€ ($11–$27) for 4:30 and 8pm concerts. Métro: porte de Pantin.

Maison de Radio France   This is the site of many of the performances of the **Orchestre Philharmonique de Radio France** and the somewhat more conservative **Orchestre National de France.** The concert hall's box office is open Monday to Saturday from 11am to 6pm. 116 av. Président-Kennedy, 16e. © **01-56-40-15-16.** Tickets 7.60€–18€ ($6.75–$16). Métro: Passy-Ranelagh.

Opéra Bastille   This controversial building—it has been called a "beached whale"—was designed by Canadian architect Carlos Ott, with curtains by

Japanese designer Issey Miyake. Since the house's grand opening in July 1989, the Opera National de Paris has presented works like Mozart's *Marriage of Figaro* and Tchaikovsky's *Queen of Spades*. The main hall is the largest of any French opera house, with 2,700 seats, but music critics have lambasted the acoustics. The building contains two other concert halls, including an intimate 250-seat room that usually hosts chamber music. Both traditional opera performances and symphony concerts are presented here, as well as both classical and modern dance. Several concerts are given for free in honor of certain French holidays. Write ahead for tickets. Place de la Bastille, 120 rue de Lyon. (℃ **08-92-69-78-68**. Tickets 9.10€–105€ ($8.15–$94) opera, 4.55€–76€ ($4.05–$68) dance. Métro: Bastille.

Opéra Comique This is a charming venue for light opera, on a smaller scale than Paris's major opera houses. Built in the late 1890s in an ornate style that might remind you of the Opéra Garnier, it's the site of small productions of operas like *Carmen, Don Giovanni, Tosca,* and *Palleas & Melisande.* There are no performances from mid-July to late August. The box office, however, is open year-round Monday to Saturday from 11am to 7pm. 5 rue Favart, 2e. (℃ **08-25-00-00-58**. Tickets 6.85€–91€ ($6.10–$81). Métro: Richelieu-Drouot.

Opéra Garnier Once the haunt of the Phantom, this is the premier venue for dance and once again for opera. Charles Garnier designed this 1875 rococo wonder during the heyday of the French Empire; the facade is adorned with marble and sculpture, including *The Dance* by Carpeaux. Following a year-long renovation, during which the Chagall ceiling was cleaned and air-conditioning was added, the facade is gleaming as it did for Napoleon III. You can see the original gilded busts and statues, the rainbow-hued marble pillars, and the mosaics. The Opéra Garnier combines ballet and opera, and offers one of the most elegant evenings you can spend in the City of Light. Because of the competition from the Bastille, the Garnier has made great efforts to present more up-to-date dance works, like choreography by Twyla Tharp, Agnes de Mille, and George Balanchine. The box office is open Monday to Saturday from 11am to 6:30pm. Place de l'Opéra, 9e. (℃ **08-92-69-78-68**. Tickets 9.10€–105€ ($8.15–$94) opera, 4.55€–68€ ($4.05–$61) dance. Métro: Opéra.

Moments The Music of Angels

If you're so inclined, some of the most moving music in Paris echoes through its churches, some of the sounds taking you back to the Middle Ages. At **Eglise de St-Eustache,** rue Rambuteau ((℃ **01-42-36-31-05**; Métro: Les Halles), High Mass with the organ playing and the choir singing is at 11am on Sunday. In summer, concerts are played on the organ, marking the church's role in holding the premiere of Berlioz's *Te Deum* and Liszt's *Messiah* in 1886. Tickets to these special concerts sell for 12€ to 26€ ($11 to $23).

The **American Church in Paris,** 65 quai d'Orsay, 7e ((℃ **01-40-62-05-00**; Métro: Invalides or Alma Marceau), sponsors free concerts from September to June on Sunday at 6pm. You can also attend free concerts at **Eglise St-Merri,** 78 rue St-Martin, 4e ((℃ **01-42-71-40-75**; Métro: Hotel-de-Ville). These performances are staged September to July on Saturday at 9pm and again on Sunday at 4pm.

Théâtre des Champs-Elysées This Art Deco theater, attracting the haute couture crowd, hosts both national and international orchestras (perhaps the Vienna Philharmonic) as well as opera and ballet. The box office is open Monday to Saturday from 1 to 7pm. There are no performances in August. 15 av. Montaigne, 8e. ① **01-49-52-50-50**, or 01-49-52-07-41 for box office. Tickets 9.10€–114€ ($8.15–$102). Métro: Alma-Marceau.

Théâtre National de Chaillot Part of the architectural complex facing the Eiffel Tower, this is one of the city's largest concert halls, hosting cultural events that are announced on billboards in front. Sometimes (rarely) dance is staged here, or you might see a brilliantly performed play by Marguerite Duras. The box office is open Monday to Saturday from 11am to 7pm and Sunday from 11am to 5pm. 1 place du Trocadéro, 16e. ① **01-53-65-30-00**. Tickets 23€ ($20) adults, 16€ ($15) seniors over 60, 11€ ($10) under age 25. Métro: Trocadéro.

2 The Club & Music Scene

Paris is still a late-night mecca. Both the quantity and the variety of nightlife still exceed that of other cities. Nowhere else will you find such a huge, mixed array of nightclubs, bars, dance clubs, cabarets, jazz dives, music halls, and honky-tonks.

A MUSIC HALL

Olympia Charles Aznavour and other big names appear in this cavernous hall. The late Yves Montand appeared once, and the performance was sold out 4 months in advance. Today you're more likely to catch Gloria Estefan. A typical lineup might include an English rock group, Italian acrobats, a French singer, a dance troupe, juggling American comedians (doing much of their work in English), and the featured star. A witty MC and an on-stage band provide a smooth transition. Performances usually begin at 8:30pm Tuesday to Sunday, with Saturday matinees at 5pm. 28 bd. des Capucines, 9e. ① **01-47-42-25-49**. Tickets 21€–61€ ($19–$54). Métro: Opéra or Madeleine.

CHANSONNIERS

Chansonniers (literally "songwriters") provide a bombastic musical satire of the day's events. This combination of parody and burlesque is a time-honored Gallic amusement and a Parisian institution. Songs are often created on the spot, inspired by the "disaster of the day."

Au Caveau de la Bolée To enter this bawdy boîte, you descend into the catacombs of the early-14th-century Abbaye de St-André, once a cafe that attracted Verlaine, who slowly snuffed out his life in absinthe here. The singing is loud and smutty, the way the predominantly student audience likes it. Occasionally, the audience sings along. You'll enjoy this place a lot more if you can follow the thread of the French-language jokes and satire, but even if you can't, there are enough visuals (magic acts and singers) to amuse. The fixed-price dinner is followed by a series of at least four entertainers, usually comedians. In lieu of paying admission for the cabaret, you can order dinner. If you've already had dinner, you can order just a drink. 25 rue de l'Hirondelle, 6e. ① **01-43-54-62-20**. Admission to show, including a set-menu dinner, 46€ ($41). Admission to show only, including 1 drink, 23€ ($20). Dinner Mon–Sat 8:30–10:30pm; cabaret Mon–Sat 10:30pm–1:30am. Métro: St-Michel.

Au Lapin Agile Picasso and Utrillo patronized this little cottage near the top of Montmartre, then known as the Cabaret des Assassins, and it has been painted by many artists, including Utrillo. You'll sit at carved wooden tables in a dimly lit room with walls covered by bohemian memorabilia and listen to French folk tunes, love ballads, army songs, sea chanteys, and music-hall ditties. You're encouraged to sing along, even if it's only the *"oui, oui, oui—non, non, non"* refrain of "Les Chevaliers de la Table Ronde." 22 rue des Saules, 18e. ℂ 01-46-06-85-87. Cover, including 1st drink, 24€ ($21). Tues–Sun 9pm–2am. Métro: Lamarck-Caulaincourt.

Théâtre des Deux Anes   Since 1920, this theater has staged satires of the foibles, excesses, and stupidities of French governments. Favorite targets are President Jacques Chirac and other mandarins of the *héxagone française*. Cultural icons, French and foreign, receive a grilling that's very funny and sometimes caustic. The place considers itself more of a theater than a cabaret and doesn't serve drinks or refreshments. The 2½-hour show is conducted in rapid-fire French slang, so if your syntax isn't up to par, you won't appreciate its charms. 100 bd. de Clichy, 18e. ℂ 01-46-06-10-26. Tickets 33€–35€ ($29–$31). Performances Tues–Sat at 8:30pm. Matinees Sat at 4:30pm and Sun at 3:30pm. Closed July–Sept. Métro: Place de Clichy.

NIGHTCLUBS & CABARETS

Decidedly expensive, these places give you your money's worth by providing lavishly spectacular floorshows. With the exception of Café Concert Ailleurs, they generally attract an older crowd. They are definitely not youth-oriented.

Chez Michou   The setting is blue, the MC wears blue, and the spotlights bathe performers in yet another shade of blue. The creative force behind the color coordination and a dollop of cross-genderism is Michou, veteran impresario whose 20-odd cross-dressing belles bear names like Hortensia and DuDuche; they lip-synch in costumes from haute couture to haute concierge, paying tribute to Americans like Whitney Houston and Tina Turner, and French stars like Mireille Mathieu, Sylvie Vartan, and Brigitte Bardot. If you don't want dinner, you'll have to stand at the bar, paying a compulsory 31€ ($28) for the first drink. 80 rue des Martyrs, 18e. ℂ 01-46-06-16-04. Cover (including dinner, aperitif, wine, coffee, and show) 95€ ($85). Dinner nightly at 8:30pm (reservations required); show begins nightly at 10:30pm. Métro: Pigalle.

Crazy Horse Saloon   Since 1951, this sophisticated strip joint has thrived thanks to good choreography and a sly, coquettish celebration of the female form. The theme binding each of the 5-minute numbers (featuring gorgeous dancers in erotic costumes) is La Femme in her various states: temperamental, sad, dancing/bouncy, or joyful. Dance numbers that endure season after season include "Le Laser" and "The Erotic Lesson." Dinner, costing 125€ to 155€ ($112–$138) is a tasteful event served at Chez Francis, a restaurant under separate management a few steps away. Shows last just under 2 hours. 12 av. George V, 8e. ℂ 01-47-23-32-32. Reservations recommended. Cover 69€–110€ ($62–$98) including 2 drinks at a table; 49€ ($44) including 2 drinks at the bar. Shows Sun–Fri 8:30 and 11pm; Sat 7:30, 9:45, and 11:50pm. Métro: George V or Alma-Marceau.

Folies-Bergère   The Folies-Bergère has been an institution since 1869. Josephine Baker, the African-American singer who danced in a banana skirt and threw bananas into the audience became "the toast of Paris" here. According to legend, the first GI to reach Paris at the 1944 Liberation asked for directions to the club. Don't expect the naughty skin-and-glitter revues of the past. In 1993 that ended with a radical restoration under new management. Today, it's a 1,600-seat theater devoted to a roster of big-stage performances in French, many of which are adaptations of Broadway blockbusters. Recent examples have included *Fame* and *Saturday Night Fever,* and a revue of male strippers inspired by an American-style *Chippendales* review. There's even been a relatively high-brow re-enactment of one of the classics of the French-language repertory, *L'Arlésienne,* by 19th-century playwright Alphonse Daudet. True, there's always an acknowledgment of the nostalgia value of the old Folies-Bergère, and reminders of the stars of yesterday (especially Josephine Baker), but if you're looking for artful nudity presented with unabashed Parisian permissiveness, head for the Crazy Horse Saloon or the Lido instead. There's an on-site restaurant serving dinners, but most spectators opt just for the show. 34 rue Richer, 9e. ℭ 01-44-79-98-98. Cover 14€–53€ ($13–$48); dinner and show 58€–84€ ($52–$75). Hours and days vary according to performance, but shows are usually Tues–Sat at 9pm, Sun at 3pm. Métro: Grands-Boulevards or Cadet.

L'Ane Rouge   This red-and-black minitheater has been a showcase for French satire and humor since it opened shortly after World War II. You'll enjoy a well-flavored dinner of French specialties, followed by a 2-hour medley of French-language standup comedy, ribald stories, and politicized jokes. If your knowledge of French is zero, you won't enjoy this place, and if you hate being singled out by a comedian in front of a crowd, stay away. 3 rue Laugier, 17e. ℭ 01-43-80-79-97. Reservations recommended. Dinner and show 50€–60€ ($45–$54). Dinner at 8pm; show from 10pm–midnight. Métro: Ternes.

Le Canotier du Pied de la Butte   The worst thing you can say about this place is that it's touristy, but the visitors share a genuine appreciation of the nuances, lyricism, and poetry of popular French songs. Each performance includes appearances by two men and two women, who interact with their own versions of the hits made famous by Piaf, Montand, Brel, and Chevalier. The byword is nostalgia, unleashed by the bucketful in a cozy red, black, and white theater with room for no more than 70. 62 bd. Rochechouart, 18e. ℭ 01-46-06-02-86. Reservations required. Cover 38€ ($34) including 1st drink. Performances daily 7:30–9pm. Métro: Anvers.

Le Paradis Latin   Built in 1889 by Alexandre-Gustave Eiffel, with the same metallic skeleton as the famous tower, Le Paradis Latin represents the architect's only venture into theater design. The place is credited with introducing vaude-ville and musical theater to Paris. In 1903 the building was a warehouse, but in the 1970s it was transformed into a successful cabaret whose singers, dancers, and special effects extol the fun, frivolity, and permissiveness of the City of Light. The show includes tasteful nudity (they contrast their more dignified nudity—breasts only—with the more blatant and unabashed nudity at Crazy Horse), a ventriloquist, and a trapeze artist. The MC speaks in French and English. 28 rue Cardinal-Lemoine, 5e. ℭ 01-43-25-28-28. Cover 75€ ($67) including half bottle of champagne; dinner and show 109€–200€ ($97–$179). Dinner Wed–Mon 8pm; revue at 9:30pm. Métro: Jussieu or Cardinal Lemoine.

Lido de Paris   The Lido's $15-million current production, *C'est Magique,* is a dramatic reworking of the classic Parisian cabaret show, with eye-popping special effects and new themes, both nostalgic and contemporary, including aer-ial and aquatic ballets using more than 60,000 gallons of water. The show, the most expensive ever in Europe, uses 80 performers, $4 million in costumes, and a $2 million lighting design with lasers. There's even an ice rink that magically appears and disappears. The legendary topless Bluebell Girls are still here, how-ever. Now that celebrated chef Paul Bocuse is a consultant, the cuisine is better than ever. 116 bis av. des Champs-Elysées, 8e. ✆ **800/227-4884** or 01-40-76-56-10. Cover for 10pm or midnight show 85€ ($76) including half bottle of champagne; 8pm dinner dance, including half bottle of champagne, and 10pm show 124€–154€ ($111–$138). Space at bar 59€ ($52). Métro: George V.

Moulin Rouge This is a camp classic. Toulouse-Lautrec immortalized the Moulin Rouge and its habitués in his works, but he'd probably have a hard time recognizing it today. Colette created a scandal by giving an onstage kiss to Mme de Morny, but it's harder to shock today's audiences. Try to get a table, as the view is much better on the main floor than from the bar. The emphasis on the strip routines and sexiness of the Belle Epoque and Paris between the wars keeps drawing crowds. Handsome men and women, virtually all topless, contribute to the appeal. The finale usually includes 2 dozen of the belles ripping loose with a topless cancan. Place Blanche, 18e. ✆ **01-53-09-82-82.** Cover 79€–89€ ($71–$80) including champagne; dinner and show from 125€ ($112). Seats at the bar, cover 60€ ($53), including 2 drinks. Dinner nightly at 7pm; shows nightly at 9 and 11pm. Métro: Blanche.

Villa d'Este In the past, this club booked Amalia Rodrigues, Portugal's leading *fadista* (singer of traditional Portuguese music), and French chanteuse Juliette Greco. Today you're more likely to hear French singer François de Guelte or other top talent from Europe and America. Villa d'Este has been around for a long time, and the quality of its offerings remains high. You'll probably hear some of the greatest hits of beloved French performers like Piaf, Aznavour, Brassens, and Brel. 4 rue Arsène-Houssaye, 8e. ✆ **01-42-56-14-65.** Cover 29€ ($26) including 1st drink; dinner (including wine) and show 42€–115€ ($38–$103). Daily, doors open at 8pm, the orchestra plays from 8:30pm, the show begins at 9:45pm, and dancing after the show lasts until 2am. Métro: Charles de Gaulle-Etoile.

JAZZ, SALSA, ROCK & MORE

The great jazz revival that long ago swept America is still going strong here, with Dixieland or Chicago rhythms being pounded out in dozens of jazz cellars, mostly called *caveaux.* Most clubs are between rue Bonaparte and rue St-Jacques on the Left Bank. The crowds attending clubs to hear rock, salsa, and the like are definitely young, often in their late teens, twenties, or early thirties. The exception to that is in the clubs offering jazz nights. Lovers of jazz span across all ages.

Au Duc des Lombards Comfortable and appealing, this jazz club replaced an earlier club several years ago and has thrived ever since. Artists begin playing at 9pm and continue (with breaks) for 5 hours, touching on everything from "free jazz" to more traditional forms like "hard bop." Unlike many of its competitors, tables can be reserved and will usually be held until 10:30pm. 42 rue des Lombards, 1er. ✆ **01-42-33-22-88.** Cover 14€–20€ ($12–$18). Daily 9pm–3am. Métro: Châtelet.

Baiser Salé This musically varied cellar club is lined with jazz-related paintings and has a large central bar and an ongoing roster of videos showing great jazz moments from the past. There's no food or even any particular glamour—everything is very mellow and laid-back. Genres featured include Afro-Caribbean, Afro-Latino, salsa, merengue, R&B, and sometimes fusion. 58 rue des Lombards, 1er. ✆ **01-42-33-37-71.** Cover 6.10€–15€ ($5.45–$14). Daily 6pm–6am; music daily 10pm–3am. Métro: Châtelet.

Bus Palladium In a single room with a long bar, this rock temple has varnished hardwoods and fabric-covered walls that barely absorb the reverberations of nonstop recorded music. You won't find techno, punk rock, jazz, blues, or soul. It's rock for hard-core, mostly heterosexual, rock wannabes ages 25 to 35. 6 rue Fontaine, 9e. ✆ **01-53-21-07-33.** Cover 15€ ($13) Fri–Sat. Tues–Sat 11pm–6am. Métro: Blanche or Pigalle.

Caveau de la Huchette   This celebrated jazz *caveaux*, reached by a winding staircase, draws a young crowd, mostly students, who dance to the music of well-known jazz combos. In prejazz days, Robespierre and Marat frequented the place. 5 rue de la Huchette, 5e. ✆ **01-43-26-65-05.** Cover 9.10€ ($8.15) Sun–Thurs, 11€ ($10) Fri–Sat; students 8.35€ ($7.45) Sun–Thurs, 11€ ($10) Fri–Sat. Sun–Thurs 9:30pm–2:30am; Fri–Sat and holidays 9:30pm–4am. Métro/RER: St-Michel.

La Chapelle des Lombards *(Finds*   The club's proximity to the Opéra Bastille seems incongruous, considering the African/Caribbean jazz and Brazilian salsa that's the norm. It's a magnet for South American and African expatriates, and the rhythms and fire of the music propel everyone onto the dance floor. 19 rue de Lappe, 11e. ✆ **01-43-57-24-24.** Cover 11€–18€ ($10–$16) including 1st drink. Women free Thurs before midnight. Thurs–Sat 10:30pm–1am. Métro: Bastille.

L'Arbuci   Smoky, dimly lit, and artfully chaotic, this basement-level establishment functions primarily as a restaurant offering jazz 5 nights a week. Don't be put off by the way it looks from the outside—once you enter and have a drink or two, you're likely to have fun, enjoying the jazz produced by players from the Philippines, Southeast Asia, Africa, and virtually everywhere else in between. If you don't want dinner, you'll pay between 5.30€ and 11€ ($4.75 and $10) per drink, depending on what you order. 25-27 rue de Buci, 6e. ✆ **01-44-32-16-00.** No cover. Set-price menus 23€–61€ ($20–$54). Restaurant open daily noon–1am. Live music is presented Wed–Sat 10:30pm–2:30am. Bar remains open till 3am nightly. Métro: Mabillon or St-Germain-des-Prés.

Le Bilboquet/Club St-Germain   This restaurant/jazz club/piano bar, where the film *Paris Blues* was shot, offers some of the best music in Paris. Jazz is played on the upper level in the restaurant, **Le Bilboquet,** a wood-paneled room with a copper ceiling, brass-trimmed sunken bar, and Victorian candelabra. The menu is limited but classic French, specializing in lamb, fish, and beef. Dinner is 46€ ($41). Under separate management is the downstairs **Club St-Germain** disco, where entrance is free, but drinks cost 15€ ($13). You can walk from one club to the other but must buy a new drink each time you change venues. 13 rue St-Benoît, 6e. ✆ **01-45-48-81-84.** No cover. Le Bilboquet 8:30pm–midnight; jazz music 10:30pm–2 or 2:30am. Club St-Germain Tues–Sun 10:30pm–4am. Métro: St-Germain-des-Prés.

Le Petit Opportun *(Finds*   Cramped and convivial, with a sense of the 13th-century masons who built the cellar, this is a jazz club seating no more than 45 patrons, many of whom are regulars. Its specialty is the traditional back-to-basics "hard bop" that avoids the dissonance and irregular rhythms of "free jazz." Artists come from Europe and North America and perform for 3-hour sessions. The rest of the time, the place is an arts-conscious cafe/pub. 15 rue des Lavandières Ste-Opportune, 1er. ✆ **01-42-36-01-36.** Cover 12€–15€ ($11–$13). Tues–Sat 9pm–5am; live music 10:30pm–2:30am. Métro: Châtelet.

Les Etoiles   Since 1856, this red-swabbed music hall has shaken with the sound of performers at work and patrons at play. Its newest incarnation is as a restaurant discothèque where the dance music is exclusively salsa and merengue and the food South American. Expect hearty portions of fried fish, shredded pork or beef, white rice, beans, and flan, with meals costing 18€ ($16). 61 rue du Château d'Eau, 10e. ✆ **01-47-70-60-56.** Cover for nondiners 15€ ($13), including 1st drink. Thurs–Sat 9pm–4:30am. Métro: Château d'Eau.

A Bar Crawl in Trendy Ménilmontant

If **rue Oberkampf** (11e) were any hotter, it would melt. How did it happen so fast? Longtime residents shake their heads and worry that the quirky authenticity of the neighborhood may disappear under the swarms of night crawlers who've migrated north from the Bastille. "Too many *banlieusards* go to the Bastille," the owner of Café Cannibale told us, referring to the reluctance of trendy Parisians to socialize with the suburban crowd.

The success of ultrahip **Café Charbon,** 109 rue Oberkampf (① 01-43-57-55-13), open daily from 9am to 2am, encouraged entrepreneurs to renovate abandoned factories and bars for the artists flowing into the neighborhood and for the crowd that was tiring of the Bastille. Some of the new spots are intentionally dilapidated, while others evoke the elegance of 19th-century watering holes. The walls often exhibit the work of local artists, the music is fairly low-key, and the drinks are reasonably priced (a glass of mint tea makes a refreshing alternative to alcohol). You can have a salad, snack, or hot plat du jour, but the food is secondary to the ambience.

Start from the Ménilmontant Métro stop and head down rue Oberkampf. Your first stop should be the divey **Le Scherkhan** at no. 144 (① 01-43-57-29-34), where you can sink into an easy chair under the fangs of a stuffed tiger, inhale the incense, and dream of equatorial Africa. It's open daily from 5pm to 2am. Stop in at the live-music club **Le Cithéa** at no. 114 (① 01-40-21-70-95). Here you get a show ranging from funk reggae to jazz fusion and house. Later continue on to **Café**

Le Sunset/Le Sunside   A staple on the Parisian jazz circuit since 1976, it maintains two separate bar areas, one on street level and one in the cellar, where separate jazz shows—each 3 hours in duration—begin at 9:30pm and 10:30pm, respectively. Expect a decor that (in the cellar) emulates a Métro station thanks to a sheath of gloss-white tiles, and a roster of French, Italian, and U.S.-derived artists that have included Roy Haynes, Aldo Romano, Richard Galliano, and, more recently, Steve Grossman, Mark Turner, and Simon Goubert. Whereas Le Sunset is dedicated to electric jazz and world music, Le Sunside is a temple of acoustic jazz, forming a unique complex in Europe with two clubs situated side by side and open daily with two live concerts every night. 60 rue des Lombards, 1er. ① 01-40-26-46-60. Cover 8€–20€ ($7.15–$18). Doors open nightly at 8:30pm. Concerts at 9:30 and 10:30pm. Métro: Châtelet.

New Morning   Jazz maniacs come to drink, talk, and dance at this long-enduring club. It remains on the see-and-be-seen circuit, so you might see Spike Lee or Prince. The high-ceilinged loft was turned into a nightclub in 1981. Many styles of music are performed, and the club is popular with jazz groups from Central and South America. Call to find out what's going on the night you plan to visit. Sometimes it's open on Sunday. 7-9 rue des Petites-Ecuries, 10e. ① 01-45-23-51-41. Cover 15€–27€ ($13–$24). Call ahead, but hours are generally Mon–Sat 8pm–1:30am. Métro: Château d'Eau.

Mercerie at no. 98 (② **01-43-38-81-30**), open Monday to Friday from 5pm to 2am and Saturday and Sunday from 3pm to 2am. At the end of the grungy bar is a tiny back room lined with long sofas. Across the street at no. 109 is **Café Charbon,** set in an early-1900s dance hall with a stunning Art Nouveau interior; it makes a relaxed place to hang out during the day and a crowded hotspot at night. Farther down on the same side of the street at no. 99 is the plush **Mecano Bar** (② **01-40-21-35-28**), open daily from noon to 2am. Mysterious old implements on the wall are left over from its days as a tool factory. The spacious back room has a palm tree, a skylight, and murals of seminude ladies lounging about in fin-de-siècle naughtiness.

Backtrack a few steps and turn left onto rue St-Maur to nos. 111-113, the **Blue Billard** (② **01-43-55-87-21**), open daily from 11am to 2am. This camera factory turned into an upscale bar/pool hall has 18 billiard tables under a mezzanine and skylight. A few steps farther on at no. 117 is a local favorite, **Les Couleurs** (② **01-43-57-95-61**), open daily from noon to 2am. It's outfitted with tacky posters, chrome-and-plastic chairs, and kitschy rec-room lamps. Live bands regularly play "free jazz," alternative rock, and anything experimental. Turn right at rue Jean-Pierre-Timbaud and at no. 93 you'll find **Café Cannibale** (② **01-49-29-95-59**), open daily from 9am to 2am. This softly lit beauty shimmers with candles, mirrors, and chandeliers. Set-price menus, usually priced at between 8.35€ and 10€ ($7.45 and $9.25) include a good-value Sunday brunch for 12€ ($11).

Slow Club   One of the most famous jazz cellars in Europe, capped with medieval ceiling vaults that give a marvelous acoustic intimacy, Slow Club presents a revolving set of artists who tend to focus on New Orleans jazz. Patrons, mostly in their thirties and early forties, appreciate the music's cross-cultural diversity. 130 rue de Rivoli, 1er. ② 01-42-33-84-30. Cover 9.10€–14€ ($8.15–$12). Tues and Thurs–Sat 10pm–3:30am. Métro: Châtelet.

DANCE CLUBS

The nightspots below are among hundreds of places where people in their twenties or early thirties go to dance—distinct from others where the main attraction is the music. The area around the church of **St-Germain-des-Prés** is full of dance clubs, but they come and go so quickly you could arrive to find a hardware store in the place of last year's white-hot disco—but, like all things in nature, the new spring up to take the place of the old. Check *Time Out: Paris* or *Pariscope* to get a sense of the current trends. Most of these clubs don't really get going until after 10pm.

Batofar   Self-consciously proud of its status as a club that virtually everybody views as hip, Batofar sits within a converted barge that floats beside an embankment on the Seine, sometimes with hundreds of gyrating dancers, most of whom are in their twenties and thirties. House, garage, techno, and live jazz from groups that hail from (among other places) Morocco, Senegal, and Germany sometimes add to the creative mix. Come here for an insight into late-night Paris at its most raffish and counterculture, and don't even try to categorize many of the after-dark denizens you're likely to meet. Tapas can be ordered for prices that begin at 3.05€ ($2.70) each, and beer will cost around 6.10€ ($5.45) a bottle. It faces 11 Quai François Mauriac, 13e. © 01-56-29-10-33. Tues–Sat 6pm–3 or 4am, depending on business. Cover 6.10€–15€ ($5.45–$13). Closed Nov–Mar. Métro: Quai de la Gare.

Club Zed *Finds* This popular nightspot in a former bakery with a vaulted masonry ceiling may surprise you with its mix of musical offerings, including samba, rock, 1960s pop, and jazz. There are also specific theme parties, such as the one at Halloween, where virtually everyone comes in costume. 2 rue des Anglais, 5e. © 01-43-54-93-78. Cover 7.60€–17[eu[($6.80–$15) including 1st drink. Wed–Thurs 10:30pm–3am; Fri–Sat 11pm–5:30am. Métro: Maubert-Mutualité.

La Balajo Opened in 1936, this dance club is best remembered as the venue where Edith Piaf first won the hearts of thousands of Parisians. Today it's easy to compare Le Balajo to New York City's Roseland—an old-fashioned venue steeped in nostalgia that sometimes manages to shake the dust out for special parties and events that can sometimes be hip and cutting-edge. Sessions held three afternoons a week focus on tangos, *paso dobles,* and waltzes, and are a lot more staid than their late-night counterparts. Then you get a younger crowd, lots of hot merengue and salsa (Tues–Thurs nights) and disco (Fri–Sat nights). 9 rue de Lappe, 11e. © 01-47-00-07-87. Cover 7.60€–9.10€ ($6.80–$8.15) for afternoon sessions; 15€–17€ ($13–$15) for nighttime sessions. Entrance includes the first drink. Mon, Thurs, and Sun 2:30–6:30pm; Tues–Sat 10:30pm–5am. Métro: Bastille.

La Coupole This landmark cafe has a basement ballroom that's a popular place to waltz and tango to orchestra music as well as bump and grind to "disco retro" (the best tunes of the 1960s, 1970s, and 1980s). Usually, the venue is house, garage, and rock-and-roll music, but Tuesday nights the focus is on salsa. The upstairs cafe is covered in "The Top Cafes" in chapter 6. 102 bd. Montparnasse, 14e. © 01-43-20-14-20. Ballroom cover 15€ ($13) for evening sessions, 12€ ($11) for matinees. Tues 9pm–3am; Fri–Sat 3–7pm and 10pm–5am; Sun 3–9pm. Métro: Vavin.

La Flèche d'Or *Finds* The setting for this hip and countercultural nightclub is a small railway station, adjacent to the Père-Lachaise cemetery, built in the 1890s and decommissioned by the SNCF in the 1950s. You're likely to have a radically different experience here depending on the night. Tuesdays focus on whatever amateur group wants to volunteer: as many as 20 different bands— some talented, others less so—perform. Wednesday is for electronic live and recorded music, Thursday is for reggae, Friday is for ska, Saturday focuses on live bands from everywhere, especially Africa, and Sunday is for salsa and merengue. The walls of this place are often hung with (for sale) paintings from temporary art exhibitions, and every Sunday morning, beginning at 11am, there's some kind of political forum and debate. 102 bis rue de Bagnolet, 20e. © 01-43-72-06-87. Cover free to 4.55€ ($4.05). Tues–Sun 7pm–2am. Métro: Alexandre Dumas.

La Java This dance hall used to be one of the most frequented in Paris, and the great Piaf and Chevalier made their names here. Today, you can still dance the waltz and perhaps even tango on a Sunday afternoon. Brazilian and Latin themes predominate on some nights. 105 rue du Faubourg du Temple, 10e. © 01-42-02-20-52. Cover 7.60€–17€ ($6.80–$15). Wed–Sat 11pm–5am; Sun 8pm–2am. Métro: Belleville.

Le Saint Occupying three medieval cellars deep in Paris's university area, this place lures 20- and 30-somethings who dance and drink and generally feel happy to be in a Left Bank student dive. The music melds New York, Los Angeles, and Europe and often leads to episodes of "Young Love Beside the Seine." 7 rue St-Severin, 5e. ✆ **01-43-25-50-04.** Cover 8€–15€ ($7.15–$13) including 1st drink. Tues–Sat 10pm–6am. Métro: St-Michel.

Les Bains The name, "The Baths," comes from this hotspot's former function as a Turkish bath, once attracting gay clients, none more notable than Marcel Proust. It may be hard to get in if the doorman doesn't think you're trendy and très chic. Yes, that was Jennifer Lopez we saw whirling around the floor. Dancing begins at midnight, and a supper-club–like restaurant lies upstairs. Meals cost 38€ to 46€ ($34–$41). On certain nights this is the hottest party atmosphere in Paris, and Mondays are increasingly gay, although sexual preference is hardly an issue at this club. "We all walk the waterfront," as one DJ enigmatically told us, as he played soul, house music, or whatever. 7 rue du Bourg-l'Abbae, 3e. ✆ **01-48-87-01-80.** Cover 15€–18€ ($13–$16). Daily midnight–6am. Métro: Réaumur-Sebastopal.

Les Coulisses/La Bohème Its premises combine a cellar-level disco with a street-level restaurant that bears two names. During the day, from 7:30am to around 8pm, it's known as La Bohème; from 8pm to 5:30am, it becomes a bit more formal and is called Les Coulisses. The food remains the same, with a set-price menu at 27€ ($24). Most nighttime patrons eventually filter down to the disco, where the decor is a cross between a feudal château and a scene from the Italian *Commedia dell'Arte*. The crowd ranges in age from 20 to around 45. 5 rue Ste-Rustique, 18e. ✆ **01-42-62-89-99.** Cover 24€ ($22) Fri–Sat, but free for patrons of either restaurant. Restaurants Tues–Sat 8pm–2am; disco Tues–Sat 11pm–5am. Métro: Abbesses or Funiculaire.

New Riverside If thoughts of Woodstock fill you with nostalgia and you want to meet Parisians between 25 and 40 who feel the same, this is the place for you. The Left Bank cellar club attracts droves of people who appreciate the indestructible premises and nostalgic music. You'll hear a range of 1970s rock and pop, especially The Doors. 7 rue Grégoire-de-Tours, 6e. ✆ **01-43-54-46-33.** Cover for men 14€ ($13) including 1st drink, but women pay cover only after midnight Fri–Sat. Daily 8:30pm–dawn. Métro: St-Michel or Odéon.

Theatre Rex Club This echoing blue-and-orange space emulates the techno-grunge clubs of London, complete with an international mood-altered crowd enjoying the kind of music only someone 18 to 28 could love. A host of DJs is on hand, including appearances from techno-circuit celeb, Laurent Garnier. 5 bd. Poissonière, 2e. ✆ **01-42-36-83-98.** Cover 7.60€–12€ ($6.80–$11) including 1st drink. Wed–Sat 11:30pm–6am. Métro: Bonne Nouvelle.

3 Bars, Pubs & Clubs

WINE BARS

Many Parisians now prefer the wine bar to the traditional cafe or bistro. The food is often better and the ambience more inviting. For cafes, see "The Top Cafes" in chapter 6.

Au Sauvignon This tiny place, with ceramic tiles and frescoes done by Left Bank artists, has tables overflowing onto a covered terrace where wines range from the cheapest Beaujolais to the most expensive St-Emilion Grand Cru. A glass is 3.35€ to 4.85€ ($3–$4.35), and it costs an extra .30€ (25¢) to consume it at a table. To accompany your wine, choose an Auvergne specialty, like

ⓘ More After-Dark Diversions

On a Paris night, the cheapest entertainment, especially if you're young, is **"the show"** staged at the southeaster tip of Ile de la Cité, behind Notre-Dame. A sort of Gallic version of the Sundowner Festival in Key West, it attracts just about everyone who ever wanted to try their hand at performance art. The entertainment is spontaneous and usually includes magicians, fire-eaters, jugglers, mimes, and music makers from all over, performing against the backdrop of the illuminated cathedral. This is one of the greatest places in Paris to meet other young people in a sometimes moderately euphoric setting.

Also popular is a **stroll along the Seine** after 10pm. Take a graveled pathway down to the river from the Left Bank side of pont de Sully, close to the Institut du Monde Arabe, and walk to the right, away from Notre-Dame. This walk, which ends near place Valhubert, is the best place to see spontaneous Paris in action at night. Joggers and saxophone players come here, and many Parisians show up to take part in impromptu dance parties.

To quench your thirst, wander onto Ile St-Louis and head for the **Café-Brasserie St-Regis,** 6 rue Jean-du-Bellay, 4e, across from pont St-Louis (ⓒ **01-43-54-59-41;** Métro: Musée du Louvre). If you want to linger, you can order a plat du jour or a coffee at the bar. But try doing as the Parisians do and order a 2.15€ ($1.90) beer to go (*une bière à emporter*) and take it with you on a stroll. The little cafe is open daily from 7am to 2am.

If you're caught waiting for the Métro to start running again at 5am, try the **Sous-Bock Tavern,** 49 rue St-Honoré, 1er (ⓒ **01-40-26-46-61;** Métro: Pont Neuf), open Monday to Saturday from 11am to 5am. Young drinkers gather here to sample some 400 varieties of beer. If you want a shot of whiskey to accompany your brew, you face a choice of 150 varieties. The dish to order is a platter of mussels—curried, with white wine, or with cream sauce; they go well with the brasserie-style fries.

---

goat cheese or a terrine. The Poilâne bread is ideal with ham, paté, or goat cheese. 80 rue des Sts-Pères, 7e. ⓒ **01-45-48-49-02.** Mon–Sat 8:30am–10pm. Métro: Sèvres-Babylone.

Aux Négociants   Ten minutes downhill from the north facade of Sacré-Coeur, this *bistro à vins* has flourished since 1980 as an outlet for wines produced in the Loire Valley. Artists, vendors, and office workers come here, linked by an appreciation of wine, costing 2.45€ to 4.85€ ($2.15–$4.35) per glass, and the allure of the plats du jour, costing 8.80€ to 12€ ($7.85–$11). 27 rue Lambert, 18e. ⓒ **01-46-06-15-11.** Mon–Fri noon–10:30pm. Métro: Lamarck-Caulincourt or Château Rouge.

Juveniles   This is a British-owned spin-off of one of Paris's most successful wine bars, nearby Willi's. Louder, less formal, less restrained, and (at least to wine lovers) more daring than its older sibling, it prides itself on experimenting with a wide roster of wines from "everywhere." High-quality but lesser-known wines from Spain, France, California, and Australia decant for 2.75€ to 7.30€ ($2.45–$6.50) per glass. Anything you like, including the "wine of the week,"

If you're looking for the most flamboyant drag in Paris, head to **Madame Arthur,** 75 bis rue des Martyrs, 18e (© **01-42-54-40-21**; Métro: Abbesses or Pigalle). It's the longest-running transvestite show in town, attracting both straights and gays. The creative force behind it is Mme Arthur, who's no lady and whose stage name during her shticks as MC is Chantaline. The performances include 9 to 11 artists with names like Vungala, Lady Lune, and Miss Badabou. You can visit just to drink or dine from a fixed-price menu (reservations required). The club is open daily from 8:30 to 10:30pm for dinner, with the show beginning at 10:30pm. After the last show, around 12:30am, the place becomes a disco. Cover (including the first drink) is 25€ ($22); dinner and the show is 45€ ($40) Sunday to Thursday and 60€ ($54) Friday and Saturday.

If drag shows aren't your cup of tea, how about *The Last Tango in Paris?* At **Le Tango,** 13 rue au Maire, 3e (© **01-42-72-17-78**; Métro: Arts et Métiers), memories of Evita and Argentina live on. This dive with a bordello decor features zouk music from the French Caribbean and Africa, as well as house, garage, and virtually every form of high-energy dance music known in New York and Los Angeles. Most patrons are gay and lesbian and in their twenties and thirties. The cover is 6.10€ ($5.45). It's open Friday and Saturday from midnight to 5am.

If you're looking for a sophisticated, laid-back venue without the high-energy exhibitionism of nightclubs, consider the **Sanz-Sans,** 49 rue du Faubourg St-Antoine, 4e (© **01-44-75-78-78**; Métro: Bastille). Testifying to the unifying power of jazz, it's a multiethnic playground where the children of prominent Parisians mingle. In this red-velvet duplex, the most important conversations seem to occur over margaritas on the stairway or the back-room couches. The later it gets, the sexier the scene becomes. There's no cover. It's open daily from 9am to 2pm and there's no cover.

can be hauled away uncorked from the wine boutique here. There's also an assortment of tapas-inspired platters for 9.10€ to 12€ ($8.15–$11). 47 rue de Richelieu, 1er. © 01-42-97-46-49. Bar Mon–Sat noon–1am; restaurant Mon–Sat noon–3pm and 6–11:30pm. Métro: Palais Royal.

La Tartine   Mirrors, brass detail, and frosted-globe chandeliers make La Tartine look like a movie set of old Paris. At least 60 wines are offered at reasonable prices, including seven kinds of Beaujolais and a large selection of Bordeaux by the glass. Glasses of wine cost 1.50€ to 2.75€ ($1.35–$2.45), and the charcuterie platter costs 6.85€ ($6.10). We recommend the light Sancerre wine and goat cheese from the Loire Valley. 24 rue de Rivoli, 4e. © 01-42-72-76-85. Thurs–Mon 9:30am–10pm and Wed noon–10pm. Métro: St-Paul.

Le Sancerre   Engagingly old-fashioned, with an agreeable staff and food prepared fresh every day, this wine bar specializes in vintages from the Loire Valley, and Sancerre. Produced in red, rosé, and white, it's known for its not-too-dry fruity aroma and legions of fans who believe it should be more celebrated. Other wine choices include Chinon and Saumur wine (both from the Loire Valley) as well as Pinot de Bourgogne (from Burgundy) and Gamet (from the Ardèche Valley in France's southwest). Food items usually include *andouillette* (chitterling sausages), omelets with flap mushrooms, fresh oysters, and quiche. Glasses of wine cost 2.45€ to 4.25€ ($2.15–$3.80); simple platters of food cost 7.75€ to 12€ ($6.90–$11) each. 22 av. Rapp, 7e. 𝒞 01-45-51-75-91. Mon–Fri 8am–9:30pm; Sat 8:30am–4pm. Métro: Alma-Marceau.

Les Bacchantes Les Bacchantes prides itself on offering more wines by the glass (at least 50) than any other wine bar in Paris and also does a hefty restaurant trade serving well-prepared *cuisine bourgeoise*. Amid exposed beams, Belle Epoque posters, and old-fashioned paneling, chalkboards announce a great list of vintages and platters. The wines, at 2.45€ to 4.85€ ($2.15–$4.35) per glass, are mainly French. Platters of food cost 9.10€ to 15€ ($8.15–$13). 21 rue Caumartin, 9e. 𝒞 01-42-65-25-35. Mon–Sat noon–midnight. Métro: Opéra or Madeleine.

Willi's Wine Bar Journalists and stockbrokers patronize this increasingly popular wine bar in the center of the financial district, run by Englishman Mark Williamson. About 250 kinds of wine are offered, including a dozen wine specials you can taste by the glass for 3.35€ to 15€ ($3–$13). Lunch is the busiest time—on quiet evenings you can better enjoy the warm ambience and 16th-century beams. Daily specials are likely to include lamb brochette with cumin and Lyonnaise sausage in truffled vinaigrette, plus spectacular desserts like chocolate terrine. A set-price lunch costs 25€ ($22), with a fixed-price dinner going for 32€ ($29). 13 rue des Petits-Champs, 1er. 𝒞 01-42-61-05-09. Bar Mon–Sat noon–11pm. Meals Mon–Sat noon–2:30pm and 7–11pm. Métro: Bourse, Pyramide, or Palais Royal.

BARS & PUBS

These "imported" places try to imitate American cocktail bars or masquerade as British pubs—most strike an alien chord. But that doesn't prevent fashionable Parisians from barhopping (not to be confused with cafe-sitting). Many bars in Paris are youth-oriented. But if you're an older traveler who prefers to take your expensive drink in one of the grand luxe bars of the world, Paris has that waiting for you, too. The bars at the Plaza Athénée, Crillon, and Ritz, for example, are among the grandest in the world and form an experience uniquely Parisian for those who want to don their finest apparel and take along a gold-plated credit card. In general, bars and pubs are open daily from 11am to 1:30am.

Académie de la Bière *Value* The decor is paneled and rustic, an appropriate foil for an "academy" whose curriculum includes more than 150 kinds of beer from microbreweries. Stella Artois, Belgium's best-selling beer, isn't available, though more than half of the dozen on tap are from small-scale breweries in Belgium that deserve to be better known. Snack-style food is available, including platters of mussels, assorted cheeses, and sausages with mustard. 88 bis bd. du Port-Royal, 5e. 𝒞 01-43-54-66-65. Daily 11am–2:30am. Métro: Port Royal.

Bar at the Plaza Athénée The hotel that contains this bastion of international chic appeals to media moguls from Europe, New York, and California, and to the expensive tastes of the patrons of the world-class shops that flank both sides of the hyperglamorous street (avenue Montaigne) on which it sits. In 2000 the hotel moved its bar from a time-honored position in the cellar (the Bar Anglais) to new, contemporary digs on the street level. Short of renting a room on the premises, it's the most practical (and cheapest) way to actually experience this legendary hotel. In the Hôtel Plaza Athénée, 25 av. Montaigne, 8e. 𝒞 01-53-67-66-65. Daily 6pm–3:30am. Métro: Alma-Marceau.

Bar du Crillon   Though some visitors consider the Bar du Crillon too stiff and elegant to allow anyone to have a good time, its social and literary history is remarkable. Hemingway set a climactic scene of *The Sun Also Rises* here, and over the years it has attracted practically every upper-level staff member of the nearby American embassy, as well as heiresses, stars, starlets, and wannabes. Under its new owner, the Concorde Group, designer Sonia Rykiel has redecorated the bar. Down the hall is the Edwardian **Jardin d'Hiver,** where, amid potted palms and upscale accessories, you can order tea, cocktails, or coffee; it's open daily from noon to 9pm. In the Hôtel du Crillon, 10 place de la Concorde, 8e. ℂ **01-44-71-15-00.** Daily 11am–2am. Métro: Concorde.

Bar Hemingway/Bar Vendôme   In 1944, during Paris's liberation, Ernest Hemingway and a group of Allied soldiers made history by "freeing" the Ritz from the Nazis and ordering a round of martinis. The Ritz commemorates this event in the **Bar Hemingway** with bookish memorabilia, rows of newspapers, and stiff drinks served in a woodsy English-club setting. Look for its entrance, and homage to other writers, close to the hotel's rue Cambon entrance. The Bar Hemingway is more fun than the Bar Vendôme. The Hemingway is virtually a singles bar—unfussy, chic, and often filled with attractive women, many of them newly single, and spending their divorce settlements taking classes at the on-site cooking school. The Vendôme, in contrast, retains its old-world stateliness. Between 5:30 and 8:30pm, it's wise to reserve a table. In the Hôtel Ritz, 15 place Vendôme, 1er. ℂ **01-43-16-30-30.** Bar Hemingway Tues–Sat 6:30pm–2am. Bar Vendôme noon–3pm for lunch, 4–6pm for tea, 6pm–1am bar. Métro: Opéra.

Barrio Latino   It would be easy to spend an entire evening at this multistoried emporium of good times, Gallic flair, and Latino charm. You won't be finished with this place until you've done a bit of exploring, so here's what you can expect: Tapas bars and dance floors on the street level (*rez-de-chausée*) and 3rd floor (*2eme étage*); a Latino restaurant on the 2nd floor (*1er étage*); and a private club on the top floor. Staff members roll glass-covered carts loaded with tapas around the floors, selling them like hot dogs at an American baseball game. The restaurant (open daily noon–3pm and 7:30pm–12:30am) specializes in food that jaded French palates sometimes find refreshing. Main courses range from 8.35€ to 26€ ($7.45–$23) and include Argentinean steaks, Brazilian fejoiada, and Mexican chili con carne, all of which taste wonderful with beer, caipirinhas, Cuba Libres, and/or rum punches. You'll be surrounded by a recorded cocoon of marvelous Latino music everywhere you go. Clientele is very mixed, mostly straight, partly gay, and 100% blasé about matters such as an individual's sexuality. 46 rue du Faubourg St-Antoine, 12e. ℂ **01-55-78-84-75.** Cover 7.60€ ($6.80) but only for nondiners, non-VIPs, and only on Fri–Sat after 9pm. Daily 11am–2 am. Métro: Bastille.

China Club   Designed to recall France's 19th-century colonies in Asia or a bordello in 1930s Shanghai (on the ground floor) and England's empire-building zeal in India (upstairs), the China Club will allow you to chitchat or flirt with the singles who crowd into the street-level bar, then escape to calmer, more contemplative climes upstairs. You'll see regulars from the worlds of fashion and the arts, along with a pack of postshow celebrants from the nearby Opéra Bastille. A street-level Chinese restaurant serves dinner daily from 7pm to 12:30am, and in the more animated (and occasionally raucous) cellar bar, live music is presented every Friday and Saturday from 10pm to 3am. 50 rue de Charenton, 12e. ℂ **01-43-43-82-02.** Daily 7pm–2am. Métro: Bastille or Ledru Rollin.

La Belle Hortense   There are dozens of other bars and cafes near this one, but none maintains a bookstore in back, and few seem so self-consciously aware of their roles as ersatz literary salons. Come for a glass of wine and participation in a discussion within what's defined as "a literary bar." It's named after a pulpy 19th-century romance (*La Belle Hortense*) set within the surrounding neighborhood. Glasses of wine cost 2.75€ to 5.30€ ($2.45–$4.75). 31 rue Vieille du Temple, 4e. ☎ **01-48-04-71-60.** Daily 5pm–2am. Métro: Hotel de Ville.

Le Bar de L'Hôtel   This is the hyper-artsy and theatrically decorated bar of a hotel that has wooed film-industry types who want to avoid the more mainstream luxury of Paris's palatial hotels. The rose-filter cheeriness is deceptive: This is the hotel where Oscar Wilde died, disgraced and impoverished. In 2000, the bar, along with the rest of the hotel, was renovated by decorating bigwig Jacques Garcia. Expect a high-Victorian color scheme of terra-cotta and dark green, marble columns, an imposing marble-topped bar, and an appealing sense of baroque (or Byzantine) intrigue. Drinks here sometimes segue into the nearby on-site restaurant, which is open Tuesday to Saturday from noon to 3pm and 8 to 10:30pm. In L'Hôtel, 13 rue des Beaux-Arts, 6e. ☎ **01-44-41-99-00.** Daily 4pm–1am. Métro: St-Germain-des-Prés.

Le Forum   Its patrons, who include frequent business travelers, compare this place to a private club in London. Part of that comes from the polished oak paneling and ornate stucco and part from its store of single-malt whiskeys. You can also try 240 cocktails, including many that haven't been popular since the Jazz Age. Champagne by the glass is common, as is that social lubricant, the martini. 4 bd. Malesherbes, 8e. ☎ **01-42-65-37-86.** Mon–Fri 11:30am–1:30am; Sat 5:30pm–1:30am. Métro: Madeleine.

Le Fumoir   At Le Fumoir, the well-traveled crowd that lives or works in the district provides a kind of classy raucousness. The decor is a lot like that of an English library, with about 6,000 books providing an aesthetic backdrop to the schmoozing. A Danish chef prepares an international menu featuring meal-size salads (the one with scallops and lobster is great), roasted codfish with zucchini, and roasted beef in red-wine sauce. More popular are the stiff mixed drinks, the wines and beers, and the dozen or so types of cigars for sale. 6 rue de l'Amiral-de-Coligny, 1er. ☎ **01-42-92-00-24.** Daily 11am–2am. Métro: Louvre-Rivoli.

Le Web Bar   Occupying a three-story space at the edge of the Marais, Le Web Bar echoes with the sound of people schmoozing and with silent computer partners thousands of miles away. On the street level is a restaurant; on the second floor is a battery of at least 18 computers you can use for 3.05€ ($2.70) per hour. On the top floor is an art gallery. To keep things perking, there's daily entertainment beginning around 7pm. Menu items stress comfort food like *boeuf bourguignonne*, with plats du jour costing 7.90€ to 8.95€ ($7.05–$8). 32 rue de Picardie, 3e. ☎ **01-42-72-66-55.** www.webbar.fr. Mon–Fri 8:30am–2am; Sat–Sun 11am–2am. Métro: République or Temple.

Maito Habana   The macho brown-and-green decor evokes a men's club. You can drink Cuba libres, cognac, or coffee or eat platters of food, with main courses costing 13€ to 18€ ($12–$16). You can also puff away at any of the cigars stocked for the pleasure of the patrons (regulars sometimes store their cigars in a safe originally designed as a safety-deposit vault). Live music is presented at 11pm Tuesday to Saturday. 19 rue de Presbourg, 16e. ☎ **01-45-00-60-63.** Cafe and cigar service Mon 9am–8pm; Tues–Fri 9am–5pm; Sat 8pm–5am. Meals Mon noon–3:30pm; Tues–Sat 8pm–midnight. Métro: Etoile.

Man Ray   This chic rendezvous off the Champs-Elysées is dedicated to Man Ray, the famous photographer and American Dadaist, who usually felt more comfortable roaming Montparnasse than the 8th. Many of Man Ray's photos decorate the club. The club is a media favorite, mainly because some of its owners are Johnny Depp, Sean Penn, and John Malkovitch. Entry is discreet, through large wrought-iron doors and virtually no sign. In the basement is a bustling restaurant presided over by two winged Indonesian goddesses. Here main courses begin at 23€ ($20). The bar upstairs is big and bustling. Jazz is presented Monday to Thursday from 7 to 9pm in the bar, and every night after 11pm a DJ provides musical animation. On Fridays the place is transformed into a disco after 11pm, with an entrance cost of 15€ ($13), including the first drink. 34 rue Marbeuf, 8e. ℂ 01-56-88-36-36. Restaurant Mon–Fri noon–2:30pm; daily 7:30pm–12:30am. Bar daily 6pm–2am. Métro: F. D. Roosevelt.

Pub St-Germain-des-Prés   With 9 rooms and 650 seats, this is France's largest pub, offering 200 brands of beer, 15 on draft. The battered decor consists of leather booths, faded gilt-framed mirrors, hanging lamps, and a stuffed parrot in a gilded cage. The atmosphere is usually quiet, relaxed, and posh. Featured beers change frequently but usually include Amstel, various Belgian brews, Whitbread, and Pimm's No. 1. If frat houses turn you on, it gets really fun from 10:30pm to 4am. You can also order food here at any time, with set menus costing from 14€ to 24€ ($12–$22) each. 17 rue de l'Ancienne-Comédie, 6e. ℂ 01-43-29-38-70. Daily 24 hours. Métro: Odéon.

4 Gay & Lesbian Bars & Clubs

Gay life is centered around **Les Halles** and **Le Marais,** with the greatest concentration of gay/lesbian clubs, restaurants, bars, and shops between the Hôtel de Ville and Rambuteau Métro stops. Gay dance clubs come and go so fast that even the magazines devoted to them—*E-mail* and *Illico,* distributed free in the gay bars and bookstores—have a hard time keeping up. For lesbians, there is *"Lesbian Magazine."* Also look for Gai Pied's *Guide Gai* and *Pariscope's* regularly featured English-language section, "A Week of Gay Outings." Also important for both men and women is *Têtu Magazine,* sold at most newsstands.

For all you need to know about Paris's gay and lesbian scene, read *Frommer's Gay & Lesbian Europe.*

Café Cox, 15 rue des Archives, 4e (ℂ 01-42-72-08-00), gets so busy in the early evening that the crowd stands on the sidewalk. This is where you'll find the most mixed gay crowd in Paris—from hunky American tourists to sexy Parisian men. A new hot place in Les Halles is **Le Tropic Café,** 66 rue des Lombards, 1er (ℂ 01-40-13-92-62; Métro: Châtelet-Les Halles), where the trendy, good-looking crowd parties until dawn. **Le Gibus,** 18 rue du Faubourg du Temple, 11e (ℂ 01-47-00-78-88; Métro: République), opens every night as a late-night disco, entertaining diverse collections of counterculture Parisians. But Friday and Saturday nights are deliberately and exclusively gay, attracting some of the most drop-dead gorgeous men in the city. Drag shows, at least on weekends, form part of the entertainment. It's open nightly from midnight to 7am. Weeknight entrance costs from 1.50€ to 11€ ($1.35–$10), depending on the venue, but on gay nights the charge is 15€ ($13) including the first drink.

A restaurant with a bar popular with women is **Okawa,** 40 rue Vieille-du-Temple, 4e (ℂ 01-48-04-30-69; Métro: Hôtel de Ville), where trendy lesbians (and some gay men) enjoy happy hour. **Les Scandaleuses,** 6 rue des Ecouffes, 3e

(✆ **01-48-87-39-26;** Métro: St-Paul), is a bar for gay women where an attached female can usually find a drinking buddy to tell her troubles to.

Amnesia Café   The Amnesia's function and crowd may change during the day, but you'll always find a cadre of local gays. This cafe/tearoom/bistro/bar includes two bar areas, a mezzanine, and a cellar bar, **Amni-Club,** open in the evening. The drinks of choice are beer, cocktails, and *café amnesia,* a specialty coffee with cognac and Chantilly cream. Deep armchairs, soft pillows, and 1930s accents create an ambience conducive to talk and laughter—it's not as sexually charged as the nearby bars. 42 rue Vieille-du-Temple, 4e. ✆ **01-42-72-16-94.** Daily noon–2am. Métro: Hôtel de Ville.

Banana Café   This popular bar is a stop for gays visiting or doing business in Paris. Occupying two floors of a 19th-century building, it has walls the color of an overripe banana, dim lighting, and a policy of raising the drink prices after 10pm, when things become really interesting. There's a street-level bar and a cellar dance floor that features a live pianist and recorded music—sometimes with dancing. On many nights, go-go dancers perform from spot-lit platforms in the cellar. 13 rue de la Ferronnerie, 1er. ✆ **01-42-33-35-31.** Daily 5pm to between 4 and 5am. Métro: Châtelet-Les Halles.

La Champmeslé   La Champmeslé—with dim lighting, background music, and comfortable banquettes—is a cozy meeting place for lesbians (and even for "well-behaved" gay men). It's housed in a 300-year-old building with exposed stone and ceiling beams and 1950s-style furnishings. On Thursday and Saturday, one of the premier lesbian events of Paris, a cabaret, begins at 10pm; every month there's a well-attended exhibit of paintings by mostly lesbian artists. The bar honors a celebrated 17th-century actress, La Champmeslé, who was instrumental in interpreting the fledgling dramatic efforts of celebrated playwright Racine. 4 rue Chabanais, 2e. ✆ **01-42-96-85-20.** Mon–Wed 2pm–2am; Thurs–Sat 2pm–5am. Métro: Pyramides or Bourse.

Le Central   Established in 1980 in a 300-year-old townhouse, Le Central is a staple of gay men's life in the Marais. Outfitted with an indestructible decor of battered paneling and windows that wrap around it on two sides, it attracts local residents who make the place their local hangout, and goodly numbers of attractive male tourists and the Parisians who appreciate them. Don't be surprised if the friendships you forge here are with other Yanks, Aussies, or Brits, as the clientele here includes lots of expatriates. A small gay hotel is upstairs (see "Gay-Friendly Hotels" in chapter 5). 33 rue Vieille-du-Temple, 4e. ✆ **01-48-87-99-33.** Mon–Fri 4pm–2am; Sat–Sun 2pm–2am. Métro: Hôtel de Ville.

Le Pulp   This is one of the most popular lesbian discos, looking like a burgundy-colored 19th-century French music hall. It's best to show up before midnight. The venue, as the French like to say, is très cool, with cutting-edge music played in a setting that just happens to discourage the presence of men. 25 bd. Poissonnière, 2e. ✆ **01-40-26-01-93.** Cover 7.60€–12€ ($6.80–$11). Thurs–Sat 11:30pm–dawn. Métro: Rue Montmartre.

Le Queen   Should you miss gay life à la New York, follow the flashing purple sign on the "main street" of Paris, near the corner of avenue George V. The place is often mobbed, primarily with gay men and (to a lesser degree) models, actresses, and the like. Look for go-go boys, drag shows, muscle shows, and everything from 1970s-style disco nights (Mondays) to Tuesday-night foam parties in summer, when cascades of mousse descend onto the dance floor. Go very late. 102 av. des Champs-Elysées, 8e. ℂ **01-53-89-08-90.** Cover 9€ ($8.05), including 1st drink, Sun–Mon, 18€ ($16) Fri–Sat. Daily 11pm to between 4 and 5am. Métro: F. D. Roosevelt.

5 Literary Haunts

Harry's New York Bar   The ads tell you to instruct your cab driver, "Sank roo doe Noo." Opened on Thanksgiving Day in 1911 by a bearded Hemingway precursor by the name of MacElhone, it's sacred to Papa disciples as the spot where members of the ambulance corps drank themselves silly during World War I. White Lady and sidecar cocktails were invented here in 1919 and 1931, respectively, and it's the alleged birthplace of the Bloody Mary and the headquarters of a fraternity of drinkers known as the International Bar Flies (IBF). In the street-level bar, daytime crowds draw from the area's insurance, banking, and travel industries; evening crowds include pre- and post-theater groupies and night owls. In the cellar, a pianist plays daily from 10pm to 2am. 5 rue Daunou, 2e. ℂ **01-42-61-71-14.** Daily 10–4am. Métro: Opéra or Pyramides.

Rosebud   The popularity of this place, known for a bemused and indulgent attitude toward anyone looking for a drink and some talk, hasn't diminished since the 1950s, when it attained its fame. The name refers to the beloved sled of Orson Welles's great *Citizen Kane.* Around the corner from Montparnasse's famous cafes, and thick in associations with Sartre and de Beauvoir, Ionesco, and Duras, Rosebud draws a crowd aged 35 to 65, though the staff has recently remarked on the appearance of students. Drop in at night for a glass of wine, a shot of whiskey, or a hamburger or chili con carne. 11 bis rue Delambre, 14e. ℂ **01-43-35-38-54.** Daily 7pm–2am. Métro: Vavin.

11

Side Trips from Paris

Paris, the city that began on an island, is the center of a curious landlocked island known as the **Ile de France.** Shaped roughly like a saucer, it's encircled by a thin ribbon of rivers: the **Epte, Aisne, Marne,** and **Yonne.** Fringing these rivers are forests with famous names—**Rambouillet, St-Germain, Compiègne,** and **Fontainebleau.** These forests are said to be responsible for Paris's clear gentle air and the unusual length of its spring and fall. This may be debatable, but there's no argument they provide the capital with a fine series of day trips, all within easy reach.

The forests surrounding Paris were once the domain of royalty and the aristocracy, and they're still sprinkled with the magnificent châteaux of their former masters. Together with ancient villages, glorious cathedrals, and cozy country inns, they make the Ile de France irresistible. In this chapter, we offer only a handful of the possibilities for day jaunts. For a more extensive list, see *Frommer's France 2003.*

1 Versailles ⭑

21km (13 miles) SW of Paris, 71km (44 miles) NE of Chartres

For centuries, the name of the Parisian suburb of Versailles resounded through the consciousness of every aristocratic family in Europe. The palace here outdazzled every other kingly residence in Europe—it was a horrendously expensive scandal and a symbol to later generations of a regime obsessed with prestige above all else.

Back in the *grand siècle,* all you needed was a sword, a hat, and a bribe for the guard at the gate. Provided you didn't look as if you had smallpox, you'd be admitted to the **Château de Versailles,** where you could stroll through salon after glittering salon—watching the Sun King rise—and dress and dine and do even more intimate things while you gossiped, danced, plotted, flirted, and trysted.

Today, Versailles needs the return of Louis XIV and his treasury. You wouldn't believe it when looking at the glittering Hall of Mirrors, but Versailles is down-at-the-heels. It suffers from a lack of funds, which translates into a shortage of security; this budget crunch was made even worse in 1999 when a windstorm wreaked havoc here (see "Your Own Tree at Versailles" below).

You get to see only half of the palace's treasures; the rest are closed to the public. Some 3.2 million visitors arrive annually; on average they spend 2 hours.

ESSENTIALS

GETTING THERE To get to Versailles catch the **RER** line C at the Gare d'Austerlitz, St-Michel, Musée d'Orsay, Invalides, Ponte de l'Alma, Champ de Mars, or Javel stop and take it to the Versailles Rive Gauche station, from which there's a shuttle bus to the château. Priced at 4.70€ ($4.20) round-trip,

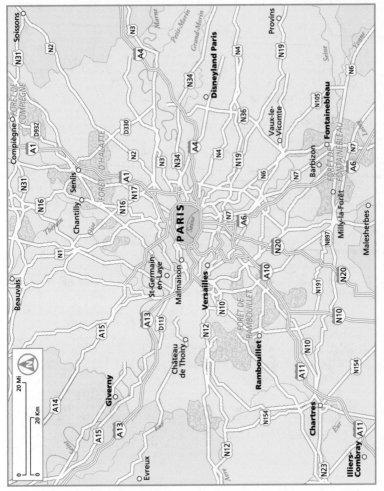

the transit takes 35 to 40 minutes; Eurailpass holders travel free on the RER, but they'll need to show their Eurailpass at the kiosk near any RER entrance to receive a ticket that will open the turnstile leading onto the RER platforms.

An alternate method of reaching Versailles from central Paris involves regular **SNCF trains,** which make frequent runs from two railway stations (Gare St-Lazare and Gare Montparnasse) to Versailles. Trains departing from Gare St-Lazare arrive at the Versailles Rive Droite railway station; trains departing from Gare Montparnasse arrive at Versailles Chantiers. Both stations lie within a 10-minute walk from the château, and we highly recommend the walk as a means of orienting yourself with the town, its geography, its scale, and its architecture. If you can't or don't want to walk, you can take bus B, bus H, or (in midsummer) a shuttle bus marked "Château" from any of the three stations directly to the château for a fee of 1.50€ ($1.35) each way, per person. Again, because of the vagaries of each of the bus schedules, we highly recommend the walk. Directions to the château are clearly signposted from each of the three railway stations.

A Weekend in London

Of course, Paris offers a seemingly endless list of wonderful things to see and do, but now that transit between the French capital and the British capital is easier than ever, why not take a weekend jaunt to London?

The **Eurostar** train roars through the **Channel Tunnel (Chunnel)**, reducing the travel time between Paris's Gare du Nord and London's Waterloo Station to 3 hours. With some restrictions, fares between London and Paris begin at $139 for one-way transport and at $158 for round-trip in second class. First-class transit begins at $219 one-way and $248 round-trip, per person. Additional discounts, in many cases, are offered to holders of Eurail and Britrail passes, youths under 26, students, and persons over 60. And for passengers looking for additional perks to first-class transport, packages can be bought beginning at $369 per person each way, that allow access to first-class waiting lounges in Paris and London, enhanced cuisine onboard, and taxi service between the station of your final destination and your hotel. If you need a hotel in London or Paris, the staff at one of Eurostar's affiliates can set up a rail/hotel package at a discounted rate. For round-trip transport plus a night in a hotel in London or Paris, plus a sightseeing package, rates begin at $595 per person in first class and $435 per person in second class. If, during your dialogues with Eurostar, you ask about special promotions, you may discover some surprising discounts. Examples include a departure from and a return to either city on the same day, at round-trip rates that can be about the same as a one-way ticket.

From North America, call the **Eurostar** division of Rail Europe at ⓒ **800/EUROSTAR.** For details about hotel packages, contact **EuroVacations** at ⓒ **877/387-6822.** If you're already in Paris, contact any travel agency, talk to your concierge, or check www.raileurope.com.

As a last resort, and frankly, we do not recommend it; you can use a combination of **Métro and city bus.** Travel to the Pont de Sèvres stop by Métro, then transfer to bus no. 171 for a westward trek that'll take 35 to 60 minutes, depending on traffic. The bus will cost you three Métro tickets and deposit you near the château gates.

If you have a **car,** take N-10, following the signs to Versailles, and then proceed along avenue de Général-Leclerc. Park on place d'Armes in front of the château.

VISITOR INFORMATION   Three main avenues radiate from place d'Armes in front of the palace. The **tourist office** is at 2 bis av. de Paris, 78000 Versailles (ⓒ **01-39-24-88-88**).

TOURING VERSAILLES

Château de Versailles ✯✯✯   Within 50 years, this residence was transformed from Louis XIII's simple hunting lodge into an extravagant palace. Begun in 1661, the construction of the château involved 32,000 to 45,000 workmen, some of whom had to drain marshes—often at the cost of their lives—and move

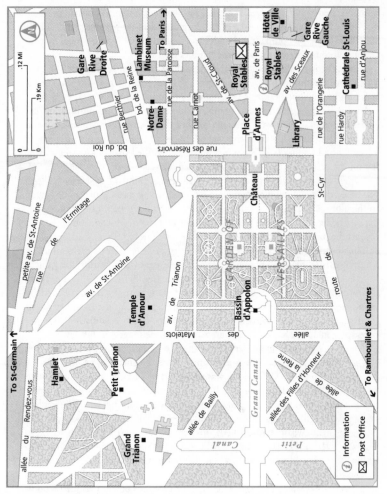

forests. Louis XIV set out to build a palace that would be the envy of all Europe, and he created a symbol of pomp and opulence that was to be copied, yet never quite duplicated, all over Europe and even in America.

So he could keep an eye on the nobles of France (and with good reason), Louis XIV summoned them to live at his court. He amused them with constant entertainment and banquets and balls, and amused himself with a roster of mistresses, the most important of whom was Mme de Maintenon (he secretly married her after his queen, Marie-Thérèse of Spain, died). To some he awarded such vital tasks as holding the hem of his ermine-lined robe. While the aristocrats played away their lives, often in silly intrigues and games, the peasants on the estates, angered by their absentee landlords, sowed the seeds of the Revolution.

When Louis XIV died in 1715, he was succeeded by his great-grandson, Louis XV, who continued the outrageous pomp, though he's said to have predicted the outcome: *"Après mois le déluge"* (After me, the deluge). His wife, Marie Leszcynska of Poland, was shocked by the court's blatant immorality. When her husband tired of her, she lived as a nun, and the king's attention turned to Mme de Pompadour, who was accused of running up a debt far beyond that of a full-scale war. Mme de Pompadour handpicked her successor, Mme du Barry, who was just about as foolhardy with the nation's treasury.

Louis XVI found his grandfather's and father's behavior scandalous—in fact, on gaining the throne in 1774 he ordered the "stairway of indiscretion" (secret stairs leading up to the king's bedchamber) be removed. This dull, weak king (who was virtuous and did have good intentions) and his Austrian-born queen, Marie Antoinette, were well liked at first, but the queen's excessive frivolity and wild spending soon led to her downfall. Louis and Marie Antoinette were at Versailles on October 6, 1789, when they were notified that mobs were marching on the palace. As predicted, *le déluge* had arrived.

Napoleon stayed at Versailles but never seemed fond of it. Louis-Philippe prevented the destruction of the palace by converting it into a museum dedicated to the glory of France. To do that, he had to surrender some of his own not-so-hard-earned currency. Many years later, John D. Rockefeller contributed heavily toward the restoration of Versailles and work continues to this day.

The six magnificent **Grands Appartements** ✦✦✦, each of them suites of rooms outfitted by various potentates and their entourages during the palace's heyday, are in the Louis XIV style, each named after the allegorical painting on their ceilings. The largest is the **Hercules Salon,** with a ceiling painted by François Lemoine depicting the Apotheosis of Hercules. In the **Mercury Salon** (with a ceiling by Jean-Baptiste Champaigne), the body of Louis XIV was put on display in 1715; his 72-year reign was one of the longest in history.

The most famous room at Versailles is the 71m (236 ft.) long **Hall of Mirrors** ✦✦✦, built to link the north and south appartements. Begun in 1678 by Mansart in the Louis XIV style, it was decorated by Le Brun and his team with 17 large arched windows matched by corresponding beveled mirrors in simulated arcades, plus amazing chandeliers and gilded lamp bearers. The vaulted ceiling is covered with paintings in classic allegorical style depicting key episodes (some of them lavishly embellished) from the life and career of Louis XIV. On June 28, 1919, the treaty ending World War I was signed in this corridor. Ironically, the German Empire was also proclaimed here in 1871.

The royal appartements were for show, but Louis XV and Louis XVI retired to the **Petits Appartements** ✦✦ to escape the demands of court etiquette. Louis XV died in his bedchamber in 1774, a victim of smallpox. In the second-floor **King's Appartements,** he stashed away first Mme de Pompadour and then Mme du Barry. Attempts have been made to return the **Queen's Appartements** to their appearance in the days of Marie Antoinette, when she played her harpsichord for audiences of specially invited guests.

Her king, Louis XVI, had an impressive **Library,** designed by Gabriel. Its panels are delicately carved, and the room has been restored and refurnished. The **Clock Room** contains Passement's astronomical clock, encased in gilded bronze. Twenty years in the making, it was completed in 1753 and is supposed to keep time until the year 9999. At the age of 7, Mozart played for the court in this room.

Gabriel designed the **Opéra** ✦✦ for Louis XV in 1748, though it wasn't completed until 1770. In its heyday, it took 3,000 candles to light the place. Using harmonies of gold and white, Hardouin-Mansart built the **Royal Chapel** ✦✦✦ in 1699, dying before its completion. Louis XVI, when still the dauphin, married Marie Antoinette here in 1770. Both the bride and the groom in this arranged marriage between rival empires (France and Austria) were teenagers.

You'll be confronted with three alternatives in how to experience the main palace at Versailles. An unguided visit, where you can tour the Grands Appartements at your own speed, costs 7.45€ ($6.65) per person (free for persons under 18). If this is your interest, address yourself to Porte (Entranceway) A. If you prefer a group tour, with guided commentary in English and French, of the same terrain plus some additional areas of the château, including the Opera House and the Chapel, expect to pay the 7.45€ ($6.65) entrance noted above, plus a supplement of either 3.95€ or 5.95€ ($3.55–$5.30), depending on whether you opt for a 60-minute or a 90-minute tour. If the guided group tour of either duration appeals to you, go to Porte D. The final option involves renting a portable cassette player with a recorded tour in English or French, which will allow you to tour the Grands Appartements plus the Opera and Chapel, for a fee of 11€ ($10). Visitors with ample amounts of time may prefer this method of touring the château. Depending on how quickly you move through the château's vast labyrinth, the prerecorded option will take between 1 and 4 hours. If the prerecorded option appeals to you, go to Porte C.

Your visit will include access to the **Musée de l'Histoire de France** (© 01-39-67-07-73), a suite of rooms containing mostly framed historical paintings and engravings. Accessible via Porte D in the château, it traces the history of the parliamentary process in France following the collapse of the monarchy in 1789, with exhibits on how laws are made and enforced.

Place d'Armes. © **01-30-83-78-00**; fax 01-39-24-88-89. Admission to the château 7.45€ ($6.65) adults, free for those under 18 and over 60. Reduced rates for adults after 3:30pm. May–Sept Tues–Sun 9am–6pm (to 5pm the rest of the year). Closed Dec 25 and Jan 1.

Gardens of Versailles ★★★ The Gardens of Versailles were laid out by the landscape artist Le Nôtre, who created a Garden of Eden using ornamental lakes and canals, geometrically designed flower beds, and avenues bordered with statuary. At the peak of their glory, 1,400 fountains spewed forth. *The Buffet* is exceptional, having been designed by Mansart. One fountain depicts Apollo in his chariot pulled by four horses, surrounded by tritons emerging from the water to light the world. On the 1.5km-long (1 mile) Grand Canal, Louis XV—imagining he was in Venice—used to take gondola rides with his favorite of the moment.

On Christmas Day 1999, the most violent windstorm in France's history thundered through Paris, causing extensive damage to parks and gardens in the Ile de France. At Versailles, the wind toppled 10,000 trees and blew out some windows at the magnificent château. The palace has now reopened, but the difficult task of replanting the thousands of trees will take some time, and it'll be years before

---

Fun Fact **Your Own Tree at Versailles**

The gardeners of Versailles claim (in French, of course) that it's an ill wind that doesn't blow some good. Before the crippling storm at Christmas in 1999, many of the trees were weak, aged, and diseased. The storms took care of that, uprooting such classics as Marie Antoinette's Virginia tulip tree planted in 1783. With $40 million in funds allocated, the park is being restored to the way it was in the heyday of the Sun King. When the work is completed, the grounds will look more spectacular than ever. For a donation of $155, you, too, can sponsor a new tree for the park. For more details, visit www.chateauversailles.fr.

Impressions

When Louis XIV finished the Grand Trianon, he told [Mme de] Maintenon he had created a paradise for her, and asked if she could think of anything now to wish for. . . . She said she could think of but one thing—it was summer, and it was balmy France—yet she would like well to sleigh ride in the leafy avenues of Versailles! The next morning found miles and miles of grassy avenues spread thick with snowy salt and sugar, and a procession of those quaint sleighs waiting to receive the chief concubine of the gaiest and most unprincipled court that France has ever seen!

—Mark Twain, *The Innocents Abroad* (1869)

---

they return to their lush grandeur. Nonetheless, there is still much that remains to enchant, and the gardens get better and better every month.

Place d'Armes (behind the Palace of Versailles). ℭ 01-30-83-78-00. Free admission, except during fireworks or fountain displays (see below). May–Oct daily 7am–sundown; Nov–Apr daily 8am–sundown.

The Trianons & The Hamlet   A long walk across the park will take you to the **Grand Trianon** ★★, in pink-and-white marble. Le Vau built a Porcelain Trianon here in 1670, covered with blue and white china tiles, but it was fragile and soon fell into ruin. So, in 1687, Louis XIV commissioned Hardouin-Mansart to build the Grand Trianon. Traditionally, it has been a place where France has lodged important guests, though de Gaulle wanted to turn it into a weekend retreat. Nixon once slept here in the room where Mme de Pompadour died. Mme de Maintenon also slept here, as did Napoleon. The original furnishings are gone, of course, with mostly Empire pieces there today.

Gabriel, the designer of place de la Concorde in Paris, built the **Petit Trianon** ★★ in 1768 for Louis XV. Louis used it for his trysts with Mme du Barry. When he died, Louis XVI presented it to his wife, and Marie Antoinette adopted it as her favorite residence, a place to escape the rigid life and oppressive scrutiny at the main palace. Many of the current furnishings, including a few in her rather modest bedchamber, belonged to the ill-fated queen.

Rousseau's theories about recapturing the natural beauty and noble simplicity of life were much in favor in the late 18th century, and they prompted Marie Antoinette to have Mique build her a 12-house **Hamlet (Le Hameau)** on the banks of the Grand Trianon Lake in 1783. She wanted a chance to experience the simplicity of peasant life—or at least peasant life as seen through the eyes of a frivolous queen. Dressed as a shepherdess, she would come here to watch sheep being tended and cows being milked, men fishing, washerwomen beating their laundry in the lake, and donkey carts bringing corn to be ground at the mill. The interiors of the hamlets cannot be visited, but their informal landscapings—in obvious contrast to the formality of the other gardens at Versailles—and bizarre origins make views of their exteriors one of the most popular attractions here.

Follow the signs from the Place d'Armes (to the immediate right after entering the Palace of Versailles). ℭ 01-30-83-78-00. Entrance to both Trianons 5€ ($4.50) for adults, 3.05€ ($2.70) for senior citizens, free for children under 18. After 3:30pm, entrance to both Trianons reduced to 3.05€ ($2.70) for adults. May–Sept daily noon–6pm; Oct–Apr daily noon–5pm.

SEASONAL EVENTS

SUMMER EVENING SPECTACLES   The **Fêtes de Nuit de Versailles (Rêve de Roi)** is a government-sponsored summer program of evening fireworks and illuminated fountains. These always capture the heightened sense of the glory of France's *ancien régime*. At randomly scattered Saturday evenings in July and September, with exact dates for 2003 not yet established at press time for this guide, 200 actors in period costume portray Louis XVI and members of his court against a backdrop of exploding fireworks. You sit on bleachers clustered at the château's boulevard de la Reine entrance, adjacent to the Fountain (Bassin) of Neptune. Depending on the location of your seat, tickets cost between 20€ ($18) and 38€ ($34) each. Gates that admit you into the bleacher area open 90 minutes before showtime, and the show itself lasts 90 minutes.

You can buy tickets in advance at the **tourist office** in Versailles (see above)—inquire by phone, fax, or mail—or in Paris at any of the **FNAC** stores (p. 266). You can also take your chances and buy tickets an hour prior to the event from a kiosk adjacent to the boulevard de la Reine entrance. Call ✆ **01-30-83-78-00** for general info about any of the nighttime or afternoon spectacles on the grounds.

AFTERNOON PROMENADES IN THE PARK *(Moments* Every Sunday between early April and mid-October, and every Saturday between July and September between 11am and noon and between 3:30pm and 5:30pm, classical music is broadcast through the park and the fountains are turned on. (Virtually every fountain in the park is turned on in stages. The most charming displays occur between 3:30 and 5:30pm.) These **Grandes Eaux Musicales** duplicate the aesthetic vision of the 18th-century architects who designed Versailles. During these sessions, hundreds of visitors walk freely around the park, enjoying the grand architecture, lavish waterworks, and recorded music of the same period as the palace's construction. The cost of admission to the park during these events is 5€ ($4.50) for adults, free for persons under 18.

WHERE TO DINE

Le Potager du Roy *★* FRENCH Philippe Letourneur cooks from the heart, specializing in a simple cuisine with robust flavors. His restaurant occupies an 18th-century building in a neighborhood known as the Parc des Cerfs ("Stag Park," where courtiers could find paid companionship with B- and C-list courtesans). The skillfully prepared menu is reinvented with the seasons and may include foie gras with vegetable-flavored vinaigrette, roasted duck with a navarin of vegetables, macaroni ragout with a persillade of snails, and roasted codfish with roasted peppers in the style of Provence. For something unusual, order the fondant of pork jowls with a confit of fresh vegetables. Try to save room for the chocolate cake, flavored with orange and served with coconut ice cream.

1 rue du Maréchal-Joffre. ✆ 01-39-50-35-34. Reservations required. Fixed-price menu 23€ ($20) at lunch, 30€–44€ ($26–$39) at dinner. AE, V. Tues–Fri noon–2:30pm and 7–10:30pm; Sat 7–10:30pm.

Le Quai No. 1 *(Value* FRENCH/SEAFOOD This informal bistro occupies an 18th-century building overlooking the château's western facade. Lithographs and wood paneling spangle the dining room, and outside is a terrace. Though the cuisine isn't as opulent or expensive as what's served in chef Gérard Vié's grander Les Trois Marches (below), it's charming and dependable in presentation. The fixed-price menus make Le Quai a bargain. Specialties are grilled sole, grilled sea bass, seafood paella, bouillabaisse, home-smoked salmon, and an upscale version of North American surf and turf, with grilled lobster and sizzling sirloin. Care and imagination go into the food, and the service is professional and polite.

1 av. de St-Cloud. ✆ 01-39-50-42-26. Reservations required. Main courses 14€ ($12); fixed-price menu 15€–30€ ($14–$27) at lunch, 19€–30€ ($17–$27) at dinner. MC, V. Tues–Sun noon–2:30pm; Tues–Sat 7:30–11pm.

Les Trois Marches ★★★ FRENCH   This is one of the best restaurants in the Ile de France. The Hôtel Trianon Palace became famous in 1919 when it served as headquarters for signatories to the Treaty of Versailles, and the dining room retains an old-world splendor. Gérard Vié is the most talented and creative chef in town, attracting a discerning crowd that doesn't mind paying the high prices. His *la cuisine de la gastronomie française* is subtle, often daring, and the service is smooth. A warm *parmentier* (potato preparation) of crayfish and oysters, both ingredients *en tartare* and both of them "salted" with caviar; a tartare of lobster that's minced, then poached, then fried, and served with aromatic herbs; scallops cooked on their shell with a covering of braised endives and exotic mushrooms; and rack of suckling veal pierced with truffles and served with a reduction of artichokes and salsify. In autumn, you might find pennelike pasta, tossed with morels, mushrooms, and Parmesan and blended in a butter sauce with white Alba truffles. Dessert might include a deliberately undercooked (*très fondant*) coffee-flavored chocolate cake served with a chicory-flavored ice cream.

In the Hôtel Trianon Palace, 1 bd. de la Reine. ℂ **01-39-50-13-21.** Reservations required far in advance. Fixed-price menu 58€ ($52); 129€ ($115) set menu available anytime. AE, DC, MC, V. Tues–Sat 12:30–2pm and 7:30–10pm. Closed Aug.

2 The Forest & Château of Rambouillet ★

55km (34 miles) SW of Paris, 42km (26 miles) NE of Chartres

Once known as La Forêt d'Yveline, the **Forest of Rambouillet** ★ is one of the loveliest forests in France. More than 47,000 acres of greenery stretch from the valley of the Eure to the high valley of Chevreuse, the latter rich in medieval and royal abbeys. Lakes, copses of deer, and even wild boar are some of the attractions of this "green lung." Most people, however, come here to see the château, which you can visit when it's not in use as a "Camp David" for French presidents.

ESSENTIALS

GETTING THERE   It takes 2 hours to see the château at Rambouillet. **Trains** depart from Paris's Gare Montparnasse every 30 minutes throughout the day. One-way passage costs 6.40€ ($5.70) for about a 35-minute ride. Information and train schedules can be obtained by contacting **La Gare de Rambouillet,** place Prud'homme (ℂ **01-53-90-20-20**). By **car,** take N-10 southwest from Paris, passing Versailles along the way.

VISITOR INFORMATION   The **tourist office** is at the Hôtel de Ville, place de la Libération (ℂ **01-34-83-21-21**).

SEEING THE CHATEAU

Château de Rambouillet ★   Dating from 1375, the château is surrounded by a park in one of the most famous forests in France. Superb woodwork is used throughout, and the walls are adorned with tapestries, many from the era of Louis XV. Before it became a royal residence, the marquise de Rambouillet kept a house here; it's said she taught Paris's cultured ladies and gentlemen how to talk, introducing them to poets and painters. François I, the Chevalier king, died of a fever here in 1547 at age 52. When the château was later occupied by the comte de Toulouse, Rambouillet was often visited by Louis XV, who was amused (in more ways than one) by the comte's high-spirited wife. Louis XVI eventually acquired the château, but Marie Antoinette found it boring and called it "the toad." In his surprisingly modest boudoir are four panels representing the continents.

Moments **Through an Enchanted Forest**

Rambouillet and its forests can provide a verdant interlude. If you've exhausted the idea of a ramble through the gardens that surround the château (or if they're closed because of a visit from the President of France), consider a visit to the **Rochers d'Angennes,** rocky hillocks that remain as leftovers from the Ice Age. To reach them, park your car on the D107, about 4km (2½ miles) north of the hamlet of Epernon. At the site, where you'll see a sign pointing to the **Rochers et Etang d'Angennes,** you can park your car and walk along a clearly marked trail, through a pine forest, before you eventually reach a rocky plateau overlooking the hills and a pond (*l'Etang d'Angennes*) nestled into the surrounding country-side. Round-trip, from the site of your parked car to the plateau and back, your promenade should take between 30 and 45 minutes.

In 1814, Napoleon's second wife, Marie-Louise (daughter of Francis II, emperor of Austria), met at Rambouillet with her father, who convinced her to abandon Napoleon and France after her husband's defeats at Moscow and Leipzig. Afterward, she fled to her original home, the royal court in Vienna, with Napoleon's 3-year-old son, François-Charles-Joseph Bonaparte (also known as l'Aiglon, the young eagle, and, at least in title, the king of Rome). Before his death in Vienna at age 21, his claim on the Napoleonic legacy was rejected by France's enemies, despite the fact that his father had had a special annex to the château at Rambouillet built especially for his use. Before his final exile to the remote island of St. Helena, Napoleon insisted on spending a final night at Rambouillet, where he secluded himself with his meditations and memories.

In 1830, the elderly Charles X, Louis XVI's brother, abdicated the throne at Rambouillet as a mob marched on the château and his troops began to desert him. From Rambouillet, he embarked for a safe but controversial haven in England. Afterward, Rambouillet fell into private hands. At one time it was a fashionable restaurant attracting Parisians by offering gondola rides. Napoleon III returned it to the Crown. In 1897, it was designated a residence for the presidents of the Republic. In 1944, Charles de Gaulle lived here briefly before giving the order for what was left of the French army to join the Americans in liberating Paris.

Parc du Château. (*C*) **01-34-83-00-25.** Admission 5.45€ ($4.90) adults, 3.50€ ($3.10) students 12–25, free for children 11 and under. Wed–Mon 10–11:30am and 2–5:30pm (to 4:30pm Oct–Mar).

WHERE TO DINE

La Poste TRADITIONAL FRENCH   On a street corner in the town's historic center, this restaurant dates from the mid–19th century, when it provided meals and shelter for the region's mail carriers. The two dining rooms have rustic beams and old-fashioned accents that complement the flavorful old-fashioned food. Good-tasting menu items include a fricassee of chicken and crayfish; noisettes of lamb "prepared in the style of a roebuck," with a *Grand Veneur* sauce (that's made with red wine, autumn berries, a touch of vinegar "to make it acidic," and crème fraîche). Also popular are civets of both female venison (*une bîche*) and rabbit.

101 rue du Général-de-Gaulle. (*C*) **01-34-83-03-01.** Reservations recommended Sat–Sun. Main courses 17€–19€ ($15–$17); fixed-price menu 19€–30€ ($17–$27). AE, MC, V. Tues–Sun noon–2pm; Tues–Wed and Fri–Sat 7–10pm.

3 The Cathedral at Chartres ⓐⓐⓐ

97km (60 miles) SW of Paris, 76km (47 miles) NW of Orléans

Many observers feel the architectural aspirations of the Middle Ages reached their highest expression in the glorious Cathédrale de Chartres. Come to see its soaring architecture, highly wrought sculpture, and, above all, its stained glass, which gave the world a new color: Chartres blue.

ESSENTIALS

GETTING THERE   It takes a full day to see Chartres. From Paris's Gare Montparnasse, **trains** run directly to Chartres, taking less than an hour and passing through a sea of wheat fields. **By car,** take A10/A11 southwest from the *périphérique* and follow the signs to Le Mans and Chartres.

VISITOR INFORMATION   The **tourist office** is on place de la Cathédrale (© 02-37-18-26-26).

SEEING THE CATHEDRAL

Cathédrale Notre-Dame de Chartres ⓐⓐⓐ   Reportedly, Rodin once sat for hours on the sidewalk, admiring this cathedral's Romanesque sculpture. His opinion: Chartres is the French Acropolis. When it began to rain, a kind soul offered him an umbrella, which he declined, so transfixed was he by this place.

The cathedral's origins are uncertain; some have suggested it grew up over an ancient Druid site that later became a Roman temple. As early as the 4th century, there was a Christian basilica here. An 1194 fire destroyed most of what had by then become a Romanesque cathedral but spared the western facade and crypt. The cathedral you see today dates principally from the 13th century, when it was rebuilt with the efforts and contributions of kings, princes, churchmen, and pilgrims from all over Europe. One of the world's greatest high Gothic cathedrals, it was the first to use flying buttresses to support the soaring dimensions within.

French sculpture in the 12th century broke into full bloom when the **Royal Portal** ⓐⓐⓐ was added. A landmark in Romanesque art, the sculptured bodies are elongated, often stylized, in their long flowing robes. But the faces are amazingly (for the time) lifelike, occasionally winking or smiling. In the central tympanum, Christ is shown at the Second Coming, with his descent depicted on the right, his ascent on the left. Before entering, walk around to both the **North Portal** and the **South Portal,** each from the 13th century. They depict such biblical scenes as the expulsion of Adam and Eve from the Garden of Eden.

Inside is a celebrated **choir screen;** work on it began in the 16th century and lasted until 1714. The niches, 40 in all, contain statues illustrating scenes from the life of the Madonna and Christ—everything from the *Massacre of the Innocents* to the *Coronation of the Virgin.*

But few rushed visitors ever notice the screen: They're too transfixed by the light from the **stained glass** ⓐⓐⓐ. Covering an expanse of more than 3,000 square yards, the glass is unlike anything else in the world. The stained glass, most

⟨ *Moments*   Music of the Spheres

If you're visiting Chartres on a Sunday afternoon, the cathedral features a free 1-hour organ concert at 4:45pm, when the filtered light of the Ile de France sunset makes the western windows come thrillingly alive.

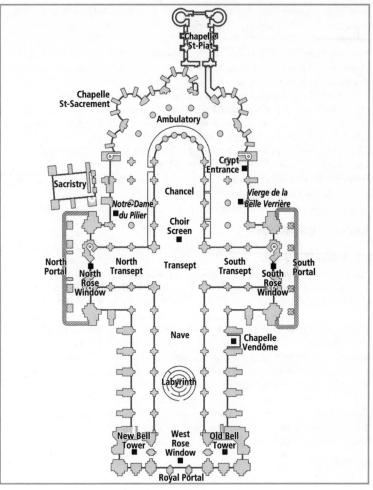

of which dates from the 12th and 13th centuries, was spared in both world wars by painstakingly removing it piece by piece. See the windows in the morning, at noon, in the afternoon, at sunset—as often as you can. Like the petals of a kaleidoscope, they constantly change. It's difficult to single out one panel or window above the others, but an exceptional one is the 12th-century *Vierge de la belle verrière* (**Our Lady of the Beautiful Window**) on the south side. Of course, there are three fiery rose windows, but you couldn't miss those if you tried.

The **nave,** the widest in France, still contains its ancient floor labyrinth, which formed a mobile channel of contemplation for monks. The wooden *Notre-Dame du piller* (**Virgin of the Pillar**), to the left of the choir, dates from the 14th century. The crypt was built over 2 centuries, beginning in the 9th. Enshrined within is *Our Lady of the Crypt,* a 1976 Madonna that replaced one destroyed during the Revolution.

Try to take a tour conducted by **Malcolm Miller** (© **02-37-28-15-58;** fax 02-37-28-33-03), an Englishman who has spent 3 decades studying the cathedral, who leads tours in English with a rare blend of scholarship, enthusiasm, and humor. He usually conducts 75-minute tours at noon and 2:45pm Monday to Saturday for 6.10€ ($5.45). Tours are canceled in the event of pilgrimages, religious celebrations, and large funerals. French-language tours at 5.30€ ($4.75) are conducted by other guides from Easter to late October at 10:30am and 3pm and the rest of the year at 2:30pm.

If you feel fit enough, don't miss the opportunity, especially in summer, to climb to the top of the **New Bell Tower.** Open the same hours as the cathedral, except for a closing between noon and 2pm, it costs 3.80€ ($3.40) for adults and 2.30€ ($2.05) for students. The **crypt,** gloomy and somber but rich with a sense of medieval history, can be visited only as part of a French-speaking tour conducted whenever there's enough demand. The cost is 1.65€ ($1.50).

After your visit, stroll through the **Episcopal Gardens** and enjoy yet another view of this remarkable cathedral.

16 Cloître Notre-Dame. © 02-37-21-59-08. Admission free. Mon–Sat 8:30am–7pm; Sun 8:30am–7pm.

EXPLORING THE OLD TOWN

If time remains, you may want to explore the medieval cobbled streets of the **Vieux Quartier** (Old Town). At the foot of the cathedral are lanes containing gabled houses and humped bridges spanning the Eure River. From the pont de Bouju, you can see the lofty spires in the background. Try to find **rue Chantault,** which boasts houses with colorful facades, one 8 centuries old.

A highlight of your visit will be **Musée des Beaux-Arts de Chartres** , 29 Cloître Notre-Dame (© **02-37-36-41-39**), next to the cathedral. A former Episcopal palace, the building at times competes with its exhibitions—one part dates from the 15th century and encompasses a courtyard. This museum of fine arts boasts a collection covering the 16th to the 20th centuries, including the work of masters like Zurbarán, Watteau, and Brósamer. Of particular interest is David Ténier's *Le Concert.* From October 31 to May 2, it's open Wednesday to Monday from 10am to noon and 2 to 5pm; the rest of the year, hours are Wednesday to Monday from 10am to noon and 2 to 6pm. Admission is 2.45€ ($2.15) for adults and 1.20€ ($1.10) for students, and free for children under 12.

WHERE TO STAY

Hotel Châtelet   This modern hotel has many traditional touches. The rustic guest rooms are inviting, with reproductions of Louis XV and Louis XVI furniture. The larger, more expensive rooms face a garden and avoid street noise. Many windows along the back garden side of the hotel open onto a view of the cathedral. The baths are boxy, without a lot of shelf space. In chilly weather, there's a log-burning fire in one of the salons. Breakfast is the only meal served, but there are numerous restaurants close by.

6-8 av. Jehan-de-Beauce, 28000 Chartres. © **02-37-21-78-00.** Fax 02-37-36-23-01. www.hotelchatelet. com. 48 units. 59€–75€ ($53–$67) double. 3rd person 9.10€ ($8.15) extra. AE, DC, MC, V. Free parking. *In room:* TV, minibar, hair dryer.

Le Grand Monarque Best Western   Chartres's leading hotel occupies a mid-19th-century building around a courtyard. It attracts people who enjoy its old-world charm, with its Art Nouveau stained glass and Louis XV chairs in the dining room. The guest rooms are decorated with reproductions of antiques, and most have sitting areas. The baths are motel standard. The hotel also has an anachronistic restaurant (a local critic found the kitchen trapped in an "*ancien régime* time warp").

22 place des Epars, 28005 Chartres. ✆ **800/528-1234** in the U.S., or 02-37-21-00-72. Fax 02-37-36-34-18. www.bw-grand-monarque.com. 55 units. 96€–141€ ($86–$126) double; 192€ ($171) suite. AE, DC, MC, V. Parking 7.60€ ($6.80). **Amenities:** Restaurant; brasserie; bar; room service; laundry/dry cleaning. *In room:* TV, minibar.

WHERE TO DINE

La Vieille Maison 🏵🏵 MODERN FRENCH   Even if the food here wasn't superb, the 14th-century building that contains it could be visited for its historic value. The dining room, outfitted in the Louis XIII style and tones of deep reds and soft green, is centered around a narrow ceiling vault, less than 2m (6 ft.) across, crafted of chiseled white stone blocks during the 800s. Cuisine is supervised by Bruno Letartre, who is the only *maître cuisinier de France* in Chartres. The menu changes between four and five times a year, reflecting the seasonality of the Ile de France and its produce. Recent examples that have impressed local critics include foie gras of duckling; roasted crayfish with Indian spices; *profiterolles* stuffed with a mixture of snails and frog's legs served with a parsley-flavored cream sauce; crisp-roasted sea bass with a confit of tomatoes and rice; supreme of turbot with saffron, baby vegetables, and saffron; and noisettes of venison fried with both Jamaican and Szechuan pepper and wild mushrooms. Dessert raves go to an apple-and-fig tart served with walnut-flavored ice cream.

5 rue au Lait. ✆ **02-37-34-10-67.** Reservations recommended. Set-price menus 27€ ($24) and 43€ ($39). Main courses 23€–43€ ($20–$39). MC, V. Tues–Sun noon–2:15pm; Tues–Sat 7–9:15pm. Closed 1 week in Aug.

Le Buisson Ardent *Value* TRADITIONAL FRENCH   Housed in a charming 16th-century house in the most historic section of town, this restaurant is one floor above street level in the shadow of the cathedral. The fixed-price menus change with the seasons. The least expensive is one of the town's best luncheon values, and an excellent break on your day trip. Everything is made with fresh meats, produce, and fish. The most popular dishes are escalope of foie gras with apples and Calvados, and émincée of roasted pigeon with sweetbreads and honey sauce. Other dishes are simpler, like codfish flavored with coriander and served with parsley flan. A dessert specialty is crispy hot pineapples with orange and passion fruit salad.

10 rue au Lait. ✆ **02-37-34-04-66.** Reservations recommended. Main courses 14€–23€ ($13–$20); fixed-price menu 16€ ($15) at lunch Mon–Fri or 21€–29€ ($19–$26) available anytime. MC, V. Thurs–Tues noon–2pm and 7:30–9:30pm.

4 Giverny 🏵

81km (50 miles) NW of Paris

On the border between Normandy and the Ile de France, **Giverny** is home to the Claude Monet Foundation, in the house where the Impressionist painter lived for 43 years. The restored house and its gardens are open to the public.

ESSENTIALS

GETTING THERE   It takes a full morning to get to Giverny and to see its sights. Take the Paris-Rouen **train** from Paris's Gare St-Lazare to the Vernon station, where a taxi can take you the 4km (2½ miles) to Giverny. Perhaps the easiest way to go is on a full-day **bus tour,** costing 96€ ($86) per person, whose focal point is Monet's house and garden. In summer, tours depart at 8am on Sunday and Wednesday. Arrange them through **Cityrama,** 4 place des Pyramides, 1er (✆ **01-44-55-61-00;** Métro: Palais Royal), or year-round by contacting **American Express,** 11 rue Scribe, 9e (✆ **01-47-14-50-00;** Métro: Opéra).

By **car,** take the Autoroute de l'Ouest (Port de St-Cloud) toward Rouen. Leave the autoroute at Bonnières, then cross the Seine on the pont de Bonnières. From here, a direct road with signs will bring you to Giverny. Expect about an hour of driving; try to avoid weekends. Another way to get there is to leave the highway at the Bonnières exit and go toward Vernon. Once in Vernon, cross the bridge over the Seine and follow the signs to Giverny or Gasny (Giverny is before Gasny). This is easier than going through Bonnières, where there aren't many signs.

SEEING MONET'S HOUSE & GARDEN

Claude Monet Foundation ✯✯✯ French painter Claude Monet was a spiritualist of light, brilliantly translating its effects at different times of the day. In fact, some critics claim he "invented light." His series of paintings of the Rouen Cathedral and of the water lilies, which one critic called "vertical interpretations of horizontal lines," are just a few of his masterpieces.

Monet came to Giverny in 1883, at age 43. While taking a small railway linking Vetheuil to Vernon, he discovered the village at a point where the Epte stream joined the Seine. Many of his friends used to visit him here at Le Pressoir, including Clemenceau, Cézanne, Rodin, Renoir, Degas, and Sisley. When Monet died in 1926, his son, Michel, inherited the house but left it abandoned until it decayed into ruins. The gardens became almost a jungle, inhabited by river rats. In 1966, Michel died and left the house to the Académie des Beaux-Arts. It wasn't until 1977 that Gerald van der Kemp, who restored Versailles, decided to work on Giverny. A large part of it was restored with gifts from American benefactors, especially the late Lila Acheson Wallace, former head of *Reader's Digest.*

You can stroll through the garden and view the thousands of flowers, including the famous *nymphéas* (water lilies). The Japanese bridge, hung with wisteria, leads to a dreamy setting of weeping willows and rhododendrons. Monet's studio barge was installed on the pond.

Rue Claude-Monet Parc Gasny. ✆ 02-32-51-28-21. Admission 5.30€ ($4.75) adults, 3.05€ ($2.70) ages 7–18, free for children under 7. Apr–Oct Tues–Sun 10am–6pm.

WHERE TO DINE

Auberge du Vieux Moulin TRADITIONAL FRENCH This stone-sided restaurant is a convenient lunch stop where the Boudeau family maintains a series of cozy dining rooms filled with Impressionist paintings. Because you can walk here from the museum, leave your car in the museum lot. Specialties include appetizers like snails in puff pastry with garlic-flavored butter sauce, guinea fowl braised in cider, chicken with shrimp, and escalope of salmon with sorrel sauce. Dessert might be a *tarte Normande* with apple slices and Calvados. The kitchen doesn't pretend the food is any more than it is: hearty country fare with panache.

21 rue de la Falaise. ✆ 02-32-51-46-15. Main courses 12€–15€ ($11–$13); fixed-price menu 20€–24€ ($18–$22). MC, V. Tues–Sun noon–3pm and 7:30–10pm. Closed Sat–Sun in Nov (same hours).

5 Disneyland Paris

32km (20 miles) E of Paris

After provoking some of the most controversial reactions in recent French history, the multimillion-dollar Euro Disney Resort opened in 1992 as one of the world's most lavish theme parks, situated on a site about one-fifth the size of Paris in the suburb of Marne-la-Vallée. In 1994, it unofficially changed its name to Disneyland Paris. In its early days, European journalists delighted in belittling

Sizing Up Monsieur Mickey

In terms of how Disneyland Paris compares to Disney's parks in the United States, it's in the middle of the pack, with top honors going to Florida's Walt Disney World and California's Disneyland running a distant third. The layout of Disneyland Paris resembles the Orlando Magic Kingdom, but the French property is smaller and has fewer attractions and rides. Disneyland Paris expanded in 2002 with the addition of Walt Disney Studios (see below).

it and accusing it of everything from cultural imperialism to the death knell of French culture. But after a rough start, the resort is on track.

In fact, it's now the number one attraction in France, with 50 million annual visitors. MONSIEUR MICKEY TRIUMPHS! the French press headlined. Disney surpasses the Eiffel Tower and the Louvre in numbers of visitors and accounts for 4% of the tourism industry's foreign currency sales. Disneyland Paris looks, tastes, and feels like its parents in California and Florida—except for the European flair (the use of pastel colors rather than primary colors) and the $10 cheeseburgers *"avec pommes frites."* Allow a full day to see the park.

ESSENTIALS

GETTING THERE   The resort is linked to the **RER** commuter express rail network (Line A), which maintains a stop within walking distance of the park. Board the RER at such Paris stops as Charles de Gaulle-Etoile, Châtelet-Les Halles, or Nation. Get off at Line A's last stop, Marne-la-Vallée/Chessy, 45 minutes from central Paris. The round-trip fare from central Paris is 12€ ($11). Trains run every 10 to 20 minutes, depending on the time of day.

Each of the hotels in the resort connects by **shuttle bus** to both Orly and Charles de Gaulle. Buses depart from both airports at intervals of 45 minutes. One-way transportation to the park from either airport costs 14€ ($12).

If you're coming by **car,** take A-4 east from Paris, getting off at exit 14, marked PARC EURO DISNEYLAND. Guest parking at any of the thousands of parking spaces is 6.85€ ($6.10) per day. An interconnected series of moving sidewalks speeds up pedestrian transit from the parking areas to the theme park's entrance. Parking for guests at any of the resort's hotels is free.

SPENDING THE DAY AT DISNEY

Disneyland Paris ★★★   The resort was designed as a total vacation destination: Included within one enormous unit are the Disneyland Park with its five entertainment "lands," six hotels, a campground, an entertainment center (Village Disney), a 27-hole golf course, and dozens of restaurants, shows, and shops. Peak season is mid-June to mid-September, as well as Christmas and Easter weeks. Entrance to Village Disney is free, though there's usually a cover charge for the dance clubs.

In the park, **Main Street, U.S.A.** features horse-drawn carriages and street-corner barbershop quartets. From the Main Street Station, steam-powered trains leave for a trip through a Grand Canyon Diorama to **Frontierland,** with paddle-wheel steamers reminiscent of the Mississippi Valley described by Mark Twain. The park's steam trains chug past **Adventureland**—with swashbuckling 18th-century pirates, the tree house of the Swiss Family Robinson, and a roller coaster called Indiana Jones and the Temple of Peril . . . Backwards! that travels in

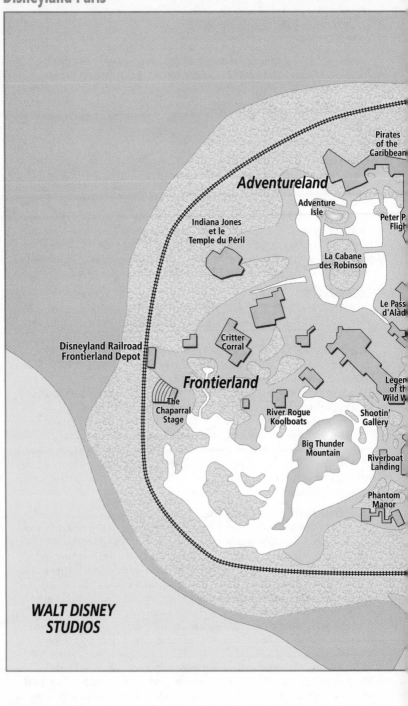

Disneyland Railroad
Fantasyland Station

Casey Jr.
Le Petit
Train du Cirque

Festival
Stage

Labyrinth

Dumbo the
Flying Elephant

Mad Hatter's
Tea Cups

Le Pays des
Contes de Fées

Les Pirouettes
du Vieux Moulin

Fantasyland

It's a Small World

Le Carrousel
de Lancelot

es Voyages
e Pinocchio

lanche-Neige
les Sept Nains

Le Château
du Belle au
Bois Dormant

Le Théâtre
du Château

Le Visionarium

Disneyland Railroad
Discoveryland Station

Vidéopolis

Star Tours

CinéMagique

Central
Plaza

Orbitron

Space
Mountain

Autopia

Les Mystères
du Nautilus

Main Street,
U.S.A.

Discoveryland

Liberty
Arcade

Discovery
Arcade

Main Street
Vehicles

Horse-Drawn
Streetcars

isneyland Railroad
Main Street Station

Guest Relations
Window

Park Entrance

reverse—to **Fantasyland.** Here you can see the symbol of the park, the Sleeping Beauty Castle (*Le Château de la belle au bois dormant*), whose soaring pinnacles and turrets are a spectacular idealized interpretation of the châteaux of France.

Visions of the future are displayed at **Discoveryland,** whose tributes to human invention and imagination are drawn from the works of Leonardo da Vinci, Jules Verne, H. G. Wells, the modern masters of science fiction, and the *Star Wars* series. Discoveryland has proven among the most popular of all the areas and is one of the few that was enlarged (in 1995) after the park's inauguration. A noteworthy addition was a new roller coaster called **Space Mountain,** which emulates an earth-to-moon transit as conceived by Jules Verne. Another popular attraction here is an in-theater experience, **Honey, I Shrunk the Kids,** where 3-D and animation gives the illusion that the audience has been shrunk.

As Disney continues to churn out animated blockbusters, look for its newest stars to appear in the park. The fact that the characters from such films as *Aladdin, The Lion King,* and *Pocahontas* are actually made of celluloid hasn't kept them out of the Ice Capades, and it certainly won't keep them out of Disneyland Paris.

Disney also maintains an entertainment center, **Village Disney,** whose indoor/outdoor layout is a cross between a California mall and the Coney Island boardwalk. Scattered on either side of a pedestrian walkway, illuminated by overhead spotlights, it's just outside the boundaries of the fenced-in acreage containing the bulk of Disneyland's attractions. The complex accommodates dance clubs, snack bars, restaurants, souvenir shops, and bars for adults who want to escape from the children for a while. Unlike the rest of the park, admission to **Village Disney** is free, so it attracts night owls from Paris and its suburbs who wouldn't otherwise be particularly interested in the park itself.

Disneyland Paris recognizes that long lines tend to frustrate families. In 2000 the park inaugurated the **Fast Pass** system, where participants go to various popular rides and receive a reservation for a 1-hour time block within which they should return. Within that 1-hour period, waiting times are usually no more than 8 minutes. This system is presently used for five of the most popular rides: Space Mountain (Discoveryland), Indiana Jones and the Temple of Peril . . . Backwards! (Adventureland), Big Thunder Mountain (Frontierland), Star Tours (Discoveryland), and Peter Pan's Flight (Fantasyland).

The park places height restrictions on only three rides. Riders of Big Thunder Mountain roller coaster must be at least 1m (3 ft., 3 in.) tall; and riders of both Space Mountain and Indiana Jones and the Temple of Peril . . . Backwards! must be at least 1 meter, 40 centimeters (4 ft., 7 in.) tall.

Other than that, age suggestions for individual rides become meaningless, because many adults seem to adore rides that are safe for even the youngest children, like Peter Pan's Flight and Snow White's Ride. The official guide to the park, distributed free at the resort's hotels and at City Hall on Main Street U.S.A., gives subtle suggestions, but it's anything but dictatorial (in fact, it's deliberately vague) about delineating which rides are suitable for which age groups.

Guided 3½-hour tours for 20 or more people can be arranged for 7.60€ ($6.80) for adults and 5.30€ ($4.75) for children 3 to 11. In view of the well-marked paths leading through the park and the availability of printed information in any language, the guided tours aren't really necessary. You can rent coin-operated lockers for 1.50€ ($1.35) and can store larger bags for 2.30€ ($2.05) per day. Children's strollers and wheelchairs rent for 4.55€ ($4.05) per day, with a 4.55€ ($4.05) deposit. Babysitting is available at any of the hotels if 24-hour advance notice is given.

Marne-la-Vallée. ℂ **01-60-30-60-53** (Disneyland Paris Guest Relations office, in City Hall on Main Street, U.S.A.). www.disneylandparis.com. Admission to park for 1 day, depending on season, 27€–36€ ($24–$32) adults, 23€–28€ ($21–$25) children 3–12, free for children 2 and under. Oct–May daily 9am–8pm; June–Sept daily 9am–11pm, depending on school and public holidays.

FOR THOSE WITH AN EXTRA DAY: WALT DISNEY STUDIOS

Next to Disneyland, **Walt Disney Studios** opened in the spring of 2002, offering a full day's experience as it takes guests on a behind-the-scenes interactive discovery of film, animation, and television. The audience is put right in the heart of the action. The four production areas of the studio are based on the real thing, and the park offers guests the chance to step through the screen and experience a world of attractions, entertainment, special effects, and never-seen-before shows.

The main entrance to the studios, called the Front Lot, consists of "Sunset Boulevard," which is an elaborate soundstage complete with hundreds of film props. The Animation Courtyard allows visitors to learn the trade secrets of Disney animators, and the Production Courtyard lets guests take a look behind the scenes of film and TV production. At Catastrophe Canyon guests are plunged into the heart of a film shoot. Finally, the Back Lot is home to special-effects and stunt workshops. A live stunt show features cars, motorbikes, and jet skis.

Marne-la-Vallée. ℂ **01-60-30-60-53**. Admission 27€–36€ ($24–$32) adults, 23€–28€ ($21–$25) children. Oct–May daily 9am–8pm; June–Sept daily 9am–11pm, depending on school and public holidays.

WHERE TO STAY

The only reason it's necessary to spend the night here is if you didn't get enough of Mickey Mouse the first day and want to hang out for another Disney adventure the following morning. Otherwise, you can easily make Disney a day trip from Paris because the transportation links are excellent.

The resort's six hotels share a reservation service. In North America, call ℂ **407/W-DISNEY.** In France, contact the **Central Reservations Office,** Euro Disney Resort, S.C.A., B.P. 105, F-77777 Marne-la-Vallée Cedex 4 (ℂ **01-60-30-60-30**).

VERY EXPENSIVE

Disneyland Hotel ★★ Mouseketeers who have rich daddies and mommies check in here at Disney's poshest hotel, charging Paris Ritz tariffs. At the park entrance, this flagship four-story hotel is Victorian, with red-tile turrets and jutting balconies. The spacious guest rooms are plushly furnished but evoke the image of Disney, with cartoon depictions and a candy-stripe decor. The beds are king, double, or twin; in some rooms armchairs convert to day beds. Paneled closets, large mirrors, and safes are found in some units. Accommodations in the rear overlook Sleeping Beauty's Castle and Big Thunder Mountain. Some less desirable units open onto a parking lot. The luxurious combination baths have marble vanities, tubs, and twin basins. On the Castle Club floor, you get free newspapers, all-day beverages, and access to a well-equipped private lounge.

Disneyland Paris, B.P. 105, F-77777 Marne-la-Vallée Cedex 4. ℂ **01-60-45-65-00.** Fax 01-60-45-65-33. www.disneylandparis.com. 496 units. 251€–509€ ($224–$455) double; from 760€ ($679) suite. Rates include breakfast. AE, DC, MC, V. **Amenities:** 2 restaurants; bar; health club with indoor/outdoor pool; whirlpool; sauna; room service; babysitting; laundry/dry cleaning. *In room:* A/C, TV, minibar, hair dryer, safe.

EXPENSIVE

Hotel New York ⊛   Picture an Art Deco New York of the '30s. Inspired by the Big Apple, this hotel is designed around a nine-story central "skyscraper" flanked by the Gramercy Park Wing and the Brownstones Wing. (The exteriors of both wings resemble row houses.) More interested in convention bookings, this hotel is less family-friendly than the others in the park. Guest rooms are comfortable, with Art Deco accessories, New York–inspired memorabilia, and roomy combination baths with twin basins and tub-and-shower combos. Try for one of the units fronting Lake Buena Vista instead of those facing the parking lot.

Disneyland Paris, B.P. 100, F-77777 Marne-la-Vallée Cedex 4. ⓒ 01-60-45-73-00. Fax 01-60-45-73-33. www.disneylandparis.com. 563 units. 155€–281€ ($138–$251) double; from 485€ ($433) suite. Rates include breakfast. AE, DC, DISC, MC, V. **Amenities:** 2 restaurants; bar; indoor and outdoor pool; exercise room; sauna; room service; babysitting. *In room:* A/C, TV, minibar, hair dryer, safe.

Newport Bay Club ⊛⊛   You expect to see the reincarnation of old Joe Kennedy walking along the large veranda with its slated roofs, awnings, and pergolas. It's very Hyannis Port here. It's also the biggest hotel in France. This hotel is designed with a central cupola, jutting balconies, and a blue-and-cream color scheme, reminiscent of a harbor-front New England hotel around 1900. The layout is irregular, with nautically decorated guest rooms in various shapes and sizes. The most spacious rooms are the corner units. The combination baths are roomy, with deluxe toiletries and tub and shower. The upscale **Yacht Club** and the less formal **Cape Cod** are the dining choices.

Disneyland Paris, B.P. 105, F-77777 Marne-la-Vallée Cedex 4. ⓒ 01-60-45-55-00. Fax 01-60-45-55-33. www.disneylandparis.com. 1,093 units. 135€–200€ ($120–$179) double; from 350€ ($312) suite. Rates include breakfast. AE, DC, MC, V. **Amenities:** 2 restaurants; bar; indoor and outdoor pool; health club; sauna. *In room:* A/C, TV, minibar, safe.

Sequoia Lodge   Built of gray stone and roughly textured planking and capped by a gently sloping green copper roof, this hotel resembles a lodge in the Rockies. The design, with parquet floors and giant chimneys, evokes the Prairie Houses of architect Frank Lloyd Wright. The hotel consists of a large central building with six chalets nearby, each housing 100 rooms. The guest rooms are comfortably rustic, with tiled baths with tub and shower (hair dryers available on request). **The Hunter's Grill** serves spit-roasted meats carved on your plate. Less formal is the **Beaver Creek Tavern.**

Disneyland Paris, B.P. 100, F-77777 Marne-la-Vallée Cedex 4. ⓒ 01-60-45-51-00. Fax 01-60-45-51-33. www.disneylandparis.com. 1,011 units. 164€–214€ ($146–$191) double; from 363€ ($324) suite. Rates include breakfast. AE, DC, MC, V. **Amenities:** 2 restaurants; bar; indoor/outdoor pool; health club; sauna; Jacuzzi. *In room:* A/C, TV, minibar.

MODERATE

Hotel Cheyenne/Hotel Santa Fe (Kids)   Next door to each other near a re-creation of Texas's Rio Grande and evoking the Old West, these are the resort's least expensive hotels. The Cheyenne accommodates visitors in 14 two-story buildings along Desperado Street; the Santa Fe, sporting a desert theme, encompasses four "nature trails" winding among 42 adobe-style pueblos. The Cheyenne is a particular favorite among families, offering a double bed and bunk beds. An array of activities are offered for children, including a play area in a log cabin with a lookout tower and a section where you can explore the "ruins" of an ancient Anasazi village. There's a mariachi atmosphere in the **Rio Grande Bar,** and country music in the **Red Garter Saloon Bar.** The only disadvantage, according to some parents with children, is the absence of a pool.

Tex-Mex specialties are offered at **La Cantina** (Santa Fe), and barbecue and smokehouse specialties predominate at the **Chuck Wagon Cafe** (Cheyenne).

Disneyland Paris, B.P. 115, F-77777 Marne-la-Vallée Cedex 4. ✆ **01-60-45-62-00** (Cheyenne) or 01-60-45-78-00 (Santa Fe). Fax 01-60-45-62-33 (Cheyenne) or 01-60-45-78-33 (Santa Fe). 2,000 units. Hotel Cheyenne 95€–155€ ($85–$138) double; Hotel Santa Fe 80€–132€ ($71–$117) double. Rates include breakfast. AE, DC, MC, V. **Amenities:** 2 restaurants; bar; 2 tennis courts; health club; sauna; hammock; room service; massage; babysitting. *In room:* A/C, TV, hair dryer, safe.

WHERE TO DINE

Disneyland Paris offers a gamut of cuisine in no less than 45 restaurants and snack bars. You can live on burgers and fries at this place, or you can experiment with vaunted cuisine that's best appreciated at the following upscale restaurants.

Auberge de Cendrillon TRADITIONAL FRENCH   This is a fairy-tale version of Cinderella's sumptuous country inn, with a glass couch in the center. A master of ceremonies, in a plumed tricorner hat and wearing an embroidered tunic and lace ruffles, welcomes you. There are corny elements here, but the chefs do go out of their way to make a big deal out of French cuisine. For the most part, they succeed admirably. The appetizers set the tone. Our favorites are their warm-goat-cheese salad with lardons or their smoked-salmon platter. Either choice will put you in the mood for some of the classics of the French table, especially loin of lamb roasted under a zesty mustard coating or tender sautéed veal medallions that are like nuggets of flavor. An aromatic chicken is also perfectly roasted in puff pastry. Because the restaurant follows the park's seasonal schedules, lunches are usually easier to arrange than dinners.

In Fantasyland. ✆ **01-64-74-24-02.** Reservations recommended. Main courses 17€–21€ ($15–$19); fixed-price menu 27€ ($24) for adults, 9.90€ ($8.80) for children. AE, DC, MC, V. Wed–Fri 11:30am–4pm; Sat 11:30am–7pm; Sun 11:30am–5pm.

California Grill ★★ CALIFORNIAN/FRENCH   This is the showcase restaurant of this vast Disney world. At the California Grill, the cuisine is the equivalent of a one-Michelin-star restaurant. Focusing on the lighter specialties for which the Golden State is famous, with many concessions to French palates, this elegant restaurant manages to accommodate both adults and children gracefully. Even French food critics are impressed with the chef's oysters prepared with leeks and salmon. We also embrace the appetizer of foie gras with roasted red peppers, and rate as "Simply fabulous" the entree of roasted pigeon with braised Chinese cabbage and black-rice vinegar. Another winning selection is fresh salmon roasted over beechwood and served with a sprinkling of walnut oil, sage sauce, asparagus, and fricassee of forest mushrooms. Many items, such as "Mickie's pizzas," spaghetti Bolognese, and grilled ham with fries, are specifically for children. If you want a quiet, mostly adult venue, go here as late as your hunger pangs will allow.

In the Disneyland Hotel. ✆ **01-60-45-65-00.** Reservations required. Main courses 15€–34€ ($13–$31); children's menu 14€ ($12). AE, DC, MC, V. Sun–Fri 7–11pm; Sat 6–11pm.

Inventions *(value* INTERNATIONAL   This might be the only buffet restaurant in Europe where animated characters, including Mickey and Minnie, go table-hopping in a way you'd expect from a family-friendly restaurant in Los Angeles. With views over a park, the restaurant contains both smoking and nonsmoking sections, and four enormous buffet tables devoted, respectively, to starters, shellfish, main courses, and desserts. Selections are wide, portions can be copious, and absolutely no one leaves this place hungry. Don't expect *grande* *cuisine*—that's the domain of the more upscale (also-recommended) **California Grill,** within the same hotel. What you'll get is a sense of American bounty and culinary generosity, with ample doses of cartoon fantasy thrown in for seasoning.

In the Disneyland Hotel. ℂ **01-60-45-65-83.** Reservations not necessary. Lunch buffet 30€ ($26) adults, 17€ ($15) children 7–11, 15€ ($13) children 3–6; dinner buffet 40€ ($35) adults, 22€ ($20) children 7–11, 17€ ($15) children 6–4 and under, free for children under 3. AE, DC, MC, V. Daily noon–3pm and 6–10:30pm.

DISNEYLAND AFTER DARK

The premier theatrical venue of Disneyland Paris is **Le Legende de Buffalo Bill** in the Disney Village (ℂ **01-60-45-71-00**). This twice-per-night stampede of entertainment recalls the show that once traveled the West with Buffalo Bill and Annie Oakley. You'll dine at tables arranged amphitheater-style around a rink where sharpshooters, runaway stagecoaches, and dozens of horses and Indians ride fast and perform alarmingly realistic acrobatics. A Texas-style barbecue, served assembly-line by waiters in 10-gallon hats, is part of the experience. Despite its corny elements, it's not without its charm and an almost mournful nostalgia for a way of life of another continent and another century. Wild Bill himself is dignified and the Indians suitably brave. Two shows are staged at 6:30 and 9:30pm costing (with dinner included) 49€ ($44) for adults, 30€ ($26) ages 3 to 11.

6 Fontainebleau ✦

60km (37 miles) S of Paris, 74km (46 miles) NE of Orléans

Within the vestiges of a forest that bears its name (the Forêt de Fontainebleau), this suburb of Paris has offered refuge to French monarchs throughout the country's history. Kings from the Renaissance valued it because of its nearness to rich hunting grounds and its distance from the slums and smells of the city. Napoleon referred to the Palais de Fontainebleau, which he embellished with his distinctive monogram and decorative style, as "the house of the centuries." Many pivotal and decisive events have occurred inside, perhaps none more memorable than when Napoleon stood on the horseshoe-shaped exterior stairway and bade farewell to his shattered army before departing for Elba.

After the glories of Versailles, a visit to Fontainebleau can be a bit of a letdown, especially if followed immediately on the day after you saw Versailles. Fontainebleau, although a grand château, actually looks like a place a king could live, whereas Versailles is more of a production.

ESSENTIALS

GETTING THERE If you stay for lunch, a trip to Fontainebleau should last a half-day. **Trains** depart from Paris's Gare de Lyon. The trip takes between 45 and 60 minutes each way and costs 6.40€ ($5.70) each way. Fontainebleau's rail station is 2km (3 miles) from the château, in Avon. A local bus (it's marked simply A/B Château) makes the trip to the château at 15-minute intervals Monday to Friday, and at 30-minute intervals every Saturday, for 1.45€ ($1.30) each way. By **car,** take A-6 south from Paris, exit onto N-191, and follow the signs.

VISITOR INFORMATION The **tourist office** is at 4 rue Royale (ℂ **01-60-74-99-99**).

SEEING THE PALACE

Palais de Fontainebleau ✦✦✦ Napoleon's affection for this palace was understandable. He followed the pattern of a succession of French kings in the

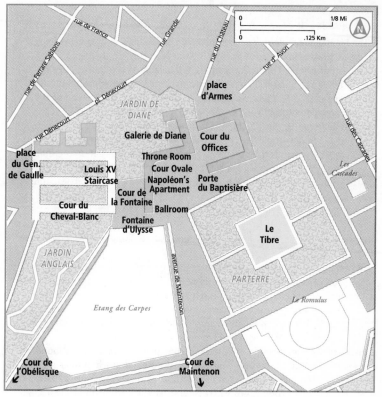

pre-Versailles days who used Fontainebleau as a resort and hunted in its forests. François I tried to turn the hunting lodge into a royal palace in the Italian Renaissance style, bringing artists, including Benvenuto Cellini, there to work for him. Under this patronage, the School of Fontainebleau gained prestige, led by painters Rosso Fiorentino and Primaticcio. The artists adorned the 63m (210-ft.) long **Gallery of François I** ★★★, where stucco-framed panels depict such scenes as *The Rape of Europa* and the monarch holding a pomegranate, a symbol of unity. The salamander, the symbol of the Chevalier king, is everywhere.

Sometimes called the Gallery of Henri II, the **Ballroom** ★★★ displays the interlaced initials "H&D," referring to Henri and his mistress, Diane de Poitiers. Competing with this illicit tandem are the initials "H&C," symbolizing Henri and his ho-hum wife, Catherine de Médicis. At one end of the room is a monumental fireplace supported by two bronze satyrs, made in 1966 (the originals were melted down during the Revolution). At the other side is the balcony of the musicians, with sculptured garlands. The ceiling displays octagonal coffering adorned with rosettes. Above the wainscoting is a series of frescoes, painted between 1550 and 1558, which depict mythological subjects such as *The Feast of Bacchus*. An architectural curiosity is the richly adorned **Louis XV Staircase** ★★. The room above it was originally decorated by Primaticcio for the bedroom of the duchesse d'Etampes, but when an architect was designing the stairway, he simply ripped out her floor. Of the Italian frescoes that were

Moments Hiking the Trails of French Kings

The Forest of Fontainebleau is riddled with hiking trails originally made by French kings and their entourages, who went hunting in the forest. A guide to the trails, *Guide des Sentiers*, is available at the tourist information center (see above). Bike paths are also cut through the forest. You can rent bikes at the Fontainebleau-Avon rail depot. At the station, go to the kiosk, **Location Mulot** (© **01-64-22-36-14**). Bike rental is 9.10€ ($8.15) per half-day, going up to 18€ ($16) for a regular bike for a full day. Open Monday to Friday from 10am to 6pm and Saturday and Sunday from 10am to 7pm. The most scenic route in our view is to take the trail on the map leading to Tour Denecourt, lying 5km (3 miles) northeast of the château. Along the way you can take in good views of the beeches, birches, and pines, a truly idyllic setting.

---

preserved, one depicts the queen of the Amazons climbing into Alexander the Great's bed.

When Louis XIV ascended to the throne, he neglected Fontainebleau because of his preoccupation with Versailles. However, he wasn't opposed to using the palace for houseguests, specifically such unwanted ones as Queen Christina, who had abdicated the throne of Sweden in a fit of religious fervor. Under the assumption that she still had "divine right," she ordered the brutal murder of her companion Monaldeschi, who had ceased to please her. Though Louis XV and then Marie Antoinette took an interest in Fontainebleau, the château found its renewed glory under Napoleon. You can wander around much of the palace on your own, visiting sites evoking the Corsican's 19th-century imperial heyday. They include the **throne room** where he abdicated his rulership of France, his **offices,** his monumental **bedroom,** and his **bathroom.** Some of the smaller Napoleonic Rooms contain his personal mementos and artifacts.

After your trek through the palace, visit the **gardens** and, especially, the **carp pond;** the gardens, however, are only a prelude to the Forest of Fontainebleau.

In the Forêt de Fontainebleau. © 01-60-71-50-70. Combination ticket for *grands appartements* 5.45€ ($4.90) adults, 3.65€ ($3.25) students 18–25, free for children under 18. Ticket to *petits appartements* and Napoleonic Rooms 3.05€ ($2.70) adults, 2.15€ ($1.90) students 18–25, free for children under 18. June–Sept Wed–Mon 9:30am–6pm; Oct–May Wed–Mon 9:30am–5pm.

WHERE TO STAY

Grand Hotel de l'Aigle-Noir (The Black Eagle) ★ Once the home of Cardinal de Retz, this mansion stands opposite the château. It was built with a formal courtyard entrance, using a high iron grille and pillars crowned by black eagles. It was converted into a hotel in 1720 and has recently been remodeled, making it the finest lodgings in town. The guest rooms are decorated with Louis XVI, Empire, or Restoration antiques or reproductions with plush mattresses and elegant bathroom amenities. All but four units have tub-shower combinations. The remaining four units have showers only. Have a drink in the Napoleon III–style piano bar. Later, you can dine on elegant French cuisine with formalized service in the grand dining room, **Le Beauharnais.**

27 place Napoléon-Bonaparte, 77300 Fontainebleau. © 01-60-74-60-00. Fax 01-60-74-60-01. www.hotel aiglenoir.fr. 56 units. 198€–230€ ($177–$205) double; from 380€ ($339) suite. AE, DC, MC, V. Parking 8.35€ ($7.45). **Amenities:** Restaurant; bar; indoor pool; exercise room; sauna; room service; babysitting; laundry/dry cleaning. *In room:* A/C, minibar, coffeemaker, hair dryer.

WHERE TO DINE

Le Caveau des Ducs TRADITIONAL FRENCH Beneath a series of 17th-century stone vaults, this restaurant occupies what was once a storage cellar for the château. Wood and flickering candles preserve the illusion. In terms of grandeur, it's not in the same league as Le Beauharnais, but it offers somewhat less pretentious food in a dramatic setting. Menu items are supervised by owner/chef André Murith, a longtime resident of Fontainebleau who's noted for his sense of humor. Examples include an excellent version of onion soup with a cheesy crust; marinated salmon with olive oil; a fried combination of foie gras with apples; a sweet and salty magret of duckling with caramelized apples; and a filet of rump steak served with Brie sauce. Desserts might include frozen nougat with red berries, or apple tart flambéed in Calvados and served with vanilla ice cream.

24 rue de Ferrare. ℂ **01-64-22-05-05.** Reservations recommended. Main courses 13€–20€ ($12–$18); fixed-price menu 20€–38€ ($18–$34). AE, MC, V. Daily noon–2pm and 7–10pm. Closed 2 weeks in Aug and 2 weeks at Christmastime.

Le François-Ier ✦ TRADITIONAL FRENCH The premier dining choice attracts with a Louis XIII decor, winemaking memorabilia, and walls the owners think are about 200 years old. If weather permits, sit on the terrace overlooking the château and the Cour des Adieux. In game season, the menu includes hare, roebuck, duck liver, and partridge. Other choices may be cold salmon with *cèpes* (flap mushrooms), *rognon de veau* (veal kidneys) with mustard sauce, and a salad of baby scallops with crayfish. The cuisine is meticulous, with an undeniable flair. The *magrêt de canard* (duck) flavored with cassis is delicious.

3 rue Royale. ℂ **01-64-22-24-68.** Reservations required. Main courses 13€–21€ ($12–$18); fixed-price menus 15€ ($13) at lunch Mon–Fri, 26€ ($23) available anytime. AE, DC, MC, V. Daily noon–2:30pm; Mon–Sat 7:30–10pm.

Appendix A:
Paris History 101

IN THE BEGINNING

Paris emerged at the crossroads of three major traffic arteries on the muddy island in the Seine that today is known as Ile de la Cité.

By around 2000 B.C., the island served as the fortified headquarters of the Parisii tribe, who called it Lutétia. The two wooden bridges connecting the island to the river's left and right banks were among the region's most strategically important, and the settlement attracted the attention of the Roman Empire. In his *Commentaries,* Julius Caesar described his conquest of Lutétia, recounting how its bridges were burned during the Gallic War of 52 B.C. and how the town on the island was pillaged, sacked, and transformed into a Roman-controlled stronghold.

Within a century, Lutétia became a full-fledged Roman town, and some of the inhabitants abandoned the frequently flooded island in favor of higher ground on what is today the Left Bank. By A.D. 200, barbarian invasions threatened the stability of Roman Gaul, and the populace from the surrounding hills flocked to the island's fortified safety. Over the next 50 years, a Christian community gained a foothold there. According to legend, St. Denis served as the city's first bishop (around 250). By this time the Roman Empire's political power had begun to wane in the region, the cultural and religious attachment of the community to the Christian bishops of Rome grew even stronger.

During the 400s, with the decline of the Roman armies, Germanic tribes from the east (the Salian Franks) were

Dateline

- 2000 B.C. Lutétia (Paris) thrives along a strategic crossing of the Seine, the headquarters of the Parisii tribe.
- 52 B.C. Julius Caesar conquers Lutétia during the Gallic Wars.
- A.D. 150 Lutétia flourishes as a Roman colony, expanding to the Left Bank.
- 200 Barbarian Gauls force the Romans to retreat to the fortifications on Ile de la Cité.
- 300 Lutétia is renamed Paris; Roman power weakens in northern France.
- 350 Paris's Christianization begins.
- 400s The Franks invade Paris, with social transformation from the Roman to the Gallo-Roman culture.
- 466 Clovis, founder of the Merovingian dynasty and first non-Roman ruler of Paris since the Parisii, is born.
- 800 Charlemagne, founder of the Carolingian dynasty, is crowned Holy Roman Emperor and rules from Aachen in modern Germany.
- 987 Hugh Capet, founder of France's foremost early medieval dynasty, rises to power; his family rules from Paris.
- 1100 The Université de Paris attracts scholars from throughout Europe.
- 1200s Paris's population and power grow, though it is often unsettled by plagues and feudal battles.
- 1422 England invades Paris during the Hundred Years' War.
- 1429 Joan of Arc tries to regain Paris for the French; the Burgundians later capture and sell her to the English, who burn her at the stake in Rouen.
- 1500s François I, first of the French Renaissance kings, embellishes Paris but chooses to maintain his court in the Loire Valley.
- 1549 Henri II rules from Paris; construction of public and private residences begins, many in the Marais.

continues

able to invade the island, founding a Frankish dynasty and prompting a Frankish-Latin fusion in the burgeoning town. The first of these Frankish kings, Clovis (466–511), founder of the Merovingian dynasty, embraced Christianity as his tribe's religion and spearheaded an explicit rejection of Roman cultural imperialism by encouraging the adoption of Parisii place names like "Paris," which came into common usage during this time.

The Merovingians were replaced by the Carolingians, whose heyday began with Charlemagne's coronation in 800. The Carolingian Empire sprawled over western Germany and eastern France, but Paris was never its capital. The city remained a commercial and religious center, sacred to the memory of St. Geneviève, who reputedly protected Paris when the Huns attacked it in the final days of the Roman Empire. The Carolingians came to an end in 987, when the empire fragmented because of the growing regional, political, and linguistic divisions between what would become modern France and modern Germany. Paris became the seat of a new dynasty, the Capetians, whose kings ruled France throughout the Middle Ages. Hugh Capet (ca. 938–996), the first of this line, ruled as comte de Paris and duc de France from 987 to 996.

THE MIDDLE AGES

Around 1100, Paris began to emerge as a great city, boasting on its Left Bank a university that attracted scholars from all over Europe. Meanwhile, kings and bishops began building the towering Gothic cathedrals of France, one of the greatest of which became Paris's Notre-Dame, a monument rising from the beating heart of the city. Paris's population increased greatly, as did the city's mercantile activity. During the 1200s, a frenzy of building transformed the skyline with convents

■ 1564 Construction begins on Catherine de Médicis's Palais des Tuileries; building facades in Paris move from half-timbered to more durable chiseled stonework.

■ 1572 The Wars of Religion reach their climax with the St. Bartholomew's Day massacre of Protestants.

■ 1598 Henri IV, the most eccentric and enlightened monarch of his era, endorses the Edict of Nantes, granting tolerance to Protestants; a crazed monk fatally stabs him 12 years later.

■ 1615 Construction begins on the Palais du Luxembourg for Henri IV's widow, Marie de Médicis.

■ 1636 The Palais Royal is launched by Cardinal Richelieu; soon two marshy islands in the Seine are interconnected and filled in to create Ile St-Louis.

■ 1643 Louis XIV, the "Sun King" and the most powerful ruler since the Caesars, rises to power; he moves his court to the newly built Versailles.

■ 1776 The American Declaration of Independence strikes a revolutionary chord in France.

■ 1789 The French Revolution begins.

■ 1793 Louis XVI and his Austrianborn queen, Marie Antoinette, are publicly guillotined.

■ 1799 Napoleon Bonaparte crowns himself Master of France and embellishes Paris further with neoclassical splendor.

■ 1803 Napoleon abandons French overseas expansion and sells Louisiana to America.

■ 1812 Napoleon is defeated in the Russian winter campaign.

■ 1814 Aided by a coalition of France's enemies, especially England, the Bourbon monarchy under Louis XVIII is restored.

■ 1821 Napoleon Bonaparte dies.

■ 1824 Louis XVIII dies and Charles X succeeds him.

■ 1830 Charles X is deposed and the more liberal Louis-Philippe is elected king; Paris prospers as it industrializes.

■ 1848 A violent working-class revolution deposes Louis-Philippe, who's replaced by autocratic Napoleon III.

continues

and churches (including the jewel-like Sainte-Chapelle, completed in 1249 after just 2 years). During the next century, the increasingly powerful French kings added dozens of monuments of their own.

As time passed, Paris's fortunes became closely linked to the power struggles between the French monarchs in Paris and the various highly competitive feudal lords of the provinces. Because of this tug-of-war, Paris was dogged by civil unrest, takeovers by one warring faction after another, and a dangerous alliance between the English and the powerful rulers of Burgundy during the Hundred Years' War. Around the same time, the city suffered a series of plagues, including the Black Death. To the humiliation of the French monarchs, the English army invaded the city in 1422. Joan of Arc (ca. 1412–31) tried unsuccessfully to reconquer Paris in 1429, and 2 years later the English, supported by a tribunal of French ecclesiastics, burned her at the stake in Rouen. Paris was reduced to poverty and economic stagnation, and its embittered and greatly reduced population turned to banditry and street crime to survive.

Despite Joan's ignominious end, the revolution she inspired continued until Paris was finally taken from the English in 1436. During the following several decades, the English retreated to the port of Calais, abandoning their once-mighty French territories. France, under the leadership of Louis XI (1423–83), witnessed an accelerating rate of change that included the transformation of a feudal and medieval social system into the nascent beginnings of a modern state.

THE RENAISSANCE & THE REFORMATION

The first of the Renaissance monarchs, François I (1494–1547), began an enlargement of Paris's Louvre (which had begun as a warehouse storing the

- **1853–70** On Napoleon III's orders, Baron Haussmann redesigns Paris's landscapes and creates the Grand Boulevards.
- **1860s** The Impressionist style emerges.
- **1870** The Franco-Prussian War ends in the defeat of France; Paris is threatened by Prussian cannons placed on the outskirts; a revolution in the aftermath of this defeat destroys the Palais des Tuileries and overthrows the government; the Third Republic rises with its elected president, Marshal MacMahon.
- **1878–1937** Several international expositions add monuments to the Paris skyline, including the Tour Eiffel and Sacré-Coeur.
- **1914–18** World War I rips apart Europe.
- **1940** German troops invade Paris; the French government, under Marshal Pétain, evacuates to Vichy, while the French Resistance under Gen. Charles de Gaulle maintains symbolic headquarters in London.
- **1944** U.S. troops liberate Paris; de Gaulle returns in triumph.
- **1948** The revolt in the French colony of Madagascar costs 80,000 French lives; France's empire continues to collapse in Southeast Asia and equatorial Africa.
- **1954–62** War begins in Algeria and is eventually lost; refugees flood Paris, and the nation becomes divided over its North African policies.
- **1958** France's Fourth Republic collapses; General de Gaulle is called out of retirement to head the Fifth Republic.
- **1968** Paris's students and factory workers engage in a general revolt; the French government is overhauled in the aftermath.
- **1981** François Mitterrand is elected France's first socialist president since the 1940s; he's reelected in 1988.
- **1989** Paris celebrates the bicentennial of the French Revolution.
- **1992** Euro Disney opens on the outskirts of Paris.

continues

archives of Philippe Auguste before being transformed into a Gothic fortress by Louis IX in the 1100s) to make it suitable as a royal residence. Despite the building's embellishment and the designation of Paris as the French capital, he spent much of his time at other châteaux amid the hunting grounds of the Loire Valley. Many later monarchs came to share his opinion that Paris's narrow streets and teeming commercialism were unhealthy, and chose to reside elsewhere.

In 1549, however, Henri II (1519–59) triumphantly established his court in Paris and successfully ruled France from within its borders, solidifying the city's role as the nation's undisputed capital. Following their ruler's lead, fashionable aristocrats quickly began

- **1994** François Mitterrand and Queen Elizabeth II ride under the English Channel in the new Chunnel.
- **1995** Jacques Chirac is elected over Mitterrand, who dies the following year; Paris is crippled by a general strike; terrorists bomb the subway.
- **1997** Authorities enforce strict immigration laws, causing strife for African and Arab immigrants and dividing the country; French voters elect Socialist Lionel Jospin as Chirac's new prime minister.
- **1998** Socialists triumph in local elections across France.
- **1999** The Euro is introduced; on Christmas Day a violent storm assaults Paris and the Ile de France, damaging buildings and toppling thousands of trees.
- **2002** France replaces its national currency, the franc, and switches to the euro, the new European currency.

to build private residences (*hôtels particuliers*) on the Right Bank, in a marshy low-lying area known as Le Marais (the swamp).

It was during this period that Paris, as the world knows it today, came into existence. The expansion of the Louvre continued, and Catherine de Médicis (1518–89) began building her Palais des Tuileries in 1564. From the shelter of dozens of elegant urban residences, France's aristocracy imbued Paris with its sense of architectural and social style, as well as the Renaissance's mores and manners. Stone quays were added to the Seine's banks, defining their limits and preventing future flood damage, and royal decrees established a series of building codes. To an increasing degree, Paris adopted the planned perspectives and visual grace worthy of the residence of a monarch.

During the late 1500s and 1600s, Protestants were persecuted by the French kings. The bloodletting reached a high point under Henri III (1551–89) during the St. Bartholomew's Day massacre of 1572. Henri III's tragic and eccentric successor, Henri IV (1553–1610), ended the Wars of Religion in 1598 by endorsing the Edict of Nantes, offering religious freedom to the Protestants of France. Henry IV also laid out the lines for one of Paris's memorable squares: place des Vosges. A deranged monk infuriated by the king's support of religious tolerance stabbed him in 1610.

After Henri IV's death, his second wife, Marie de Médicis (1573–1642), acting as regent, planned the Palais du Luxembourg (1615), whose gardens have functioned ever since as a rendezvous for Parisians. In 1636, Cardinal Richelieu (1585–1642), who virtually ruled France during the minority of Louis XIII, built the sprawling premises of the Palais Royal. Under Louis XIII (1601–43), two uninhabited islands in the Seine were joined together with landfill, connected to Ile de la Cité and to the mainland with bridges, and renamed Ile St-Louis. Also laid out were the Jardin des Plantes, whose flowers and medicinal herbs were arranged according to their scientific and medical category.

THE SUN KING & THE FRENCH REVOLUTION

Louis XIV (1638–1715) was crowned king of France when he was only 9 years old. Cardinal Mazarin (1602–61), Louis's Sicilian-born chief minister, dominated the government in Paris during the Sun King's minority. This era marked the emergence of the French kings as absolute monarchs. As if to concretize their power, they embellished Paris with many of the monuments that still serve as symbols of the city. These included new alterations to the Louvre and the construction of the pont Royal, quai Peletier, place des Victoires, place Vendôme, Champs-Elysées, and Hôtel des Invalides. Meanwhile, Louis XIV absented himself from the city, constructing, at a staggering expense, the Château de Versailles, 21km (13 miles) southwest. Today the palace stands as the single most visible monument to the most flamboyant era of French history.

Meanwhile, the rising power of England, particularly its navy, represented a serious threat to France, otherwise the world's most powerful nation. One of the many theaters of the Anglo-French conflict was the American Revolution, during which the French kings supported the Americans in their struggle against the Crown. Ironically, within 15 years, the fervor the monarchs had nurtured crossed the Atlantic and destroyed them. The spark that kindled the fire came from Paris itself. For years before the outbreak of hostilities between the Americans and the British, the Enlightenment and its philosophers had fostered a new generation of thinkers who opposed absolutism, religious fanaticism, and superstition. Revolution had been brewing for almost 50 years, and after the French Revolution's explosive events, Europe was completely changed.

Though it began with moderate aims, the Revolution had soon turned the radical Jacobins into overlords, led by Robespierre (1758–94). On August 10, 1792, troops from Marseilles, aided by a Parisian mob, threw Louis XVI (1754–93) and his Austrian-born queen, Marie Antoinette (1755–93), into prison. Several months later, after countless humiliations and a bogus trial, they were guillotined at place de la Révolution (later renamed place de la Concorde) on January 21, 1793. The Reign of Terror continued for another 18 months, with Parisians of all political persuasions fearing for their lives.

THE RISE OF NAPOLEON

It required the militaristic fervor of Napoleon Bonaparte (1769–1821) to unite France once again. Considered then and today a strategic genius with almost limitless ambition, he restored to Paris and to France a national pride that had been diminished during the Revolution's horror. After many impressive political and military victories, he entered Paris in 1799, at the age of 30, and crowned himself "First Consul and Master of France."

A brilliant politician, Napoleon moderated the atheistic rigidity of the early adherents of the Revolution by establishing peace with the Vatican. Soon thereafter, the legendary love of Parisians for their amusements began to revive; boulevard des Italiens became the rendezvous point of the fashionable, while boulevard du Temple, which housed many of the capital's theaters, became the favorite watering hole of the working class. In his self-appointed role as a French Caesar, Napoleon continued to alter Paris's face with the construction of the neoclassical arcades of rue de Rivoli (1801), the Arc du Carrousel and Arc du Triomphe, and the neoclassical grandeur of La Madeleine. On a less grandiose scale, the city's slaughterhouses and cemeteries were sanitized and moved away from the center of town, and new industries began to crowd workers from the countryside into the cramped slums of a newly industrialized Paris.

Napoleon's victories had made him the envy of Europe, but his infamous retreat from Moscow during the winter of 1812 reduced his formerly invincible army to tatters as 400,000 Frenchmen lost their lives. After a complicated series of events that included his return from exile, Napoleon was defeated at Waterloo by the armies of the English, the Dutch, and the Prussians. Exiled to the British-held island of St. Helena in the remote South Atlantic, he died in 1821, possibly the victim of an unknown poisoner. Sometime later, his body was returned to Paris and interred in a massive porphyry sarcophagus in the Hôtel des Invalides, Louis XIV's monument to the ailing and fallen warriors of France.

In the power vacuum that followed Napoleon's expulsion and death, Paris became the scene of intense lobbying over the future fate of France. The Bourbon monarchy was soon reestablished, but with reduced powers. In 1830, the regime was overthrown. Louis-Philippe (1773–1850), duc d'Orléans and the son of a duke who had voted in 1793 for the death of Louis XVI, was elected king under a liberalized constitution. His prosperous reign lasted for 18 years, during which England and France more or less collaborated on matters of foreign policy.

Paris reveled in its prosperity, grateful for the money and glamour that had elevated it to one of the world's top cultural and commercial centers. Paris opened its first railway line in 1837 and its first gas-fed streetlights shortly after. It was a time of wealth, grace, culture, and expansion, though the industrialization of certain working-class districts produced great poverty. The era also witnessed the development of French cuisine to the high form that still prevails, while a newly empowered bourgeoisie reveled in its attempts to create the good life.

THE SECOND EMPIRE

In 1848, a series of revolutions spread from one European capital to the next. The violent upheaval in Paris revealed the dissatisfaction of members of the working class. Fueled by a financial crash and scandals in the government, the revolt forced Louis-Philippe out. That year, Emperor Napoleon's nephew, Napoleon III (1808–73), was elected president by moderate and conservative elements. Appealing to the property-owning instinct of a nation that hadn't forgotten the violent revolution of less than a century before, he established a right-wing government and assumed complete power as emperor in 1851.

In 1853, Napoleon III undertook Europe's largest urban redevelopment project by commissioning Baron Eugène-Georges Haussmann (1809–91) to redesign Paris. Haussmann created a vast network of boulevards interconnected with a series of squares that cut across old neighborhoods. While this reorganization gave the capital the look for which it's now famous, screams of outrage sounded throughout the neighborhoods that the construction split apart. By 1866, the entrepreneurs of an increasingly industrialized Paris began to regard the Second Empire as a hindrance. In 1870, during the Franco-Prussian War, the Prussians defeated Napoleon III at Sedan and held him prisoner along with 100,000 of his soldiers. Paris was threatened with bombardments from German cannons, by far the most advanced of their age, set up on the city's eastern periphery.

Although agitated diplomacy gained a Prussian withdrawal, international humiliation and perceived military incompetence sparked a revolt in Paris. One of the immediate effects was the burning of one of Paris's historic landmarks, the Palais des Tuileries. Today, only the gardens of this once-great palace remain.

The events of 1870 ushered in the Third Republic and its elected president, Marshal Marie Edme Patrice Maurice de MacMahon (1808–93), in 1873.

Under the Third Republic, peace and prosperity gradually returned, and Paris regained its glamour. Universal Expositions held in 1878, 1889, 1900, and 1937 were the catalyst for the construction of such enduring monuments as the Trocadéro, the Palais de Chaillot, the Tour Eiffel, the Grand Palais and the Petit Palais, and the neo-Byzantine Sacré-Coeur. The *réseau métropolitain* (the Métro) was constructed, providing a model for subway systems throughout Europe.

WORLD WAR I

International rivalries and conflicting alliances led to World War I, which, after decisive German victories for 2 years, degenerated into the mud-slogged horror of trench warfare. Industrialization during and after the war transformed Paris and its environs into one of the largest metropolitan areas in Europe and undisputed ever since as the center of France's intellectual and commercial life.

Immediately after the Allied victory, grave economic problems, coupled with a populace demoralized from years of fighting, encouraged the rise of Socialism and the formation of a Communist party, both movements centered in Paris. Also from Paris, the French government, led by the vindictive Georges Clemenceau (1841–1929), occupied Germany's Ruhr Valley, then and now one of that country's most profitable and industrialized regions, and demanded every centime of reparations it could wring from its humiliated neighbor, a policy that contributed to the outbreak of World War II.

THE 1920S—AMERICANS IN PARIS

The so-called Lost Generation, led by American expatriates Gertrude Stein and Alice B. Toklas, topped the list of celebrities who "occupied" Paris after World War I, ushering in one of its most glamorous eras. The living was cheap in Paris. Two people could manage for about a year on a $1,000 scholarship, provided they could scrape up another $500 or so in extra earnings. Paris attracted the littérateur, bon viveur, and drifter. Writers like Henry Miller, Ernest Hemingway, and F. Scott Fitzgerald all lived here. Even Cole Porter came, living first at the Ritz, then at 13 rue de Monsieur. James Joyce, half blind and led around by Ezra Pound, arrived in Paris and went to the salon of Natalie Barney. She became famous for pulling off stunts like inviting Mata Hari to perform a Javanese dance completely nude at one of her parties, labeled "for women only, a lesbian orgy." Novelist Colette was barred, though she begged her husband to let her go.

With the collapse of Wall Street, many Americans returned home, except hard-core artists like Henry Miller, who wandered around smoking Gauloises and writing *Tropic of Cancer,* which was banned in America. "I have no money, no resources, no hopes. I am the happiest man alive," Miller said. Eventually, he met the diary writer Anaïs Nin, and they began to live a life that gave both of them material for their prose. But even such diehards as Miller and Nin eventually realized 1930s Paris was collapsing as war clouds loomed. Gertrude and Alice remained in France, as other American expats fled to safer shores.

THE WINDS OF WAR

Thanks to an array of alliances, when Germany invaded Poland in 1939, France had no choice but to declare war. Within a few months, on June 14, 1940, Nazi armies marched down the Champs-Elysées and passed beneath the Arc de Triomphe. Newsreel cameras recorded the French openly weeping at the sight. The city suffered little from the war materially, but for 4 years it survived in a kind of half-life—cold, dull, and drab—fostering scattered pockets of fighters who resisted sometimes passively and sometimes with active sabotage.

During the Nazi occupation of Paris, the French government, under Marshal Henri Pétain (1856–1951), moved to the isolated resort of Vichy and cooperated (or collaborated, depending on your point of view) with the Nazis. Tremendous internal dissension, the memory of which still simmers today, pitted many factions against one another. The Free French Resistance fled for its own safety to London, where it was headed by Charles de Gaulle (1880–1970), who became president of France's Fourth Republic after the war.

POSTWAR PARIS

Despite its gains in prestige and prosperity after the end of World War II, Paris was rocked many times by internal dissent as domestic and international events embroiled the government controversy. In 1951, Paris celebrated the 2,000th anniversary of the city's founding and poured much energy into rebuilding its image as a center of fashion, lifestyle, and glamour. Paris became internationally recognized as both a staple in the travel diets of many North Americans and as a beacon for art and artists.

The War of Algerian Independence (1954–58), in which Algeria sought to go from being a French *département* (an integral extension of the French nation) to an independent country, was an anguishing event, more devastating than the earlier loss of France's colonies. The population of France (Paris in particular) ballooned as French citizens fled Algeria and returned with few possessions and much bitterness. In 1958, as a result of the enormous loss of lives, money, and prestige in the Algerian affair, France's Fourth Republic collapsed, and de Gaulle was called out of retirement to form a new government, the Fifth Republic. In 1962, the Algerian war ended with victory for Algeria, as France's colonies in central and equatorial Africa became independent one by one. The sun had finally set on the French Empire.

In 1968, a general revolt by Parisian students, whose activism mirrored that of their counterparts in the United States, turned the capital into an armed camp, causing a near-collapse of the national government and the very real possibility of total civil war. Though the crisis was averted, for several weeks it seemed as if French society was on the brink of anarchy.

CONTEMPORARY PARIS

In 1981, François Mitterrand (1916–96) was elected the first Socialist president of France since World War II by a very close vote. Massive amounts of capital were taken out of the country, and though the drain slowed after initial jitters, many wealthy Parisians still prefer to invest their money elsewhere.

Paris today still struggles with social unrest in Corsica and from Muslim fundamentalists both inside and outside of France. In the mid-1990s, racial tensions continued to nag at France, as the debate over immigration raged. Many right-wing political parties have created a racial backlash against North Africans and against "corruptive foreign influences" in general.

On his third try, Jacques Chirac (b. 1932), a longtime mayor of Paris, won the presidency of France in 1995 with 52% of the vote. Mitterrand turned over the reins on May 17 and died shortly thereafter. France embarked on a new era, but Chirac's popularity faded in the wake of unrest caused by an 11.5% unemployment rate. In the spring of 1998, France ousted its Conservative parties in an endorsement of Prime Minister Lionel Jospin (b. 1937) and his

Socialist-led government. The triumph of Jospin and his Communist and Green Party allies represented a disavowal of the center-right Conservatives. This was a stunning blow to Chirac's Neo-Gaullists and the center-right parties led by François Leotard, and certainly to Jean-Marie Le Pen's often fanatical National Front.

By putting the Left back in charge, the French had voted against all the new ideas proposed to them for pushing their country into competitiveness and out of its economic doldrums. In spite of this resistance to change, Jospin is still ever so gently moving France into the new millennium. Without breaking the budget or losing public favor, the prime minister has picked his way through the minefields of French politics—militant unions, a public wedded to generous benefits, and widespread resistance to change. Jospin refers to his path as "leftist realism."

In 1999, France joined with 11 other European Union countries in adopting the euro as its standard of currency, though the French franc remained in circulation until March, 2002. The new currency, it is hoped, will accelerate the creation of a single economy, comprising nearly 300 million Europeans, with a combined gross national product approaching, by some estimates, $9 trillion, larger than that of the United States.

Appendix B:
Glossary of Useful Terms

It is often amazing how a word or two of halting French will change your hosts' disposition in their home country. At the very least, try to learn a few numbers, basic greetings, and—above all—the life-raft phrase, *Parlez-vous anglais?* (Do you speak English?). As it turns out, many people do speak a passable English and will use it liberally, if you demonstrate the basic courtesy of greeting them in their language. Go out, try our glossary, and don't be bashful. *Bonne chance!*

1 Useful French Words & Phrases

English	French	Pronunciation
Yes/No	**Oui/Non**	wee/nohn
Okay	**D'accord**	*dah*-core
Please	**S'il vous plaît**	seel voo *play*
Thank you	**Merci**	*mair*-see
You're welcome	**De rien**	duh ree-*ehn*
Hello (during daylight)	**Bonjour**	bohn-*jhoor*
Good evening	**Bonsoir**	bohn-*swahr*
Good-bye	**Au revoir**	o ruh-*vwahr*
What's your name?	**Comment vous appellez-vous?**	ko-*mahn*-voo-za-pell-ay-voo?
My name is	**Je m'appelle**	*jhuh* ma-pell
How are you?	**Comment allez-vous?**	kuh-mahn-tahl-ay-voo?
So-so	**Comme ci, comme ça**	kum-*see*, kum-*sah*
I'm sorry/excuse me	**Pardon**	pahr-*dohn*

GETTING AROUND/STREET SMARTS

English	French	Pronunciation
Do you speak English?	**Parlez-vous anglais?**	par-lay-voo-ahn-*glay?*
I don't speak French	**Je ne parle pas français**	jhuh ne parl pah frahn-*say*
I don't understand	**Je ne comprends pas**	jhuh ne kohm-*prahn* pas
Could you speak more loudly/more slowly?	**Pouvez-vous parler plus fort/plus lentement?**	Poo-*vay* voo par-lay ploo for/ploo lan-te-*ment?*
What is it?	**Qu'est-ce que c'est?**	kess-kuh-*say?*
What time is it?	**Qu'elle heure est-il?**	kel uhr eh-*teel?*
What?	**Quoi?**	kwah?
How? or What did you say?	**Comment?**	ko-*mahn?*
When?	**Quand?**	kahn?
Where is?	**Où est?**	ooh-eh?
Who?	**Qui?**	kee?
Why?	**Pourquoi?**	poor-*kwah?*
here/there	**ici/là**	ee-*see*/lah
left/right	**à gauche/à droite**	a goash/a drwaht
straight ahead	**tout droit**	too-drwah
Fill the tank (of a car), please	**Le plein, s'il vous plaît**	luh plan, seel-voo-*play*

English	French	Pronunciation
I want to get off at	**Je voudrais descendre à**	jhe voo-*dray* day-son-drah ah
airport	**l'aéroport**	lair-o-*por*
bank	**la banque**	lah bahnk
bridge	**pont**	pohn
bus station	**la gare routière**	lah gar roo-tee-*air*
bus stop	**l'arrêt de bus**	lah-*ray* duh boohss
by means of a car	**en voiture**	ahn vwa-*toor*
cashier	**la caisse**	lah *kess*
cathedral	**cathedral**	ka-tay-*dral*
church	**église**	ay-*gleez*
driver's license	**permis de conduire**	per-*mee* duh con-*dweer*
elevator	**l'ascenseur**	lah sahn *seuhr*
entrance (to a building or a city)	**une porte**	ewn port
exit (from a building or a freeway)	**une sortie**	ewn sor-*tee*
gasoline	**du pétrol/de l'essence**	duh pay-*trol*/de lay-*sahns*
hospital	**l'hôpital**	low-pee-*tahl*
luggage storage	**consigne**	kohn-*seen*-yuh
museum	**le musée**	luh mew-*zay*
no smoking	**défense de fumer**	day-*fahns* de fu-may
one-day pass	**ticket journalier**	tee-kay jhoor-nall-ee-*ay*
one-way ticket	**aller simple**	ah-*lay* sam-pluh
police	**la police**	lah po-*lees*
round-trip ticket	**aller-retour**	ah-*lay* re-*toor*
second floor	**premier étage**	prem-ee-*ehr* ay-*taj*
slow down	**ralentir**	rah-lahn-*teer*
store	**le magasin**	luh ma-ga-*zehn*
street	**rue**	roo
subway	**le métro**	le may-tro
telephone	**le téléphone**	luh tay-lay-*phone*
ticket	**un billet**	uh *bee*-yay
toilets	**les toilettes/les WC**	lay twa-*lets*/les vay-*say*

NECESSITIES

English	French	Pronunciation
I'd like	**Je voudrais**	jhe voo-*dray*
a room	**une chambre**	ewn *shahm*-bruh
the key	**la clé (la clef)**	la clay
How much does ?	**C'est combien?/**	say comb-bee-*ehn?*/
it cost	**Ça coûte combien?**	sah coot comb-bee-*ehn?*
That's expensive	**C'est cher/chère**	say share
Do you take credit cards?	**Est-ce que vous acceptez les cartes de credit?**	es-kuh voo zaksep-*tay* lay kart duh creh-*dee?*
I'd like to buy	**Je voudrais acheter**	jhe voo-dray ahsh-*tay*
aspirin	**des aspirines/ des aspros**	deyz ahs-peer-*een*/ deyz ahs-*proh*
condoms	**des préservatifs**	day pray-ser-va-*teef*
dress	**une robe**	ewn robe
envelopes	**des envelopes**	days ahn-veh-*lope*
gift	**un cadeau**	uh kah-*doe*
handbag	**un sac**	uh sahk

hat	**un chapeau**	uh shah-*poh*
map of the city	**un plan de ville**	unh plahn de *veel*
newspaper	**un journal**	uh zhoor-*nahl*
phonecard	**une carte téléphonique**	uh cart tay-lay-fone-*eek*
postcard	**une carte postale**	ewn carte pos-*tahl*
road map	**une carte routière**	ewn cart roo-tee-*air*
shoes	**des chaussures**	day show-*suhr*
soap	**du savon**	dew sah-*vohn*
stamp	**un timbre**	uh *tam*-bruh
writing paper	**du papier è lettres**	dew pap-pee-*ay* a *let*-ruh

IN YOUR HOTEL

English	French	Pronunciation
Are taxes included?	**Est-ce que les taxes sont comprises?**	ess-keh lay taks son com-*preez?*
balcony	**un balcon**	uh bahl-cohn
bathtub	**une baignoire**	ewn bayn-*nwar*
hot and cold water	**l'eau chaude et froide**	low showed ay fwad
Is breakfast included?	**Petit déjeuner inclus?**	peh-*tee* day-jheun-*ay* ehn-*klu?*
room	**une chambre**	ewn *shawm*-bruh
shower	**une douche**	ewn dooch
sink	**un lavabo**	uh la-va-*bow*
suite	**une suite**	ewn sweet
We're staying for . . . days	**On reste pour . . . jours**	ohn rest poor . . . jhoor

NUMBERS & ORDINALS

English	French	Pronunciation
zero	**zéro**	*zare*-oh
one	**un**	oon
two	**deux**	duh
three	**trois**	twah
four	**quatre**	*kaht*-ruh
five	**cinq**	sank
six	**six**	seess
seven	**sept**	set
eight	**huit**	wheat
nine	**neuf**	noof
ten	**dix**	deess
eleven	**onze**	ohnz
twelve	**douze**	dooz
thirteen	**treize**	trehz
fourteen	**quatorze**	kah-*torz*
fifteen	**quinze**	kanz
sixteen	**seize**	sez
seventeen	**dix-sept**	deez-*set*
eighteen	**dix-huit**	deez-*wheat*
nineteen	**dix-neuf**	deez-*noof*
twenty	**vingt**	vehn
forty	**quarante**	ka-*rahnt*
fifty	**cinquante**	sang-*kahnt*
one hundred	**cent**	sahn
one thousand	**mille**	meel

English	French	Pronunciation
first	premier	*preh*-mee-ay
second	deuxième	*duhz*-zee-em
third	troisième	*twa*-zee-em
fourth	quatrième	*kaht*-ree-em
fifth	cinquième	*sank*-ee-em
sixth	sixième	*sees*-ee-em
seventh	septième	*set*-ee-em
eighth	huitième	*wheat*-ee-em
ninth	neuvième	*neuv*-ee-em
tenth	dixième	*dees*-ee-em

THE CALENDAR

English	French	Pronunciation
Sunday	dimanche	dee-*mahnsh*
Monday	lundi	luhn-*dee*
Tuesday	mardi	mahr-*dee*
Wednesday	mercredi	mair-kruh-*dee*
Thursday	jeudi	jheu-*dee*
Friday	vendredi	vawn-druh-*dee*
Saturday	samedi	sahm-*dee*
yesterday	hier	ee-*air*
today	aujourd'hui	o-jhord-*dwee*
this morning/ this afternoon	ce matin/ cet après-midi	suh ma-*tan*/set ah-preh mee-*dee*
tonight	ce soir	suh *swahr*
tomorrow	demain	de-*man*

2 Food/Menu/Cooking Terms

English	French	Pronunciation
I would like to eat	Je voudrais manger	jhe voo-*dray* mahn-*jhay*
Please give me	Donnez-moi, s'il vous plaît	doe-nay-*mwah*, seel voo play
a bottle of	une bouteille de	ewn boo-*tay* duh
a cup of	une tasse de	ewn tass duh
a glass of	un verre de	uh vair duh
a plate of breakfast	une assiette de le petit-déjeuner	ewn ass-ee-*et* duh luh puh-tee day-zhuh-*nay*
a cocktail	un apéritif	uh ah-pay-ree-*teef*
the check/bill	l'addition/la note	la-dee-see-*ohn*/la noat
dinner	le dîner	luh dee-*nay*
a knife	un couteau	uh koo-*toe*
a napkin	une serviette	ewn sair-vee-*et*
a spoon	une cuillère	ewn kwee-*air*
Cheers!	A votre santé!	ah vo-truh sahn-*tay*!
fixed-price menu	un menu	uh may-*new*
fork	une fourchette	ewn four-*shet*
Is the tip/ service included?	Est-ce que le service est compris?	ess-ke luh ser-*vees* eh com-*pree*?
Waiter!/Waitress!	Monsieur!/ Mademoiselle!	mun-*syuh*/mad-mwa-*zel*
wine list	une carte des vins	ewn cart day *van*

appetizer	une entrée	ewn en-*tray*
main course	un plat principal	uh plah pran-see-*pahl*
tip included	service compris	sehr-*vees* cohm-*pree*
sample of the chef's best	menu dégustation	may-*new* day-gus-ta-see-*on*

MEATS

English	French	Pronunciation
beef stew	du pot au feu	dew poht o *fhe*
beef with red wine and vegetables	du boeuf à la mode	dew bewf ah lah *mhowd*
chicken	du poulet	*dew poo*-lay
rolls of baked chicken, veal, or fish	des quenelles	day ke-*nelle*
chicken with mushrooms and wine	du coq au vin	dew cock o vhin
frogs' legs	des cuisses de grenouilles	day cweess duh gre-*noo*-yuh
ham	du jambon	dew jahm-bohn
lamb	de l'agneau	duh lahn-*nyo*
rabbit	du lapin	dew lah-pan
sirloin	de l'aloyau	duh lahl-why-*yo*
steak	du bifteck	dew beef-*tek*
steak with peppercorn and a cognac sauce	un steak au poivre	uh stake o *pwah*-vruh
double tenderloin	du chateaubriand	dew *sha*-tow-bree-ahn
stewed meat with cream and eggs	de la blanquette	duh lah blon-*kette*
veal	du veau	dew *voh*

FISH

English	French	Pronunciation
fish (freshwater)	du poisson de rivière, or du poisson d'eau douce	dew pwah-sson duh ree-vee-*aire,* dew pwah-sson d'o *dooss*
fish (saltwater)	du poisson de mer	dew pwah-sson duh *mehr*
soup with tomatoes, garlic, and olive oil	de la bouillabaisse	duh lah booh-ya-*besse*
herring	du hareng	dew ahr-*rahn*
lobster	du homard	dew oh-*mahr*
mussels	des moules	day *moohl*
mussels with herb, wine, and shallot sauce	des moules marinières	day moohl mar-ee-nee-*air*
oysters	des huîtres	dayz hoo-*ee*-truhs
shrimp	des crevettes	day kreh-*vette*
smoked salmon	du saumon fumé	dew sow-mohn fu-*may*
tuna	du thon	dew tohn
trout	de la truite	duh lah tru-*eet*

SIDES/APPETIZERS

English	French	Pronunciation
butter	du beurre	dew bhuhr
bread	du pain	dew pan

goose liver	du foie gras	dew fwah grah
potted minced pork	des rillettes	day ree-*yett*
rice	du riz	dew ree
snails	des escargots	dayz ess-car-*goh*

FRUITS/VEGETABLES

English	French	Pronunciation
cabbage	du choux	dew *shoe*
eggplant	de l'aubergine	duh loh-ber-*jheen*
grapes	du raisin	dew ray-*zhan*
green beans	des haricots verts	day ahr-ee-coh *vaire*
lemon/lime	du citron/du citron vert	dew cee-*tron*/dew cee-tron *vaire*
pineapple	de l'ananas	duh lah-na-*nas*
potatoes	des pommes de terre	day puhm duh *tehr*
potatoes au gratin	des pommes de terre dauphinois	day puhm duh tehr doh-feen-wah
french fried potatoes	des pommes frites	day puhm *freet*
spinach	des épinards	dayz ay-pin-*ards*
strawberries	des fraises	day *frez*

SOUPS/SALADS

English	French	Pronunciation
fruit salad	une salade de fruit/ une macédoine de fruits	ewn sah-lahd duh *fwee*/ewn mah-say-doine duh fwee
green salad	une salade verte	ewn sah-lahd *vairt*
lettuce salad	une salade de laitue	ewn sah-lahd duh lay-tew
onion soup	de la soupe à l'oignon	duh lah soop ah low-*nyon*
mixed vegetables and fish salad	une salade niçoise	ewn sah-lahd nee-*swaz*
sauerkraut	de la choucroute	duh lah chew-*kroot*
vegetable soup with basil	de la soupe au pistou	duh lah soop oh pees-tou

BEVERAGES

English	French	Pronunciation
beer	de la bière	duh lah bee-*aire*
milk	du lait	dew *lay*
orange juice	du jus d'orange	dew joo d'or-*ahn*-jhe
water	de l'eau	duh lo
red wine	du vin rouge	dew vhin *rooj*
white wine	du vin blanc	dew vhin *blahn*
coffee (black)	un café noir	uh ka-fay *nwahr*
coffee (with cream)	un café crème	uh ka-fay *krem*
coffee (with milk)	un café au lait	uh ka-fay o *lay*
coffee (decaf)	un café décaféiné (slang: un déca)	un ka-fay day-kah-fay-*nay* (uh *day*-kah)
coffee (espresso)	un café espresso (un express)	uh ka-fay e-*sprehss*-o (un ek-*sprehss*)
tea	du thé	dew *tay*
herbal tea	une tisane	ewn tee-*zahn*

Index

See also Accomodations and Restaurant indexes, below.

ACCOMMODATIONS

RESTAURANTS

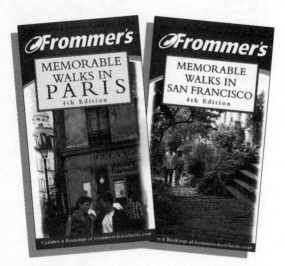

Frommer's® Complete Travel Guides

Alaska
Alaska Cruises & Ports of Call
Amsterdam
Argentina & Chile
Arizona
Atlanta
Australia
Austria
Bahamas
Barcelona, Madrid & Seville
Beijing
Belgium, Holland & Luxembourg
Bermuda
Boston
Brazil
British Columbia & the Canadian Rockies
Budapest & the Best of Hungary
California
Canada
Cancún, Cozumel & the Yucatán
Cape Cod, Nantucket & Martha's Vineyard
Caribbean
Caribbean Cruises & Ports of Call
Caribbean Ports of Call
Carolinas & Georgia
Chicago
China
Colorado
Costa Rica
Denmark
Denver, Boulder & Colorado Springs
England
Europe
European Cruises & Ports of Call
Florida

France
Germany
Great Britain
Greece
Greek Islands
Hawaii
Hong Kong
Honolulu, Waikiki & Oahu
Ireland
Israel
Italy
Jamaica
Japan
Las Vegas
London
Los Angeles
Maryland & Delaware
Maui
Mexico
Montana & Wyoming
Montréal & Québec City
Munich & the Bavarian Alps
Nashville & Memphis
Nepal
New England
New Mexico
New Orleans
New York City
New Zealand
Northern Italy
Nova Scotia, New Brunswick & Prince Edward Island
Oregon
Paris
Philadelphia & the Amish Country
Portugal
Prague & the Best of the Czech Republic

Provence & the Riviera
Puerto Rico
Rome
San Antonio & Austin
San Diego
San Francisco
Santa Fe, Taos & Albuquerque
Scandinavia
Scotland
Seattle & Portland
Shanghai
Singapore & Malaysia
South Africa
South America
South Florida
South Pacific
Southeast Asia
Spain
Sweden
Switzerland
Texas
Thailand
Tokyo
Toronto
Tuscany & Umbria
USA
Utah
Vancouver & Victoria
Vermont, New Hampshire & Maine
Vienna & the Danube Valley
Virgin Islands
Virginia
Walt Disney World® & Orlando
Washington, D.C.
Washington State

Frommer's® Dollar-a-Day Guides

Australia from $50 a Day
California from $70 a Day
Caribbean from $70 a Day
England from $75 a Day
Europe from $70 a Day

Florida from $70 a Day
Hawaii from $80 a Day
Ireland from $60 a Day
Italy from $70 a Day
London from $85 a Day

New York from $90 a Day
Paris from $80 a Day
San Francisco from $70 a Day
Washington, D.C. from $80 a Day

Frommer's® Portable Guides

Acapulco, Ixtapa & Zihuatanejo
Amsterdam
Aruba
Australia's Great Barrier Reef
Bahamas
Berlin
Big Island of Hawaii
Boston
California Wine Country
Cancún
Charleston & Savannah
Chicago
Disneyland®
Dublin
Florence

Frankfurt
Hong Kong
Houston
Las Vegas
London
Los Angeles
Los Cabos & Baja
Maine Coast
Maui
Miami
New Orleans
New York City
Paris
Phoenix & Scottsdale

Portland
Puerto Rico
Puerto Vallarta, Manzanillo & Guadalajara
Rio de Janeiro
San Diego
San Francisco
Seattle
Sydney
Tampa & St. Petersburg
Vancouver
Venice
Virgin Islands
Washington, D.C.

Frommer's® National Park Guides

Banff & Jasper
Family Vacations in the National Parks
Grand Canyon

National Parks of the American West
Rocky Mountain

Yellowstone & Grand Teton
Yosemite & Sequoia/ Kings Canyon
Zion & Bryce Canyon

FROMMER'S® MEMORABLE WALKS

Chicago	New York	San Francisco
London	Paris	Washington, D.C.

FROMMER'S® GREAT OUTDOOR GUIDES

Arizona & New Mexico	Northern California	Vermont & New Hampshire
New England	Southern New England	

SUZY GERSHMAN'S BORN TO SHOP GUIDES

Born to Shop: France	Born to Shop: Italy	Born to Shop: New York
Born to Shop: Hong Kong,	Born to Shop: London	Born to Shop: Paris
Shanghai & Beijing		

FROMMER'S® IRREVERENT GUIDES

Amsterdam	Los Angeles	San Francisco
Boston	Manhattan	Seattle & Portland
Chicago	New Orleans	Vancouver
Las Vegas	Paris	Walt Disney World®
London	Rome	Washington, D.C.

FROMMER'S® BEST-LOVED DRIVING TOURS

Britain	Germany	Northern Italy
California	Ireland	Scotland
Florida	Italy	Spain
France	New England	Tuscany & Umbria

HANGING OUT™ GUIDES

Hanging Out in England	Hanging Out in France	Hanging Out in Italy
Hanging Out in Europe	Hanging Out in Ireland	Hanging Out in Spain

THE UNOFFICIAL GUIDES®

Bed & Breakfasts and Country	Southwest & South Central	Mid-Atlantic with Kids
Inns in:	Plains	Mini Las Vegas
California	U.S.A.	Mini-Mickey
Great Lakes States	Beyond Disney	New England and New York with
Mid-Atlantic	Branson, Missouri	Kids
New England	California with Kids	New Orleans
Northwest	Chicago	New York City
Rockies	Cruises	Paris
Southeast	Disneyland®	San Francisco
Southwest	Florida with Kids	Skiing in the West
Best RV & Tent Campgrounds in:	Golf Vacations in the Eastern U.S.	Southeast with Kids
California & the West	Great Smoky & Blue Ridge Region	Walt Disney World®
Florida & the Southeast	Inside Disney	Walt Disney World® for Grown-u
Great Lakes States	Hawaii	Walt Disney World® with Kids
Mid-Atlantic	Las Vegas	Washington, D.C.
Northeast	London	World's Best Diving Vacations
Northwest & Central Plains		

SPECIAL-INTEREST TITLES

Frommer's Adventure Guide to Australia &
  New Zealand
Frommer's Adventure Guide to Central America
Frommer's Adventure Guide to India & Pakistan
Frommer's Adventure Guide to South America
Frommer's Adventure Guide to Southeast Asia
Frommer's Adventure Guide to Southern Africa
Frommer's Britain's Best Bed & Breakfasts and
  Country Inns
Frommer's Caribbean Hideaways
Frommer's Exploring America by RV
Frommer's Fly Safe, Fly Smart
Frommer's France's Best Bed & Breakfasts and
  Country Inns
Frommer's Gay & Lesbian Europe

Frommer's Italy's Best Bed & Breakfasts and
  Country Inns
Frommer's New York City with Kids
Frommer's Ottawa with Kids
Frommer's Road Atlas Britain
Frommer's Road Atlas Europe
Frommer's Road Atlas France
Frommer's Toronto with Kids
Frommer's Vancouver with Kids
Frommer's Washington, D.C., with Kids
Israel Past & Present
The New York Times' Guide to Unforgettable
  Weekends
Places Rated Almanac
Retirement Places Rated

America Online Keyword: Travel
Booked seat 6A, open return.
Rented red 4-wheel drive.
Reserved cabin, no running water.
Discovered space.